GOOD TIMES, BAD TIMES

GOOD TIMES,
BAD TIMES

Harold Evans

WEIDENFELD AND NICOLSON
LONDON

The author and publishers are grateful for permission to use the
photographs listed on p. vii and those from the following sources
on p. xiii: Syndication International, Popperfoto, *The Age*,
Camera Press, Sally Soames/*The Sunday Times*, Keystone and
Universal Pictorial Press (3)

First published in 1983 in Great Britain by
George Weidenfeld & Nicolson Ltd
91 Clapham High Street, London SW4 7TA
Reprinted December 1983

ISBN 0 297 78295 9

Printed in Great Britain by Butler & Tanner Ltd
Frome and London

CONTENTS

ILLUSTRATIONS

To Tina

ACKNOWLEDGEMENTS

I express my gratitude first to the hundreds of readers and the many members of the staff of *The Times* and *The Sunday Times* who wrote to me during March 1982, when I resigned the editorship of *The Times*. All the messages were, and still are, deeply appreciated.

In writing this book I have had the benefit not only of my own diaries and contemporaneous notes but also those of others, past and present, at Times Newspapers and I thank them all for their generosity and courage. Edwin Taylor's records were especially helpful. I have not attempted a detailed history of my years at *The Sunday Times*, but the passages of this book relating to that newspaper owe a debt, as did the original adventures, to Hugo Young, Phillip Knightley, Bruce Page, Paul Eddy, Elaine Potter, Ron Hall, David Blundy, Patrick Forman, Marjorie Wallace, John Whale, Peter Roberts, David Leitch, Chris Ryder, Magnus Linklater, James Evans, Bob Ducas and especially George Darby, and also to my former managerial colleague Donald Cruickshank. I must make special mention of my personal assistant at *The Sunday Times*, Joan Thomas, who sustained me with loyalty and resource in all our years together at *The Northern Echo* and *The Sunday Times*.

Gordon Phillips, the former archivist of *The Times*, read the historical passages in draft with a critical eye. For additional research I thank Tracey Scoffield, Royce Haimann, Jacqueline Lloyd and my assistant, Brenda Haddou, who, along with Alex MacCormick, senior editor at Weidenfeld, superintended everything with cool precision. I was fortunate in the dedication of Dunn, Frank, my indexer, and in the printers Butler & Tanner. For assistance in Australia, I gratefully acknowledge Mrs Nan Rivett, Sir Theodor Bray, and Colin Chapman, who was, for forty-eight hours in 1982, the Editor of *The Australian*.

I am deeply indebted to John Heilpern for his critical overview and his many thoughtful improvements. Oscar Turnill edited the manuscript with meticulous skill, and I also thank Tanya Schmoller.

Much of *Good Times, Bad Times* was written while I was a visiting professor at the Poynter Institute for Media Studies, St Petersburg, Florida. I thank Eugene Patterson, President of the Poynter Institute and editor-in-chief of the *St Petersburg Times*, for his invitation and Marion Poynter for her hospitality.

This is not an autobiography, but I take the opportunity to place on record my gratitude to those who have given me my professional opportunities and encouraged and guided me. First the late Tom Henry at the *Manchester Evening News*; Lord Gibson, the late Charles Fenby, and Shannan Stevenson at the Westminster Press and *The Northern Echo*; and, of course, at *The Sunday Times*, from 1966 to 1980, Roy and Ken Thomson, Gordon Brunton and pre-eminently Denis Hamilton, first as my editor and then as editor-in-chief of Times Newspapers.

HAROLD EVANS

DRAMATIS PERSONAE

Rupert Murdoch
chairman, News International/
Times Newspapers

Gerald Long
managing director, Times
Newspapers

Richard Searby
Australian legal adviser to Rupert
Murdoch

Charles Douglas-Home
deputy editor, *The Times*

Frank Giles
deputy editor/editor, *The Sunday
Times*

William Rees-Mogg
editor (1966–81), *The Times*

Lord Robens
(formerly Sir Alfred) national
director, Times Newspapers

Sir Edward Pickering
national director, Times
Newspapers

Sir Denis Hamilton
chairman and editor-in-chief, Times
Newspapers

This is a list of the people who - in addition to the author - were involved significantly in the principal events described in this book. It is given alphabetically by surname; some groups (e.g. trade unions) are also included. The list is not exhaustive: a fuller one appears in the index. In many instances titles and roles changed (that is part of the story) and the description here, as in the photograph captions on the previous page, is that relevant at the time. Most of those mentioned now hold different appointments (or none) both inside and outside Times Newspapers.

Ken Ashton, general secretary, NUJ

John Barry, managing editor features/NUJ chapel official, *The Sunday Times*
Ken Beattie, circulation director, Times Newspapers
John Biffen, Secretary of State for Trade
Reg Brady, NATSOPA chapel official, *The Sunday Times* machine room
Arthur Brittenden, corporate relations director, Times Newspapers
Tina Brown (Mrs Harold Evans)
Gordon Brunton, Thomson chief executive in UK

James Callaghan, former Prime Minister
John Collier, general manager, Times Newspapers
Donald Cruickshank, finance director, Times Newspapers

Lord Dacre (Hugh Trevor-Roper), national director, Times Newspapers
Richard Davy, leader-writer, *The Times*
Les Dixon, president, NGA. Died November 1983
Bernard Donoughue, political consultant, *The Sunday Times*/assistant editor, *The Times*
Robert Ducas, US president/manager, Times Newspapers

Richard Eddis, legal adviser to Harold Evans
Roy Ekberg, company secretary, Times Newspapers
Fred Emery, home editor, *The Times*
James Evans, *Sunday Times* lawyer/chairman, Times Newspapers executive board, and director Thomson Organisation

Barry Fitzpatrick, NATSOPA clerical chapel official, *The Sunday Times*

Peter Gibbings, chairman, *The Guardian*
Bill Gillespie, assistant/managing director, Times Newspapers
John Grant, managing editor, *The Times*
Lord Greene (Sidney Greene), national director, Times Newspapers

Sir William Haley, former editor, *The Times*

Ron Hall, editor, *The Sunday Times* Magazine

Adrian Hamilton, business news editor, *The Times*

Michael Hamlyn, executive editor, *The Times*/manager, Murdoch newspapers' news services, New York

Louis Heren, deputy editor, *The Times*

Owen Hickey, assistant editor, *The Times*

Anthony Holden, features editor, *The Times*

Brian Horton, foreign editor, *The Times*

M. J. (Duke) Hussey, chief executive/consultant, Times Newspapers

Eric Jacobs, labour editor/NUJ chapel official, *The Sunday Times*

Frank Johnson, parliamentary writer, *The Times*

JOTT: Journalists of The Times Ltd

Bill Keys, general secretary, SOGAT/chairman, TUC print industry committee

Michael Leapman, New York reporter, *The Times*

Brian MacArthur, executive editor, *The Times*/deputy editor, *The Sunday Times*

Anna Murdoch (Mrs Rupert Murdoch)

NATSOPA: National Society of Operative Printers and Assistants, union for clerical staff, machine-room assistants and others

NGA: National Graphical Association, principal printing craft union, also including machine-room pressmen

Dugal Nisbet-Smith, managing director, Times Newspapers

Geraldine Norman, chairman JOTT/sale-room correspondent, *The Times*

NUJ: National Union of Journalists

Owen O'Brien, general secretary, NATSOPA

Bill O'Neill, general manager, Times Newspapers

Peter Roberts, managing editor, *The Sunday Times*

Paul Routledge, labour reporter/NUJ chapel official, *The Times*

Lord Roll (formerly Sir Eric), national director, Times Newspapers/chairman, S.G. Warburg, merchant bankers

Michael Ruda, advertisement director, Times Newspapers

Liz Seeber, editor's secretary, *The Times*

James Sherwood, chairman, Sea Containers
Geoffrey Smith, leader-writer, *The Times*
Godfrey Smith, chief accountant, Times Newspapers (not to be
    confused with Godfrey S., *Sunday Times* writer, or Geoffrey S., *qv*)
SOGAT: Society of Graphical and Allied Trades, union for various
    newspaper staffs, including distributors
Peter Stehrenberger, finance director, Times Newspapers

Edwin Taylor, design editor, *The Times* and *The Sunday Times*
Margaret Thatcher, Prime Minister
Ken Thomson (2nd Lord Thomson), chairman, Thomson
    Organisation
Roy Thomson (Lord Thomson of Fleet), chairman, Thomson
    Organisation
Joan Thomas, editor's personal assistant, *The Sunday Times*
Gary Thorne, marketing director, Times Newspapers
Oscar Turnill, assistant editor, *The Times*

Joe Wade, general secretary, NGA
Antony Whitaker, legal manager, Times Newspapers
Peter Wilsher, foreign editor, *The Sunday Times*

Hugo Young, deputy editor, *The Sunday Times*

# FOREWORD

Early in 1982, ten months after he had taken over *The Times* and *The Sunday Times* Rupert Murdoch went to see the Prime Minister, Mrs Thatcher. They shared a problem: it was me.

I was the editor of *The Times* and Murdoch's difficulty was how to dispose of me. *The Times* was supposed to be protected from political interference, and its editor from dismissal, by a spectacular series of pledges Murdoch had given in 1981. The irony was still fresh on them: they were given to Mrs Thatcher's Government and they were her justification for sparing Murdoch an investigation by the Monopolies Commission. Prominent Tory MPs, as well as the Opposition, believed the fair trading laws demanded a Monopolies hearing on Murdoch's bid and the alternatives to it. It was not an unreasonable view of the law and it chimed with Conservative principles of competition, since the man who sought permission to acquire the biggest selling quality Sunday newspaper and Britain's most famous daily newspaper already owned the biggest selling daily newspaper, the *Sun*, and the biggest selling Sunday newspaper, the *News of the World*. These newspapers, however, happened to have campaigned for Mrs Thatcher in the 1979 general election and it was Mrs Thatcher's will which prevailed in the Government discussions on the take-over in 1981. I heard on 22 January that she had insisted there would be no Monopolies inquiry. Murdoch had stood by her in the dark days and she was going to stand by him. The new Secretary of State for Trade, John Biffen, put it differently when he rose in the Commons five days later, but it added up to approval for Murdoch on condition that he gave various undertakings of editorial independence, which he readily did. I could not fail to be impressed by the guarantees; I had helped in their formulation in Times Newspapers. I knew that Murdoch issued promises as prudently as the Weimar republic issued marks; but the Secretary of State entrenched some of the *Times* undertakings with criminal sanctions. 'Hell, I'll go to prison if I speak a word to you,' Murdoch said to me the day after the Commons debate and it seemed a huge joke. 'What if I found a way of tearing up all those guarantees and firing an editor?' he asked the assembled staff of *The Times*. 'The answer is there would be a terrible public stink and it would destroy the paper.'

Murdoch had an idea he put to Mrs Thatcher for solving the Evans problem. It was that I should be offered some grand and improving public post. Mrs Thatcher was intrigued by Murdoch's ploy and mooted it with the chairman of the Conservative party, Cecil Parkinson. Murdoch's stance was that I was not a good daily newspaper editor, but his central point was that I was not a Tory. 'And that is what matters from our point of view,' Parkinson told a colleague. My offence in the eyes of the Prime Minister and the chairman of the party was unreliability: there was a doubt, aggravated by Murdoch, whether *The Times* under Evans would back Mrs Thatcher and the Tories wholeheartedly. Deviationist tendencies had been noted; and this was pre-Falklands, when nerves in No. 10 and Tory Central Office were stretched tight by the rise of the Social Democrats and Mrs Thatcher's low standing in the polls. Parkinson looked around and reported that there was a search for a chairman of the Sports Council to succeed Dicky Jeeps, the former England rugby player, whose five-year term was up by the end of 1982. Ski-ing, the amiable Parkinson observed, was Evans's second passion to newspapers. It was, as it happened, not considered a bait I would take and I am grateful for that; I would not have cared to tangle with a scrum-half of the calibre of Jeeps, who was reappointed. I was fifty-three and I did not, in any case, contemplate an early retirement from journalism. Murdoch, who had been looking for a justification for my sacking, came up with another idea which was more in the conventions of Fleet Street. He found a weapon within *The Times* by exploiting the disquiet at changes which he himself had encouraged, by denying me the editorial freedom he had guaranteed to Parliament, and by disaffection in the form of my deputy, Charles Douglas-Home.

Murdoch's wish that *The Times* should be valiant for Thatcher in Britain and stalwart for Reagan in the United States had been obvious from the start of my editorship; it gradually developed into warfare only with the rise of the Social Democratic Party, though there were some odd events on the way to Tyburn. There was a brawl on the doorstep of my home about the virtues of monetarism, a smear campaign among Tory MPs to the effect that I was a spendthrift and probably a socialist, and Murdoch's general manager, Gerald Long, demanded in writing to know why I allowed *The Times* to report that the recession was not over when the Government had said it was. It was in the New Year of 1982 that Murdoch escalated his campaign to open personal hostility, coupled with secret briefings of politicians and well-placed journalists. He went out of his way in talking to the Tory back bench media group of MPs to say I had gone overboard on the SDP. Not everyone swallowed the Murdoch line. 'We knew you better than that,' the chairman, Geoffrey Johnson-Smith, said later. But nobody knew what to make of Murdoch's charges that I had overspent; it remained useful groundwork should there be a public scandal. He was shrewder with me on politics at this stage, prefacing his assaults with disclaimers that he was making them. He couched his political campaign in terms of criticizing me for 'lack of firm convictions' and 'a conscience'. I had heard the code before. Shortly after Murdoch acquired the papers and while I was still at *The Sunday Times*, I wrote a prominent leading article headed 'Wrong, Mrs Thatcher, Wrong, Wrong, Wrong'. It was not a new statement of the paper's position. It summarized the theme of economic leaders I had written during the previous year, but it was a highly critical point-by-point analysis of her public economic statements and it drew an enormous response. There were hundreds of letters, mostly critical of the leading article at first and then swinging the other way. Two weeks later, when my appointment to *The Times* had been announced, Henry Brandon, the *Sunday Times* correspondent in Washington, wrote to me about a conversation with Mrs Thatcher:

> When I talked to the PM at the British embassy party for the President your new appointment came up and I suggested to her that *The Times* needed someone like yourself to break the old moulds. She said she liked you and that *The Times* needed a facelift, but she wondered whether you 'had enough anchor, enough firm convictions', because that is important with a newpaper like *The Times*.

Brandon commented: 'She is probably worried that you might not support her as did William. At any rate, I pass this on to you–it was a private conversation but Henry Grunwald [editor-in-chief, *Time* magazine] listened in on it – because it is always useful to know what a PM thinks of one.'

I could understand the anxiety in February 1981, but I would have been surprised and, frankly, shocked at the way it had developed a year later. Murdoch was right that I was not a Tory, but I was not a Social Democrat either, or Labour or Liberal or a Welsh Nationalist. I have voted several ways according to my judgements. In the 1979 general election I voted for Mrs Thatcher. But my personal voting record is less relevant than my professional conviction, which has always been that a news journalist should not engage in active party politics and that there is supreme value in the independence of a newspaper. This has meant the sacrifice of a chance to lose a deposit in a general election. The second year William Rees-Mogg stood as a Conservative candidate in miners' territory at Chester-le-Street, County Durham, in 1959, I refused a similar glittering opportunity as a Liberal in a Tory seat in Cheshire. I can understand why some journalists find it hard to shed party affiliation and for the most part I have not known it affect their work as reporters. I find it impossible, however, to congratulate editors who, during their active invigilation of a supposedly independent newspaper, take political honours from a government. I edited *The Sunday Times* as a newspaper independent of party; in my fourteen years we endorsed the Conservative party twice and Labour once. For *The Times* independence of party seemed to me even more of an imperative and for several reasons. For a start it deals in news every day; and the daily news in print in Britain is more brilliantly polluted by partisan judgements than the press in most other democracies and certainly by comparison with the press of the United States.

The arithmetic favours the Conservative party: if the *Sun* on the right and the *Mirror* on the left cancel each other out, the *Daily Mail* and the *Daily Express* are net in the balance for the Tories, and it shows in the selection and presentation of news as well as in features and leading articles. In the serious press of opinion, *The Financial Times* is more neutral than right, but the conservative *Daily Telegraph* has three times the readership of the liberal *Guardian*. This does not mean that *The Times* should regard itself as political ballast, which would be a dereliction of duty, or be frightened of robust support for any party on its merits, but it does mean it is a national loss if its judgements in news and opinion are in any way affected by party allegiance. Loyalty to party may be acknowledged as something of a virtue and it is clearly rewarded, but independence is a higher ideal and it is worth the effort. It serves the readers, it keeps the politicians on their toes, it is more interesting. For *The Times* there should be the example of its history. One of the greatest editors of *The Times*, Thomas Barnes, broke with the tradition of supporting the party in power. He was accused of lacking conviction by those who wanted *The Times* to take a definite line and stick to it as an administration or opposition journal, but he saw himself as beholden to public opinion rather than to party and dominated by neither. It was Barnes who bequeathed the very idea of a newspaper as an independent authority. The most famous disaster for *The Times*, the appeasement of Nazi Germany, had its roots as surely in Geoffrey Dawson's personal loyalty to the Prime Minister, Stanley Baldwin. The years in which *The Times* saw itself as an extension of government and party are the years of a measured mediocrity.

I would not have thought that the expression of this idea of independence in 1981-2 had been notably hostile to Mrs Thatcher and the Conservative Government. The policies were described in excruciating detail. Some concerning the economy were attacked, many were supported: the Chancellor of the Exchequer told us the support of *The Times* had been critical in the public pay battle with the civil service. The ordeal of the Opposition Labour party was unsparingly documented. But I ensured as well that the rise of the Social Democratic Party was thoroughly reported and fairly assessed, and that the Tory critics of Mrs Thatcher had a platform.

My personal relations with Mrs Thatcher seemed tolerable until *The Times* reported the affair of Denis Thatcher's intervention in a planning appeal. I had never, as a newspaper editor, made a point of trying to see a Prime Minister or Leader of the Opposition frequently, but I met Mrs Thatcher at various functions over a decade. I admire her resolution. She has only one voice, in public and in private. But she is limited in her appreciation of dissent. She can understand total opposition more easily than she can accommodate friendly criticism. Enemies are expected to obstruct; everyone else is expected to rally round. There is no such thing as disagreement; it is lack of faith. She could not understand why, if I opposed trade union restrictions and especially the closed shop in journalism, I did not agree with her as passionately on everything else. It must be equivocation. Evans was not quite 'solid'.

If Mrs Thatcher is not the ideal participant in an exercise of editorial independence, she is not the first Prime Minister to prefer a favourable press. Harold Wilson conducted a campaign against Nora Beloff, the political correspondent of *The Observer*, whose editor and owner David Astor repulsed him. When Roy Thomson's bid for *The Times* was being considered by the Monopolies Commission, Wilson suggested over dinner at Chequers that he ought to get rid of David Wood, its political correspondent. The suggestion was ignored. The difference at *The Times* between 1967 and 1982 lies in the character of the two owners, Roy Thomson and Rupert Murdoch. There are superficial resemblances: colonial boy makes good in newspapers in Britain, works hard, charms people, diversifies successfully and rejoices in money and conservative opinion. But the differences between the men are more revealing. Thomson's most memorable quality was an instinct for truth. He got into all sorts of scrapes for it; he seemed to enjoy letting the cat out of the bag. He meant what he said about the virtue of editorial independence and the duty of newspapers to serve their communities. He was incapable of dissembling. He counselled his business colleagues, but never issued directives or sought to be flattered as the boss. He could be caustic but he did not deal in fear. In 1963 *The Sunday Times* was critical of Prime Minister Harold Macmillan's policies at a time when Thomson knew he was being considered for an honour by the Prime Minister's committee. He never uttered a word. 'I would have bitten my

tongue first,' he said in his autobiography. When politicians or businessmen complained he blinked genially at them through his pebbled glasses,
and sometimes deflected them to Denis Hamilton, his scrupulous
editor-in-chief. It would have been unthinkable for him to attack one of
his own editors before a group of MPs: he was loyal and straightforward.
Only once in fourteen years did Denis Hamilton, as editor-in-chief, seek
to guide me on a political line the proprietor would like. In the general
election of 1974 he mildly suggested to me that Roy Thomson would be
unhappy if *The Sunday Times* came out for Labour. I told Thomson
himself, in one of our Saturday night telephone conversations, that we
were going in that direction. He took it in his stride, made some shrewd
comments on the characters of Heath and Wilson, and concluded, 'Well,
Harold, it's up to you ... How's the run tonight?' Hamilton never
mentioned it again. He had not been carrying a message; it was his own
initiative, an example of his prudence rather than Thomson pressure.

Thomson would bet his business judgement against anyone, but he
did not expect any great weight to be attached to his political views. He
was conservative, but his conservatism was homespun Samuel Smiles.
Murdoch's is factory fresh. Thomson's amounted to a few pioneer
principles about honesty, humility and thrift drawn from the hard life of
the self-made man surprised at his own success; it was instinctive rather
than ideological. It was a bit quirky and prejudiced, something he wore
comfortably himself, but did not expect everyone else to copy. Murdoch's conservatism has nothing to do with a homely philosophy of
self-reliance; its wellsprings are the retention of power and money, its
methods are manipulation and the adroit manufacture of alliances. It
has a wider political expression, but it is for all that less deep-rooted; it
can be jettisoned at any moment for advantage. Politicians are endorsed
when the calculation is that they will win power and patronage. A
newspaper independent of the proprietor's needs at any moment has no
place in such a scheme of things. It is a personal tool.

Thomson, like Murdoch, saw newspapers as a way of making money,
but, as Francis Williams observed, Thomson's enduring contribution
was to show how the profession of journalism might be carried on
within the increasingly complex business of the press. For Murdoch the
business of the press is more business for Murdoch. It is the subjugation
of journalism to marketing and personal power-broking which is offensive; and this need not be a feature of an interventionist proprietor. Lord
Hartwell, the editor-in-chief of the *Daily Telegraph* and *Sunday Telegraph*, is also the proprietor, but his standards as editor-in-chief are
those of journalism. So were those of the editor-proprietor of *The Observer*, David Astor. It is customary to portray Thomson's disassociation
from editorial as the product of a preoccupation with money. It is a false

explanation. There were numerous occasions when editorial material in *The Sunday Times* and *The Times* affected Thomson's pocket. I recall in particular a *Sunday Times* editorial and series of articles which raised the whole issue of the early licensing arrangements for North Sea oil exploration in a manner damaging to Thomson commercial interests. There was never a murmur. An Insight exposé of CIA involvement in elections in Guyana was published the day before a Thomson team selling a television station met the government; they were asked to leave the country forthwith. We showed a similar felicity when the chief executive, Gordon Brunton, was in South Africa. It was typical that I heard about these repercussions only years later and by chance. But I was present, and somewhat apprehensive despite the record, when I thwarted a business deal Roy Thomson personally made. He phoned me on a Saturday to say he had been told by Mormon friends that *The Sunday Times* could have the autobiography of the reclusive millionaire Howard Hughes. It was at the time when a fake autobiography of Hughes had been written by Clifford Irving. Howard Hughes, Thomson was tipped off, was ready to come out of his years of seclusion to tell his own story. We were in Miami the next day. Hughes's lawyer, Chester Davis, and Mormon aides shuttled between Thomson's room and wherever they were keeping Hughes, whom we were never allowed to see. I was astounded at Thomson's cheek in the financial talks, but he gauged it right. He was tickled pink when our offer for book and serial rights was accepted. But two or three days later, when the detailed papers were drawn up, I saw the Hughes people had not yielded to us on editorial control of the book. I told Thomson this was not acceptable and, when the Hughes people resisted, he nonchalantly tore up the deal. Months later, when our own book on the hoax came out, the Hughes people complained to Thomson. 'Well,' I heard him say, 'it's a good read, a lot of fun and I enjoyed it.' The legend is that Thomson only read the advertisements in newspapers, editorial being the stuff in between. He liked to count the ads, but again, unlike Murdoch, he did have the patience and the interest to read long articles. When I travelled with him to Miami, he read both *The Observer* and *Sunday Times* from cover to cover and gave the soundest judgements on them. (It was also typical of him that, when I appeared for breakfast with both the *Miami Herald* and the *Wall Street Journal*, he roasted me for extravagance.)

The truth is that passing from Thomson to Murdoch was a transition from light to dark; and all of us involved were diminished by the shadows. It was not simply a question of editorial independence being absolute and unthreatened under Thomson, father and son: it was celebrated. Journalism had a chance to show what might be achieved with reasonable freedom and resources. The freedom of the press is commonly discussed in relation to government and law. These external restraints are important. I spent a considerable amount of my career as an editor finding ways round them. In 1974 in the Granada Guildhall lectures, frustrated by laws of contempt and confidence, I characterized the British press as 'half-free' by comparison with the press of the United States. The comparison remains, in my judgement, substantially as valid today as then. But *The Sunday Times* was able to operate with some success in the public interest despite these external restraints because we had a firm base of internal freedom and, crucially, we had the staff with the skills to make good use of the opportunity. We had the steadfast support of Thomson and Hamilton. When there were legal attempts to suppress what we thought ought to be revealed, and we were the judges, they uncomplainingly made the money available. Most importantly, the atmosphere they created nourished and developed the talents of a remarkable group of journalists. Truth is an elusive quarry, but the staff knew it was the only authority they had to satisfy.

Towards the end of the Thomson era the internal freedom was eroded by the guerrilla warfare of the print unions; there was a collapse of spirit at the top of the Thomson Organisation; and in 1981 the internal freedoms that had been enjoyed for twenty years fell under siege to Rupert Murdoch. This book first describes the style and values of the Thomson era during my editorship of *The Sunday Times* and gives a taste of some of the stories and investigative campaigns we undertook. Then I move to the Murdoch era and its traumatic inner reality during my editorship of *The Times*.

I

THE SUNDAY TIMES AND THE CROSSMAN DIARIES

Roy Thomson never came to *The Sunday Times* on a Saturday. We always talked on the telephone. It was doubly unusual to have both Roy and his son Kenneth in my office as I did on the evening of Saturday, 25 January 1975. They said there was nothing special on their minds. I told them they had chosen quite a night. The presses were running, but at any moment I expected a court order to stop them – and at the behest of the Government. The Attorney-General's office was threatening action. Our lawyer was standing by. A Downing Street dispatch rider had just picked up two copies of the first edition at the request of the Prime Minister, Harold Wilson, who was at Chequers.

The cause of official consternation was four pages I was publishing in *The Sunday Times* in defiance of the Cabinet Secretary and at risk of criminal prosecution under the Official Secrets Act. They contained what I announced as the first of a series of long extracts from the diaries of Richard Crossman, the former Labour Minister, whose dying instruction to his wife and literary executors was to fight the official pressure he knew would be brought to suppress them. I had taken the decision to publish in great secrecy, fearing an injunction to stop us. Only six other people at *The Sunday Times* knew our intentions: Denis Hamilton, the editor-in-chief; two *Sunday Times* lawyers; my deputy editor, Frank Giles; the head printer; and Ron Hall, who planned the pages. Working alone at night, the head printer himself set the 10,000-word extract. Galley proofs were not distributed. When printing started, I held back the copies normally sent down to Whitehall early on Saturday evenings.

Ken Thomson looked concerned. His father blinked behind his pebble glasses: 'You happy in your own mind, Harold?'

'I am,' I replied, as if I were already in the dock. 'It's the full story of Cabinet meetings, but there's no breach of national security. It's in the public interest. People should know how they're governed . . .' I assured him that the lawyers had advised on strategy.

'A good read, eh?' said the owner.

I saw Lord Thomson happily to the front entrance of the building with his combustible *Sunday Times* in his hand, and impulsively told the commissionaire to bolt the big double doors. I had the fleeting notion that we might thereby delay receipt of an injunction against the paper and gain time to distribute more copies. Any court order could actually be telephoned through by the duty judge: all the same, I left the doors locked as a symbol of our embattlement.

In the fourteen years I was editor of *The Sunday Times*, from 1967 to 1981, I came to know well the routes from my office in Gray's Inn Road to the law courts in the Strand. My hours in court were rarely necessary because of something *The Sunday Times* had published. We had to defend very few libel cases. I went before the judges because Government or corporations or individuals tried to find reasons in law for preventing *The Sunday Times* printing what it knew to be true. 'News', as Lord Northcliffe said, 'is what somebody somewhere wants to suppress. Everything else is advertising.' Few people would disagree with the first sentiment. At *The Sunday Times* we did not seek trouble with the law; it happened because the journalism Roy Thomson made possible ran into conflict with arbitrary power. It was not abstract or remote power, but the power that is capable of building an airliner knowing it will fall out of the skies, or of cheating small savers, or concealing plans to rob communities of their railways, or selling a deforming drug and refusing to compensate reasonably for the shattered lives, or even of bringing the weight of the state against the publication of a politician's diaries.

We won all of these battles in the end, though the news was sometimes a little late getting through to our readers – anything from one week to eight years. The portent of resistance arrived at *The Sunday Times* very early in my editorship. It was a man in a bowler hat. He sought me out in the composing room one Saturday with an order from Mr Justice Sebag Shaw that I must not publish information from a document we had secured from Athens. It was a copy of a report by a London public relations firm, Maurice Fraser and Associates, to their clients, the Greek military junta. The part which interested us was Fraser's claim secretly to have enlisted a British MP to work on behalf of the Greek Government 'behind the scenes in order to influence other British MPs'. I sat through two trials before the order was lifted by the Appeal Court. The case itself – Fraser *v*. Evans – was hardly memorable, but it introduced me to the law of confidence which was to be deployed against us on graver matters, including Crossman and Thalidomide, and which remains one of the unique restrictions on the freedom of the press in Britain.

I came to be alert to the danger of the last-minute injunction, sought out of court and without chance of pleading our case. Edward Heath objected in 1977 to a report we were about to make on his connection with the financial company Slater Walker, and he sought a court order at 7 p.m. on a Saturday to stop the presses and have the report removed. His solicitor refused to say where the judge lived in the hope that we would not be able to contest the injunction. We managed to locate the judge, but a Keystone Cops scene thereby ensued with *The Sunday Times* cars full of lawyers trying to reach the judge's home before Sir Peter Rawlinson, representing Heath, could arrive in his car. Then the judge found he could not hear the application, because it so happened he had a connection with the Royal Yachting Association, which also had a connection with Slater Walker. Then the judge's dog bit Bruce Page of *The Sunday Times*. And the chase was on to the second duty judge's home, who offered us sherry and refused the injunction.

In 1972, two Scotland Yard detectives came to my office to caution me formally for a prosecution under the Official Secrets Act. We had published a confidential copy of a civil service report to the Minister of Transport advocating the closure of one third of the country's railway system. In the end no charges were brought. It was part of the necessary warfare with a secretive Executive which used among many weapons those of injunction, Parliamentary privilege and contempt. We were sustained by our readers; whatever the story, the sense of embattlement was real when we were not. Our criticisms of Enoch Powell's 'rivers of blood' speech brought thousands of protests. Our massive coverage of Ulster caused political and public offence, and produced political pressures. John Barry and the Insight team in Ulster wrote 50,000 words (and a best-selling book). Other newspapers suggested our reports on torture of internees had been fabricated (the Compton Report corroborated our evidence) and a delegation of Conservative MPs called on me to denounce our coverage as unpatriotic. Roy Thomson was assailed by politicians and others when we attempted difficult and contentious journalism like this. He always had an answer. It was printed on a card he carried in his pocket for twenty-five years. He called it his 'creed':

> I can state with the utmost emphasis that no person or group can buy or influence editorial support from any newspaper in the Thomson group. Each paper may perceive this interest in its own way, and will do this without advice, counsel or guidance from the central office of the Thomson Organisation.
>
> I do not believe that a newspaper can be run properly unless its editorial columns are run freely and independently by a highly skilled and dedicated professional journalist.
>
> This is and will continue to be my policy.

When anyone protested to Roy Thomson about his newspapers he would produce his creed or calling-card from his pocket and silence the critic by adding, 'You wouldn't expect me to go back on my word, would ya?' He never did. As he came to own more and more newspapers, he grew more emphatic about editorial independence: 'I still refused to believe that I knew as well as the editors what was best, editorially', he wrote in his 1975 autobiography. 'Apart from being the way that produced the best and most honest newspapers, it was the only sensible way for a man to run as many newspapers as I owned.'

When I first got to know him in 1966, he was seventy-two. The barber's son from Timmins, Ontario, owned scores of small papers in North America when he bought the *Scotsman* in 1953, but he made the bulk of his fortune after he was sixty. He would arrive at 8.45 a.m. at *The Sunday Times* offices in Gray's Inn Road, a black Homburg tilted on the back of his head. He wore shiny double-breasted suits with wide-bottomed trousers: he begrudged spending money on clothes. When he was created Baron Thomson of Fleet in 1964, he celebrated by queuing at Burberrys for a cashmere coat reduced from £75 to £40. He loved being a lord, and had his coat of arms engraved on the double glass doors at *The Sunday Times*. He was a creative proprietor: the first colour magazine in British journalism was 'Thomson's folly' at *The Sunday Times* and he expanded the paper to 64-page and 72-page issues. Among many enterprises, he began a group of local evening newspapers when everyone said the industry was dying. (They did well at first.) He liked the introduction that Times Newspapers gave him to the great and powerful. Anybody could say anything to him and he felt he could say anything to anyone. He could get away with murder, stopping a lunch of eminent political figures with a risqué joke: 'Say, have you heard this one?' In personal meetings he tried hard to sell banking to Chou En-lai and capitalism to Khrushchev (with whom he got along famously). Balance-sheets and budgets were his favourite reading, next to 'whodunits', of which he had 3,000. The numbers he was most interested in with me were circulation figures. There was a ritual telephone call every Saturday night. 'How's the run going, Harold?' Then: 'What's the figures?' He liked the challenge that *The Sunday Times* might one day surpass the circulation of *both The Observer* and the *Sunday Telegraph* combined. He grumbled when price rises set us back, but it was good-natured. There was no pressure to seek circulation by any means. He disapproved of sex and violence in newspapers. He had a similar antagonism to trendy hairstyles. Lewis Chester had an Afro hairstyle when he was working on *Hoax*, our book about the fake Howard Hughes autobiography. To appease Roy, we had Chester specially shorn for his photograph on the dust-jacket.

In June 1976 we realized his ambition for *The Sunday Times*. On June the 20th the paper had a sale of 6,000 copies above the combined sale of *The Observer* and *Sunday Telegraph*. I could not tell him on the telephone. He was in hospital and I wrote to him there. He died shortly afterwards. His son – called Mr Thomson in Canada and Lord Thomson in Britain – took over and continued his father's tradition. It was five years before Rupert Murdoch succeeded to the company that Roy Thomson founded. On his death I wrote in a leader for *The Sunday Times*:

Lord Thomson was not a journalist, but he was the best friend journalism ever had. Not many of his editorial colleagues shared his views on numerous issues of the day, such as capital punishment or the role of trade unions. This is one of his contributions to journalism: his willingness, early in his career, not to treat a newspaper he owned as a weapon of personal power or propaganda. But his contributions to journalism were deeper than that. Simply stated he made good journalism possible and he knew what it was. He chose to detach himself from the editorial conduct of his newspapers and that is often seen as his principal virtue, because there have been too many owners, here and in North America, who have been erratic meddlers with no scruples about the loftier pretensions of journalism. Roy Thomson's distinction is that he created a new kind of ownership. He never once imposed his opinions on *The Sunday Times*, nor, remarkably, ever once sought a single editorial favour for himself, his friends or any of his companies. He was the antithesis of the bully or the manipulator. He was a free trader in ideas and enthusiasms. He was the most uncorrupt and incorruptible of men. But, above all, there was his homely regard for truth, the source of journalism's moral energy and the precept we love and remember him by.

He also believed that the 'social mission' of every great newspaper is to provide 'a home for a large number of salaried eccentrics'. That is not a description anyone would apply to his friend and colleague Charles Denis (C.D.) Hamilton, my predecessor as editor of *The Sunday Times* for six years and my chairman and editor-in-chief of Times Newspapers for fourteen years. Far from eccentric, 'C.D.' appears to be the acme of convention. He has moved all his adult life in exalted circles, the confidant of Field Marshal Montgomery, the friend of Harold Macmillan and of Louis Mountbatten. His dress and style are reminiscent of the younger Anthony Eden and his manner is altogether restrained and diplomatic. Conversation he seems to regard as a courtesy, something not to be ruffled by argument or opinion. That is the first of many contradictions in him. His aura discourages what he most relishes: the provocations of talent and youth. He recruited and promoted at *The Sunday Times* an eccentrically varied group of young people and gave them creative freedom. When I arrived in 1966, Godfrey Smith, Michael Rand, Nicholas Tomalin, Peter Wilsher, Ron Hall, Bruce Page, Mark Boxer, Hugo Young, John Barry, Lewis Chester, Charles Raw, Cal McCrystal, Stephen Aris, David Leitch and Stephen Fay were already there. Their common denominator was that they were all certain to cock a snook at one convention or another.

The indispensable, elegant Hamilton, as Cyril Connolly described him, comes from a humble background. His father was an engineer in a steelworks and they lived in a terraced house in Middlesbrough, where he went to high school and started work at sixteen as a reporter on the *Evening Gazette*. His university, he was proud of saying, was the British Army. 'Leff, right, leff, right', he would command me sometimes, encouraging the double-quick marching step of the Durham Light Infantry he had led at Dunkirk. He led the DLI back to Normandy in 1945 and through the charred hedges of the Bessin as the commander of the 11th battalion. He won a DSO for bravery. He was a Colonel at twenty-five and an acting Brigadier. The story goes that he raided other units for the best men. I believe it. He did the same thing in journalism. He was only twenty-eight when Lord Kemsley made him editorial director of the Kemsley group with a seat on the board. Kemsley was editor-in-chief of *The Sunday Times* and his editor was H.V. (Harry) Hodson, a Fellow of All Souls, whom Hamilton succeeded in the second year of Thomson's acquisition. 'He's a fellow that doesn't display himself,' Thomson said of Hamilton, 'but I reckon he's the best man for the job.'

Hamilton brought to *The Sunday Times* first of all a talent for delegation and a battlefield commitment to personal loyalty. But there were other elements to his personality and style. He was a King's Scout: 'Have you done your good deed for the day, Harold?' A consoling note to someone in misfortune would satisfy him as much as a scoop. He valued civility and discretion. Here is a memo of his to me during my first months as editor:

> Lord Trevelyan, whom I respect more than any other ex-diplomat, told me last week that suddenly this year the *Observer* was doing a better job on foreign affairs, particularly European and Russian, and that our regular and former deep coverage of the USA had been curtailed. I would like to get a researcher to look at this, but I will only do it with your knowledge. Perhaps we should compare the *Sunday Telegraph* as well. Strangely enough Harold Macmillan mentioned a similar thing three weeks ago. I am, as you know, extremely happy at the general run of events at *The Sunday Times*. It is an excellent, forceful paper. From every point of view we must watch we don't lose first place as an interpreter of serious events, or overdo the sex.

The man of action was rarely displayed, however. Hamilton was frequently absent on inward journeys, presenting a withdrawn, introspective persona. Young men arriving briskly for interview were disconcerted by his long silences. Later, after they had babbled away, they thought it was a device to catch them out. But it was natural, not tactical; he did it with his family, with everyone. Harold Macmillan remarked upon it; so did his fellow commanders in the war. Hamilton the CO was noted for long, awkward silences before delivering a disciplinary judgement. He was credited with always getting it right, but he had to brood on his intuitions first. Over the telephone his pauses would run into minutes. He fretted a great deal, skirting the edges of a decision, sniffing the air, advancing and retreating. But his silences were also the mark of a dreamer. He had visions of advances in public taste that newspapers might nurture. It was he who, as a trustee of the British Museum and editor-in-chief of Times Newspapers, brought the great Tutankhamun and Chinese exhibitions to London. He was knighted in 1976, but agonized before accepting. He disapproved strongly of newspapermen who accepted political rewards, fearing it would compromise their in-dependence. In the end he accepted the honour for services to the arts.

It was Hamilton who brought me to London as his chief assistant and later managing editor when I was thirty-seven. I had been editor of *The Northern Echo* for nearly five years, sitting in the chair of the great nineteenth-century editor-campaigner W.T. Stead. I could see Stead's letter accepting his appointment still standing framed on a bookcase: 'What a marvellous opportunity for attacking the devil!' Like Hamilton, I began in newspapers at the age of sixteen. (I was a reporter on a Lancashire weekly newspaper.) After the RAF and Durham University, I joined the *Manchester Evening News*, becoming a leader writer and assistant editor. A Harkness Fellowship allowed me to study foreign policy for two years in the United States at Chicago and Stanford universities: while there I also worked on American newspapers and filed reports for *The Guardian*. Hamilton had noticed a prolonged campaign I was undertaking as editor of *The Northern Echo* for an official inquiry into the hanging of Timothy Evans for the mass murders committed by John Christie. At the time the country was debating the issue of whether to abolish capital punishment. I had been in London to see Chuter Ede, the Home Secretary who had signed Evans's death warrant. 'I did it on the best advice,' he told me. 'We hanged the wrong man.' Our campaign had become national news with huge support in Parliament. I had the pleasure of writing its conclusion for Hamilton's *Sunday Times:* a Royal pardon for Timothy Evans and the abolition of the death penalty.

After a year, I was appointed editor. The other principal candidate for the editorship, Frank Giles, the foreign editor, became my deputy. He is a graceful and cultivated man, educated at Wellington School, a history scholar at Brasenose College, Oxford, bilingual in French, fluent in Italian, and a biographer of Henri de Blowitz, *Prince of Journalists*. He had been Ernest Bevin's private secretary at the Foreign Office and served in Moscow with Sir Archibald Clark Kerr. Some of the new young Turks at *The Sunday Times* regarded his debonair style with suspicion, comparing him to the actor Ian Carmichael. But he was a steadfast and calming influence on the paper, and remained my deputy for fourteen years. *The Sunday Times* I inherited in 1967 at the age of thirty-eight was vivid with personality and excitement. We held our conferences in the office designed by Snowdon for Hamilton as an intimate book-lined drawing-room with sofas, silk cushions and an Eames chair. The paper was sustained in its glittering artistic and literary traditions by Cyril Connolly, Raymond Mortimer, Leonard Russell, J.W. Lambert, Dilys Powell, Desmond Shawe-Taylor, Richard Buckle, Harold Hobson and Maurice Wiggin. I brought in John Carey, Claire Tomalin, David Cairns, James Fenton, John Mortimer, Alan Brien, Russell Davies, Jonathan Raban and Julian Barnes. Hamilton had begun the tradition of lengthy book serializations, beginning with Montgomery's memoirs. Godfrey Smith was the editor of the colour magazine. He sprang from his bath one morning with the idea of running sections of the magazine which could be collected into a book: our first partwork was 'A Thousand Makers of the 20th Century'. I was able to develop the paper's adventurous authority in foreign reporting with Nicholas Tomalin (who was killed by a Syrian rocket in the Yom Kippur war), Philip Jacobson, Murray Sayle, David Blundy, Ian Jack, Antony Terry, David Leitch and David Holden (who was murdered in Cairo by espionage agents).

The Insight unit was then just three reporters in a tiny office with a researcher (Parin Janmohamed) who had mainly been writing short background features, but they had also begun to explore investigative reporting with help on the nature of legal proof from a new *Sunday Times* lawyer, James Evans. In the 'bogus Beaujolais' story, they exposed how false labels were put on cheap wine; in the story of 'the Chippendale commode', they proved the existence of antique dealers' rings; and they had, most ambitiously, written 6,000 words on the Profumo scandal. Among my ambitions for the paper, I wanted to develop the Insight unit, and reflect W.T. Stead's 'governing functions' of the press – its 'argus-eyed power of inspection'. Ron Hall was the editor of Insight; educated at Pembroke College, Cambridge, and the *Daily Mirror*, he was a highly sceptical man who had already created a sensation with his story of unscrupulous landlords in 'The Life and Times of Peter Rachman'. His deputy was Bruce Page, an Australian of voracious intellect who had learned his craft in Melbourne with Adrian Deamer (later sacked by Rupert Murdoch as editor of *The Australian*). I soon added another Australian, Phillip Knightley, who was to become celebrated in 1981 for exposing that Britain's richest family, the Vesteys, paid no tax on income running into millions of pounds, and a wily and fertile former army officer and antique dealer, Colin Simpson. Hall burned on a slow fuse; Page, who was to succeed him, was eager to slay dragons. Hall, the Cambridge man, camouflaged intellect with an air of boredom; Page called on Machiavelli, Marx, Coleridge and Keynes with all the vehemence of the autodidact. It was Page I worked with on the first big Insight investigation after I joined the paper – the bogus car insurance company of Emil Savundra – and it was Page who was to spearhead the major investigations of the next decade. Savundra was my first brush with the law on *The Sunday Times*. We were rebuked from the bench for prejudicing his trial – at a time when he had not even been charged.

When Denis Hamilton became editor-in-chief of *The Times* and *Sunday Times*, he described his relationship to the individual editors in the words of Bagehot: to 'advise, encourage and perhaps warn'. In all my years with Hamilton, he never deviated from Bagehot. He believed, as Thomson did, in the independence of editors. 'You'll have total freedom with Roy,' he told me, and then added, 'so long as you don't attack the Queen.'

It was therefore permissible to take on Her Majesty's Government. The challenge to the Government we made in publishing the diaries of Richard Crossman was to the convention, regarded for decades by all governments as having the force of law, that Cabinet Ministers must submit to official censorship if they wished to publish a documented account of their experiences within thirty years. Crossman was in the Labour Cabinet from 1964 to 1970. He had an observant eye and a relish for biting personal comment and gossip. He was also a compulsive communicator, a former Oxford don with an obsessive interest in the British constitution, and he analysed its working as he operated within it. His diaries were not exciting because of scoops and stories, though they were 'a good read', but because they realized his ambition to show how the British system of government really works in practice, for good and for ill. The mass of detail of Prime Ministerial and Cabinet manoeuvres and Ministers' arguments with civil servants showed the extent to which the doctrine of collective responsibility is a mask for Cabinet ignorance and impotence. Such is the power of the permanent officials that a Minister without the backing of the Prime Minister or Chancellor cannot hope to appeal against an interdepartmental paper produced by civil servants. And a much-debated constitutional change of significance had indeed taken place. The Prime Minister is not first among equals. He (or she) has become all-powerful. Or, as Crossman put it in conversation: 'He can now snuff out an opponent in his own party more easily than any Soviet leader can demote or dismiss anyone opposed to him.'

It was this sense of seeing the political machine exposed with all its pulleys and levers and clanking parts which I found fascinating when I took a proof of the first volume of Crossman's diaries with me on a holiday in August 1974. He had asked my view on two draft chapters while he was alive, worried about criticism that he was going into too much detail. I had urged him on. I was thrilled with the result. The

volume covered the years 1964-6. There was a revealing account of how
the Cabinet dealt with the economic crisis of July 1966, but the unique
accomplishment was the picture it gave of what it was like to be a
Cabinet Minister in the 1960s. It was unthinkable that the diaries might
be suppressed or truncated. Walking on the Scottish moors, I conceived
a notion of how they might break through a series of barriers already
erected against them. Of course I knew the political gossip would cause a
stir and increase the sales of *The Sunday Times*, and I had no objection to
that, but the book had more enduring value. If we could reflect the full
range of the diaries by publishing a great deal of them in proper sequence,
resisting the temptation to go for all the juicy bits, we would show their
true nature as being one of great seriousness. That would be worth doing
in itself, but it would also make it harder for the Government to
suggest state secrets were at risk. Crossman was his own best advocate.

The Cabinet Office was the censor the diaries had to get past, the
agent of the power of the Prime Minister and of ministerial protocol.
Crossman had died on 5 April 1974. On 28 April I had announced in
The Sunday Times that we would serialize the first volume of his diaries
in the autumn, when it was to be published jointly by Jonathan Cape
and Hamish Hamilton. The Cabinet Secretary, Sir John Hunt, sent a
letter at once to Dr Janet Morgan, the Oxford historian who had been
Crossman's editorial assistant. 'Like many other people I am looking
forward to reading Dick Crossman's Diaries,' he wrote. 'But I was a
little surprised at the report in *The Sunday Times* ... Mr Crossman
recognized the need to submit the manuscript to us. I trust that you (and/
or his executors) will submit for scrutiny the text which it is proposed to
publish.' Crossman had chosen three literary executors: his wife Anne
and two friends, Michael Foot and Graham Greene. Greene was also the
managing director of Jonathan Cape, the co-publisher. They sent Hunt
proofs of the book on 10 June and on 21 June were summoned to his
splendid office looking over the Prime Minister's garden. They were met
with a simple pronouncement: the diaries could not be published for
thirty years. Excision would not do. The diaries were riddled with
detailed accounts of Cabinet and Cabinet committee meetings, and
accounts of the advice of senior civil servants. Publication would destroy
the mutual trust and confidence on which the British system of government was based.

It was deadlock; it was a case for Goodman. Graham Greene felt sure
that Lord Goodman, Britain's most famous conciliator and also, use-
fully, Prime Minister Harold Wilson's own lawyer, would be able to find
a way out. Hunt was indeed persuaded to relent on his outright rejection
of the whole book. He agreed to consider an edited version; in return
Goodman promised that the literary executors would give fourteen days'

notice of any intention to publish, plenty of time for Hunt to secure a court injunction banning publication. It was at this point that *The Sunday Times*, as owner of the serial rights, was brought into the affair. It was a bold decision by the executors. They were under no obligation to involve us; we had serial rights only when the book was 'ready' for publication. The key figure was Greene in his triple role as friend of Crossman, executor and the leader in the publishing arrangement with Hamish Hamilton. At his suggestion I was invited to Goodman's office on 1 July and shown a sample of the kind of cuts they thought were necessary to appease Hunt. As he guessed I would be, I was dismayed. But the gulf between Crossman and what Hunt would approve was even greater. The eunuch version was sent to Hunt on 6 August and rejected in September. Goodman despondently recounted what had happened. 'Well,' said an exasperated Goodman to Hunt, 'what *can* we say? Can we say that Crossman sat at this Cabinet table and looked out at St James's Park?' Hunt reflected. 'Yes,' he said finally, 'provided you don't indicate who else was sitting with him.'

All accounts of Cabinet meetings, all advice by civil servants and policy discussions were taboo, or as Hunt preferred to put it, they fell within forbidden 'parameters'. Ministers and civil servants, he argued, would not talk frankly if they knew their views would sooner rather than later become public knowledge. It was a claim and an argument that would be unthinkable in the United States where Presidents and Secretaries rapidly and in detail account for their period in office. But Crossman's executors were stymied. Lord Lloyd of Hampstead, a noted constitutional lawyer, and Brian Neill Q.C. acting for Times Newspapers said proceedings under the Official Secrets Act were sure to succeed in stopping or punishing publication. So did our *Sunday Times* lawyers. And Goodman, as part of his fourteen-day deal with Hunt, had said he would tell him if *The Sunday Times* had any plans to publish Crossman.

That was just what I had in mind. The only way out of the impasse, I concluded on my holiday, was to get into a position where *The Sunday Times*, exploiting the swiftness of newspaper publishing, was free to take the Government by surprise. This was tricky. Crossman's third literary executor, Michael Foot, had become a Minister. Crossman had chosen Foot because he thought that as a journalist he would be passionate for publication. He was not. His reverence for the House of Commons and Cabinet government was greater. He was honourably trying to do his duty. 'I promised Dick,' he said. But I did not want to embarrass him as a Minister or complicate matters, so I took only Anne Crossman and Greene to separate lunches. They, too, were bound by the promise to Hunt, so what I put obliquely to Anne and rather more directly to Greene was that there might just possibly come a moment when, without being asked their permission, they would wake up to find the diaries in *The Sunday Times* and, if that were to happen, it would be intended to help book publication. Of course, they should understand I had no such intention at present and that I preferred to seek the agreement of the Cabinet Secretary, as they had, to edited extracts. . . .

We went ahead at *The Sunday Times* producing a second eunuch to show to Hunt. He said he would consider our version if I gave him fourteen days' notice of any intention to publish, as Goodman had done. I refused, saying I was legally bound to the executors, who were in turn still bound by their undertaking to him. I knew our editing exercise was doomed from the start. The purpose was to show we had tried. I was already preparing for a legal battle. I mounted an elaborate exercise with John Barry, a former Insight editor, to justify publication by exploring the precedents back to Lloyd George and in particular by comparing Crossman's diary in exhaustive detail with Harold Wilson's approved memoir of the same period. All I needed was the opportunity and it came when I reported to the executors that Hunt had rejected the *Sunday Times* editing of the diaries; he had budged not an inch. We all of us assembled in a small committee room at the Commons – Anne Crossman, Foot, Greene, Goodman, with Denis Hamilton, our lawyers and John Barry. It was a long and tense meeting. Foot proposed they should simply tell Hunt they were going ahead. It was bold but fatal to my secret plans. It was sure to provoke an injunction before the public had any idea what Crossman represented; and on the legal advice we had, the book was sure to be banned for thirty years. It was Goodman who came to the rescue with the proposal that *The Sunday Times* should be left to talk to Hunt without having to come back to the executors. As soon as Hunt heard of this, he wrote to warn me that 'in certain circumstances the matter would pass out of my hands'. He concluded: 'I have no alternative to requiring of you an undertaking that *The Sunday Times* will not publish any extracts from the Crossman Diary which have not been cleared with me without giving me at least seven clear days' notice, and I should like to have this by Monday, 27th January.' I received his letter on Thursday, 23 January. It was an interesting Friday and Saturday at *The Sunday Times*.

I could not have been more pleased with Hunt's letter. The form of his request gave me one weekend when I was free of commitments or legal restraint. That concentrated the mind. I had no doubt we should seize the opportunity to publish without warning and risk the consequences. This was not merely to challenge Hunt on Crossman or have an exciting scoop: it was to challenge the absolute faith in clandestine government which he faithfully represented. Britain had a record of bad decisions secretly arrived at. Margaret Gowing's history of nuclear development provided one staggering example. Concorde, again, was a project which would not have begun if full and informed public debate had preceded the decision. The account in Crossman of the 1966 economic crisis demonstrated vividly that nothing was gained by the secrecy and absence of informed debate on the real choices then between deflation and devaluation. None of the habits of mind which produced this preference for announcing, rather than debating, policy would be easily changed.

I told Denis Hamilton my plan to publish without permission or warning that weekend. I did not have to put my arguments in detail. We had discussed the general issues many times. I knew the way he had resisted the Government's attempt in 1966 to suppress a series of articles on the conduct of sterling policy and how Roy Thomson had refused to be nobbled. Hamilton called in James Evans, the senior lawyer in the company, and Antony Whitaker, the *Sunday Times* lawyer. Denis Hamilton had bought Crossman while he was editor, but he was uneasy. He wondered about the propriety of divulging detailed Cabinet discussions. He objected (as I did) to Crossman's critical identification of minor civil servants. James Evans pitched in with the view that prosecution was likely. As Michael Foot had done, he suggested we might seek a judge's ruling. I said it would be intolerable to give the courts an opportunity to reinforce the already unacceptable tendency to impose prior restraint on publication of various kinds. At this point Hamilton went out for a few minutes. 'For heaven's sake, don't say any more,' I hissed at James Evans, dousing him with the frustration of months of manoeuvre. When Hamilton came back, Evans allowed Antony Whitaker to take up the argument. Whitaker was in favour of publication. Crossman ineradicably in print would help us more in any future trial than Crossman the vague menace to the peace of the realm.

'Are you in a position to defend the case?' Hamilton asked me.

I told him of all the preparations we had made. There was one of those long pauses for which he was celebrated. 'Well, go ahead,' he said, and left at once for Canterbury Cathedral. I thought that was overdoing it a bit. I saw in the next day's *Times* that he had been at the enthronement of the Archbishop.

So we published.

The Monday after that Saturday visit by Roy Thomson and his son to *The Sunday Times*, the Attorney-General, amid general outcry, pondered an immediate prosecution. I had begun the launch in a way which would have enabled the law officers and Government to avoid such a public confrontation. I had not announced in the paper that we were defying the Government. I wrote a paragraph of introduction to our Crossman pages, saying truthfully that the extracts 'have been seen by the Cabinet Office and their views taken into account'. It gave them an opportunity to save face and for us to go ahead with serialization by stealth. Instead, they let it be known that a prosecution had not been ruled out. Then I had a call at my home from the Cabinet Secretary, Sir John Hunt: 'Look, I don't want to fall out with you, could I see your next extract?' I did not want a trial so soon with only one week of Crossman in the open. I agreed on the explicit understanding that the final right of decision each week was mine. With great courtesy Hunt asked to see our Crossman extracts for weeks ahead. With great regret I explained that this was impractical.

The next nine weeks of our serialization were an extraordinary tactical contest. Week by week I sent Hunt more material than I could possibly publish. Ticking away in the bulk of it were paragraphs of forbidden material. When he identified and challenged five of them I would with-hold two and publish three. In early extracts of Cabinet meetings I would include Crossman's record of a division of opinion, but keep out the names, deleting, for instance, 'I suspect Jim Callaghan had done a great deal of quiet lobbying. On my side I had George Brown, the Lord Chancellor, Frank Cousins, Fred Peart and Jim Griffiths, but very little other support.' But the week after that I would publish names. The telex lines were hot between London and Ottawa, Washington and Moscow as Hunt accompanied the Prime Minister on official visits and tried to control what we were doing. 'There are a number of passages which cause me concern and which I must ask you to exclude or amend....'

I deleted one of four accounts of Cabinet meetings, amended another and for the first time without amendment printed two others recording detailed Cabinet discussions on immigration policy and public expenditure. This was a calculated risk. It produced a letter from the Treasury Solicitor:

> I am writing to you on the instructions of the Attorney-General ... Under the headings of 'July 8', 'July 17', and 'July 20', *The Sunday Times* published in detail the late Mr Crossman's accounts of what occurred and what was said during meetings of the Cabinet. The Attorney-General regards publication of such accounts as being contrary to the public interest. The Attorney-General has instructed me to inform you that if the *Sunday Times* should again include passages from the *Diaries* which include similar details proceedings for an injunction may be taken against Times Newspapers Ltd without further notice.

It was my turn to retreat. I aimed to publish nine extracts in chronological order and there were four more before we reached Crossman's riveting account of the July 1966 economic crisis. Hunt objected to six passages in the fifth extract. I deleted four and amended two. The following week I was less conciliatory. I spent hours in my office with Antony Whitaker, the legal adviser, and John Barry, going line by line through Crossman, debating how far we might go. On 10 March we reached our goal and over Hunt's protests *The Sunday Times* published without any editing at all Crossman's full account of the crisis Cabinet. By the end of the series we had broken every single parameter – and given the public the right to judge.

We had published nearly 100,000 words. I thought we had secured full release for the unexpurgated diaries to be published but as soon as the book was announced the Attorney-General moved to ban it by court order. Having let us go free, he was determined to block the publisher and executors. They decided to fight and risk the heavy legal costs of doing so. I could not see our allies singled out like this and I contrived a way to get us into court. The following week I ran unpublished Crossman material without showing it to the Cabinet Office and I exploited the work we had long prepared comparing the Wilson and Crossman versions of the same event. Hugo Young and John Barry interviewed other Ministers in case studies of decisions on pensions and race. The Ministers' recollections differed in some respects from both Crossman and Wilson, an emphatic reminder I thought of the value of free publication. I announced that more case studies would follow. This time I was sure the Attorney-General would act. The Ministers we interviewed were adding to the challenge to the Hunt parameters. I had a substitute page ready for the presses with big white spaces saying: 'The extract from the Crossman diaries which was to have appeared at this point has had to be deleted following an injunction granted last night by a High Court judge as a result of an application by the Attorney-General.'

This time there were no late-night telephone calls from the Treasury Solicitor but two days after publication our *Sunday Times* lawyer, Antony Whitaker, announced: 'They're going for an injunction to stop us doing any more.' I shocked him with a cheer. If we could win the court battle, we would not only stop censorship of the book but constrain Government secrecy.

However, when we went along to the law courts in the Strand, we found that the Attorney-General's writ went a great deal further than Crossman's diaries. In an attempt to stop us interviewing Ministers, it claimed a power for the Cabinet Secretary to scrutinize and censor the reporting of any discussions, past or present, where this reporting revealed how policy was being formed or executed. This was a restriction that guaranteed all the enlightenment afforded a diligent reader of the Albanian *People's Daily*. We learned that these extravagant extensions had been written in at the last moment not by Hunt or the Attorney-General, but spontaneously by lawyers on the case. 'That's sure to get thrown out,' I whispered to our side. But Mr Justice Ackner on 26 June granted in full an injunction which, for a brief period, prohibited contemporary political reporting as well as the Crossman diaries. On appeal, we got this all-embracing injunction reduced to the Crossman diaries provided we did not publish further extracts before a full trial took place. The newspaper and the executors became joint defendants. We had one month, till the end of July, to prepare. All our early work now came to fruition, though it remained a prodigious task for lawyers, newspaper and executors: we analysed more than 300 sets of memoirs and other books to plot the way the parameters had been applied in the past, if at all, to Lloyd George, Winston Churchill, Anthony Eden, Harold Macmillan and Harold Wilson, and assorted Field Marshals. We sought out affidavits from scores of scholars, lawyers and former Cabinet Ministers who would testify for Crossman. Hamilton and Thomson recognized it would be costly. We were determined to go all the way to the House of Lords if necessary, which would cost a minimum of £100,000.

The Chief Justice, Lord Widgery, took the trial. It had obvious echoes of the Pentagon Papers, though in our case nothing had been stolen. To everyone's surprise, the Attorney-General did not wheel on the howitzer of the Official Secrets Act, which would have meant a criminal trial with a jury. He appealed for Crossman to be banned in the public interest on grounds of an arcane law of confidence. It is unheard of in the rest of the world, but for fifteen years it was a darkening shadow across my path and its bizarre outline had better be sketched. The law of confidence was originally invented to stop a man called Strange publishing a catalogue of privately printed etchings made by Queen Victoria and Prince Albert. It then developed over such great issues as to whether it was Peter Pan Manufacturing Corporation or Corsets Silhouette Ltd which invented a bra cup. Sitting in the High Court in 1975 and hearing the Attorney-General solemnly cite these trade cases in support of the suppression of Crossman was disorienting. How could bras and glue and patent medicine have any relevance to the political issues at stake in the trial? The bridge was made in 1967, when a judge extended confidence beyond commercial secrets and into private rights. An injunction then was granted to prevent the Duke of Argyll revealing, in a Sunday newspaper, what it was like to be married to the Duchess. The Attorney-General now sought another leap forward to extend confidence from marital to public affairs, i.e. from the private life of a duchess to the conduct of a government. We argued that the growth of the role of the state and the power of the bureaucracy had been accompanied by an increase in secrecy, and we fought the law of confidence as an irrelevant vulgarity.

Would Widgery buy it? Everyone was in court to find out after a two-month recess, Hunt affably across the aisle from Anne Crossman, Graham Greene and me. It was a cliff-hanger. Not until the last few minutes of his long judgment did he tell us. Yes, confidence could apply to government. No, the first volume of the diaries would not be banned. Everything in it could be published. 'I cannot believe', said Widgery, 'that the publication at this interval of anything in Volume I would inhibit free discussion in the Cabinet of today even though the individuals involved are the same and the national problems have a distressing similarity with those of a decade ago.'

It was a bigger victory than I appreciated at the time. We were caught on Widgery's fork. He extended the law of confidence into public affairs, but volume one of the Crossman diaries could be published without even one of the cuts the Cabinet Secretary had been demanding. The extension of confidence was a scaffolding erected on a stage bare of legal precedent. Widgery, having put it there, chose not to use it; I thought others might. None the less, the judgment destroyed the principle of Cabinet secrecy and it curbed the Cabinet Secretary's power. Shortly afterwards the Government accepted the recommendation of a committee of inquiry, to which I gave evidence, not to regulate ministerial memoirs by statute. It was left, basically, to the sense of obligation of a Minister with no possibility of common-law restriction after fifteen years.

So it was that *The Sunday Times* defeated one of the many inter- ferences with open democratic government in Britain. The Crossman case was a landmark. His further volumes and many other political memoirs have been freely published since. I was exhilarated by what we had done, but depressed by how many people thought it was tasteless and dangerous for people to know what is going on. We had no great support. 'You've done a terrible thing,' one political journalist told me, looking over his shoulder for the barricades in the streets. Several news- paper editorials supported suppression. Fewer than a handful of MPs took an interest. John Griffith observed in the *New Statesman*:

> Executive secrecy was fought out in the courts amid an overwhelming and deafening silence from the politicians in and out of Westminster ... Richard Crossman was trying deliberately to break the oligarchy of political power. Nothing in recent times demonstrates more conclusively the decline in the power of the House of Commons than the failure of its Members to support the most significant constitutional protest of our generation.

However, change did flow from the Crossman case and more from others which feature in this part of my book where journalism ran into conflict with arbitrary power. The Thalidomide victims' families won redress after a decade; the cause of the DC-10 air disaster was finally exposed. But the legal and political institutions which should have prevented such ills not only allowed them to happen: they were active in preventing redress. The law failed the Thalidomide families and it nearly defeated *The Sunday Times* when it tried to come to their assistance. The DC-10 families were properly compensated only because they were able to sue in the United States; and we were able to shed light on the origins of the disaster only because America is a more open society than ours. I believe that the press in Britain failed for a generation effectively to challenge extensions of corporate and executive power which produced an erosion of human rights; and that the courts in Britain, where there is no Bill of Rights, have always been concerned to enforce property rights above personal rights. In a political democracy it is the cellular changes which matter – the barely perceptible accretion of case law and the careless application of its makeshift principles, the seduction of public temper, the effrontery that goes unchallenged or unchecked until finally it becomes an accepted custom. Post-war journalism in Britain was ignorant of this trend, its horizons limited. The popular press might occasionally cause a fuss by running a political campaign or more often by bad taste and intrusion into privacy. The popular Sunday press exposed vice and petty fraud. The quality press practised invertebrate journalism. It recycled speeches and statements, and delivered stylish opinions on routine public affairs. It mistook solemnity for seriousness, and by seriousness I mean a serious scrutiny of institutions and activities which affect the lives, safety and happiness of millions of people.

It did not ask questions. It criticized politicians, but it did not challenge so much as become an accomplice in the conventional jousts of opinion. It did not make an issue of anything that was not already an issue. At Kemsley's *Sunday Times* in the 1950s, before Thomson and Hamilton, it was a sackable offence to provoke a solicitor's letter. (Not until the 1960s did *The Sunday Times* deploy a full-time reporting staff.) In the 1970s the sequence of trials and injunctions in which *The Sunday Times* figured most prominently did not happen because journalism had suddenly decided to challenge the law and political institutions. It was because in the cases we investigated the law and the political institutions had failed the public. Who would have predicted that a commercial case to protect Queen Victoria's etchings in the nineteenth century would be used in the twentieth to suppress the diaries of a politician, the bribery of an MP, and the Thalidomide documents? Expert commissions recommended reform; Parliament was unwilling to respond. As Hugo Young of *The Sunday Times* noted in his study of the Crossman case, and as I found with a variety of investigations, the cult of discretion and secrecy had embedded itself so deeply in British life that even to challenge it was to shock.

2

DC-10 DISASTER

The worst air crash the world had then seen occurred just outside Paris on a fine Sunday. Ten minutes after taking off for London from Orly Airport, at 12.30 p.m. on 3 March 1974, a DC-10 airliner operated by Turkish Airlines plunged 11,500 feet into the Forest of Ermenonville at 497 miles per hour. There were 346 victims. They died violently because the DC-10 had a lie in it.

It took *The Sunday Times* nearly two years to trace that lie, and with it the disaster that should never have happened. It brought us into conflict in a California court with McDonnell Douglas which built the doomed DC-10, their Ship 29, and it raised the question, as did the Thalidomide tragedy, of how far the press should go on behalf of the citizen in challenging corporate power. It was piquant that in this contest with McDonnell Douglas they quoted the Thalidomide campaign as an example of our irresponsibility.

I could never have imagined these ramifications that Sunday, but I was sure at once it was a story we had to explore as thoroughly as any: how could a $17 million airliner so catastrophically fall out of a clear sky? Here was an aircraft built by perhaps the best-run aerospace company in America, drawing on the expertise of the vast American subcontracting industry representing the supremacy of American technology, and all approved by the Federal Aviation Administration. I did not know then, but there was an apex on bewilderment. In 1972 there had been a dress rehearsal for just such a disaster: how could its lessons have failed to save Ship 29 in 1974?

When I heard the news from Paris I happened to be visiting a friend of Durham University days, Brian Scrivener, who was flying 707s across the Atlantic for British Airways: his questions multiplied my own. As it was Sunday we were not manning the office, but by the time I called the news editor, Del Mercer, at his home, he already had Antony Terry on his way to Ermenonville from our Paris office and Paul Eddy was flying out from London at his own suggestion. Eddy was to be the principal reporter on Ship 29 with someone not yet assigned, Elaine Potter. They made as complementary a couple as you could find. Potter is a Doctor of Philosophy of Oxford University; Eddy left school at 16. Potter, born in Durban, had had a little holiday-work experience on the *Rand Daily Mail* and ten months on the Kent *Messenger*. Eddy was the news room's most admired hard-news reporter. He learned his trade in three years on a small daily in Warwickshire, and another four years grafting as a freelance. I took him on to *The Sunday Times* when he kept coming in with a series of accurate aviation stories. Potter came by way of an introduction from the historian Max Beloff. She is fluent, vivacious, obviously determined. Eddy masks his street smartness and his feelings. When, in later months, the going became difficult he was animated by the memory of the smouldering forest where Ship 29 came down, but it was mostly a private emotion.

The early start was valuable, not so much for what could be learned in the rush and confusion, but for two important contacts. Eddy and Terry established a good working relationship first with the gendarmerie captain, Jacques Lannier, who was in charge at the site, and later in the week with Charles (Chuck) Miller, then head of the US Bureau of Aviation Safety, who flew out from Washington. Like most experts, Miller had an innate distaste for journalists and a fear of their demand for simple explanations. 'A bomb' was the explanation in several news-papers; the *Daily Telegraph* ran it for two days.

Eddy was helped here by the arrival of a third staffman, Patrick Forman. He is a pilot himself with an instrument rating on multi-engined planes and a solicitor. He returned to journalism after a spell doing investigations for the Consumer Council as chief legal adviser. Forman and Miller got on famously, talking about safe flying. Miller, reassured that we were not seeking instant answers, shared his suspicions with them in confidence. Gradually he also provided our first insights into the effect on the agencies concerned with air safety of President Nixon's attack on the power and independence of the federal civil service. There was an ambiguity in the role of the Federal Aviation Administration as both the promoter of the industry and also its policeman. Nixon's appointment in 1969 of John Shaffer as head of the FAA had skewed this dangerously. Whereas previously almost all the safety recommendations made by the National Transport Safety Board had been adopted by the FAA, by 1971 nearly half were being rejected. There was a political dimension to the crash of Ship 29 as well as an engineering failure.

The prime cause of the latter was soon established when one of the controllers at Orly replayed the video tape of the radar screen and noticed that a minute before the dot of Ship 29 disappeared a tiny sliver had broken from it. Nine miles from the crash they found the sliver in a field, a four-foot-square cargo door, and the bodies of six passengers who had been ejected from the plane while strapped to their seats.

By midweek it was possible to read what had happened: when the airliner climbed, the air pressure inside the fuselage was maintained as it decreased on the outside. At just over 11,500 feet the pressure differential was such that five tons of air pressed against the inside of the door. The latches, only partially secured, burst open; there was an outward rush of pressurized air so rapid as to resemble an explosion, and part of the passenger cabin floor collapsed, severing or jamming the control cables from the cockpit to the tail. The captain lost control over his rudders which help to steer the aircraft and had little control over the elevators which make it climb or descend.

It was possible to read about this because it is what happened to another DC-10 over Windsor, Ontario, on 12 June 1972, and by mid week we had the report of the inquiry into the Windsor accident. When that cargo door blew off, a coffin and the corpse it contained fell through the hole two miles to earth and a flight attendant could see the clouds rushing beneath her feet as she struggled to avoid following it. No lives were lost. The plane had only 67 passengers and by brilliant use of his engines Captain Bryce McCormick was able to regain partial control, descend and land at Detroit.

'They are supposed to have fixed that door,' said Chuck Miller in Paris. But when Lannier showed him Ship 29's cargo door it was at once clear that one of three modifications to the door latch system advised after Windsor, the fixing of a support plate to prevent faulty closure, had not been made. Back in London we were able to add to Miller's dismay. Freddie Laker had taken delivery of a DC-10 for Laker Airways and a reporter phoned in: 'There is definitely no support plate. But the paperwork from Douglas says the job was done.' Forman went off to examine aircraft cargo doors and came back saying that the DC-10 rigging reminded him of the man hearing the clock strike thirteen: 'It throws everything that has gone before into disbelief.'

It was clear it would take time to elucidate the mysteries, and to help cover the costs and justify the efforts I signed a contract for a book and engaged a television crew to make a documentary as we went along. Bruce Page was eager to take the inquiry into his special projects unit, which was sensible, and I asked the news room to release Paul Eddy 'for a few months' to work with Elaine Potter, who had played a key role in the Thalidomide inquiry.

There was a beneficial consequence of the Thalidomide campaign. During it I had invited to London two Los Angeles lawyers, James Butler and Bob Fry, whose firm had won a big settlement of an American Thalidomide case. In the week of the Paris crash Fry telephoned us to canvass the idea of Ship 29's families avoiding the Thalidomide ordeal by mounting their case for compensation in California, where the DC-10 was made. Of the 346 victims, 177 were British, 56 Turkish, 48 Japanese and 25 American, and the rest other nationalities. Many of the British passengers had been prominent in medicine, law, science, government and labour. Page got in touch with Mary Hope, the widow of one of the British victims, Francis Hope, Paris correspondent for *The Observer* and the *New Statesman*; I thought with sadness of the exhilarating high spirits of Francis when I had had lunch with him a few weeks previously. He was thirty-five. Almost two thirds of those who died were under forty. Mary Hope responded at once to Page's call. She was keen to file suit in the United States. She was incensed that the compensation for wrongful death in air travel everywhere except the United States was arbitrarily limited so that families stood to be devastated financially as well as emotionally. But she was a journalist herself, with the BBC, and she had another reason for preferring America: 'I want the truth to come out.' She believed the American courts were likely more quickly to compel more facts in an action for wrongful death.

Fry flew into London with Stuart Speiser, one of the men who first made that belief possible. Once an aerial crop duster in Florida and Cuba, Speiser founded the first lawyer-pilot law firm to contest cases of wrongful death. He has a passionate concern for the individual which is directed with great forensic ability; he helped Ralph Nader win his privacy action against General Motors. Less than four weeks after the crash the firm of Speiser, Krause and Madole, working in partnership with Jefferson, Butler and Fry, filed Mary Hope's claim in the Central District of California. It was a crucial move in the affair of Ship 29 and a brave action by Mary Hope. It made her the focus of attention. London is the international centre of the world's aviation insurance market. The lawyers for McDonnell Douglas and Lloyd's, the principal insurers of Douglas and Turkish Airlines, were trying to induce all the other families to settle in Britain with immediate cash offers. Speiser met dozens of English solicitors. He felt their chill of moral disapproval for the contingent fee system whereby Mary Hope would pay a proportion of damages to his firm and nothing if she lost. He did not conceal his criticism of English neglect of personal rights and the reverence for property rights: 'Your lawyers expect people to bear wrongful death bravely but develop a strong sense of justice for redress for a lost painting or an injured racehorse.' But the English solicitors were impressed by Speiser, the author of eighteen law books and a long way from the image of an ambulance chaser. Mary Hope's lead was followed by almost everyone, though with several other firms involved as well as Speiser's. Eventually, with the freer American attitude to public interest litigation and class actions, 339 further claims were consolidated under the title Hope *v.* McDonnell Douglas.

McDonnell Douglas and Lloyd's lawyers were not pleased with our role. On 24 March we published an analysis demonstrating how much better families would fare if their claims could be tried in the United States. Nobody took up the offer to settle out of court in Britain. We were accused of prejudice. What we had done publicly, as some other newspapers did, was disseminate information. Even so, I had no qualms after Thalidomide about our close relationship with the plaintiffs' American lawyers. The passengers in Ship 29 were in the same position as the unborn children whose mothers took a poisonous tranquillizer: wholly without guilt. It was possible to be impelled by a sense of their innocence and the plight of their families while respecting all the canons of fair and accurate journalism. We were eager to hear what McDonnell Douglas and Turkish Airlines had to say about the disaster. Our first ambition was to find out what had happened, but we never thought there would be a simple explanation.

The first question was why a DC-10 which was still in a McDonnell Douglas hangar when near-disaster occurred at Windsor was none the less delivered to Turkish Airlines six months later without modifications to the cargo-door lock which the makers themselves were recommending to the airlines. Three weeks after the crash John Brizendine, the president of the Douglas division, acknowledged that the work had not been done, but said the company's records showed it had been. It was, he said, 'a circumstance for which we do not yet have an explanation'. But the McDonnell Douglas line was to deflect criticism to other people. They had blamed a baggage-handler for Windsor. On 17 April Sanford McDonnell, the corporation's president, told his annual general meeting that the Paris crash had been caused by an 'illiterate' baggage-handler at Orly who had failed to close the door properly. We interviewed the man, Mahmoud Mahmoudi, literate but not an English-speaker, and satisfied ourselves he had done nothing wrong: one of the lethal weaknesses of the door was for it to appear to be locked when it was not. This is one of the defects the modifications after Windsor were supposed to have removed.

The second question was why these modifications were not made part of an Airworthiness Directive from the FAA, which would have had the force of federal law.

And, third, there was the question of how in the first place the risks of the cargo-door lock failing, and consequently of explosive decompression collapsing a floor, were overlooked in an industry with a record of safety and sophistication. Whatever the answers, all would have to be seen in a context which was the fierce competition for sales and for survival between McDonnell Douglas developing the DC-10, and Lockheed the TriStar, in the jumbo-jet market dominated by Boeing and the 747. Douglas needed to sell between 350 and 400 aircraft to break even.

This was the scale of inquiry planned that March. Bruce Page immersed himself in the technology of aircraft engineering in Britain and the United States; he spent time with Boeing in Seattle. Eddy practically lived with Lockheed in Los Angeles. Patrick Forman followed the service lives of DC-10s with other airlines and travelled on the flight deck of a surviving Turkish Airlines DC-10. But first Eddy and Potter took the questions to Washington. They were impressed, as all visiting journalists are, by the flow of information and the status of the press. Eddy attended hearings in the Senate and the House of Representatives and talked freely with the Senate investigators, Don Gray and Jim Kelly. 'They're so frank. No cold shoulders. I feel part of the human race,' he rang back. An answer of sorts emerged to the first question on Ship 29. After Windsor, Miller's bureau advised that the door and the vulnerable cabin floor should be modified. The Western regional officials of the FAA, who had approved the original designs, did then prepare Airworthiness Directives (ADs) for immediate action. But their chief, John Shaffer, overruled them. He reached a 'gentleman's agreement' with Jackson McGowen, then president of Douglas, that McGowen would fix his 'goddam plane'. All that happened was that Douglas and the airlines beefed up the electric wiring on the door; later Douglas sent out three service bulletins, among scores of others, which recommended more changes to the door-locking mechanism without in any way suggesting they were life or death matters. Eddy concluded that if the ADs had been issued, Ship 29, still then sitting in a McDonnell Douglas hangar, would not have crashed – but the grounding of all DC-10s for modification would have jeopardized the aircraft's commercial career. It was this which influenced Shaffer. He said he would 'never have sat around fat, dumb and happy' at the FAA if he had known aircraft were coming out of Douglas with lethal cargo doors; but the conclusion had to be that at the time he so identified with the industry he let this happen.

Eddy's expectation that Washington would answer the other questions on Ship 29 was short-lived. For all the comparative openness, and criticism of the FAA by the House, Congress did not persist. Watergate was on the boil, five months from Nixon's resignation. It did not help that the safety agencies had had their confidence shaken by the programme of Nixon's White House to make public servants more responsive. Later in the year Chuck Miller, an indiscreet critic of laxness, was forced out of the Bureau of Aviation Safety.

The search for truth moved west to the trial in Los Angeles. There it did not synchronize perfectly with the search for justice. The doughty Judge Pierson (Pete) Hall, then in his eightieth year, was asked by the defendants to seal all the internal documents they were producing to the court, so that they would remain secret at least until the end of the case. He agreed. He was not a friend of the industry. His first air-crash case took eight years to settle. He determined thereafter to 'do a lot of innovating' to speed things up. He was sensitive to the hardship delay could inflict on widows and children because his own father had died shortly after he was born and he had been brought up in an institution. He set rigorous schedules for the discovery of documents and settled eight other major cases in two years each. His hope in agreeing to seal the documents was that it would persuade the companies to reach an early settlement without a trial of liability which they were denying: McDonnell Douglas, Turkish Airlines, and the Convair division of General Dynamics, which made the fuselage, were all blaming each other. An infinity of argument seemed in prospect.

I understood Judge Hall's motive. But for us it was awkward. The informal understanding in London, following our assistance to Stuart Speiser and James Butler and Bob Fry, was that there would be an exchange of information. Speiser's firm represented most of the British families but somewhat under half the total. Half a dozen other law firms were involved. Judge Hall conscripted them into a committee. By no means all of the lawyers had the same enthusiasm for the participation of *The Sunday Times* in the discovery process even before the judge's ruling. The plaintiffs' various lawyers did not in any event easily find the harmony they required for them to act as a group. On one occasion a plaintiffs' lawyer objected to Potter reading a document and took it from her and all the other documents she had. Eddy and Potter worried about this. A certain tension was generated by the fact that everyone was on different floors of the same glass-fronted office block on Wilshire Boulevard – the lawyers for the plaintiffs and for the defence happened to share the same building and it was also agreed that pre-trial interrogations would take place here. One set of the thousands of documents was kept in the offices of Jefferson, Butler and Fry, who provided headquarters for all the plaintiffs' lawyers. A further set was in a room retained in the building for common access to the originals of the documents.

It was impossible to contemplate the possibility that the truth about Ermenonville lay in those mounting bundles of documents in two rooms but might never emerge if the issue of liability did not go to trial. Clearly, the plaintiffs' lawyers had their duty to obtain the best compensation, preferably without the anxiety, delay and expense of a trial. Clearly, *The Sunday Times* had a wider duty, which it had to try to discharge without hampering the plaintiffs' lawyers in any way. Eddy and Potter began copying every single document. I approved of their action. We engaged Mark Hurwitz of Hurwitz and Hurwitz, Orange, California, who was then defending an American reporter under pressure to disclose his sources in an article on the Manson murders. Hurwitz advised that we would not be acting illegally if we (a) did not publish during the case; (b) had legitimate access to where the documents were stored; (c) paid for our own copying; and (d) did not deprive the interested parties of their use. We met all these conditions. We had access to the building and we acquired a key to the official repository. In the evenings and at weekends and during adjournments Eddy and Potter took in suitcases, loaded them up and took the contents to a photocopying shop run at unusual hours by students from the University of California at Los Angeles. Exhibits that were too large to be copied were mounted on the wall of Eddy's apartment and photographed. They told no one in Los Angeles other than our lawyers what they were doing. They ensured that the exhibits were always back in place before they could be missed.

There is no doubt that if this activity had been known to McDonnell Douglas they would have asked Judge Hall to rule us in contempt of court. It is highly likely he would have done so. We were ourselves breaking no injunction. We had been party to no agreement. We had taken legal advice. We had no intention of publishing anything at this point. But the risk to me, the reporters and the company was serious, and we took it only because of the greater risk that the truth would never emerge. All the information in the documents would be revealed at a full trial, but if there was a settlement out of court the documents would stay sealed. That summer, as it happened, was when I was contesting in an English court the right of Distillers to suppress all the documents in the Thalidomide case, which we possessed. We lost and unhesitatingly obeyed the court ruling, and I would have unhesitatingly obeyed any similar ruling against *The Sunday Times* in a California court. Fortunately there was none. We were able to operate in a grey area, ready to justify our action and ready to face any consequences.

There were at least 50,000 pages to copy, and later ship to London. It was a huge task. It was also nerve-racking. One night Eddy carried two suitcases of documents to his car in the supposedly deserted car park beneath the building. He put them in the boot but the catch had jammed and his attempts to force it shut brought a security guard.

'Sir, can I help?'

'I'm having trouble with the catch.'

Fortunately for the project, the guard had no curiosity as to what was inside the boot; he merely tied it down.

There was never the slightest intention of rushing into print with anything we discovered on this exercise. Prudence apart, we wanted to see everything in context. That was why Page and Eddy had spent so much time with aircraft companies, to understand the engineering and the commercial and regulatory environment in which the documents were created. It was necessary, for instance, to be able to analyse the faults in the door and the successive modifications. The blueprints in the disclosure documents were important to this. They took us beyond the sketches that had appeared in technical aviation magazines. When the blueprints arrived in London, Page pinned them up on his office wall. Thorpe's of Gray's Inn Road made a working model for us.

The documents formed, as Stuart Speiser put it, the most minute legal examination of an aircraft history ever made. Potter forgot about the coyotes and snakes she could view from her temporary home in Benedict Canyon, Beverly Hills, as fairly early on she read a memorandum by F.D. (Dan) Applegate, the Director of Product Engineering of the Convair division of General Dynamics in San Diego, California. Convair were responsible for carrying out the detailed design of the fuselage of the DC-10 and its doors. This is the opening of what Applegate wrote on 27 June 1972, fifteen days after the graphic warning of Windsor:

Subject: DC-10 Future Accident Liability
The potential for long-term Convair liability on the DC-10 has caused me increasing concern for several reasons.
1. The fundamental safety of the cargo-door latching system has been progressively degraded since the program began in 1968.
2. The airplane demonstrated an inherent susceptibility to catastrophic failure when exposed to explosive decompression of the cargo compartment in 1970 ground tests.

Referring to Windsor, Applegate wrote: 'It is only chance that the aircraft was not lost. Douglas has again studied alternative corrective actions and appears to be applying more "Band-aids".'

He argued that the fundamental deficiency of the DC-10 was the liability of the cabin floor to collapse on explosive decompression which might be caused by sabotage, mid-air collision or other hazards in addition to the flawed cargo door. He observed that the 'fundamental failure mode' of the door was being discussed yet again by Douglas and Convair, and it appeared that Douglas was waiting and hoping for government direction or regulation in the hope of passing costs on to Convair or their customers. And there was this paragraph:

My only criticism of Douglas in this regard is that once this inherent weakness was demonstrated by the July 1970 test failure, they did not take immediate steps to correct it. It seems to me inevitable that, in the twenty years ahead of us, DC-10 cargo doors will come open and I would expect this to usually result in the loss of the airplane.

When I read this in London I felt more than ever justified in what we had done, and keenly concerned to know what had happened to the Applegate memorandum. Eddy and Potter found out. On 3 July 1972 there was a memorandum from Applegate's superior at Convair, J.B. Hurt. He did not take issue, he said, with the facts or the concern expressed, but he rejected an approach to Douglas: 'We have an interesting legal and moral problem,' he concluded, 'and I feel that any direct conversation on this subject with Douglas should be based on the assumption that as a result Convair may subsequently find itself in a position where it must assume all or a significant proportion of the costs that are involved.'

I was shaken by Hurt's resolution of the legal and moral problem, but the documents took one back and forth in degrees of culpability. In 1969, we found, Convair supplied Douglas with a Failure Mode and Effects Analysis (FMEA) which included warnings of sequences very similar to what happened over Windsor and outside Paris: 'Door will close and latch but will not safety lock.' Since, then, the certificate of airworthiness depended on the cargo door being fail-safe (when in fact it was positively dangerous), how did the new jumbo jet get through the inspection procedures? Douglas did not show the Convair analysis to the FAA nor reply to Convair. As for the FAA, we came to appreciate a central flaw: much of its inspection work is done by engineers it designates from within the manufacturing company. A Douglas engineer approved the cargo door for the company, changed into an FAA hat and approved it for its airworthiness certificate. The FAA told us it did not have the manpower to inspect every one of the thousands of parts and systems of a modern airliner. Of 42,950 conformity inspections on the DC-10 no fewer than 31,895 were carried out by Douglas employees.

Slowly the elements of the disaster fell into place. But crucially the documents did not explain how Ship 29 contained a lie, flying without modifications that McDonnell Douglas records said had been done. In September the first witnesses arrived on Wilshire Boulevard to give depositions. Eddy and Potter were eager to hear the testimony of John Brizendine on how far he had got with the mystery. Pre-trial depositions are given informally without the presence of court officials, though they are on oath and recorded. For Ship 29 the proceedings were held in the offices of Robert Packard, representing McDonnell Douglas, with lawyers for both sides sitting round a table with the witness. Potter walked in. The McDonnell Douglas lawyer faltered in his tracks when he saw her, then recovered: 'You are trespassing. I must ask you to leave.'

We could not leave it at that. In the Granada lecture, in London's Guildhall, which I had given – as it happened – the day after the Paris crash, I had characterized the British press as half-free by comparison with the American. But I was well aware that the American press maintained its superior freedoms only by constant vigilance. No American newspaper had the inside track that we had on the proceedings in Los Angeles; none had attempted to attend the deposition-taking. I told my friend Tim Hays, of the Riverside Press, California, then President of the American Society of Newspaper Editors, that we would pick up the challenge and accordingly on 12 September we filed a complaint in Judge Hall's court. We asked Judge Hall to grant us an injunction restraining McDonnell Douglas so that the pre-trial examination of witnesses would be open to the press. The plaintiffs' committee of lawyers backed us. Packard insisted on his territorial rights. When the court agent went to serve our summons, he accused him, too, of trespass: 'Get off the premises or I will call the police.'

This was the first time a British newspaper had attempted in this way to exert rights to information under the American constitution. I was not deterred by our alien status. It lies at the heart of American history to afford to aliens in the United States the freedoms of speech, press, religion, assembly and association afforded to citizens. My advice on pre-trial depositions was that several US courts had ruled they should be public; Stuart Speiser said that in aviation cases he had never known an American newspaper try to gain admission.

Judge Hall's court hardly rang with the clash of great constitutional principles when McDonnell Douglas contested our application. 'I'm going to get you today,' said the lawyer nominated by Lloyd's, James Fitzsimons, as he rapped the edge of the witness stand with a rolled-up copy of *The Sunday Times*. Judge Hall reprimanded him for being threatening. The man in the box was Robert Ducas, then President of Times Newspapers in America, who stood in for me for a four-hour cross-examination; I was heavily involved in London in negotiations on the Crossman diaries. The hearing went on for three days and was followed by written argument. All the British press was savaged by Fitzsimons for making the relatives think the streets of America are paved with gold. *The Sunday Times*, said Fitzsimons, was the prime leader. It was 'one of the evils standing at the door of a right to a fair trial'. It was notorious for trying to conduct trial by newspaper. It had been condemned for this by the House of Lords and found guilty of contempt of court in the Thalidomide case. Now it came to California to pass judgment on a case that belonged to an American jury. And it came into court with dirty hands. It had been doing deals and trade-offs with the plaintiffs' lawyers. With a dramatic flourish he produced a photocopy of a Telex message from Eddy to Don Madole, Speiser's Washington partner, and another sent to Elaine Potter, care of Jim Butler's office. The message Eddy gave Madole was from Patrick Forman, who had somehow managed to penetrate military-style security to listen to the flight deck recording of the last exchanges between Ship 29's crew;

it vividly confirmed what rear decompression did to the control of a DC-10.

We did not deny having passed information to the families' lawyers. Principally we argued along the lines of one of the leading cases 'that the widest possible dissemination of information from diverse and antagonistic sources is essential to the welfare of the public'. If the hearings were secret, an out-of-court settlement might result in the true cause of the disaster being obscured for ever. Robert Packard announced that if we won he would still refuse to allow the press to attend the hearings in his office. If pre-trial hearings were moved to another venue, he would refuse to produce McDonnell Douglas witnesses unless the court issued a contempt order. 'They're acting this way because they feel so guilty about what's in the evidence,' Jim Butler remarked. McDonnell Douglas made every effort to frustrate us. Two attorneys of the FAA who had agreed to continue discussions cancelled after an objection by McDonnell Douglas. Eddy and Potter became a little jumpy when Mark Hurwitz cheerfully told them: 'You've got to assume you're under surveillance. This case involves millions of dollars. You can get a phone tapped round here for $250.' They took to calling us only from public telephone booths. They were still copying and shipping documents – and by now these began to include written statements taken from the witnesses in the depositions.

This was, again, a grey and hazardous area with a ruling awaited on our right to attend the actual examinations. I was resolved not to publish anything which would prejudice our ability to tell the full story or which would damage the relatives. The test of the resolve came when confronted with the lie in Ship 29 – microfilm photographs of three stiff cardboard forms. Each of the forms described one of the critical modifications to the cargo latch system that McDonnell Douglas had agreed to do as part of the gentleman's agreement with Shaffer. Only one of them, meaningless by itself, was certainly done. Yet all three cardboard forms were stamped by five Douglas inspectors to certify that the modifications were executed, inspected and passed as airworthy on 18 July 1972.

Eddy and Potter read the secret testimony of three of the inspectors, Edward M. Evans, Henry C. Noriega and Shelby G. Newton, examined under oath. Not one of them could recall working on the cargo door of any DC-10 in 1972, none of them could recall working with the others at any time and they were all certain they could not have done so on 18 July. Noriega and Newton were working on other planes, only Evans could theoretically have been on Ship 29. Their stamps were personal to them, issued under strict security. They denied lending or losing them. They could not explain how they came to be affixed to fraudulent paper.

Elaine Potter, who had secured the names of the witnesses early on, tried to find the men to talk to them herself, especially Evans, who was also the only full-time inspector. There were no home addresses in any of the directories. She spent long hours drinking with the union bosses at Long Beach; finally she gave the job to a private detective in Los Angeles. He came up with their addresses within a few days. She went to see Evans, a stooped, studious man of twenty-nine who left home each day at 6.30 a.m., went to college after work and did not return home to his wife and small child until 10.30 p.m. Every day at 7 a.m. he would get an inspector's assignment and collect the relevant documents and his stamp. 'I kept my own stamp in my pocket all day and never let anyone use it.' He had nothing to add save bewilderment and depression.

John Brizendine's secret testimony over seven days and 1,500 pages shed no more light on the mystery. McDonnell Douglas lawyers told the other side that there had been an internal investigation but because it was conducted by qualified lawyers its results were privileged and need not be revealed in litigation. Brizendine was offhand: 'I don't recall what was ever determined precisely.' Steadfastly he refused to accept that his company was to blame. He could not deny that the support plate was missing, but he asserted as confidently as Turkish Airlines denied it that Turkish Airlines misrigged the locking device on the cargo door In such a way as to make it absurdly dangerous. As for taking heed of the terrible warning of Windsor, he thought it irrelevant beyond showing the DC-10 to fly very well.

'But McDonnell Douglas sent a special message to Captain McCormick congratulating him on his performance,' said an examining lawyer.

'I would also tell the guy who waxes the floor in my lobby that he has done a great job too,' Brizendine replied.

It was as well we were such good customers of the UCLA students' copying business. We failed to gain access to the interrogations. One of the plaintiffs' lawyers told us he had a conversation with the judge. He wanted to rule in our favour but he was worried that McDonnell Douglas would appeal and would also try to use the verdict to get him removed from the case. Both of these things would delay settlement of the relatives' claims. 'And I would be against you on those grounds, too,' the lawyer told us. 'Our first duty is to our clients.' Fortunately our nightly access to the documents made the conflict between truth and justice academic.

In May 1975 McDonnell Douglas, General Dynamics and Turkish Airlines gave in. After more argument $62 million was shared by a total of 1,122 claimants on behalf of 340 of the 346 victims. The specialist and technically expert lawyers had done a prodigious job. They and the American legal system gave innocent individuals a chance against powerful industrial and financial interests in a way barely aspired to in

Britain, a striking contrast with the Thalidomide débâcle and thousands of personal injury injustices.

But what of the truth Mary Hope sought? After every effort we never solved the mystery of the false records. Even in the more open American society there is a limit to what journalism can discover. The best guess is that it happened in a delivery panic at the end of 1972. Turkish Airlines ordered three DC-10s in September and insisted on having two before Christmas for the big numbers of Turkish workers travelling home from Western Europe (and also, it seems, for Turkey to have military air capacity handy for the trouble brewing between Turkey and Greece over Cyprus). In the rush to meet that order someone in McDonnell Douglas must have filled out the blanks on the records retroactively.

The settlement out of court ended any hope of testing that theory and placing the final personal responsibilities behind the corporate shield. Nobody could blame the relatives for settling when they did. Mary Hope thought just about enough had come out and she had a concern for plaintiffs poorer than herself. I had a moving letter from the widow of an eminent medical man killed in the crash. She wanted my advice on how to go on. 'I am not interested in compensation. I will do anything I can to bring a trial in order that the truth may be heard.' It was too much of a burden to impose on her or any of the victims. Politics and public opinion had to assume that wider responsibility.

For our part, we published *Destination Disaster* by Paul Eddy, Elaine Potter and Bruce Page; we serialized it and the articles were widely syndicated across the United States. I sent copies of the book to every member of Congress with a *Sunday Times* leader urging, among other things, a resumption of the Ship 29 inquiry. Congress did make some improvements. The National Transportation Safety Board became an independent agency; and in July 1975 the FAA ordered makers and airlines to modify every single jumbo jet, the 747s and the 1011s as well as the DC-10s, so as to prevent catastrophic floor collapse from any cause, at a cost of $60 million. But there was another DC-10 disaster at Chicago when an engine fell off, fatally disrupting not only control lines but communication systems in a way not possible on the Boeing 747. There was not the inquiry we would like to have seen into the risks of safety in the competitive pressures which produced three rival jumbo jets. And ambiguity remained in the role of the Federal Aviation Administration. These are still issues of world-wide importance, since nearly 80 per cent of the passenger aircraft in service in the West are of American origin. It is some reassurance that, in addition to federal regulation and a generally superb level of technical skill, there is in the United States a proper enforcement of personal as well as property rights and a recognition of the value of a free flow of information.

3
PHILBY

I had been editor of *The Sunday Times* for only two months in 1967 when I picked up an idea which plunged us into a conflict most starkly epitomized by this question: when is it right to suppress the truth on the grounds of national security? The investigation was the most intensive the paper had ever then undertaken. For eight months it focused the energies and intellects of many people on understanding the mind of one man and the institution he betrayed.

It started with a casual remark at lunch with Jeremy Isaacs, later to be the first head of Channel Four Television and at that time head of current affairs at Thames Television. How interesting it was, said Isaacs, that Guy Burgess and Donald Maclean, who spied for the Soviet Union, and 'that other man Philby', who defected, were all educated at Cambridge University in the early 1930s. When I got back to the office, I remarked to Bruce Page that we knew little about Philby. I had just regrouped Insight, under Page's control, so that the four reporters could concentrate full-time on complex inquiries instead of having to produce a page of short features weekly.

'Perhaps, if you trace the careers of all three, you'll find the man who recruited them while they were at Cambridge,' I told him. I added, by way of a spur, that I had heard Patrick Seale of *The Observer* was writing a book with Philby's third wife, Eleanor.

All that was known about Philby at the time was that he was a low-ranking diplomat and later a journalist who had defected to the Soviet Union ten years after resigning from the Foreign Service. I had a look at our library clippings on Harold Adrian Russell Philby, known more usually as Kim Philby. They showed that he first surfaced as a news subject in 1955, four years after the diplomats Burgess and Maclean fled to Moscow. Only then was an official report made on the affair. An MP suggested Philby might have been the 'third man' who tipped them off. Where he had got the idea from was then something of a mystery, though we solved it later. The Foreign Secretary, Harold Macmillan, cleared

Philby. He had been asked to resign from his diplomatic post, but, Macmillan added, 'I have no reasons to conclude that Mr Philby has at any time betrayed the interests of this country, or to identify him with the so-called third man, if indeed there was one.' Photographs and a television transcript of Philby's subsequent press conference revealed a polished, upper-class man with a stammer who captivated the reporters in his respectable grey, pin-stripe suit as an amused martyr of national security. It was too bad that he had put up his old Cambridge friend Burgess in his house in Washington just before Burgess fled with Maclean.

Our files contained a few articles about the Middle East that Philby had written for *The Observer* from Beirut. He had become a correspondent for both that newspaper and the *Economist* after leaving the Foreign Service. Early in 1963 he had vanished from Beirut, leaving a bewildered Eleanor Philby not knowing whether he was dead or alive. Six months later he had turned up in Moscow. There was a clip of Edward Heath, Lord Privy Seal, answering questions in the Commons. Yes, before his defection, Philby had confessed to having 'warned Maclean, through Burgess'. Despite the admission, it was a low-key affair. A one-time diplomat of humble status and journalist had, after all, helped his friend to escape and he had also had some earlier contacts with the Russians. He was considerably less important and interesting than the high-powered Maclean and the colourful Burgess. Or so it seemed.

This was the universal understanding at the time, hard though it is to realize in the light of the reality we exposed. We deduced early on that Philby had not been a diplomat like Burgess and Maclean but a member of the British Secret Intelligence Service (SIS, also referred to as MI6). This might make him considerably more important. Secrets, after all, would be his daily business, whereas Burgess and Maclean were mostly engaged in routine diplomatic work. So what had Philby done inside British intelligence? How long had he been there? What had gone wrong with our security services that they could let Burgess and Maclean escape, and harbour another defector of their own? I suggested that this should be our theme, with Philby as the human exemplar. We made a feasibility study of attempting to answer these questions and I said that Page could have more people when necessary. It became an all-absorbing, full-scale investigation only after two months – and the Six-Day War in the Middle East in June diverted energies for a time – but at its peak a total of eighteen *Sunday Times* reporters were at work in Britain, the United States and the Middle East.

Page was the animating genius. It appealed to something deep in his own character. Partly this was his Aussie contempt for the British establishment, a contempt the Philby story perfectly supported: 'We're dealing', he would say, 'with a lot of unemployable twerps selling off the old country to any old bidder.' Partly it was his own complex mind, which has continually exhibited a fascination with other people's duplicity, supposed or actual. He needed no urging to try to open the Chinese boxes of Philby's life. Early in the morning and late at night, ringed in cigar smoke, he was at his typewriter recording the notes of his own interviews, collating the work of others into a longer and longer 'state of knowledge' memorandum, turning hunches into hypotheses to test on me and on Hugo Young, Phillip Knightley, David Leitch and John Barry, his principal aides. Young brought a wealth of political contacts to the inquiry, and Knightley a talent for winning confidences, based on his unassuming nature and manifest integrity. But it could be disconcerting talking about the KGB when Knightley was around: he has an uncanny physical resemblance to Lenin.

It was a slow beginning. We wrote to Sir Stewart Menzies, who in 1939 took over as 'C', the head of SIS, and had retired to Wiltshire. He courteously declined to see us, but added, 'What a blackguard Philby was'. Intriguing. But how does one find the other SIS officers whose paths might have crossed the blackguard's? Page found a clue in the ordinary reference books. Various people who had been in Philby's ambit were in Who's Who as having been 'attached Foreign Office' or the more gnomic 'FO'. When Page checked these names against the official Foreign Office list of diplomats, they were not there. One had a picture of these intelligence officers, for that is what they were, pausing over the career section of their entry when they filled in the Who's Who form: 'Spying for HMG' hardly seemed right. Another typical clue would be an entry like: '1st Sec. Istanbul 1950–53. Retired 1958'. Five missing years.

David Leitch went to see Cyril Connolly, the writer and Sunday Times reviewer who had known Burgess and Maclean intimately and had written a book about them, The Missing Diplomats, in 1953. He pulled a copy from a glass cabinet; annotated in the margins were the names of his sources. He was delighted to be drawn into the chase of journalism. We went through all the other literature and that of wartime espionage abroad (SIS) and counter-espionage in Britain (MI5).

We began calling people. A number of them at once said, 'Sorry, Official Secrets Act', and put down the phone. Some talked happily and mostly irrelevantly about blowing up bridges for Special Operations Executive, or looking for Germans in haystacks for MI5. Those who had met Philby, the rising star in SIS bridging the gulf between the former Indian Army policemen and the influx of intellectuals, were impelled by curiosity, recalling his charming stammer. Others with more recent experiences would talk only in generalities. I became used to the expression of apology and depression worn by a reporter back from a fruitless day. The general pattern that emerged was that we learned nothing of the post-war period unless we knew something. 'What did you do?' or 'What did Philby do?' ended the interview. Areas where we displayed reasonable knowledge were 'in court', especially when we added some fresh item for our interviewee. Bits of information were denied and others corroborated, sometimes only implicitly. The fragments were carried into the next interview, where a little extra might be gleaned. It helped to be referred from one person to the next, or sometimes a dozen more. Scraps of insight accumulated. Another *Sunday Times* reviewer, Hugh Trevor-Roper (now Lord Dacre), the Oxford historian who had been in war-time intelligence, related a moment in a conversation with Philby. Trevor-Roper, like everyone else, had found him charming but detached. Then, one day over a drink, when they fell to discussing historical analysis, Philby abruptly and with great force declared: 'Of course, when it comes to historical analysis, there is nothing that compares with Marx's Eighteenth Brumaire of Louis Bonaparte.' The guard was swiftly restored. There was more to Philby than anyone had appreciated.

We built up a picture of a double life. David Leitch, who had been at Cambridge himself, went back to explore the Cambridge of the 1930s, the young ex-public-schoolboys in their flannel bags and tweed jackets cosseted by the college servants but inflamed, some of them, by Ramsay MacDonald's 'betrayal' of the working classes. Leitch returned with the story that Philby had been a vehement Marxist and after Cambridge rode his motorcycle to Vienna, racked by street fighting between the Left and the Fascists. Page called Eric Gedye, who had been in Vienna as a newspaperman when Philby was there in 1933–4, to find out what the young graduate had been up to. The answer was that he had helped to smuggle out Socialists and Communists, mixed with Communists and married one. But, when he came back to England in 1934, he gradually shed his left-wing opinions. He joined an upper-class pro-Nazi organization, and reported the Spanish Civil War from Franco's side for *The Times*. 'Look, here he is building a new identity,' said Page excitedly coming into my office with a photograph of Philby at a swastika-bedecked dinner of the Anglo-German Fellowship in 1936. 'He must have already been working for the Russians, recruited in Vienna, I bet.' Languid confirmation of long service was provided by a former Foreign Office man, a specialist in Anglican liturgy, whom John Barry saw in his apartment: 'Oh, dear,' he said, 'why does no one read our statements with the care with which we drafted them?' This was a reference to a line in Heath's 1963 statement which said that the British were 'now aware' that Philby had 'worked for the Soviet authorities *before* 1946' (italics added). In other words, they had known for some unspecified time that he was a Russian agent after 1946 and had then just discovered that Philby had been working for the Soviet Union before that, i.e. all along. This made the question of what he was doing in British intelligence from 1940 onwards more pressing, and we knew nothing beyond the war.

Leitch thought a way forward might be to ask a former colleague, Alun Gwynne Jones, the defence correspondent of *The Times* who had become Lord Chalfont and a Minister at the Foreign Office. He invited Leitch and Page to his room at the Foreign Office. 'You must stop your inquiries,' said Chalfont. 'There is the most monstrous danger here. You will be helping the enemy.' It was the first signal of the official campaign to kill the Philby story. I told Denis Hamilton about it and about the way I was tackling the inquiry. I could understand his blanching. He had a highly developed sense of patriotism. It would have been unnatural if he had not indulged in one of his long pauses and if I had not had to justify what we were doing, only a few months into my editorship.

'There's been a terrific cover-up,' I said. 'We don't know what it is, but there's something scandalous in the Philby affair. It may be as bad as Burgess and Maclean, and it's time the intelligence services got a shake-up.'

'But how can you be sure you won't help the Russians?' he asked.

'Well, we can't tell them more than Philby must have already told them. Denis, we're the ones in the dark.'

'And what about the Official Secrets Act?'

'Can't we judge the risks at the end?'

'Let me think about it.'

He came back to me a few days later. 'I can tell you I've seen the PM and the head of the Service in very great secrecy. I've told them that you are not a man who would want to damage his country. But I've seen too much slaughter in my life, Harold. Will you let them see a draft to make sure we don't put anyone at risk? All I've said is that you will consider representations.'

I said I would. None of us wanted to risk anyone's life by some unwitting reference. Hamilton said he had arranged that I should see Chalfont and also Sir Denis Greenhill, who was a deputy under-secretary at the Foreign Office and, I discovered later, the main link between the Foreign Office and SIS.

'But you must take great care in all this,' Hamilton cautioned. 'Say nothing to anyone. The Foreign Office is alarmed. It all needs very careful handling.'

I had a drink with Chalfont at the Garrick club. He was bland. I thought the Hamilton initiative meant that the Foreign Office would answer our questions. 'Afraid not,' said Chalfont, 'but we'll not stand in your way.' Greenhill left no doubt that, despite Hamilton's testimonial on my behalf and Chalfont's blandness, we were going to be opposed all along the line. Greenhill was then fifty-four, a man of contained vigour, muscled in his double-breasted pinstripe like an American football player and ready to block any run. He was not an orthodox Foreign Office man. His early schooling before Oxford University was at Bishop's Stortford, not Eton or Harrow. He had entered the Foreign Service in 1946, after serving as a Colonel in the Royal Engineers in the war, and had been in Washington running the Embassy's Middle East department while Philby and Burgess were there. Burgess had been foisted on the department just before his get-away, and Greenhill later remembered him* as an idle, shambling man with an Eton bow tie who dropped cigarette ash on other people's papers, drank other people's whisky and told entertaining tales to discredit the famous: 'I have never heard a name-dropper in the same class.'

For Burgess he had amused contempt, for Philby detestation.

'You'll make a hero out of him,' he accused.

'Of course not. The whole idea is to show the damage he did.'

'That's what disturbs us. You'll do more damage with the Americans if you write about Philby. Who is this fellow Page? What's *his* game?'

This was the first of a number of meetings with Greenhill, usually at his club, the Travellers', sometimes at his unpretentious house in West London, and once grandly at the Foreign Office. The pattern was the same. Why were we persisting with this damaging inquiry? Who was behind it? I expected the pressure, always with steely courtesy. I thought I would gain some information. I gained none. If I asked him a question about Philby, his eyes clouded.

We were making a little headway on Philby's role in British intelligence. He had gone out to Instanbul in 1947 as 'temporary' First Secretary, a cover for being a field agent. He made surveys of border areas with the Soviet Union. A message from Beirut said that in his final years there he loved displaying a large photograph of the double-humped Mount Ararat on the Turkish–Soviet border. Its uniqueness lay in the fact that it could have been taken only from the Soviet side. The conclusion we drew was that SIS had allowed him to be a double agent in Turkey. He had come back to England to take a course at a spy school near Gosport, proving himself good at pistol shooting, unarmed combat and night sabotage: added to his reputation with women, it would have gone with the James Bond image Greenhill hated, except for the universal testimony that he would drink raki as greedily as Burgess drank Taittinger Blanc de Blancs.

---

* *The Times*, 7 September 1977.

However, establishing that he pottered about on the Turkish border with a pistol scarcely explained the tremors of fear we were getting from the Foreign Office. 'They're like jelly,' Hamilton remarked. 'But we've nothing to shake them yet,' I grumbled.

Two conversations transformed the inquiry. Michael Frayn, the novelist and playwright, has been a friend of mine since he came down from Cambridge to work on *The Guardian* in Manchester. He called me fairly early on to say a bright acquaintance of his wanted to enter journalism and would I meet him. Frayn's tips are always good; when he said his friend was from the Foreign Office I was doubly intrigued. His name was John Sackur, an earnest, intelligent man in his thirties. He wanted a foreign post, preferably Africa, about which he was particularly knowledgeable. I told him I had a possible vacancy only in the Middle East. I took my time talking to him on several occasions. One day in my office I said:

'By the way, we're looking into the life of one of your old Foreign Office colleagues. Kim Philby.'

'Philby?' said Sackur, incredulously. 'Philby? You'll never be able to print it.'

He was tense.

'Why not?' I asked.

'It'll get stopped. D notices, the Queen. It goes to the highest in the land.' And then he bit out: 'Philby was a copper-bottomed bastard.'

It emerged that he had written a report on the damage Philby had done. He would not say any more. It was startling and frustrating. Philby was very important, but why? I introduced Sackur to Frank Giles, my deputy, who had himself once worked at the Foreign Office. 'We can't appoint him to anything,' said Giles. 'I asked him if he was a "friend"*. He said he was.'

I unleashed Bruce Page on Sackur. Beyond saying we were wasting our time looking at Philby's doings in the Middle East, he gave us no more clues. I could not work it out. If Sackur had been sent to scare us off, what he said only whetted our appetites. Page believed Sackur's disgust was real and that he was sincere in wanting to leave the Foreign Office. He had a passionate interest in black Africa and disliked British links with South Africa.

I drafted in more help for Insight. Everything went much faster. Shortly after the Sackur bombshell, Phillip Knightley tracked down the real name of 'John Whitwell', who had written a book called *British Agent* in 1966. It was tame stuff about 'Whitwell's' thirty-five years as a lowly member of SIS, but there were publishing rumours that the book

---

* By Whitehall tradition SIS men are known as 'The Friends'.

had been edited for clearance under the Official Secrets Act. Knightley found 'Whitwell' living in two rooms above a seedy café in East London. His real name was A.L. (Leslie) Nicholson, and he was down on his luck without much of a pension. Knightley took him for a slap-up lunch in an Italian restaurant of Nicholson's choice, but sitting there amid the City types and listening to Nicholson's reminiscences about the 'Old Firm', he began to think he was wasting his time. Knightley had begun with oblique questions, because he did not want to reveal how little we knew, but frustration made him bolder. It became clear to Nicholson that for all our efforts we did not know what Philby's SIS job had been. He was aware that the illness he had was serious (he died two years later) and in a nice, unassuming manner, after coffee and over his second brandy, he revealed to Knightley what Philby had really done.

Page and Knightley came into my office coolly.

'How do you like this?' asked Page. 'In 1945 old Kim was made head of the anti-Soviet section of British intelligence.'

Knightley capped him: 'The man running our operations against the Russians was a Russian agent himself!'

Our inquiry had been going on for four months in a curious parallel with the piecemeal and clandestine methods of the world we were exploring. Not a line, of course, had yet appeared in *The Sunday Times*. There was an entirely different atmosphere, as we knew there would be, when Phillip Knightley and Hugo Young carried the inquiry to the United States. If Philby was important in 1945, what was he doing when he was 'temporary' First Secretary in Washington from 1950? Surely not spying on the Americans.

We should probably have begun in the United States, which is a much more open society with a free press built into its Bill of Rights and with attitudes to journalism and inquiry utterly different from those habitual in Britain. It is not surprising in a way, since newspapers carried the torch of independence from the British in the eighteenth century, but always refreshing to the reporter accustomed to the closed doors of Whitehall. Of course, at the beginning, we had no idea that Philby was so important.

Knightley went to the campus of Brown University, Rhode Island, to see a man who had been an assistant director of the fledgling Central Intelligence Agency when Philby was in Washington. Lyman B. Kirkpatrick had become a professor of politics on his retirement with polio; he was in a wheelchair when Knightley asked him about Philby. Kirkpatrick combined secret knowledge with an intellectual zest for freedom of speech. On detail he was reticent, but he did not equivocate about Philby: 'He was your liaison officer with the CIA and the FBI.'

This was an even more astounding piece of information than what Knightley had learned in the East End café. It meant that Philby, for three years of the Cold War, had been at the heart of Western intelligence operations.

In Washington Hugo Young, who knew his way around Capitol Hill, having been a Congressional Fellow, went into the offices of the Senate Foreign Affairs Committee and asked to see various papers. Certainly. Have a chair. He could not take them away, and there were then no proper copying facilities, but he was welcome to sit all day and read them. He flicked through and stopped. There, on file, was a documentary assessment of the damage done to the United States by Burgess and Maclean. It was in the form of a letter from the State Department answering questions from Senator James Eastland, chairman of the Senate Internal Security Sub-committee. Eastland's comments were scribbled in the margin. 'Nuts!' he wrote against diplomatic glosses on disaster. Suddenly, Young found himself reading that Maclean was a major atomic spy: nobody before had known what value he might have been to the Russians. He had been allowed, among other things, to see information on uranium purchasing, which would have enabled the Russians to calculate how many bombs the West proposed to make. Knightley, sitting in a North Virginia farmhouse at about the same time, heard Admiral Lewis Strauss, former chairman of the Atomic Energy Commission, say: 'I'll be bitter to my dying day that Maclean had a pass to get into our building without an escort.'

But what damage had Philby done in his unique position? Following three separate hints, we discovered a murderous betrayal which made the jumpiness of the Foreign Office even easier to understand. 'Have a look at Albania,' said Kirkpatrick. 'Philby lost us a lot of lives in Eastern Europe', a former SIS man in Rome told Leitch. Something on Albania, we learned from Tom Driberg MP, was expunged from his own book at the request of the Foreign Office. It was only a paragraph saying there had been a débâcle, a titbit he had picked up from Burgess declaiming against Western meddling in Eastern Europe. Behind those few lines there was a vast ambition and a vast tragedy. Unknown to the world, the British and the Americans had been engaged in subversive operations to try and roll back the frontiers of Communism in Eastern Europe. It had begun with the British in 1947 infiltrating anti-Communist guerrillas into Albania for raids and sabotage. In 1949, when Albania was still unsettled, and Yugoslavia had broken with Russia, and the anti-Communist rebels in Greece were on the point of defeat, the Americans had had the idea that a Communist collapse in Albania might ripple throughout the Balkans. Nobody can say what might have happened. But the whole enterprise was doomed, because at the centre of the campaign against Albania, sitting in Washington on the Anglo-American Special Policy Committee, was Kim Philby.

We pieced together the story of the Albanian expedition, which had lain secret for seventeen years, by finding survivors: at least 300 men lost their lives. One of the Insight researchers tracked down a group of Albanians working for the Forestry Commission. A small army of them had been assembled, they told us, including the entire Royal Guard to King Zog in exile in Cairo. The army was trained in guerrilla warfare in Malta and the first big 'drops' of men who would lead the revolution were infiltrated into Albania by sea and air in spring 1950. 'They always knew we were coming', one of the few who lived told *The Sunday Times* researcher. The infiltrators were shot, the local people who helped them were forcibly resettled in another area. Yet the final stages of the Albanian operation went ahead after the defection of Burgess and Maclean and the recall of Philby to London for questioning. How did he get away with it all?

Knightley and Barry asked for a meeting with William Skardon, MI5's lethally sympathetic interrogator who had made Fuchs 'sing'. They met in the old Lyons teashop at Charing Cross station – more Le Carré. *The Sunday Times* men had been waiting for a little while when a moustached, middle-aged man slid in on them from an adjoining table. He had been there some time, listening, sizing them up. He stalked in conversation too. He believed he could have cracked Philby, but he had been given less than half a chance: Philby slipped through in the gap of class and style between the 'jumped-up coppers' of MI5 and the country gentlemen at the top of SIS loyal to their man. We knew by now that there had been a compromise between the spy-catchers of MI5, who were sure he was guilty, and SIS, who could not believe that Philby, who had, after all, done dangerous double work in Turkey, was a man to betray his service, his class and his country. Instead of a prolonged interrogation, Philby was given a secret trial with quasi-judicial procedures. Ripples of despair remained in legal circles at what had happened when Helenus Milmo, then a QC and later a judge, had been brought in as prosecuting counsel at the trial in MI5's Leconfield House off Curzon Street. Using his stutter to effect, Philby had half mockingly slipped through the loops of circumstantial evidence which was all 'Buster' Milmo had to fasten round his neck.

We knew enough by now to call off cagey fishing expeditions and ask precise questions of political leaders. A Tory Minister told us how, on arriving at the Foreign Office, he was briefed that SIS was protecting Philby and keeping him on their books. As the Anglican liturgist cautioned us, 'read carefully'. Both Macmillan in 1955 and Heath in 1963 said Philby had resigned from 'the Foreign Service', and this was true, but irrelevant. His diplomatic status had only been a cover for his real employment as an officer in the SIS and this was maintained right to the end. Beirut was an encore for the double agent. His employment by *The Observer* had followed an approach from the Foreign Office. John Wyndham, Macmillan's private secretary, defended Macmillan's record in the affair by describing the shake-up of SIS and MI5 he had enforced. The SIS had had imposed on it as 'C' the head of the despised MI5, Dick White, an intellectual and career officer, who had all along been morally certain of Philby's guilt. It was an appointment so secret that a new CIA man in London was told that his first task was to find out who 'C' was.

There was, therefore, a tale of reform as well as of disaster. I could not enthuse Greenhill nor George (later Lord) Wigg, then Paymaster General and adviser to the Prime Minister, whom I saw in his office at 10 Downing Street. They would not tell us about changes in the Service nor confirm Philby's role in the Albanian débâcle. Hamilton may have conveyed that we had honourable intentions, but official hostility never relaxed. There were frequent insinuations that Page was a Communist. I developed a standard reply: 'Well, he's safely locked up in a slave labour camp on the Gray's Inn Road.' Page was confined at all hours to a project X office, driving everyone as hard as himself to evaluate what we had and to follow up the proliferating leads.

Towards the middle of September, Page's long state-of-knowledge memorandum was almost publishable in itself as a study of Philby's treachery and its context: the record of why, for a period, the British Secret Service was vulnerable to a man of his intentions. It was a contribution to the unwritten history of two decades. David Leitch added icing. He looked up Philby in the telephone book, that prime source for investigative journalists, and came across Philby, J., who was Kim Philby's eldest son by his second marriage, to Aileen. John Philby turned out to be a quiet man in his early twenties, living in a basement flat in Hampstead with a couple of pet Alsatians. He had ambitions to be a war photographer. 'Would you like to take a picture of your father?' asked Leitch, reflecting on the poignancy of the relationship between the exiled traitor and a son with the natural affections for a father. John Philby went to Moscow. He returned with a photograph of his father standing in Red Square, and a few remarks about his past which were merely confirmatory of facts we had already established: 'I was given the task of penetrating British intelligence in 1933', he told his son, 'and told that it did not matter how long it took.'

'Philby's a bore. Drop him and do an article on the KGB,' said Greenhill. 'It is more interesting and we can give you information.' I told Greenhill I intended to publish something soon on Philby, but I was not averse to writing about the KGB, and I arranged for Hugo Young to see Greenhill. They had lunch at the Travellers'; Greenhill brought a man called Terence Leckie. It became apparent that Leckie was either an MI6

man or a functionary in the Information and Research Department of
the Foreign Office, the group set up after the war to counter Soviet
propaganda. As they walked back to the Foreign Office across St James's
Park, Greenhill impressed on Young the need to portray Philby as 'a
copper-bottomed bastard'. In the afternoon he was put in an empty
room at the Foreign Office with Leckie and treated to a long, elementary
but always polite piece of education in the iniquities of the KGB. This
was followed a few days later by an unmarked envelope addressed to
him at *The Sunday Times* which contained a massive drawing of the
KGB's structure, as MI6 supposed it to be. The letter bore neither the
name nor address of its sender.

Young thought the authorities had given up hope of trying to stop
publication altogether and were concentrating on seeing that Philby was
not presented as any kind of hero, and reminding everyone, unexcep-
tionally, that the KGB has its fingers everywhere in modern Britain. But
on 22 September I received a warning notice about British intelligence
services from the Services, Press and Broadcasting D Notice Committee.
It said in part:

> You are requested not to publish anything about:
>   (a) secret activities of the British intelligence or counter-intelligence services
> undertaken inside or outside the UK for the purposes of national security;
>   (b) identities, whereabouts and tasks of persons of whatever status or rank
> who are or have been employed by either Service [MI5 and MI6]...

D notices are issued only when the press representatives on the committee agree the official case for censorship. They are a warning that this
is where the ice is thin on the Official Secrets Act. The Attorney-General
would cite non-observance in a prosecution, but the notices have no
legal force in themselves. I decided to ignore the request. The D notice
on intelligence was sent to all editors as part of a review, said the
Secretary of the Committee. James Evans, *The Sunday Times*'s robust
lawyer, was exceedingly anxious about its relationship to Philby and
wrote me a memorandum. I told Hamilton that I proposed to ignore it,
because the two paragraphs would wipe out every line of our eight-
month inquiry.

There was a serious problem, however. The Insight draft by Page told
how Philby took a chance in recruiting into wartime intelligence someone
of undoubted patriotism who knew his past opinions, a Westminster
and Oxford schoolfriend who had travelled Europe with him in the early
1930s. Conversely, it was an example of the personal loyalty Philby
attracted that, when he was in the cold after 1951, the man was willing
to act as a witness to his marriage in 1959 to Eleanor at Holborn Register
Office. The trouble was that, as we approached publication, the man

was on active duty for the Secret Intelligence Service in Hong Kong. Page nevertheless wanted the name kept in for credibility; he was not impressed with the argument that it exposed the British agent to danger. I was. Page also thought it absurd to be writing about 'C' instead of Dick White. I was inclined to agree. Hamilton wanted both matters kept secret.

I decided to go for a drive into the country. My destination was Hampton Lucy House, Warwickshire. It was an exceptionally fine early autumn day and I admired the garden of my host, Cyril John Radcliffe, a former Lord of Appeal in Ordinary. It was good to be away from the shadows and inversions of intelligence. I had gone for advice. Radcliffe had chaired a number of security inquiries; he had also given the Reith lectures on the problems of power. I sketched our findings for him. He listened gravely. I said I was open to argument on whether publication would damage national security in ways I could not presently conceive. He offered none. I asked him about the names. He did not think it would be a serious matter to mention the London chiefs in the circumstances, but he questioned the necessity and the wisdom of naming the active SIS officer. This confirmed my own judgements. Hamilton accepted them on my return. Page did not. As I knew we were nearing publication, I showed Greenhill the reference to Ian 'Tim' Milne (he retired in 1968 to become a Senior Clerk at the House of Commons). He insisted it would ruin Milne's work and hazard his life. He still had a hope that I would abandon the series of articles I planned; I told him that I would not expose Milne to risk.

All that remained to be resolved was the date of publication. Insight kept picking up traces of another big Philby betrayal. Page wanted to find it. 'What's a few more weeks after all this time and effort?' I gave him two. John Philby, who frequented the office with Leitch on his return from Moscow, had dinner one night with Patrick Seale. The first edition of *The Observer* of the following Saturday evening, 30 September, arrived in our office around 6 p.m. with the Eleanor Philby story of life with a spy. I had ours on the presses by 6.30 p.m. 'Insight reveals that top Russian spy was being groomed to head Britain's secret service'. It dominated the front page with John Philby's photograph of his determinedly casual father in Red Square in an open-necked shirt, one hand in his jacket pocket. Our story, the first of a long series, was vastly superior, as it should have been given the resources put into it; but in a curious way the simultaneous publication probably weakened the effect of both in the public consciousness, as if everyone had known about Philby all along.

There was, none the less, an immediate hue and cry in the press and Parliament – against *The Sunday Times* rather than Philby or the Foreign

Office cover-up. Philby was not important and his story was not worth telling; or alternatively, Philby was so important that to tell his story would endanger national security. Several newspapers, not discouraged by official sources, asserted or implied that our Philby story could be nothing but a Russian plant. Sir Stewart Menzies, who had retired as 'C' in 1953, declared that Philby was not important in the SIS. Yet it was hardly credible that he himself would send to Washington an unimportant man to have the free run of CIA headquarters. The Frost programme staged a debate on Philby and newspaper ethics. George Wigg fulminated that *The Sunday Times* was seeking to discredit the British Secret Service. 'Bunk', said Roy Thomson for all of us.

Publication produces information. I had two messages after our first news story and the announcement of the serial, which resulted in strange contrasting journeys for two *Sunday Times* men. The first message was a letter from the heart of England:

> I am wondering whether next week's issue will mention an incident which occurred in Istanbul in August 1945 and in which both Philby and I were involved. If so, and I am mentioned by name, I should be grateful for a preview of the text before it is published. The incident convinced me that Philby was either a Soviet agent or unbelievably incompetent and I took what seemed to me at the time the appropriate action.

It was Knightley again who set off the next day for a remote part of Shropshire, arriving eventually at a great house set in acres of forest. The door was opened by a Sheriff of the county, a former diplomat by the name of John Reed, who ushered Knightley into his study.

'I was First Secretary in our embassy in Turkey in the summer of 1945,' he began. 'We moved for the summer from the embassy in Ankara to the consulate in Istanbul ...' They had a visitor one morning, Konstantin Volkov, ostensibly the Soviet consul, in reality the area head of NKVD (later KGB, the Soviet Secret Service). He wanted to defect. John Reed, as a Russian-speaker, but not an intelligence officer, interviewed him. Volkov said he had been attached to the Soviet secret service headquarters in Moscow only five months before and there was a lot he had to tell in return for a safe passage to Cyprus. For instance, among the Soviet agents in government departments in London were two Foreign Office diplomats and an officer in counter-intelligence. 'It seemed there was very important material. I wrote down the outline by hand,' said Reed, 'and I sent it away to London by courier the next day.' One week passed, then another, then at last an agent arrived from London. It was Philby.

'I asked him why the hell someone could not have come out sooner. "Sorry, old man," he said, "it would have interfered with leave arrangements".' Philby returned to London empty handed. All Reed's attempts to contact Volkov failed. Sometime later a Russian military aircraft made an unscheduled and irregular landing at Istanbul airport. It quickly took off again with a heavily-bandaged figure, lifted in from a stretcher.

'I made a point of contacting an intelligence officer to tell him my suspicions of Philby,' said Knightley's host. 'But nothing appeared to happen.' The memory of the betrayal still made his voice shake.

The second message I had was from Kim Philby himself. He offered me his memoirs. Send sómeone with powers to negotiate, he said in a telegram. I was strongly averse to publishing articles from a book by Philby, but it would be interesting to see what he was up to. Murray Sayle was the man to send, a deceptively convivial hard reporter from Australia who later reported Vietnam, climbed Everest and sailed the Atlantic. He had a visa to see a Russian space-shot. I asked him to call on Philby in Moscow. It was easier said than done. He had given no address; even John Philby did not have it. Sayle rang the KGB when he arrived. Philby was a non-person. Then he remembered that Philby was a keen cricket follower. Sometime he would be forced to come out into the open to pick up his copy of *The Times* at the post office for overseas mail.

'Mr Philby,' said Sayle to the man with *The Times*.

'Wh-Wh-Where are you st-staying.' The stutter was back.

'At the Leningradskaya.'

'I'll c-call you.'

Back in his room Sayle answered the phone. There was a strange choking sound as if someone was trying to say something. Then the caller hung up. It happened again five minutes later, the same sound, a click and silence.

The third time Sayle said, 'Mr Philby?'

'Speaking,' said Philby quite clearly.

They arranged to meet in Room 436 at the Minsk Hotel on Gorky Boulevard. Men with bulges in their blue suits stood idly by at either end of the corridor. 'I have naturally taken precautions against any rough stuff,' said Philby. 'You would not get ten yards.'

The room was bare except for two chairs and a table with a briefcase on it. Inside were a bottle of vodka, two glasses and a pistol. Sayle asked Philby how he reacted to the charge that he was a traitor. He replied:

To betray you must first belong. I never belonged. I have followed exactly the same line the whole of my life. The fight against fascism and the fight against imperialism were fundamentally the same fight ... I am a serving officer of the KGB. Undoubtedly ours is the best intelligence service there has ever been. We have a tradition of foresight and patience laid down by that brilliant man Feliks Dzerzinsky [who founded the Cheka, forerunner of the KGB]. When I first started to work for the Soviet Union, for example, I used to meet my contact once a week for two whole years when absolutely nothing happened at all. We were patiently waiting for an opportunity.

Philby took Sayle to a restaurant, where the waitors had the shape of a mountain printed on their jackets. 'It's Ararat, which side?'

He floated a remarkable offer. 'There was an interesting suggestion in the *Economist*. The idea was that I would be prepared to withdraw my manuscript if the Krogers were exchanged for Brooke. If that were, in fact, a condition of the Krogers' being released, of course I would withdraw my book.' (The Krogers were sentenced in Britain in March 1961 to twenty years for espionage; Gerald Brooke was sentenced in Russia in July 1965 to a year's imprisonment and four years in labour camp.)

The idea of Philby writing a book agitated the Foreign Office, when I told Greenhill about it.

'You cannot take it.'

'Maybe not, but someone will.'

'But we can't have Philby in *The Sunday Times*. That's putting him on Broadway.'

I was interested to read what Philby had to say, but I was even more opposed than Greenhill to running the Philby book in *The Sunday Times*, and Hamilton was too. I had three reasons. First, I wanted nothing to contaminate our wholly original reporting effort: enough attempts had been made to smear it by the ignorant and the jealous. Second, I was loth to spend manpower and time combing the manuscript for the lies and distortions Greenhill insisted it would contain. Third, I could not defend paying a penny for it; that would be rewarding treason. I told Greenhill I would think about what he had said. I was disinclined to jump to attention after the run-around we had been given. But my mind was made up; I thought he read it.

The Foreign Secretary, George Brown, disabused me. There was a call to my home from Denis Hamilton: 'You've just been denounced as a traitor.'

Hamilton was very upset. He had been at a dinner given by Roy Thomson for American and British business leaders. Introducing the Foreign Secretary, Thomson had made a joke Brown did not find amusing. As soon as he got to his feet he pitched into Thomson generally and then, without saying Philby, homed in on the subject:

I understand *The Sunday Times* is somehow in your control. If I may say so, my dear Roy, we would be much happier if you would exercise a little control. You are doing, your papers are doing, a very great disservice to this country. Some of us think it is about time we stopped giving the Russians a head start on what we are doing – I ask you and *The Sunday Times* to take this into account and for God's sake stop.

Thomson rang me the next morning: 'Don't worry about George.' At the dinner he had passed off Brown's remarks as 'a very good picture of the man who is Foreign Secretary'. Hamilton advised me to sit in the Commons press gallery. He thought there was a good chance I would be denounced from the floor of the House. It turned out to be a quiet afternoon; the Prime Minister carpeted his Foreign Secretary instead of me.

In due course I turned down the Philby book without seeing it. It was serialized in the *Sunday Express*, whereupon Greenhill greeted me with a typically Foreign Office response: 'It's all jolly accurate,' he said.

The Philby investigation was a proving-ground for Insight as a group and creative in another way. The strain on our resources had been considerable, without a murmur from Hamilton or Thomson. We relieved it in a way that was creative for future endeavours: we produced a book about it, the first of about thirty from our major efforts in the following fifteen years. It was well received and commercially successful. In this way we were able to present the public with the full fruits of our work, stimulate the staff and finance some expensive journalism.

Despite the furore, I have never for a moment regretted the Philby investigation. The 'very great disservice' was done by Philby and by those who protected him and concealed their own incompetence. Our work showed that class solidarity is not a satisfactory basis for trust and that too much secrecy perpetuates error and inefficiency. Demonstrably in Philby's case it cost many innocent lives. As a former provincial editor, it was my first prolonged experience of dealing with central government. I was charmed by the courtesies, but unimpressed by the philosophy. The exposure of past blunders, culminating in the mammoth blunder over Philby, was not something that could be left to the conscientious decision of the Foreign Office or the Government.

There was, in the end, no real excuse for the evasions and falsehoods. The press shouted a lot over the missing diplomats at the time, but the shouts were ineffective, because nobody did the work of inquiry on the three traitors which alone was capable of making the Government sit up. Our inquiries were admittedly beset with frustration and they were costly. Yet, if the press will not do this work, who else can? Individual MPs are easily misled, without resources and ill matched against the executive. A degree of public accountability is incumbent on the intelligence services, at least the same degree that is acknowledged in the United States. The Philby saga showed beyond doubt that it will not come spontaneously.

4
THALIDOMIDE

James Evans, the lawyer at *The Sunday Times*, set a piece of foolscap paper on the kitchen table of his tiny flat near St Pancras station and tried his hand at something new – writing a leading article. He was faced in September 1972 with what seemed to be an impossible demand from me, and he had an idea which seemed best tried out in the form of a leader. The sentences he wrote and crossed out and wrote again that lunchtime were to transform a large number of lives and change the laws of England, though not without the spilling of a great deal more legal ink: in the end no fewer than thirty-seven judges were called on to consider the words scratched at James Evans's kitchen table.

What I had instructed Evans to do was to find a way for *The Sunday Times* to begin a campaign for the Thalidomide children. Most of them had reached the age of eleven without receiving a penny of compensation for the appalling injuries inflicted on them by the poisonous nature of the Thalidomide sleeping pill their mothers had taken during pregnancy. Some of the children were without arms, some without legs, and some were limbless trunks. There were more than 450 of them in Britain. Only sixty-two claims had been settled against the giant liquor and spirits firm, Distillers, whose subsidiary Distillers (Biochemicals) made the drug under licence from Chemie Grunenthal of Germany. Pitiable sums amounting on average to around £16,000 had been agreed. The children's plight was a national scandal, but a secret one. The problem James Evans faced was to keep me out of prison long enough to make it a public one. Publication of any material that might prejudice the legal proceedings would violate the law of contempt of court. This was why there had been silence in the press and Parliament for a decade. Everybody had forgotten about the Thalidomide children.

James Evans had the subtlety to find a way through this brick wall. He had learned his law at Cambridge and in the Gray's Inn libel bar but also as a part-time adviser dealing with the risks in the rum stories produced by Kemsley's *Empire News* and *Sunday Graphic*. He had been drawn into *The Sunday Times* as a full-time adviser when Insight began probing into Rachman and the Profumo affair. He brought with him some of the grand court-room style. Such was his gilded manner of speech that it would not have been surprising to hear him address a reporter, 'May it please your Lordship', as he took the man gently through what he had written, but there was a hard edge on the frills. He tested the evidence as it would be tested in court and he was well liked; he had always wanted to be a journalist. With Thalidomide he was in an unenviable position. Five years before a slip by a journalist and a misjudgement by one of his Saturday libel readers had landed me in court before the Lord Chief Justice. We had by accident published the previous convictions of a man who was to stand trial. I was personally exonerated, but the paper was fined £5,000. 'I will never mention that case to you again,' said Denis Hamilton on my acquittal, and he never did, but none of us could lightly contemplate a challenge to the law. Yet James Evans knew I was at the end of my patience with Thalidomide. I had been waiting for three years to publish articles on how the drug was made in the first place, based on internal Distillers' documents I had acquired without their knowledge. He had worried about the risks in 1968, when I published a four-page investigation on the reckless deceits of Chemie Grunenthal. David Hirst QC had advised that it would be a flagrant contempt because it touched on issues that would be canvassed if the English cases came to trial. I had gone ahead following a somewhat more optimistic opinion from Peter Bristow QC and there had been no reprisals. But Evans was insistent that I would face a committal order if I published anything about Distillers' making the drug in Britain until every single case had been settled. Nobody had any doubt Evans was right. He disliked the restriction as much as any of us. At one stage he came up with the idea that we should set our articles in page-proof form and take them round to Distillers' grand headquarters in St James's Square in the hope that the sight of newspaper pages about to go to press would galvanize them to comment and so acquiesce in publication. We had started this exercise, but I came to think it futile. In John Wilmers QC Distillers had one of the sharpest of legal minds and they had always shown themselves zealous in asking for the Attorney-General's protection. We would be shown the door or, worse, face a court injunction banning publication altogether.

The delay was aggravating, but it seemed tolerable at the time because we assumed that the cases would shortly be settled out of court and settled fairly. Our principal concern was to shed light on how the disaster had occurred: there had never been a public inquiry. Since the cases were unlikely to be tried, there would be no exposure of the documents in court. I took the view that the public was entitled to know how a dangerous drug came to be produced and whether new safety regulations were sufficient. This remained an aim throughout the Thalidomide battle, but in 1972 our priorities changed for two reasons. James Evans suddenly had to contend with more than our desire to write history that might be held to prejudice a case. I told him I wanted to intervene at once and directly in the litigation with the simple and undeniable purpose of winning more money for the parents. 'There's a real contempt challenge for you, James,' I told him, and I gave him a copy of the first and fundamental reason for my insistence that we had somehow to publish. It was a long memorandum full of the arithmetic of pain and suffering and deprivation of the amenities of life. It showed for the first time just how ridiculous were the sums of money the court had decided were enough for the Thalidomide children. The curiosity was that all this information, collated by a brilliant investigative journalist, had been freely available to anyone in 1969. It was the work of Bruce Page, whom I had diverted from other features to lead the Thalidomide project. Page had read two long, complex articles in the *Modern Law Review* by John Prevett, an actuary with the London firm of Bacon and Woodrow, and went to see him because Prevett used the 1969 settlements to attack the way judges fix damages by rule of thumb. The lawyers for the children, believing they had a weak case, had settled with Distillers on the basis of the company paying 40% of what it would have paid if the children had been able to win a negligence action in court. Mr Justice Hinchliffe had rejected actuarial evidence and refused to allow for inflation. Prevett showed how the full award for the armless and legless boy in the test case would run out when he was twenty-seven – and he was receiving only 40% of that.

John Wilmers for Distillers had pointed out that the Government had, after all, promised to control inflation and the judge agreed that talk about rising prices was 'speculation' and 'hearsay'. Thus a child who Prevett calculated needed £106,000 to cover loss of income and special care for life was awarded just £24,000 – and of this he received only 40%, making a final award of £9,600.

This was staggering, yet all the information had been available in 1969. Prevett gave evidence in the hearings. Routine court reporting should have been enough to expose the disaster. But Prevett got short shrift in the press and, when the awards were announced, they fell foul of Fleet Street stereotyping: the children were given the cheerful 'fortune' headlines associated with pools winners. *The Sunday Times* criticized the settlements at the time, before new writs against Distillers made everything *sub judice* again. There was a leader page article under what we thought was the bold headline 'What Price a Pound of Flesh?'. This was exceptional, but it was inadequate in the light of the Prevett-Page memorandum: the Thalidomide story concerns some shortcomings in journalism as well as a legal débâcle.

The second impetus that early autumn came from Phillip Knightley. He had been trying to monitor the secret negotiations between Distillers and the other 389 families who had sued late. They were frightened. Their lawyers had warned them that if word leaked into the newspapers they would not get a penny: Distillers would withdraw the offer. Others were told they would lose their legal aid certificates entitling them to assistance from public funds. But Knightley had won some confidences, just as he did in the Philby inquiries. He is a phlegmatic personality, but he was agitated when he came into my office: 'Can't we do something? Most of them are ready to sign up and yet it's only for *half* what the 1969 families got. Half 1969!' Earlier in the year there had been a brief sensation when David Mason, a successful and self-confident Mayfair art dealer, had refused to go along with all the other parents in accepting a trust fund of £3.25 million. The solicitors acting for all the parents, Kimber Bull, and their counsel, James Miskin QC, had accepted Distillers' condition that their offer was dependent on every family accepting it. Mason refused. To him it was charity and niggardly charity. The parents' legal team took him to court and Judge Hinchliffe removed him, and five other families, as 'next friends' to their children. This meant that the right to decide, on legal matters, what was best for their children passed to a Treasury solicitor. The decision was overturned by Lord Denning in the Appeal Court. Everyone thus acquired the right to refuse Distillers' offer. Knightley's news was that this freedom and months of more negotiation had made no difference. Behind the silence imposed by contempt laws and fear, an outrageous settlement was about to take place. Half of 1969, said Knightley. And in every case 1969's full award was half, Prevett and Page proved, of what was necessary. And that half-award was itself cut by 60% ... The end of the regression was an armless girl entering her teens with a sum for pain, special care and loss of amenity of no more than £6,000.

I reported all this at the Tuesday editorial conference which began the week at *The Sunday Times* and at the end I called in James Evans, who did not normally attend. 'We can't let it happen, James', I told him. I had the Page-Prevett memorandum and I had a long article in draft by Knightley based on the trawl through 10,000 Distillers' internal documents which Evans had checked for libel. 'I'm going to publish, come what may.' In a further effort to disturb his celebrated equanimity I added: 'And I want to go on publishing week after week. This is it. Please advise me how best to do it.'

'I have the picture perfectly,' he responded. 'Alpine tourist asks guide to take him to the top of the Eiger by the safe route ... Let me think about it, mm?' He went off to his flat. I called in Bruce Page from holiday and asked him to convert his memorandum into an article. My request to James Evans to find a way of enabling us to publish week after week was a long shot, but a vital one if we could manage it. There are occasions when it is no use publishing the truth once. I realized this early on in my career, when I thought a single article in the *Manchester Evening News* would do the trick. In the campaign I began at *The Northern Echo* for an inquiry into the wrongful hanging of Timothy Evans I published something every day for months before there was any effect, though a few of the staff there were exasperated by the repetition. The great Horacę Greeley of the New York *Tribune* had it right: 'The moment a newspaperman tires of his campaign is the moment the public notices it.' Nobody had taken any notice of our single article in 1969 'What Price a Pound of Flesh?', published before the second round of legal cases made everything *sub judice* again. When David Mason rebelled, he told his story to the *Daily Mail*. It printed three dramatic articles and then it was silenced by a warning from the Attorney-General. So was everybody else. There was another flurry of news headlines when Mason and the other five families were removed as 'next friends', but once again there was no ripple effect. It was largely, but not entirely, fear of contempt. The BBC Television programme *Twenty-four Hours* planned to interview parents, but cancelled the programme when Distillers threatened to protest. David Mason stopped giving interviews, which always ended on the newspaper lawyer's spike.

The erratic nature of the interest in the Thalidomide children was also a reflection of the way newspapers and television news programmes work. 'News' is defined too episodically and too topically. It was the same in 1959–62, when Thalidomide was found to have affected 8,000 children round the world. There was an outcry, but then concern was allowed to evaporate. Nothing 'new' happened, nobody made speeches or marched down Whitehall, so there was no 'news' and the Thalidomide victims were gradually forgotten. The unconscious assumption was that our institutions functioned the way they are supposed to function: the law was seeing that justice was done. But it wasn't; and journalism had not learned how to write about processes, rather than about events. The process of legal disaster and the gradual disintegration of the families was ignored. I include myself in this retrospective criticism. I had an interest in the Thalidomide children at *The Northern Echo*. I had published some frank pictures and been told by readers who were disturbed by them, 'We don't want to know'. Then I forgot about the children, like everyone else. A *Sunday Times* campaign might have to keep going for a long time to redress the balance of power between isolated and frightened families and a powerful corporation with no limit to its legal life. I had no doubt we could maintain momentum, if James Evans could find a way. There were many unanswered questions. Why had there been no public inquiry? Just how was it that the scandal had been allowed to languish for so long? What had happened to 450 families in eleven years and what was happening to them now? Who, for that matter, were Distillers and what was their side of the story? How good were the Health Service provisions for disabled people generally? What had really gone wrong in the manufacture of the drug and how good were the improvements in drug control? Had the parents' lawyers done all they could?

James Evans, sitting at his kitchen table, did have an idea of a route up the Eiger. It came from something he had read in *The Sunday Times*. We had reported Lady Hoare, founder of a charitable trust, as saying: 'It is a tragic and deplorable situation. Many parents feel ground down by prolonged litigation, degraded by the detailed form filling they have had to undergo and deeper resentment of being made to feel they were going cap in hand for charity, rather than moral justice from the wealthy Distillers.' That phrase 'moral justice' had been nagging at James Evans and he began to write:

> The peculiar agony of this saga is that no one should feel a sense of relief that at last a settlement may be in sight. One should feel only a sense of shame. First, it shames our society that a decade should have passed ... Secondly, it shames the law that the compensation should be so low ... Thirdly, the Thalidomide children shame Distillers. It is appreciated that Distillers have always denied negligence and, if the cases were pursued, the children might end up with nothing. It is appreciated that Distillers' lawyers have a professional duty to secure the best terms for their clients. But at the end of the day what is to be paid in settlement is the decision of Distillers, and they should offer much, much more to every one of the Thalidomide victims. It may be argued that Distillers have a duty to their shareholders and that, having taken account of skilled legal advice, the terms are just. But the law is not always the same as justice. There are times when insistence on the letter of the law is as exposed to criticism as infringement of another's legal rights. The figure in the proposed settlement is to be £3.35 million spread over ten years. This does not shine as a beacon against pre-tax profits last year of £64.8 million and company assets worth £422 million. Without in any way surrendering on negligence, Distillers could and should think again.

The crucial distinction Evans had defined was between moral liability and legal liability. 'Do you think, Harry, you could hold your horses on legal liability, mmm, eh?' he said, handing me a couple of sheets of paper. He was slightly flushed with suppressed excitement, but he spoke coolly as always. 'I've had a stab at putting our defence in the form of a leader. Make what you like of it as a leader, of course. I think it enables us to plead that we are not prejudging the legal case of liability.' For this reason, said Evans, it was prudent to start with the Page memorandum indicting the original settlements. It was essential to keep this quite distinct from the Knightley article on the making of the drug. That went to the heart of the issue of legal liability. It was bound to be challenged and the campaign would be stopped dead in its tracks with the paper heavily fined and its editor with time on his hands in Wormwood Scrubs.

I adopted the James Evans strategy at once for the start of the campaign in the issue of 24 September 1972. I told Denis Hamilton. He was very relaxed about it. I also told the advertising manager, Donald Barrett. 'Distillers are our largest single advertiser. As a group, they spend £600,000 a year,' he told me. 'I know that won't stop you and it shouldn't,' he added. (Distiller's withdrew all their advertising after the beginning of the campaign.) I planned three pages on the history of the litigation, the demolition of the financial terms and the effect on the families. James Evans's kitchen manifesto needed very little work to make it the *Sunday Times* leader. I headlined it 'Children on our Conscience', and placed next to it a photograph of an armless Philippa aged ten. As a slogan for the campaign, I picked up James Evans's theme of shame: 'The Thalidomide Children', I wrote, 'A Cause for National Shame'. At the last minute I changed that to 'Our Thalidomide Children'. When the presses started to run, I took two visitors into the machine room to watch. They were David Mason and his wife Vicki, whose daughter Louise was in hospital with only flippers where her legs and arms should have been. 'Until now I never believed it would happen,' Mason called over the din. Whirling on the presses was one paragraph that was to be the subject of years of contention. 'In a future article', it said, '*The Sunday Times* will trace how the tragedy occurred.' It was a device. If nobody objected to the first article, we would publish the second; if we were prosecuted for the first article, however, we would reinforce our moral-legal distinction by demonstrating how different it was from the unpublished article. Originally I had intended to announce the second article for the second week. 'May I say that it would be wise', said James Evans, 'to give yourself and the courts a little more time to sort that out?'

The first noticeable sequel to the launch of our campaign was the silence. Apart from a BBC radio interview with me on the Sunday with a BBC lawyer hovering in the control room, every newspaper and television news programme ignored it. For two or three days I thought Distillers and the law officers of the Crown were going to do the same. The Attorney-General, Sir Peter Rawlinson, was in Strasbourg. It was on the following Friday that I noticed the official embossed seal on an envelope handed to me and read a letter written at the instigation of the

Roy Thomson

How *The Sunday Times* revealed on 1 October 1967 that Kim Philby was a Russian spy.

After a four-year battle, *The Sunday Times* is finally able to publish the history of Thalidomide.

The editor questions reporters on medical and legal points in a draft report for *The Sunday Times* – Patricia Ashdown-Sharp (left) and Marjorie Wallace.

Lord Denning, Master of the Rolls, presents the gold medal of the Institute of Journalists for services to the freedom of the press, February 1980.

Victory line up, October 1975, after the Lord Chief Justice rejected the Attorney-General's request to ban the Crossman Diaries: (left to right) Harold Evans, Mrs Anne Crossman, widow of the former cabinet minister, and Graham C. Greene, the publisher.

The editor and the *Sunday Times* printers prepare a page in metal.

Farewell: leaving the composing room in March 1981 for the editorship of *The Times*.

Solicitor-General, Geoffrey Howe (later the Chancellor of the Exchequer), by Thomas Hetherington, the Legal Secretary to the Attorney-General. A formal complaint had been made about *The Sunday Times* and my radio interview, he said; he did not say then it was Distillers, but it was. 'There may be grounds for claiming that the articles taken as a whole constitute contempt. The Solicitor-General would be grateful for your observations on this matter. In the meantime you will no doubt wish to consider your position in the light of the complaint that has been made, particularly in view of the reference already made to a future article on this subject.'

My private reply was a long letter pointing out that the cases were all civil actions to be tried by a judge alone, and that we had avoided canvassing the issue of negligence. 'I was at great pains', I wrote, 'to make it clear that I urged the defendants to reconsider their offer on moral and not on legal grounds, emphasizing that this was entirely consistent with the maintenance of their denial of negligence.' My public reply was to continue the campaign on the moral issues. Harry Street, Professor of English Law at the University of Manchester, savaged the arbitrariness of the way judges assessed damages without regard to actuarial evidence on need and inflation. Since Judge Hinchliffe's 1969 awards, the inflation which he regarded as mythical had reduced the value of them by a fifth. The father of David Jones, who received one of the highest sums, £20,800, for loss of arms and legs, spoke of their dismay on realizing that what looked like a large sum of money had gone nowhere: 'Had I fully appreciated the problems we are facing now, I would have stood up in the court and shouted. . . .' The mother of Patrick Pope wrote movingly of her son's bravery; he had had forty-two operations and they had still not received a penny.

There was still not a line in any other newspaper and nothing on television; there were no more radio invitations. It was demoralizing. But there was one reader of *The Sunday Times* who made up for the sense of isolation. He came on the telephone to me at home the first Sunday morning. The conversation was a little slow because Jack Ashley MP is deaf; he converses on the telephone by lip-reading the silent enunciation of his wife, Pauline, who listens on an extension. Ashley came to the Commons in 1966 as a Labour MP by way of crane-driving in Widnes, Lancashire, scholarships to Ruskin College, Oxford, and Caius College, Cambridge, and producing radio and television programmes for the BBC. He was about to be offered a ministerial post when he had an operation to clear up a minor affliction in one ear and ended up without hearing in either. He stayed in the Commons because of the surge of affection and support for him, and he was chairman of the All-Party Committee on the Disabled, when he read our Thalidomide articles in his garden in the sunshine. On the following Tuesday he met in my office with Page and Knightley, he asked questions, and at the end he said: 'Well, that's decided. I'll give up writing my autobiography until we've won.' I reprinted our three pages and sent them to every MP, editor and television producer. Ashley wrote to the Prime Minister, Edward Heath, who brushed him off ('Legal matters are not a matter for this or for a Labour Government'). He wrote to the responsible Minister, Sir Keith Joseph, who took the same line: 'There is a case before the courts and the issue raised must be left to them.' He tabled an Early Day motion, a device for collecting signatures, saying the Distillers' settlement was inadequate, and the clerks to the House of Commons rejected it on legal grounds. We reprinted our second week's material and dispatched copies again into the void. At *The Sunday Times* we were receiving hundreds of letters of support, but with Parliament and the Press apparently shut off, and Distillers in its trench, the outlook for raising hell seemed bleak.

It was at this point that the felicity of James Evans and his strategy were confirmed. He had been having a difficult time making sure that nothing crept into our pages at any stage of production from any source which looked remotely like the sharp end of legal liability. I put in bold paragraphs announcing that Distillers had always denied negligence and that our information was presented in support of a moral argument. This care enabled Evans to maintain the validity of the distinction when he spoke on the telephone with the Attorney-General's office, as he did several times. He came to an understanding with Hetherington that he would supply a copy of the draft article, if I approved, provided they would agree either to give us a fair wind or seek an adjudication in court. He persuaded me that it was better than publishing and risking committal, because it helped to emphasize the moral–legal distinction on which we were mounting the whole campaign. On 9 October Hetherington wrote: 'The Attorney-General instructs me to say that he has now considered the material published in *The Sunday Times* on the 24th September and 1st October. He instructs me to say that he does not propose to take any action over the matter already published.' But the letter asked me to send the draft article to Distillers. I did. They complained, and on 12 October the Attorney-General issued a writ against *The Sunday Times*.

It was the beginning of a prodigious legal battle to define the balance between public interest in the freedom of the press and in the administration of the law. The hearing was set down for 7 November before the Lord Chief Justice. It put our draft article at risk, but I was sure a High Court trial would make the press sit up and take notice – and everyone was now free to join our moral campaign without fear of prosecution.

The day I received the Attorney's letter, I spoke on the telephone with Jack Ashley at the Commons. He was on his way to a private appointment with the Speaker to protest at the Parliamentary restrictions. I was just in time to tell him about the Attorney-General's implicit acceptance of our moral-legal distinction. That afternoon the Speaker allowed Ashley to put his case for free speech for MPs on the floor of the Commons: 'Moral justice', Ashley declared, 'is not a question of law and therefore cannot be *sub judice*.' The Speaker said he would rule the next day. Ashley saw him later in his room and they discussed the terms that might be used in a 'moral' Early Day Motion. The Speaker had to be convinced that it was feasible to draw the line. The following day he ruled that he would accept Ashley's motion if it concerned itself with moral justice. The way was open not only for MPs to join the campaign – 265 soon signed Ashley's critical motion – but also for a range of Parliamentary activity.

I knew fairly early on that we would go down in the High Court. I had learned enough from various appearances in court to gauge the way the wind is blowing by the questions from the bench. Mr Justice Brabin and Mr Justice Melford Stevenson, who sat with the Lord Chief Justice, Lord Widgery, made a few barbed comments. When it seemed to be suggested that we wanted to publish the article because it had a commercial value to us, I asked Brian Neill QC to object. Melford Stevenson responded dryly: 'I am approaching the case on the basis that everybody is very high-minded.' It was uncomfortable climbing into the witness box at eye-level with the bench to add to a long affidavit I had given. I wanted to provide new information on Thalidomide settlements in Sweden, but, when Neill put the question, the Lord Chief Justice intervened.

'Really, Mr Neill. We are starting on a fresh case now. What is all this about the Swedish settlement?'

Mr Neill: 'If your Lordship does not think it assists the Court ...'

The Lord Chief Justice: 'I certainly do not think you are entitled at this stage to bring in new matters.'

I taxed their Lordships' patience further. The Attorney-General had dwelt on the pressure Distillers would be under if our draft article were published. In response to a question from Neill, I said to the bench: 'My Lord, there is great public dismay that after ten years the law has not yet produced justice. I am speaking from the many letters I have received. There is great anxiety that the parents after all this time are subject to enormous pressures.'

Lord Chief Justice: 'You have spoken about the parents being at breaking point in your affidavit.'

'Yes, my Lord.'

Lord Chief Justice: 'We have got to remember every word said in this court can be published to the world tomorrow and much of the purpose of this application might be defeated if we develop facts of this kind. I think you may take it that your attitude is very clear in your affidavit. You should understand that further taxing of the investigation would not be right.'

The judgment banned the draft article. There could be no balance of competing interests between a free press and a fair trial once legal proceedings had begun. No 'pressure on a party' could be allowed. This is what the Attorney-General had argued, though he had chosen not to proceed against our articles and they certainly brought pressure. The court was not asked to rule on what we had already published, but it was clear they would have found us in contempt on everything: 'We see no distinction in this case between persuasion directed to a legal obligation, and persuasion directed to a moral obligation.' It was lucky that a different view had already been taken in Parliament; it makes its own *sub judice* rules, but it would not have been helpful to have had an earlier ruling from the court.

We said we would appeal. We were discovering more about the tragedy all the time and it drove us on; more about the strong case that could have been mounted and the utter failure of the legal investigation on behalf of the parents; and more about the wrecked lives. The drug disappeared from the market in 1961, but the problems it left behind were only just coming into perspective. We had conducted a handful of interviews with parents at various times before we began the campaign, but in September I engaged the journalist Marjorie Wallace to join us. She has a degree in pyschology, had been a director with BBC Television and was on maternity leave when I asked her to interview some parents for two weeks. She was still deeply involved with the Thalidomide families ten years later. She wrote a fine book, and scripted an award-winning BBC documentary. Marjorie is not the conventional image of a sentimentalist. She asked hard questions. It was an immense strain for her to plunge into the emotional havoc; families began to ring her constantly for advice. She visited and revisited more than a hundred. She found them in a patchwork of environments – Tudor mansions in Kent, terraced houses in Glasgow, semi-detached houses on ring roads, caravans and bleak Highland cottages (and curiously few in London). But there was one common feature: they were in little camps pitched on the outskirts of society. They had lived through ten years of isolation and guilt. The mothers blamed themselves for taking a sleeping pill: many of the marriages had broken under the strain. Few had the money to make life a little easier. There was no help with the exhausting task of lifting overweight limbless children entering their teens. The National Health Service wheelchairs were primitive canvas contraptions not designed for such dramatic afflictions. They had not been able to turn much to their doctors, many of whom felt guilty at having prescribed the pill and were fearful of litigation; they had found the hospitals bewildered by the uniqueness of their injuries, with staff in some places refusing to help. Marjorie Wallace found that the distribution of the compensation had been amateur and inhumane. A child who was blind and deaf with severe brain damage and in need of constant attention had received the same £16,000 as a bright young girl with foreshortened arms and in a good home. There were many obvious discrepancies. But there were some instances where the Thalidomide families put a neglectful society to shame by their courage and endeavour. On a dark November afternoon Marjorie Wallace took the train to Huntingdon and a dilapidated two-up two-down cottage to meet the adoptive parents of one of the five most severely damaged children. 'Come and meet Terry,' said Len Wiles cheerfully, and they drove to the local school. Terry was nowhere to be seen. 'Ah, there you are, you rascal!' exclaimed Wiles, picking up a tiny bundle of humanity without arms or legs and no more than two feet high. Marjorie Wallace found herself holding the boy on the drive back, and was pummelled with questions by him. 'Where do you come from? Which paper? Ugh! Not that one! What length of article?' At the cottage, Leonard Wiles proudly presented his invention that had transformed Terry's life. From scrap metal and old army surplus he had made a 'supercar', a chair that worked on the principle of the forklift truck. Shuffling into the seat from the floor, Terry could press a knob with his shoulders and raise himself to any level to talk to people face to face. He could drive himself through the narrow doors of his cottage and into the fields. He was happy.

Terry Wiles and his inventive foster-father caught the imagination of the public. I was publishing the story of one family a week at this stage. There was none of the rejection by readers that I had experienced in the early 1960s at *The Northern Echo*; letters with cheques came in, and people telephoned asking what they could do. I told them to write to Distillers and their MP. *The Sunday Times* itself was drawn into Parliamentary activity. We briefed Ashley's all-party committee; I went alone to see the Minister of Health, Sir Keith Joseph, in his gloomy office at the Elephant and Castle and tried to impress on him that if we were bringing pressure on Distillers it was mild to the pressure the parents had endured in the past ten years from a drug distributed by the National Health Service. Joseph and the Prime Minister, Edward Heath, were still taking a hard line, insisting that the Government could not intervene in a private dispute and refusing a day for a full debate. An important group of Tory MPs, and notably two medical men, Tom Stuttaford and Gerard Vaughan, let Heath know he faced rebellion. The climax came on 29 November, two months from the start of our campaign. The Labour Opposition gave up a day of its time for a full-scale debate and I was invited to Harold Wilson's room at the Commons with Jack Ashley, Alf Morris and Sir Elwyn Jones to discuss the wording of the motion calling on Distillers to face up to its moral responsibilities and for the Government to set up a trust fund for the children. It was a moving debate led by Ashley in a packed House, where speaker after speaker criticized Distillers. Heath relented with the announcement of a Government trust fund of £3 million for congenitally disabled, with a further £3 million for the Thalidomide children at the end of the litigation. He went further a few weeks later, setting up a Royal Commission under Lord Pearson to examine the whole question of personal injury damages.

This was the turning-point. For the first twenty-three days of the campaign we had had no coverage at all from press and television. I wrote letters, telephoned, and sent reprints of every *Sunday Times* article. Nothing much appeared. Even the *Daily Mail*, which began publishing news items after a month, did not comment editorially until the eighth week of our campaign. There were three elements in the combustion – the banning of the article; the Parliamentary debate; and Distillers' obduracy. On the eve of the debate there was the first sign of a response from the company. Heath's Parliamentary Private Secretary, Timothy Kitson, stopped me in the lobby of the Commons to ask whether I thought the move by Distillers would end the campaign. I said 'No'. It was an increase in their offer from £3.25 to £5 million. I told Kitson our advice was that the children needed £20 million on any realistic assessment. The £5 million was swept aside in the emotions of the Commons debate and suddenly the campaign was self-sustaining. It was a national issue, on every front page and high in every news bulletin. A supermarket chain announced a boycott of Distillers' products. David Mason was fertile in providing news in his own way – a call for the withdrawal of the Royal warrant, a visit to Ralph Nader in the United States. But the most important impetus came from a small group of individual shareholders and, in time, the financial institutions of the City of London. The impetus was provided by three shareholders among a quarter of a million: Tony Lynes, the journalist, and two neighbours of Knightley's, Roger and Sarah Broad. They formed a shareholders' committee with the ultimate aim of challenging the basic stand of the Distillers' board, headed by Sir Alexander McDonald. The board believed that it was not the board's money to give away; it was the shareholders'. McDonald was supported in his sense of principle by the conviction that legally the company owed the parents nothing; he was not entirely to be blamed for that view in the light of the failure of the parents' lawyers to assemble the strong case they should have done. *The Sunday Times*, with the help of the Rowntree Trust, bought the thirty-two volumes of shareholders' names from Distillers. I published hundreds of names of the bigger holders in a page resembling a telephone directory. It was avidly read. Such was the interest from the press, with the telephones ringing from early morning to the early hours, that I engaged half a dozen researchers under Knightley to help the committee. Local authorities, trade unions, and churches who held shares were rung by local and national newspapers. Many said they would support a call for an extraordinary general meeting. It would have taken some time to get the 10% of signatures needed, for it represented 36 million shares, but for a curious City parallel to the James Evans analysis. *The Guardian* rang Legal and General, the second largest life assurance company in Britain, which held 3.5 million Distillers shares. Ron Peet, the chief executive, thought about it and concluded that powerful corporations had moral as well as legal responsibilities. He said so. He added that Distillers were also provoking consumer hostility and prejudicing their own commercial interests. But it was Peet's moral censure that cata-pulted his statement into the limelight. It was front-page news. Other big shareholders, insurance companies and merchant banks joined in; so did the Greater London Council with 350,000 shares and a score of other cities and towns. On 3 January 1973 Distillers gave in. It announced that it would pay £20 million to compensate all the families. The money available was now nearly ten times the original offer.

This was not quite the end of the compensation story. So much had gone wrong before, so suspicious were the parents of their lawyers, that with Jack Ashley I called a meeting in the board room at *The Sunday Times* and we set up a liaison committee with parents, expert advisers from the City, law and medicine. John Prevett, the original questioning actuary, came in to approve the final scheme: it involved Distillers in a liability of £28.4 million, for all the children including the 1969 cases. Things happened more quickly than they used to do. Jack Ashley rang me on a Saturday to say he had discovered that the Treasury proposed to tax the money the children received. I wrote a leader for the Sunday. The following week the new Prime Minister, Harold Wilson, topped up the charitable trust with £5 million from Government funds to pay the tax.

The future of the Thalidomide children was now secure, but our ambitions had always been wider. Some lasting benefits to society might be gained from their sufferings if we could identify the medical and legal weaknesses which had betrayed them. Nor was it a small matter for the freedom of the press that our draft article was still banned. We could not accept the High Court's narrow view that the discussion of public affairs was always at the mercy of a single writ, issued as they are as a mere formality in the course of any serious human conflict. Two activities followed from these thoughts. First, I set out to pursue our case for the freedom of the press to the highest judicial level. That took eight years. Second, Bruce Page and Elaine Potter began to reconstruct the Thalidomide history so that we could publish as soon as we were legally free. That was not until almost four years from the date we announced that in 'a future article' we would examine how the tragedy occurred.

There was a room at *The Sunday Times* which was full of Thalidomide documents: three filing cabinets containing the documents in German of Chemie Grunenthal, originators of the drug, and another set of cabinets with the Distillers' documents which I acquired in 1968 from Dr Montagu Phillips, the pharmacological adviser to the parents. The Distillers' documents revealed how little research of their own they had done in acquiring the drug from Chemie Grunenthal, how they had unwarrantably taken Grunenthal's scientific reputation on trust, and had continued selling the drug after a danger warning. At least two, and possibly six, employees in Australia had known four months before the drug was withdrawn that Dr William McBride, a leading Sydney obstetrician, believed it was the cause of deformation in babies he had delivered. This information was in our banned article. Early in 1973 we began an investigation independent of this material to test the validity of the commonest assertion about Thalidomide. This was that Thalidomide was properly tested according to the knowledge of the time, when drugs were thought not to reach the foetus. The then Minister of Health, Enoch Powell, said this, the newspapers repeated it, and the parents' lawyers believed it, which was why they settled for so little. Our critics shouted it during our campaign – the *Economist*, the *Daily Telegraph* and its city editor, Kenneth Fleet, the Law Society's *Gazette*, and Peregrine Worsthorne in the *Sunday Telegraph*. 'It was standard medical dogma that the foetus was effectively isolated', Fleet declared on 8 January 1973. They were all wrong.

When I went to Bruce Page's offices in the months after the end of the compensation campaign, I was likely to be accosted by a molecular structure. Page studied the organic chemistry of Thalidomide so as better to understand the mechanism of disaster. He drew me a one-dimensional sketch of the pattern that had caused so much human distress. Robert Jones, whom we engaged as scientific adviser, went deeper into the pharmacology. We began a search of the scientific literature of the period. Page and Potter visited laboratories. There was no question about it: reproductive studies were routinely done in the 1950s (Thalidomide was produced in Britain from 1958). Elaine Potter went to the laboratories of Hoffmann–La Roche in New Jersey, producers of

Librium, Valium, and Mogadon, and saw the records. It had been routine procedure since 1944. In Raleigh, North Carolina, she met Robert Hitchings, the inventor of Daraprim, the break-through anti-malarial drug, who told her they had done reproductive studies since 1950. Furthermore, the studies on Daraprim were done in Britain. The list added up – Hoffmann-La Roche, Lederle, Burroughs Wellcome (in Britain), Pfizer, Smith, Kline and French, and ICI in Britain where Dr Edward Paget did reproductive studies for an anaemia drug in 1955. If these had been done with Thalidomide, they would not have shown precisely what deformities it produced, but they would have shown it might endanger unborn children. Nor was any of this a secret at the time. The tranquillizers in direct competition with Thalidomide were tested for their effects on pregnant animals and the results published.

So why did the press, the Minister of Health, and the parents' lawyers fail to discover the strength of the children's case? Because Distillers told them what to believe. This was the 1950s and journalism was at a high level only in the standard of its credulity. There were astonishing similarities in important articles in *The Times*, *The Guardian* and in the letters the Ministry of Health sent to parents. Dr Alfred Byrne in *The Guardian* stated frankly that his information was from Distillers; we found the author of *The Times* report, its industrial correspondent Duncan Burn, and he, too, had recycled Distillers. To understand how the Ministry of Health formed its view, Elaine Potter called on Dr E. Conybeare, a senior medical officer at the Ministry, who had retired. He was engagingly frank, saying that he had briefed Enoch Powell after he himself had been briefed by a Distillers medical adviser.

We only began to understand the scale of the failure of the lawyers when Dr Phillips died. Elaine Potter went to see his widow, who allowed her to search through his files. They documented Phillips's exchanges over the years with the lawyers. They revealed how little evidence had been gathered, how inadequate legal aid had been in sustaining a proper case, and how hopeless it was to have Phillips as the solitary expert adviser. Nobody, for instance, had done a straightforward laboratory test to check the British patent specification for Thalidomide. *The Sunday Times* did and the laboratory reported that three out of four methods given by Grunenthal failed to function – an important clue to the sloppiness of Grunenthal. Most critically of all, Potter came across a copy of the culminating opinion of Desmond Ackner QC, who advised settling for 40% of the full damages. Ackner wrote that there was 'no evidence' to suggest that prudent drug manufacturers in 1958 tested their drugs on pregnant animals. He was misinformed. But additionally his opinion reported that Dr Edward Paget, formerly of ICI, had refused to give evidence and that, even if he had, it would not necessarily have been helpful. Potter went to see Dr Paget, director of Inveresk Research Institute, a member of the Medicines Commission and the World Health Organisation expert committees, and author or joint author of some forty-eight distinguished publications, and he told her something different. First, he had no recollection of being approached, except by Distillers, who did not want his evidence. Second, he would have given evidence as a professional duty. And third, he would have said that he, as a toxicologist, and others like him world-wide, were testing drugs on pregnant animals in the 1950s. Of Ackner's summary of what he would have testified, he said: 'I totally reject this account.' Ackner had said Paget would testify that ICI would not in 1959 have tested a sedative or hypnotic. Without any doubt at all, said Paget, he would have testified to the contrary: any ICI drug likely to be used by pregnant women would have been tested for its effect on pregnant animals.

In a few months in 1973 Page, Potter, and Jones assembled the strong legal case on drug manufacture that had eluded the lawyers. Phillip Knightley flew to see Dr McBride and reported back that he had not been asked for evidence until after the 40% settlement had been agreed. All this would have given a different course to the Thalidomide story. It has also to be said that the information we had by midsummer 1973 was superior to our draft article of 1972; in particular, the draft accepted Dr Phillips's unsound idea that Thalidomide's dangers might have been predicted from its organic structure.

However, all this knowledge was confined within *The Sunday Times*. A few weeks after Distillers had made their new acceptable offer, I sat in the Appeal Court to contest the ban on our draft article. Once again the interventions pointed the way. The Master of the Rolls, Lord Denning, Lord Justice Phillimore and Lord Justice Scarman unanimously reversed the order of the Divisional Court. They rejected the notion that a writ must always silence discussion. 'Besides the interest of the parties in litigation,' said Denning, 'there is the interest of the public in matters of national concern and the freedom of the press to make fair comment.' It was a short-lived victory. Denning refused leave to appeal, but the Attorney-General won it from the House of Lords itself and the arguments took place in May 1973. Legal cases are heard only by five eminent Law Lords. The awesome sound of 'Law Lords' is belied by the informality: no wigs, no court ceremonial, and a teasing method of questioning. I liked the way the revered Lord Reid, at eighty-two, stopped the Attorney-General with a hypothetical. It would be contempt, said the Attorney, to tell a grocer you would stop buying from him unless he dropped a legal action.

'Wait a minute,' said Lord Reid. 'What if he doesn't tell the shopkeeper, but simply does not send in his weekly order? Is that contempt?' But in July 1973, when I went along to pick up the printed judgments, I found: 'It is Ordered, by the Lords Spiritual and Temporal in the Court of Parliament of Her Majesty the Queen Assembled, That the Cause be....' I found that all five Law Lords declared the pending article contempt of court because it prejudged the issues. I was acutely depressed. Our case and their judgments met each other only as an express on the up-line meets an express on the down, flashing past each other in a blur.

Lord Cross talked of Thalidomide being 'in the early stages of litigation'. Two of the Lords refused to accept the possibility of there sometimes being greater public benefit from free speech than from preserving the legal cocoon intact. It was contempt to tug Shylock's sleeve on the Rialto and beg him not to seek his pound of flesh. Only by six judges to five was our original moral campaign regarded as legitimate, a damned close-run thing. There was no sign of concern that for twelve years it had been impossible to discuss the causes of the disaster and its lessons for public policy in civil liability, drug testing, and advertising. None of the judgments acknowledged the principal reason why *The Sunday Times* involved itself in the first place. This was the plain failure of the legal system to provide a remedy which was remotely acceptable. The judges took the case as if it were a newspaper gratuitously throwing sand in the smooth mills of the law. Lord Simon said that 'dwelling on the peculiar horror of this particular case is apt to cloud judgment'. That such eminent deliberations could have concluded with barely a reference to the human realities seemed to me a measure of the insulation of the legal profession. So as to leave no doubt in my mind, Mr Justice Talbot ruled against us in another action with Distillers. Some time after the Lords' ruling I told Distillers I was ending the tactical understanding I had given during the contempt hearings not to use the Distillers' documents. Distillers sought an injunction on grounds that publication would be a breach of confidence. Mr Justice Talbot heard the case. Many old lags were present – Prince Albert and Strange (etchings); Fraser and Evans (Greek Government); Saltman Engineering and Campbell Engineering (leather punches); Argyll and Argyll (marriage confidences). We argued the towel case (Initial Services *v.* Putterill), where an employee disclosed unfair trading and Denning ruled that such confidential information could be disclosed in the public interest. Surely, we said, there was a higher public interest than confidentiality in learning how the Thalidomide disaster had been inflicted on innocent people. Mr Justice Talbot disagreed: 'There is no crime or fraud or misdeed on the part of the plaintiffs [Distillers] and in my view negligence, even if it could be proved, could not be within the same class so as to constitute an exception to the need to protect confidentiality.'

It meant that there was a double lock on the draft article, one on the grounds of contempt by the Lords and one on grounds of confidence. Marjorie Wallace came to the rescue against the Lords. She was in Ireland, where an unknown number of mothers had been affected by Thalidomide. She had gone to a gloomy Victorian house in Clonskeagh outside Dublin to meet a famous Irishman and jurist, Sean MacBride, who was going to act for the parents. 'I have an idea,' he told her. 'I've just been with the judges on the European Commission of Human Rights. I know their feelings on free speech. I think *The Sunday Times* could win a major victory for human rights.' So began our adventure to draw succour from a convention born out of the idealism of the war against Hitler. Britain has been bound since 1953 to respect the European Convention for the Protection of Human Rights, which it has ratified though not yet incorporated into our law. In January 1973, I complained to the commission on behalf of Times Newspapers and myself, Bruce Page, Phillip Knightley and Elaine Potter that we had been deprived of our rights under Article 10. This guarantees everyone the right to free expression and to receive and impart information and ideas without interference by public authority.

James Evans had moved from *The Sunday Times* to the Thomson Organisation, though he maintained a keen interest. Our legal work was now in the hands of Antony Whitaker, a Wykehamist who read law at Oxford and was a member of Gray's Inn. If James Evans was a smooth round circle, Antony Whitaker was a nervous vertical line of jagged energy. He had come to us from the leaner legal pastures of the *Sunday Mirror* and he fell ravenously on the complexities of the European case. His first task was to have our case admitted. Somewhat less than 5% of complaints to the European Commission are accepted; the vast majority are rejected as groundless or outside its authority; a few it settles by reconciliation between the parties. It is a slow business. It was not until September 1974 that the Government argued against the admissibility of our complaint and not until December 1975 that Antony Whitaker took the first of many bumpy journeys to Strasbourg. He argued *in camera* against Gordon Slynn QC for the Government, who relied on Article 10's provision that the exercise of free speech might be subject to such restrictions as are necessary in a democratic society for the protection of the reputation or rights of others and 'for maintaining the authority and impartiality of the judiciary'. Whitaker was able to cite the Phillimore–Cameron inquiry which in December 1974 advocated reform of the British laws of contempt so as to liberate discussion, especially in civil cases such as Thalidomide. The European Commission adjourned for five months to study the case. In the intervening period I had an offer it was thought I could not refuse. 'I've had the Treasury Solicitor's office on the line,' said Antony Whitaker, bursting in. 'The Attorney-General says, if we withdraw our European application, he'll ask the Court to discharge the injunction against us.' There were by this time only a handful of Thalidomide cases unsettled, but on the logic of the original injunction it should not matter whether there was one or four hundred. It was a *volte-face*. If I agreed, I would be able to publish our long-delayed account of the origins of the tragedy. The Distillers' documents, which formed a large part of the original banned article, were under the separate confidentiality injunction imposed by Mr Justice Talbot. But we had available the results of the impressive investigation by the special projects unit. I told Whitaker no. We would continue the fight in Europe. That meant more delay for the Thalidomide article, but a resolution of all the cases could not be long delayed now, and what was at stake in Europe was more important even than our disclosure of the origins of tragedy. If we lost in Europe, we were no worse off than we would have been still stuck with the House of Lords ruling. But if we eventually won we would be enlarging the freedom of the press. It would be that much harder for any similar scandal to languish in secrecy.

I did not, in any event, have to wait long. The Attorney-General did what he had proposed. He did not have his deal with us, but no doubt with the intention of impressing the Commission, he acted on his own. He went before the Lord Chief Justice, Lord Widgery, and asked him to lift the injunction he had imposed in 1972. There were still four cases, but Widgery did it in a hearing that lasted only four minutes and on 27 June 1976 we published a six-page report documenting the powerful and scientifically sound case that the parents might have had all along. On 18 May 1977 the European Commission of Human Rights concluded by eight votes against five that the restrictions imposed on our right to freedom of expression were in breach of Article 10 of the Convention:

> If the public interest to clarify matters of great importance cannot be satisfied by any kind of official investigation, it must, in a democratic society, at least be allowed to find expression in another way. Only the most pressing grounds can be sufficient to justify that the authorities stop information on matters, the clarification of which would seem to lie in the public interest.

The stage was set for a full trial before the international group of judges of the European Court of Human Rights. Anthony Lester QC joined Antony Whitaker for the oral arguments in April 1978. It was one of the most memorable days of my life when, a year later, I sat in Strasbourg on 26 April 1979 and listened to the conclusions of '*l'affaire Sunday Times*'. Twenty judges of the European Court had deliberated. They sat in a great semi-circle in black gowns. It was only in the last sentences of the judgment that the declaration came. Nine of them were against us, including the British judge, Sir Gerald Fitzmaurice, but eleven carried the court: 'We find there has been a violation of Article 10.' It meant the House of Lords injunction had infringed our rights to free speech and that the law of contempt would have to be liberalized in Britain in the spirit of the Convention. In 1982 an Act of Parliament re-defined the law. Among other reforms, it changed the starting-point of *sub judice* so that it did not start from the issue of a writ but from the much later time when a case is set down for trial. Had this been the law before, the Thalidomide scandal could not for so long have remained secret.

It was the first time the European Court had reviewed a decision of the House of Lords. The narrow victory was the finding that their ban on *The Sunday Times* was disproportionate. 'The Attorney-General moved the knight and left the queen exposed,' said Whitaker pointing to the Court's comment on Widgery's 1976 discharge of the injunction: 'Discharge in these circumstances prompts the question whether the injunction was necessary in the first place.' But the European Court ruling went beyond Thalidomide and beyond even a repudiation of our archaic law of contempt. It put its judgment in a way which appealed to me, not so much on the right of the press to publish as the right of an individual to information which may affect his life, liberty and happiness. That is a powerful weapon against many of the censorships that have grown up in my generation in Britain. The same robust attitude on individual rights could affect many areas where bureaucratic, corporate or trade union power or common-law judgments have in Britain eaten into our liberties, in each case without reference to a written Bill of Rights of the kind which protects the American citizen. Many of our freedoms in Britain depend on judge-made common law. Sometimes, with a Denning, they are stoutly defended, sometimes they are repu-diated, frequently they are frayed and always they are subject to legis-lative interference. The case for incorporating the European Convention into our own law was unanswerable, said Lord Scarman after our victory. It was 'a milestone in English law'.

The elation at *The Sunday Times* at these events was tempered by a harsher reality. As we fought against external restraints, our freedoms began to be eroded from within. It was the print unions, or more specifically a number of militants, who carelessly holed the vessel. In July 1977, when the European Commission reported, it added the banned draft article as appendix, so making it available for publication. I had the exciting news by telex from Strasbourg at noon on Friday. I asked for the paper to be increased in size. The NGA machine managers de-manded six more men to make up a crew of 101 as part of a running battle with management, and then said it was too late to call them in.

When the run began on Saturday they operated only eight of the nine presses – depriving whole areas of the country of *The Sunday Times* and with it the climax of our entire Thalidomide campaign. At midnight, I sat in my office pleading with the union committee, led by a stocky and taciturn man called Vic Dunn. For forty minutes we debated their claim against management for extra crewing 'costing only £300 a week' against my desire for the long-banned article to reach all the readers. Most of them were sympathetic, though they would not run the ninth press. I implored them to run into paid overtime to get out as many copies as possible on the eight presses. I thought this would happen. It did not. We lost 540,000 copies, one third of the print.

There was far worse to come. When we won the Thalidomide victory in the European Court, there was no *Sunday Times* in which to report it. Times Newspapers had suspended publication in the midst of industrial chaos in November 1978. Suspension was principally an attempt to control guerrilla warfare in the press room, and also to restore a semblance of efficient working in the clerical areas where the dominant and obstructive union figure was the persuasive Barry Fitzpatrick. The NGA machine managers were one main cause of disruption in the press room. Another was the machine assistants in NATSOPA, led by a permanently bronzed man with a lupine grin who relished a fight, Reg Brady. These two sets of workers were constantly in dispute with each other and with management. Week after week, month after month, the work of hundreds of people in all departments was thrown away. In April, when management appealed for normal working, 3.5 million copies had been lost. By November the number of lost copies had tripled. We had become *The Sunday Sometimes*.

The year's suspension solved nothing. I spent it trying to find a middle ground between management and unions; it proved a quicksand. The frustration and heartbreak began again the moment we resumed publication in November 1979 after losing nearly £40 million. Petty disputes continued in key departments. Millions of pounds of revenue and millions of copies were lost on *The Sunday Times*. In August 1980 the journalists of *The Times* went on strike for a 21% pay rise. By October press room squabbles had lost us copies on twenty occasions, a total of 4 million homes deprived of the paper. In October, Brady and Dunn were competing over differentials. There was a loss of 788,000 copies of *The Sunday Times* on 12 October. Times Newspapers management made its usual protest. On 18 October there was a loss of 328,000 copies. 'It can't go on, can it, sir?' said the commissionaire as I left dispiritedly for home that Saturday night. I thought of pleading again with the union men in the press room and decided against. Nobody seemed to care any more.

5
SALE OF THE
CENTURY

It is not every day that news is delivered personally to one's doorstep by the editor of *The Times*. Early in the evening of Monday 20 October, when I returned to London from walking in Kent still downcast by Saturday's disastrous production run of *The Sunday Times*, William Rees-Mogg called in unexpectedly at my home. We lived only half a mile apart in the Westminster area, but we had not made a habit of calling on each other.

'It's all over,' he said and delivered his scoop. 'Thomsons are pulling out.'

There was to be a public sale of all the titles, but the news was to be kept secret until Wednesday 22 October. It had all been decided at an informal meeting at Thomson's headquarters, at Stratford Place off Oxford Street, with the Thomson directors Gordon Brunton, James Evans, Michael Brown, Denis Hamilton, and Rees-Mogg. There had been attempts all day, he said, to call me in. I was puzzled by that, since an afternoon message would have reached me, but I let it pass. Nobody was to know about the decision, not even other members of the executive board: Dugal Nisbet-Smith, Derek Jewell, Garry Thorne, Jack Bryers, Paul Crowe and Donald Cruickshank, the general manager of *The Sunday Times*. As Rees-Mogg spoke, my telephone rang. Cruickshank, proving that he had a nose for journalism as well as for accountancy, was on the line to say something odd was happening. The executive board members at Printing House Square simply could not gain approval for any kind of action and statement about the Saturday night disaster. I said I had a visitor and could not talk.

Rees-Mogg was effervescent rather than stunned, fizzing with criticism for the way the sale was being organized. 'They're mad, quite mad.' He had demonstrated, he said, how they could have done a reverse deal for *The Times* with the *Birmingham Post*, relieving Thomson of the burden of ownership and escaping the anarchic greed of the London print unions. As for *The Sunday Times*, they could have sacked Brady and saved millions in redundancy money if everybody else had walked out.

It was frustrating not to have been at the Thomson meeting, but it would not have made a scrap of difference about closure. The Thomson board, which had supplied us with £22 million in cash in 1980, had set a tripwire in September, when further *Sunday Times* disruption had followed the demoralizing strike of *Times* journalists at the end of August. Brady had triggered the action. Brunton then became as committed to a particular strategy as the Prussian Field Marshal Schlieffen had once been: Thomson would make an open and spectacular retreat. The option of selling *The Times* and keeping *The Sunday Times* was briefly discussed; so was an immediate closure of both papers, dismissing the bulk of the workforce for misconduct and saving on redundancy payments. Denis Hamilton disliked the idea of a public auction. He would have preferred to talk privately to potential new owners with the right attitude to the titles: something might be arranged with Lord Barnetson, chairman of the rival *Observer* and also chairman of the provincial group United Newspapers, an ingenious financier and newspaperman. Such an approach would ensure that undesirables did not get into the act, but Hamilton had not prevailed. James Evans thought the sale of *The Times*, above anything, had to be an open affair; private deals seemed to him to smack of the furtive. Brunton relished the idea of finding unexpected contenders whom he could lock in negotiation.

Rees-Mogg, as he left me, said he was thinking of trying to form a consortium to buy *The Times* from Thomson. 'A single proprietor', he pronounced, 'is best for *The Sunday Times*.'

It was not the moment to argue; I said we must talk more soon, and hastened to see Denis Hamilton at his flat in Palace Street. He would never forgive the print union militants Brady and Fitzpatrick and company, he said, but most of all it was due to *The Times* journalists being on strike; that was what had decided it with Ken Thomson. Hamilton showed me the statement that had been drafted at Stratford Place that afternoon. It indicted the unions, fairly, for disruption and broken agreements, which were expected to produce a pre-tax loss of £15 million in 1980. The Thomson Organisation had spent £70 million on the papers since the 1967 merger. It would finance them until next March, which allowed just over four months for a transfer of ownership. It was not, at that stage, dogmatic about a package sale: 'Whilst it may be preferable for Times Newspapers to be kept together as an entity, it is possible that interest will be shown in individual titles or parts of the company. Any such proposals would be carefully examined.'

Hamilton said he had succeeded in having written into the statement various commitments about which the Thomson Organisation was not enthusiastic, in particular that bidders for the titles would have to pass a set of criteria devised by the four national directors, the editor-in-chief and the two editors. I read the statement through, suggesting various points and drawing his attention to a curious omission: the new owners were not to be asked, in the draft, for a commitment to editorial independence. It was an oversight he agreed he would put right next day with Gordon Brunton.

He was plainly exhausted. He had spent his life building up *The Sunday Times* and the marriage with *The Times*; now it was seed to the wind. At the end of our year's shut-down, when our hopes were renewed, he had spent hours in this same room with Brady in a heart-to-heart attempt to reach an understanding, and he thought he had succeeded; week after week since our return to publication, that understanding had been hurled in his face, hundreds of thousands of copies at a time.

I felt deeply for him in his desolation. He was drained of anger, beyond tears, sustaining himself by the procedures of sale in the numbed manner of a householder totting up the remnants of a fire. *The Sunday Times* would be all right, he murmured: it was such a strong and profitable paper if it could be produced properly. Everyone would want it, but *The Times* had to be saved, too. I shared his sense of sadness and betrayal, but I was buoyed up, I found, by relief that the guerrilla warfare was at an end and by the vague hope that something might yet be built on the wreckage. It was with this in mind that, when I left Hamilton, I invited Donald Cruickshank to dinner. I thought it was wrong that he, as the general manager of *The Sunday Times*, had not been told. I still did not tell him. I kept the secret. But on the basis of a spurious shared ignorance of what was happening, we canvassed various scenarios and determined that we would try to continue our formal partnership as editor and general manager, and try to save *The Sunday Times*.

I thought it would be harder to put on a poker face with my closest editorial colleagues at the Tuesday conference which opened the week's work. It was attended by journalists with seismological ears, alert for any kind of tremor. They were intent on knowing the cause of the latest production disaster, which I told them, and on knowing what management would do, at which point I dissembled and diverted their attention to the week's new excitements. Their spirit in all this time was extraordinary; despite week after week of botched production, with good stories as well as copies lost, they maintained a marvellous enthusiasm for the paper.

Rees-Mogg came over in the evening. We co-ordinated our plans for telling our respective staff the next day and reminisced about how enjoyable it had been working together. In the light of what was to happen to our papers, we could have spent the time more wisely. We might have deliberated on how we could help each other to acquire separate possession of the titles. We assumed too readily that the goal of independence could be reached only by independent action. We might have questioned this assumption then; we should certainly have questioned it later as the Thomson preference for a package sale hardened into a condition.

The only explanation for our going our separate ways is that Rees-Mogg and I had become too disillusioned by attempts to co-ordinate the interests of *The Times* and of *The Sunday Times* in Times Newspapers. We had campaigned within the Thomson Organisation for separate operating companies. We had succeeded only in having separate executive committees set up for each title, but our experience with these had reinforced our views: discussion and decisions in these bodies seemed crisper, and they held out the hope of reanimating old title loyalties amongst the staffs. Rees-Mogg saw the sale as an opportunity for *The Times* to be published outside London much more economically and to be rid of the infections of *Sunday Times* labour troubles. I saw it as an opportunity for *The Sunday Times* to shed the demoralizing incubus of *Times* losses, to tackle our overmanning and to concentrate management attention. These views were shared by our staffs; I never heard a single voice advocate continuing the marriage and I heard many denounce it.

All the same, it came as a surprise to me the next afternoon, following the morning announcement of the sale, to look down from my office on to the front entrance of *The Times* and see Rees-Mogg standing in the drizzle in his double-breasted suit proclaiming our divorce to a gaggle of television crews and pressmen. There is an emotional and showy side to Rees-Mogg which is disguised by his solemn demeanour and revealed only occasionally by an impulsive command or a schoolboy giggle. He was going to try to form a syndicate, he announced, to buy *The Times* and break away from *The Sunday Times*. On Monday he was off to Canada to see Lord Thomson and convince him that the proposal was a practical one. The logic of this was not altogether apparent, since the power of sale had been clearly delegated to Brunton and the British management. He clearly risked offending the sensibilities of Brunton, Hamilton and James Evans (which he certainly did when BBC Television's *Panorama* showed a film starring Rees-Mogg on his North American travels to save *The Times*). Hamilton was angry. How could William launch off on his own without consulting his chairman and editor-in-chief; how could he denounce in such sweeping terms the 1967 merger in which he had assisted? Thomsons in Canada were upset, Brunton was cross. If he would not fall into line they would have to consider sacking him.

This was meant perhaps more as a warning to me than a real threat to Rees-Mogg, who was only doing what he thought best for *The Times*. I had decided, in any event, to proceed quietly in an effort to secure *The Sunday Times* in independent ownership. Even if I had not, I guessed rightly that the organizations whose support I might want to seek would require confidentiality. None of the names canvassed in the press reports as purchasers in 'the sale of the century' was immediately attractive. Seven were featured early on: Rupert Murdoch, the Australian owner of the *Sun* and the *News of the World*; Lord Rothermere, owner of the *Daily Mail*; Lord Matthews of the Express group; Sir James Goldsmith, proprietor of *Now!* magazine; Robert Anderson of Atlantic Richfield (Arco), the American oil company which then owned *The Observer*; a secret City consortium rumoured to have something to do with the Australian entrepreneur Robert Holmes à Court, who has since acquired Associated Communications Corporation; and Robert Maxwell of Pergamon Press, an old *Sunday Times* antagonist. Who were these seven dwarfs, I asked a staff meeting, to seek the hand of Snow White? In the 1979 shutdown some of the journalists in the NUJ chapel had congregated in a bedroom at the Howard Hotel overlooking the Thames to discuss with Lord Rothermere – visiting Britain from tax exile in Paris – the possibility of his acquiring the entire editorial staff of *The Sunday Times*. When they pressed him on whether he would interfere as proprietor of a new Sunday paper they would produce, he said – graciously – he would not if he had Harold Evans as his editor. *The Sunday Times* men found Rothermere congenial, but they shied away when he added what they saw as a chilling qualification: 'The *Daily Mail* is us and me, so to speak, it is our right arm and leg.' They feared this meant they would be the left arm and leg. Lord Matthews was a more likely interventionist; so was Rupert Murdoch; but both of them had too many newspapers to hope to get round the Monopolies Commission, even if we wanted them.

Going it alone was not, as I saw it, a last resort. It was a first choice. *The Sunday Times* was not a cripple which needed to accept restrictions on its freedom. As a Thomson spokesman said that first week, it was 'very, very rare for a profitable paper like *The Sunday Times* to come on the market. Given uninterrupted production – as it had in the Sixties and early Seventies – photocomposition and an uplift in the economy, it has a profit potential of £10 million a year.' I believed that this potential, to say nothing of editorial independence, was unlikely to be achieved by the simple purchase of *The Sunday Times* as the subsidiary of a commercial company. Always up against the clock, always vulnerable to the smallest hitch, a newspaper requires an unremitting spirit of teamwork. At *The Sunday Times*, management and unions had failed to achieve it. A new framework for co-operation was required which, without debilitating decision-making, would dramatize and focus the common interest of management and staff. Editorially we had to give permanent life to the vision of a dead man; we could not expect to find another Roy Thomson.

What I envisaged, vaguely enough at this stage, was raising money from a small group of investors, offering stock to the staff, and creating an editorial trust. Easier said than done, and it obviously could not be attempted by the editor without two essentials: the support of the journalists and professional advice. At this point the NUJ chapel had as father (chairman) John Barry, the managing editor of features. A former Insight editor, matching intellectual range with urbanity, he also had a taste for Byzantine negotiation and an unexploited capacity for making speeches. Before the shutdown, he had defeated one of my proposals in the house agreement on working conditions by depicting me as Napoleon rendered by the artist David, a despot astride a gleaming white charger, while the infantry were expected to trot mutely behind.

The chapel also elected a committee of senior men, departmental heads and the like to guide them. They became known as 'the cardinals'; their 'pope' was Peter Wilsher, the foreign editor and the editor of Business News in the 1970s, a versatile, acerbic man with an equal ability to spot a dud accountant or a good poet. For my part, I turned to Cruickshank and also to Bernard Donoughue.

Cruickshank relished his appointment as general manager of *The Sunday Times* at the age of thirty-six. For five years, before he joined the Times Newspapers board, he had counselled other people as a McKinsey business consultant, a navigator at the captain's elbow, and that was the role he had when he first joined us as a director without portfolio just before the year of suspension. He had a sharp, flinty look and he aligned himself with the hawks. Taking over the day-to-day running of *The Sunday Times* appealed to him because it was a command, and one that called on all his skills and experience. He had qualified as a chartered accountant, after graduating from Aberdeen and the Manchester Business School; he had worked in the high-technology aerospace business of Alcan. He had rapidly absorbed the spirit of *The Sunday Times*. The journalists liked his canniness as well as his readiness to expose any decision to argument. He and I worked well together.

Cruickshank was in a difficult position. Once the sale was announced, we agreed that it would be unthinkable to await events. But Cruickshank, as well as being general manager of *The Sunday Times*, was finance director of Times Newspapers, and in that position responsible to the managing director, Dugal Nisbet-Smith, and the chairman, James Evans. Evans was too new to the post to have a complete grasp of detail; Nisbet-Smith specialized in labour and production. Cruickshank was bound to be drawn into helping Warburgs prepare the financial prospectus for the Thomson sale, a prospectus, moreover, which would give the figures for a unified company sale rather than one of individual titles. He did not know whether he could divide his loyalties: what view would Gordon Brunton, James Evans and Duke Hussey, the former chief executive, make of his participation in a bid to purchase *The Sunday Times*? He would have to ask them at some stage – he had no talent or taste for subterfuge – and he was worried also about a possible conflict of interest. He might well be a member of the negotiating team which would meet a potential purchaser. How could he do it if he were himself part of a purchasing group?

Even without Cruickshank's hesitations I knew I had to enlist Bernard Donoughue. I have never met anyone whose appearance is more deceptive. He looks like a tough centre forward in professional football, heavy-boned and lean. He has a gap tooth and his hair sits tightly on his head in orderly rows of crinkly black like the paper one finds in boxes of chocolates. It would not be a surprise if he spoke with a heavy Irish brogue. The clue to his merit lies in the wariness in his light blue eyes. It is more than the vigilance and tactical cunning of the soccer player, though he was a vigorous weekend combatant on Hampstead Heath; it is the mark of a prudent, analytical and reflective intelligence which took the Northamptonshire son of a metal polisher in a car factory to a first-class honours degree at Lincoln College, Oxford, in 1957 and then, at thirty-nine, into 10 Downing Street as the senior policy adviser to two Prime Ministers. Harold Wilson appointed him as the first head of the policy unit in 1974 and James Callaghan kept him on as the only survivor of Harold Wilson's 'kitchen cabinet'.

I got to know him before those days. He was then a lecturer at the London School of Economics; he had been a reporter on Hamilton's *Sunday Times*. I met him as a Highgate neighbour and a mutual friend of William Rodgers, the former Labour Minister; he had been with him in the Campaign for Democratic Socialism which helped Hugh Gaitskell defeat the Left. He enjoyed the war of grassroots political intrigue, which drew on the dual character traits I observed in him – an intellectual zest for manœuvre matched by an emotional willingness to commit himself to a cause or a person.

When he was at No. 10, his loyalty to Wilson, Callaghan and the Government was such that he was a poor source of news; he was a good friend, but friendship was secondary to his idea of duty. What constantly surprises me is his acute sense of public opinion. In 1974, when we went on a skiing holiday – we shared passions for music and sport – I passed the time on the journey by expounding on what I thought the likely course of events would be in the confrontation between Edward Heath and the coal-miners. I thought I was at the centre of things and he at the periphery. He listened patiently and corrected me; he analysed Heath's errors, forecast an election, the way it would be fought and what would happen. It was exactly right, just as William Rees-Mogg was exactly wrong.

It was his political judgement which led me to invite Donoughue to spend one day a week at *The Sunday Times* when Labour lost the election in 1979. He joined the Economist Intelligence Unit and Grieveson Grant, the stockbrokers, for four days a week, and discussed political issues with us on Fridays. He knew his way round the City, so he was a natural ally in the search for honest money. I raised the question with him amid the turmoil of the first day of the news and he agreed to help. He would take soundings on which merchant banks we should approach for advice. It was an advantage that he was not on the full-time editorial staff; I imagined he would not be the focus of hierarchical jealousy within the paper.

The first day produced an ally I would never have thought of approaching. My personal assistant Joan Thomas ribbed me with, 'Can't you do something to create some excitement like Rees-Mogg?' and shortly afterwards put through a call that would have made some ripples had we announced it. The caller was James Callaghan. What could he do to help? He knew nothing of the business, he said, but he knew the print union leaders and he admired *The Sunday Times*. Would I like to meet him at the Commons the next morning in confidence and put him in the picture?

I hardly knew Callaghan then; we had not as a paper been particularly kind to him and would not, I think, have supported him in the election of 1979 had we been publishing. This would not have deterred him, I recognize now. Former Prime Ministers tend to fidget a bit when they are retired in good health with a sense of what they might still achieve in public affairs. The involvement of a party political leader clearly had some risks, but at the very least he might help privately with the unions. Jim will fix it, the headlines used to say. Well, there was a lot to fix. For *The Sunday Times* to stand alone there would have to be robust negotiation with the print unions on manning, disruption and technology. I had no hesitation in saying I would call on him.

Donald Cruickshank thought it was all right for him to come with me, so we briefed Callaghan together in his room at the Commons. I had last seen him grey and dejected after the election and when he had been in hospital; now he looked apple-cheeked and fit, a genial Sussex farmer in town for the day. As an initiation present to the dark side of Fleet Street I gave him a copy of *Stop Press*, the book by Eric Jacobs on the dramas of our year of shutdown. He promised to read it. What had happened was a bloody shame, he said. He knew Ken Thomson as a decent man. He did not know the ins and outs, but the print unions had much to answer for in this year's disruptions. He was not concerned about *The Times*; *The Sunday Times* had a broader appeal, it was fairer and it had done good things, 'Insight and all that'. Its traditions should be maintained. Had we thought, he asked, of offering shares to the unions or workers so that they could feel involved, or of printing outside London?

The answer was 'yes' to both. We were keen on shares for the staff, provided we were not being asked to run the paper as a co-operative. The second idea was attractive but awkward. The machines in Gray's Inn Road thundered at full stretch through the night until 5 a.m. to run off 1.5 million copies of a 72-page *Sunday Times*. No other printing plant in Britain could do this. We could split the printing between a number of provincial centres but, despite our overmanning, this was no cheaper page for page. We had to make sense of Gray's Inn Road. The best solution, we thought, lay in a radical restructuring of the print arrangements. We were too reliant on Saturday night 'cowboys', the 500 or so casual workers who had no loyalty to the paper. We were too reliant on a mechanically perfect run, too vulnerable to mishap or mischief. If we employed a smaller permanent staff we could begin printing the Review section (serial, leisure, books and women's features) on Thursday or Friday, and so increase the number of pages and advertising revenue.

Callaghan said that he would, if we wished, talk privately to the print union general secretaries on all these matters to see if there was any point in going further. It would all have to be confidential. We were relieved he said it first; we took it as a mark of his sincerity. The last thing we wanted was a public relations exercise. We felt we were walking on eggs.

I went that evening to see Denis Hamilton at his flat. A solitary light cast a shadow on the fireplace painting of his hero Nelson; Hamilton was in low spirits, looking out into the dusk across rooftop turrets towards Westminster Cathedral. I told him I was thinking of putting together a group to bid for *The Sunday Times*; I respected Cruickshank's sensibilities and did not mention him. There were various possible allies and backers, I said. I had one in mind which I felt it premature and possibly awkward to mention to him, but I told him of Callaghan's initiative. Something might emerge from that or the other lines I was thinking of following. Would he like to be the chairman? I would be happy to do the legwork.

He winced. 'I couldn't possibly go through all that again with the unions. Oh, no, no, no, Harold. . . . How could you expect me to?'

I felt guilty. How indeed could I expect this shy, introspective man to gird himself yet again for negotiation? Events might well have taken a different turn had he said 'yes', but I sympathized with him and thought I understood. He wanted to conserve his energy for possible battles with Gordon Brunton over the detailed editorial criteria for the sale. These had yet to be decided, and Warburgs wanted them for their preliminary sieve. Should Thomson insist that a buyer must keep on all the editors? What should we say about editorial independence? 'You must think about them urgently,' he said.

It was the evening after Hamilton's refusal that I decided to take the plunge with the possible ally I had not mentioned: *The Guardian*. Roy Thomson had agreed to print it under contract on our *Sunday Times* presses in 1961; in 1965, two years before the Thomson rescue of *The Times*, the latter's then chief proprietor, Gavin Astor, and his editor and chief executive, Sir William Haley, had talked to Laurence Scott about a *Times–Guardian* merger, an idea which was abandoned in the light of the objections of the editor of *The Guardian*, Alastair Hetherington, that it would leave the serious centre-left reader nowhere to go. Despite the antecedents, nobody in all the comment, so far as I know, canvassed the possibility of *The Guardian* as a partner for *The Sunday Times*. *The Guardian* was seen, no doubt, as a competitor by Times Newspapers Ltd because of its rivalry with *The Times*. But the game had changed. William Rees-Mogg was determined to leave what he called 'the snake pit' of Gray's Inn Road; so was the executive committee of Journalists of The Times Ltd (JOTT), in which most of *The Times*'s editorial staff had banded together with the object of buying the paper (we now began to talk of a JOTT–Mogg consortium). Printing and distributing a mere 270,000 copies of a 28-page *Times* outside Gray's Inn Road was exactly ten times more feasible than attempting it with *The Sunday Times*. It would at least halve the daily's setting, composing and machine-room costs. Of course, printing outside London could be attempted with *The Times* in the same company, but it was more likely to be achieved if there was a legal separation. Lord Barnetson's United Newspapers, Lord Cowdray's Westminster Press, the *Birmingham Post* and several other provincial groups all had the capacity.

The Guardian, unlike a JOTT–Mogg *Times*, seemed committed to London. The idea I wanted to explore with the *Guardian* management was that they would invest in *The Sunday Times* and assist us with management and entrepreneurial skill. They would tighten the security of their printing contract with us in Gray's Inn Road, and we would have the security of that revenue. Also *The Guardian* could assist us in finding other customers: there was enough spare capacity to print both the *Daily Mail*, say, and *The Guardian* during the week. I was conscious that this might all seem like adultery to Denis Hamilton, who was the best man at *The Times–Sunday Times* wedding, but I had no doubt that early rescue for *The Times* required the divorce Rees-Mogg had filed. There were also, in an association with *The Guardian*, compensations in personal affection and in professional philosophy. I was a Manchester man who had cut his teeth on the political and literary pages of the *Manchester Guardian*. I had worked for the company as an assistant editor of the *Manchester Evening News*, I knew the people, and writing for the paper, a good test, had been satisfying. More important than mere nostalgia was the knowledge that the remarkable Scott Trust, which owned the company, had given genuine freedom to a succession of provocatively independent editors.

I knew the then editor of *The Guardian*, Peter Preston, but as the business was managerial I arranged to meet Peter Gibbings, the chairman, at his Chelsea home. He is a barrister who began in newspapers by answering questions in the Anne Temple Human Casebook in the *Daily Mail* ('my boy friend won't kiss me, what shall I do?'). He went into general management for Associated, joined *The Observer* as circulation manager and was deputy managing director when he was recruited to run *The Guardian* in 1967. He is in his fifties, as smooth-looking as the racing thoroughbreds he kindly appraised for me in the paddock at Ascot one summer with the head of the Thomson Organisation, Gordon Brunton, an owner with a box. It had been said at one of our Times board meetings that Gibbings was 'unreliable', but that was during some tiff. Donoughue spoke highly of him and so did Hetherington, *The Guardian*'s former editor. Gibbings was the quietest of Fleet Street managers. Somehow, without creating panic or hostility, he had made *The Guardian*'s losses the basis for continuous cost-cutting; the style was not of hand-to-mouth poverty but of stylish economy, the leather patch on the old cashmere jacket. He had recruited Gerry Taylor as advertisement director to bring revenue *The Guardian* had never seen; and, with hardly anyone noticing, he had acquired profitable batches of small papers in Surrey and Greater Manchester.

He was even better informed than I expected about Times Newspapers. He knew the identities and degrees of bloody-mindedness of our tormentors in the chapels, he knew who on the management side could kick an own goal, and, when I sketched out my ideas, he put flesh on them almost at once. How would it be, he mused, if *The Guardian* took 24.5% of the new *Sunday Times*, just 0.5% under the monopolies legislation definition of a controlling interest which would require approval of the Secretary of State? We could set up a trust similar to the Scott Trust, and perhaps linked to it, to guarantee editorial independence. But, if we were to go ahead with our exploration, there would have to be some understandings. It would have to be in secrecy. He would have to take his closest colleagues with him, and there would have to be a clear understanding between us on firm management, sensible practices and pay; he was not about to open a vein for the infections of the old *Sunday Times*.

I was encouraged by his cheerful perception of the opportunities that lay beyond the obvious problems. His interest had mounted to enthusiasm when we met seven days later at my home with Cruickshank and Jim Markwick from *The Guardian*. We both had some explaining to do: he that he had met Gordon Brunton at the races, who had spontaneously asked him if he was interested in Times Newspapers, and he had been obliged to say he was, without divulging the nature of the interest. For my part I explained the Cruickshank dilemma: he would not have much to say for fear that he might suddenly materialize on the other side of a negotiation. I reported that I had heard from Callaghan. The union general secretaries had welcomed his call and our initiative. He had told them bluntly he was not getting involved unless they were going to deliver. He had read *Stop Press* had been horrified. I wondered if Gibbings and Markwick would agree that we should tell Callaghan of *The Guardian*'s involvement. Gibbings was a little uneasy about Callaghan. He recognized that he might be able to do much to encourage union co-operation, but would the price be a public feeling that both papers had embraced Labour? Shares for the staff was a good idea, but would Callaghan in particular understand that when we got down to the nitty-gritty of jobs and demarcation it was management work? Would he feel he had been taken for a ride if he were not in charge of the company? Gibbings said he was making the points out of prudence. Callaghan could be trusted with the confidence about *The Guardian*. He thought, and I did not dissent, that we should otherwise keep the boxes separate for the time being. We left it that *The Guardian* would apply for the prospectus from Warburgs and I would look for the remainder of the investment. Gibbings said he thought their bankers, Hambros, would gladly raise it, in addition to their 24%, but I preferred not to increase our dependence on *The Guardian*. Donoughue was scouting the City, Harold Lever, the former Paymaster-General, had promised to put on his thinking-cap for us, and there were American connections I had in mind for a visit the following week.

It was time to talk to 'the cardinals'. I was apprehensive. Would they give their backing to initiatives that must inevitably sound vague? If they did so, would the staff as a whole endorse them and stand by them as the weeks slipped away? They valued the independence and freedom of the paper every bit as much as the editor; it was their work, after all, which made the idea manifest week after week. How safe was it, though, to assume that as the date for closure neared they would all reject a conventional Fleet Street proprietor who was prepared to make a few genuflections? One of the senior men on the paper wrote to me: 'A lot of people are more frightened than they care to admit.'

We met over lunch after the Tuesday editorial conference. It was a talented, well-balanced group, including the chapel militant Peter Wilby, who was education correspondent, Eric Jacobs, who was labour editor and a moderate with Whitehall experience, and several heads of departments: Ron Hall, the editor of the colour magazine, a formidable personality with no time for union politics; the Old Etonian Magnus Linklater, a former editor of the magazine and now associate features editor; Tony Bambridge, the irrepressibly cheerful editor of Business News; two men of the solid centre, John Lovesey, originator of the Fun Run and a former father of the chapel, and Peter Harland, an ex-provincial editor then in charge of the editorial side of new technology, who had been at Cambridge with Hall; and two natural conciliators in Derrik (Del) Mercer, head of Home News, and Peter Roberts, the managing editor who dealt with the union on management's behalf.

Wilsher was in the chair and in his high, cracked voice opened with what I thought was a menacing observation. I would recall, he said, that in the shutdown they had discussed whether they should present themselves to a proprietor as a going concern 'with or without H.E.'. Did I have any thoughts on that? Well, yes. I was not excited by the idea of *Sunday Times* journalists being hawked around Fleet Street as a job lot. As for H.E., he had to admit he was not wild about the possibility of being the conductor who raised his baton to an empty stage. But I was being oversensitive. They were entitled to look at all the options and, when I told them I was launched on two separate secret initiatives, they were full of ideas. Ron Hall said he would report on whether, in the event of the closure of Gray's Inn Road, we could convert *The Sunday Times* into a news magazine produced at Watford by Sun Printers. Roberts agreed to come back with ideas, his own and others, on ownership and management structure with an emphasis on participation. Wilby perked up at that. Harland undertook to report on printing the newspaper.... We needed to be sure we could not escape Gray's Inn Road and to examine how quickly we might move *The Sunday Times* on its own to the new technology. Hall's and Harland's work was necessary because I could not be sure at this stage that I would be able to call on any management knowledge.

I discussed these matters also with John Barry. He thought the chapel would go along, but there might be some support for a dissident view from Lewis Chester, another ex-Insight editor and one of the most forceful personalities in the chapel. Chester, who had been one of the authors of our book on the fall of the house of Beaverbrook, had become convinced that energy and personal presence were what counted in dealing with the print unions. He felt that for *The Sunday Times* a good old-fashioned Cockney proprietor, living above the shop, was better than any kind of consortium. It was a refrain I was to hear from other sources with rather more power; most immediately it came on my North American fund-raising trip from Mrs Katherine (Kay) Graham, the owner of the *Washington Post*.

I had known Kay and her editor, Ben Bradlee, who had run the Watergate exposure in the *Post*, for years; I had admired in particular how they had run the presses and flown in their newsprint by helicopter to defeat a savage pressmen's strike. The *Post*, I thought, would be an admirable partner for us with the *Guardian*; but it was not to be. Mrs Graham thought a consortium crazy; we needed a single strong personality. It was the same answer at the *New York Times*. Sydney Gruson gracefully declined the opportunity to get London printers' ink on their hands, but pointed me in the direction of Sy Newhouse, one of the two Newhouse brothers running Condé Nast magazines and Newhouse newspapers, who were thought to be in an expansionist mood and certainly had the money. I was not able to call on the Newhouses, as I had to go to Hartford, Connecticut, and Boston to see two of the world's biggest insurance companies, and Tom Winship, the editor of the *Boston Globe*. I left the Newhouses to the redoubtable energies of Bob Ducas.

Ducas, then forty-three, was the president of Times Newspapers of Great Britain Inc. He was half-English, half-American, an Old Etonian and junior tennis star who had graduated from selling millions of dollars' worth of advertising to take charge, while still in his twenties, of all the business operations of Times Newspapers in North America. In his early days in administrative control of the elegant Times office on 42nd Street his abrasive efficiency did not endear him to the journalists, but they came to appreciate his ability to fix things. He was a wizard at selling Times book projects. No door remains closed for long to Ducas, whose Hooray-Henry drawl can penetrate two-inch steel plate. He had been busy talking to his Wall Street contacts. Within minutes of my arriving in his office he had wheeled in a smooth American-Lebanese executive from the merchant bankers Kidder Peabody. They would organize the whole thing for us. 'To hell with letting Thomson sell to the crap merchants,' Ducas barked. 'It's a staff buy-out we want. The Yanks know much more about buy-outs than the Brits. We'll revolutionize Fleet Street.' However, it was too early to commit us to a banker; nor did I feel able to let Kidders begin approaching their client investors. Some of their money would be from the Middle East, which might complicate the question of editorial independence. Roy Thomson told me once of an occasion when an oil sheikh had offered him all the gold he would need to buy the *New York Times*. 'Of course', the sheikh had murmured, 'we would want you to make it anti-Zionist.'

There was no money for us in Hartford. I was made to feel I was reducing the life expectancies of the executives even by mentioning the London print unions. But in Boston there was enthusiasm for a link with *The Sunday Times*, and no question that here was another ideal partner for us in terms of editorial empathy. For several years the *Globe* and *The Sunday Times* had exchanged journalists. Winship introduced me to Bill Taylor (who turned out to be a relation of Ducas). He ran the company and his family owned one third of it. He took a hard-headed view of what might be achieved with our unions; he liked the possibilities of the editorial connection in foreign reporting and book publishing, and we arranged a London visit.

When I got back there was another intriguing serenade. A letter merely said: 'Well! Any chance of you coming round to have a drink to discuss your problems?' I thought it might merely be an offer of publicity, but when I arrived to see Denis Forman, the chairman of Granada Television, his first words were: 'We want to buy *The Sunday Times*.' With him in his Golden Square office, adorned with modern paintings, were Alex Bernstein, the nephew of Sidney and the chairman of the whole group, and David Plowright, the managing director of Granada Television. I knew them all well. I had enjoyed doing many television programmes for them; twenty years earlier Plowright's career had survived producing me on *What The Papers Say*. I admired Granada's creativity and tenacity. Here was yet another ideal partner, but Granada were not inclined to think small. 'We must have control,' said Bernstein. 'We must close down and start again on a green field site with all the new technology,' said Plowright. I explained that this would entail closing down for a long time with a paper the size of *The Sunday Times*; as for control, I had begun talks with 'other interested parties'. Forman said they would think again about control; it might be that the IBA would prefer them to have a minority holding in our consortium. They would like to have the financial facts.

They were not the only ones. Talks with the *Guardian* and with the *Globe* were promising, but marking time. During the next few weeks the murmur at the end of every meeting with leading bankers was that it was all jolly interesting but they would, er, naturally appreciate seeing a few, ahem, figures. With Donoughue I visited Morgan Grenfell, the Queen's banker; Barclays Merchant Bank; and Schroder Wagg. In a separate operation James Callaghan, who was making reasonable progress with the general secretaries, arrived at my house with two Manchester directors of the Co-op Bank and Insurance Society and an armed guard; I was not sure whether he was to look after Callaghan or to make sure the directors didn't make a run for it when we asked for money.

In the meetings with the merchant bankers, in which Callaghan was not involved, Donoughue did most of the talking. He quite brazenly said we were offering the privilege of their acting as the lead banker without immediate fee. The chairman of Barclays Merchant Bank, Francis Dolling, came up with the intriguing idea of putting some shares in trust for the print unions conditional on their good behaviour. At Morgan Grenfell the deputy chairman, Christopher Reeves, reminded us that their chairman, Lord Catto, had acted for Murdoch in his bids for the *News of the World*, *Sun*, *Express* and *Observer*, but he had not approached them and they were probably free and interested. At Schroder Wagg we were made to feel as if we were casing the joint.

The requirement for figures was running up against two obstacles. First, Gordon Brunton had instructed directors of Times Newspapers not to give 'financial or other information to any third party'. Second, Thomson had told Warburgs that for the prospectus Times Newspapers was to be treated as a single asset; the financial consequences of splitting *The Times* and *The Sunday Times* were not to be set out. Beyond this there was a dislike, amounting to open hostility at times, of any consortium. It was aggravated by Rees-Mogg's public statements, but it was there before these were made and it principally reflected the feeling of Brunton. Ken Thomson had given him *carte blanche*. Five years earlier the relations of Hamilton with Roy Thomson had been such that, if he chose, he could have had an influence on the chief shareholder. He had at this stage none with the son. Though Hamilton was editor-in-chief, Ken Thomson had made no effort to consult him. The journalists' strike at *The Times* had not merely disenchanted Thomson with Times Newspapers, it had destroyed Hamilton's special relationship with the family.

Brunton was the dominant figure, the one the successful bidder for Times Newspapers would have to please. He had escaped odium for the £40 million failure of the year's shutdown. He was seen as the architect of the fortunes of Thomson British Holdings in North Sea oil, holidays, books, magazines and North American acquisitions, and as a brilliant negotiator. Roy Thomson himself brought him in after losing the 1961 take-over battle for Odhams to the *Mirror*; Odhams' chairman, Sir Christopher Chancellor, tipped him off to steal the thrusting young man from London's East End with the LSE degree whom he had been grooming as his successor. Brunton was quickly successful, buying up companies in Britain, South Africa and Australia, and later investing in travel against all the accounting advice. But perhaps what had most impressed Roy Thomson, who saw himself as champion cheeseparer of the world, was the occasion when Brunton had argued him into making the offer for Thomas Nelson, the publishers, on the basis of earnings rather than assets, which Thomson preferred, and saved £600,000. It was legend in the company how Roy had suggested a celebration dinner and left Brunton to pay the bill.

Nobody would have risked doing that to Gordon Brunton in 1981. He is a generous man, but not one to trifle with. He has a habit, when opposed, of lowering his large, domed forehead as if about to charge. He is open-minded politically, but on business affairs he does not change his mind easily and most people, seeing the glint behind his horn-rimmed glasses and the set of his jaw, are not minded to try. It was not without trepidation that I raised the question of the sale when I was his guest on 18 November at a Thirty Club dinner of newspaper executives at Claridge's. 'Don't worry, my boy,' he boomed. 'These papers won't die. But it's got to be a company deal. We are not going to split the titles.' I was depressed enough to record in my diary: 'Gordon bounced me on sale. Made me think it's not unions so much as TTO [the Thomson Organisation] which is going to be our problem.' So I called him at home the next day to try again. Newhouse was interested in buying, he said – in the end they did not want to be absentee owners of a troublesome enterprise – and so was Boston University, Lonrho, Sir James Goldsmith and Robert Maxwell. Murdoch had let it be known he intended to wait till everything collapsed and then he would pick up the pieces. I told Brunton I thought *The Sunday Times* could be saved on its own and that at some stage I would want to put our propositions to him personally. His response was discouraging. 'Barnetson is putting together a consortium. I am not prepared to give any information at the moment to consortia.'

It was a rebuff, though in one sense I was privileged. The next day, at a joint lunch of the boards of Times Newspapers and Thomson, Brunton would only say he had given various undertakings of confidentiality and so could not say what 'fine corporations' wanted to buy us. Hamilton sat dejected throughout; he was still hurt and angry with Rees-Mogg. He suggested, when we talked privately, that I should make an approach to Lord Barnetson, who was chairman of *The Observer* as well as of United Newspapers. 'The trouble with Murdoch', he suddenly volunteered, 'is that he is too quixotic. You would get no continuity from him and continuity is what a quality newspaper is all about.' It was, in truth, what Hamilton had provided.

This was now the third reference to Murdoch. Rees-Mogg had told me over lunch on 14 November, on his return from the United States, that he had been to have tea with Murdoch in his *New York Post* office: I was surprised, because he had previously expressed a poor opinion of him. 'Rupert says he's not interested in *The Times*,' William said to me now, 'but he is in *The Sunday Times*. He thinks you might be against him and he's been wondering if he should ring you. Why not call him yourself?' I resolved that that was one thing I would never do.

I did sound out Barnetson, as Hamilton had suggested. The late Bill Barnetson, resplendent in waistcoat and gold fob watch, was one of the shrewdest men in Fleet Street. He pooh-poohed Brunton's story that he was part of a consortium. He discounted the prospect of a bid for Times Newspapers by Atlantic Richfield and *The Observer* or by United Newspapers. Rees-Mogg was right to want to take the printing of *The Times* out of London: Barnetson had advised him how it could be done for £7 million a year which would at once make it profitable. *The Sunday Times* should stand on its own as a title, but lease its presses during the week to *The Financial Times* as well as *The Guardian*. This would enable *The Financial Times* to realize the real-estate value of its premises.

Somehow I had not thought of *The Financial Times*; it could make a significant contribution to the printing overheads of an independent *Sunday Times*. I called Alan Hare, the managing director. He was not overjoyed at the idea of risking his paper with our press-room chapels: it was not on. He would be interested only if the *Daily Telegraph* joined in too, in Duke Hussey's old dream of creating one printing centre for the quality papers. This was too complex an ambition, I thought, at this particular time, and I could not anyway take it further myself for the sake of the secret alliance with *The Guardian*. The presses could take the *Telegraph* and *FT* but only at the cost of squeezing out *The Guardian*. I reported it all, however, to Hamilton in case he wished to pursue it himself.

It was hard to work out what was going on behind the scenes at Thomson. Hamilton had not exaggerated the annoyance Rees-Mogg had created by going public with his consortium; I thought the criticism of him was absurd. I lost only half a halo by leading a consortium; the other half was preserved by the discretion enjoined by our partners. Brunton was certainly in a genial mood when he invited me and Tina to dinner at the end of November at his Elizabethan farmhouse near Godalming in Surrey. He had been riding across his acres. He looked fit and happy, proclaiming in front of a great log fire that union negotiations would begin with the new owner in ten days' time. He did not attach a name then, but over dinner spoke warmly of Atlantic Richfield, owners of *The Observer*. I took this as a clue, because during the shutdown Brunton had vowed he would never forgive Anderson of Arco for exploiting the absence of *The Sunday Times*. 'They'll run the two papers separately for a bit, then merge them,' said Brunton confidently. 'But who do you want, Harry?' I said I would like to be in a position to run

The Sunday Times. He dismissed the thought. 'That's not for you. You don't want to go into management. You're a creative journalist. It's *The Times* you should do. The Thunderer hasn't thundered for a long time. But don't worry about *The Sunday Times*. I have a few principles about the editorial conduct of the paper.'

In the next few days a take-over by Arco gained credence. The *Daily Mirror* said Anderson was in town to decide between J.R. and Bobby Ewing, that is between Harold Evans and Donald Trelford. Conor Cruise O'Brien had to be restrained from launching an immediate campaign against the idea of a combined *Sunday Times–Observer*.

Other characters in the melodrama were beginning to shuffle about in the wings. Lord Rothermere used the occasion of the funeral of his nonagenarian London *Evening News* (merged with the *Standard*) to say he would be interested in buying *The Sunday Times*, but would like to see it closed first. With a carelessness about figures that comes painlessly to millionaires, he said, 'Anyone would have to be mad to buy *The Sunday Times* as it exists now losing £15 million a year.' (The sum represented the losses of the whole company including *The Times*.) John Barry reported that this had been followed up by a private call from a Rothermere assistant to say they wanted discussions: they, too, had some idea of using Gray's Inn Road, moving the *Daily Mail* there and realizing the millions of pounds of real estate locked up in their old premises at Carmelite House on the Embankment.

One night in Paris another of the contenders mentioned by Brunton entered the arena with a bravura display of capework. Not for Sir James Goldsmith the stealth of Murdoch or the geniality of Barnetson. He was then, in his mid-forties, the proprietor of *Now!* magazine (which he closed the following year). The son of an English Jewish father, who had sent him to Eton, and a French Roman Catholic mother, he had earned himself the title of Britain's No. 1 Grocer, building Cavenham Foods with ferocious energy into the third largest food company in Europe. An excitable man of radical right-wing opinions, he was eager to add a newspaper title to his Bovril, Marmite, and Maypole and Lipton stores. In 1976 he had tried to buy *The Observer* and been beaten off by Lord Goodman. He had then tried to control the *Daily Express* by buying stock, and had been beaten off by Sir Max Aitken. The following year he had joined forces with Tiny Rowlands of Lonrho to oppose Rothermere's bid, and lost to Victor Matthews of Trafalgar House.

His connections with *The Sunday Times* had been equally unhappy, though for different reasons. Richard Milner of Business News had enraged him by asking questions about his deals; so had Charles Raw. He had asked Roy Thomson to tell me to stop, and he had complained to Brunton. I had seen Goldsmith and told him he was certainly entitled to have allegations fairly put to him, but not to expect either an acquaint-anceship with Thomson or Brunton or an incidental business connection in insurance and legal publishing to have any influence on *The Sunday Times*. I did not at the time think I had bowled him over. Subsequently, he had defamed one of the best *Sunday Times* reporters, Phillip Knight-ley, and paid libel damages. Also, he had most famously featured in *The Sunday Times* scoop disclosing that Sir Harold Wilson's retirement honours list was held up because there were objections in Whitehall and Buckingham Palace to the inclusion of Goldsmith and other friends of Lady Falkender.

It did not surprise me, then, to hear in November that he was a critic. However, as a bidder and possible proprietor, his views had piquancy and he made them known with a certain panache on a day of double celebration: he resigned from the CBI and his wife was delivered of a baby. David Leitch, a former Paris correspondent of the paper who still contributed, was in the Paris Travellers' Club when Goldsmith arrived. Leitch reported back to me:

Goldsmith delivered his blast in front of several Travellers' members who listened indulgently as if Jimmy sounding off were a regular feature of club life (it seems it is). I don't think he had any special reason for this performance, which he launched into the moment he arrived. He wasn't drunk, though he had been drinking champagne. He began by saying that the *ST* was journal-istically a very impressive paper but that he would 'buy it for ten million [sterling] for the pleasure of shutting it down'. This was because Business News 'was a cancer' which would finally infect the whole organism and therefore, by way of elaborate medical metaphor, the paper had to be killed off. He said he would be prepared to back someone who would act 'as a real proprietor', that is to say, someone who used the paper to propagate political and other ideas. He said this Beaverbrook tradition of the proprietor's role was healthy and honest; much preferable to what he eccentrically sees as Roy Thomson's approach – that is, acquiring the papers as a means to oil leases and other commercial benefits.

Goldsmith said he would be prepared to put up money to back *The Times*, though – except for the Business News, naturally – it was journalistically inferior to the *ST*. William, however, he saw as an honest, sincere man whom he would be happy to assist. Again because of Business News and also some rambling history of TV debates, Goldsmith is convinced that you fall far short of this accolade. Indeed, most damagingly in his eyes, you are the ally and patron on Charles Raw who 'isn't a journalist at all, though he pretends to be. He's an ideologist and an anti-free enterprise crusader masquerading as an investigative reporter'.

The subject of investigative reporting stimulated a fine, conspiratorial blast in the course of which he claimed, most exotically, that Larry Stern (of the *Washington Post*) had been a Cuban agent. He said he had a very good source for this and he was sure Stern had been the guiding spirit behind Woodward and Bernstein. He mentioned that he'd had a dinner *à deux* with Richard Nixon at La Grenouille in New York a few nights previously; whether this was meant to hint at the source I'm not sure. He believed the likeliest purchaser of TNL was Vere Harmsworth [Lord Rothermere] who would use the presses to print a *Sunday Mail*. He did not think any serious bidding would take place until after closure. By the end he had calmed down a bit and specifically exempted Tony Bambridge ('unobjectionable') from his strictures against Business News. He said there were a lot of good reporters, as opposed to ideologists and so forth on the paper. Lewis Chester exemplified a life-style and 'extreme left-wing political position' he disagreed with but he was impressed by the accuracy of reporting in the Chester-Fenby book, *The Fall of the House of Beaverbrook*.

The paranoid loathing he feels for the Business News and Charles Raw goes back to the period when Arnold Wesker visited the paper and wrote a play and article. He believes that Wesker uncovered an anti-Semitic vendetta levelled against himself and that you are somehow part of it. He knew I worked for the *ST* and that was the pretext. He said he was making a point of repeating his remarks about Charles Raw's 'ideological' bias in different places because he wanted either Charles or the *ST*, it wasn't clear which, to sue him.

Shortly after Leitch's message I had a call from Harold Lever. Goldsmith had told him he wanted to meet me over lunch at Lever's house to 'bury the hatchet'. I bore Goldsmith no ill-will. I declined for the same reason I had not responded to Murdoch's invitation to phone. The sale was a chance to create something new in Fleet Street; none of the seven dwarfs was as attractive as the ownership we were losing. At just about this time, in mid-November, things began to click into place at last. First, we settled on bankers. Donoughue and I had been impressed with Morgan Grenfell; they said they would be our lead bankers and act without fee. Slaughter and May became our solicitors. Second, it became possible to construct a plan for an independent *Sunday Times*. At a Times Newspapers board meeting on 19 November, when we approved the Times Newspapers prospectus for Warburgs, the marketing director, Garry Thorne, who was also general manager of *The Times*, raised the sensitive issue of staff who wanted to take part in consortia. Senior advertising and marketing men had formed themselves under him into a group called TREE – Times Revenue Earning Executives. Thorne wanted them for one thing to be able to give advice to JOTT; it was ridiculous that JOTT was contemplating hiring an outside marketing consultant. To my surprise, James Evans did not demur, nor try to clamp down on information. Consequently the way became clear for Cruickshank to work with our executive committee. Neither consortia nor splits of the company had suddenly become popular with Thomson; but it must have been decided that it was prudent not to block them at this stage.

I had an opportunity to bolster the case for separating the titles when, on 1 December, the national directors came to lunch with us, followed by a special meeting of Times Newspapers Holdings, the top-tier non-executive board. Rees-Mogg and I were called in separately in the afternoon to give our views on the criteria the new ownership should be asked to accept. In addition to the four national directors, Lords Dacre, Greene, Robens and Roll, there were Lord Keith and Tommy Emblem (for the Astors); James Evans and Duke Hussey; and Sir Denis Hamilton in the chair. I had heard from Rees-Mogg, who was flushed with annoyance by it, that Hamilton had taken the deputy editor of The Times, Louis Heren, to lunch and told him how wrong it was for consortia to be formed for the separate titles. In the board interview Hamilton asked if I had anything to say on the 'hot potato' of the sale of the company, as opposed to the sale of separate titles. I replied that Times Newspapers had had some successes and it was wrong to portray it as a total failure, but I did believe that Times Newspapers had problems of size and loyalties. We needed to draw on title loyalties and involve the staff more (vigorous nods from Keith). I did not rule out a continuation of single ownership, but I preferred devolution. My group would be in a position to save The Sunday Times on its own. This led to an exchange with Lord Roll, who was present in a dual capacity as a national director and the chairman of Warburgs.

LORD ROLL: That is well in the terms of the remit. You should not think it is excluded.

EVANS: No, but the procedure which has been adopted effectively puts it as a second choice.

LORD ROLL: I imagine several things will be going on at the same time.

I was invited to comment on the draft of criteria for Warburgs. It included a clause that the new owners should be asked if they would give a written guarantee of independence for the editors 'on similar lines to that which they had enjoyed under the Astor and Thomson ownership', and what the terms should be if the appointments of the present editors were continued. I responded that the terms for the present editors were a side matter; what was vital was to institutionalize the way the editors were protected. This need not be by the present convention, but it needed to be set down in detail. It was important also to get a pledge that the unique character of The Sunday Times would be preserved; in the news area this meant a willingness from time to time to stake resources on inquiry and to take calculated risks. Nobody dissented. Another clause said that 'the new owners should be of good reputation' and should of preference be British but 'Commonwealth and North American would not be excluded'. Lord Keith was keen on British ownership. Duke Hussey suggested, unsuccessfully, that Europeans should be excluded because the EEC was unpopular. Everyone agreed that Arab and Israeli interests should be excluded. It was a cheerful enough meeting with Hamilton saying that all the directors would like me to compliment the staff of *The Sunday Times* on its continued success in the face of our difficulties.

In these favourable breezes I applied to Warburgs for a copy of the Times Newspapers Information Memorandum. I knew, as a director, what was in it, but formal application was the act of a potential bidder. I notified Brunton and Hamilton I was doing so. I half expected a rebuke and a rejection, or possibly a request to leave the vetting committee, for it was a formal notice of intention to keep on uttering the dirty words 'single title' and 'consortium'. We had heard that a consortium headed by Sir Richard Marsh with Peter Jay and David Frost in it had been refused the document 'at this time', and Warburgs were attaching four pages of conditions, which had to be signed, to any release of the document. The second paragraph sought a promise not to 'initiate or accept or engage in any contacts of any kind with the staff, union representatives or employees at Times Newspapers'. I told Geoffrey Elliott of Warburgs that I could not accept this. He did not press it. Morgan Grenfell received the document. I did accept the first clause of the conditions, which was an undertaking not to reveal that we had expressed an interest in buying 'Times Newspapers Limited and/or that company's titles or assets'. There did not seem much point at the time; it was a condition *The Guardian*, *Boston Globe*, and Granada all wanted anyway.

Secrecy was becoming a way of life. Meetings with *The Guardian* were in my home. When I talked with 'the cardinals' it was still about 'x' and 'y' and 'z'. James Callaghan and the union leaders were extremely anxious that their negotiations should not leak. The union men were leading double lives, talking to Callaghan in 'private capacities' at meetings that 'had not taken place' so that they did not have to risk the enterprise by reporting prematurely to their executives. When a meeting was finally fixed between us all for 8 December in his office in Old Scotland Yard I fancied that I had scuttled undetected through the portico in the manner of Moriarty, but I had made an error so elementary I nearly blew the whole thing. Bill Keys, the general secretary of SOGAT, arrived in Callaghan's office complaining that when he had visited the gents on his way he had found himself next to a SOGAT member who had interrogated him on what he was up to. Was it perchance something to do with Harold Evans? It was my driver, nature having overruled my instruction to return to the office. Keys, fortunately, was used to bluffing his way out of awkward situations.

The others present in Callaghan's room were Owen O'Brien, the general secretary of NATSOPA, and the top two of the NGA, general secretary Joe Wade and his president Les Dixon. These were the key unions, the ones who had most jobs to lose by closure, and the ones with most to give in the way of manning, efficient practices and continuous production. Callaghan and Keys (also chairman of the print industry committee of the TUC) had agreed that they should do everything they could to ensure that *The Times* and *Sunday Times* did not fall under the personal control of a millionaire or anyone who would wish to use them as a source of propaganda or power. Callaghan had made it clear he would not do anything unless the unions were going to give 'copper-bottomed guarantees' on production and be realistic about manning and new technology. Keys had made enough progress for us to meet to discuss Callaghan's proposal that a trust should be formed to acquire the business. It would offer the workers directly, and through their chapels and trade unions, a chance to buy shares; it would use their guarantees and new operating agreements to attract outside investment; and the trustees would be pledged to defend editorial independence in the manner of the Scott Trust at *The Guardian*. Major investors would have representation on the trust, and so would the unions, but there would be professional management.

All this, everyone recognized, was only the outline of a bramble bush. There was one simplification in that nobody wanted to do anything with *The Times*; *The Sunday Times* was seen as potentially a very profitable newspaper. This preference for concentrating effort on saving titles singly was contrary to their representations to Brunton that they preferred a company sale because it saved more jobs. There was variable enthusiasm about the unions themselves putting money into *The Sunday Times*. Wade, to Callaghan's displeasure, was discouraging: 'How can I put my members' money into something that's likely to yield a lower return than the Trustee Savings Bank? Anyway, most of them are not in Fleet Street.' His president, Dixon, liked the idea; O'Brien thought NATSOPA might go along with something nominal like £80,000 from each union; Keys was keen, remarking that his union had put some money into local radio. Everyone agreed that the unions had to control what Dixon called the 'cowboys', the Saturday night casuals. Keys proclaimed that SOGAT had easily the best record, which inflamed the others, and before Callaghan could intervene we were in the middle of a shouting match about which was the worst union. Then Wade had another bout of frankness: 'Jim, you must understand that general secretaries cannot necessarily deliver anything, not even continuous production.' Callaghan responded sharply: 'Well, in that case I am not going to write to Ken Thomson putting down a marker.' O'Brien came to the rescue, pulling from his pocket a draft of a disputes procedure which the others thought they could accept.

It was agreed that Callaghan should formally register the interest of the group by writing (as he did) to Ken Thomson, Gordon Brunton, Warburgs and Morgan Grenfell, and that in early January I would show them a management plan for a solo *Sunday Times*, with the implications in manning and practices spelled out. Bill Keys was to co-ordinate the union side. Unfortunately, said Callaghan, the January meeting would have to go ahead without him. He was committed to leaving for Australia and Singapore on 9 January, returning on 15 February. This left only three weeks between his return and closure. Clearly we would hope by then to be well into negotiations, certainly with Thomsons and probably with the unions too. This was a pity, because Callaghan, while not being knowledgeable, had already demonstrated he could bang heads together. I consoled myself with the thought that at least it would make dealing with *The Guardian* easier. Peter Gibbings had grown jumpy about Callaghan.

We did not get anywhere that afternoon with Callaghan's ideas on a trust. This did not worry me at this stage. *The Guardian*, Granada and the *Boston Globe* would all want their say, and Donoughue was conferring with Morgan Grenfell. There were all sorts of possibilities. It was nice to think we might achieve something like the set-up at the *Milwaukee Journal*, where a successful employee partnership scheme had been carried through by a visionary publisher on the death of the founder; or like *Le Monde* or the John Lewis Partnership. But these were pipedreams. The main capital assets involved had in those cases effectively been given away to the employees. I had once been emboldened by the environment of our meeting to suggest to Roy Thomson that he should do just that as his final contribution to British journalism. We were dining with a group of Chinese Communist leaders, and the talk was about how capitalism might be improved. Roy had given it short shrift. 'No, the workers would just sell their stock; that's what they do in ICI.'

A number of *Sunday Times* specialist staff had also put up schemes, notably Graham Serjeant, the financial columnist; Alastair Brett, one of the lawyers; and Colin Simpson, the investigative journalist, who was normally looking at balance sheets to see how the money had been stolen. Peter Wilsher was acting as catalyst and cold-water bath. Nobody favoured simple workers' control. The most popular idea was to encourage employee shareholdings by giving shares as bonuses for good performance and by inviting subscriptions for a special class of employee share (including management) which would be discounted in return for restricting resale to other staff. These employee shareholdings were not envisaged as taking up more than 5% of the initial capital. They were seen as incentives rather than as industrial democracy.

Bob Ducas reported that the Taylor family had been unable to carry the other trustees of the *Boston Globe*, but he had been in touch with more of his friends. Henry Keswick, the owner of the *Spectator* and taipan of Jardine Matheson & Muir, the biggest trading company in Hong Kong, expressed a personal, but not a corporate, interest. Raymond Mason, the chief executive of Charter company, the large independent oil group, who was an admirer of *The Sunday Times* and a personal friend of Peter Jay as well as of Ducas, acted quickly. Charter owned the *Philadelphia Bulletin*, which was not doing well, and he despatched to London its president and publisher M.S. (Buddy) Hayden. He caught the next Concorde, a dark compact man firing questions as he hit the tarmac. Fortunately, Cruickshank had done his sums, for Hayden was a master of every detail of newspaper production. Finally he said they would like 50%. We demurred. He had 'no problem' with our concept of a trust guaranteeing editorial independence, but we felt too large a share for Charter might unbalance the consortium and possibly create difficulties with *The Guardian*; and we still had to accommodate Granada. The last word from Denis Forman, after they had seen the Cruickshank draft plan for the paper, was that they were still interested, provided I promised to stay, but they would consider only a controlling interest.

Relating all these groups was clearly going to be a complex and delicate matter, but Morgan Grenfell refused to be fazed. Nonchalance in the face of anarchy was very much their style in everything, as if displays of energy or raised voices invited rebuke from the whiskered and waistcoated founders preserved in sepia on the walls of their parlours. The languor of the young men in their nice, chalk-striped blue suits alarmed me at first. Had Donoughue deceived himself? But always they had done a lot more work than they cared to acknowledge, producing papers on the best tax arrangements for our ideas for employee stock and an outline of our formal bid letter. They had reservations about the Callaghan trust, but recognized that it might prepare the ground for the union agreements that would assure the future of *The Sunday Times*. The Cruickshank draft management plan predicted that sudden inheritance of the overheads currently shared with *The Times* would reduce the profit of nearly £5 million projected in the Warburg prospectus to one of around £1 million in our first year, on a revenue of no less than £69 million. But the 1982 profit would be in the region of £8 million and thereafter it would run at around £11 million. This made healthy reading against the Morgan Grenfell guess that we might acquire the business for about £10 million; they and we regarded the figure mentioned in the press of £50 million or more as either a wild guess or a Thomson leak for the purposes of bargaining. Cruickshank's 1982 plan included concentrating the paper in the one building at 200 Gray's Inn Road, so saving on our share of the rent of the new building, and the offer of full-time jobs to smaller permanent production crews. The pattern of shifts proposed for NGA and NATSOPA regular staff gave us the chance to gain extra revenue by printing 32 pages on a Friday to produce 88-page newspapers, 16 pages more than the maximum then. We would still need casual drivers and packers in SOGAT, but the main 'cowboy' problem would be removed; disruption by casual workers had cost Times Newspapers £2 million loss of trading profit in 1978 and nearly £1.5 million in 1980.

We could go it alone. The print workers at *The Sunday Times* knew nothing of my meetings, but it was an article of faith that it had been a bad marriage and the physical consummation at Gray's Inn Road a disaster. The *Sunday Times* men blamed *The Times* for the odium of losses; *The Times* men blamed *The Sunday Times* for a plague of disruption. Wherever I went on Fridays and Saturdays back at the newspaper I was drawn aside by Linotype operators, comps, foundry men, messengers and drivers eager for a fresh start. 'I'd take a stake myself in *The Sunday Times*. . . . The union won't get me out again. . . . We'll deal with the bovver boys, don't you worry.' In the news room one day Peter Wilby warned me, 'I hope you're getting somewhere ... they'll bolt in favour of anyone turned up by TTO', but editorial morale seemed high. They were certainly producing some very good newspapers.

On 11 December, when I called on Denis Hamilton in his office, he was a deeply troubled man. He was hurt that Ken Thomson was not consulting him – Hamilton was, of course, chairman of Times Newspapers. Thomson, treading heavily during a company after-dinner speech, had also just wounded him by expressing his relief at getting rid of Times Newspapers. Hamilton created Times Newspapers; it was his life. In an extraordinary incident, the Hamiltons, who normally endure much for protocol, had felt strongly enough to walk out of the dinner. Rees-Mogg's open criticisms of Times Newspapers' structure still rankled as 'sabotage'. Though I had refrained from seconding Rees-Mogg in public, Hamilton in his isolation felt let down. I could understand his disillusionment, since both Rees-Mogg and I owed our chairs to his creation of the company.

At a Reuters board meeting that week, he told me, Murdoch had said he was interested in the company. He did not want to apply to Warburg for a prospectus so he, Hamilton, was giving him one. 'Murdoch asked if he would be acceptable to you', Hamilton said casually, 'and I told him that he would, subject to certain guarantees.' He was standing by his desk, looking out of the window into Gray's Inn Road. 'Perhaps I should have asked you first, so I'm asking you now.'

I was astounded. The only explanation was that Hamilton thought he could tame Murdoch as he had tamed Kemsley and Thomson. He had not been willing to consider our consortium for *The Sunday Times* since he had turned down my invitation to him to lead it, but his attitude to Murdoch represented a staggering reversal. For most of Murdoch's London career, Hamilton had been his sternest critic. He had softened his attitude to him recently, when Murdoch joined the Reuters board, but only a few weeks before he had volunteered the judgement that Murdoch was unsuitable. The way Hamilton raised Murdoch with me now was wholly out of character. In the fifteen years I had known him, he avoided stressful argument, but, when there was something grave to discuss, he always made it a formal matter. Yet here he was casually pre-empting the most crucial decision on our future.

I could scarcely believe it. 'But, Denis, we have our consortium. That's the way *The Sunday Times* wants to go.'

The meeting seemed a torment to him. He stared out of the window, saying nothing again.

'Murdoch?' I went on. 'What guarantees? They'd have to be something special.'

It was an inadequate expression of my shock. Having dropped his bombshell, he did not want to discuss Murdoch. He moved off the subject, inconsequentially I thought at the time, asking, 'Have you ever thought of editing *The Times*?' Yes, of course I had, I said, but perhaps he should do it, now that Rees-Mogg had announced he would leave after the sale. He had always said he wished he had never given up editing in 1966. He could easily do it for four years. He brooded. 'No, what *The Times* needs is a new marketing strategy and a young man in his thirties full of energy . . .'.

A few days later, at a Christmas party in the colour magazine offices, a senior *Sunday Times* man, Peter Harland, remarked to Hamilton that he thought our consortium was the best thing since Reuter's pigeons. He was startled by Hamilton's scorn. I had not discussed my consortium activities in any detail with Hamilton following his refusal to join the Callaghan talks. The truth was that we both shied away from a subject that would jar our friendship. I deliberately did not tell him about *The Guardian*. Peter Gibbings's wishes apart, the time for this was when the bids for both an independent *Sunday Times* and an independent *Times* were in place, and the move could not in any way be regarded as damaging to *The Times*.

The finishing touches to our application were made in a long meeting in my office with Bernard Donoughue, Donald Cruickshank, and Tony Richmond-Watson of Morgan Grenfell. A six-page letter from Morgan Grenfell to Warburgs, outlining our proposals, but not naming a price yet, was prepared and held back until 31 December, the Thomson deadline. I had asked 'the cardinals' and a number of other people in the office if they wished to be associated with it, which they did, so Morgan Grenfell told Warburgs they were making a proposal for purchase 'on behalf of Harold Evans, Editor of *The Sunday Times* and Chairman of the Sunday Times Executive Committee, and his close associates on the Staff'.

The letter (text in appendix) began:

> At the time of purchase the shareholders of the Company will consist principally of substantial and reputable investment institutions. Shares will be made available to the employees of the Company generally as well as to Mr Evans and his Associates. It is possible that there will be at least one significant trade investment in the shares of the Company, but such holdings are not expected to represent a majority of the share capital ...

Morgan Grenfell concluded that they looked forward to a response from Thomson at their earliest convenience.

I felt cheered, as I went on holiday, by how far we had come. We had established that an independent *Sunday Times* was a realistic proposition. We had prepared the ground for two sets of negotiations. We knew what we wanted from both Thomson and from the unions, and what we could offer them. Brunton and Hamilton had hardly been encouraging, but the game was about to change. In January, according to Peter Gibbings's plan, there would be a press conference when, with our bankers, Morgan Grenfell and Hambros, we would announce the basic *Sunday Times–Guardian* alliance. The Callaghan initiative might have borne fruit for display. By then, crucially, Thomson would have two proposals from long-time colleagues and directors of Times Newspapers for both *The Sunday Times* and *The Times*. Rees-Mogg and Lord Barnetson had told me how it was planned to print *The Times* outside London for a total cost of £7 million a year, one-third of the current cost. This would make it immediately profitable and ensure not merely its survival but also its ability to carry out its proclaimed historic role as a newspaper of record. The heady thought was that both papers could be reborn in freedom and security. It would make worthwhile all the sacrifices of the Thomson family, the agonies of their managements and the frustrations of the staffs.

As I went on holiday, I had Christmas greetings from Ken Thomson in Canada. I did not suppose there was any symbolic significance in his traditional present: a box of hard cheese.

6

THE GUARANTEES

There were blizzards in the French Alps in the early days of 1981. I was in one of them, at the top of a mountain in Les Arcs, when James Callaghan telephoned from London. I doubt whether I would have skied down in one piece, as I just about did, had I known the message that was waiting for me at the bottom. 'It's a disaster,' said Callaghan when the French telephone system eventually delivered him. 'The Thomson management are thick in secret negotiation with Murdoch. And I've got to leave for Australia.' Bill Keys of SOGAT was the source of his intelligence.

The afternoon's ski run in a blizzard had been an unhappy omen. The slope was too steep, the snow too deep, the visibility treacherous. Gullies vanishing into infinity awaited every false move. The large lumps known as 'moguls' loomed up in the mist, removing breath and confidence. Friendly paths through the trees ended in ice walls. Nothing was to be trusted.

The first alarm, when I cut short my holiday on Thursday 8 January, was to read what Brunton had told union leaders. The unnamed new proprietor would be acceptable, he said, to the unions, to Thomson, to the national directors 'and the editor-in-chief'. There was no mention of the two editors of *The Times* and *Sunday Times*. Neither Hamilton nor Brunton responded to a message I had sent on ahead that I would be back in the office on Friday and available for discussion. But Eric Jacobs, who was writing a report for *The Sunday Times*, did reach Brunton, who told him the editors could not expect to be on the vetting committee because they were competitors for the titles.

The danger that this might become the Thomson view had concerned us all ever since we made the decision to put in an independent bid for *The Sunday Times*. It was not all that unreasonable. I had, indeed, discussed with 'the cardinals' whether I should resign from the vetting committee myself so as to be free to lead opposition publicly to an unacceptable bidder. The consensus had been that the vetting committee was a better place to defend editorial freedoms; it was a place in the company's trenches rather than no-man's-land. So Peter Wilsher set out to protest to as many national directors as he could reach, and I tried to find out what was going on. We had heard nothing from Warburgs or Thomson since our proposal had been submitted. Hamilton had gone to earth, but I ran down James Evans at home. He was reassuring. Was it Murdoch? Oh, nothing was happening yet, and of course our consortium had not been excluded. It was a matter for Denis Hamilton; I should talk to him.

A completely different picture emerged when I spoke with Bill Keys. He had met Murdoch on the Monday. There was no doubt he was Thomson's choice. He was bidding for all titles. He had put proposals to Brunton and been promised a response within three days. 'He's frightfully confident of success,' said Keys, who was dismayed by the social and political implications of a Murdoch take-over. I sent telegrams to Hamilton's London and country homes. Finally on Sunday evening he called. It was a painful conversation. What was I doing in London? I should not have broken my holiday without consulting the editor-in-chief. How dare Wilsher try to reach the national directors. My staff was impossible. As for the vetting committee, that was a matter for him, not Brunton. 'There may be some public disagreement, but I am bound to consult the editors.' He sounded strained; I was somewhat reassured about the vetting and there seemed no point in tormenting him with Thomson's secret preference for Murdoch over our consortium. This was, I now think, carrying consideration too far, but I was excited at the time by the imminent prospect of announcing the alliance with *The Guardian*. Battle could then commence.

Clearly, if Bill Keys were right, we would have to move fast on all fronts, but the meeting with *The Guardian* and our bankers was arranged for Monday 12 January, and it was to be followed the next day by one with the Callaghan group of union general secretaries. We would have to decide, among other things, how to publicize our bid so that it could not be swept under the carpet: Warburgs had insisted that applicants for the prospectus should agree to keep quiet about their interest.

Murdoch himself made this less of a problem by breaking the rule. On that Sunday he gave an interview from Washington to BBC radio's *The World This Weekend* in which he said he was seriously 'considering' a bid. His original interest had been in *The Sunday Times*, one of the world's finest newspapers edited by one of the great editors, etc., but now he 'might' consider the purchase of all five titles in Times Newspapers. He had asked for figures. Thomsons, for their part, refused to answer press queries as to whether Murdoch was their favoured bidder. It was all window-dressing, though far more blatant than I realized at the time. Murdoch, I learned later, had seen Brunton in London as early as 8 December to declare an interest in all five titles. Thomsons had jumped to it. Warburgs' document had been sent round to News International. For the next three weeks Murdoch was constantly on the telephone with questions. On 30 December he put in an opening bid of a derisory £1 million – cheeky, but the kind of poker Brunton relished. Lonrho and Associated Newspapers had also put in proposals.

The week of 12–19 January was an urgent round of consultations in Fleet Street and the City, with Ducas keeping in touch with Buddy Hayden and Standard Oil of America. Some of them had been planned before Christmas in the happy belief that they would just about coincide with negotiations with Thomson-Warburg. Some were improvised as the week took a nasty turn. Every day we expected some word from Geoffrey Elliott at Warburgs or from Brunton himself. Richmond-Watson at Morgan Grenfell had called Warburgs at the end of the first week in January to see how our proposals had been received. It was made clear to him that they were preoccupied with proposals to buy the whole company. He responded that we might be able to meet Thomson's desire to dispose of the whole company: he was thinking of a link with the JOTT-Mogg consortium at *The Times*. He was surprised, in any event, that we had not been invited to explain our own proposals in detail. So much for Lord Roll's assurance at our directors' meeting that several things would be going on at the same time. Only one thing was going on. Still, we thought, this will not survive what we have in mind for the week.

The *Guardian* and Callaghan group meetings were arranged out of our offices, in Room 343 at the Charing Cross Hotel, a subterfuge to which the hotel management contributed by announcing 'Times Newspapers meeting' in white plastic letters on a stand in the main lobby. The *Guardian* board was meeting there and Gibbings came in with Peter Preston, the editor; Donoughue and Richmond-Watson joined us. The first item, I suggested, was how we could force ourselves into serious consideration by Thomson, and especially how we could cope with their insistence on selling the whole company in a single package. Well, said Gibbings, perhaps they had better explain that unfortunately they had been unable to carry the *Guardian* board with them. ...

It was a devastating moment. Donoughue's eyes popped and I suppose he would say my jaw dropped. Preston, who likes to ponder before he speaks, bit on his pipe, folded his arms, and left the talking to Gibbings. 'We are as keen as ever we were,' said Gibbings, 'but we have spent the morning looking at our forecasts for revenues for 1981. They're disastrous. We have to offer the workforce almost no wage increases. We just don't see how we can do that and justify spending several millions buying shares in *The Sunday Times*.'

I wondered whether the rumours about Murdoch had upset them. No, but he was a disaster. 'Don't trust a single word he says,' said Gibbings, and Preston was moved to nod his endorsement. Gibbings had been powerfully affected by Murdoch's treatment of managers.

Preston recalled how editors who resisted Murdoch's interventions vanished like managers of Crystal Palace football club. *The Guardian* would do what it could to help. Gibbings made the gesture of offering £250,000 for the independent bid, and Preston was to write a brilliantly derisive editorial on the central issues of press freedom and diversity.

These were not issues to cut much ice with the Callaghan group of general secretaries when we met at teatime in the jinxed Room 343. They thought Murdoch had it in the bag. They competed in banter about which of them Murdoch had sent for first. 'Come clean with me, I met him in Eaton Square last Monday,' said Les Dixon of the N G A. 'He's got all the figures, he knows what he wants.' He added to me, 'He's going to sack all your top management.' A Reuters man was coming to run Times Newspapers with Murdoch. Dixon and Owen O'Brien (N A T S O P A) exchanged bromides on how nice and easy it would be to have someone take over the whole company and most of the jobs: 'We can make a deal with him.' Only Keys joined me in pressing fidelity to the alliance we had so painfully put together, which would give their members a chance to take shares. Dixon doodled while Keys spelled out Murdoch's political prejudices. I told them I understood the attraction to them of preserving the whole company. How would it be if we linked up with Rees-Mogg's consortium? Everyone hooted.

It was hopeless. The best I could do was ask them to press for guarantees of editorial freedom. Keys and O'Brien said they would. Dixon fell in, then remembered his lines: 'Murdoch is high in his praise for you, Harry. He says he will pull out of the whole deal if you won't go on editing *The Sunday Times* for him.' Keys rounded off a jolly evening by saying Murdoch was flying in from Washington to see Brunton on Friday and to get a final answer the following Monday, 19 January.

Thus, in the space of a few days, much of the planning of the previous autumn had been destroyed. The atmosphere in the company was one of a family plot. Hamilton was evasive about the schedule. He was surviving on finesse and feeling the strain. I saw him several times in his office in the week of 12–19 January. He was pale and tense, wearing a surgical collar and silk scarf. He patently wanted the whole deal to go through without any argument. He avoided telling me directly that he, Brunton and James Evans had plumped for Murdoch. One day I walked in when he was talking to Evans and there followed one of those awkward conversations when two people try to go on talking without letting the third know what it is all about. There was not much meat, said Evans, on 'those people' who came yesterday. He would be seeing 'him' again on Friday.

Hamilton spoke about Murdoch as one would about a royal prince; polite society assumed an automatic succession of the blood royal in the undefined fullness of time. Harmsworth (Lord Rothermere) and Lonrho were beyond the pale; Harmsworth was only interested in a sordid property deal. It was eerie how everyone had been programmed on Murdoch-speak. 'He thinks the world of you,' said Hamilton, on the defensive. 'No, no, it isn't just soft soap. He thought highly of you long before this; he told me in Beirut [a reference to a Reuters meeting]. He will want to discuss with you who should edit *The Times*.' Murdoch's tactics were now transparent. 'He has asked me to stay on as chairman,' Hamilton said, and added severely: 'I won't take a penny from him. There will be national directors, there will be assurances. I won't let you down. But you've got to stop your staff talking to national directors. I won't have it. *I* am the vetting committee.'

It was hard to take, not least from Hamilton, who had played so determining a role as the creator and guardian. This was not the Hamilton I knew and admired, the editor-in-chief whose prudence we had so often found exasperating when we wanted to dive from the twenty-foot board before checking whether there was water in the pool. I announced that I would have to consider my position on the vetting committee and as editor of the paper. And the staff had a right to be anxious. My implicit threat of resignation was an unrealistic way of expressing frustration; I had been thinking, it was true, of leaving *The Sunday Times* for television, but I could hardly pull out in these circumstances. Nor was it sensible to sacrifice a position on the vetting committee. Hamilton reacted more strongly than I thought he would: 'You can't do that. You will sabotage the whole deal.' And he added, 'Of course you must stay on the vetting committee. Don't push me.'

He did not want to talk about our consortium at any time in the week. He had been sent the Morgan Grenfell letter, but affected an air of puzzlement as does a man hearing of some exotic custom. He had, he said, seen and heard nothing of the JOTT-Mogg group. It was, he supposed, a safety net 'like yours' in case everything else fell through. I said, 'No', ours was our distinct first preference.

In meetings with 'the cardinals', Donoughue and Cruickshank we reviewed the wreckage. Two efforts were worth making, it seemed. The first was to reinforce our bid for *The Sunday Times*. The second, anticipating failure, was to exert every bit of pressure we could to entrench the editorial freedoms which Roy Thomson had conferred and which his successors placed at risk.

Nothing that we knew about Murdoch encouraged the idea that he would develop what Roy Thomson had bequeathed. Unimpeachable sources, as lobby men would say, told us impeccable stories about his mischievous tendencies. His cousin, Ranald Macdonald, the publisher of the excellent Melbourne *Age*, suggested on a visit to London that after Murdoch acquired the Ansett airline, his papers ran stories to promote it. 'You must not trust him. I'll make that plain to Brunton.' His solicitor, the inestimable Lord Goodman, pronounced in his Johnsonian manner: 'Of course Harold Evans cannot work for Murdoch. He will interfere too much.' I had not asked Goodman for a view. He was intervening in a spirited debate between Lady Harlech (anti) and Lady Pamela Hartwell (pro: he's so lovable) which threatened the civilized equanimity of a dinner party at the Eaton Square home of Harold and Diane Lever.

'The cardinals' decided that Wilsher should seek a meeting of senior editorial men with Hamilton to make three points. First, that they would object to the idea that national directors should be in purdah; lacking any long or direct experience of the paper and its staff, they ought to welcome some discussion of editorial hopes and fears. Second, he would record the staff's expectation that there would be a vetting committee and the two editors would be retained on it. And third, they would appeal for a reconsideration of Thomson-Warburg selection procedures so that our consortium received a fair hearing. Donoughue undertook to brief John Smith M P, the Shadow Secretary of State for Trade, so that he might press for Murdoch's bid, or that of any other large group, to be referred to the Monopolies Commission. Cruickshank reported that Murdoch's acquisition of Times Newspapers would yield him 31 million readers of national morning newspapers, or 41%, and 34 million of the national Sunday newspaper market or 45%. Even so, 'the cardinals' reported that a majority of the journalists' chapel might not stand out against Murdoch; the view was that a bit of ruthless cynicism was just what the doctor ordered for the more disruptive of the print chapels.

As for our own bid, there was no doubt where the difficulty lay. It was not in alliances or money, maddening though *The Guardian*'s eleventh-hour retreat had been: disappointment with the union leaders was less because expectations were lower. The difficulty lay squarely with our own colleagues in the Thomson Organisation. It was a bitter thought that they should favour an outsider, and one for whom they had expressed contempt in the past. There was some talk that I should go to see Ken Thomson, who had proclaimed right at the beginning that the sale would not be an auction: 'We will take into account the policy and responsibility of the buyer as well as the interests of the employees, shareholders, readers, and advertisers.' I discounted it for the same reason I had not followed Rees-Mogg to Toronto. The power lay in

London, and Brunton and Hamilton would be antagonized by any such move. We had to deal with the excuse for favouring Murdoch: that he was the only bidder prepared to take the whole company off their hands. We developed the idea of constructing a bid for the whole company jointly with another group, and separating afterwards into two title companies. We called it the railway train option, coupling and uncoupling around Gordon Brunton's marshalling yard. I reckoned we had a week or ten days to talk to possible bidders and go back to Granada Television and Standard Oil.

There were four potential coaches to which we could hook up. There were two newspaper groups, the *Daily Mail* and *The Observer*, who had played with their cards close to their chest. I made arrangements to talk to them. And there were two groups which had made bids for *The Times* – the consortium put together by William Rees-Mogg and JOTT, which had attracted all the publicity, and one formed by an extraordinary company called Sea Containers, which had surfaced only in a paragraph in *The Sunday Times* that had Brunton bewildered: 'There are only two copies of their application, one I carry around with me and one Warburgs have locked up in their safe.' Though we had carried the story on Sunday 11 January, we quite failed to appreciate the significance of the Sea Containers bid. It was a failure of journalism and of enterprise, because it was an imaginative, solidly financed proposal which merited public examination.

Sea Containers is a group with London headquarters founded by an innovative American in his forties, James Sherwood. Its largest business is the owning and leasing worldwide of marine cargo, containers and container ships. He started his business in the early 1960s at the beginning of the container revolution, based on ideas formed while serving as a navy officer keeping supplies flowing to the troops in the Korean War. More glamorously, Sherwood has branched out into leisure. It is one of Sea Containers' companies which with great style and sophistication has recreated the Venice Simplon-Orient-Express. It owns the Hotel Cipriani in Venice, Harry's Bar in London, the Villa San Michele in Florence, The Lodge at Vail, Colorado, a housing estate in Hong Kong and the King's Reach development on the South Bank of the Thames opposite the *Daily Mail* building. In September 1980 it had assets of nearly $700 million, shareholder funds of $223 million, and more than $100 million in spare cash.

The letter which Sherwood wrote to Warburgs on 22 December offered £4 million for the title of *The Times*, with Thomson paying for redundancies. It was a very fair opening offer for a paper predicted by the Warburg prospectus to lose £8·9 million in 1981, £4·4 million in 1982 and £1 million in 1983. Sherwood pledged to maintain the character and quality of *The Times*, in particular the independence of the editor, and to accept the system of national directors.

The most important feature, however, of the Sea Containers proposal was in the prospect it offered of ending once and for all the financial sickness of *The Times*. Some of this would have struck a discordant note with Brunton: 'We believe it is necessary to separate the ownership of *The Sunday Times* and *The Times*. *The Times* must make maximum use of the new technology and must sharply cut staffing to survive. This can only be accomplished if the composing room, plate making, printing and distribution processes are moved well out of London. It would appear that *The Sunday Times* has greater profit potential and must be printed in London. It seems unlikely to us that a common owner of *The Times* and *The Sunday Times* could move the production of one paper outside of London without risking industrial action against the other paper. Also, we believe the two publications have little in common and complete separation would enhance productivity.'

Sherwood sketched the Sea Containers plan for efficient newspaper production. Journalists and classified advertising staff working from the King's Reach site by the Thames would write at electronic terminals which would transmit by line to the composing room outside London. Three locations in Britain and one abroad would be fed by facsimile techniques similar to those in use at the *Wall Street Journal*. It was not an anti-union operation. Other than management Sea Containers expected all operations to be carried out by members of the traditional print unions. Of course one of these unions, the National Graphical Association (NGA), had resisted the introduction of direct photocomposition entry by journalists and advertising staff throughout the 1979 Thomson shutdown. To that extent the Sea Containers proposal was a risk, and it had the disadvantage of requiring a gap in publication of about three months. But if ever there was a moment for a new beginning, and if ever there was a chance of *The Times* riding to security on a crest, it had surely arrived. The Thomson decision to sell had shaken the union leadership, as I knew from my meetings; their members were ready, some of them eager, to make a fresh start. The NGA would have been under tremendous pressure, not least from other unions, to accept what similar unions all over the world had accepted. And separation of the titles would have meant that *The Times* clearly had to make its own way in the world.

In the week starting 12 January we did not know enough to appreciate the value to us of an alliance with Sea Containers. We went, naturally enough, to the Rees-Mogg and JOTT consortium. Sir Michael Swann, former chairman of the BBC, had come in as chairman of the group, and the spadework was being done by Hugh Stephenson, the Winchester scholar who edits the *New Statesman* and was then editor of the *Times Business News* and a leading figure in JOTT. Rees-Mogg, who was leaving the chair at *The Times* to be an antiquarian bookseller and a director of GEC, did not seem to be making the running any longer. He was certainly in a genially relaxed mood about it all when we met for lunch on 15 January, glad to be handing over *The Times*, which had begun to bore him: 'always a sign it is time to go'. Someone of national reputation, he said, would succeed him. I proposed Peter Jay, the *Times* columnist and former ambassador to Washington. 'Oh, no,' he giggled, 'he's got feet of clay up to his Adam's apple.'

As for Murdoch, *laissez faire* was the best course. It was imprudent to antagonize him when we would have to negotiate conditions of editorial independence. And he would fail anyway. The unions, whose learning curve he regarded as a horizontal line, were bound to 'blow it' in the negotiations, which meant our separate consortia would get a chance. I thought this was whistling in the dark, but Rees-Mogg perceived something about the situation which made me feel I had been naïve: 'Brunton is determined to go ahead with a man he regards as an equal. If he wanted our consortia to be linked as railway carriages he would have put them together himself.' It was a depressing thought, but Rees-Mogg agreed I could try to act as yard marshal. Hugh Stephenson was not ablaze with enthusiasm. In his view, Stratford Place disliked our consortium more than his. His suspicion was that we wanted to exploit JOTT-Mogg on the theory, far from reality, that they were favoured by Brunton and would be the preferred bidder when Murdoch failed with the unions: association with them was our only hope of a seat at the peace table. It took several approaches by Donoughue and Cruickshank to get talks going.

In the meantime, proving that paranoia is not confined to Wyke-hamists, I had come to doubt the viability as well as the verve of the JOTT-Mogg consortium, and had approached both Atlantic Richfield, then owners of *The Observer*, and the *Daily Mail* for exploratory talks. Neither Associated nor Arco was the best solution for *The Times*, still less *The Sunday Times*. Both implied a continuance of traditional and extravagant London printing for *The Times* with the consolation of uninterrupted publication: both JOTT-Mogg and Sea Containers required a suspension. The crucial point was to find a way of satisfying Brunton's technical and psychological requirements. It was our intention to bring JOTT into these discussions if they got off the ground.

The meeting with Thornton Bradshaw, then deputy chairman of Arco (and now chairman of RCA), had been set up on Sunday 11 January, when I met him at a drinks party at the home of Donald Trelford, the editor of *The Observer*. Still numbed by my Thomson-Murdoch news,

I lectured Bradshaw on the public interest hazards of one man owning four British national newspaper titles, perhaps not the most appealing argument to an international tycoon, but I thought Arco had a disembodied conscience about these matters; they had certainly kept their promises to respect the independence of *The Observer*.

Bradshaw agreed to a meeting at Claridge's on 14 January, and in a suite freshened by early daffodils I sought with Donoughue and Cruickshank to sell him our railway train idea. A link with the JOTT-Mogg consortium was one possibility, but another was for Arco to bid with us for the company on the understanding that they would publish and print *The Times*, and be rewarded with a share of our *Sunday Times* profits. Printing *The Times* on *The Observer* presses would also make a contribution to their overheads; I knew they were interested in this. Cruickshank demonstrated with prolific figures how *The Sunday Times* was a rich prospect even allowing for the extra overheads with the return of *The Times* to its historic site. Of course, we said, it was a novel idea for two competitors to co-operate, but it was not unique; there were joint production agreements between competitors in many cities in the United States. If they secured *The Times*, they could offer shares to JOTT. I was sure Thornton Bradshaw had fallen asleep, poleaxed by Cruickshank's bingo-calling. He did eventually respond wearily. He was leaving the next day for Germany. He would have a look at Cruickshank's sums. It seemed more out of politeness than real interest.

At the *Daily Mail* Mick Shields, Lord Rothermere's managing director, was candid. 'My God, what have I got to do to stop the chairman wanting to acquire more newspapers? We've only just paid off half the *Evening News* staff.' Rothermere, directing operations from Paris, had instructed his Associated Newspapers directors to make a bid. They were seeing Brunton again later that week. Some of them, including David English, the editor of the *Mail*, were keen, but Shields regarded *The Times* with horror. The only solution for it was to award six dukedoms annually in return for the privilege of paying the bills. He just did not see how it could be made profitable in Fleet Street. Shields acknowledged the industrial and financial logic of the *Daily Mail*'s acquiring the plant and premises at Gray's Inn Road. Richmond-Watson said he thought £12 million would be enough to offer. Peter Harland, who had been checking printing for us, confirmed there was enough capacity to print the *Mail* as well as *The Times* and *Guardian* during the week. Associated could sell off Carmelite House and have cash in hand after the deal. One could see Shields reflecting, too, that the share in *The Sunday Times* which we offered might divert Rothermere from his risky pet project of a *Mail on Sunday*. Shields and his colleagues had no doubt that *The Sunday Times* was very much a going concern; we should be making even bigger profits than we had been. They were keen on *The Sunday Times*, too keen. They were not content with joining the railway train. They wanted to drive it. I thought that it might be possible for them to have as much as 40% of *The Sunday Times* if they would join in a bid for the whole company. There might be some formula for sharing ownership of *The Times* and its losses. It was not enough. Shields wanted control. We agreed to keep in touch.

There was more dispiriting news at the office. Denis Forman of Granada had been to see the IBA to clear the way for an announcement of their participation. Sir Brian Young, the Director General, had made it clear the IBA would not approve. The grounds were that it was the IBA which had stopped Murdoch from writing the programme schedules at London Weekend Television because, as a press tycoon, he already had excessive control in the media. How could the IBA approve Granada's extending its influence into national newspapers? 'We stayed up into the small hours', said Forman, 'trying to think if we could launder our link through a trust. We would have been prepared to make a fight of it against the IBA, but for the Murdoch point, which is pretty compelling.' I had to concede that it was. It was a pity. The investment could be replaced. What hurt was that we had lost another partner with proven regard for editorial freedom and with a high profile. Even the phlegmatic Cruickshank was becoming alarmed at the momentum of Thomson's covert dealings with Murdoch. We were in danger of being swept away unnoticed in an avalanche. Press reports were saying that negotiations were 'about to begin', but every bit of intelligence we could gather suggested that things were further ahead than anyone had cared to indicate. Cruickshank reported that the general manager, Dugal Nisbet-Smith, was briefing Murdoch men for negotiations with the unions: 'He's beginning to wonder if he's knitting a noose for himself.'

I decided on Thursday 15 January to try to cut through the secrecy by asking Brunton. He was more open than I had expected. It was none the less a disturbing conversation. Yes, they were talking to Murdoch. He was seeing him again that day. 'I've been to the Department of Trade. There's no need for a Monopolies Commission inquiry. There's an exemption under Section 58 for a loss-making company.' Sensing that I was not overjoyed, Brunton denied that it was all cut and dried. He was still talking to Rothermere. 'I'm worried that Murdoch won't pay enough. I've had a hard job keeping out the undesirables. You don't know what pressure I've been under, pressures nobody knows about.' I took this as a reference on the one hand to Lonrho, Goldsmith and Maxwell, and on the other to Canada's desire to recoup some of its losses. Hamilton had already suggested as much. The consortium disappeared under the Brunton steamroller. I should relax. I wouldn't really like to deal with the bloodyminded Times Newspapers unions would I? As for editorial freedom, he was going to insist on trustees, I would have his 'additional personal guarantees', and anyway Murdoch wanted me to stay as *Sunday Times* editor. He was high in his praises, etc.

'The cardinals' saw Hamilton the same day. They came back spitting blood. He had not been reticent with them about our consortium; he had denounced it as a 'journalists' ramp', which was a curious notion since ours was the only proposal which from the start envisaged shares for all the workforce. Their anxieties about Murdoch were misplaced, he said. He would leave them alone. Everyone had been terrified when Roy Thomson took over, but in three months everything was in balance. When it was remarked that Thomson hardly had Murdoch's form sheet, Hamilton had replied that he would make editorial independence a personal issue. He would threaten to resign and it would be a credible threat, he said, because he already had his pension. In the evening he called me, ostensibly to discuss the meeting, but also to say I should keep my diary free for an important unspecified meeting the following Tuesday morning at Stratford Place. I took it to be the vetting committee.

It helped to know the nearness of the precipice. Donoughue and Hugo Young briefed Members of Parliament on what was happening. Phillip Whitehead, the Labour M P for Derby North, and Jonathan Aitken, the Tory M P for Thanet, put down a Commons motion calling for a bid by Murdoch to be subject to stringent examination by the Monopolies Commission. I gave Wilsher a rundown on the consortium and its history so that he might take my place if it became impossible to reconcile my role as a bidder with that of a director and presumptive member of the vetting committee.

Most importantly, the *Sunday Times–Times* train at last managed to get up a bit of steam. Cruickshank and Donoughue had a meeting with Hugh Stephenson at the offices of the J O T T adviser, John Jackson of Philips. There were differences in the approaches of the two consortia. J O T T-Mogg wanted Thomson to pay everyone off before they took over *The Times*; we intended to have no break in publication. We offered to help them finance their own redundancies from the greater *Sunday Times* cash flow. We wanted to wean them from relying on a Murdoch nego-tiating failure or of continuing to present themselves as buyers of second resort. The conclusion was that it was too difficult at this stage to construct a single joint bid, but the bankers for both sides, Barings for J O T T and Morgan Grenfell for us, would go to Warburgs with a bid which combined the two separate bids for *The Times* and *The Sunday Times*.

This was the position in the middle of the week when I had a telephone call from Gerald Long, the managing director of Reuters, who was to play a curious role in my life. His message, in deadly secret, was that Murdoch had asked him to become managing director of *The Times*. I had already guessed this from the remark by Dixon of the NGA about a Reuters man being with Murdoch. But what Long really wanted to say was that Murdoch had been trying to telephone me and could not get through my security screen. Would I speak to him?

I kept him talking while I decided. It was true I had avoided speaking to Murdoch. I had never responded to Rees-Mogg's November message that he would like a chat and I had told my private office not to put him through if he came on. Two considerations competed in my mind. Was it realistic to shun someone who might win control of the company? On the other hand, was it prudent to meet someone who might have to appear before the vetting committee? Was Murdoch, as it were, *sub judice*? Curiosity won. I gave Long my home number. That evening Murdoch called and Tina answered. I took the telephone.

'It's all mine,' he said at once. 'Unless Harmsworth comes along with a bigger offer. What do you hear?'

He did not wait for an answer: 'I'm going to make a clean sweep of management. I'm fixing the redundancies tomorrow with James Evans.'

I was fighting for air. Was it all over? I found myself in a reflex action picking on the word redundancies as if he already had control.

'There's some good people in management,' I commented. 'Cruickshank is first-class for one.'

He came back at me: 'He didn't do very well with Fitzpatrick.'

That was an insider's remark. It was a reference to agreements made in the 1980 negotiations to resume publication when Barry Fitzpatrick of NATSOPA and *The Sunday Times* had played a stalling game, and everyone had been screaming at Cruickshank to make a deal. It meant Thomson was in cahoots with Murdoch, it meant that behind the hints, evasions and equivocations of the last weeks and maybe months there had been briefings and business intimacies of the kind only given to *a new owner*.

'We ought to meet,' he said. 'How about a bite to eat tomorrow?'

'I've got a board meeting.'

'How often', he asked in a critical tone, 'do you have those things?'

I said I would try to make lunch, unhappy but impelled by the need to know just what was going on. Murdoch had become a prime source. At 1.30 p.m. the next day, he opened the door of his house in Eaton Place, Belgravia.

'Good to see you. Come in,' he breezed. 'I've just had Arnold Goodman on the phone with a message from Thornton Bradshaw. *The*

Observer would like to take *The Times* off my hands. I've turned them down.'

The Times ... He must have won both *The Times* and *The Sunday Times*. And *The Observer* and Thornton Bradshaw? They must think so, too. And were they also doing a deal behind our back when we had offered partnership?

For years I had read about Murdoch's style in take-overs; as I will relate in the next chapter, *The Sunday Times* had said he kept a bordello of newspapers. I had followed his trail of one supposed outrage in journalism after another. It had been interesting, like watching wild game at a safe distance.

We sat at opposite ends of a sofa in an impersonal living-room, a few bold abstracts on the walls, no books, none of the clutter of sentiment, the house of a visiting fireman done up by an interior decorator. I tackled him at once.

'Why are you bidding for the whole company? Rees-Mogg said you told him you didn't want *The Times*.'

'Rees-Mogg! He's got it wrong. I've wanted *The Times* all along. *The Sunday Times* is great, but such a lot needs to be done to *The Times*. Of course the business plan in the Warburg paper is bullshit.' Then he was off again, talking as the owner: 'The Thomson people say they're good at getting ad money. Huh. Those guys ought to get out and sell *The Times* on the back of *The Sunday Times*. We're going to print *The Sunday Times* in two sections, Friday and Saturday – go up in size.'

He affected to find Brunton's salesmanship a joke. 'He keeps tapping his briefcase saying he's got five more top-class names in there.' A big grin. 'I'll bet he has!'

For all the fast talk he kept wanting to know if there was any news about 'Harmsworth' and his price. I gave him none about anybody; I knew nothing of Rothermere's price and kept to myself the knowledge of coolness at the *Daily Mail*. If he was so eager for news, perhaps he did not have the company after all.

We went into lunch.

Murdoch took the initiative again: 'Would you like to edit *The Times*?'

It was time to put him right on a few things. I was quietly angry at the way he kept choosing to ignore our bid.

'*The Sunday Times* isn't yours yet. We want to succeed with our consortium. ['Sure, sure'.] We know more than you about *The Sunday Times*. We've worked out everything that needs to be done for a Friday-Saturday print. You might fail. And whatever happens with Brunton and his sale, you'll have to get through the vetting committee and it'll be tough, I can tell you. What about those stories of using your paper to push your airline?'

He interjected. 'They're wrong, wrong, wrong. Just look at the papers. I don't use influence like that.'

'Well, if you get there, you're going to have to satisfy us on independence, on the idea of public trusteeship ['Sure, sure'.], and no commercial interference. We want to maintain *The Sunday Times* as a campaigning, investigating paper.'

He was unfazed. 'Sure, *The Sunday Times* is great. How about Denis Hamilton for chairman, and for trustees what about Arnold Weinstock and Sainsbury and James Callaghan? And Lord Drogheda? And Lord Catto?' He laughed. 'I'm going to watch Brunton's face when I fish a list out of my pocket.'

He said he was going to set up a separate company for Times Newspapers. He surprised me by taking a swipe at his friend Larry Lamb, his editor at the *Sun*: '*Sir* Albert won't have anything to do with this. We'll keep him miles away....'

Over coffee he returned to the subject of *The Times*. Who should edit it? Did he want a national political figure, I asked, rebuking myself again for falling in with his presumption.

'My God, it needs a *journalist*. Isn't it a terrible paper!'

'There's Hugh Stephenson.'

'You must be joking, look at his Business News. Deadly!'

'We'll give you a run with our consortium,' I said, standing up to go. 'But I won't campaign against you with the unions, because we'll need just as big a cut in jobs.'

'Of course,' he grinned. 'I understand about your consortium. You want a piece of the action. Don't blame you.'

He did not understand at all. 'It's not that. We want to be away from *The Times* and to try something different with our staff. We'll need manning cuts, but we know we can make a go of it. We can even make a profit with fewer pages.'

He nodded, 'Yeah, yeah.' It made me still more impatient to act on what he had told me.

As soon as I could get to a telephone I told Donoughue and Cruickshank about *The Observer*, and I rang Roger Harrison, one of its two managing directors. He had not been present at our meeting with Thornton Bradshaw, but I had met him at the end of December with Donald Trelford, the editor of *The Observer*, and they had said they would like to print *The Times*, but could not recommend to Atlantic Richfield that they own it. 'What is going on?' I asked. I told him of the later meeting where Thornton Bradshaw had said he would come back to us after examining our figures. Harrison did not know what was going on, and

neither did Brian Nicholson, the other managing director. I phoned him
from a dinner given by SOGAT's London branch at which the officials
were dropping heavy hints about Murdoch and *The Sunday Times*.
Nicholson said he would try to reach Bradshaw or Robert Anderson,
the chairman of Arco, wherever they were in the world.

I urged Donoughue and Cruickshank to get the whip out on our joint
Sunday Times–Times consortia. The sooner the bankers for the two
groups went to Warburgs with a joint proposal the better. Clearly we
should have united our efforts earlier, and more publicly. But the different mood in the two groups was demonstrated by a statement JOTT put
out on 16 January through Hugh Stephenson, Geoffrey Smith and Malcolm Brown. We believed our *Sunday Times* consortium was easily the
best solution and never stopped saying so. The JOTT statement was
different. Their offer, they said, provided '*a* viable way' (my italic) of
ensuring the continued publication of *The Times* and the supplements.
But it went on: 'The members of JOTT are not, however, opposed to the
sale to an alternative proprietor, providing that he is prepared to guarantee the editorial integrity of the papers.'

Murdoch, having made contact, was soon on the phone again. Tina
and I had dinner with him in Eaton Place on Saturday 17 January, and
she noted his alarming charm in her diary:

> I had to admit I liked him hugely. He was in an American country gentleman's
> three-piece suit and heavy shoes, and was by turns urbane and shady. His
> face seems to have been made for the cartoonist's distortion – the gargoyle
> lips, deep furrows in the brow, the hint of five o'clock shadow that gives him
> such an underworld air when he's sunk in thought. But when he was standing
> by the fire with one foot on the fender laughing uproariously he seemed
> robust and refreshing. There's no doubt he lives newspapers. They are not
> merely seen by him as assets, as Ken Thomson sees them. At 8 o'clock, when
> the first editions arrived, he fell upon them with childish excitement. I warmed
> to him when he read *The Observer*'s hostile account of his bid and instead of
> being cross burst into gales of laughter: 'The bastards!' he shouted, throwing
> it to the floor.
>
> The truth is that, although he'll be trouble, he'll also be enormous fun and
> H. has had so many years of Thomson greyness this vivid rascal could bring
> back some of the jokes. 'I sacked the best editor of the *News of the World*,'
> he said at one point. 'He was too nasty even for me. Shrimsley had to ask
> himself what the ordinary man wanted to read that week. Stafford Somerfield
> *knew*!'

I had a call the next day from Nicholson. The approach to Murdoch
and also one to Thomson was an Arco initiative, nothing to do with the
local *Observer* management. Apologetically he added: 'Arco sometimes
does things without telling us.' (A few months later Arco verified this by

selling *The Observer* without telling the *Observer* board.) The *Mail* was playing its own game too. Seeking control of *The Sunday Times*, they bid £20 million for the whole company with its losses and put in a separate bid of £25 million for the profit-making *Sunday Times*.

So, at what was clearly the last bend in the week of 19 January, it was Murdoch way out in front, pursued by the *Daily Mail*, with Atlantic Richfield somewhere behind. The promising Sea Containers was out of sight. Brunton, I learned later, disqualified Lonrho, Goldsmith, Maxwell, the Aga Khan, Robert Holmes à Court (who bid for *The Times* alone), and about forty others, a number backed by Arab oil money.

It was clear we had no hope of thwarting Murdoch at this stage, but I thought it was time his proximity to control was made known. When, on Sunday 18 January, I did a short BBC television trailer for a series of programmes I had prepared on newspapers I broke the news that Murdoch was going to be Thomson's choice. Hamilton and Brunton were not pleased, but I was fed up with the equivocations.

We had to be ready to take Murdoch's place if he fell at any one of three fences – financial, editorial and unions – and this meant being in a position to offer for the whole of Times Newspapers. We also had to devise the best structures for preserving editorial independence should Murdoch succeed and I made this my priority in the week of 19 January, while Cruickshank and Donoughue proceeded with JOTT and the bankers. I was at home trying to do this when there was a call which precipitated a showdown with Brunton. It was from Billy Hamilton, the public relations adviser. He was speaking on behalf of his client Jim Sherwood of Sea Containers, who thought it would be a good idea if we got together. I knew little about the Sea Containers bid then. They were obviously not aware how far things had gone with Murdoch. None the less I said I would tell Donoughue and Cruickshank who would be in touch. They were calling on me that afternoon.

About an hour after the Sea Containers call, Brunton was on the line. Somehow he had heard about it. He was menacing. 'You have been talking to Sea Containers. I am not prepared to deal with Sea Containers. I am not prepared to deal with consortia. I am selling to Murdoch. Is that straight? I have a situation in which all the titles can survive. Do I make myself clear? Murdoch is not pleased there is opposition to him, and you are a key factor. I want assurances you are not moving in another direction.' I told him the same as I had told Murdoch about my position. What was wrong with our consortium, I asked. We knew the business, we knew the people, we knew what editorial independence meant. 'Consortia', he snapped, 'cannot deal with unions. And I am not selling single titles. I will not see *The Times* shut down.' (It was still a weakness of our position that the JOTT plan envisaged a temporary shutdown of *The Times*.) While the *blitzkrieg* was on, he bombed Rothermere as well. 'I can get more than double the money out of him. But they would be a disaster. And they won't give me the necessary guarantees for the production of *The Times*.' He rounded off with assurances about Murdoch: 'Rupert will make promises he will keep.'

I was still shaken by Brunton's vehemence when Cruickshank and Donoughue came in that afternoon with a simple proposition. I should lead the paper in a public campaign against the Murdoch deal and accept the loss of a place on the vetting committee. It was against the public interest to concentrate so much power in one man and his record was against him. Thomsons were making a shabby deal with bogus arguments.

There was force in what they had to say; in the light of events they were right, and I was wrong to resist them. A public campaign might have failed, but one should have been fought. What I argued, though, and they took with good grace, was that the deal was going through, like it or not, and the best thing was to use the vetting powers to tie Murdoch's hands as they had never been tied before. He might even jib so much that he would be disqualified, which would be ideal. Secondly, a public campaign would so anger Brunton that it would kill whatever last chance we had of taking over the paper should Murdoch fail with Thomson, the unions or the law. I know now that Brunton positively would not have sold us our paper or *The Times* to JOTT. I still had hope then, and three days later on Thursday 22 January sufficient progress had been made by our group and JOTT for Richmond–Watson of Morgan Grenfell and Jim Peers of Barings to go round to Warburgs and make a joint proposal worth around £8 million. They asked for negotiations on the price and argued that a joint double bid would implement in full the disposal which Thomson wanted to achieve. Thomson would keep the freehold in Gray's Inn Road and we would pay a commercial rent. Sufficient funds would be available for working capital for both papers.

Geoffrey Elliott of Warburgs came up with a feeble excuse for the way they had frozen us out. He had been told by Thomson that both editors had said they were putting forward proposals of last resort only to be considered after commercial proposals had failed. Richmond–Watson said this was certainly not, and had never been, the case with our group. Our letter made this plain. Peers, for JOTT, said that might originally have been their position, but since talking to us they had changed it; they were not now going to require redundancies to be paid to all *Times* employees before acquisition.

Elliott, to our bankers' annoyance, would not enter into specific discussion. All he would say was that he would inform Thomson. The marker was in place, but that was all it could have been at that stage. It had not then been announced, but the boards of Thomson and Times Newspapers had already approved the conditional sale to Murdoch.

The crucial vetting procedures, unique in newspaper history, began the day after Brunton's telephone call. The time on Tuesday that Hamilton had asked me to keep free was for a lunch when he could consult the two editors. We had not met as a threesome since the start of the sale and the strains. There was no hint of tension. Hamilton was much more relaxed. There was an air of unreality about the proceedings in which we were asked to choose between Murdoch, Associated, Arco and Lonrho. The real question was whether at the eleventh hour we were prepared to object to the choice that had already been made.

Murdoch's relative attraction lay in his reputation as an international publisher willing to commit resources and be tough and effective in dealing with the unions. As Rees-Mogg put it, there had been an extraordinary disassociation about the editorial process: 'as the King castles, the roof lifts off'. So we said that among those choices Murdoch was preferred, though he would have to satisfy us on editorial guarantees. And we would keep our consortia bids in place. (In a crude poll on these proprietors taken after a *Sunday Times* NUJ chapel meeting Murdoch won 37 first and second preferences, Rothermere 32, Tiny Rowlands and Lonrho 11. But the journalists made it clear they overwhelmingly preferred their consortium.) Hamilton concluded lunch with the news that there would be a meeting of the vetting committee probably some time the next day at which we would decide on the guarantees we wanted and interview Murdoch.

The exercise about to begin required a process of legal and editorial imagination. The practices of *The Sunday Times* under the Thomsons and Hamilton, and of *The Times* in the Astor and Thomson periods represented the largest degree of editorial freedom imaginable, but they were not written down. Nor is editorial independence in a commercial undertaking easily reduced to rules. There was no single blueprint we could turn to. There are plenty of horror stories in the annals of Britain and the United States of political and commercial corruption, but on the positive side little beyond rhetoric. There were useful references to an editor's rights against management, as Hugo Young pointed out, in the memorandum of his requirements that Geoffrey Dawson had submitted to the Astors when asked to return as editor of *The Times* in 1922, but the language was descriptive, not prescriptive. The Scott Trust deed at *The Guardian* was admirable, but not concerned with detail. And, of course, we had our own constitution of Times Newspapers, which everybody assumed was all we needed to get Murdoch to sign. Yet, when our in-house lawyers Antony Whitaker and Alastair Brett looked at our Articles of Association for me, they reported that they were far too loose.

The idea had grown up that the independence of the editors of *The Times* and *Sunday Times*, and through them of the reporters and commentators, was protected in the last resort by four national figures on the main board of the company. These figures were the creation of Denis Hamilton and Roy Thomson when Thomson's application to buy *The Times* went before the Monopolies Commission in 1966; two of them were nominated by Thomson and two by the minority shareholder Gavin Astor. What had been forgotten in the happy years since 1966, because it had not been necessary to remember, was that the four national figures were a minority on the board with no effective powers against the ownership. The Monopolies Commission, indeed, had dismissed their original appointment as 'window-dressing', at best no more than a declaration of good intent by Thomson. It did not think it was realistic to give them powers of veto over the dismissal of an editor: 'The national figures, however eminent they may be, could not be expected to intervene effectively in the highly technical business of producing a newspaper. Moreover, in the event of a dispute about the authority of an editor or the appointment or dismissal of an editor, there would be no assurance that national figures would take any different view of the best interests of the company from that of their fellow directors.'

For Murdoch to agree to continue 'our system' was, therefore, no defence at all if he chose to behave differently from the Thomsons. This was one glaring gap in a statement of principles drawn up by JOTT on 16 January. It waffled about there needing to be a shared spirit of confidence, but on the issue of editorship merely said the appointing board should include 'a proportion' of independent public figures.

The lawyers helping me identified an even more basic weakness. In a company wholly owned by Murdoch there was nothing to prevent his altering the Articles of Association in any way he chose to increase his personal power, dispose of the titles, or further emasculate or even dismiss the national directors. They proposed that, in spite of the 1966 Monopolies Commission doubts, I should seek to specify and entrench the powers of national directors. The appointment or removal of an editor of *The Times*, *The Sunday Times* or the supplements should require the prior consent of all the national directors (or possibly just a majority of them), and the sanction of the national directors should be enshrined in their exclusive ownership of a special class of share which alone should have voting rights on appointment, dismissal and disposal of the papers.

I went further than this in a memorandum I prepared for the vetting committee and discussed with 'the cardinals'. I suggested that the national directors should appoint themselves, with the owner having a right to veto up to three names in any three-year period, and that a series of formal undertakings should be contained in the contract of sale and lodged with the Department of Trade, as the minority report of the 1966 Monopolies Commission had recommended. The undertakings I had in mind were no more than an attempt to codify the customs of the successful Hamilton–Thomson years: 'In the Thomson era', I said,

> The Sunday Times has never had to worry about the reporting of holidays and oil and Yellow Pages [in which Thomson had important interests]. It has had complete independence, irrespective of the commercial repercussions for the Thomson Organisation. This must be maintained. Each editor has been free to run his paper within the budgets agreed with management. The allocation of the budget between the different departments and priorities has been a matter for him, once the overall total has been agreed. It is of course the business of the proprietor and management to say what the paper can afford in staff and salaries; and there will always be overlaps and arguments here. But it must be recognized that the maintenance of the high quality of The Times and Sunday Times in home and foreign reporting, investigation and cultural coverage has required an editorial allocation higher than in popular newspapers, and a willingness to invest in quality. The ability of The Sunday Times in particular to risk unpopularity and financial or circulation losses has been fundamental in its success in pursuing inquiries and causes in the public interest: Thalidomide, the Crossman diaries, the DC-10 air disaster, Slater Walker, Enoch Powell, and more recently Vestey.

I argued that the tradition and therefore the requirement in future was that the editor should have complete and final control of political policy, all editorial appointments, the selection and balance of news, and the right to refuse to publish an advertisement. Written down, it sounded autocratic. In reality an editor is influenced by his staff, but a recognition of the editor's authority is the constitutional mechanism for maintaining professional standards and for protecting the staff who observe them. In management relations, drawing on some of the language of Dawson, I asked for the continuation of equality of status, in their respective spheres, of the chief managing executive of the newspaper and the editor; equality of access to the proprietor on matters of editorial budget and space; and a recognition that the management had no business making editorial representations to the staff or anyone other than the editor.

Hamilton, as chairman and editor-in-chief, and representing ownership, had promised the Monopolies Commission in 1966 that nothing would be done to infringe the direct authority of the editors over their staffs. He would naturally talk to the editors on public policy or other matters, though it would be in each instance for the editor to determine the attitude of the paper, but the editor's independent authority would be made plain to all senior staff members. Hamilton had been scrupulous in honouring this promise. He knew from long experience how essential it was if an editor were to maintain standards and command respect; erosion of the principle inevitably led to intrigue and anarchy. In my notes to the vetting committee I drew attention to Hamilton's conduct of the office: 'He has always made his views known directly, privately and personally, to the editor and has never, as Mr Murdoch is said to do, walked into the news room giving instructions. Nor has the editor-in-chief attended editorial conferences. Practices such as these may be acceptable in other newspapers or other countries, but they would be unacceptable in the tradition of *The Sunday Times* and *The Times*.' There had never been the slightest risk of either editor being confronted with instructions given to a member of staff by editor-in-chief or management.

The JOTT statement, which Hamilton gave Murdoch to study at lunch on Wednesday a few hours before the vetting committee, had satisfactory language on politics and interference with the staff. It was adopted by *The Sunday Times* journalists' chapel, which called additionally for a senior member of editorial staff and a distinguished independent journalist to be appointed national directors. Murdoch was invited to subscribe to a statement of principles that the papers would be free from party political bias and attachment to any sectional interest. I liked the way JOTT summarized the principle of non-interference. The sentence, which I was to have engraved on my heart, read simply: 'Instructions are to be given to journalists only by their editor or by those to whom he has delegated authority.'

The JOTT statement had a second flaw, in addition to the major one on the powers of national directors. It failed crucially to grasp the significance of having an agreed budget and discretion to spend within it. This is not a question of more or less money, but more or less creative freedom. JOTT too readily presumed an editorial budget and merely asked for an annual allocation of space within the paper: not much use if an editor had to seek management approval every time something unexpected happened. There was one final clause I wrote on my shopping list – that we should get an undertaking from Murdoch not to allow the establishment at Times Newspapers of a closed shop in journalism, an infringement of press freedom and an infection he had been unable or unwilling to withstand at the *Sun*.

Thus armed, I went to Stratford Place around 6 p.m. to find already assembled in one of its pretentious conference rooms, all chandeliers and polished mahogany, Hamilton, Rees-Mogg, and three national directors,

Lords Dacre, Greene and Roll, Lord Robens being abroad. Six against one: were we any match for the champion?

Murdoch was upstairs arguing about money with Brunton. Teams of negotiators were eyeball to eyeball in several rooms. Periodically our door would open and one of the lawyers, lost in the maze of mahogany, would stare at us and scuttle out again. We had an extract from the draft contract before us. It was hopeless on protecting editorial freedom. It simply asked Murdoch to continue the present system of national directors and to maintain the papers as editorially independent and of high quality. I brought forward my proposals for redefining and protecting the powers of the national directors. Roll supported me: 'Let's try it.'

Hamilton was emphatic that the shares of Times Newspapers should not be owned by News International or subsidiaries; he wanted financial as well as editorial and managerial control to be in Gray's Inn Road, not Bouverie Street. I raised the question of staff participation, bearing in mind the *Sunday Times* chapel's wish to have a senior member of the paper made a national director, and JOTT's request that the board appoint as editor someone 'acceptable to the body of journalists as a whole'. Agitation ensued. Would it not lead to the staff electing the editor? None of us favoured that. Surely it was up to the journalists' chapel to press Murdoch on participation, not us. At Roll's suggestion, again, it was left that we would mention the dirty word and see how he responded.

Nobody dissented from our asking Murdoch to accept the current and past relationships between editors and managers and the owner. Of the national directors, Roll had done most of the talking, Dacre saying barely anything and Greene nothing at all. This was to be the pattern of the evening, though just before Murdoch came in Roll remarked: 'We don't understand much about some of these things. It's up to the editors to make the points.'

Bill MacLeod, the company secretary, was taking minutes and Hamilton's assistant, Enid Knowles, had a notebook. I kept a full and precise record of my own.

Murdoch came in like someone visiting a friend in hospital, walking quietly, speaking softly. He was well groomed. I noticed, for the first time, the thick black hair on the back of his hands. He sat opposite me across the table, next to Rees-Mogg. He kept his eyes on Hamilton in the chair, who thought he had to put him at his ease.

'We set criteria, very high, which have eliminated a lot of people. Out of seven possibles you have emerged as the most suitable bidder. So you won't find any great hostility here at all. It's just in all our interests to ask you some questions.' Perhaps Mr Murdoch would like to say something? Before the candidate could attempt the question, however, Hamilton then took ten minutes to sketch how the editors since 1966 had worked in a climate of 'very considerable, well total, freedom. They've had no interference on content. They have always felt that if the proprietor or editor-in-chief wished to remove them from office they had the protection of the national directors.'

Murdoch nodded gravely. He finally got a chance to say his piece. He had not, he said, prepared a statement. Things would come out in questioning. But he did want to say how very much he respected the place of *The Times* and *Sunday Times* in British life. If he were to be the favourite, he would respect that and put all his energies and resources into them, though they were not as great as Lord Thomson's.

The manner was diffident still, but there was pride in what he had to say:

Perhaps it would help if I gave a little bit of my own background. I come from a newspaper family. I was brought up by my father, who was a journalist and editor before becoming a publisher, and I learned the traditions of editorial freedom from him. I started by running a very small newspaper in Adelaide and I was ambitious and over-reaching, and took the first step that came to me, buying not the best and greatest newspapers available, but what was around and what I could afford. I built up the company over twenty-eight years in Australia, this country and now America, with very different products. Basically we're a newspaper company with some interest in associated media and television.' (He smiled.) 'I accidentally bought a half-share in an airline last year and it turned out to be too good a business to sell. I've learned a great deal about the business of producing different newspapers for different publics. A particular feature which should be taken account of is that I have stayed with difficult situations. When I started the national daily *The Australian*, people were convinced I'd go bankrupt, but I never did. It has been a big drain on us for many years. It is only now becoming viable. It's a very different type of paper from my New York *Post*. We're not running away from it. We're going to see it out. Just look at my record. I've been in situations where we've been losing a lot of money and I've not been frightened to stand up to my directors and shareholders, and say, 'Stay with it'.

As for the role of this board and the national directors, I see them as a court of appeal. If the proprietor should interfere in an unethical manner to try to protect a big advertiser from being exposed in the paper or to force political judgement on an editor or to run vendettas, I think the editors would come and seek relief. If there is anything of value in newspapers, it is the goodwill position they have in the community. Obviously to do anything which would prompt an editor to go to the national directors and create a public row would be totally destructive. At all times there must be editorial independence. Just as they should be preventing me from interfering, I don't think directors should interfere either.

Roll opened for us. He hoped Murdoch would understand that we had to form a judgement of him, but we were bound to put down some words. There had to be something in writing, proper documentation to put in to the Government. 'It's unfortunate,' he murmured. He hoped Murdoch would not take offence. 'I can live with that,' said Murdoch, 'though I'm nervous about legislating too much.' Hamilton ventured obliquely into the critical area of the powers of the national directors. Murdoch had said he intended to confirm the present structures. What did he think they were? If the intention was to get Murdoch to confirm something that did not exist but which we hoped to achieve, it failed. Hamilton had to say that the powers of the national directors were not in a single legal document; they were dotted about, defined in statements to the 1966 Monopolies Commission and speeches. Murdoch said he could see expansion of the board to increase the number of national directors to six. He himself would be chairman of Times Newspapers and on the board of the Holdings company with the national directors.

Roll secured the right of national directors to control appointments to their own ranks: 'They have the initiative of suggesting names, but you have the veto.' Murdoch nodded his agreement. Hamilton followed up and secured three-yearly, rather than annual, terms for them. The powers of the national directors over the appointment and removal of editors was achieved on the nod, almost too casually for my liking.

> ROLL: Editors to be appointed, etc. with the approval of the board and a majority of national directors?
> MURDOCH: I accept that fully.
> ROLL: We'll draft it into the Articles of Association.
> EVANS: You have understood that, have you? It does involve the proprietor giving up certain power.
> MURDOCH: I'd be very disappointed if I could not keep the confidence of this board.
> EVANS: It is an advance in terms on what has gone before.
> ROLL: It isn't in practice. I can't believe a proprietor wanting to get rid of an editor would not be sure that the national directors with some sort of not clearly defined responsibility were not really behind him. Of course, the national directors would not take responsibility for that themselves. It would be unthinkable that they should say, 'You ought to get rid of so and so.'
> MURDOCH: Absolutely.
> ROLL: Checks and balances.
> EVANS: I just wanted to be sure Mr Murdoch knows what he is saying.

Murdoch said he saw himself as chairman of Times Newspapers and, 'You know who I would like as managing director.' He would appoint Lord Catto of Morgan Grenfell to the Holdings board and he very much hoped that Harold Evans would stay as editor of *The Sunday Times*.

Hamilton raised the statements by JOTT and the *Sunday Times* chapel.

Murdoch rejected the JOTT idea of appointing editors 'acceptable to the staff as a whole'. He was not prepared to have anything like the election of an editor, but he went along with the spirit, he said, of representing staff views. Perhaps the appointment – selected not elected – of a really responsible journalist to the board would meet this point.

Hamilton, suddenly decisive, encouraged him to think of two staff-men. It would help to establish trust. Then, all deference gone, he pitched into Murdoch about separating *The Times* company from News International, which controls the *Sun* and *News of the World*. It had clearly become an issue behind the scenes. Hamilton recoiled from the ideal of the journalistic and managerial talent of Times Newspapers being subordinate to Bouverie Street. The way he put it, with uncanny prescience, was that it would be 'unacceptable' for the titles of *The Times* to be subservient to News International. Rees-Mogg supported him. Murdoch muttered, 'Yes, yes,' but added that he must have one holding company, because there were tax implications. Finally, after more havering, he agreed. He would talk to his lawyers and accountants.

Rees-Mogg was anxious to go through the points on editorial integrity drafted by JOTT. I had remedied the oversight on the editors' right to a budget. Where Clause (f) said the executive board was to be responsible after consultation with the editors for fixing an annual budget for editorial space, I added the words 'and expenditure'. Rees-Mogg concurred. The weak clause on the appointment of editors (Clause [d]) had obviously been overtaken by Murdoch's ready acceptance of the superior power of national directors – or so I thought. Murdoch let his eye drift down the single page. He said nothing about the first clause, which acknowledged that *The Times* and *Sunday Times* would continue to be papers free of party political bias and sectional interests irrespective of Murdoch's politics or commercial interests. But he jibbed at being asked to say the editors would not be subject to instructions from either the proprietor or the management on the content of the paper. It was hard to redraft, because Murdoch could not define what it was about the wording he found difficult. Three lords, a knight and two editors stared down at the paper with him. Wisely Hamilton diverted us: we would put that clause aside for the moment. What about Clause (c) on the sole right of the editor to give instructions? 'Of course I'll work only through the editor,' said Murdoch. 'But I'd like to be able to walk through the news department and talk to people and encourage them from time to time. A personal focus of loyalty.' Rees-Mogg chipped in: 'My committee thinks it will be all right for you to praise a reporter, but not to criticize him.' I trusted he was joking. It was a false and foolish distinction.

Murdoch had moved on, recognizing the rights of the editors of the supplements and enjoying himself: 'I happened to be in Oxford last

Saturday and my history don had *Literary Supplements* piled high right
to the ceiling in his bedroom, every issue since he had been at Worcester.'
He was quite forthcoming on management matters. He even volunteered
an improvement on the budget clause. An editor would certainly have
discretion within an agreed budget and it could be reviewed every six
months. Of course there would be direct access to him and equality of
status with the managing director.

Yes, appointments and dismissals were a matter solely for the editor,
though he would like to be consulted on senior appointments. So that
left us with the second unresolved clause, on the content of the paper. I
thought there was good language in the 1966 Monopolies Commission
report and read out paragraphs, basically Hamilton's original testimony.
This led to Murdoch's accepting the editor's exclusive control not of 'the
content' of the paper but of the selection and balance of news and
opinion. 'I find that a lot easier.' He had been troubled, it seemed, by the
fact that 'content' included advertising and he did not want to yield
management authority in determining the proportion between editorial
and advertising. It was a fair point. We settled for the editor's right to
refuse to publish any particular advertisement: advertising managers
universally regard editors as squeamish on matters of politics and sex.

Hamilton sent me a note with the single word 'Politics'. I was glad of
the reminder to reinforce the understanding under the first clause of the
JOTT statement. I asked Murdoch if he would subscribe to paragraph 84
in the 1966 Monopolies Commission report as depicting the proper
relationship on politics between editor and proprietor in Times Newspapers. It was, in fact, Hamilton's promise, faithfully carried out over
fifteen years: 'Each of the two editors would make his own decisions on
matters of opinion in leading articles; each would be free to disagree
with the other and each newspaper would continue to take separately its
own lines of policy'. I said that it would mean seeing *The Times* and
Sunday Times disagree with each other, and both of them with the *Sun*
and the *News of the World*. He responded to Hamilton: 'I'd not like to
be barred from discussing politics with the editor,' but he added as he
turned to me: 'Of course you have the final say.'

Hamilton rounded things off with a 'do-you-take-this-man' question.
Would he promise to maintain the character of *The Times* as a paper of
record in sickness and in health, and of *The Sunday Times* as a paper of
investigation and special features? He would. I reminded him that journalism in the public interest such as the Thalidomide and DC-10 investigations, and the publication of the Crossman diaries could be costly
in terms of litigation and sometimes loss of sale. He was nonchalant. 'I
face this all the time with my other newspapers.' The comparison with
his other newspapers was not blindingly obvious, but we were dotting

the i's now. He briskly agreed not to have a closed shop in journalism. I had only one nagging doubt, which was the entrenchment of the rights of the national directors, but I did not raise it when Murdoch assured Hamilton, at the conclusion, that he was fully prepared both to see the Secretary of State and to lodge with him the amended Articles of Association. It had been an impressive performance. We had been engaged for nearly ninety minutes. We seemed to have achieved what we had set out to achieve; and Murdoch's answers and demeanour had been such that, when he left, there was no argument. All that remained was to set it down in writing. It was easier said than done.

It was 9 p.m. Murdoch had gone off upstairs to Brunton's room. Dinner was being served in the main boardroom for the vetting committee and the directors of Times Newspapers Holdings who had been called to approve whatever was agreed. This meant we were joined by Lord Keith and Tommy Emblem, the two directors representing the Astor 15% holding, and Duke Hussey, vice-chairman to Hamilton. Keith was cross: the Astors had not told him they were selling. But this was only the first of a series of upsets as the evening wore on. Rees-Mogg and I undertook to draft the statement for the press of what had been agreed, and went into an ante-room to do it. He began to write in his customary longhand and got stuck at the first sentence, the first literary eclipse of Rees-Mogg known to man. I went to an unfamiliar electric typewriter and got stuck too. We were both too excited, acutely conscious of the significance of every comma. I had never imagined we would be attempting to define the new constitution of Times Newspapers in these circumstances. I suggested to Rees-Mogg that I should do a solo run. He went off to dinner and half an hour later I had finished a draft. I listed the undertakings in order of importance: first a paragraph on the national directors, their manner of election, and the enhancement of their powers; second, one on their powers in relation to the appointment and dismissal of editors; and third on the disposition of titles. I followed that with a fourth section on the maintenance of editorial independence over staff, news and option and political policy. I rounded off by listing the points from the JOTT statement that had not already been covered.

I went in to dinner, gave Rees-Mogg the draft, and tried the Thomson claret. I did not get very far. Rees-Mogg objected to the draft. He did not like the way I had opened with four sections before the JOTT points. He objected to the consequent renumbering. I was saying we could adjust that, when he flushed and raised his voice: 'And you've left out Clause (d). JOTT is an agreed text. You don't understand anything.' A bewildered Eric Roll looked on as we argued. Clause (d) in JOTT said: 'The board is to appoint the editor who is to be acceptable to the body of journalists as a whole.' We had already agreed it was too weak, in that it did not refer to the superior power of the national directors. What we had secured with Murdoch was set out in the second paragaph in my draft: 'The editors, to be appointed by the board, may only be appointed or removed by the agreement of a majority of the national directors.' Rees-Mogg reinstated the JOTT clause and amended it to read: 'The editors are to be appointed by the board, including at least a majority of the national directors.' I thought it was inferior: it said nothing about the dismissal of an editor (nor staff acceptability for that matter). Rees-Mogg was angry. We were getting nowhere, our normal tolerances brittle. He thought I was stupidly hazarding Murdoch's approval; I thought he was playing to the JOTT gallery. I went back to the annexe. I had eaten nothing. The sound of merriment next door was not much help. Working alone again, however, I soon completed my second draft. I retained all the opening sections, because I was sure that was the right priority, but I raised and renumbered the JOTT points in sequence, except for Clause (d) on the editorships. Surely Rees-Mogg would see there was no sense in retaining a duplication and one that was clumsier and weaker?

Not so. He reinserted Clause (d), and, where I had said that the national directors should perpetuate themselves, he wrote instead: 'They will be required to approve subsequent nominations to their membership.' It was not the same thing at all. It was not an accurate record of what Murdoch had just accepted. It took the power of nomination from the national directors and put it back into Murdoch's hands, but I felt too exhausted to argue any more. I reassured myself that the national directors would themselves hold fast to the power they had heard Murdoch grant them. I told Roll about it.

The dinner table had been cleared and it looked as if we were in for a long night. There were traumas upstairs. The atmosphere was nasty, and waves of it drifted downstairs. Murdoch had offered £10 million and then £12 million on the understanding that were net assets of £17.9 million in addition to the building. Then he and his team became suspicious. They accused Ian Clubb, the Scottish financial director of Thomson, who had once been finance director at Times Newspapers, of cheating on the figures. 'Bloody well apologize to him,' said Brunton to Murdoch. His lawyer, Richard Searby, made pacifying movements. Michael Brown, one of Brunton's two deputies, was brought in and said he would put in writing not only that the assets were worth £17.9 million but also that current losses would not exceed £14.5 million. 'There was blood on the walls,' said Brunton later. Hamilton interrupted all this with my draft of the editorial constitution, seeking Murdoch's approval of the record.

The board waited downstairs. As midnight approached, I took the air in Stratford Place with Eric Roll; he predicted that we would soon all be able to go to bed. It was part of the psychology of negotiation that both sides needed a midnight session; he had thought of demonstrating it on graph paper. The Thomson-Murdoch deal fitted Roll's diagnosis. Once we had passed midnight, things moved quickly. The deal was closed at £12 million; one of the directors came down and said Murdoch was 'literally shaking with excitement' at his acquisition. There would be redundancies costing perhaps £10 million, which Murdoch would have to pay, but the more paid out here, the quicker the return to profit. And after Murdoch had made an aggregate profit of £20 million from the group, Thomson would for the next ten years receive 25% of any profits over £5 million a year. It was very much in Murdoch's favour. The freehold of the *Sunday Times* building in Gray's Inn Road was alone worth the purchase price; Murdoch himself boasted later that he had paid less than half the book value of its tangible assets. Then Hamilton announced there was agreement on the editorial guarantees as well, and we joined the crowd opening bottles in Brunton's room. Murdoch, looking exhausted, said: 'Yeah, it's OK. But it's a lousy subbing job. You could have made it shorter. See.' And he gave me back my draft. He had deleted Rees-Mogg's Clause (d) from the press statements. There was not a peep out of Rees-Mogg. I did not know whether to laugh or cry.

I felt pleased with what we had accomplished, but there was a sour taste to it next day. Donoughue said it had been a waste of time, Murdoch would find ways of getting round it all. I went over the fine print with a staff lawyer and sent Hamilton a note on how the powers of the national directors might be entrenched when the Articles of Association came to be revised. Hamilton was interested. To my surprise, in the light of his sustained advocacy, he had developed doubts: 'I don't trust Murdoch.'

Donoughue told me that he and Cruickshank had, in the meantime, made big strides with the JOTT consortium; this was the day, in fact, that Morgan Grenfell and Barings went to Warburgs with the double proposal. They still had a hope that Murdoch would be blocked by the Monopolies Commission; most of the staff did not see how a reference could be avoided. Mrs Thatcher had answered questions in the House by saying application for consent, when received, would be considered in accordance with the law, the Fair Trading Act of 1973. The Leader of the House, Francis Pym, said the importance of the issue was understood.

But this was Murdoch's day. I reported his success to a staff meeting in the afternoon, saying I still preferred our consortium, but that I would stand by my approval of the bid in the light of the new editorial constitution.

The packed press conference which followed in the curtained and floodlit ballroom of the Portman hotel was an unhappy experience. I had a momentary consolation in being able to say to Geoffrey Elliott how badly I thought Warburgs had treated our bid. But I now felt bound to lend public support to Murdoch. It was what I had said I would do if he became a conditional purchaser who met us on the editorial constitution; and he had done both. He had won because Brunton saw Murdoch as the avenger of Thomson's defeat by the unions in the shutdown of 1979, because the JOTT-Mogg consortium predicted a break in publication of *The Times*, and because Murdoch had been single-minded by comparison with the shilly-shallying of Arco and the *Mail*; and he had flattered the right people. However, it was one thing to acknowledge failure privately and another to symbolize it by appearing on the platform with Murdoch, Brunton and Hamilton. I thought I had avoided it, arriving late from my staff meeting and sitting at the back in a tangle of television cables.

Murdoch, in pin-stripe suit with silk tie and a pocket handkerchief, was in a fidget, taking his glasses off and on, pouring glasses of iced water and bristling at the questions. His impatience testified to his dislike of the working press. What was his object? Success. How would it be attained? By much hard work. What would he do himself? Work hard. Newspaper reports that he had originally wanted only *The Sunday Times* were 'totally inaccurate'. Then Hamilton said the editors were in the hall and Rees-Mogg and I were propelled onto the platform. There was pandemonium as photographers, snarling to one another, 'Call yourself a professional?' jostled to get a shot of us with Murdoch. They caught me looking foolishly to heaven as Murdoch glowered.

Yet one had to admire the man's drive. Around 8.30 p.m. the same day, before he even had an office, he was in Gray's Inn Road as the proprietor-designate, telling Ron Hall that any magazine with too many ads cheated the public, collecting a proof of Rees-Mogg's leader on the deal from the executive editor of *The Times*, Michael Hamlyn, and over dinner at the Ivy with his smooth Australian lawyer, Richard Searby, pumping me about *The Sunday Times*. At his request I took him through the paper department by department, and was extolling the strength of the book and arts reviews when he cut me short: 'Never read those kind of pages.' It was here Searby spotted a small technical error in *The Times* leader, which I phoned through to Hamlyn. He had already corrected it, but it led to the legend that on his first day Murdoch had altered a *Times* leader even before the vetting committee's ink was dry. The next day, when of course he turned up as *The Sunday Times* went to press, Murdoch did alter a leader with his own hand. Since this, too, has entered the lore of Fleet Street, and it was not without significance, the facts should be related.

I had written a leader on the deal, which I will outline shortly, and in it had mentioned other concentrations of ownership in Fleet Street, including Express Newspapers 'which owns the *Daily Express*, the *Sunday Express* and half the *Evening Standard*'. Murdoch, having walked through various departments, lingered in his shirt-sleeves in the composing room where the pages were being made up. I was busy seeing the leader page and page one to press, and Peter Roberts, the managing editor, introduced him to the reading desk, where finished proofs were being piled. 'You might care to read the leader,' said Roberts, helpfully. Murdoch did, asked for a pen and made a mark on the proof which he gave to Roberts for processing. Roberts brought it over to me, asking if he should give it to the printer, and I told him to forget it. The mark Murdoch made was to insert 'the *Star*' in the list of Express Newspapers. He was right that the *Star* was in the Express stable, but I did not consider it worth delaying the first edition for such a minor correction and I was not enchanted that Murdoch should make a mark on a leader proof affecting his own interests. I made the insertion myself when the leader page went to press again later. It was a trivial incident, but it made a deep impression on the staff that, so soon after the vetting committee's essays in drawing the line, Murdoch should make a mark in a leader and give what was tantamount to an instruction to a journalist. The hapless Roberts, one of the kindliest and most courteous of men, was made to feel he had let the regiment down. I might have done nothing more about this, but senior executives were so upset that I put a note through Murdoch's door not far from my home on Sunday saying it would not do. He must make any observations to the editor, he must not make marks on proofs at any time, and we must go through the ground rules together again. Within minutes he was on the telephone: 'Gee, I'm sorry. The adrenalin got going and, after all, I was only making a correction.' When we discussed it again the following day, he repeated his regrets like a schoolboy caught smoking and promised to restrain himself. I began to feel I was a heel to raise it at all.

7
BIFFEN'S
MISSING MILLIONS

Mrs Thatcher wanted Rupert Murdoch's acquisition of Times Newspapers to avoid a reference to the Monopolies Commission. The Minister who had to take the decision, John Biffen, is regarded by all sides of the House of Commons as a fair and pleasant man, but not a Minister with an iron grip, nor one to stand up to the Prime Minister. Times Newspapers was the subject of his first major decision as Secretary of State for Trade and he made it with surprising dispatch. When he was Chief Secretary of the Treasury, he agonized where Ministers like Nigel Lawson wielded the axe with pleasure and he did not have a reputation for detailed application. The case of *The Sunday Times* and its capacity to survive as a separate newspaper required this, but his consent to Murdoch's take-over was swift. A newspaper merger unprecedented in newspaper history went through in three days. In such a rapid process it is perhaps understandable that he overlooked, or his officials allowed him to overlook, £4·6 million of revenue and £700,000 of *Sunday Times* profit, so that as regards *The Sunday Times* he failed to apply the provisions of the Fair Trading Act of 1973.

Time and the play of special interests and inhibitions all conspired to handicap the debate on Murdoch's acquisition of Britain's most famous daily newspaper with its distinguished supplements and of the leading Sunday newspaper.

The print unions wanted to get on with the manning negotiations, as I knew they would, but I was surprised more than I should have been at the way people on the political left declared that monopoly did not have a nasty taste after all. Norman Atkinson MP made a distinction between mere sordid commercial diversity, which would concern the Commission, and editorial diversity, over which the vetting committee had done a superior job. Bill Keys had written to me on 22 January saying: 'This continued concentration of ownership in the Press cannot be for the good of the nation nor for press freedom'; but he went along with Owen O'Brien of NATSOPA and Joe Wade of the NGA in asking Michael Foot not to press for an inquiry, and Ken Ashton of the National Union of Journalists went along with them. The reason, as I knew from my conversations, was the notion that they could preserve most of their members' jobs in a straight transfer of Times Newspapers to Murdoch. On the public interest point, they said that, if Harold Evans had declared himself satisfied with the editorial guarantees, what better could emerge from an inquiry? What those in favour of an inquiry wanted, of course, was for the way to be opened for proper consideration of alternative bids which would also have carried editorial seals of good housekeeping.

Time was on a ratchet. Biffen was in India when the application for his consent was formally requested on 23 January. Brunton had seen the officials earlier, but Biffen did not have the papers until his return to the Department on Tuesday 26 January. Twenty-four hours later he rose in the Commons to announce his approval forthwith, without reference to the Monopolies Commission. He was propelled, he argued, in part by the Thomson timetable. The papers would be closed in March unless sold. The Monopolies Commission could not report in under two months and this would leave time neither for Murdoch to negotiate with the unions nor for a new buyer to make a deal with Thomsons.

Members of Parliament on both sides of the House said the Thomson timetable was a phoney pistol at the Minister's head; he himself declared it was a disturbing aspect of the sale. But it was no more disturbing than the figures Biffen used to portray *The Sunday Times* as a bankrupt newspaper. It was for me, sitting gagged and bound in the House of Commons press gallery, perhaps the most bitter and frustrating moment in the whole affair.

I was inhibited in two ways: one, by having been part of the procedure which approved Murdoch; and two, by the way I had decided to try to reconcile the irreconcilables in my position as a bidder, a director and an editor – a buyer whose only chance was for Murdoch to fail, but who would lose that chance by doing anything which upset the seller; a director who had a duty to stand by the decisions of his board in which he had taken a full part; but an editor with a duty to public policy and to the views of his staff. The strains of this were manifest when I came to write the leading article for *The Sunday Times* the day after the press conference. Rees-Mogg's leader in *The Times* pretty well hauled down the flag of his own consortium on the grounds that it would not have avoided a break in publication. 'That reinforced the Thomson preference for a single bidder and the staff too have a strong preference for unbroken publication.' His reference to the monopolies law was dismissive: 'Murdoch's purchase could be referred to the Monopolies Commission, though there is a ministerial discretion in cases where papers are under imminent threat of closure.' This leader was disliked among the *Sunday*

Times staff. They were incensed at the way the alternatives to Murdoch had been brushed aside and the timetable fixed by Thomson without regard to the need for public debate. Many of them objected to being swept into what they saw as a large, alien publishing group on the sole grounds that it was necessary to save *The Times*. They passed a resolution calling for a Monopolies Commission inquiry; so did the *Times* journalists' chapel, though 100 of the 280 dissociated themselves from it.

I did not think I could go all out for an inquiry in my *Sunday Times* leader. It would have amounted to initiating the public campaign I said I would forswear if the editorial guarantees were satisfactory, and they were. The risk of *The Times*'s closing down bothered me, yet I was loath to duck the issue. I therefore wrote a long leader canvassing the arguments. I said that the journalists' move was not a mark of hostility to Murdoch personally; they admired his energy, directness and publishing flair. But their anxieties about concentration of proprietorial power were understandable: 'The risk is that the power of ownership could be abused, as it has so often been abused in Fleet Street, to impose a common political line. This is too substantial a question to be brushed aside because of the brinkmanship imposed by the Thomson timetable. The decisions made now will be a more or less permanent feature of our landscape.' Then I set out three 'legitimate, though not conclusive' points against a monopolies reference: the greater degree of competition between national daily newspapers in London than in any other capital city; the break in *Times* production; and, overwhelmingly, the editorial guarantees. They did not make the papers more free – one cannot extend a circle beyond 360° – but they did inscribe that freedom in decisive and unique detail. The most useful thing Parliament could do, I concluded, was to scrutinize the security of the guarantees.

I was less than happy with the leader when it went to press. I regretted that I had fallen in with the prompting of my deputy, Frank Giles, that I was the only person who could write the leader and we could thus save the time which Friday's editorial conference would spend debating our line. Donoughue was soon in my room. He thought the balance of the leader was to oppose a monopolies reference. Did I really want to do that? Giles thought it was fine, but now the political editor Hugo Young entered and agreed with Donoughue. He was followed by Eric Jacobs, the labour editor. What was this, I asked, a jamboree of leader writers? But Jacobs deserved a hearing too. He had played a leading part in the staff deliberations and he was a member of the editorial policy group. He was, he said, 'rather disappointed'. His manner was agitated, yet concealed a still greater degree of anxiety and concern. He wanted me to make more of our consortium. Giles disagreed: how could one canvass one's own case in the columns of the paper? We debated it for some time and I decided the critics had the better of it. I deleted the word 'over-whelmingly' in the reference to the guarantees because of the implication that they were so important they overwhelmed all other considerations. I rewrote the conclusion: 'There is thus a very good case for the Murdoch proposal; but it is for the Minister to apply the monopolies law and for Parliament to satisfy itself that the viable and unobjectionable alterna-tives have been properly considered and that the Murdoch guarantees are sound.' Hugo Young thought it was brave. Murdoch, who had noted the change between editions, growled his disapproval. He was not sure then that Mrs Thatcher would get her way.

The press debate was restricted and soon curtailed. *The Guardian, Financial Times* and *Telegraph* all urged a reference to the Monopolies Commission. The important questions for a free press needed to be brought into the public domain, said *The Financial Times*, and to be fully and thoroughly aired before the Murdoch bid went through. It was clearly the intention of the Fair Trading Act that only in the most exceptional circumstances should newspaper mergers not be referred. The *Telegraph* was not impressed with the case for speed: 'it is arguable that a temporary closure might make it easier for a future owner to resolve the formidable problems of relationship with the printing unions'. The *Economist* came down every time on both sides of the fence. A reference was mandatory under the law, but it was not worth bothering about because the Monopolies Commission would be the Keystone Cops sent to police Dodge City. Murdoch was an intervention-ist 'likely after a while to treat any fastidious guarantee-waving in Printing House Square with healthy expletives', but what, asked the *Economist*, was wrong with that? *The Guardian* was clear: it would be a disgrace if the Government were induced to waive its monopoly investigations when the owner of the largest-selling Sunday newspaper and of the largest-selling daily newspaper might also control Times Newspapers with considerable political sensitivity attached. The Thom-son timetable had been constructed to discourage alternatives, but there were two substantial alternatives in the consortia put together by the two editors: 'Mr Rupert Murdoch is not the Emperor Ming in a world devoid of Flash Gordons.'

A vigorous case for an inquiry was made also in the advertising trade press. *Marketing Week* said the accretion of power and influence, un-known in Fleet Street since Northcliffe's time, cried out for a reference. It could not be said that Murdoch was the only way of keeping the business going, because there were other financially viable offers. A separation of the titles would be a good idea as well, because it would bring a chance to increase the number of owners in Fleet Street instead of reducing them. Editorial guarantees or not, this was the only way of preserving press freedom under the rules of the game. It was the essence of our case. Philip Kleinman in his column in *Campaign* pitched into me for staying loyal to the board in the year of shutdown, and condemned the extraordinary and repulsive secrecy of the sale, and the political offensiveness of allowing Murdoch to concentrate so much influence. He thought nothing of our labours in the vetting committee: 'Editorial independence at Times Newspapers will remain what it has always been in Fleet Street and elsewhere – the freedom of editors to be whatever the proprietor wants, or at least does not object to.'

There were a number of horror stories about Murdoch's record which made us glad we had battened down the hatches. Labour and Tory MPs competed to add to the indictment in the emergency debate. Jonathan Aitken, who had condemned Murdoch's record in an article in the *Daily Express*, spoke from experience in Australia to accuse him of regarding journalism as a way to further his commercial interests. He had strewn worthless assurances and safeguards on newspaper and television ownership around the world like confetti. Christopher Price cited the Australian Broadcasting Tribunal and Phillip Whitehead the Australian Press Council for evidence of Murdoch showing newspapers and television stations persistent bias, and for misleading and unfair reporting to gain an unfair advantage. The trouble with this line of attack was that the Minister had an answer ready. It was not to deny any of the charges – how could he? – but to announce that his conditions for approval of the deal would be entrenched, with Murdoch risking a jail sentence if he broke them. The editorial safeguards we had achieved in the vetting committee would be incorporated in the Articles of Association of Times Newspapers, changeable only with the Minister's approval. The formula had been worked out the night before with the Solicitor-General, Sir Ian Percival, and Denis Hamilton, after Biffen had seen delegations of journalists from both papers as well as Brunton and Murdoch. It neatly drew tight, though with a different knot, the loophole our lawyers had pointed out to me. It was an excellent move and, sitting in the gallery with Hamilton, I did not see what more could be done on editorial independence.

However, Murdoch's record was only one aspect of the case for a Monopolies inquiry. The other was the very fact of concentration. Biffen's handcuffs were a spectacular diversion. The real point was whether the law was being enforced. And it was not.

Newspaper mergers are treated differently in the Act from other mergers in industry and trade. They are the only instances where, by law, references must be made for a judgement on public interest – except in two defined cases. The Minister has discretion only when he is satisfied that a newspaper is otherwise in imminent danger of dying because either it is not economic as a going concern or not economic as a separate newspaper. Biffen might well argue that the facts about *The Times* justified his using his discretion to avoid an inquiry. It was not a going concern. It might otherwise close. JOTT-Mogg and Sea Containers both envisaged a short break in publication, though Arco and Associated did not. Biffen was exaggerating when he talked about the possibility of permanent closure of *The Times* if the Murdoch deal fell through, but he was within his discretionary rights in refusing to have *The Times* deal examined.

No such argument supported the refusal to refer *The Sunday Times* for inquiry. This did not stop Biffen's relying on it. He said his accountants had carried out a detailed investigation of the financial position and future prospects of the paper. They had concluded that *The Sunday Times* was not economic as a going concern. 'What rubbish!' I whispered urgently to Hamilton, the architect of its success. He said nothing. I felt like shouting the roof off. Here we had all been – Murdoch, Rothermere, Tiny Rowlands and us – bidding millions of pounds to buy a paper and here was Biffen, on a cursory study of the business, writing it off. He had not declared merely that *The Sunday Times* lost £600,000 in 1980 – which it did not and I will come to that. He had pronounced to be unviable a business with a turnover of £53 million, which Warburgs forecast would make a profit of £4·8 million in 1981, £11·9 million in 1982 and £13 million in 1983. Biffen had two defences for his convenient definition of bankruptcy.

Since the future looked as bright as most of the past, he wrote off the future, too: 'I do not believe that I am entitled to take a view on future prospects upon existing experience.' But the Fair Trading Act, as Mr Delwyn Williams at once pointed out, did not say the judgement should be on the current state of a newspaper. It referred to a going concern, which must on any use of language mean considering where the paper might be going beyond the present. Some estimate of future prospects is hardly esoteric. One would not buy a corner shop in Grantham without looking at the next few years' figures. Biffen fell back again on his professional advisers. This time the lawyers in the Department were to blame for there being no tomorrow. One senses he became uneasy with his demolition of modern capitalism; in Biffenland many blue-chip companies, such as ICI when he spoke, would not be going concerns. He retreated, under the pressure which was less than he should have received, to the arcane matter of overheads. He confused everyone including himself, which was easy enough since a proper consideration would have required two sets of figures for overheads and he produced no details in the Commons.

Peter Emery, who took part in the debate as the Minister responsible for getting the Act on the statute book, intervened to help Biffen by saying that the overheads would be higher for *The Sunday Times*, the *cause célèbre*, as a separate newspaper than as part of Times Newspapers. Again, there was no discussion of how much higher and for how long. Everyone was making judgements about numbers without the numbers. It was this which made the debate a farce. Phillip Whitehead did his best with profit forecasts for a stand-alone *Sunday Times*, supplied by Cruickshank to Donoughue, and he made a spirited contribution, mentioning our consortium as an exciting departure in British journalism. Jo Grimond, a director of *The Guardian*, thought anyone ought to be able to see *The Times* and *Sunday Times* consortia represented a badly needed new departure in Fleet Street. Jonathan Aitken advocated Lonrho, Associated or Arco. The bidding process had not been fairly or openly conducted according to general commercial rules. He had that very morning been denied a copy of the prospectus by the 'Thomson-Warburg plotters'. But Biffen sidestepped any discussion about alternatives by falling back on the Thomson timetable. And, to complete his afternoon's breach of the peace, he used his last few seconds to call on 'a more formidable participant in this debate than I, namely, Mr Harold Evans'. His assistants had been adept. They had taken from the tapes the statement I had made to the Press Association that afternoon: 'No editor or journalist could ask for wider guarantees of editorial independence on news than those Mr Murdoch has accepted and which are now entrenched by the Secretary of State.'

I had opened the statement by saying: 'I would still prefer our consortium.' Biffen censored that bit. All in all it was an appropriate way for a bad afternoon to be wrapped up.

Five Tories voted against Biffen – Jonathan Aitkin, Peter Bottomley, Hugh Fraser, Barry Porter and Delwyn Williams – but he got his way by 281 votes to 239.

It was more than two weeks after the debate, when Murdoch's purchase was final and formal, that Biffen told the Commons he had placed in the Library the memorandum setting out the material on which he based his decision. Nobody took it further at the time, but an examination of it I have made since reveals extraordinary treatment of what Biffen called 'the main question ... whether I was wise in my judgement that *The Sunday Times* was not an economic and going concern as a separate newspaper'.

There are three main features: an omission of revenue and profit which alone put *The Sunday Times* at break-even point in 1980; the treatment of overheads; and the novel use of interest charges. The responsibility is Biffen's, but the Thomson Organisation encouraged him in that direction because it wanted to sell to Murdoch (who went to the Department of Trade himself and made a considerable impression). Neither Cruickshank, as finance director and general manager of *The Sunday Times*, nor I, as chairman of the executive committee, was consulted by the Department of Trade on the newspaper we managed, nor on the detailed work we had done with Morgan Grenfell for a stand-alone *Sunday Times*. But Cruickshank, as finance director as well as general manager, was asked to supply figures to Thomson. It was, as he put it, an exercise in reverse alchemy: an attempt to translate gold into lead.

The first point is that even for the year 1980, which Biffen eccentrically chose to regard as the single test, he mis-stated the position. *The Sunday Times* did not lose £600,000; it broke even. Biffen's figures overlooked the non-newspaper business run very profitably by Times Newspapers. Most of this depended on *The Sunday Times* and received free advertising and promotion in the paper – *The Sunday Times* Selective Marketplace, a direct-mail business bringing in more than £3 million, and the Wine Club are two of the best-known examples. These were listed in the Warburg prospectus – but they were easy to overlook because they were not with the main appendix on *The Sunday Times*. Biffen ignored even obvious newspaper revenues like the syndication of *The Sunday Times* work around the world, and also the contract to print *The Guardian* on three *Sunday Times* presses. In all, he missed out £4·6 million of revenue, yielding more than £700,000 of profit in 1980. (Profits from the ancillary activities were £800,000 in 1977 and £600,000 in 1978.) Nowhere in this memorandum did he account for these profits.

Biffen chose the single year 1980 to justify his demolition of *The Sunday Times*, but the paper had made profits in seventeen out of twenty years. A single difficult year does not change the basic economics of any business with such a record. Even so, Biffen allowed the House to be misled about 1980. In the Commons he said it was a period 'relatively free from the adverse impact of the shutdown'. On the contrary, it was the adverse impact of being off the streets for eleven months which persuaded the board of Times Newspapers to spend several million pounds on promotion, and to give me more editorial space to the exclusion at times of even the most lucrative appointments advertising. Furthermore, £2 million was lost in production shortfalls. Without these factors, which Biffen ignored, *The Sunday Times* would have made the substantial profit of £5·3 million in 1980.

As for the rest, the accounting is complicated, but surely not too complex for Biffen's advisers. The crucial numbers are all set out in the Table. This shows the trading profit of *The Sunday Times* before charging interest on the capital employed in the business, and taxes. It covers

The Sunday Times: trading profit before charging interest and tax
£ million

	1977	1978	1980	1981	1982
1 Warburg prospectus estimate with *ST* as part of TNHL – but excluding other *ST* trading income	2·3	2·9	(0·7)	4·8	11·9
2 Biffen in Annex C with *ST* as part of TNHL	2·1	2·6	(0·7)	2·5	8·1
3 Biffen in Commons Library papers for stand-alone *Sunday Times* – but excluding other *ST* trading income	2·1	2·6	(0·7)	(0·1)	5·5
4 Cruickshank in forecast for stand-alone *ST* and including *ST*'s other trading income	2·9	3·2	Break even	1·1	8·3

the actual period 1977 to 1980, omitting 1979 when the paper was published for only five weeks, and the profit we forecast at the time of the sale for 1981 and 1982. Cases 1 and 2 are for *The Sunday Times* as part of Times Newspapers, paying its share of overheads. The first is from the Warburg prospectus, the second from Biffen's working papers; both exclude the income from other *Sunday Times* trading. Cases 3 and 4 are for *The Sunday Times* on its own. Biffen (3) has again overlooked the other *Sunday Times* income. This oversight is amended in Case 4, which is the prospectus Cruickshank agreed with Morgan Grenfell for a *Sunday Times* on its own.

It will be seen that Biffen's figures (2) reduced the *Sunday Times* profits by comparison with the Warburg prospectus. They did this even for the actual results of 1977 and 1978. This was achieved, with the help of Thomson, by arbitrarily increasing the rent that had been charged three years previously by Thomson for 200 Gray's Inn Road, the building that housed *The Sunday Times*. There were substantial disagreements within the board of Times Newspapers and between the board and Thomson over the profit forecasts for *The Times*: Thomson wanted the profit potential inflated. But the profit for *The Sunday Times* had been accepted by Thomson and Warburgs. It had never been an issue, yet Biffen's advisers, again with Thomson's agreement, reduced the 1981 profit forecast from £4·8 to £2·5 million and the 1982 forecast from £11·9 to £8·1 million. These adjustments flowed mainly from eliminating estimates of demanning, incidentally savings which Rupert Murdoch later achieved. Biffen's figures also arbitrarily sliced £7 million off the forecast advertising revenues for 1981 – though the 1980 forecast was dead on. Nevertheless, even after these adjustments, the picture is of a newspaper which was profitable in 1977 and 1978, suffered a modest loss in 1980 in exceptional circumstances, and was forecast to return to profitability within two years and to be as profitable as any newspaper in Fleet Street. All this still without crediting *The Sunday Times* with any of the profit from other trading which would certainly have continued.

Biffen's advisers made the figures worse, again, by making a huge charge of £2 million and more against *The Sunday Times* for the capital employed in the business. We never paid interest, in fact, to Thomson for any advances. Biffen's notional charge in the future depended entirely on the assumption one made about the sums that would have to be borrowed as opposed to the amount subscribed as equity capital. This was a most unusual approach which, if applied to many of our blue-chip companies, would result in reported losses year after year. What Biffen was doing was calling the shareholders' return a charge on capital, deducting it from the trading profit of the business and calling the resultant figure the profit or loss of the business. Nowhere else have I seen this presentation, nor heard a robust argument in its favour. It was, in reality, a device to support the assertion that *The Sunday Times* was unviable.

Now for cases 3 and 4 in the Table, the position of *The Sunday Times* on its own, which is what our consortium proposed, and which Biffen was obliged to consider since the law refers to single newspaper titles. This does raise the question of overheads, those costs which are incurred whatever the level of business activity, the cost of accommodation, support staff such as doormen and cleaners, depreciation on the machinery, and services such as electricity. Biffen in the Commons mixed up the overheads of *The Sunday Times* as part of Times Newspapers and as a separate company, but in the Library paper he gives a figure of an additional cost of £2·6 million in overheads by 1983. Geoffrey Robinson in the debate asked for full disclosure of the Department's working papers. This would have revealed, I believe, how superficial the study had been. But Cruickshank had done immensely detailed work on overheads for the Morgan Grenfell prospectus. He proposed to concentrate the new *Sunday Times* in one building, sharing with Thomson the costs of removing *The Times* and its supplements. Interestingly, he proposed to spend on promotion, because he thought demand would be less than predicted in the Warburg prospectus, and in the event his forecast was very close to what occurred under Murdoch.

It is simpler to compare Biffen's and Cruickshank's forecasts without Biffen's theoretical £2·6 million, but of course with Cruickshank's real overhead costs. Cruickshank/Morgan Grenfell (4) includes the profits Biffen overlooked from the *Sunday Times* Wine Club, direct mail, syndication and so on. The 1981 profit for *The Sunday Times* comes out at £1·1 million, small enough but hardly a definition of unviability. The Cruickshank/Morgan Grenfell profit forecast for 1982 was £8·3 million, taking account of the improvements in productivity which could be achieved and the costs of running 200 Gray's Inn Road just for *The Sunday Times*. Very much a going concern.

Biffen and Thomson got away with it. Jonathan Aitken said in the Commons that Biffen's decision was likely to be challenged in the courts. Mick Shields, the managing director of Associated, had told him they were likely to test it by issuing a writ of mandamus, demanding, in effect, that the Secretary of State should fulfil his obligations under the Act. The *Sunday Times* journalists took up this cudgel and filed a suit. A lawyer asked to advise on the validity of our precious guarantees remarked: 'If you put a mad bulldog on a leash, it's still a mad bulldog.' On Biffen's accountancy, they went to Gerhard Weiss, a senior partner in the firm of Cork Gully, the liquidators, who has specialized in all forms of insolvency, including receiverships, since 1952. Weiss has great experience in trying to judge whether the business of a company or a particular part of its business is economic as a going concern. 'In my opinion', he told them, 'the most significant question is the estimate of the future profitability of *The Sunday Times*.' He looked at the results and forecasts – I helped by letting John Barry have the draft management plan for 1981 – and declared: 'I consider *The Sunday Times* is economic as a going concern.' He swore an affidavit which concluded: 'If I were the receiver of Times Newspapers Ltd and decided to close down *The Sunday Times* instead of continuing it and trying to dispose of it as going concern, I should expect a claim against me for negligence as a receiver.'

The action was set down for Monday 9 February. Murdoch was beside himself. He was never off the telephone to me and Hamilton. What was the latest state of play? What could be done? Who were John Barry and Eric Jacobs leading the action? What did they want? All I could tell him was that the journalists saw it as a matter of principle rather than personality. All this stuff about the uneconomic *Sunday Times* had offended their pride and sense of fairness. I was not encouraging the court action; on the contrary, it was a matter for the chapel. He must know from their resolution that they had several demands: they wanted a senior *Sunday Times* journalist to be made a national director, and a veto power on the appointment or dismissal of their editor, though

not the power of choice. Hamilton said the *Sunday Times* journalists
were threatening the future of *The Times*.

I was impressed by the spirit of the chapel. Jonathan Aitken, I learned
later, was their intermediary with Associated. They were talking to
Associated, because the costs of fighting the court action were put at
£60,000: they needed subvention. They also had a meeting in the Savile
Club with James Evans. He told them that, if they succeeded in thwarting
Murdoch, Thomsons would not choose the consortia. They would invite
Rothermere next, though Brunton had been critical of Associated's
approach: 'It seemed rather fluffy, about as substantial as a snowfall in
June'. Anything but the consortia, it seemed. Despite the fact that he was
next in line, Rothermere shied away from helping to pay the court costs.
Mick Shields, true to the attitude he had displayed to us, persuaded
Rothermere against. The *Sunday Times* chapel had therefore to decide
whether to pay all the costs itself by raising a levy on its 150 or so
members of £400 each, minus what might be raised from the *Times* staff
of 280. 'I've just discovered', a *Times* man reported, 'that the size of
every man's soul is a little smaller than his mortgage.'

It was at this point on Saturday 7 February that the *Sunday Times*
men had the first of two meetings with Murdoch: Eric Jacobs (the chapel
father), who had led the delegation to see John Biffen, whom they had
asked for an inquiry and an entrenchment of the powers of the national
directors; the persuasive John Barry, the managing editor of features and
former father who had led the chapel into battle; John Frayer, the labour
reporter, a hard-headed wary man (now with BBC Television); and Peter
Wilby, who tended to speak for the more militant staff.

It would be an exaggeration to say the business of putting out the
newspaper went on as usual. The space barons had their impromptu
Saturday huddles to resolve priorities, but there were also others ex-
changing opinions on the credibility of the designated new owner, who
was brooding alone at that moment in Hamilton's office in *The Times*
building. The production of newspapers in Australia, of course, had
stopped entirely so that their staffs could tell the Poms what they were
letting themselves in for if they let 'Rupie' in. Costs apart, there was a
division in the chapel between those who saw the court action as a
weapon to open up the whole question of the sale, and others who
perceived it simply as a means of improving staff participation. I was in
my room writing a leader on Mrs Thatcher and Keynes between frequent
telephone interruptions from Murdoch. I began to think he had no idea
of the pressure of deadlines. He was continually bearing down on me as
if I could drop everything and deliver the chapel to him. The bashful
Murdoch of the vetting committee had shed his veil. It was around
5 p.m., just after we had put the first edition to bed, when Jacobs and

Barry came back and reported to the chapel. As the editor, I did not attend chapel meetings. This one was held in the Business News department. It was packed and passionate. The chapel's team had secured Murdoch's agreement on the appointment to the board of the Holdings company (though not as national directors) of one working journalist from *The Sunday Times* and one from *The Times*. Two other journalists 'of independence and distinction' would be among the national directors, who would be six rather than four. These were the responses Murdoch had told the vetting committee he thought he might offer to meet calls for participation. The chapel was fiercely divided about whether this was enough to end the court action. Barry, to the surprise of many, spoke against going on with it, and so did Hugo Young. Fear of a closure and the loss of *The Times* in the end carried the meeting.

Nobody was really happy with the outcome. The minority printed a tee-shirt for the fourteen members of the Gravediggers' Club: 'Don't Blame Us. We Voted Against.' Even the peacemakers felt uneasy. Barry came to my room to say that he had decided he would leave the paper and write a book on NATO. Though he had quixotically helped to sell the compromise to the chapel, he could not work for Murdoch. This was a loss to the paper and I asked him why he had chosen to quit. As a former Insight editor and veteran of many a confrontation with the artful dodgers of politics and commerce, Barry had been impressed by Murdoch's guile. He had put on a country-boy air, hurt that they did not trust or like him. He had told them engagingly that he had not thought much of the vetting process: old codgers, he implied, whereas he could talk man to man with the journalists. 'But he knew exactly what structures would turn him into a constitutional monarch at Times Newspapers and he was quite determined to be absolute. The man's charm is *lethal*.' Barry wafted his hand in front me like a shark's tail. 'One minute he's swimming along with a smile, then snap! There's blood in the water. Your head's gone.'

8

THE TENTH
PROPRIETOR

I did not have a settled view of the designated tenth proprietor of *The Times*, who was also the owner of newspapers selling 50 million copies a week round the world. I had been acquainted with Murdoch for twelve years. I was forty and had been editor of *The Sunday Times* for two years when, in 1969, he took over the *News of the World* at thirty-seven. So we had arrived in positions of authority in Fleet Street at about the same time and age, though by rather different paths. I knew something of him from Australian newspaper friends. I heard every jolly swagman's yarn which placed him somewhere between Ned Kelly and Citizen Kane. I followed his doings after he left London for America in 1973 and met him occasionally in those years. But the image I formed wobbled. There was something wrong with the negative or my fixing solution: just when the outline of an open countenance was coming into focus it would emerge darkly smudged or a grimace would dissolve into a disarming grin.

The conventional image, which is constantly repeated in newspaper profiles, is that on the death of his sixty-six-year-old father, Sir Keith, Rupert Murdoch found himself robbed of his inheritance on the *Melbourne Herald*, but, fired with revenge and trained by Beaverbrook, he single-handedly took over a failing newspaper in Adelaide and bombarded the country with sex and scandal. The true facts are, however, slightly different. Keith Murdoch never held more than a paltry number of shares in the *Herald* empire he built, and Murdoch, though a confident twenty-three, was not presumptuous enough to expect to follow his father as managing director. He had retired anyway. At the same time, it was hardly penury that faced the Murdoch family. Murdoch's beginnings are a family album of grand houses, horses and servants, and a boy with fine eyes at the knee of a famous father. He was the only son – there were three daughters – of Sir Keith, who made his name sixteen years before the birth of his son. In 1915, at the age of twenty-nine, Keith Murdoch, a Melbourne parliamentary reporter, wangled his way to

Gallipoli on a mission for the Australian Government. He broke a promise to respect military censorship so as to expose to the British and Australian Prime Ministers the tragic futility of the Dardanelles expedition. A friendship followed with Lord Northcliffe, then the owner of *The Times*, and the editorship of the *Herald* in Melbourne, where he put Northcliffe's counsel to good use. He reinvigorated a solid newspaper and went on to run the company and the largest newspaper group in Australia. He was forty-two when he married Elisabeth Greene, aged nineteen. For their only son, the connection of journalism, politics and privilege was umbilical; the leading politicians were suitors at his father's house in Melbourne and at their country estate.

The valuable legacy Keith Murdoch left was a controlling personal interest in the Queensland Newspaper Company, publishers of papers in Adelaide and Brisbane. One of my close Australian newspaper friends, the late Rohan Rivett, was Murdoch's first editor and another, Sir Theodor Bray, narrowly escaped being a second at the *Brisbane Courier Mail*. Both men were appointed by Keith Murdoch and were there when Rupert Murdoch arrived to claim his inheritance. It was Rivett who made the *Adelaide News* and Rivett was the first editor Murdoch fired.

Bray told me that, as chief executive, Keith Murdoch respected the editor's independence; nobody was quite so sure with the raw young Rupert Murdoch, to whom the Brisbane executives swiftly commended the attractions of Adelaide. In any event Murdoch sold the Brisbane interest to pay death duties and launched himself in the dignified southern city of Adelaide. With his mother and sisters he had 57% of the tabloid *News* and *The Sunday News*, plus a radio station in the mining city of Broken Hill, where he indulged his taste for gambling.

The *News* company was in profit and it had in Rohan Rivett, only seven years older than Murdoch, a professional editor-in-chief of great flair, experience and courage, hand-picked by Keith Murdoch a year before his death. He was a graduate of Melbourne and Oxford universities; he had reported from China, Malaya and London; and he had been a Japanese prisoner of war. He was captured when, as a war correspondent, he volunteered to keep broadcasting on Singapore Radio. I was moved by his book about his adventures and ordeals. He came from a celebrated liberal family, his grandfather, Alfred Deakin, was a great Australian Prime Minister and his father, Sir David Rivett, one of the most famous Australian scientists. Murdoch was lucky to have Rivett. He himself had negligible newspaper training. He had used his father's connections to spend short spells during Oxford vacations with the *Melbourne Herald* and the *Birmingham Gazette*, and, after graduation, three months with Beaverbrook's slick sub-editing team at the

Daily Express, where the managing editor was Edward Pickering. But
that was all. It was Rivett who turned the *News* from a humdrum rag
into a paper with a crusading intelligence on local issues and a sense of
the wider world. He upset the Adelaide Establishment, who regarded
him as something of a Red, but he was more a libertarian humanist than
an ideological left-winger. Keith Murdoch had asked Rivett to befriend
his son, who went from Geelong Grammar School, the hearty Australian
equivalent of Eton, to Worcester College, Oxford, when Rivett was his
father's London correspondent. Rivett and his wife, Nan, had the young
Murdoch down for weekends in Sunbury-on-Thames and took him on
a European motoring holiday. They were to become close over the years;
Murdoch visited the Rivetts' home in Adelaide a great deal and spent
time with the family at the beach. The Rivett children were fond of him
too. In the early days Murdoch looked up to Rivett and shared his radical
views. Rupert was known as 'Red Rupert' at Oxford, where he was by
all accounts restless with no taste for studies and had a cocky attitude
towards authority. He collected a third-class degree in politics and
economics, and was banned from the Labour club for canvassing for
office – quite attractive achievements. It was on the seven-year partnership with Rivett and an early mastery of the commercial side that
Murdoch built the success of the *News*.

Murdoch's individual and spectacular achievement was in the way he
used this increasingly profitable Adelaide base. He secured a licence for
the Channel Nine television station and, in 1960, he induced the over-
confident Fairfax Group to let him buy the *Sydney Daily* and *Sunday
Mirror*. It was here, rather than in Adelaide, and with the later purchase
of the sex and crime weekly *Truth* in Melbourne and Brisbane, that
Murdoch made his reputation for buying and hyping titles, and engorg-
ing his acquisitions with crime and cheesecake. 'Leper Rapes Virgin,
Gives Birth to Monster Baby' sold in Sydney as it was to sell in London
and San Antonio, Texas. But he learned something else too: 'The way to
operate', he became fond of saying, 'is with OPM – other people's money.'
He was able to operate on the scale he did only because he convinced the
government-backed Commonwealth Bank of Australia, the biggest trading bank in the country, that he was a fair bet. By the time he arrived in
London late in 1968 to win a bruising take-over brawl with Robert
Maxwell for the *News of the World* he had built a financial pyramid by
which he controlled newspaper, magazine and television interests worth
an estimated $50 million. Every Australian I knew, and Fleet Street had
quite a number, wanted Murdoch to beat Maxwell. Maxwell was distrusted; Murdoch was then seen as a fresh impulse. Everyone liked his
attempt in 1964 to establish Australia's first national newspaper, the
seriously inclined *Australian*. The more outrageous stories of his conduct

amused the British and relieved the Aussies individually of the burden of living up to the national bushwhacker image.

My friendship with Rivett, though, had given me sight of another side of Murdoch. Rivett told me how 'the young Murdoch' gradually tried to erode his authority over the editorial side of the *Adelaide News*. The most serious matter was the Stuart affair, which happened nine years before Murdoch's triumphant entry into Fleet Street. Rivett was in anguish when he arrived in Tokyo for the 1960 annual conference of editors organized by the International Press Institute. He was on bail, and he felt betrayed by Murdoch. In January, Rivett and News Ltd had gone on trial facing nine charges of libel, including the rare and grave one of seditious libel, with a conviction on any one of them carrying the chance of imprisonment. Rivett had become convinced that an aborigine, Robert Max Stuart, sentenced to hang for murdering a girl of nine, had had a raw deal and was not necessarily guilty. There was a dubious confession, there were the doubts of a Catholic priest who saw Stuart in prison before one of the seven successive dates set for his execution, and there were new witnesses found by Rivett who testified that Stuart was in fact working at a funfair when the murder most probably occurred. Rivett campaigned for an inquiry before Stuart was hanged. Murdoch became equally caught up in the crusade. It became a campaign against the crusty Sir Thomas Playford and his anti-Labour state government, which retained power by a gerrymander giving two out of every three seats to the minority country voters. Playford was forced to set up a Royal Commission, but two of the three commissioners were judges involved in Stuart's trials, including the Chief Justice, Sir Mellis Napier.

During the hearings, the QC for Stuart, Jack Shand, protested that Napier's attitude to his cross-examination of a policeman meant there was not going to be a thorough investigation, so he walked out. Rivett wrote a contents bill on this: 'Shand Quits: "You Won't Give Stuart Fair Go"'. Murdoch suggested the headline for the front page of the *News*: 'Mr Shand, QC, indicts Sir Mellis Napier: These Commissioners Cannot Do the Job'. Later Murdoch gave Rivett the wording for a new contents bill: 'Commission Breaks Up: Shand Blasts Napier'. It was the Murdoch wording in both instances which infuriated the Prime Minister. He denounced the *News* in Parliament for undermining public faith in judges. The atmosphere in the city was heated and apprehensive, and the day after the debate, when Rivett was away, Murdoch took the unusual step of writing an editorial. It maintained the *News*'s position that Stuart should not hang until the new evidence had been tested – his sentence was finally commuted to life – but it conceded that on the headline and the poster the *News* was wrong: they should never have been published and they regretted them. Murdoch conceded too much.

Rivett thought so, I thought so when I looked at the circumstances, and so did the jury. Eventually Rivett was acquitted on eight of the libel charges and the ninth was withdrawn. He properly took responsibility as editor for the words Murdoch had suggested, and he defended them as he was right to do. In Tokyo he was distressed because he felt that Murdoch had let him down when the going got rough and when the established politicians were out for his blood. Murdoch declined to answer questions in court; Rivett made a statement from the dock.

Rivett was a red-haired lance of a figure, warm and impulsive. His friends were sad to see him so downcast in Tokyo. After three and a half years on the Burma railway under the Japanese, it was all a bit too much for him. Two months later and five weeks after the last charge against Rivett and the company had been withdrawn, Murdoch sacked him. He did it by sending round a three-line letter.

Publicly, both Rivett and Murdoch refused to connect the dismissal with the Stuart case. I knew the case to be part of it. Murdoch had had enough of tackling Playford and the Establishment; he had also developed a distaste for independent editors. The libel trial, a fright for him and an ordeal for Rivett, was a milestone in his conversion from sympathetic liberal to scourge of the 'bleeding hearts'.

My first experience of Murdoch was under cover. In April 1969, four months after Murdoch acquired the *News of the World*, his defeated rival, Captain Robert Maxwell, a naturalized Briton, scientific publisher, propagandist and former Labour MP, offered to take the ailing *Sun* newspaper off the hands of Hugh Cudlipp at IPC and to run it as a non-profitmaking Labour daily. An affable Murdoch rang me to say he had documents on Maxwell. It was all hush-hush and I could have them if I did not announce who had passed them on. I had not yet met Murdoch. 'Why don't you run them yourself?' I asked. 'Nobody here', he responded, 'can look at it as well as your Insight guys.' This was not the whole truth. For a third party to discredit Maxwell was more useful to Murdoch, who had his own eyes on the *Sun*, but was biding his time.

We had been curious for some while about the origins and adventures of Maxwell, and Insight collected the file from Murdoch. His papers turned out to be flimsy stuff, but we continued our own inquiries into Maxwell and were well placed to write about him when, in August, in a City sensation, the £25 million sale of his Pergamon Group to the American Saul Steinberg's Leasco collapsed because of doubts about Pergamon profits and accounts. However, it was print-union hostility more than anything which persuaded Maxwell to withdraw his bid for the *Sun*, which left the way open for Murdoch to make his most triumphant acquisition so far. He relieved IPC of the title for the historically paltry sum of £50,000 down.

My memory of the Rivett case took some of the gloss from Murdoch for me, but a decade had passed and I did warm to his derring-do in Fleet Street. I was curious to meet the man who was taking on Hugh Cudlipp and the *Daily Mirror*. In November 1969 I invited him to a dinner-party in my home in Highgate, but, by the time the day came, I found I was entertaining London's most notorious pariah. Not only was it a few days after he had started striptease in his revamped *Sun*, but he had simultaneously outraged everyone's sense of fair play by raking over the ashes of the affair of John Profumo, Secretary of State for War, who had lied to the House of Commons about his secret relationship with the call-girl Christine Keeler. It had all been done to death in 1963, when the *News of the World* paid £20,000 for her story. The disgraced Profumo redeemed himself in the public eye by taking up good works with his wife – and a decent obscurity that was suddenly menaced six years later by the *News of the World*'s proclamation that it would serialize extracts from Christine Keeler's autobiography. To everyone it seemed like the hand of that brash new Australian owner; in fact, Stafford Somerfield, the paper's editor, had bought the series and would have defended it on the disarming grounds that he wanted to sell papers, but for Murdoch stepping forward to say it was his decision and he did it to show up politicians who lied. It was an answer that was six years too late. Denis Hamilton was prominent in drafting a motion of censure by the Press Council; he seemed to take Murdoch's conduct as a personal affront and the *Sun* as a daily insult. Murdoch was shunned by polite society and roasted by David Frost on his television chat show. Short of sending him back in irons, England could not have been less welcoming.

When he arrived for dinner, I found myself greeting a plumpish man of my own height (5'8") with an unlined, soft, round face. He was counterpointed by the slim, crystalline beauty of his second wife, Anna, a former reporter on his Sydney tabloid. She was talkative, vivacious and open, whereas he was apparently crippled by shyness. He shuffled, smiled and left sentences in mid-air. He seemed too diffident to be a tycoon and too inarticulate to be a journalist. This was as appealing as it was surprising. It was hard to put him at ease. He was bashful with the other guests, Woodrow and Verushka Wyatt, Frank and Lady Kitty Giles, and Nigel Ryan, the new editor of ITN's *News at Ten*, who had been at Oxford at the same time as Murdoch. He murmured something half-apologetic to them about the Keeler affair, that he had not quite realized how much had been told before; it was an attractive admission, more for the manner of its delivery than its content. Everyone fell over themselves to say they quite understood. It was the Frost show for London Weekend Television which had most upset him. He had been misled, he said, that it was all to be 'a pally chat'. In an aside to me, which seemed out of character at the time, he steamed that Frost would regret that deception. He had told Frost: 'You'll keep, David.'

All of this was over before the first course. Murdoch talked a little about his ambitions for *The Australian*, but it was Woodrow Wyatt who dominated the evening with a belligerent defence of the war in Vietnam. Giles and I supported him against the scepticism of the others including Murdoch. At the end of the evening, Murdoch stood in the living-room leafing through a copy of the eighth issue of his *Sun*, which had been specially delivered by his driver, and pointed with some pride to a news story on the front page that the *Sun* had to itself.

I was glad we had invited the Murdochs. We were touched when they said we had made them feel at home and that ours was their first invitation to a journalist's home. Enid, my first wife, remarked that they seemed to have had a rotten time in England. But a neighbour of ours in Highgate, Charles Fenby, who had been my editorial director at the Westminster Press when I was the editor of *The Northern Echo*, reproved me in his icy and languid manner for entertaining Murdoch: 'You should know better. The man's a shit and he'll never change.' Fenby had been the editor of the *Birmingham Gazette* when Murdoch's father prevailed on the company chairman, Pat Gibson (later Lord Gibson), to give young Rupe a vacation job there. 'I took him in, befriended him and showed him all I could', said Fenby, 'and what did he do? He wrote a filthy letter to Pat afterwards saying I should be fired.' Many years later I mentioned this to Murdoch: 'Sure I did. Silly old Fenby, a lousy editor.'

More than a year passed before I had contact with Murdoch again. In the autumn of 1972, while I was in the middle of *The Sunday Times* campaign for the Thalidomide children, I was asked if I would succeed Hugh Cudlipp as the head of IPC's newspapers, including the *Daily Mirror*. Murdoch came on to me at home. 'I hear IPC want you. You're crazy if you work for Ryder,' he said, referring to Don Ryder, the chairman of Reed International, which controlled IPC. 'He's impossible. You're going great at *The Sunday Times*. How's the Thalidomide thing?' I told him how dismayed I was by the failure of the rest of the press to report the campaign. We were walking a legal tightrope, but things could be reported and it would all help to focus attention on the plight of the families. He responded at once: 'Fuck the judges, fuck the law. We'll help.' Nothing appeared in the *Sun* and nothing in the *News of the World*. But something else did: lurid posters began to appear all over the country calling for a boycott of whisky and gin produced by Distillers (who had made the drug and were being slow over compensation). The Attorney-General declared that they were illegal and that Scotland Yard was investigating who was responsible. Police ripped them down when overnight they were plastered on the door, windows and railings of

Distillers' discreet headquarters in St James's Square. They were savage: a bottle of Distillers' gin was featured with a deformed baby: 'Mother's ruin ... children's poison'. The undetected sponsor of the posters, I learned later, was Murdoch. He released a senior *News of the World* executive to organize them as a private individual and then take leave in Australia. Murdoch's idea, apparently, was that the *News of the World* and other papers would then be able to reproduce the posters as news without risk of prosecution for contempt. The lawyers advised that this was a strategem without a hope; it was also one which almost torpedoed *The Sunday Times*, because we were arguing in court and in Parliament that our campaign was justified because it was based on moral persuasion rather than unfair pressure. The Attorney-General tried to put the posters before the High Court as evidence of coercion; fortunately the judges accepted they were not our work.

The incident left me puzzling again about Murdoch. He talked tough and he gambled in business dealings, but he had shied away from taking a minor risk in his papers on behalf on the Thalidomide children at a time when *The Sunday Times* was isolated and fully exposed. He was not at all exceptional in this; but the timidity fitted oddly with the bravado of his telephone talk. Was it the fear of losing money in court? Or a hangover from Rivett's trial? I thought at first that the crude poster campaign was at least evidence of some concern on Murdoch's part, giving the lie to the reputation he has now acquired for despising sentiment and compassion. Yet, as soon as the posters failed to provide an excuse for Murdoch's papers safely to share or steal *The Sunday Times*'s thunder, the idea was abandoned. Supplies of the posters ran out after a week.

He could have afforded to take risks. His British company pulsated with the profits of the 'soar away *Sun*'. The paper had earned him the nicknames of 'the Dirty Digger' and 'Thanks for the Mammary Murdoch', but it had found new newspaper readers. By the end of 1972 the *Sun* has passed three million daily sales from the 800,000 of 1969. He had bought a 40% stake in London Weekend Television and doubled his provincial newspaper titles. Shortly after the poster incident, we decided it was time to assess Rupert Murdoch. He had done much for the newspaper business, but had he done anything for journalism? The *Sun* was a commercial success and lustily edited by Larry Lamb, but it was a formula of the 1930s. Murdoch's serious flagship, *The Australian*, had drifted down market; he had fired a distinguished liberal editor, Adrian Deamer. His *Sunday Australian* had been amalgamated with his tabloid *Sunday Telegraph* in Sydney. We were encouraged in our assessment by another distinguished Australian editor who knew Murdoch and Australian journalism, and gave us guidance. Graham Perkin was the editor of the Melbourne *Age* from 1966 until his death at the age of forty-five in 1975, and was dedicated in a deceptively breezy manner to the public service idea of journalism. He was at odds with Murdoch in what he saw as his contempt for political objectivity and professional standards. Perkin thought Australia needed a Press Council to adjudicate on fairness, truth and privacy; Murdoch derided the idea as interference by failed editors and retired schoolmasters. For all that, Perkin was fascinated by Murdoch. He knew him well. He had declined an invitation to work for him, but he thought that within this impulsive man there might still be found the lost idealist. Perkin drew hope from two periods: Murdoch's first seven years in Adelaide with Rivett, before the break, and the three years from 1968 to 1971, when Adrian Deamer gave *The Australian* a conscience. Murdoch had sacked Deamer, as he had sacked Rivett, and had devoted himself to expanding a wholly commercial empire, but Perkin had not written him off: 'Perhaps when he has enough economic security, which in his terms means millions, the idealism will break out again.' In subsequent years, many people believed this; the idea was still around in 1981, when Murdoch acquired *The Times*. One was left with the thought that, if economic security compelled Murdoch to be a multi-millionaire many times over, the wells of personal insecurity must run deep.

We reflected Perkin's view in our *Sunday Times* profile, but we had a great deal of trouble with Murdoch before it was published. He refused in November 1972 to see the colour magazine writer Peter Dunn, and there was a clamp-down in his company. This was an odd posture for a newspaper man, given that *The Sunday Times* had not been notably hostile to him or his papers. Dunn found the wall of silence exasperating and, inevitably, his first draft reflected the bias of some of the sources who did want to say something about Murdoch. This was only to be expected and Dunn, as an experienced profile writer, was aware of the problem. Then someone made a mistake and sent this first draft to Murdoch. The magazine's idea was that their manifest readiness to receive corrections at an early stage might encourage Murdoch and others to give their versions of events, but it was far too early a draft. It merely reinforced Murdoch's defensiveness that he was to be the victim of character assassination. There was talk of an injunction, which was absurd, since I had no intention of publishing what Murdoch had seen, nor had Dunn the slightest expectation that it would be printed in that form. Murdoch's editorial director, Larry Lamb, declaring he had not consulted Murdoch, wrote me a letter saying that the *News of the World* had higher standards than *The Sunday Times*: he would not demean himself by correcting the so-called 'facts' nor would he talk to the author. Fortunately the premature draft proved a useful exercise. I sent it to

Perkin and also to Rohan Rivett. Dunn readily incorporated their amendments and others. Rivett, showing professional objectivity, thought it 'a
bit unkind' about Murdoch and too laudatory of his mother. I sent
Murdoch a version I was ready to publish, but on which, again, we were
ready to consider corrections. Dunn vividly described Murdoch's rise
and some of the rows on the way. He depicted him as a loner whose
self-doubt demanded unquestioning loyalty from subordinates. He saw
him, rather than a journalist or inspirer of journalists, primarily as a
businessman of entrepreneurial nerve with a flair for swift bulldozing.
He credited him with an original talent evident in the pungent and racy
television commercials for the *Sun* which had transformed the way
newspapers were advertised on television. This skill had done as much
for the paper, Dunn suggested, as the exposure of acres of flesh in his
'bordello' of newspapers. Fleet Street, he concluded, was to some extent
in his debt for the aggressive optimism he brought from Australia: 'He
has shown that newspapers can be saved and revived. Whether more
than this can be expected from Rupert Murdoch is still a matter of
speculation.'

Murdoch wrote to me: 'Although I think it is still full of malice and
pretentious sneering, I must admit that you seem to have cut out the
author's more extreme ravings which were in the original draft.' Then
he listed thirty-one corrections. He did not eat sausages, certainly never
any bought from his own canteen. He seldom used his quarter-interest in
a box at Covent Garden. He was not aware of Lord Goodman's having
introduced him to any important person that he would not have met in
the normal course of events. He was not a sacker of editors. 'I admit
I have a reputation for firing editors, but the facts do not support
it ... I have only ever sacked one editor of *The Australian* – although
I admit I sacked him twice. I suggest that is evidence of a forgiving
nature!'

More substantively he said he had 'never done a deal with any political party for anything', and he was at pains to deny any second thoughts
about criticism of his papers. Most recently the *News of the World* had
collected another rebuke from the Press Council for photographing Lord
Lambton, a Government Minister, in bed with a prostitute. I had written
a personal article for *The Sunday Times* critical of the pornographic
surveillance and the sloppy way the paper had allowed the unpublished
photographs, instruments of blackmail, to be taken away by a petty
crook. Four of Murdoch's corrections were on this subject: 'You must
be joking if you think there are any long shadows from the Lambton
affair ... I was not away when the scandal broke. ... The Press Council
has no bearing on my happiness or 'sunshine'. By the way, does it have
any on yours? ... I do not hate the Press Council. I just think they are a

pussy-footing arm of the establishment.' We got the message – he wanted it to be known he didn't give a damn.

I heard nothing after publication, but Murdoch later said he had refused to give *The Sunday Times* an interview because we were part of a 'conspiracy to do him in, a conspiracy by elitist snobs who don't like an Australian coming to Britain'. It was good knock-about stuff. Bare breasts in the *Sun*? There were more, he claimed, in *The Sunday Times* colour magazine. He had done a nipple count to prove it. *The Sunday Times* was just a popular newspaper with small headlines. *The Observer* was smuttier than the *News of the World* because it wrote about 'women masturbating on horseback'. There was nothing suggestive about a *Sun* series called 'How to get your husband to come home early', which was illustrated by a girl, naked except for woollen stockings, lying on her back waving her legs in the air. It was a clean, fun picture that one could look at over breakfast; it made you feel better about the day ahead.

I did not hear again from Murdoch for several years. He opened his North American bridgehead in 1973, buying the San Antonio *Express* and *News* in an airport lounge for $19 million and reviving them with a formula of gore and guts, and soon afterwards he launched his national tabloid the *Star*. Five editors and $12 million later he had established it as a supermarket paper about life after death, receding hairlines and risible menace ('ferocious swarms of man-killing bees are buzzing their way towards North America'). But in early December 1976 he called me in London and asked to have dinner with me, so I invited him to the Garrick. It was a week or so after he had bought the tabloid *New York Post*, his eighty-fourth newspaper, at the end of November. At almost the same moment he had just failed to acquire *The Observer*.

He breezed into the Garrick bar to give me a handshake from the hip and a wide chuckling grin as if we were old friends: 'Hi, Harry. We'd have given you a run for your money with *The Ob*.' There was no mention of the famous colour magazine profile. His main purpose, it seemed, was to pump me about talent in Fleet Street, notably Derek Jameson of the *Daily Mirror* (later his editor of the *News of the World*). It was our first private social meeting since the Highgate dinner. The slight shock on seeing that the babyface of 1969 had become a relief map of canyons and gorges was mitigated by his boyishness. He was alight with self-assurance; the shyness of the 1969 dinner had vanished. He was cynical in a droll way as he described what he would have done with *The Observer*: 'All that third world garbage would have gone. It doesn't sell papers. So would Trelford,' – a reference to the editor, Donald Trelford, who had resisted him and whom he had designated to be crushed by two Murdoch editors, Bruce Rothwell and Anthony Shrimsley. He had clearly drifted to the right since the *Sun* had supported

Harold Wilson and the Labour Party, though he evinced little interest in British politics. He was preoccupied then with New York personalities and the permutations of ethnic and religious voting patterns. Later, when the *Post* supported Edward Koch for Mayor over Mario Cuomo, he was quoted as saying: 'It's very simple. There are two-and-a-half million Jews in New York and one million Italians.'

A few months after our dinner, I read that fifty of the sixty reporters on the *Post* had petitioned him alleging news distortion in the *Post* in favour of Koch (which a study by the journalism magazine *More* confirmed) eliciting from Murdoch the memorable remark: 'They think it's their paper. Well, they're wrong. It's mine.' It was a further example of a trend in Murdoch's approach to journalism rather more disturbing than tits on page 3 and man-killing bees. In New York, a former managing editor of the *Post* told me of the way Murdoch indicated which politician was up and which was down for the purposes of news treatment. In Sydney, Murdoch personally directed the coverage in the 1972 Australian general election and did 'some dreadful things', in his later words, to opponents of Gough Whitlam and the Labour Party. The Australian Press Council criticized the *Adelaide News* for bias in 1974. And in the 1975 general election journalists on three Murdoch dailies staged a twenty-four-hour strike in protest at 'blind ... biased ... relentless' campaigning for the Liberal Party and Malcolm Fraser with slanted headlines, distortion and suppression of dissent. Demonstrators burned copies of *The Australian* as they came off the presses. Murdoch's editorial aide, Bruce Rothwell, excelled in his zeal to please, solemnly depriving readers of *The Australian* of knowledge of the rate of New Zealand's inflation in case it damaged Fraser.

I visited New York quite frequently in the late 1970s. If the British Establishment had been hostile to Murdoch, the New York one was murderous. His peers in newspaper publishing were still spitting blood years after his 'me too' deal in the newspaper strike of 1978. He was supposed to be leading the employers, but he got his *New York Post* on the streets first through secret negotiations with the print unions in which, adding insult to injury, he promised he would match any concessions they might wring out of the other publishers. Punch Sulzberger, the publisher of the *New York Times*, refused to attend any function at which Murdoch was present. Murdoch was also excoriated everywhere for what he was doing to the *Post* as the 'hands-on' chief editor. 'Headless Body in Topless Bar' was the style, the ultimate parody of the macho tabloid. Everyone's distaste for the *Post*'s salivation over crime, gossip, sport and Wingo (the *Post*'s equivalent of Bingo) was made tolerable by their certainty that he would fail because the New Yorker was more sophisticated than the sex-ridden and credulous Londoner. The memory of the old *New York Post* was absurdly exalted in this process by people who had stopped reading it years ago when it had lost its way. The predictions of Murdoch's foundering on the rock of New York sophistication were belied by sales increases. They were expensively obtained – the *Post* was not getting the big advertising and it was losing an annual $20 million – but its progress sapped the confidence of the *New York Daily News* for a time, something unimaginable to anyone who could recall its heyday. The editor of the *New York Times*, Abe Rosenthal, predicted in *Esquire* magazine: 'He'll be out of town in a couple of years', and he was wrong. Within a couple of months of his acquisition of the *Post*, *Time* magazine proclaimed Murdoch's emergence as a major figure in American journalism. In what was best described as a spaghetti Eastern, he manœuvred control of the magazine group of *New York*, *Village Voice* and *New West* away from their founder-editor, his friend Clay Felker. *Time* magazine featured Murdoch on its cover as King Kong clutching the betrayed Felker. There was a court case and there was a staff walk-out at *New York* magazine, but only the iconoclastic boulevard newspaper *Village Voice*, pledging staff unity, maintained an irreverent editorial independence.

If time thwarted Rosenthal as a prophet, it recompensed him as a critic. He attacked Murdoch as 'a bad element practising mean, ugly, violent journalism'. Murdoch retaliated by harrying him about his private life in the *Post* gossip page. But Rosenthal, a much admired editor, had the satisfaction of seeing his criticism ricochet in all the leading journals of opinion and analysis, and be endorsed by the powerful figure of Otis Chandler, publisher of the *Los Angeles Times*. They were all capped by the *Columbia Journalism Review*, which devoted a lead editorial in 1980 to declaring that the *Post* had gone beyond the anathemas of press critics and entered a moral universe in which judgements of an altogether different order were required. The *Post*, it declared, was appealing to the basest passions and appetites of the hour. This was not another lament about bared breasts: 'The front pages regularly play to two emotions: fear and rage. And all too often what follows is meant to turn white against black, the comfortable against the poor, the First World against the Third. Murdoch has learned that exploiting the really grand social passions pays better than pandering to the small private ones. The *New York Post* is no longer merely a journalistic problem. It is a social problem – a force for evil.'

I was in New York at the time of one of the more notorious examples of excess, when the *Post* wallowed in the terror and gore of the 'Son of Sam' murders: 'No One is Safe from the Son of Sam', said a *Post* headline. When David Berkowitz was arrested as the suspected mad killer 'Son of Sam', and before his trial, the *Post* ran letters he had written years before to a girl-friend under the headline 'How I Became a Mass Killer, by David Berkowitz'. The condemnation the *Post* provoked by this treatment was thoroughly justified; but it has to be said that the *Daily News* was little better on this issue, and that the police and mayor aided and abetted in the contempt for the processes of fair trial.

Murdoch conceded in a critical interview that he had been wrong to approve the Berkowitz headline. However, he said he took pride in having reversed the *Post*'s support for the death penalty. He gave almost as good as he had been receiving: 'I've gotten a bit sick of being the whipping boy for every trendy liberal in town. I don't give a damn what the media critics say. It's what your readers say. If you haven't got any readers, you're only talking to yourself, which is what so many American editors are doing.' He showed himself still sensitive about page-three girls. It would be tasteless in America, but 'every other newspaper' was doing it in London: 'It's only done with very glamorous girls who don't look suggestive.'

Murdoch's isolation was palpable. The last time I saw him before his arrival in London to close the deal for Times Newspapers was at a seminar at Princeton in 1977 organized by the Ford Foundation. It was to discuss the relationships between business and the press, and it was attended by editors, publishers and the heads of some of the largest corporations in the United States. The organizers were on tenterhooks about how Murdoch might behave towards his colleagues from the press. He came with Anna; it was the return of the shy man. He was cold-shouldered by most of the senior journalists. On the final day he found his San Antonio paper under attack by a company chairman for supposedly printing unchecked and false allegations. He was in good company. Similar criticisms were made of the *Wall Street Journal*. Murdoch defended what had been done, but Fred Taylor, the executive editor of the *Wall Street Journal*, did not care to keep him company. 'One of the misapprehensions here on the part of the businessmen', said Taylor, 'is that there is this great monolith of the press.' He distanced himself: 'There is the *Wall Street Journal* and there is the New York *Post*. Mr Murdoch is perfectly able to defend the New York *Post*. I'll be damned if I will.'

Later the same evening Murdoch asked me jokingly if I would take over the *Village Voice* and teach the journalists the meaning of responsibility. The next invitation was to edit *The Times*.

9

QUESTIONS
OF TRUST

New York, Sydney and London might fret about Rupert Murdoch's record and his intentions; Gerald Long did not. The chief executive of Reuters news agency and the man designated managing director of *The Times* and *The Sunday Times* dealt only in absolutes. He had no doubt, not a scintilla of doubt, that Murdoch was a great man and one dedicated to restoring a derelict national institution to glory. Since he would run the company in Murdoch's absences on three continents, Long's judgement, character and abilities were crucial to us all. He was to be a brooding and perplexing personality in my life and that of Times Newspapers.

Almost the first words Long said to me, when he telephoned early in January 1981, were to emphasize that there would be no threat to editorial freedom while he was around. 'Rupert knows who he has asked to join him. I've spent my life in defence of the independence of journalists and I am not about to change. Harry, no Reuters reporter has ever been told what to say in a story. No, my God!' He took the opportunity to express admiration for *The Sunday Times* and in particular for the way we were following a story on cuts being imposed on a BBC Television series about intelligence agencies. Secret activities, he said with sudden vehemence, were dangerous and foolish, and should be exposed. I could not hope to match his level of outrage.

Murdoch was a new boy as a director of Reuters, which is owned by the national newspapers. He was appointed only in 1980, but he and Long had known each other for much longer. It was after a Reuters board meeting as early as 10 December that Murdoch told Long he was thinking of bidding for Times Newspapers. Without Denis Hamilton's knowledge – Hamilton was chairman of both Reuters and Times Newspapers – Murdoch had asked Long to be managing director. 'After a full three second pause I said, "Yes," and I've still not discussed terms,' Long told me in the first week in February. 'The combination of *The Times* and Rupert is irresistible! We've talked a lot about *The Times* over the years. He always said he would never do it, but we both knew he'd love to. He was just arguing with himself.'

The occasion was a lunch cooked by Long at his terraced home in a corner of Myddelton Square, five minutes' walk from the Gray's Inn Road office where Murdoch's men were negotiating with the unions. He was then fifty-seven, with a black, walrus moustache, a red flare on his cheek, bristling hair and big, thrusting jaws and eyebrows. He was very much the Governor of a Victorian colony. 'Rupert wants you to do *The Times*,' he said as he stood in the kitchen seeing to a salad. 'Hasn't he told you? He went on to say that I must appreciate that Rupert was a much misunderstood man. He would not try to interfere with editorial matters. The guarantees we had made such a fuss about were not needed. They were simply Murdoch promising not to do things he had never intended to do.

Long had had a brilliantly successful career over thirty years at Reuters, nearly twenty of them as chief executive. He had a vision of the enormous demand for business information and what computer-based electronics might do to satisfy it. When he took over in 1963, the agency was running hard to stand still with its traditional reporting service from 350 full-time foreign correspondents round the world. It showed a loss of £51,000 that year. Long made a crucial deal with a US company, Ultronics, which financed Reuters in the purchase of its video terminals. These enabled subscribers punching a code on a keyboard to have instant access to US stock and commodity prices. Long gained the right to sell this service outside North America. He moved into the foreign exchange and money markets with the Monitor system, offering instant video information on prices from information on their own positions fed in by banks and dealers. It was nothing less than the creation of an electronic 'floor' for trading. He also took the momentous step of setting up a North American news network. Previously Reuters had taken most of its US news through the American news agency Associated Press. It was not mere editorial ego which inspired Long. Going it alone in North America freed Reuters to sell its growing financial services in the world's richest market.

Long was criticized at first for being obsessed with video games. He was triumphantly vindicated. The revenues from the business services rendered Reuters invulnerable to the fluctuations of newspaper fortunes and financed an expansion which made it the biggest of the international news organizations. Profits in 1982 were £35 million. Long was not personally popular, however. He ran the agency with an iron fist, reducing even some of the directors to mumbling about autocracy. He was thought to be hostile to journalists if not to journalism. When, in 1977, he removed Jonathan Fenby, the son of his old friend Charles, from the editorship of Reuters world service, he reconstructed the top executive committee so that the editor did not have a seat on it and the new editor reported directly to Long. He had a taste, as Anthony Robinson reported in *The Financial Times*, for occasional but sudden defenestration *pour encourager les autres*. He took no prisoners. Long saved Reuters, though, and made it a real global presence.

I had known him for fifteen years, having first met him shortly after he became chief executive in 1963. He was then only thirty-nine, but he was a Sidney Greenstreet figure of bulk and booming authority. He had a home near mine in Highgate and gave frequent dinners for Reuters clients from abroad. They always seemed to come in packs of six, which Long moved between with aplomb. He had read modern languages at Cambridge, interrupted by the Army, and polished them in ten years as a Reuters correspondent in Bonn, Paris and finally Ankara, which expelled him. He always dominated the table, which meant there was an awkward pause in the multilingual dissection of European politics whenever Long repaired to the kitchen. He liked to do the cooking. It is one of a number of unexpected passions in Long's life. He seethes with rare knowledge. It amuses him to know the libretto of every Mozart opera; anyone who does not is a fool. A conversation with Long is alarming. One might travel over great areas of human interest without provoking more than a polite raising of an eyebrow or a series of gloomy nods, but as soon as one strays into pretension, reckless in the desire to elicit a response, there is an ambush. French canals, dictionaries, poached eggs, the guillotine, Zen Buddhism, sea legs ... the areas of danger are as unpredictable as his ferocity.

Extremism is a feature of all aspects of his personality. He wears his hair not merely cropped short but in a last-of-the-Mohicans scalp. His laugh is supersonic. You see it first, a mute accelerating convulsion ('Remember what M. Joseph Prudhomme remarked about Napoleon's ambition,' he likes to say. ' "If only he had stayed an artillery lieutenant, he would have still been on the throne!" '). It is seconds before the roar shakes the listeners and sometimes minutes before the sound fades. It is never in proportion to the stimulus. It is embarrassing at first experience, since it is impossible for anyone else to sustain such a performance; one learns simply to take pleasure in his pleasure.

Long is scored only for percussion. He is polarized on all subjects, grave or trivial. He has no tolerance for half measures; moderation is the ultimate vice. He brought certainty and a fine intelligence to the business of newspapers. It did not bother him that he knew next to nothing about it; he had known next to nothing about electronics. He was responsible for producing newspapers when he was oppressing the Germans, as he put it, but the special knowledge required was confined to supplying the German printers with kegs of beer amid the scarcities of Cologne in 1945. For thirty-five years he had been only a spectator in Fleet Street. He looked forward to running newspapers. They dealt in words by which men conveyed thought, and were therefore a Good Thing, unlike mass audience television, which purveyed pictures and was, therefore, a Menace to Civilization.

In all his high-wire performances as a manager, Long maintained on his passport and in his mind that he was a journalist first. His interest in professional matters was typically fitful and vehement. I was concerned in the 1970s about the danger of government interference implicit in a charter proposed by UNESCO to regulate newspapers and reporting, the so-called 'new information order'. So were other editors in the International Press Institute, set up to defend press freedom round the world. All hot air, said Long. Imbecilic to waste time worrying about it. Reuters would stay aloof from the row. UNESCO set up a commission under Sean MacBride, the former Irish statesman and winner of the Nobel and Lenin Peace Prizes. In June 1978, at a committee meeting of the British committee of IPI, Rosemary Righter of *The Sunday Times* reported on the activities of MacBride's commission in Britain and mentioned the participation of the sociologist press critic, Professor James Halloran of Leicester University. Long went purple. Henceforth there was no holding him. He appeared on the platform in Athens in 1979 when the IPI arranged a debate between editors and MacBride. I thought I had done rather well picking holes in MacBride's case. It was a mere draught compared to the whirlwind Long summoned up. He glared across at MacBride throughout his denunciation: 'You have produced a monster that reflects a hatred of free information.' Some thought it was a polemic of such offensiveness that it would rebound, but it certainly made the corridors buzz with excitement.

For all his career triumphs, Long became a sad man over the years. He had a problem with a delinquent son which his rectitude would not allow to be kept out of the newspapers. He was appalled when it was suggested that this might be attempted. He fell ill and was ordered to lose weight. He took to running round the streets of Islington at dawn. It was effective, but his friends thought his temper had become more brittle. He could sit at a dinner-party in utter silence, without a single word throughout for the person on either side. His concern for standards in journalism shaded into an animosity towards journalists. He denounced Robert Fisk of *The Times*, a reporter I admired, for holding a Soviet gun in Afhganistan. The circumstances were that Fisk was in a Soviet convoy which was ambushed by Afghans and a Soviet officer thrust the weapon into Fisk's hands. He did not fire or point it, but to Long he had compromised the independence of journalism: 'Fisk is a cowboy.' He was altogether critical of *The Times* and gave vent to it that day at Myddelton Square. 'The paper has lost all authority. My God, we're going to get it back.' I pricked up my ears at 'we'. For periods of its history the editor of *The Times* had deferred to the manager, notably in foreign affairs. I took the view of C.P. Scott of the *Manchester Guardian*: 'The editor and business manager should march hand in hand, the first, be it well understood, just an inch or two in advance.' But Long was not making any bid. He hoped I would not mind his passing on comments from his experience and I did not, once the lines of command were clear. I said that if I did, after all, edit *The Times*, I would need all the help I could get, and I listened to his views on the quality of various foreign correspondents. 'The man you need for authority', he said, in a moment of final reflection reminiscent of Lord Copper, 'is Penning-Rowsell of *The Financial Times*', and he plucked a book by him from his shelves. I scribbled a note of it, *The Wines of Bordeaux*.

If there is to be ambiguity, Long would have said, let it be maximum ambiguity. There was indeed over the editorship of *The Times*. It was not clear that it was on offer; and I was not clear I wanted it, if it were, nor even that I would work for Murdoch as editor of *The Sunday Times*. It was obvious that I was being teased about *The Times*. Murdoch, Brunton and Hamilton had all floated the idea at different periods, Murdoch at that first January meeting a few days before the deal with Thomson was clinched. Then he had said publicly he hoped I would stay at *The Sunday Times* and there was talk of ten candidacies for *The Times* chair. I commended Hugo Young of *The Sunday Times* for it.

I heard nothing more until the week of the Long lunch, when Murdoch asked me over to the office Ken Thomson used to inhabit. 'What would you do with *The Times*, Harry?', he asked, spreading out the paper. I leafed through it, making comments about various sections and concluding with ideas for the back page. He said he would like to start a Friday arts and entertainments section like the *New York Times*. I had heard that Charles Douglas-Home, Louis Heren and Hugh Stephenson, three of *The Times* executives, had each been formally interviewed. I did not regard my meeting with Murdoch as either an application or an interview. When Hamilton sounded me out again, I made it clear I was not applying for the editorship, but would have to be invited. 'I would not do that job without the enthusiastic backing of the national directors.' Conversations followed with Murdoch which required the assumption on his part that he had offered to nominate me to the national directors, and on mine that I had accepted. On Saturday 7 February he interrupted me in the middle of a leader to ask me to go over to his office with my deputy, Frank Giles, for pork pie and sandwiches to talk about staff on both newspapers. Then Tina and I were invited to dinner with Anna at his house in Belgravia on the eve of his settlement with the unions. She was exactly as she had been when she walked through my door in Highgate twelve years before, warm and animated, and she entertained us with poise as we waited for Murdoch to get out of a meeting with the union general secretaries. 'I don't want Rupert to take *The Times*,' she said, 'hurtling about the world to three different cities, three different time zones, but when he sets his heart on something nothing can stop him.' They had one child at school in Australia and two in New York. She was taking university courses there, but she worried about New York. Her nine-year-old instructed her to walk on the edge of the pavement because muggers waited in doorways. 'The Americans carry money for muggers. That's why they got into trouble with the Ayatollah. They've learned to give in to muggers.'

Murdoch came in laughing about the cynicism of the union officials. He talked about *The Times* again, floating the idea of a column by Norman St John Stevas, whom Mrs Thatcher had just sacked from the Cabinet. Again it was ambiguous whether I was being addressed as a journalist or as editor-designate.

The more I thought about *The Times*, the more tantalized I became. Here was the oldest newspaper, the most famous newspaper, and one which might be made the best daily there could be. It had six opportunities for excellence to every one *The Sunday Times* had. Its past was full of inspiration; there was no limit to what it might achieve in the future. Its readers were intelligent and influential. It had no obligations except to be truthful, relevant and interesting to them. Its opinions were its own; it was traditionally nobody's mouthpiece. It had unlimited scope to report the world and Britain, to explore science and enhance the arts, and above all to be serious in purpose, monitoring the use of power and exposing its abuses. In so far as it had editorial and commercial problems, that was stimulating. There was plenty of sail that might be filled. I had begun my editing career with a great provincial daily. I saw *The Times* as a pinnacle.

But what of Murdoch?

He had pulled off a great commercial and political coup. He had the worst reputation regarding editorial quality and independence, but he had won the newspapers with the best reputation. He had more titles, and more titles of low quality, than any other proprietor. But he had avoided the reference to the Monopolies Commission which informed opinion had thought inevitable. He had persuaded the Thomson Organisation to turn its back on imaginative proposals from its own staff, including the two editors and other directors. He had acquired a flourishing Sunday newspaper and the most renowned daily for half the money his principal rivals offered. Rees-Mogg commended him to the British public as 'a man in love with newspapers, a newspaper professional but even more a newspaper romantic'. He might have added 'and a man in love with money and power'. Murdoch had gained access to a huge cash flow of £100 million a year, with sure profits from *The Sunday Times* and the *Times Educational Supplement*, and prestige from *The Times*. What this coup represented more than anything was Murdoch's supreme skill in manipulation. It was a talent which had been remarked on even when he was a teenager. A senior master of Geelong Grammar School had told Rohan Rivett that in a lifetime of teaching he had never known a boy in his mid-teens so able and astute at manipulating others – masters, prefects and schoolfriends.

The appetite that this skill served could not be his love of newspapers in the sense Rees-Mogg then admired. Murdoch is always portrayed as the great shirt-sleeves journalist, excited by deadlines and news. It was a credible view perhaps when he owned a handful of newspapers in his early days and started *The Australian*. It has become threadbare as an explanation of his drive and ambition. It is not necessary to own eighty newspapers to satisfy a love of journalism. His incessant accumulation of titles does not bring him closer to his supposed passion; it removes him further from it. Adolph S. Ochs, the founder of the modern *New York Times*, thought no man big enough to run more than one newspaper. Certainly no man can be deeply involved in daily journalism in more than one place. Murdoch might occasionally try; it explained some of the gaffes. Nor does a newspaper romantic necessarily find satisfaction, as Murdoch does, in buying into such diverse interests as airlines, television stations, publishing houses, oil and mineral interests, and satellites, whilst undertaking the lobbying associated with business that depends on government favour. There is no common denominator between these businesses and journalism. It is acquisiton that excites Murdoch and calls on his considerable abilities as an organizer and manager of finance, and as a manipulator of men and companies. 'It is no fun running newspapers,' he once said, 'the fun is in owning them.' In the early days it was said that his driving force was to out-perform his father. Later, with the extension of his interests into the United States, it was said he had set himself the goal of building a mightier empire than that achieved by Roy Thomson. Perhaps this is so, but his management of journalism is vastly different from that of both his father and Thomson.

Gerald Long thought Murdoch 'a genius', but they could not have been more different in their approach to running newspapers. It could be said of them, as the great Victorian journalist W.T. Stead once remarked of his editor on the *Pall Mall Gazette*: 'We disagreed on

everything from the existence of God to the make-up of a newspaper.'
Murdoch acted on impulse and intuition. Long called in consultants.
Everything had to be written down, said Long, and he typed memos on
his portable typewriter. Murdoch always reached for the telephone or
jumped on Concorde. Long commanded by orderly delegation; he had
an acute sense of hierarchy. Murdoch's reputation was for intervening
at all levels at all times. There were other things in life for Long than
newspaper sales and business dealings. To Murdoch, business was life.
He indulged Long's passion for opera by agreeing to the company
purchase of seats at Covent Garden, but he never went himself, just as
he never read arts reviews. It saddened Long that Murdoch's interests in
life did not extend to noticing what he ate.

Murdoch deploys charm. His manner is convivial and disarming. He
has a rough sense of fun (if one is not the victim of it). He is assiduous
and adept at flattery, beguiling when relayed by a third party, but his
particular talent is to suggest that the listener is part of a privileged inner
circle of exclusive intimacy and mutual understanding. He chuckles at
his cheerful little betrayals: 'We'll both have to stroke Denis [Hamilton]
a lot,' he told me, 'he's so super-sensitive.' He does not stand on ceremony. His appearance is formal in his dark, pin-stripe suits, always with
a meticulously folded white handkerchief in the breast pocket. But his
movements are shambling and loose. He comes at you with speed,
interjecting his light Australian accent with Americanisms, creating the
impression of openness and candour. 'Gee, I'm sorry,' he might say, 'I
really boobed.' The flip side of the charm is a bleak hostility expressed
through highly charged language or brutal curtness. He is well aware of
his ability to win or to frighten and exploits this by switching persona
unpredictably to create insecurity. There is a cold centre. He genuinely
is not afflicted by a personal embarrassment or sensitivity towards
others. What makes him formidable is that, even knowing this, one can
find him likeable.

Was he Gerald Long's 'genius' or the sinister influence perceived by
the editor of the New York Times? His record in popular journalism
was unappealing, though commercially profitable. All his papers ran
political propaganda. He had courted political figures. William Safire
had publicly censured him in the New York Times: 'When journalism
and government get too close, both suffer.' On the other hand, there was
at least this to be said for Murdoch: he brought confidence and determination to deal with the running sore of Times Newspapers – the print
unions. Disruption and demarcation disputes had cost The Sunday
Times millions of pounds in lost revenue and millions of lost copies. The
journalists had been left demoralized. If anyone could deal with the
unions, Murdoch could. He knew the union leaders. He had dealt most

effectively with them in the past. He would not be an absentee landlord; his style in negotiation was to do it himself on the spot, and his toughness was believed. In his talk about the future, everything seemed possible: eighty pages for *The Sunday Times*, a reinvigorated *Times* with access to the new technology, an end to the frustration and ruin of lost copies. He was utterly confident he could succeed.

He offered a vigorous partnership. As I contemplated *The Times*, my hope was that we could be partners who respected each other's prerogatives: his the control of the business and mine the responsibility for the integrity and independence of the journalism. Why had he bought the paper if it was not to maintain and enhance its reputation? No doubt the cachet of acquiring it gave him pleasure, one in the eye for the Establishment he thought had snubbed him. However, except as a qualification for bankruptcy, ownership was not enough: he would have to restore it to profit; he would have to sort out the unions and the high-cost inefficiencies, and galvanise the commercial departments. We had an identity of interest here. He had said he would not meddle, but this was the perpetual dilemma with Murdoch. In his presence it was barely possible to believe he would break his word; away from him, it was barely possible to believe he would keep it. He was incontinent in breach of promise.

The outgoing editor of *The Times* was sure. When Murdoch completed his union deals on 12 February, Rees-Mogg wrote a celebratory leader which hailed the fifth proprietorship* in the 196 years of the paper and, referring to the far-reaching assurances of editorial independence Murdoch had given, declared 'there is no reason to doubt that he will abide by them'. But reasons for doubt there certainly were. This was why we had all regarded it as essential to have the assurances in the first place. Only a few days before, in the *New Statesman*, Bruce Page tracked what happened to Murdoch's promises in his News Ltd acquisition of the TEN-10 television station in Sydney. Murdoch had assured the Australian Broadcasting Tribunal that no changes were contemplated, that 'it would be madness to contemplate any changes at all', that TEN-10's 'magnificent' chairman, Sir Kenneth Humphreys, would remain, and that News Ltd was not interested in adding a television holding in Melbourne. Not to have been misleading, the evidence should have been given in a strait-jacket. All the acts of madness were swiftly carried out.

The most charitable explanation of Murdoch's attitude to a promise was that he meant it when he made it; only circumstances changed, as they had rather more honourably done for his father in the Dardanelles.

---

* Murdoch was the tenth individual chief shareholder; previously the paper had been controlled by the Walter family (4 people), Northcliffe, the Astors (2), and the Thomsons (2).

A doyen of Australian journalism was quoted anonymously in *The Financial Times*: 'I am sure Rupert means well and has a genuine desire to give those guarantees. . . . I am equally sure it will require almost super-human restraint on Rupert's part not to interfere.' Shortly after the incident of Murdoch's mark on the leader proof, and again before he was the owner, I found Frank Giles about to cancel a visit to Jordan at Murdoch's request so that, quite unnecessarily, he could be on hand in London. Murdoch had not asked me and, since the visit was one I had personally urged on Giles for an exclusive interview with King Hussein at a propitious moment, I reinstated it. Murdoch was equable; at the time I felt sure he would not do that again.

These were early manifestations of what I came to call the 'Graham Perkin syndrome', after my Australian editor-friend. Everyone ached to believe, as Perkin did, that there was a decent man inside Murdoch struggling to get out. David Astor, Arnold Goodman, John Freeman, Denis Hamilton, all believed they could do business with him (though Roy Thomson never did). In all the meetings at this time, and especially before the vetting committee, he impressed everyone with his apparent sincerity. He seemed to all of us to mean what he said. Perhaps that was how it had been before, but this time it would be different. Murdoch is like the philanderer who convinces each new girl that she's the one who'll change him. I rang my friend Mrs Kay Graham, owner of the *Washington Post* and *Newsweek*. She knew Murdoch well. She had lost to him in the take-over battle for the *New York* magazine interests on the side of Clay Felker, but she was not identified as a public enemy. The skeleton this time was a report in a magazine which said Mrs Graham had sobbed to Murdoch on the telephone when the *New York* magazine battle was lost. 'He lied about me, we know the story could have come only from him.' But Mrs Graham, none the less, thought the risk of working with him was worth taking. 'You can stand up to him. You know, I believe he may just be ready to behave.' In keeping with 'the Perkin syndrome', I wanted to believe that myself.

Bernard Donoughue saw the way my mind was moving and tried hard to put it into reverse. 'You're simply being tempted from your power base,' he argued. He had talked, I learned later, with Ranald Macdonald, the publisher of *The Age* in Melbourne, who is Murdoch's cousin. Mac-donald had told him: 'It's always the same. Everybody thinks that this time Murdoch will behave, that they are the ones he will get along with. I played with him as a boy. I *know* him. It will never work.' And there were other soothsayers. Clay Felker rang from New York to say Murdoch was inevitably treacherous. Tina came back unhappy from a lunch with Sir John Junor, the editor of the *Sunday Express*. 'Rupert wants Harry away from *The Sunday Times* because he is well established there.

The Times will be the bait,' Junor warned. 'He'll offer it to him and he'll give him just one year there. You'll see, one year.'

Confronted with a Cassandra, I fell back on our constitution. Murdoch had never had to contend with anything like it before. The odds turned somewhat on the national directors. There were four, to be increased to six. The senior pair, who had been directors since the Thomson take-over in 1967, were Lord Robens, then aged seventy-one, and Lord Roll, who was seventy-four. Alf Robens is more foxy than his bluff air suggests. He began in Manchester as a trade union official for shop assistants and rose to become Minister of Labour and later chairman of the National Coal Board. My first acquaintance with Eric Roll was between the covers of his economics textbook when I was an undergraduate; it was pleasant twenty years later to resume the course. 'Eric', as Roy Jenkins put it, 'is one of the great ballbearings of British society.' He helped things to go round more smoothly than anyone imagined possible when he was Under Secretary to George Brown at the Department of Economic Affairs in the white-hot 1960s days of the National Plan. He took his genius for intelligent compromise into the banking parlours of S.G. Warburg in 1967 and became chairman in 1974. The quartet was completed by the intellectual and the trade union leader, both playing to type. The historian Hugh Trevor-Roper (Lord Dacre), eyes screwed up behind pebble glasses, was permanently sniffing the air for *non sequiturs*. He had worked in British Intelligence and wrote the classic book *The Last Days of Hitler* by putting German officers through his Oxford tutorial. In 1981 he had not yet been called for a resit himself on his authentication of the forged Hitler diaries. He was sixty-seven and the Master of Peterhouse, Cambridge, having recently defected from Oxford. Lord Greene, seventy-one, joined the railways in 1924, when he left elementary school, and stayed all his life, first as a railwayman for twenty years and then as a union organizer for the National Union of Railwaymen. Sidney Greene was a shrewd General Secretary from 1957 to 1974. He always had a reputation for being as straight as the line from York to Darlington, but he rarely spoke in board meetings.

I sat with these directors on the main board of Times Newspapers. Could they be counted on to see fair play? I thought they could. They kept calm, under Denis Hamilton's leadership, when articles in *The Sunday Times* made waves. I was only twice disappointed in them, both of which were occasions when the Thomson engine was running full speed. First, they acquiesced in Thomson's choice of Murdoch. Roll as chairman of Warburgs, the bank advising Thomson, was in a difficult position, but none of them pressed for a report on the alternatives including the consortia. Second, there was their role in the 1979 confrontation with the print unions, the year of suspension. The executive directors, of whom I was one, could not claim to have been brilliant, but the national directors, with the possible exception of Robens, accepted the decisions of the executive board more readily than I thought they would. I expected them to use their freedom as non-executive directors to put our tactics and our strategy to critical examination. They were all loyal. They showed strong nerves as the stoppage continued and the money poured out. The trouble was we were on a mistaken course, at the cost of £40 million and eventually of the company. Shortly before we closed, Robens raised some awkward questions such as, 'What if the unions dig in?' but he did not persist in the face of the icy indication from Gordon Brunton that it was not a matter for that board. The surprise was Dacre (Trevor-Roper), who had been lobbied to raise questions by journalists critical of the closure: he kept his head down. The image is still vivid in my mind of the crucial main board meeting, at which Dacre barely looked up from correcting the proof of a *Sunday Times* book review. But I knew him to be hostile to Murdoch, and I felt even more confidence in the national directors when it was announced that Denis Hamilton would be joining these four and would also become chairman of the Times Holdings board. He had let Murdoch in, and he would want to find the choice vindicated. He would not be able to live with himself if he failed to uphold the ideals of decency and independence he had maintained in his own years at *The Times*.

These were the men, and their formal powers were extensive and backed by government. To what extent did they believe in Murdoch's guarantees of editorial independence? There are two reports of Dacre's view. One version claims that he said, 'We have put a paper hook through the nose of Leviathan.' The version I heard, however, was, 'We have Leviathan by the nose.'

There is a technique in photography called directional blur, which is used to give an impression of speed. On Tuesday 17 February I was in Amsterdam as the president of the international jury in the World Press Photo contest when I was formally invited to be the twelfth editor of *The Times*, and I soon felt I had been very much directionally blurred. Murdoch reached me in Amsterdam to say he was about to nominate me if I agreed; I did. I returned and had lunch with him at the Savoy, I spoke to the *Sunday Times* staff the same afternoon; three weeks later I was editing *The Times*. I had imagined there would be an interview with the national directors, as there had been when I was appointed editor of *The Sunday Times*, and a period of discussion, preparation and handover. Murdoch had other ideas: 'I can't wait to get an active editor in that graveyard.'

I ended my speech to my *Sunday Times* staff that afternoon unable to hold back the tears. It was time for me to move on, but I had only an hour previously committed myself irrevocably to crossing the bridge to *The Times* and our crowded news room had been the scene of fourteen years of happy turmoil. It was abrupt and painful.

The sentiment and nostalgia of the afternoon were soon lost. In the evening Murdoch gave a dinner at the Café Royal. Richard Searby, his urbane lawyer from Melbourne, was there with his wife Caroline, Gerald and Anne Long, Tina and I, but not Anna Murdoch, who would have changed the chemistry, or Frank Giles and his wife, Kitty. It was the first time I had been with Murdoch and Long together. It was bad news. They egged each other on in cynicism and animosity. If the entertainment flagged, Searby added mockery. I was engaged by Caroline Searby and missed some of the exchanges, but that night Tina wrote in her diary:

> I was disconcerted by Long with his Lucky Lucan moustache and impene-
> trable inward stare, and I was unhappy about the savagery with which he
> and Murdoch rubbished William Rees-Mogg and Denis Hamilton. I stuck up
> for Hamilton by saying that he had good taste in people and once had the
> courage to appoint Harry. Murdoch ruggedly conceded this. Long just re-
> iterated, 'He's a bloody pompous old fool'.

Hamilton, resigning as editor-in-chief, wrote me a gentlemanly and stylish adieu referring to his Saturday night telephone calls of 'fond memory'. He was appointed a national director and chairman of the supervisory Times Newspapers Holdings board, with Murdoch as vice-chairman. Louis Heren, deputy editor of *The Times*, and Peter Roberts, managing editor of *The Sunday Times*, joined as staff members following Murdoch's deal with the *Sunday Times* chapel. The others were Searby, Lord Drogheda, Lord Astor of Hever, and Lord Catto, chairman of Morgan Grenfell.

Frank Giles, at the age of sixty-two, was appointed editor of *The Sunday Times*. He had been an accomplished and faithful deputy, but did not put himself forward for the editorship. He had planned to retire at about this time and certainly did not fancy a reprise as number two. I had commended Hugo Young, the political editor, as a leader in public affairs, and Ron Hall, the editor of the magazine, as a newspaperman. Murdoch veered to Hall, then he told me that Denis Hamilton had objections to Hall and Young, and Frank's appointment until 1985 would give time to make a longer-term choice. Hall and Young were appointed joint deputy editors.

The managing director, Dugal Nisbet-Smith, and all the executive directors were fired, though Duke Hussey, the managing director for most of the previous decade, was given a consultancy, and Garry Thorne, the marketing director, was given a bone in the form of *The Times* advertising account. Donald Cruickshank, my *Sunday Times* general manager and the finance director of the company, was fired too. He knew more than anyone about the profitable running of the papers. 'Think so?' said Long when I told him. Derek Jewell had built up the company's other revenues – half of the £1 million profit that Biffen mislaid – and I told Murdoch that he was a money-maker. But he, too, was fired. A shake-out of top management was inevitable, but the sword remained unsheathed. Murdoch abolished the marketing departments and sacked almost all the senior advertising men. I could hardly walk along a corridor without seeing another familiar face strained and shattered. The vocabulary of the purge was frank enough. Nobody was allowed to think he had been 'let go'. Murdoch 'severed' and 'terminated' people. So many staff lists had names erased that anyone sacked was later said to have been 'Tipp-Exed'. A central judgement seemed to be whether somebody was 'with us', which meant showing an indiscriminate contempt for all that had gone before.

It was the first take-over I had experienced. It was not merely insensitive and unjust: it was reckless in its consequences for the company, notably in the loss of good sales people. One of the salesmen 'terminated' by Michael Ruda, the new advertising director from the *News of the World*, alone brought in more than £1 million-worth of Middle East business per year. He was snapped up by the *International Herald Tribune*. Revenue was lost in both advertising and syndication. 'Mike says they have been sitting on their arses, not out selling,' Murdoch told me one evening, when he dropped into my *Sunday Times* office. He went on to say that he was merging the advertising departments of *The Times* and *Sunday Times*. This meant that one salesman would sell space for both papers. It sounds logical. It works for popular newspaper companies where the papers being sold are very similar, delivering x million housewives to the advertiser. But it had never worked in the quality market. We tried it in 1968 with an advertising director new to the press. The salesmen sold the easiest one first, *The Sunday Times*. All the computer print-outs made *The Sunday Times* an attractive advertising medium. But then to sell *The Times* the salesman had to tell the client to forget all about that computer rubbish and think of prestige: never mind the width, feel the quality. The forked-tongue act raised a smile, but lost too much revenue for *The Times* without any gain for *The Sunday Times*.

I recited the history to Murdoch. He brushed it aside. 'Mike's boys will tell the big advertisers that they're out of *The Sunday Times* unless they go in *The Times*. We did it with the *News of the World* and the *Sun*.' I could not agree. This would be overtly making *The Times* look weak, whereas in some markets it had unique strengths and by definition we would be discounting *The Times* rates, which was unnecessary and demeaning. I cannot say I made the slightest impression. 'Mike's really making them jump over there,' said Murdoch gleefully. The subject was closed. Donald Barrett, the advertisement director who had been with the company for twenty-six years, was fired and given two days to get out of the building. Bryan Todd, head of *The Times* advertising, received special treatment: he was sacked on Thursday by Long and again by Ruda on Friday.

The scythe stopped short of the print unions. Reg Brady, the press-room chapel leader who had done more than anyone to disillusion Thomson, remained and so did Barry Fitzpatrick, the militant leader of the clerical chapel. Murdoch met the Thomson deadline of 12 February for the union agreements, but he had to relent on his hard line. He won a lifesaving victory for *The Times* supplements in removing their production from Gray's Inn Road, but there was no significant reduction in the overmanning of *The Times* and *Sunday Times*. The savings announced were less than they appeared. Of the 130 cuts in the 800-strong clerical chapel of NATSOPA, 110 were unfilled 'vacancies'. It was an opportunity forgone, an expensive one that would have to be taken up another day.

The deal on new technology was one that had been on the table for Thomson to pick up. It perpetuated the keyboard monopoly for the NGA. It consigned to an indefinite future, perhaps for ever, access to the computer for all the originators of material, journalists, researchers, tele-ad girls. It meant that we were perpetuating into the 1980s a system of double keystroking which had already for a decade been progressively abandoned round the world. The computer system in Gray's Inn Road, the only one of its kind in Fleet Street, was designed to translate key-strokes made at the visual display terminal into direct commands for a photocomposing machine, so that they emerged in the form of a photographic bromide ready for insertion on the page. Murdoch's acquiescence locked off this dramatic facility. Hundreds of thousands of keystrokes made daily by journalists and tele-add girls would be made all over again by printers, the fertility of happy invention denied its full fruits by the grimy rules of union demarcation. There were many losses here for the efficient production of a newspaper and for serious journalism as well.

Little, therefore, had changed in the geology of the paper I was about to edit. It was on the slide. The financial position remained more men-acing than at any time in the paper's history. A loss of £10 million in 1981 was forecast by Thomson management, to be followed by one of around £8 million in 1982. Murdoch had not achieved anything to make the losses significantly lower. Indeed, my judgement was that the advertising changes made the outlook worse. The suspension had damaged *The Times* far more than *The Sunday Times*. *The Sunday Times* recovered, *The Times* did not. Its three competitors increased sales to such an extent in the year of suspension that an advertiser could at one time reach more of his market with these three than he had before with four. There had been a sharp deterioration in the competitive position of *The Times*. On suspension in 1979 it was selling 310,000 copies daily and *The Guardian* was only 2,000 ahead. When I was appointed, the figures were: *The Guardian* 401,000, *The Times* 280,000 and the *Telegraph* more than a million ahead. *The Times* had been warmly welcomed on its return, but readers drifted away. There were 3,000 fewer daily sales than in the last year of Sir William Haley's editorship, when the firm was merged with *The Sunday Times*.

I did not believe *The Times* was irredeemably unprofitable. There had been profits in every one of the nine years before 1966, when the Astors sold to Thomson, though not enough for the development needed. That costs had to be attacked was obvious; more intriguing was the strategy that should be followed. On the Thomson take-over in 1967, Denis Hamilton and Rees-Mogg sought a daily sale of half a million copies, which would justify higher advertising rates. They did this by adding pages, including a separate business section, by promotion and by making the paper brighter. It worked to the extent that the sale reached 437,000 in 1969, and advertising improved dramatically. It is a caricature of this period to say, as it often is, that the new readers were the unwashed and unwanted lower-income groups. The profile improved, but it was costing more to acquire them than the £3 million confidently predicted to the Monopolies Commission in 1966. Thomson himself thought he might have to invest £5 million – 'my one extravagance', he would say with a grumpy twinkle – but eight years later *The Times* had taken £8 million from his private fortune as well as eating the profits of *The Sunday Times*. With rising costs and a recession, hopes of profitability receded and the strategy was changed. The expensive drive for circulation was stopped with a big increase in the cover price; newsprint costs were held back by redesigning the pages to pack more in. Advertisers were offered a more concentrated market of upper-income readers. It nearly worked. In the good year of 1973 *The Times* was barely below break-even point. But then there came the oil price crisis and the rapid rise in newsprint costs, producing losses of around £1 million, and finally the disastrous year of suspension.

I looked forward to discussing strategy with Murdoch and Long. Murdoch was certainly all for sales. I found a note on my desk at *The Sunday Times*:

Dear Harry,

   I thought this might cheer you up – we're *only* 100,000 behind The Guardian and 1,150,000 behind the Tele!

   Let's get on with it!

      Rupert

He was talking to interviewers of a sale of half a million in 'not too many years'. I saw it as part of my immediate task to improve the appeal of *The Times* so that the decline in sales, worrying on any policy, might be halted and reversed. I was sure this could be done, given time and support, without diluting the paper's authority or altering its historic character.

10
TIMES PAST AND
TIMES PRESENT

Ten days before I was due to take the chair at my first *Times* conference I took my preoccupations to a small sturdy house lying securely against the steepness of Gorey Hill on Jersey in the Channel Islands. The journey was completed in a light aircraft which dipped and bobbed over the water on a rain-streaked day, and it was good to be on solid ground again. The feeling of stability is one I shall always associate with the imposing figure who opened the door, William John Haley, the tenth editor of *The Times*, fit and vigilant on the brink of his eightieth birthday.

He has a personality very like the house he has chosen for his last years on the island of his birth. There is a stony exterior rising straight from the pavement, rather grey and uninviting, but beyond it there is a delightful surprise: the rear of Beau Site offers a panorama of Gorey Bay. William John reveals warmth and a surpassing good nature. He has a strongly sculpted head, a profile for Mount Rushmore. The legend when he ran Reuters in the war and the BBC after it, succeeding Lord Reith as Director General for eight years, was that he was the only man in London with two glass eyes, and when he does not smile he has an intimidating look. It was a perfect accompaniment to the Victorian rectitude of the leaders he wrote at *The Times* in the 1950s and 1960s ('It *is* a Moral Issue'; 'Irresponsiblity is Rife'; 'Why the £ is Weak'; 'Morons on the March'). His renown and his rhetoric chilled the hearts of the wicked and the ungodly in high places. His last words to the staff of *The Times* were these: 'There are things which are bad and false and ugly and no amount of specious casuistry will make them good or true or beautiful.' He was a very aloof editor of *The Times*. He strictly enforced the rule of anonymity on himself and the staff: 'Signed writing invites exhibitionism. I was asked by a Cabinet Minister to tell him who had written a particular leading article. When I refused to do so, he complained, "That's the worst thing about your damned *Times*. I don't need to read So-and-So [in another paper] because I know he carries no guns. I have to read your leader carefully because goodness knows who has written it." '

I had come to talk about editing *The Times*, but we reminisced for a while with his wife Susan. The first curiosity is that she was Northcliffe's secretary at *The Times*, the second that it was to Susie Gibbons that 'William John', as she calls him, reported for daily duty as a shorthand-typist foreign telegraphist when he joined at the age of eighteen in 1919. William John admired the way *The Times* staff resisted Northcliffe: 'Three editors and the staff held him at bay for fourteen years'. We had some common associations. He was the chief sub-editor of the *Manchester Evening News* in the year I was born, and for several years its editor, and twenty-five years later I sat at the same subs' table in Cross Street with the same unlikely enthusiasm for table-tennis. When I arrived they still talked about how Haley, then editor, would stride through the reporters' room after Last Extra edition and silently tap Tom Jackson on the shoulder. It was a command to leave the typewriter for a game on the office table. 'I always won, but one day I did lose to him,' Tom related. 'He never ever invited me again.' Another of life's obstacles had been overcome. Haley had an extraordinary will to excel. He did all the book reviewing at the *Evening News*; at *The Times* he wrote literary articles under 'Oliver Edwards', and he and Patrick Ryan might cover all the books. 'I had an excellent weekend, thank you. Read eight books and reviewed three of them.' He was not boasting. He was measuring himself against the exacting standards he had set.

His model for editorship was Thomas Barnes, the first real editor of *The Times*. 'Not Delane. He let the proprietor sit in his chair and alter leaders.' There were small photographs of both editors on his *Times* table in his library at Beau Site. It was not easy to induce him to talk about the modern problems of editing *The Times*. He had never said a word about the paper in all the years since his retirement. He did not want to be thought critical. Thomsons had been fine proprietors. They had kept every promise, respected the fact that *The Times* had no private role to play in politics. As we talked about the paper, however, he smelt printer's ink again. He was sorry anonymity had been abandoned in 1967. He was still sometimes asked who was 'A Conservative' who wrote a series of articles for *The Times* in 1964 on the challenges for the Tories going into opposition. He would never reveal the name. I am still curious, which reinforces one of his points: 'Anonymity can increase longevity.'

The traditions of *The Times* that mattered were three, he said: to be completely independent – '*The Sunday Times* has shown you know how to do that'; to be a journal of record; and to view issues from the national interest. People had a *right* to be sure of finding the details of the White

Papers and Blue Books, and the parliamentary and law reports, but I should not be afraid to make changes. My word, he had made many before he put news on the front page in 1966. He reflected, looking out over the terraced garden and on to the bay where sun came through, clearly wondering whether he was saying too much. 'Perhaps you can do something about the letters. The layout is ambiguous now in what *The Times* regards as the lead letter of the day.' This was a service and a signal he missed. I recalled the occasion when, just as the leader page was going to press, Fred Emery, the new boy in letters, remarked to Haley that he had been unable to speak to the professor who was the author of the lead letter. 'Take it out,' Haley instructed. The paper was delayed as a new letter was found the authenticity of which had been checked. 'Won't do that again, will you?'

He moved happily on to obituaries. 'When I was editor, I was constantly asked to include people of title or rank. I refused. My rule was that they had to have done something with their lives. Sometimes the column goes wrong, giving pride of place to show-business personalities. That confuses celebrity with attainment. I hope you will not do that.'

After lunch we went for a walk through country lanes and by the deserted shore, climbing the promontory to Gorey Castle. He barely noticed gradients, enthusing about the Edwardian authoresses Flora Annie Steel (*On the Face of the Waters*), and Lady Charlotte Guest, the writer of the Mabinogion: 'remarkable women'. He was still reviewing English fiction for *The Times*. I took the opportunity to ask him about his working day. Memos on the telephone first thing in the morning, ideas for the day, comments on the previous night's paper. Lunch at the Athenaeum or the Ritz Grill. Letters in the afternoon. A leader at 5 p.m. perhaps two or three times a week. 'I believe the editor should always write the leader if there is to be a change of the paper's policy.' He had not been a dining-out editor. Except on Thursdays, when he had six people to dinner at home, he stayed to see the proofs of the first edition and sat with the night editor going through the paper column by column. He always went to the composing room to make up the leaders and letters; he was the first editor in modern times to do that. The eleventh editor had returned to the previous tradition. I told Haley that I intended to follow him; he seemed pleased with that.

Later, when I had returned to London, I had a letter of typical consideration from William John signed in his big round hand. It said that when I looked up Lady Guest in the *Dictionary of National Biography* I should be sure to look under Schreiber, because she had married again. He also came up with the name of Henry Kaiser, the American industrialist of Liberty ships fame, as the one person we had both forgotten who had original ideas in recruiting staff. He thanked me for making 'the somewhat arduous trip' to Gorey Bay.

I agreed with all that Haley said. The definition of *The Times* as a paper of record provoked Murdoch to jeer. There was certainly a pompous vagueness about the way the phrase was often intoned, as if it solved all the problems of daily journalism. But there were two values in it. First it was a reminder that a newspaper ought to have a memory. A developing story must be followed through to the end; popular newspapers drop a story when it loses its fizz. Second, it ought to force reflection on what a responsible newspaper recorded. The full-page parliamentary report was indispensable. The *Telegraph*, *Guardian* and *Financial Times* had allowed their reports to dribble away. *The Times* was the only paper to have its own staff of parliamentary shorthand reporters. It was also the only newspaper to compile its own law reports, written by barristers and accepted as authority in court, and here again *The Times* scored. It was less vigilant than the *Telegraph* in keeping its eye to the keyhole of the matrimonial courts, while pretending to look the other way; the *Telegraph* was in a class by itself for exploiting sex by stealth. But in cases of public merit *The Times* was essential.

I looked forward to superintending the third area of record, because it meant I would no longer have to worry about death. At *The Sunday Times* I had great difficulty inducing the staff to take the subject seriously. No public figure departing on a Friday or Saturday could be sure we would notice their going. *The Times* did. I was always grateful for that as a reader. Its obituaries were an ornament in the land. The court circular, and the appointments, wills and birthdays of its page, were another part of the record, mainly routine, though the subtleties of the circular were not to be underrated. It had been used to flash political as well as social signals and might again: Queen Victoria alarmed Mr Gladstone's camp when on 13 August 1892 she put in the court circular that she accepted the resignation of her Prime Minister, Lord Salisbury, 'with much regret'. Nowhere in the world, finally, was there a feature comparable to letters to *The Times*. The best, if somewhat smug, encapsulation of their quality came from one of them in 1970: 'Sir, King George V, approached by a friend who hoped that a word in the right quarter would solve a difficulty, said, "My dear fellow, I can't help you! You'd better write to *The Times*."'

Parliament, law and obituaries were three pillars of *The Times*, and a fourth was the leader column. It was required reading because of its independence and range. I cannot assert that it was consistently superior to the other newspapers in style or argument, but I always turned to *The Times* first in the hope that Rees-Mogg might have written one of his audacious specials. I remember Denis Hamilton's consternation in having to deal with the complaints about the assertion that George Brown drunk would have made a better Prime Minister than Harold Wilson sober. One of the problems, clearly, in the absence of Rees-Mogg was going to be in providing this occasional thrill of outrage. However, there were bigger problems. The paper was vulnerable in home news, the arts, features, and sport. This was partly for reasons of space, and partly for reasons I was to discover. *The Times* was running four more pages at that time than *The Guardian*, but most of this advantage was spent on the four pillars, and a very large business news, and it had four fewer pages than the *Telegraph*. *The Guardian* ran livelier arts and feature pages, and the *Telegraph* more comprehensive home news pages. *The Times* gave almost equal space to home and foreign (or 'overseas', as the office jargon preferred), which was right since it had never been an insular newspaper; but *The Times* had not established the ascendancy in foreign news one might have expected with this space and sixteen staff correspondents, some of them outstanding. I agreed with an analysis by two French journalists carried out between April and October 1980 that the coverage looked like a long accumulation of 'raw' news, whose volume might discourage the reader and which too often lacked inter-pretation and analysis. This was especially irritating when the corres-pondents merely duplicated impersonal news agency reports. There was clearly a difficult problem here. In home news I missed detail; and I wondered about the genesis of the spectacular blunder of falsely naming Donald Beves, an innocent and kindly don, as being the KGB recruiter of Burgess, Maclean and Philby at Cambridge in the 1930s. In addition to all this, I found the paper hard to read and uninviting, a judgement supported by market research among the readers.

Among my letters of goodwill, as I thought about what I would do, was one that was to prove prescient. It was from another *Times* luminary, Donald Tyerman, a former deputy editor who had gone on to edit *The Economist*. Tyerman, who died in 1981, had a brilliant mind and was a trenchant chairman of the International Press Institute. He reminded me of Geoffrey Crowther's remark that, while the editor of *The Times* might be as free as air, there were gremlins in every corner to sit on his pen and his programme. 'In your ambition to make it a great newspaper again', Tyerman wrote, 'you will find the tradition is both a spur and a danger.'

It was partly to confirm in my mind the essential elements of the tradition that I had gone to Gorey Bay, but it required a longer journey. A postcard from Alan Coren, the editor of *Punch*, said: 'It's the best news since John Walter decided to give up the coal business.' The first John Walter founded his *Daily Universal Register* in 1785 (renamed *The*

Times in 1788) only when he went bankrupt as an underwriter, after leaving the coal trade. He spent sixteen months in 'the horrible Bastille' of Newgate and an hour in the pillory at Charing Cross for saying the King's sons were insincere in their joy when he recovered from insanity. The publication set no precedent for fearless journalism, though it happened to be true. Walter was only doing what he had been paid to do. He had £300 a year from secret service funds for inserting paragraphs with a distinguishing mark sent to him from the Treasury at the behest of the Prime Minister, the younger Pitt, who feared dismissal if the King was declared insane and a Regency installed. Walter did one brave thing, which was to refuse to confess the authorship of the paragraphs; and his original corruption was commonplace. All the newspapers of the day were in the pay of one political faction or another. Journalism was synonymous with blackmail. Scandalous paragraphs were inserted, suppressed or contradicted for fees.

The political independence that was to become the heartbeat of *The Times* began with the man who recoiled from graft and propaganda, and appointed its two most famous editors. John Walter II, who took over the direction of the paper in 1803 at the age of twenty-seven, had the revolutionary idea of making *The Times* commercially independent, and so politically and culturally free. He began with the small matter of theatre tickets: he paid for them and printed candid reviews instead of puffs. He appreciated the value of early and accurate news, and set up a proper foreign service. It embroiled him in a running battle with the Post Office and the rackets it ran in the delivery and translation of foreign journals. Postal officials boarded ships and seized packages addressed to *The Times*. Walter beat them; *The Times* prospered. In 1814 it was the first newspaper printed by steam. Then by stages from 1817, partly from a desire to spend time in the country with his 'rather pretty and chatty' second wife, but also from conviction, John Walter II gave journalism another new idea, an editor independent of his proprietor with complete editorial authority. Thomas Barnes, aged thirty-two, a barrister of the Inner Temple and Cambridge graduate, was the man he chose, as vivid a personality as any in the history of journalism, but a man of obstinate anonymity. He was not at all the popular image of an editor of *The Times*, no more than the paper he produced conformed to the stereotype of sobriety and convention. He was a born Bohemian who lived with a mistress; he loved wine and town pastimes, and, for a trifling bet, swam from the steps of the Apothecaries Garden, Chelsea, to Westminster Bridge. He was a radical. He reported and denounced the Peterloo massacre, campaigned against the new Poor Law and thundered for the Reform Act of 1832. When he walked home to dinner across Blackfriars Bridge, fat and nearsighted in middle age, he carried a bludgeon, alert to the threats of diehard Tories to have him knocked on the head. The enduring contribution of Barnes, singularly unappreciated even today, was to conceive and organize a newspaper not as a means by which government could influence people, but as one by which people could influence government. The idea that there is an entity called public opinion which can be characterized and which is the commonplace of political rhetoric today is a concept bequeathed to us by Barnes. He sought to create a healthy public opinion by supplying it with news uncorrupted by agents of court, party, ministry and embassy. He used the new turnpikes with teams of fast horses to bring him intelligence on what people in the country were thinking. He reflected that opinion, he allied *The Times* with it, but he also sought to lead it. By 1820 *The Times* was strong enough to acknowledge dependence only on public opinion, which George Canning likened to the new force of steam. Barnes was an anonymous editor even in death. All that appeared on 8 May 1841 was this classified advertisement in *The Times*: 'On the 7th inst., at his house in Soho Square, Thomas Barnes, Esq. in the 56th year of his age.'

The free and independent daily newspaper in Britain has its origins in Walter and Barnes, and its triumphant fulfilment in the thirty-six-year partnership of all the Victorian virtues which succeeded them, the third John Walter and his editor, John Thadeus Delane. There is a story of a member of *The Times* staff proudly reporting that he had seen the editor riding down Whitehall on horseback with a duke walking on each side. It serves at least as a symbol of his eminence as the best-informed man in Europe, untainted by party ties and determined to obtain 'the earliest and most correct intelligence of the events of the time and instantly, by disclosing them, to make them the common property of the nation'. Barnes stayed in, Delane went out. In the London season he dined out every night, sometimes a hundred nights in succession, listening to the ambassadors and cabinet ministers. I intended to keep my ears open, but without hope or intention of emulating Delane. 'Swelling', he called it, but he put it to good purpose, going back to his gaslit office in Printing House Square with exclusive information and staying there, reading and marking every proof, until 5 a.m., when the paper went to press. 'I have seen more sunrises', he said, 'than any man alive.' Staying until our modern first-edition time, which I was certain I would at least do, was a less onerous heritage. The pre-eminence that Delane established was such that in 1854 Lord John Russell wrote to Queen Victoria that 'the degree of information possessed by *The Times* is mortifying, humiliating and incomprehensible'. But Delane fulfilled the more difficult purpose of a newspaper in telling Ministers, as well as people, things they did not know; his newspaper was not a mere noticeboard to record events. It was investigations by *The Times* which exposed the fraud in the railway mania of the period and reporting by William Howard Russell which gave the true picture of the war in the Crimea.

Delane, as Haley noted, did not have quite the freedom of Barnes. The editor might return from dining out to find his proofs jumbled and the proprietor ensconced at his desk ready to debate a point: 'the Griff', he called him, a shortened form of 'griffin' or grim guardian. John Walter III, like John Walter II, was an MP, akin to the wets of latter-day Toryism, but the Griff never sought to impose a party line. He was a simple, religious man, his interventions were occasional, and he shared Delane's repugnance for privilege and nepotism. His central role was to sustain Delane in his independence and, with his manager, to provide commercial and mechanical advance. John Walter III took a crucial decision that determined the editorial character of *The Times* for succeeding generations to the present day. *The Times* outstripped all the other newspapers. It sold around 70,000 copies during the Crimean War, a greater sale than all its rivals put together; on the occasion of the wedding of the Prince of Wales in 1863 it sold an unprecedented 108,000 copies. In the mid 1850s, when the repressive taxes on newspapers began to be dismantled, Walter was faced with the certainty that to maintain its supremacy *The Times* would have to popularize its content and lower its price to compete with the new penny papers, the *Daily Telegraph*, the *Standard* and the *News*. He quite deliberately rejected that course. In 1861 he fixed the price of *The Times* at threepence. He saw himself not as the heir to a business but the temporary custodian of a tradition, and the tradition was to offer Englishmen 'the best possible newspaper'. This meant a newspaper with full and accurate reporting from home and abroad, ample and exact parliamentary and other reports with independent leading articles, theatrical and other sections of the paper done, as he put it, 'with as much life, spirit, classical taste as could be got for love or money'. The penny papers of London overtook *The Times* and new journals like the *Manchester Guardian*, the *Scotsman* and *The Northern Echo* challenged it for readers. In the 1880s the *Telegraph*, selling half a million, was proclaiming 'the largest circulation in the world', but *The Times* had sufficient readers and revenues. It was not inevitable that it should find itself, as it did, a beached and barnacled whale on the shores of the twentieth century.

This is what happened in the third phase of the history of *The Times*, when Arthur Fraser Walter failed to maintain its business inventiveness, and two editors and their staffs, but principally George Earle Buckle, editor from 1884 to 1912, a Fellow of All Souls, came to regard *The Times* not as a newspaper but as an institution. In the years after Delane's retirement a healthy conservatism, for want of imagination, hardened into reaction. Pride degenerated into complacency. Methods were mistaken for principles. News was too narrowly defined in a rapidly changing society. Buckle, as a young man, repulsed the overtures of Randolph Churchill, but the political line became predictably Conservative. Highminded and stiffnecked, *The Times* went its own way, looking askance alike at the newspaper subheading, the typewriter and the telephone. Its credibility was damaged during its campaign against Home Rule for Ireland by the publication of letters forged to implicate the Irish leader Charles Parnell in political assassinations; its habit of deference was demonstrated by its refusal to publish the undisputed text of a telegram from Queen Victoria deploring the Dreyfus verdict, which was secured by its famous diplomatic correspondent Henri de Blowitz. The manager, not the editor, ran the foreign service; the foreman printer slung the paper together. By 1908 the sale had dropped to 38,000, half what it had been in Delane's day. *The Times* was facing ruin.

This long period of decline produced the most controversial phase in the history of the paper and of its principles. It was bought secretly by Mr x, alias Lord Northcliffe, who remarked that it was a national monument of such character he would feel bound to leave it in time to the British Museum. There were uncanny echoes. Was Murdoch Northcliffe? Murdoch, like Northcliffe, hustled in successfully and abrasively from the popular end of the Street with money and promises. Northcliffe was his father's mentor. Were we in for a rerun and would it be disastrous if we were? I had mixed feelings. It is commonly said that Northcliffe lowered the traditional standards of *The Times*. Harcourt Kitchin sniffed: '*The Times* was a caste newspaper and Lord Northcliffe did not belong to that caste', the caste being that of the educated upper-class Englishman. But Northcliffe was right to inveigh against the 'priggish slackness' that permeated Printing House Square. 'Six hundred years ago', he said in 1912, 'there was near the site of *The Times* office a monastery, the home of the Black Friars, recluses who lived remote from the world. The same kind of men inhabit Printing House Square today.' It alarmed the Black Friars, but it did no damage to the real traditions of *The Times* to have a daily news conference, lighten the layout, take notice of aviation, introduce photographs or sharpen the headlines – on the contrary. A Barnes or Delane in the twentieth century would have done the same. Northcliffe did become obsessed with brevity for its own sake, but his campaign made *The Times* a newspaper again and his acumen put it in the black.

The record does not end there, however. The tradition Northcliffe did breach and then violate with increasing venom, as his monomania and paranoia waxed, was the independence of the paper. No other chief proprietor had ever used *The Times* as an agency for the promotion of political, still less personal, vendettas or so humiliated his editors. He was, at his death, on the point of firing his third editor; as Keith Murdoch observed: 'I value him as a friend, but would certainly quarrel with him as an employer. He cannot resist making his employees feel that they are the puppets of his will.' It was in this respect, a quite different matter from his newspaper genius, that he menaced *The Times*. Here the editor and staff were right to resist, and what a nightmare it became with Northcliffe's spies and ferrets, and his increasing rages. Yet it is to Northcliffe and Northcliffe alone, as the official *History of The Times* acknowledges, that *The Times* owed its transformation from a bankrupt Victorian relic into a flourishing twentieth-century property.

There was no threat to the independence of *The Times* and the freedom of its editors in the following fifty-nine years, the fifth phase of *The Times*. The Astors, from 1922, and then the Thomsons, from 1966, regarded it as a trust. It was Northcliffe's sacked editor of 1919, Geoffrey Dawson, who, on being asked back by John Jacob Astor and the minority shareholder John Walter IV, wrote the formal memorandum on an editor's right to edit, which was respected and on which we built our pyramid of guarantees in 1981. The freedom had a dark side when Dawson in the 1930s sold out the Austrians and the Czechs in the years of appeasement, and Major Astor stayed detached (though John Walter fulminated). But an interfering Northcliffe at the time might just as easily have got it wrong as did Dawson and his deputy, Barrington-Ward. The policy was backed by Ministers and by public opinion of all parties.

Nor was the fundamental character of the paper changed in these fifty-nine years, though there was a suspicious, not to say paranoid, constituent. William Haley faced it. When *The Times* made a trading loss in 1957, the board commissioned the chartered accountants Cooper Brothers to make a report. It advocated news on the front page and a brighter newspaper with more readers. The report was denounced in a long anonymous memorandum by senior staff: it was not the duty of *The Times* to appeal to 'the reading public'; its duty was to serve 'the governing class of Great Britain'. Haley made the changes, but slowly. News went on the front page nine years later. Ten years after Cooper, Haley's successor, William Rees-Mogg, was accused of heresy. He had gone 'quali-pop', according to twenty-nine of his senior staff who signed a round robin originating in the White Swan pub. It said:

> In view of the changes in the editorial character of the paper which are under consideration, it is appropriate that we should express our concern about certain earlier changes that have been made in the past few years.
>
> We recognise the need for innovation and evolution of style, and we agree that many of the things that have been changed needed to be changed. But

the general effect of what has been done, and of the manner in which it has been done, has been to diminish the authority, independence, accuracy, discrimination and seriousness of *The Times*. These are chief among its essential values. To the degree that they are lost *The Times* departs from its true tradition, and forfeits the principal editorial factor in its commercial success.

It is because we are sure you are determined to uphold the tradition of *The Times* as a paper of the highest quality that we now address you. We believe we can make a constructive contribution to the proposals under consideration, provided we are given an opportunity to discuss them with you and others directly involved, and provided the discussions take place at a formative stage. We accordingly ask for the opportunity.

The signatories were a very mixed group indeed: senior members of the pre-Thomson old guard, supported by some newcomers. The idea of the letter was Bob Jones's, a hard-headed business news reporter; the wording was by Owen Hickey, leader writer. The foreign editor, Teddy Hodgkin, signed and so did the heads of letters, sport and obituaries, and the parliamentary gallery. Several leader writers signed and also a group of young specialists: Innis Macbeath (labour), Charles Douglas-Home (defence), Brian MacArthur (education) and Hugh Stephenson, later the second editor of business news.*

A coalescence of grievances produced it: anxiety about popularization, the eager drive of the news-conscious deputy editor Michael Cudlipp, distaste for a men's fashion page, the wild rumour of a joint babywear advertising exercise with *The Sunday Times*, and the feeling that they could not get through to the editor. A few were upset, even, that *The Times* had exposed corruption at Scotland Yard by recording the conversations between a criminal suspect and a policeman asking for a bribe. Rees-Mogg angrily summoned the mutineers and gave them a dressing down. The paper would not have survived without Thomson. They represented no one but themselves. He was backed to the hilt by Hamilton. (When one of the dissident groups had gone to see Hamilton, he had dramatically brought the editor into the meeting from a side room. 'We have always worked closely together. We have never disagreed on policy. There is nothing I will hear that I would not wish the editor to hear.') Mutiny ended with an agreement on more consultation through the union. Later when the commercial strategy of the paper resulted in its redesign with smaller headlines and the absorption inside

* The full list was Michael Baily, Patrick Brogan, Jerome Caminada, George Clark, Charles Douglas-Home, James H. Greenwood, John Greig, Richard Harris, John Hennessy, E. C. Hodgkin, Bob Jones, Mollie Keenan, Roya Lewis, C. D. Longley, Brian MacArthur, Innis Macbeath, Kenneth Mackenzie, Hugh Noyes, A. M. Rendel, Geoffrey Smith, David Spanier, Hugh Stephenson, Colin Watson, Stuart Weir, Michael Wolfers, Alan H. Wood, David Wood, and Geoffrey Woolley.

the paper of the business section, an area of legitimate complaint for inaccuracy, the group felt vindicated; some were relieved when the newly-acquired readers were shed.

I had a lot to learn from the history of *The Times*. I was thrilled at the idea of being a part of it. All the successful periods, I noted, were when editor, staff and proprietor were in harmony on the idea of the paper with the editor free to follow an independent line and the chief proprietor fertile in sustaining journalism with engineering and commercial initiative. What settled in my mind, though, was the image of Crowther's gremlins in every corner. How frequently delusive the idea of the past had been for the present! The recurrent fear was that almost any change in the paper was a breach with tradition, and that somehow *The Times* had a special duty to resist change in society as well, that it was itself part of the established order and must help to sustain it. These perceptions flourished in the 1980s, as I was to discover, as they did in the 1880s.

I had one important appointment to make, that of deputy editor. I would have done well, in the light of events, to divert Haley from *On the Face of the Waters* to *The Discourses* by Machiavelli, with special reference to chapter XLII.

Rees-Mogg's deputy editor was Louis Heren, who combined this post, unusually, with that of home editor, overseeing all the news produced in Britain from reporters, specialists and political staff. Louis Heren was bitterly disappointed not to succeed Rees-Mogg. It would have been a romantic climax to a real newspaperman's career: Cockney Errand Boy to Editor of *Times*. He was born in dockland. His father, who had a job in *The Times* press-room, died when Heren was four years old. Jobs in the print went to sons of fathers already in the trade, but Heren's mother took him along to *The Times* and he was accepted when he left school at fifteen in 1934. He was a messenger first, running errands down the dark passages and firelit rooms of the old Printing House Square premises. It was unthinkable then that a messenger boy should become a reporter, but Heren did; forty years later he still gave the impression that he had a secret fear of being found out not to belong to *The Times*. He was suspicious, not to say hostile, with outsiders. I first met him when he was in Washington, feuding with Henry Brandon, the *Sunday Times* correspondent, and got to know him when he became foreign editor in London, feuding with Frank Giles. He saw and reported for *The Times* the massacres following the British withdrawal from India; the birth of Israel; the wars in Korea and Malaya; Adenauer's Germany and Kennedy's Washington. Adenauer called him a *Drahtzieher* or wire-puller. He escaped death for his paper in Damascus, where an army colonel was shot in mistake for the man from *The Times*, in Israel on a hazardous flight with the photographer Robert Capa, and in the paddy fields of Korea. He was the first to tell the world about the Dead Sea Scrolls; and *The Times* spiked his story that President Kennedy was going to insist on the removal of Soviet missiles from Cuba.

All foreign correspondents suffer from 'peripheritis', a condition first identified in a Hong Kong bar for me by the legendary Richard Hughes: they exist on the periphery of the paper, remote from the jokes and gossip, half-forgotten, and yet always subject to its whims. They cannot fail to acquire, with every mosquito bite and mangled story, a suspicion of the bureaucrats at base. Heren, after twenty-three years in the field, had been rehabilitated by his spell as an executive, a foreign editor himself despatching telexes to outer places, but he was convinced absurdly that he had been cheated of the editorship of *The Times* by a plot by William Rees-Mogg. There had been a poll in which the assistant editors had been asked to give their preferences for editor between Heren, Charles Douglas-Home, the foreign editor, and Hugh Stephenson, the editor of business news. Heren told everyone he had come top, but that Rees-Mogg had concealed it, because of his preference for Douglas-Home, and that was because Douglas-Home was an Etonian and a Tory: 'He's managed to offend most people who work under him. It's our class system again.'

When I was appointed, Heren sent me a letter: 'Welcome aboard. If it could not be me, then better you than anyone I can think of.' He also sent me a copy of a memorandum on the paper and its organization which he had given to Murdoch.

He made constructive criticism of the layout, features and the arts, the amount of space taken by business news, and the organization of the paper. 'William Rees-Mogg practises what he chooses to describe as a cabinet form of government. The analogy is false. We do not have the equivalent of cabinet meetings. Indeed the editor is rarely interested in the news content. His successor should be more actively concerned in the selection of news and the generation of ideas.'

Heren was then sixty-two. He had the look and style of a barefisted Corinthian pugilist of the Regency. His laugh was resonant and comradely, but the small almond eyes in the square face suggested calculation and he could look mean. It was hard to disappoint him again, but I had to. I had agreed with Murdoch that I should stay as editor for seven years until I was sixty, and in that time develop a successor. Heren was too old to succeed me and, in any event, I wanted a deputy younger than myself. I invited him to stay on as associate editor with freedom to write and travel, and with access to the editor to give his views on the development of the paper. He refused. I sympathized with his frustration, but the role I offered was a worthwhile and honourable conclusion to a gallant career, and he was being made a journalist director in the new company. I could not persuade him. He insisted on staying as deputy editor. Several people made their views known. Rees-Mogg and his managing editor, John Grant, when I met them together, counselled against keeping Heren as deputy editor. 'He'll make too much trouble for you,' said Grant. As for that wretched poll, Douglas-Home had come top with Hugh Stephenson second and there was only one vote for Heren: 'Of course, when he asked the assistant editors, nobody could bear to tell him they hadn't voted for him.' The Heren show rapidly became overcrowded. Long had worked in Bonn at the same time as Heren, competition which had not led to a lifelong friendship. He was vehement: I was being soft in letting Heren stay on at all; he should be severed. I demurred, but Long went ahead on his own and asked Murdoch to approve a settlement. 'You'll have to live with Heren,' said Murdoch on the telephone. 'Cost me too much to pay him off. Give him airline tickets round the world.'

Heren was obstinate. John Grant eventually persuaded him that being an associate editor was a good thing for a man of his age. Then it was Grant's turn. He was fifty-eight and liked the idea of redundancy money. I preferred the idea of retaining a *Times* man who, on Rees-Mogg's say so, knew the rat-runs and had the editorial budgets and administration in the palm of his hand. I induced Grant to stay.

I was ready to go outside *The Times* for the deputy editor. My first preference was Hugo Young, the political editor of *The Sunday Times*, who was the right age, forty-two, and whose pedigree was Ampleforth, Balliol, a Harkness Fellowship and the *Yorkshire Post*. He was an incisive leader writer and columnist, but a skilled reporter as well, winning awards for his political investigations with Stephen Fay. I was not sure how ingrained were some of the political attitudes among the Black Friars. Young I knew to have strong liberal principles, but an open mind on party politics. His writing would help to fill the gap left by Rees-Mogg and I trusted him. But it was not to be. Frank Giles was aghast at the idea that he would lose Young, whom he saw as his own successor. Murdoch arbitrated in favour of Giles.

Murdoch, Hamilton and Rees-Mogg all recommended Douglas-Home as deputy editor. Murdoch had interviewed him for the chair. 'He isn't editor material,' he told me, 'but he knows the paper and he'd be loyal to you in the tough task of energizing this place.'

Charles Cospatrick Douglas-Home was forty-three. He and Heren might have posed for contrary caricatures of English life. He is the second son of the second son of the 13th Earl of Home. During the week he lived in upper-class thrift in north London; at weekends he was in Gloucestershire hunting, gardening and making up a rubber. His father was Henry Montagu Douglas-Home, an ornithologist, his uncle Alec the Conservative Prime Minister for a year and his uncle William the author of the play *The Reluctant Debutante*. Douglas-Home followed the conventional course of younger sons of the aristocracy. Eton first, the Army next with a short commission in the Royal Scots Greys, and then the Empire which meant, in his case, nine months bumming in Canada and eighteen months as an aide-de-camp to the Governor of Kenya, then Sir Evelyn Baring. He failed in auditions at both the BBC and ITV to be a television commentator, which he thought his natural vocation, but his pianist brother, Robin, who later committed suicide, was reviewing records for the *Daily Express* and got him an introduction to Edward Pickering, then the paper's editor (and in 1981 appointed by Murdoch to be a national director of *The Times*).

Douglas-Home's *Who's Who* entry lists his career as starting as the military correspondent of the *Daily Express*, but he had some taste of street journalism first as a junior reporter for the *Express* in Glasgow, filing reports on car accidents and petty crime. It was a long way from Government House in Nairobi. He was then twenty-three. A year later he was called to London to stand in for the defence and science correspondent, Chapman Pincher, and then had a frustrating spell in the political department. His break came in 1964. Alun Gwynne Jones, the defence correspondent of Sir William Haley's *Times*, telephoned him to say he should apply for his job: Gwynne Jones was becoming Lord Chalfont in Harold Wilson's Government. Uncle Alec had by this time been in and out as Prime Minister, but Charlie Douglas-Home found the relationship useful in his subsequent travels – 'Foreigners gave me their confidence on the strength of the name'. His best moments were reporting from the six-day Arab–Israeli war in 1967 and getting expelled from Czechoslovakia in 1968 for going round country lanes looking for troop concentrations.

Rees-Mogg brought him on rapidly, thereafter, as features editor and home editor; he gave up his brightly coloured shirts and married stage designer Jessica Violet Gwynne, the daughter of Major John Neville Wake-Gwynne and Patricia Louisa Morrison Bell of Somerset.

As an executive, Douglas-Home had a serious blot on his copybook. Some four years earlier, when he was home editor of *The Times*, he prepared a secret dossier for his new news editor, Brian MacArthur, which recorded details of the private lives of every reporter and specialist on his staff. The dossier went beyond an assessment of professional capabilities. One of the reporters, who grew suspicious, found a key to his filing-cabinet and opened it one night. He was appalled to read about himself: 'He is subject to frequent depressions which he attributes to his conditions of work but which I blame on his chaotic love life'. One

Times reporter was described as 'not a gentleman'. The chapel of the NUJ raised a formal protest and Douglas-Home apologized. The practice would be discontinued and the records destroyed, he promised.

I met Douglas-Home for the first time when he was foreign editor. Denis Hamilton liked to mix *Times* and *Sunday Times* executives for entertaining foreign ministers or ambassadors of note. Douglas-Home briefed himself well and followed up his questions with jocular chaff. I liked his spirit. Off parade he could be infinitely relaxed and agreeable, even whimsical. He had two appearances as well. The one I saw mostly then was the young subaltern, but with his pale papyrus skin he could, when tired, look an old man. He was, I learned, plagued by a bad back from falling off a horse.

I did not know then about the dossier affair. He was in something of a reverie when he ambled across the Coley Street bridge from *The Times* to *The Sunday Times* building for the first of several talks that February. Subject to what transpired, I was ready to offer him the deputy editorship. He was said not to have Stephenson's intellect, but he had wider experience on the paper and he knew the staff well; I had begun to attach importance to this. Tony Norbury of *The Times* production staff, who did some Saturday stints at *The Sunday Times*, said the 'working' *Times* people, as he put it, were eager to have me over there; but vapours of clannishness wafted across the bridge as well. It would be sensible to have a *Times* man as an ally. As Douglas-Home chatted and mused, I thought we could establish an easy and viable relationship. 'Charlie will do a good job for you,' Rees-Mogg had said. But the candidate was in two minds. 'Oh, I don't know,' he said. 'I've been passed over this time. I'm not sure I would be allowed to succeed you at the end of the seven years.' It was part of his charm that he made it sound like a compliment rather than the lament of the lost crown prince. 'Did you see Murdoch on *Panorama*?' he asked. 'Jessica and I felt we were watching *Jaws* II.' He was thinking about taking redundancy money and writing books. He had written on Rommel and Evelyn Baring, and had one 'on the stocks' on the monarchy. He would stay only on certain conditions. 'State them,' I said. He demurred. He would think things over. He kept in touch, but without commitment or more information about his mysterious conditions. The time ran out. I said farewell to *The Sunday Times* on Saturday 7 March and was in a mood in which apprehension chased away nostalgia when Douglas-Home telephoned on the evening before I was due to start at *The Times*. He asked if he could come to see me at home.

He had questions for me, but they became rhetorical as the evening unwound in Douglas-Home's indictment of Rees-Mogg's *Times*. 'It's a sloppy paper. Michael Hamlyn runs it because William goes home at 6 p.m. Can you imagine that? Hamlyn is the secret editor of *The Times*. Would you believe it? The specialists are asleep. The layout is dull. You'd know what to do about that, I don't. Hamlyn is working on something, but it's all close to the chest. I'm foreign editor, but not in on leaders. Can you believe it? There's no flexibility on space. John Grant's in charge of it, but he only keeps the shop.' On and on it went and, as he ticked off each criticism, his spine sagged a notch, until a couple of hours later he was lying three-quarter-length on his back on my sofa. It was a fascinating insight for me into the paper and the frustration of one of its senior executives. He had been one of the signatories of the White Swan protest to Rees-Mogg in 1970, but now change was needed. 'Murdoch was right to appoint you,' he concluded. 'Coming from outside with your experience, you can do things nobody else could.'

He got round to his conditions. The deputy editor should not be sealed off from the paper. He should have the same field of action as the editor, which meant the whole paper including leaders. He should be consulted on appointments and dismissals. He should know what was going on at all times. 'And I'd like to sit with you on the back bench at night. I could learn a lot.' This was a reference to the area where the main decisions are taken during production. None of that bothered me and I told him so; I wanted it to be a partnership. He could see every memorandum I wrote. We would keep a central filing system. I would discuss all my ideas for change with him. The rhythm of a daily paper would make disputation less than on *The Sunday Times* and I would not protest about that, but I believed in an open office with opportunities for argument.

'And then there's Murdoch,' said the putative deputy editor. 'He's a wrecker of institutions. How can I trust you to be independent if I don't know what Murdoch is saying to you? Will you tell me?'

It was presumptuous and it was dangerous. There were no maps for the journey I was to begin the next day. No editor of *The Times* had ever before had such a delicate relationship with a proprietor, both exploring the constraints and opportunities of a new constitution, both with their pride and ambitions. I wanted to establish the best possible relationship consistent with independence. I had no idea what Murdoch might say to me. He was bound to have some good ideas we would want to adopt, and there would be times when I would want to bounce something off him. If it became known that something had originated with Murdoch, it could be made to look as if I were taking orders, however sensible the idea. If it became gossip that I had rejected a Murdoch proposal, as I was bound to do at some time, he might feel his editorial impotence was being paraded. There were endless possibilities for mischief, and yet, if Douglas-Home was to be trusted, the proposal had merit. I had nothing to hide from my deputy editor. I was not going to be provocative, but I was determined to be independent. My acceptance would demonstrate goodwill and good faith. Provided it was a strict confidence between the editor and his deputy, the system might well help to reinforce our determination. There would be someone with whom I could discuss the Murdoch relationship; Gerald Long would be unsympathetic. So I told Douglas-Home I would confide in him. After all, it was the independence of *The Times* that was at issue.

'Then it's a deal, and you can count on me,' said Douglas-Home and we shook hands on it. It was close to midnight. Nine hours later I was editing *The Times*.

II

FIRST EDITIONS

There are pictures of *The Times* for the year I was born which show the sub-editors of the home department sitting gravely round a polished oval table in a room with a merry coal fire in the grate, like so many directors of an old-established banking parlour shut off from the clamour of events. Claud Cockburn has described how he found a sub-editor in the overseas room translating a passage of Plato's *Phaedo* into Chinese, for a bet, while another dictated the Greek passage aloud from memory. Leader writers dined grandly in Private House, the family quarters for generations of the founding Walter family. The editorial rooms – it seems crude to call them offices – were then on the original site of the King's old printing house in Blackfriars overlooking Queen Victoria Street, where John Walter I founded the *Daily Universal Register* on New Year's Day in 1785. The spirits of Barnes and Delane still invested the premises when John Walter III rebuilt them in 1874, preserving the royal coat of arms carved in stone in the spandrel over the entrance, and they probably flitted about the board room of the new postwar block with its splendid view of St Paul's Cathedral. It is hard to imagine anyone caring to haunt *The Times* in Gray's Inn Road. The editorial offices, on the first floor above a lavish marble entrance, have the charm of an out-patients' registry. There is a large area for the reporters and another for the home and overseas subs and sport, lit dimly by fluorescent tube and drained of style or colour. The home and overseas editors are encased behind high sheet glass. For a few, there is sight of the telex room with its promise of happenings, but the nerve centre of the news desk with its telephones and television is cut off behind half-partitions of fluted glass. There are corridors with more half-partitions, behind which specialist writers conduct archaeological research on mounds of old journals. Only in the late afternoons, when the night staff take over and reporters try to meet the deadlines, is the void diminished.

I began my first day as editor with a 10 a.m. tour conducted by Charles Douglas-Home, whose appointment as deputy editor I planned to announce in the afternoon. There were signs of activity. The reporters who were in had to make quick decisions: did they talk to the new editor or answer the phone? Encouragingly they all chose the latter. Rodney Cowton, the news editor, was torn between a natural deference and the demands of the news schedule for my first conference at noon. Away from the main concourse, Philip Howard, the literary editor, stood in red braces in a small room, where he was deciding among sixty books on the half dozen for review. The arts editor, John Higgins, sat in the best cubicle, looking out with satisfaction on the grass of the inner yard. It was when we turned a corner into another area that I had my first education. At a long table there were about ten people, men and women, more than I had seen together all morning. 'What are you doing?' I asked. 'Nothing,' was the answer, and accurate it was too. Most of them were reading the morning's papers or gazing into space; one, between stabs at the crossword puzzle, was making marks on the proof of a page. Douglas-Home said this was the special reports department, which prepared the pages carrying editorial features and related advertising on Saudi Arabia, concrete mixing, and the like. It was under John Greig, and Greig materialized at that moment, a whirlwind of expostulation. Words frothed over his lips like waves on a barrier reef. I thought it was a marvellous effort to compensate for the lassitude of his department; it turned out to be his normal style. The message was that the sub-editors did indeed have nothing to do, as the next special report was not due for a week. I told Douglas-Home, as we limped away, that I had a first task for him: to redeploy the last mariners. Greig, I understood, had done well in producing the reports, but it was unthinkable to contemplate such a dissipation of journalists. Why could we not edit the special reports as part of the general production effort, integrating the sub-editors with those on the home or foreign desks? There was, I knew, a higher turnover of sub-editors. We could, in a short time, reduce staff costs and fill everyone's hours more happily.

There was more life in the obituaries department. It was, to be sure, lit in a lugubrious manner, but the two men and one woman pressed into the cluttered space were diligent in the preparation of three columns of material for the next day's paper. It exemplified the range of achievement *The Times* sought to honour – assessments of Lord Rhyl, formerly the rebellious right-wing Conservative Minister Nigel Birch, of the painter Winifred Nicholson, the Russian conductor Kyril Kondrashin and the American film critic Bosley Crowther. Lord Rhyl's obituary had been ready for some time. When a man first makes a mark in public life, his literary headstone is quietly prepared and his name inscribed in a card index. Colin Watson, the obituaries editor, explained that they liked to be ready for all eventualities. In his twenty-five years as obituaries editor he had built up a library of 4–5,000 articles with constant updating and revising by outside contributors. No one is allowed a preview of his obituary, even Sir Winston Churchill was politely turned away. Watson carried a consoling tact into ordinary conversation. 'We'd be very grateful if you hear that anyone is (cough) not, um, well, if you let us know, so that we can, um, prepare.' I did not like the way he measured my pallor; I was suffering from a lingering cold. I diverted him: did they have something ready on Rupert Murdoch? Yes, of course, but they were 'improving' it.

It is a short skip across a column rule in the newspaper and a few steps in the building to the department with powers of social life and death. The court circular is published in full exactly as it it is sent from Buckingham Palace with scrupulous regard, unlike the practice in the Telegraph, for its taste in capital letters. On the following day the reference would be to The Prince of Wales but only to the Lady Diana Spencer, the capital letter T being accorded only to members of the Royal Family who are Majesties or Royal Highnesses. Such matters and whether your birthday, like the Queen's, is publicly recognized on the court page, I found to be the responsibility of another troika. Margaret Alexander and her two ladies-in-waiting abandoned Debrett and Burke to receive me. I marvelled at their equanimity. The page is a minefield of protocol and pride. They were installed in an office whose plate glass fronted a common corridor leading to the works. They were constantly exposed to the vulgar scrutiny of streams of comers and goers of all departments, but they retained their composure and concentration as if the loss of an apostrophe in the guest list of an embassy reception would lead to an overnight declaration of war.

It was the court page which bowled me my first Times googly. A reader, who would not be put off, was demanding to know why I wanted to ruin a happy betrothal: her daughter's engagement notice had been barred from the court page. The announcement was acceptable, but the daughter, supported heart and soul by her man, insisted on calling herself Ms, and she had been told that the editor of The Times would not publish such offensive language. The rejection, I learned, was by a scrutineer in the classified advertising department; I had not realized until then that many of the announcements on the court page are paid advertising. The scrutineer said the rule originated with the editor and the court page. Mrs Alexander could not remember when or how it had been proclaimed. Calculating that it did not descend to us from time immemorial, I declared that, short of pretending to be earls, people should be free to call themselves what they liked, not least when they were paying for the privilege. Having run up the flag for both commerce and women's liberation, and without being able to discern whether it was with or without the approval of Mrs Alexander, I just had time before the noon news conference to call on the department whose favour is a matter of daily petition.

Some two hundred letters to the editor had arrived. Magisterially printed on coroneted linen wove or the work of a shaky ballpoint artist, they were in the sight of Leon Pilpel, a meticulous former chief sub-editor of the newspaper, all equal contenders until he had read every one and given an alpha, beta or gamma. There was no doubting either the efficiency with which he conducted his department or the feeling that Charles Dickens might have been responsible for staffing it. There was a very, very fat man with a hearty chuckle, and a very, very thin young man with a wan smile, and Pilpel himself, who had the profile of a happy Mr Punch with a big stick for anyone who tried to bully his way into his columns. He had, in his lead pile of letters, the chairman of the Visitors' Board to Her Majesty's Pentonville prison on their efforts to reduce the incarceration of remand prisoners, the solicitor Sir David Napley on why journalists needed to be disciplined, a Tory MP on how Britain might avoid a row over Canada's constitution, and a proposal for exhibiting the lifework of the artist Charles Tunnicliffe. There was a letter I particularly liked suggesting that duty-free goods should be available on arrival, rather than departure, to reduce the impedimenta of travel, and a promising line in indignation about Eton boys eating subsidized butter from the EEC butter mountain. Pilpel thought it was a quiet day. Every letter would be acknowledged. No letter selected for publication would be cut; if the letter was good, but too long, the writer himself would be asked to do the compression. These were sound rules, and so was another which Pilpel enforced with rigour: *The Times* would not publish any letter sent to another newspaper. I told the letters editor, as I had told obituaries and the court page, that there would be no changes in editorial policy.

I could hear Pilpel's battery of typists disappointing and delighting the correspondents through a thin partition when I arrived in my own office just before noon. It was like a railway waiting-room with cane chairs in rows in front of my table, and a view of the publishing-yard. It was a temporary one, while Rees-Mogg's was done up for me; Long had brought in the designer Theo Crosby of Pentagram, who designed the executive suite along the principal editorial corridor. There was a temporary secretary as well, a tall girl with a ponytail called Elizabeth Seeber, who was to play a role in my dramas I could never have imagined.

Promptly at noon the day executives, fifteen or so, filed in to report to the editor and each other how they were deploying the staff. Douglas-

Home sat on my right, Owen Hickey and the leader writers drifted in a little late and stood at the back. My first day in the chair was accompanied by an unparalleled one-day stoppage by civil servants over a pay dispute. Ministers in Whitehall were going without tea and sympathetic advice; the Cabinet Office was picketed and No. 10 had just had its laundry turned away. Heathrow had been brought to a standstill for the first time in thirty-five years. The collection of revenue was disrupted, so was that of foreign intelligence. Customs men had stopped frisking smugglers and they were making no money at the Mint. I told the conference that I wanted them to go through their normal routines while I settled in. John Grant produced a small-scale dummy of the following day's paper, which he had negotiated with the advertising department, and announced the space for home news, foreign, business and sport. The disproportion was glaring: forty-eight columns in all for business, against only fourteen inside the paper for foreign and eighteen for home. Foreign news and sport were mixed up on the same page, and fashion and sport on another, but I said nothing. Grant made no further contribution; he regarded his work as done. Rodney Cowton, the principal scavenger in the civil service strike, sat in his shirt-sleeves clutching a packet of messages from the Press Association news agency. He was a plump, soft-spoken man who looked about as apprehensive as I felt. He passed round copies of his home news schedule, a single page listing which of the day's events were being covered by staffmen, and the stories specialists were offering. Then, line by line, he read it all aloud *andante*. Ivan Barnes, the bearded foreign news editor, did the same *allegro*, and he was followed, *largo*, by David Young from the news desk of business news. The chorus was completed by Margaret Allen, *allegro vivace*, with the news that Bernard Levin was pacing the floor and about to deliver on the greatest legal scandal of the century.

Douglas-Home had told me it was the custom for senior departmental heads to attend conference, but to leave it to these news editors or deputies to report and answer any queries: it was something he disliked, feeling that senior officers should lead and NCOs carry out instructions. But the curious thing to me was the silence. When each reading had finished, nobody made any proposals from another department, nobody volunteered any ideas on how we might improve our coverage. It was with some diffidence that I suggested we might attempt a political profile of the leader of the main civil service union on strike, William Kendall, and that for a report on multi-racial schooling from Diana Geddes, the education correspondent, the picture editor might try to arrange a photograph of children affected.

With that the news captains departed, leaving the leading articles to be settled. Douglas-Home and Hugh Stephenson remained with Owen

Hickey and six leader writers. There was Geoffrey Smith, George Hill and Marcel Berlins for home affairs and Richard Davy, Richard Owen and Peter Strafford for foreign. I deferred to Hickey. I was anxious to encourage him. He sat, concave in his chair, rationing his words in a dry, high voice, one eye drifting behind his apothecary's gold frames. The civil service strike was the obvious leading subject for comment. At the heart of the stoppage was the government's abolition of the pay research body after twenty-five years and the civil service demand for 15% compared with the offer of 7%. *The Times* regarded civil servants as among its principal readers. The Government had offended them and the sense of fair play by abrogating the comparative method of fixing pay without first putting something else in its place. But nobody in conference saw how the civil servants could be supported in an inflationary 15% claim when they were in safe jobs with inflation-proof pensions, at a time when $2\frac{1}{2}$ million people had no jobs at all. The strike was out of proportion to the grievance and it was not an ordinary strike: it was an attack on the operations of the state by its servants, cleverly designed to do much damage for little sacrifice. Hickey volunteered to write this. I suggested that, while condemning the strike, we should give the leader more pith by suggesting a weapon for the Government and a way out of such confrontations in future. Civil servants should be reminded that their protected pensions and safe jobs were benefits which carried obligations. There should be formal recognition of this in a deal whereby vital public-sector unions renounced the strike weapon in return for the benefits in security.

Two other leaders were assigned without much discussion. Richard Davy outlined what he might say about letters from President Brezhnev on arms control and Marcel Berlins proposed to write critically on President Reagan's delay in agreeing the Law of the Sea convention. Hickey fixed the lengths in a quick trading session.

As I went to lunch with the assistant editors I had pieces of typing thrust into my hand. It was the incendiary Levin. 'Here's a present for your first day,' he cried. Chicanery and incompetence among lawyers, perjury in witnesses, partiality in the Lord Chief Justice. Here's a how d'ye do, I thought; and here, too, are the forbidding names of Lord Goodman and Peter Carter-Ruck. It was, it so happened, an innocuous reference to Goodman and it had all taken place a long time ago with most of the criticized parties dead. Levin was declaring new evidence which showed, he maintained, that the *Spectator* had not after all libelled Richard Crossman, Aneurin Bevan and Morgan Phillips by saying they had been seen drunk in Venice in 1957, because they had been. I approved it without qualm (though Lord Goodman wrote to me the next day to warn that Levin, 'the most famous *Luftmensch*' of his day, demonstrat-

Rupert Murdoch

Sale of the century: a word for the new owner of Times Newspapers from the Murdoch lawyer Richard Searby at the Thomson Press conference, January 1981.

William Rees-Mogg, the outgoing editor of *The Times*, at home in Somerset.

First edition, March 1981: Harold Evans, editor of *The Times*, pushes to press his first *Times* front page, a rare privilege accorded by the printers.

The changing *Times:* some traditional readers protested at the use of dramatic pictures in the paper.

The editor on the back bench at *The Times*, where the main news decisions were made.

Innovation: the old *Times* back page (left) was replaced in June by the Times Information Service on a page devoted to editorial. At the same time Harold Evans also restored the *Times* tradition of featuring photography on the back page on Saturdays.

Two firsts: (left) the first edition of Preview, a weekly guide to the arts and leisure, which was launched in June 1981. On 30 July the wedding of the Prince and Princess of Wales was commemorated by a full-page colour photograph, the first in the national press.

The wedding of the Prince and Princess of Wales, at St Paul's, July 29 1981
A moment of personal dedication and public devotion in ten centuries of monarchy

UNLIKELY EVENTS.

THE TIMES STARTS A COMIC STRIP.

To readers who wrote protesting at the changing *Times*, the editor's reply included a copy of this 1928 *Punch* cartoon.

Night work in 'New Printing House Square' – the name that was banned.

Inside *The Times*: editor and owner talk to night staff in the news room during the suspension of the paper, September 1981. Charles Douglas-Home is behind the editor's right shoulder. Home editor Fred Emery (*below*) engages Rupert Murdoch in discussion. David Hopkinson and John Brian centre.

ing to the new regime his undoubted genius for scurrility, had better not say it all again).

The concerns of the assistant editors, agreeably discussed in *The Times* private dining-room adorned with paintings of that great rascal Henri de Blowitz and the Balkans correspondent, James David Bourchier, were amplified and elaborated immediately afterwards when I spoke to all the staff in the reporters' area of the news room. There were a lot of people. There were messengers and secretaries, night staff as well as day, and they had squashed themselves into a circle with a space in the middle suitable for any speaker with his head on a swivel. I was almost speechless; the cold was affecting my voice. I told them facetiously that I was the victim of 'temporium bacillis quieta'; no classical scholar sprang out to debate my conjugation.

Their questions suggested to me they were divided between those who yearned for some old, non-existent order, when *The Times* did not have to worry about competition for news or nasty losses, and those who thought there was a case for change and new blood. Geraldine Norman, the saleroom correspondent and chairman of JOTT, wanted classified advertising restored to the front page. Conversely, night editor John Brian, a long-serving, silver-haired man who looked like a brigadier, wanted classified removed from the back page as well and news put in its place. Some raised fearful rumours that we might be seeking many more readers; Fred Emery, the political editor, suggested that the price should be kept down so that we could get them. Pat Davis, the foreign manager and leader of the Institute of Journalists, appealed for a ban on new words. 'Shoot out' and 'look-alike' had both appeared in *The Times*. One sub-editor, Sammy Rao, ventured to question the use of 'Mr' in headlines, and another, Paul Feldorf, one of the guardians of style, the rigid modular layout.

There was a defensive phalanx from business news. Margaret Stone and a tall man with a flaming red beard, whom I came to know as the diarist Ross Davis, wanted to be assured that there would continue to be two front pages in the paper, one on the front and the other leading business news. It was, Davis insisted, a quasi-autonomous part of the paper. There was also a body of reporters, David Nicholson-Lord and Alan Hamilton to the fore, who wanted to know where *The Times* was going wrong at the moment. How could we respond to our competitors and who were they really?

I replied to all their points. I understood their anxieties about the take-over and about my arrival. On individual points, I said no to Geraldine Norman's classified advertising, yes to back page news, and no to a republic for business staff. I would try to have clear rules on English usage. Design was being carefully studied. I would not model

The Times on *The Sunday Times*, which was necessarily a more theatrical newspaper. We were not going for a massive sale. We wanted the right kind of readers. It was not healthy to be 100,000 behind *The Guardian*, but it would be wrong to think of numbers first. If we produced the right newspaper, the right readers would follow. Yes, I would stay at night and work with the sub-editors; I essayed that it was the editing theory of maximum irritation. Accuracy and authority must be the keynotes. Nobody had mentioned our coverage of parliament, which was costly, the law report, obituaries, or the letters, but to me they were the pillars of *The Times*. They could be assured I would protect these features come what may. A few more conventional home news scoops would not go amiss – an important one a day, say, on the front page. As for rivals, it was *The Financial Times* for authority, the *Telegraph* for its range and skill in compression, and *The Guardian* for the liveliness of its feature pages. But we were not going to imitate anyone.

The question of Murdoch, his character and commitment, came up fitfully. Ross Davis said many of them had been sickened by the style of firings at an hour's notice on the advertising floors above. I said it had caused distress on *The Sunday Times*, too, and saddened me, but 'I think it would be safe to say that period is over now'. Michael Frenchman from special reports wondered if there was a deadline for viability for *The Times*. The irrepressible Ross Davis wanted to know how I got on with Murdoch personally: were we not both irritating men, he asked. I replied yes, we got on well; yes, we were irritating men. *The Observer* had it right that we had to be restraints on each other. I added that Murdoch had been very forthcoming in the vetting committee; Louis Heren should see to it, as a new editorial member on the board, that the vetting minutes were published (they never were). We had rightly insisted on editorial guarantees, but I welcomed an active proprietor. I liked his enthusiasm. He was a great hope for making *The Times* pay. He had not put a time limit on his investment, but we must do everything we could for viability consistent with retaining editorial quality. True independence required us to stand on our own feet. I had never before worked on a loss-making newspaper; I did not like the idea.

It remained for me to announce that Louis Heren was relinquishing the deputy editorship to become an associate editor. There was no more vivid reporter of the world scene, I said, no more adroit opener of closed doors and no more effective dispeller of the image of *The Times* as effete and antiquated. Those would be his three roles as associate editor. Charles Douglas-Home would succeed him with responsibilities across the floor. He would have the same free run as the editor: 'I was going to say in my absence, but even when I'm here probably,' I joked.

In my diary I noted: 'People tell me the atmosphere at the meeting was good. But does it really matter? After all, I am not seeking popularity. I must not yield to that. I've got to be tough, tough, tough and get results, improve the paper for my own sake and for the sake of *The Times*. Being popular on *The Times* is no bloody good to anybody if it continues in its present manner.'

The reporters went urgently back to their typewriters and telephones, the sub-editors in more leisurely manner at this hour unpacked their sandwiches and laid out their scissors, pencils and paste, and the editor disappeared into another conference. The 4 p.m. conference was for the night staff to learn what the day staff had proposed and what had happened to the world in the meantime. Pilpel reported on the letters chosen for publication, Hickey on the state of the leaders. The news schedules had been brought up to date, each item numbered and its length indicated. It was possible to discern what might be released to the chief sub-editors for the inside pages and what should be held back as a candidate for front-page prominence. The civil service strike had so many elements it was going to spill over on to page 2. Douglas-Home drawled, 'Let me see numbers 2, 6, 8, 9, 12 home and 6, 8, 14 foreign.' The stories were copied and sent in packages to his room. 'Can't read them all, of course,' he said, 'but it keeps them on their toes.' By the 6 p.m. conference, the editor or his deputy had to be in a position to decide which handful of stories should be run on the front page, and which should lead the paper. The night editors were impatient to plan the shape of the page, choose a photograph and supervise the detailed text editing; they hoped by 8 p.m. to have every front page story edited and 'revised': revision meant reading the work of the sub-editors before it reached the printer to make sure the sub had cut the story to the right length, had written a headline which fitted the space and the news, and had given the printer the correct instructions.

What magic there is in print. Between 6 and 7 p.m. in helter-skelter sequence I was given various scruffy bits of typed copy paper, some pages with scrawled insertions and crossings out. In the morning in three crisp columns, with the insignia aloft, the words marched immaculately on to the parade ground of public opinion as the voice of *The Times*. Hickey, I noticed, had not canvassed my idea of menacing the privileges of the civil service. I was a bit put out, but it was prudent of him to reflect on the idea; we were, at any rate, ready to endorse it at once when Christopher Patten and William Waldegrave suggested something similar in a letter we featured later in the month. Hickey's leader was brilliantly written. The body politic, he wrote, had been disabled by a kind of *locomotor ataxia*, its limbs incapable of executing the motion intended by its will. Such a large defection from duty by normally responsible public servants suggested that the habits and morality of trade unionism had now superseded any other public morality in the government of their conduct. 'And the new morality is preposterous even in its own context: the unveiling of a bust of Ernest Bevin, the greatest English trade unionist of the twentieth century, was unattended yesterday by representatives of the unions, even his own, other than by a picket to keep all the others away.'

There was a second pleasure that first evening. It lay in what happened when I made a formal visit to all the production departments and finally to the publishing warehouse, where the papers are stacked, tied and dispatched. All were so warm in their welcome. It was symbolized in the composing room, where I was invited to take over the printers' jealously guarded job of locking up the metal forme which held all the type of the front page and push it to the stereotypers for moulding. As I did this, the printers created hullaballoo, banging metal on metal, a ceremony normally performed when some long-serving printer is retired. No doubt some of the reception was an expression of relief that they had come through a period of turmoil: and no doubt some of it lay in Rees-Mogg's habit of remaining aloof from the works. But I was touched to be 'banged in' only two days after being ceremonially 'banged out' of *The Sunday Times*.

I watched the foundry men pump molten lead into the papier mâché stereotypes to create the cylindrical castings for the pages of my first edition, and, around 10 p.m., I watched in the press room as the long reels of print sped into inky blur. I shouted at the crews. They, more sensibly, coped with the din and the occasion by cupping their hands to my ear. Newspaper printing is a primitive business, noisy, messy and uncertain in comparison to electronic journalism, but there is an irreplaceable satisfaction in seeing the discrete copies of the paper emerge, a crystallization of mind and mechanics.

Some of the glow chilled on finding that the middle of the paper had been brutally mugged by the presentation of a four-page special report on inner cities: 'Urban Regeneration' some joker had written over tombstones of big black type and sooty photographs. I noted that the labour staff had done an extraordinarily thorough job of reporting the civil service stoppage, but that on page 2 it meandered in a confusing and wasteful manner; that Keith Waldegrave had successfully symbolized racially mixed schooling, finding and photographing in a Vauxhall playground a group of Cypriot, Jamaican, Anglo-Indian and Guyanese girls; and that something had gone wrong with the article on William Kendall, the leader of the striking civil servants, which was on the main feature page. It was a straightforward biography which might have been written any time; it had not assessed the man's character and pinned him down on the morality of a public service strike, which was the only reason for running a piece on him. Did this mean I would like it changed, I was asked. I said I thought that was a good idea. This led to the reappearance in the office of the Whitehall specialist writer Peter Hennessy, who had been called at home. His final edition article was a significant improvement; he had not been properly briefed, he told me later, and preferred to do the revision in the office. None the less, it became something of a talking-point that the new editor dragged reporters from their homes.

I felt as if I had hardly been home myself, such is the velocity of daily newspaper editing, when, next evening, I fretted to take a telephone call from the Chancellor of the Exchequer, Sir Geoffrey Howe. It was Budget Day and his private office had asked me if I would stand by for a talk with him at 6.30 p.m. He was late. This was awkward: the deadline for the leading article was 7 p.m. It was more than awkward: it was apocalyptic. I was down to write the main leader myself: did the Chancellor not realize how the world hung on my every word? And what a late leader would do to the health of a courteous gentleman of sixty-four called Ernest Russell, who was in charge of our production? And how the Black Friars would parse every sentence of it? I had taken on the burden in the light of morning because I wanted to wean *The Times* from Rees-Mogg's monetarism and to take the first opportunity of breaking my duck on the leader page. It was an area in which neither Hickey nor Douglas-Home was comfortable; the editor of business news, Hugh Stephenson, and the economics editor, David Blake, agreed with the general line, but Stephenson was absorbed in organizing our specialist response and Blake was writing both a personal article for the main feature page and a page 1 analysis. Blake somehow found time to give me notes, which were helpful on the arithmetic of a deflation of £3.3 billion. I was delayed in reading the Budget speech, when the door opened to admit a man in a brown porkpie hat with a red woollen scarf round his neck. I did not want to be too abrupt with the managing director, dropping off on his way home, to inspect my temporary office. Then, when I decided I had better get on with writing, Howe or no Howe, I discovered that the editor who aspired to tell the Chancellor what to do with the nation's finances had forgotten to get himself a typewriter.

I was not in much condition for three rounds with anyone when Sir Geoffrey did come on the line shortly after 7 p.m. My main concern was to deduce whether his Budget was a more subtle exercise than the headlines were bound to make it. I had no quarrel with his attack on consumption, notably the increased duties on vehicles, drink and tobacco, which would make the budget unpopular, but did he hope and intend to offset his fiscal deflation, which would on its own make perhaps 200,000 more unemployed, with non-fiscal measures that would stimulate non-inflationary investment and exports? If he did, we could endorse his strategy; if not, we would have to savage him. He had cut minimum lending rate by 2%, which was a start, but without further cuts and public investment the slump would be deepened. New telecommunications or railway electrification would have a net cost far lower than the amount committed, because, by cutting unemployment, it would reduce that fastest growing and least useful form of public spending, the payment of people to be idle. Was he ready to discriminate in the public sector borrowing requirement between current and capital spending? Or was he still a prisoner of crude monetary aggregates? His answer was hardly conclusive, but it was mildly encouraging. Yes, he wanted to see still lower interest rates. Yes, he did hope to identify 'profit centres' in the public area. There were various difficulties to do with the public sector borrowing requirement, but, yes, British Telecom was a fair case.

If we both had world enough and time we might that very evening have penetrated the mysteries of the PSBR, but I was thankful to catch the first edition. Someone had produced an eccentric typewriter and Douglas-Home gamely rushed the post-Howe pages to the printer. The leader said that the budget would merit favourable judgement if, and only if, Howe intended to follow up with non-fiscal measures and there were 'some indications' that he might. There was another sentence in midstream of the leader: 'Prudent control of the money supply is certainly required, but it is no longer an adequate prescription for policy.' *The Times* had slipped anchor on monetarism.

In these early days, Murdoch was also in a small temporary office. There had been a panic just before I arrived that he was taking a room on the first floor, in the heart of the editorial section; Douglas-Home urged me to stop it and, with visions of Murdoch nightly stalking the news room, I did not need any urging. Gerald Long, when I mentioned it, said that Murdoch had indeed spotted an office on the editorial floor he thought a useful forward position. 'No, no, Rupert, you can't do that, I told him,' said Long, amused at the incorrigibility of his charge and pleased with his own command of the situation. 'People get Rupert wrong, you know. He gets these ideas in his head, but you can tell him he's wrong and he'll laugh and agree.'

Murdoch was installing himself on the sixth floor. Pentagram, the designers, had moved in to do up Denis Hamilton's former suite adjacent to the central management. The main room, on the corner of Coley Street and Gray's Inn Road, commanded a view across the street into the sixth-floor offices of *The Sunday Times*. The room was furnished for Murdoch in light pine with a rug in front of two sofas and Australian abstracts on the walls. There was a room-length shelf behind his desk for a display of every newspaper and magazine it was possible to lay hands on. Pentagram also wished on him a standard light similar to a Belisha beacon, which went the rounds of various executives' offices when he scornfully cast it out. With Hamilton's net curtains removed and his desk in a new position, Murdoch had only to glance up and he could, if he wished, look directly into the editor's office at *The Sunday Times*. For some visitors he would stand up with a big grin and with his fingers pointed like a pistol fire bang! bang! at Frank Giles, sitting with his back to the window. It was open season on Giles from the very first day: Long had conceived one of his instant dislikes, and Murdoch was restive about *The Sunday Times*. It seemed funny at first. Ambling into my temporary office one evening Murdoch gave me a sidelong grin: 'I'm just going over to terrorize Frank.'

When Murdoch asked me to his office, I would invariably find him standing in his shirt-sleeves looking down through his big, round glasses at an open *Times*. He had curious ways of going through a paper. He would wet his thumb to turn a page and, slack-wristed, make scrawling ink marks, dyslexic ticks and crosses: 'Ahem, ye-rss (scrawl) ... mmm ... (scrawl) ye-rss ... whad'dya want overlines for (scrawl) ... nobody reads 'em (big cross).' Whereas most people would point to an item they wanted to discuss, Murdoch would lay his whole hand on it, impressing fingers and thumb possessively on the page as if having his prints taken.

The day after the budget he doodled through the two full pages of our parliamentary report. 'Mm ... I read all of that ... very intelligent ... Gerry tells me you wrote the leader yourself.' His pen lingered, then flicked a big tick. 'Best thing in the paper.' I felt as if I had been made head boy. 'Well, there's lots to do. Get to it, Harry.'

Later in the day I was asked up again. 'Sorry, sorry, you're busy I know.' He'd been thinking about staffing. We needed younger men. I should root out the old guard. But he was soon on to politics. It wasn't a bad budget. Thatcher was right to be tough. To hell with the wets. But why should the Queen get an increase of 12%? All those flunkeys at the Palace when everyone else had to batten down. Rotten example.

I had not absorbed the details about the Civil List and on the face of it 12% did not fit well with our telling the civil servants to settle for 7%. I said I'd have a look at it. It was simpler to respond to his next remark. That big tax on North Sea oil companies: why was profit a dirty word in this country? I took up the thought. My budget leader had already characterized Geoffrey Howe as Mr Hyde, in one breath announcing a pilot scheme of Government guarantees for banks so that they could help more businesses to start, and in the next imposing a £400 million tax on them. It did not make sense. But the leader reference had been cryptic: I had not attacked the fact that the tax was retrospective. I rattled on to Murdoch. The banks did not do enough for business. The *Sunday Times* series 'Banking on Britain' by Harold Lever and George Edwards had made that clear. But it was wrong for Government to take money from the banks, when it ought to be going to new companies. Perhaps I'd do a fuller leader. 'Sure, sure, Harry,' said Murdoch. I volunteered, because he seemed to have become uneasy, that I did not in the least mind talking about public affairs in this manner. I reflected later that perhaps I had bored him.

I told Douglas-Home of the talk, as I had agreed to tell him of everything; he had no comments. The morning leader conference had not been very fertile, so I discussed the subjects the same afternoon with Hickey. The odd case of the Tory Chancellor who did not like profit appealed to me, and Hickey suggested Hugh Stephenson might have a shot. He was a good choice. As a member of the Wilson committee on the City, he agreed both about the need of the banks to develop creative, long-term methods of financing new industry and about the offensiveness of Howe's tax. In quick time he delivered a crisp main editorial on both bank and oil taxation, which I headlined 'Retrospective and Retrograde'. I felt the Murdoch session had been stimulating. But the Royal finances were another matter. The hairs had risen on the back of Hickey's neck as they had on mine. In his experience, he said, these things were never quite what they seemed. He was right. We held the counterfeiter on remand for a day or two pending inquiries.

However, I had not finished with Royal finances that day. The same evening I was invited to a cocktail party at Murdoch's office in Bouverie Street, headquarters of the *Sun*. There again I heard the refrain about the Royal Family beating the pay freeze. It was the editorial director of the *Sun*, Peter Stephens, telling Murdoch how they were getting on with a blast on Royal money. The *Sun* that morning had a headline in four decks 'The Royals get a 12% no-squeeze rise in pay' and a hostile report said the Queen would receive £360,000 a year more 'despite predictions that the taxpayers' contributions to the Royal Family would be pruned'. Murdoch had moved away before I was able to tell Stephens, an old friend, that their facts were almost certainly wrong; and when I caught up with Murdoch I told him, too.

We corrected the *Sun*, and everyone else, in a *Times* leader. The headlines were based, as Hickey dryly remarked, on an annual misreading of the Civil List. First, the increase in the personal incomes of the

Queen and members of her family is only a small element of the increase in the Civil List. What it really represents is an increase in the costs of performing the public duties of the Head of State and the associated duties of members of the Royal Family. Other people's wages take most of that. In the following year, wages were to be held to 6%; other price increases, over which the Palace had no control, had to be provided for at 11%. Second, the figure for 1981 (£3,964,200 net in total) was determined on the same basis as other cash limits for the 'public sector'. The increase was 10% for the new financial year. The Civil Lists Acts deal in calendar years and it was this difference in the periods of comparison at a time of falling inflation which produced the figure of 12% for 1980 over 1981. And finally this was one cash limit that was never overrun; any deficit was made up from personal resources, usually the Queen's.

Murdoch never mentioned the 12% again, but it was only the first of many manifestations of his critical fascination with royalty. He and Long competed in declarations of virulent republicanism. I took Murdoch's at first as the badge of the Australian male, the surrogate of a hairy chest and a can of Fosters, but I was to discover it ran deeper than that. As it happened, there was, before the week was out, another example of the overlapping of Bouverie Street and Gray's Inn Road in matters Royal. When I was off on the Friday evening, Murdoch came down to the back bench where Michael Hamlyn, the executive editor at night, was examining the picture crop. He lit happily on a photograph of the Prince of Wales taking a tumble at steeplechasing. 'But there's a better one at the *Sun* you could get.' It turned out to be a freelance picture which would cost £200, much more than *The Times* would have thought of paying normally. Hamlyn, feeling that he had been bank-rolled, bought it for the front page.

There was a sense of action about the place. Board meetings were over in an hour. Within days it had been decided we would attempt the first eighty-page *Sunday Times*. *The Times* would begin the transfer to photocomposition by going live with some pages from 17 March. We would have the first ever colour magazine for *The Times* for the wedding of the Prince of Wales and colour in the paper if possible. We would see where we might produce *The Times* on the Continent, as *The Financial Times* was doing. Something would be done to improve the quality of the printing. Murdoch and Long were down in the *Sunday Times* press rooms themselves on the first Saturday night; it had come to be regarded as a no-go area for top management. They were appalled at what they observed – not enough pressmen there when they were needed, though there were hundreds on the payroll.

Long set about the administration in a rational and incisive manner. He launched a study to see whether, with the space-saving afforded by photocomposition, we could squeeze everyone into the *Sunday Times* building at 200 Gray's Inn Road, which would save £2 million a year. He talked about relieving the gloom of our offices; there was the prospect of a coffee and sandwich bar for the night editorial staff, who had to decamp to the Blue Lion pub in Gray's Inn Road: they would as soon cross the Styx as hazard the journey to the underground canteen.

There was a counterpoint to the promise of these early days. Personal animosities were hardly unknown in the Hamilton-Thomson days, but with Murdoch and Long they were cultivated like tropical plants, assuming unimagined shapes and colours, sometimes sinister, sometimes absurd.

There was a small farewell lunch for William Rees-Mogg in a boardroom annexe attended by Murdoch, Long and Hamilton and a few others. Long, scornful of the chef and kitchens he had inherited from Thomson days, went to the trouble of commissioning his wife to buy and cook a magnificent fish for the occasion, but once it had been presented on its silver tray he fell into a grumpy trance. There were long awkward silences and there was no toast from Murdoch or an embarrassed Hamilton, or even a few words of goodwill. Long's dislike of Rees-Mogg and of Giles was surpassed only by his venom for Hamilton, who had been his chairman at Reuters and resisted his transfer to *The Times*. Murdoch and Long muttered and pulled faces when Hamilton spoke at a dinner given for me to say farewell to *The Sunday Times*. He was admittedly a little self-regarding, but it was a poignant moment for him, too, still chairman of *The Times* but without any semblance of power left. 'Hamilton was a bloody disgrace. I'm going to bag him,' Long announced. 'Oh, God, Hamilton is so touchy,' Murdoch groaned. 'He goes on and on and on.' Hamilton was a ruminative chairman, indeed, but his crime seems to have been to produce an agenda and to debate whether he could or could not accept an honorarium. I was disturbed enough by all this to remind Murdoch that he owed a profound debt to Hamilton; he would never have got the papers without him. 'Don't worry,' he said, 'I know. I'll look after him.'

Murdoch and Long shared the habit of talking about politics in terms of personalities. It was a competition in machismo. To my surprise their first guests for lunch in the main boardroom in March were the Gang of Four of the SDP: Roy Jenkins, David Owen, Shirley Williams and William Rodgers. Murdoch had declared they were all crap. In the evening he came down to my room to make sure I had not caught an infection: 'Roy Jenkins didn't answer me on anything.' But at lunch he masked his feelings, asking polite, probing questions on policy to which

Rodgers responded that they were not to be tricked by people like Murdoch into premature answers. Owen delivered on toughness: the Callaghan Government should have declared a national emergency against the unions in the winter of discontent. Jenkins was nonchalantly amusing: 'I do believe the Callaghan Government did immensely better after I had gone.' But nothing could propitiate Long. He had made the mistake of arranging lunch at a table long enough for a regiment so that yards separated each person from the other; he filled the gaps with his bristling and glowering.

Long's early weapon against Giles was food and wine: he found it personally offensive that Giles knew something about France. Giles, whose French accent was better, conceded Long's superior knowledge on literature, but it was a futile gesture. Memos were hurled across the bridge to *The Sunday Times* like custard pies. 'As a devoted reader of cookery books, columns, etc.,' Long opened,

> may I say that the recipe for fried sausages and bananas with white wine, marmite and mashed potatoes given by Mme Angeloglou on Sunday was one of the most revolting I have seen for some time. Her statement that tinned soup is ideal for after-theatre suppers would not meet with universal approval either. Smoked trout soup presents a hitherto unknown hazard in dining out. I believe that sugar is the principal ingredient by weight of most tinned soups, disastrous enough for the health of the Island Race without adding more. Perhaps this is what they cook all the time in Hampstead, God help us, but it gives a rather curious picture of the readers of *The Sunday Times*.

Don't you try out the recipes yourself first, Long inquired.

The first Saturday Giles edited *The Sunday Times*, Murdoch and Long did a tour of the paper. Murdoch arrived at Giles's office shortly after the first editions had been brought up. It is quite a moment on a Sunday newspaper, five days of effort to survey and compare with the rivals. At *The Sunday Times* the tradition has been that the editor leafs through the papers in an appreciative manner, unless there is some bad error, and the senior editorial men had assembled for this when Murdoch appeared at the side door and precipitated a pantomime.

Giles asked Murdoch if he would like a drink and went on his knees to the low refrigerator by the door to get it. There was, after all, something to celebrate on the occasion of the first issue. 'Bitter lemon,' said Murdoch irritably, striding over the kneeling body of his editor to get at the newspapers on the reading table. To some of those present it was a portent. It was certainly an awkward moment. Murdoch, showing the sensitivity for editor's authority he has nurtured over many years, snapped, 'That's not right,' as soon as he got his hands on *The Sunday Times*. Giles was due to make his own tour of the works and left his

executives with Murdoch, who went through the paper in a surly manner, grumbling his comments to them. It was not perhaps 'giving instructions to a journalist' but it was queasily close. 'I stayed away,' said Hugo
Young. 'I knew what would happen.'

Giles had a companion in the pillory. Murdoch and Long, and their
lawyer Richard Searby as well, advertised an animosity for Lord Dacre,
which I was invited to share on the grounds that he had opposed my
appointment as editor of *The Times*. He had preferred Douglas-Home
as 'more academic'. His real objection appeared to be to *The Sunday
Times*, which he described, according to Murdoch, as a tearaway paper.
He had also, apparently, listened to journalists on problems that might
be raised at the Holdings board. He was too clever by half. Another of
Dacre's alleged faults, which he shared with the other four national
directors – Hamilton, Robens, Greene and Roll – was to have been
offended by Murdoch's introduction of the sixth national director, Sir
Edward Pickering. The appointment of two journalists of 'independence
and distinction' as the fifth and sixth national directors was the result of
the eleventh-hour deal between Murdoch and the *Sunday Times* chapel
in February, when they were threatening to go to court for a monopolies
inquiry. Of course, they were not consulted on names. Twenty years
previously Pickering had been a Beaverbrook editor at the *Daily
Express*, for the five years from 1957 to 1962. The rest of his career had
been spent in editorial management with IPC, owners of the Mirror
Group.

The choice may have been uninspiring, the manner of it crude, but the
event also revealed negligence in the national directors' husbandry of
their powers. In the vetting committee procedures we had elicited the
agreement from Murdoch that national directors had the power of
nomination to their ranks and he of approval only. In his alteration of
my press release, Rees-Mogg had inadvertently given the power of
nomination back to Murdoch, but when Murdoch put out his own press
release on 22 January he said that on a vacancy arising among the
national directors he had undertaken to appoint 'such a person as with
the approval of the purchaser the remaining independent directors shall
have proposed'. This left the nominating powers with the national
directors. Somebody slipped up with the Articles of Association, for
these put the power of nomination back into Murdoch's hands. Even
there, however, it said 'nominations must first be approved' by the
national directors. And this is precisely what Murdoch did not do. When
the national directors went for their meeting in the board room at
The Times, Pickering was already outside, waiting to take his place
with them. The original four had no enthusiasm for Pickering. They
were furious at Murdoch's presumption, but rejecting him at that stage

was too embarrassing and so Pickering became the sixth national director.

In a way, it was my fault that Pickering was there. He had been in the Garrick club bar one day during the final stages of Murdoch's acquisition. 'Rupert's the best thing for you all,' he said, and I mentioned this to Murdoch. There were to be times when I wished my reporting assiduity had been less.

12

THE BLACK FRIARS

Sitting down to write a leading article for *The Times* excites awkward emotions. It is as well that there is always a deadline and an irascible printer, for one begins to brood. These were the columns where Thomas Barnes drove his chariots of fire. This is where he invented the whole concept of the unsigned leading article as the soul of a newspaper. Before Barnes became editor in 1817 opinion was attributed to Junius or some such oracle. Barnes introduced the mysterious 'we' which enraged William Cobbett in the nineteenth century as much as it did Tony Benn in the twentieth. 'It gives men an idea', said Cobbett, 'that they are reading proceedings from a little council of wise men who have been sitting and deliberating on what they wish to put forth. Each paragraph appears to be a little sort of order in council; a solemn decision of a species of literary conclave.'

Cobbett was intent on exposing the 'we' as being no more than the solitary opinion of its editor, a Wizard of Oz behind the façade of Printing House Square. But readers today cannot be sure whose hand has been on the pen. The cloak of collective anonymity is passed round. Editors may dine out on omniscience but in the office they draw back from trying to demonstrate it on every modern complexity. There are many editors on all classes of newspaper who never write a leading article at all.

Denis Hamilton was an innovative editor of *The Sunday Times* but he delegated all the leader-writing to Rees-Mogg and discouraged strong opinion in the paper's name. His predecessor, H.V. (Harry) Hodson, liked leader-writing so much he continued to volunteer for it after his retirement. At *The Guardian* A.P. Wadsworth and Alastair Hetherington consulted colleagues but made their names with trenchant leaders of their own. But C.P. Scott became a frequent leader writer only in the latter part of his editorship. At *The Times* William Haley wrote one of his best-known leaders, 'Why the Pound is Weak', on the back of an envelope while being driven to work; Rees-Mogg wrote swiftly by hand, plucking his epigrams as effortlessly as refilling his fountain-pen. Yet, contrary to the common picture of his editorship, John Delane (1841–77 in the chair) never wrote leaders. He is also always wrongly credited with the authorship of the famously eloquent leader of 6 February 1852 which, in response to parliamentary attack, defined the first duty of the press as disclosure. This was the work of Robert Lowe and Henry Reeve. Delane was hardly idle or unopinionated. He had convictions and expressed them through other minds and other pens.

In the United States, by contrast, it is regarded as a mark of integrity rather than of indolence for the editor never to write a leader. There are frequently two people calling themselves 'the' editor, one responsible for opinion and another for news. At the *New York Times* and at the *Washington Post* the division is as separate as church and state. Meg Greenfield, the *Post*'s editorial page editor, sees herself and her seven leader-writing colleagues as the Vatican City inside the Italian republic, surrounded but sovereign and independent. Ben Bradlee, the *Post*'s editor, has never been to a meeting of the editorial writing group in eighteen years, and editorial writers have never attended a news meeting. This arrangement helps a newspaper reject charges of news management of the kind Governor Huey Long once levelled at *Time* Magazine's Henry Luce: 'He's the owner of a shoe shop who stocks only the shoes to fit hisself.' But schizophrenia has been observed in extreme cases, the editorial page saying perhaps that the North–South issues are a priority for the attention of all thinking people and the news pages not carrying a line about them.

An editor who oversees the whole newspaper, which is the common practice in Britain, can lay down a broad policy but he cannot hope sensibly to contribute more than a few leaders a week in a serious newspaper offering argument rather than assertion. The key question then is how he concerts the opinions of others. The custom of *The Times*, until Rees-Mogg's arrival in 1967, was for the editor to talk individually with a leader writer, which once induced one of them, E.H. Carr, to remark in the 1940s that the policy of *The Times* was decided by a committee that never met. Rees-Mogg set up a formal conference of leader writers, as I did at *The Sunday Times*. I had written leaders from very early in my career. I followed Henry Fairlie and Sidney Cursley as the leader writer for the *Manchester Evening News* in 1955 and did 750 words at 8 a.m. every day at the behest of Tom Henry, the editor, who barked out the subject as he strode through my office and often left its treatment to me.

I started a regular leader conference in my first week as editor of *The Sunday Times*. It took place in my room for between one and two hours on a Friday morning. Those I invited to attend were all Oxford men, though with mixed experience: of the private office of Ernest Bevin at the Foreign Office, Aubrey Jones's prices and incomes board, oversight of reforms in India and wartime factories in Britain, television and publishing, and the Nuremberg war trials. Everybody had other jobs on the staff, except Harry Hodson, the former editor, who brought fresh air in from outside as a Provost of Ditchley. Hugo Young and Ronald Butt came back from their beats in Westminster and Whitehall to argue politics from the liberal centre and traditional right. Young, who was also chief leader writer, wrote incisively and did most of the political leaders; he had a fine indignation. Frank Giles and, later, Peter Calvocoressi wrote on foreign affairs with competitive personal knowledge of people and places; Eric Jacobs on labour; John Whale on home issues and religion; and Peter Wilsher with bravura on anything at all.

I wrote almost all the leaders on the economy. Having lived in the stricken North-East I felt I knew the human consequences of what later became known, in Denis Healey's phrase, as sado-monetarism (I had also taken my degree in economics at Durham University). The waste of energies and talent in unemployment always appalled me. I never argued for keeping open worn-out pits and uncompetitive shipyards. I was excited by how well new industries settled in the North-East, and at *The Sunday Times* in those early years I wrote mainly about the need for incentives for industrial investment, and regional policies to build on neglected human and physical capital. *The Sunday Times* was an early advocate of incomes policies as a means of trying to increase output without inflation. I was disappointed by the short-burn of Harold Wilson's white-hot technological revolution and the failure to tackle abuses of union power which seemed to me more central to our problems. When the outgoing Chancellor Roy Jenkins asked me in 1970 why we had backed Edward Heath, I told him it was partly because of the judgement that Heath would be more radical; Iain Macleod's early death and the oil price explosion transformed the scene. Harold Lever, former Cabinet Minister and financial wizard, with whom I shared a Manchester background, then became a great influence on me. He made me appreciate the futility of trying to solve our problems in isolation from the great tides running in the world. I talked with him once a week at his flat in Eaton Square, often staying for lunch with the bankers, academics and emissaries from Europe and the United States who more and more came to ask what should be done. In the early 1970s, when I persuaded him to write articles in *The Sunday Times*, he was alone in his analysis of the way the oil price explosions in a world of floating currencies would produce slump and inflation and menace the banking and trading systems, and he was original in his prescriptions for avoiding disaster. I put Lever's views to my conference from 1973 onwards, nobody was able to counter them and we espoused them in the face of a universal complacency: William Simon, then Secretary of the United States Treasury, declared that the free market alone would prevent oil going above $10 a barrel. So did the monetarist Milton Friedman. It reached $34. In the Thatcher years I saw that inflation had to be controlled and that a shake-out of labour was necessary in many industries, not least newspapers, but I did not see why we should tolerate a persistently higher level of unemployment than any other major economy.

The procedure which grew up in my editorial conference was for me to sketch my own approach, and invite criticism, but also to ask others to expose propositions for discussion. There was almost always a real debate, not least because I wanted a clear line in the leader column. Ronald Butt and Harry Hodson led the opposition front bench on my economic views. In a generally centre-left gathering, Butt, who sided with Enoch Powell on immigration and was cool on Europe, made everyone concentrate furiously, and Wilsher was always ready to inject asperities into anything that looked like agreement. The future of Ulster, bombing in Vietnam and Cambodia, immigration, abortion law reform, Rhodesia, and the virtues of Ronald Reagan, provoked the sharpest divisions. Nothing ever raised the temperature more than the Nigerian civil war with Giles and me opposed to Biafra's split, fearing endless secessions in Africa, and Butt and Young uniting behind the Ibos and General Ojukwu. The whole paper was divided in this way. When the London Biafrans marched outside *The Sunday Times* building demanding my head there were those inside the building ready to give it to them. My practice when divisions ran this deep was to make sure the leader dealt fully with the critics' points and to allow expressions contrary to the policy of the paper to appear on the feature pages. For this reason I accepted the colour magazine's identification with the Biafran cause.

On Ulster, John Whale was always pressing political initiatives and Butt was always sceptical. Once I flew back from Europe to write a leader because Giles, as acting editor, and Young, as chief leader writer, were utterly at odds on the paper's response to the *Fearless* proposals for Rhodesia. Ordinarily, I summed up and assigned the writers, usually choosing the one who best represented the views of the conference but asking him to acknowledge minority points. There were rare occasions when I used the editor's prerogative to sum up against the drift, as Clement Attlee did sometimes at Cabinet, which meant I had to write the leader myself. We voted only at general elections and then informally; and I always wrote these leaders.

This was how *Sunday Times* policy was decided over a period of fourteen years. I imagined the same kind of thing would happen at *The Times*. I looked forward to testing my convictions on the 'Black Friars' of Northcliffe's demonology. Rees-Mogg had clearly dominated the political-economic deliberations in his conference, though it had been intriguing to note that when he became convinced we should return to the gold standard he had espoused the cause in personal articles rather than in a leader.

Rees-Mogg's *Times* backed the Conservative party in every general election, but it periodically expressed yearnings for a coalition of the right-centre. In the late 1960s it encouraged Cecil King's lunatic notion of a coup against Harold Wilson's Labour Government in favour of a government of business leaders led by Lord Robens. In the autumn election of 1974, it predicted that economic crisis would produce a coalition government of national unity well inside five years and urged one there and then between Conservatives and Liberals. (This was the election in which the final editorial in *The Sunday Times* expressed a preference for the Labour party for the first time in its history.) In his last hours as editor, in February 1981, Rees-Mogg had enjoyed another small fling and (quoting Jane Austen's *Emma*) had publicly embraced Shirley Williams of the Gang of Four as the next Prime Minister. She had a second-class mind, he pronounced, but a nice sensibility and was a peacemaker, unlike the quarrelsome Foot and the partisan Thatcher. 'I've had enough of Thatcher and Foot,' Rees-Mogg said with an engaging giggle in a brief encounter on the pavement outside *The Times*.

I did not take his quixotic display of affection seriously. My intention was to try to position *The Times* where the political parties, including the emergent Social Democrats, would earn our support according to their responses on central issues: a revival of the economy, a zest for international cooperation in free trade and Western partnership in defence, a dedication to personal liberties against state, corporate and trade-union power. The economic dialogue between Labour and Conservative was sterile. If I was critical of government by abacus, I was depressed by Labour's disorderly regression; I saw them as hostile to enterprise, insular, captive to the big unions, careless of the risks of hyper-inflation in indiscriminate public spending without control of pay. I welcomed the secession of the four former Labour Ministers and the founding in January of the Council for Social Democracy just before Murdoch's take-over. I was left in no doubt where Murdoch and Long stood. 'Did you see what that shit Rees-Mogg has done?' said Murdoch referring to the Shirley Williams leader. Long was similarly enraged. It was an attempt to tie *The Times* to the weak-kneed Social Democrats. When by way of diversion I remarked that Rees-Mogg had a point that the British single-vote system was Russian roulette, Long gave me an intensive viva on the deficiences of the German system from which I was lucky to escape alive. Both of them exaggerated the significance of the

Rees-Mogg leader; it should have been regarded as one of his political entertainments, the *jeu d'esprit* of a man in sight of the end of a long sentence to be solemn. I would aim for consistency in *Times* policy but I did not feel bound by Rees-Mogg's parting fling any more than I did by his attachment to coalitions or monetarism.

Rees-Mogg used to conduct the leader rites from the Kennedy-style rocking-chair in his cluttered office, following the noon news conference. I moved the meetings to the airy conference room. Owen Hickey, who had spent all his working life at *The Times*, was the central figure. 'He's the conscience of the paper,' said John Grant. Everyone was a little in awe of his fastidiousness. Once asked if his grounds for refusing to join the journalists' union were political, he said, 'No, aesthetic'. In appearance, certainly, he looks as people would like the editor of *The Times* to look, silver-haired, slight and forever sixty, the archetypal bachelor don, though in fact he married late. He has a delightful shy smile, but a distinct slant to the eyes under a tight-stretched brow can give a sly air and he cultivates asperity as well as reticence. Rees-Mogg used to give a Tuesday morning conference on general policy. Hickey dubbed them Moggologues. Of Haley, he said 'the old boy's not really an intellectual'. And he did not approve of my appointment to the editorship.

He was nearing his fifty-seventh birthday that March of 1981 after twenty-six years as a leader writer, appointed by Haley from *The Times Educational Supplement* which he joined in 1949 straight from Oxford, after army service. 'Journalism', he declared to another leader writer, 'is a *pis aller*. Better than being a second-class don at a second-class university.' As associate editor he was in charge of the leaders and letters, and Bernard Donoughue, when he arrived, remarked that the arrangements reminded him of nothing so much as his own days at Oxford with Hickey marking the essays brought to the tutor's room. I was both exasperated and enchanted by Hickey. I could not work it out at first. Was I speaking in Ki-Swahili? He did not respond. I made a point of opening the conference by asking if he would like to lead off, but often he had to be cranked up to say anything at all.

'You've done wonders with old Owen,' said Douglas-Home, rubbing his hands.

'I don't see it.'

'But you've got him writing again. He went on writer's strike with William. Just wouldn't write. Rees-Mogg upset him by putting in his own stuff without telling anyone what he was up to. He'd just say the leader was taken care of.' This made it decidedly puzzling. The conclusion I had come to was that Hickey had a distaste for the vigorous discussion of the kind that flourished at *The Sunday Times*. 'I have one up my sleeve,' he would say about a leader he preferred not to discuss at conference. He was cryptic. He had no difficulty debating when he wanted. He liked pricking balloons. His moods bothered me a great deal because Hickey was a brilliant writer of leaders. He could tolerate, and indeed would often produce, a leader which was all analysis and no opinion, but he had a rare skill in identifying the points of principle in a tangled issue. He had authority, he was without political prejudice and his language was always enjoyable. When, a few weeks into my editorship, a pompous reader wrote to ask which vulgar person from the *Sun* had been brought in to write *The Times* leaders, I was happy to send for inspection a few Hickey leaders including one on the prayer book which concluded with a fine flourish:

> Unless the Church takes more seriously the commission it received in 1974 and keeps the Book of Common Prayer *in* use as well as *for* use, it will carelessly abuse many loyal sons and daughters and deprive the next generations of acquaintance with an uncommon efflorescence of Christianity: a dignified, settled, devout and valid liturgy.

There were three other men on the home side.

Geoffrey Smith, a rumpled figure of fifty-one with pinched eyes, had been writing many of the political editorials, coming to the job by way of Edinburgh University, the *Edinburgh Evening News* and *Times* obituaries. He startled me by the vehemence with which he advanced middle-of-the-road opinions, Two Points this side, and Two Points that side. The Crucifixion was not a good thing, but then it was not altogether a bad thing either.

George Hill, a moustached, handsome, dreamy man just past forty who rides his bicycle erectly through King's Cross traffic as if it was the High at Oxford, had responsibility for housing, social security, the trade unions and the countryside. He realized for me in a twinkling an ambition I had to revive the celebrated *Times* fourth leader. This did not go back to the anecdotage of the eighteenth-century coffee-house, as readers like to imagine; it was an invention of Northcliffe who, in 1914, after six years of frustration trying to get things done at his *Times*, wrote a memo: 'Humbly beg for light leading article until I return.' He had enjoyed light leaders in the *Daily Telegraph* and in *Bicycling News* when he was a boy. They had continued in *The Times* until Rees-Mogg dropped them. No doubt they had become stale. But in Hill's hands, and agreed at only one a week on Saturdays, the fourth leader flowered. With others, he wrote on LBDs – little black dresses; the colour of the British passport in Europe; snowfalls; the phenomenon of a man trying to break *into* prison; insomnia; the art of political egg-throwing; the eligibility of 150 pythons for residence in England; and he explained the mystery of why the British had not gone in for Citizen's Band radio once it was legalized: 'Why should they? They had made their point, but as usual they had nothing to say to each other, particularly not to people they had not been properly introduced to, and least of all when identified as Bushy Tail of Bagshot or Caddis Fly of St Andrew's.'

The third home writer, Marcel Berlins, aged forty, was a wetback: he had swum in from across the specialists' corridor as the legal correspondent and stayed because he found it congenial. He is a South African with a rapid tongue and a sense of mischief. I had for many years admired his reporting of *Sunday Times* cases.

Foreign leaders were principally the responsibility of Richard Davy, a man of fifty permanently creased by worry, who had been twenty-six years on *The Times*. Both his father and his brother were celebrated *Observer* journalists. At Oxford he had been plagued by ill health and took only a third-class degree, but his merit showed in his acquisition of fluency in languages and the brilliance of his reporting on the Russian invasion of Czechoslovakia. He had a profound knowledge of Eastern Europe. For a spell he was executive editor at nights, but was not a success because the role required a series of brutal decisions for which Davy's mind was too finely tuned.

He was assisted by Richard Owen, at thirty-four the youngest of the group, who was writing on the Middle East; and Peter Strafford, aged forty-five, who had dominion over France, Iberia and Latin America. A large part of the globe but, as James Reston said of the American people, they would do anything for Latin America except read about it, and Strafford, a man with a talent for diffidence, had found it hard to get into the paper. It had obviously not been much help to have caned his foreign editor. Strafford had been head boy at Eton and had found cause to punish young Douglas-Home; he had joined *The Times* in 1960, five years ahead of Douglas-Home, but the young bounder had leapfrogged into positions of power.

As a group, we may have been an amusing social slice; as the voice of England we were eccentric in the manner of the archetypal civil service, short on experience of industry, science and life north of Potters Bar, but additionally with no one who had been inside government or run anything. If this was the citadel of *The Times* it was stultified by charm. Specialist contributors might cover the subject gaps, but these worried me less than an air of amiable amateurism, responding to the news well enough with intelligent analysis in moderate tone, but not driven by a will to have practical effect. At its best, with the brilliant impertinence of a Rees-Mogg, the result was enjoyable, even stimulating; at its worst it was style without substance. Somehow we had to get into the engine-room of government policy, leading as well as reacting. I was sure it could be done without losing tone.

It was both easier and harder than with *The Sunday Times*. Six days a week with two or three leaders a day gave more opportunities for definition but also for losing focus in the blur of events. I was disappointed that we did not seem ready to make the running on some central issues. George Hill, keeper of the smile, would think nothing of a weekend tramping an area in his walking boots before *The Times* pronounced on a motorway or a wood to be felled, and he did that with passion, but when it came to the crucial issue of the trade unions his good nature got the better of him. I thought this the best opportunity for many years to tackle the injustices and inefficiencies of the closed shop and seek to curtail some of the unions' privileged immunities from the damaging consequences of strikes. *The Times* had to be in the vanguard, using its independence from left and right to tilt the balance of debate. The inclination or the custom, I was not sure which, was to fix the subject for an essay rather than start with a conviction that had to be justified and elaborated. I feared the ghost of Barnes when I took part in conversations which went:

'We should do a leader on Belgium.'

'Why?' I asked. 'What's happened?'

'Nothing. Very long time since we wrote on Belgium.'

It took me a while to confess to my feeling that we ought not to write a leader unless we had something relevant to say. There was a place for analysis and updating in *The Times*, but the leader column should be about getting things done or undone and at least be an expression of values. I asked for policy papers we could discuss so that we were not always reacting to events. I did as much leader editing as I could, delegating also to Douglas-Home and Hickey. They had no taste for salvage work. I would find Douglas-Home gazing morosely at a leader and sighing, as he popped it into the pneumatic tube, '*Not* a very good leader, I'm afraid.' Hickey held the offending copy at a distance from his person. He was adept at winkling out bad sentences, reluctant to add or rewrite. Douglas-Home was good at labelling mutton as lamb; his headlines were often the only positive thing about a leader. Hickey, by contrast, was a specialist in the genre of 'Small earthquake in Chile, not many dead'.

These perplexities and depressions were eased a good deal with the arrival of Bernard Donoughue and other changes in the group. I was delighted to attract Donoughue from the Economist Intelligence Unit because of his combination of intellectual distinction and practical experience. Oxford, Harvard, the news rooms of *The Sunday Times* and *Sunday Telegraph*, the court of governors of the London School of Economics during its riotous days, No. 10 Downing Street, the ill-lit Labour committee rooms of St Pancras North. It was the ideal induction course for a *Times* leader writer. Alan Watkins in an article in the *Spectator* in 1983 criticized me for employing Donoughue 'who was not a journalist but an academic who has turned to the political advising trade'. In fact, as a glance at *Who's Who* would have shown, Donoughue began his career after Harvard as a reporter for *The Sunday Times* and later for the *Sunday Telegraph* where he wrote leaders. He has harvested insights at every stage and, though a Labour supporter most of his life, he travels without party baggage. None of the left-right labels adhere to his restless curiosity. A tic he has picked up from his time inside the secretive and paranoid world of government is a habit of taking one aside and confiding in a conspiratorial voice that it is a nice day for cricket.

The chemistry of the conference was further improved by the attendance of three men with other duties, Adrian Hamilton, editor of business news, who was especially knowledgeable about energy; Brian Horton, the foreign editor, who had run Reuters and been in business on his own account; and David Blake, the economics editor, a one-time Labour parliamentary candidate and a former Common Market correspondent. Blake shared with Donoughue a readiness to shed personal politics. The style of walking around with his shirt-tail out was his own; I decided to take it as a daily indicator of the level of sterling. Blake breakfasted on economic indices.

Something like a zest for debate began to be possible with the return as a full-time leader writer of Edward Mortimer, a Fellow of All Souls. He came back from the US where he had spent two years writing a book about the history of Islam. Rees-Mogg used to say he was the cleverest person on the paper. He joined in 1967 as No. 2 man in Paris, went back to All Souls, and then returned in 1973 at the suggestion of Douglas-Home to specialize on the Middle East. His practical experience was limited, but he was ready to give any proposition a spin on the lathe of his intellect.

We sat daily for half to three quarters of an hour round the long pine table, uninterrupted except for the cricket scores: Hickey and Smith were MCC members and next to prison overcrowding it was Berlins's favourite topic. I sat at the top with Hickey at silly mid-on, Smith mid-off, Donoughue at cover, and Douglas-Home in the slips. As I surveyed the group I thought of the remark of one of Delane's leader writers, the Reverend Thomas Mozley: 'To write a leading article may take only from two hours to two hours and a half, but then all the rest of your time you are a crouching tiger, waiting, waiting, waiting, to make your spring.'

Teeth did, after a time, emerge. Convictions surfaced. For Hickey the cause was Ulster, for Donoughue waste in the public sector, for

Douglas-Home the reintroduction of conscription, for Hamilton the Soviet gas pipeline, and for Davy relations with the Soviet Union. There were successes and reverses. 'We must back him', Donoughue declared at once when Michael Heseltine was set on forcing a referendum on councils who wished to levy a supplementary rate. 'It's unconstitutional', declared Hickey, rousing himself to battle. It was a good debate, Donoughue's priority for restraining irresponsible councils and their public sector unions competing with Hickey's for retaining freedom from central government. It was the only time in this area that Donoughue failed to carry the conference with him; but he faithfully reflected its views in the leader he wrote. Douglas-Home also came to grief early on over national service. Hickey hated the idea as much as one of Douglas-Home's arguments: 'It's a way to keep the classes in touch with each other.' Hamilton succeeded in having *The Times* back the planned Soviet gas pipeline to Western Europe with a convincing exposition of the case against it followed by an even more convincing exposition of the case for it. He was slow and painful in delivery but powerful in effect. His view chimed with Davy's attitude. Murdoch, in odd circumstances in 1982 which I will relate, wanted a declaration of economic war against the Soviet Union. It was an idea that Davy had lived with and endlessly dissected; his leaders were scrupulously argued. I agreed with his rejection of it. I had talked for hours with Henry Kissinger about his dealings with the Soviets, as the Americans put it, and I had been reinforced in my conviction that, obnoxious as the regime was, there was more danger to the world in a return to the Cold War. It was possible, with toughness and seriousness, to make progress with them; in a thermonuclear world there was an insistent responsibility to try.

As the new group settled down Donoughue joined Hickey as a writer of the more important domestic leaders. Douglas-Home and Hamilton wrote infrequently. Horton did not write at all, but challenged. Douglas-Home's style was to lob in questions, though not at quite as fast a rate as at the Hamilton lunches. It took Donoughue a month to get over what I called the Barnes effect of feeling that every sentence had to be lapidary, but then his authority broke through. Few other people could have spotted and exposed as he did a Treasury submission to the Megaw Inquiry into civil service pay which would enable civil servants to enjoy privileged exemption from cash limits and privileged access to the contingency reserve. We ran this news in the leader column only, as Delane liked to do, but with comment which maintained the momentum of our economic policy, pointing out that since Mrs Thatcher had taken office the number of jobs in public administration and defence had fallen by only 2·5 per cent while they had fallen by 8 per cent in the economy as a whole.

'Bernard's got a head of steam,' said Douglas-Home, who had been impressed that Donoughue was uninhibited on Labour party matters: he excoriated the sectarian, intolerant, anti-parliamentarian Left which had taken over the 'rotten' party organization and he suggested Michael Foot should make way. He was tough on British Telecom and British Gas, interested less in the ideology of public ownership than the effects of monopoly. But there were tensions with Donoughue's emergence. It reduced the opportunities for Geoffrey Smith, though he had a regular signed column of his own; and Donoughue and Hickey did not hit it off. Donoughue thought Hickey was negative; Hickey thought Donoughue combative and they disagreed about Ulster.

As I prepared to leave *The Sunday Times*, John Whale had said, 'You'll find Owen Hickey a good man except on Ulster.'

'Can we discuss Ireland?' said Donoughue in conference.

'Of course,' I replied. 'Owen, would you lead us?'

'What is there to talk about?'

'What we can do', Donoughue insisted, 'to re-create political life in the North. It's that or the gunmen. And there's got to be dialogue with the South.'

'We could have civil war,' Hickey interjected sharply, 'if people go on talking loosely about unification.'

Hickey and Donoughue argued to a standstill. I postponed a leader. Hickey, a Catholic with a farm in the Republic, wrote a cogent memorandum. To him the starting-point was to recognize that the nature of the quarrel was about allegiance. 'The English have difficulty in understanding this – putting it down to bigotry, or religious intolerance, or moral inferiority or national temperament because they have not suffered a crisis of that kind in their modern history.' There could be no wavering in the commitment to the majority in Ulster that their status within the United Kingdom could not be changed without their consent. It was dangerous to try to make them more amenable to the prospect of Irish unity by talk of withdrawal, timetables, blueprints for a new Ireland and the like. They would organize to resist. 'And it merely convinces the IRA it is making ground. Hope is its oxygen supply. It must be denied it.'

Donoughue's response was to say he accepted the commitment on consent but the IRA would flourish if there was no movement in Ulster; it was a way of cutting the flow of dollars from America. There had to be more attempts at power sharing, new institutions however stumbling, so that the minority could still hope for something from politics. It was really a question of a difference of emphasis between the two men. I respected both their positions. I maintained Hickey's control of Ulster leaders but asked him to acknowledge Donoughue's points. He did. His leaders were resolute on the principle of consent but they acknowledged the importance of political movement and relations with the Republic. The clash was worthwhile.

In the light of the later developments with Mrs Thatcher and Murdoch the political line that emerged needs to be described. The notable feature to me was that a consensus was fairly quickly and smoothly established. Our attitude to the three parties was one of despair for Labour as an alternative government; goodwill for the emergent Liberal/SDP Alliance; and support with vigilance and chastisement for the Conservatives. The Tories, it seemed to us, put controlling inflation first and sacrificed growth. Labour proposed to go for growth at whatever risk to inflation. The SDP Alliance was trying to define a course which offered reasonable growth with reasonable price stability, not wholly convincingly, but at least they sought to be rational instead of trying to instil faith by re-iteration. We were not far out when we wrote in October 1981: 'From what we have seen so far the central demand for Proportional Representation in elections is crucial to the party's long-term success.' We also thought fair voting was overdue and we said so. Donoughue and Smith disagreed about the way the SDP leader should be chosen. Smith preferred it to be the choice of the parliamentary party, Donoughue of the party in the country. We went with Smith. The SDP went with Donoughue.

Many people of nervous disposition believe that it is the duty and tradition of *The Times* to maintain public confidence in the Government of the day; among politicians this seems to become almost an article of faith on receiving the seals of office. It has only erratic credence. The most I felt was that Government might have the benefit of any doubt. With the Conservative Government headed by Mrs Thatcher we were stalwart in support in some difficult passages, notably over pay and hunger strikes, but critical of important aspects of economic policy. Our assessment of Mrs Thatcher was measured. The words we used most frequently about her were determination, honesty, consistency, strength, integrity, resource, courage. When I was supporting Michael Edwardes in refusing to budge from his famous 3·8% pay offer which almost shut down British Leyland for good in November 1981, I criticized Michael Foot for fudging the inescapable correlation between wages and prices and jobs and added: 'Mrs Thatcher is often accused of harshness and folly but she does not attempt to deceive the people, uncomfortable though her utterances may be.' Her controversial abolition of the Civil Service Department was praised as brave radicalism in a Donoughue leader headed 'Madame Guillotine'. We generously exempted her from our impatience over the Treasury's failure to pursue currency stability by entering sterling in the European Monetary System: 'The dithering and increasingly inelegant equivocation is not, as everyone knows, the work of Mrs Thatcher herself. It is not her style.'

On the other side, there was a lack of sensitivity which worried most people in conference. Nobody had a good word to say for Mrs Thatcher's television address during the riots. It was a time for leadership to relieve the hatreds in society and to restore confidence, not for scoring points on the ordinary battleground of politics. 'Not for the first time,' we said, 'she was unable to strike the right note when a broad sense of social understanding was required.' A more persistent misgiving was her resentment of criticism. We knew it from our own encounters with the Prime Minister and we heard it in our individual meetings with members of her Cabinet. I did not ask Douglas-Home or Donoughue or Smith who had said various things to them and they did not ask me who 'someone who should know' was. It was, in 1981, the least harmonious Conservative administrative within memory. We thought she was entitled to change it that autumn and insist that those who took posts should accept the self-discipline necessary. But the corollary was a wider debate in the party and so, in the leader columns and in ample space on the news pages, I helped Edward Heath, Ian Gilmour, Norman St John Stevas and Geoffrey Rippon to mount their attack. 'This is not because they have a wholly convincing alternative or that they represent a higher order of politician,' I wrote.

> Mrs Margaret Thatcher is the best Prime Minister we have got. It is rather because the air in the Tory house has become fetid. New thoughts must circulate. Unfortunately, given existing technologies, they have to be attached to personalities. This complicates matters when Mr Heath, say, makes a well-argued speech but he is not to be disqualified or derided merely because he is a former Prime Minister. It is doing the Tory Party a good deal of harm for it to resemble less of a Church and more of an Inquisition.

This political line was unpopular with Murdoch and Long, and the pressures to change it developed perceptibly as Mrs Thatcher's standing in the opinion polls failed to revive and the Social Democrats gained ground. Murdoch's technique was not to criticize particular leaders or, after the first week, to suggest topics, but to make what would please him unmistakably clear. A former *Times* reporter, Michael Leapman, says in a book about Murdoch that I discussed specific phrases in leading articles with him. This would be like asking Sweeney Todd for a close shave. I never did that, nor did I ever seek his opinion on a leader, and Leapman in a letter to me now says he meant to suggest that it was Murdoch who raised specific phrases with me. But this is also wrong and it misunderstands the way Murdoch operates. He is not a miniaturist. He creates an aura. The aura he created in 1981-2 was one of bleak hostility to Edward Heath and the Tory rebels, and contempt for the Social Democrats. He did this by persistent derision of them at our meetings and on the telephone, by sending me articles marked 'worth reading!' which espoused right-wing views, by jabbing a finger at head-lines which he thought could have been more supportive of Mrs Thatcher – 'You're always getting at her' – and through the agency of his managing director, Long. I published two big articles by Lord Lever on inter-national measures to control currencies and interest rates as the key to our economic revival; they supported *The Times*'s view that Mrs Thatcher should give more leadership in this area. Long exhibited a hostility quite out of proportion to the nature of the subject – on which he had expressed no previous interest. He harangued me for a whole lunchtime. Murdoch himself came more and more to object to the balanced assessment of the Government I have described, calling later in my editorship for more 'conviction', which meant more cheer-leading. When he said that the leaders were 'thoughtful' it was not a warming remark but a criticism. As the unemployment totals approached 3 mil-lion, both he and Long complained that *The Times* should be writing about the numbers of people who *were* employed. 'We have more people in employment than they do in Europe!' became a refrain. None of this represented a reasonable exchange of views between editor and pro-prietor, unexceptional on any newspaper. The tone was assertive and hostile to debate. Such incidents were not isolated. They amounted to pressures to manipulate the independent editorial policy of *The Times* and they escalated into a campaign, as I shall relate.

Inside *The Times*, by contrast, there was little argument on economic policy. Much the most serious division was over the Middle East and it is worth elaborating for the light it throws on our working methods and relationships. Edward Mortimer and Richard Owen were convinced that Yasser Arafat's Palestine Liberation Organization must be involved in any negotiations to provide a home for Palestinians on the Israeli-occu-pied West Bank of the Jordan. This was a respectable view. It was, after all, the policy that the European Community, led by Lord Carrington for Britain, had put forward at Venice in June 1980. I was sure it was wrong.

'How can you expect the Israelis to talk to the PLO when they murder them on their way home from synagogue?' I asked.

'The Americans must force them to,' was the reply. 'And look at what that madman Begin is doing to the Arabs on the West Bank: more arrests, more raids, more Israeli settlements.'

This was an issue on which *The Times* might have a real influence in London and Washington, if not Jerusalem and Damascus. President Carter's Camp David agreement between Sadat and Begin had led to Israeli withdrawal in the Sinai but it was stalled on the scope and nature of transitional Arab self-government on the West Bank. Egypt, Israel, the United States, Jordan and the Palestinian inhabitants of the West Bank and Gaza were mentioned in the accords. President Reagan was feeling his way with the Europeans hoping, and the Israelis fearing, that the United States would go along with the Venice declaration and involve the PLO.

The Jordan flowed through *The Times* conference room as Lady Eden once said the Suez Canal flowed through her drawing room. Horton and Donoughue were as passionate on the Israeli side as Mortimer and Owen on the Arab. The first two focussed on a democratic state surrounded by enemies who would not acknowledge her right to exist. The others focussed on a dispossessed Palestinian people for whom the PLO was the recognized voice. Douglas-Home was with Owen and Mortimer. As foreign editor he had organized a series on the Palestinians which enraged the Jewish lobby in Britain, but in these discussions he stayed on the sidelines. Hamilton tended to go along with them also. As the arguments waxed Donoughue felt the others were peddling a Foreign Office line with a whiff of antisemitism. Mortimer thought that I was soft on Israel. He put up a PLO poster in his room.

I approached the issue rather differently. I shared Mortimer's and Owen's sympathy for the Palestinians and their criticisms of Begin. I had talked with educated Palestinians on the West Bank. But I did not think the PLO could deliver. It was so hated by Israelis, so suspect in its formal renunciation of terrorism, that no conceivable Israeli Government would negotiate with it. America would be wasting its energies and time trying to change that. I joined a dinner with Moshe Dayan in London in April. He was fixed in his judgement that the PLO aim was to establish Palestine 'in the place of Israel, not by the side of Israel'; he said the American sale of Awacs to Saudi Arabia had stiffened Israel's determination to fight for its security. American pressure, I thought, was more realistically deployed bending Begin on the degree of autonomy for the West Bank Arabs; Abba Eban gave me some ideas on this when he called on me at *The Times*. I also had lingering hopes that Jordan could be brought into the diplomacy. It had been excluded in 1974 when an Arab summit designated the PLO as the sole voice of the Palestinians. But that might change. It was moderate. King Hussein was trusted. It was to explore these possibilities that while I was at *The Sunday Times*, as I described earlier, I had insisted that Frank Giles should carry out his interview with the King which Murdoch asked him to cancel.

As for being soft on Israel, and unfeeling about the Palestinians, I restrained myself from reminding Mortimer that at *The Sunday Times* I had endured a great deal of criticism for documenting cases of ill-treatment of Arabs on the West Bank by the Israeli military. Throughout our arguments I tried to stay pragmatic, but I began to share some of

Donoughue's emotions when the British Government found 'insuperable practical difficulties' in October to sending a British Minister to honour Dayan's funeral; he died six months after our London meeting. Actions as insensitive as that had, to me, the same consequence as *The Times* backing the PLO; they inflamed Israel's national mood of suspicion and strengthened Begin against the more moderate Israeli Labour party's support for an arrangement with Jordan leading to Palestinian self-government.

Events tended to justify scepticism about the PLO. At the Arab summit at Fez in November they vetoed, with Syria's encouragement, the eight-point peace plan devised by Crown Prince Fahd of Saudi Arabia which included the 'right of all states in the region to live in peace'. Owen wrote a leader. It was critical of the PLO and its factions, but I strengthened it by writing towards the end:

> It is worst news of all for the Palestinian people who ever since the birth of Israel have paid dearly for the extremism and intrigue of the Arab radicals who destroyed the Lebanon, nearly destroyed Jordan and will not rest, they say, until they have destroyed Israel. The Arab radicals can frustrate the Saudis and the Jordanians and would like to frustrate the Egyptians but they cannot deliver anything except what they have delivered in the past: bloodshed and futility.

Owen's leader said the ball was now in Israel's court to show that there was life in Camp David by offering a genuine measure of autonomy on the West Bank, and I agreed with him. When Begin failed to do that, I was at one with Mortimer and Owen in calling for American pressure to be exerted. In February Owen wrote presciently: 'The danger is that Israel might take advantage of Syrian weakness to launch a large-scale invasion of Southern Lebanon with the aim of eliminating Palestinian bases.' But I felt I always had to be vigilant. In January, when I did not edit a leader, a reference to the desirability of involving the PLO popped up again. It did now carry the rider that it should first give proper recognition to Israel, but I would have crossed out the reference to the PLO.

I reserved the right to make additions and alterations of this nature so that *The Times* kept close to a policy, whether over the Middle East, or the trade unions, or the economy. I regarded the clarity and consistency in *Times* policy as one of the editor's essential duties. I edited for language and emphasis as well as direction. Listening, for instance, to Geoffrey Smith decapitating the syllables prepared one for a leader dripping in blood. It was always clear, on time, and as agreed, but it never had that 'little bit of devil' Barnes thought so necessary. I never had to add or change a word in Hickey. With Davy there was only one period when he was off-colour and I had to write material into a leader on Poland. The arrangement I had with Blake and Hamilton, who had other responsibilities, was that I was glad to use a note from them as the basis of a leader: sometimes doing no more than adding a few phrases. I thought the system worked well; they seemed pleased with the result.

There was nothing unusual in my action. In Rees-Mogg's time, I was told, Hickey was irritated enough by revision to remark on one occasion: 'I've stopped reading *The Times* leaders even when I've written them.' Most editors of *The Times* have been uncompromising revisers. Delane claimed 'not a column has been published which has not had some of my handwriting in the margin'. The diaries of Barrington-Ward (1941–8) are full of reference to the need to do heavy work on this or that man's leader. On *The Guardian*, C.P. Scott encouraged diversity of expression but it had to be consistent with his vision of the moral and political unity of the paper. Leader writers whose work was rewritten or spiked never heard why. Scott's tradition was that they would learn by example.

In the autumn, however, Douglas-Home said the full-time leader writers were restive. I invited them in for a talk. It was Davy who put the point. They recognized the editor's prerogative, he said, but was there an implication in my changes to leaders that I was not satisfied with their work? I explained my approach. I did not want to maintain the tradition of discursive essays but to revive the older tradition of Barnes that leaders should be 'designed to be acted on'. I thought the meeting cleared the air. But I heard later that Mortimer attributed some of what he called my 'pro-Israeli' attitude on the Middle East to an appeasement of Murdoch, supposedly a Zionist on account of his *New York Post*'s Jewish readership. It was not so. My view was my own, right or wrong, as it had been before Murdoch ever came on the scene. And Murdoch never once raised Israel or the Middle East with me. His preoccupations were closer to home.

13
CHANGING
THE TIMES

Journalism being a predatory profession, I was fortunate in the way calamity and scandal followed my inauguration at *The Times*. Hardly had one shock been headlined than another followed. Someone tried to kill the President of the United States, and someone else the Pope; and someone did kill President Sadat. A pistol was pointed at the Queen. Our cities were shaken by riot, a mass murderer of women went on trial, there were new spy mysteries, and the political mould of fifty years was broken. Had *The Times* been the sensational newspaper its readers feared it would become in Murdoch's hands, we would have had to ransack the type cases to cope with it all. These events were a challenge to any newspaper, but within *The Times* there was a deeper issue: the paper's conception of itself. Murmuring that *The Times* is a newspaper of record was all very well, but it did not begin to answer the question of what it should record and how it should do it, nor of how it should set about recording what others insisted on concealing. I had no instant answers. They emerged in the collision of events, with bruises on the way.

News wrenched the staff of *The Times* from anxiety about the future – but it also tested their readiness to respond to a different approach. I had been editor of *The Times* for twenty-one days when President Reagan was shot in an attempted assassination on 30 March 1981. I hurried back to the office. Executive night editor Michael Hamlyn had prepared a brief lead to the paper, Douglas-Home had agreed that Geoffrey Smith in America should do a leader, and they were sitting side by side in a half-empty room awaiting the reports from four staffmen in New York and Washington. The approach I decided that night was to become the template for all our coverage of big events. First, the hallmarks of *The Times* had to be detailed documentation and authoritative explanation. This required space as well as careful briefing of the writers. Second, length without logic is a disservice. We had to organize the way we presented material very carefully. There were two elements to the universal curiosity about the Reagan story. Everyone would want as accurate and full an account as possible of what had happened, but they would also want to know about violence in America, what kind of person tried to kill the President and what would happen if Reagan died. The first curiosity was best satisfied by a crisp narrative of the shooting, the second by more discursive background reports. I was convinced the narrative in *The Times* should not be diverted and diluted by answering any questions other than 'what happened?', and similarly that the answers to the consequential questions were too interesting to be mixed up in the narrative, where they would also be vulnerable to late cuts for space. It is not as simple to carry this out as it sounds. Daily newspapers responding to big news invariably muddle the two elements. Time is one reason. Another is that the news agencies are the main bulk suppliers of news on international events and they tend to throw everything in on Jeb Stuart's American Civil War principle of 'fustest with the mostest'. Nor is it easy to impose logical divisions on a fast-developing story. Overlap and repetition are natural.

There was to be a lot of heartache in *The Times* over these problems in the following six months, but that night everything worked well. I found it easy to divide the story. In addition to the narrative, I asked for a separate report on the gunman, another on the violent history attendant upon American Presidents, and a third on the character of the next in line, Vice-President Bush. These all arrived exactly as requested to be planned into the page. I reached a second conclusion that night, which was that our response on big events was not confetti we should ask the reader to gather through the paper; it should be concentrated for ease of reference. Because the death of President Reagan would have been a momentous event for the world and because it was then a distinct possibility, I was sure all the elements of the Reagan story should be presented together on the front page, so I startled the taciturn Hamlyn by asking him to move off the front page everything not about Reagan and create a second 'front page' on page 3, shunting what was thus displaced to page 4, while reducing display so as to conserve text space. To give time for this, we merely updated the 11.15 p.m. second edition as it stood, and concentrated the major changes on the third edition (for which the printer would want the last copy before midnight to go to press at 12.15 a.m.). I planned the page, which meant doing quick sums about story lengths and sketches of how it might all come together with the news photographs. The confines of the page are a discipline which force a reconciliation of conflicting claims for space and display. Those who refer to the design of a newspaper as packaging or window-dressing are merely parading their ignorance. The page layout and the typographical dress are not something added on: they are integral to an expression of a scale of values.

The photographs demanded space, and this was to be the third strand of my approach: where they deserved it, they should have it, not as decoration but as communication. Some people on *The Times* regarded photography as a black art of tabloid journalism; but good news photographs are information too: the still image has an affinity with the way we recall scenes to mind. As I sketched and read copy, Douglas-Home and Hamlyn had debated their preferences in three dramatic photographs which showed the President looking towards the gunman, being hit, and being bundled into his car. I urged them that agreement on the best photograph was irrelevant; they were an unusual true sequence and to use one would throw away this rare quality; to use three at small size was a waste. So I schemed the three photographs six columns wide to run vertically down the page, which is the way the eye runs most naturally on a sequence. I allocated two full columns for the main text and separate spaces for the subsidiary stories, which I signalled with simple labels 'The gunman', 'The next in line' and 'The violent history'. Rather than telling everyone the 8.30 p.m. news that President Reagan had been shot, we wrote the main headline to focus on the latest news point: 'President Reagan: bullet removed from lung'. I was struck by the gameness of Reagan and used his words to his wife Nancy as a secondary small headline: 'Honey, I forgot to duck . . .'

Everyone's adrenalin was running high. The printers made up the pages in hot metal and remade them, and then began again as the news changed, groaning with big grins, 'Here they come again!' as we arrived in the composing room. The final edition was dramatic, without loss of detail; it was as good as we could make it. Murdoch, phoning from New York, said his intelligence system told him *The Times* was the best in the Street; we won praise in the trade papers from journalists and advertising agencies. But a body of *Times* readers hated the Reagan special. Some asserted that photographs were vulgar and big photographs out of place in *The Times*; some took exception to the 'Honey' headline; some disliked the conventional front page being shunted to page 3; and a small number cancelled the paper on the grounds that we overrated the importance of an American president, dead or alive. Douglas-Home was amused at my discomfiture and laughingly waved the letters aside as of no importance, but I was amazed by their ferocity: at any moment a man would arrive in the front hall with a horsewhip. I replied personally to all the letter-writers and discovered that Douglas-Home had a gauge of the readership. There were no protests when we developed the approach as the waves of big news rolled in. We did it many times, but notably for the Brixton and Toxteth riots, the Columbia space shuttle, Israel's bombing raid on Iraq's nuclear reactor at Osirak, the shooting of the Pope, the scare over the Queen's safety, the assassination of Sadat and martial law in Poland. In each case we presented a coherent narrative with every relevant detail accompanied on the same page by separate articles which sought to answer all the questions the main news was likely to arouse. In the Brixton riots, Martin Huckerby excelled with hour-by-hour observation from the violent streets, but we supplemented this narrative with a more academic study of the borough and its problems, and an authoritative comparison by Peter Evans of police methods in Brixton and Handsworth, the forerunner of a long national debate on community policing.

Eyebrows were raised that I did these pages myself, working with the subs into the small hours. I had to learn *Times* procedures and found it awkward turning from the inches *The Sunday Times* used to the *Times* centimetres; I am sure I made errors which were gratifying to all who observed them. I did the work for a number of reasons. I wanted to find out how the sub-editing system worked and who responded well, but principally I was feeling my way to the form. I was sure there was a better way than doing what the *Times* would naturally have done, which would have been to assign separate headlines to stories that were not distinct, but simply came from separate sources, so producing overlap and repetition. Despite the success of the Reagan page, I was not as sure of my formula as I made out in those early encounters with the unexpected. If it was misconceived, I wanted to find out for myself. The old habits died hard. The conceptual distinctions of the separate articles were frequently muddied on first edition, with the same aspect appearing in two or three places. I had difficulties in having subsidiary articles introduced with a simple identifying label headline. Sometimes, worst of all, we omitted essential detail. Everyone got very bored with my intoning that *The Times* lives by detail.

If the Reagan night was creative, some things I observed were not good for my blood pressure. Hamlyn and the sub-editors did well, but they worked against handicaps. There was a Bleak House air. The copy flooding in by teleprinter and telephone from the United States was jumbled on the foreign sub-editors' table with other foreign copy. *The Times* regarded the spike on which rejected copy is conventionally impaled as dangerous, and instead used wire baskets. Developments in the Reagan story were twice lost in the piles and found only when subsequent pages did not make sense: we almost missed an edition with the naming of Hinckley as the would-be assassin. All those people who needed to be close together were far apart; planning and execution were divorced. The night editors' desk, where the paper was planned, was slung at one side, isolated from the sub-editors, who had constantly to liaise on detail, and even more isolated from the home and foreign news editors, who commissioned reports. The foreign news editor, in touch with the overseas staff, was way off in a room by himself. The picture editor was in outer darkness. There was no intercom. Internal telephone numbers were a close secret. When people had queries, they walked; the more sedentary called across a crowded room. Some did neither and muttered their grievances at their desks. They had my sympathy; I found myself doing the same. One night I edited a report from Craig Seton in Belfast, introducing into his report with his approval some information from a Press Association report he did not have. The Press Association sent a correction, which was left lying on the home desk at the other side of the room, so that we published an error. It was mortifying. I thought at first that the room layout, sanctified by a decade, would have some logic that would be magically revealed to the patient novitiate. But after several frustrating weeks, finding there was none, I asked for the room to be reorganized. Most people braced themselves bravely; one or two senior people, however, had the same attitude to change as the few readers who resented the invention of the camera. At times I thought I might be qualifying for a Nobel Prize for solving the seating arrangements of the peace table between North and South Vietnamese. It took me four months of shuttle diplomacy to have the desks at *The Times* sensibly grouped. It transformed the night's work.

It was clear early on that the organization was not up to the demands I wanted to make on it. All the machinery seemed to be in place, conferences and news schedules, and an executive hierarchy satisfied with its lists that everything was in order, but it was as if a Rolls-Royce had a knock in the engine. Nothing could be taken for granted. The return of the Columbia space shuttle in mid-April was a significant and exciting event. A few of its heat-resistant tiles were damaged during lift-off and the world waited to see what would happen when the two astronauts re-entered the earth's atmosphere. I was given a proof of the page that had been prepared and took it with me to my new office to watch the dry lake landing on television with the chief foreign leader writer, Richard Davy. He was standing by to write a Columbia leader, whatever happened. The page was weak. As Columbia made its dramatic reappearance on earth, we wanted to know what its success meant for the future of space science, and this was the moment when everyone was interested to read a comprehensive account of the mission. We fulfilled neither need. There were about three hours before first edition. A news organization like *The Times* could surely catch up. As Davy went to his typewriter, I went to the news room. The science correspondent could brief Davy quickly and then write his own article.

'Let's see what we can do,' I said in the news room. 'Tell Leapman in America what we want. Kindly get the science correspondent to see Davy first and then to write a thousand words on what comes next in space. Let's have a diagram to show how a space lab might be put together and how it might work.' Embarrassment followed. Pearce Wright, the science correspondent, could not be found. They thought he had gone home at about 6 p.m. Home? I could not believe it. It was absurd that a staff specialist was not in the office for a big event in his area the timing of which was known well in advance, but the news implications unpredictable. 'Well, he'd done his piece,' said the wretched news desk man. 'And there's nobody', added the night editor with a hint of triumph, 'to do a new diagram.' We searched the incoming wire agency material for a science specialist article of the right quality; we searched the library for illustrations. None of us knew enough about the subject to be sure. Leapman filed well, but his message inevitably lacked some of the detail being supplied by news agency reporters. First edition had to go imperfectly, though Davy had managed a thoughtful leader without Pearce Wright. I did not conceal my feelings. Someone joked: 'How about some heat-resistant tiles for the editor?' Pearce Wright was found in a restaurant and returned to check what we had done, and to write himself. We knitted the agency details and Leapman's copy to produce an absorbing narrative and biographies of the astronauts, and we had a new page for the final edition. It was better than anything in the other papers, but it had been touch and go, and much of the pressure had been unnecessary.

The first priority was to get a grip on news. My heart sank in the mornings in those early months when, at home with nine newspapers spread out on the bed and floor, I set out on the daily newspaper editor's foot patrol through the newsprint, checking how we compared in coverage. A rocket launcher captured in Ulster by the police: not in *The Times*. Lord Scarman appointed to inquire into the limitations on the rights of clients to sue architects, solicitors and builders: every paper except *The Times*. A woman baby-sitter on trial for stabbing an eighteen-month-old girl to death had been tried previously for murder, but her past hidden by the Rehabilitation of Offenders Act: every paper except *The Times*. Lady Diana Spencer, in a plunging black dress, attended her first public function with Prince Charles since the announcement of their engagement: delightful pictures and good reports in all other papers, but a muddy and poorly edited photograph in a late edition of *The Times*, and no report. Rolls-Royce won an important engine order from Eastern Airlines in the United States: in other papers from first edition, but not a line in a *Times* with nearly forty columns of business news.

I expected that the office, when I arrived, would be bubbling a little about such failures, but there was not a ripple. Douglas-Home would flap his shoulders crossly that it was a damn nuisance and probably due to 'those bloody subs', and he would support me with a stern look round the room when I raised the failures at conference. Invariably nobody knew anything; very politely I was assured it would be looked into. One or two misses could be accepted, some differences of judgement were proper. What grated was the clockwork way we missed reports universally and rightly judged newsworthy. Every miss yielded a different culprit. This story missed an edition because the telephone copy-takers ended work at 1 a.m., did I not know? This one because the Manchester stringer had changed his telephone number, confounded fellow. The Scarman document had been left on the desk of Marcel Berlins, the legal correspondent, on his day off. The baby-sitter murder story had been available on the Press Association service, but was discarded by the chief sub-editor for an inconsequential staff item. Eastern Airlines? Leapman in New York does not cover business stories. Lady Diana? Sorry about that, she seems to have dropped off our news schedules. Ask me another.

Some staff reports went into print untouched by human mind. Britain was going to oppose the EEC planning code, we said, without giving one clue what was in the code. Another staff man writing about the Country-side Bill said Birmingham University had made an 'interesting survey' of an aspect of it; he kept its interesting conclusions to himself. Charles McKean's architectural reports were often rendered unintelligible by the omission of the illustration he had diligently provided. How, day after day, could things like this go through all the supposed sieves?

There were consolations. The experienced home affairs specialist, Peter Evans, secured an unpublished Home Office report documenting serious defects in the system of investigating complaints of assault by the police. Ronald Kershaw, our man in Leeds, revealed how the Yorkshire miners' leader, Arthur Scargill, was planning to oust moderate Labour MPS from coalfield seats in favour of left-wingers. Ian Bradley, following a tip I had received, exposed the Labour party unelected caucus in Manchester as giving orders to elected councillors, which was a nice jolt for The Guardian. The education correspondent, Diana Geddes, was ahead on university financing. Robert Fisk in Beirut and Michael Binyon in Moscow were filing vividly. But individual performance could not arrest decline if there were something wrong in the organization of the paper.

Some of the early disappointments could be put down to new people working together. Craig Seton was asked to write a sketch of Sir Roger Hollis, the former spymaster, for a page I was doing. When I received his copy, I wanted it done differently and went over to the news editor. He was on the telephone and gestured me to deal directly with Seton, busy at his typewriter. Later I heard that Douglas-Home had also spoken directly to Seton about his story, at slight variance to me so we were both asking Seton for something different, which was in turn entirely different from the way Louis Heren, still home editor, had briefed Seton in the first place. But 'Setonitis', as I dubbed this celebrated confusion, did not really explain why we had consistent difficulty in implementing even our own ideas.

I came to the conclusion that somewhere in those lacklustre corridors at *The Times* there was a Bermuda Triangle. Stories took off with experienced crews, we tracked them on the schedules, then they vanished without trace. When the rioters were due in court, I asked for detailed reports, emphasizing the number of human lives affected. Swallowed in the void. I tried again. Fragments of paragraphs were seen in the afternoon and lost at night in clear weather.

Launching an idea in a leader did not help. We suggested a new Riot Act: the Police Commissioner's reply in a speech dived straight into the Triangle. One successful journey seemed to increase the risks. Oxford University's decision to have a postal ballot on whether they should charge overseas students £400 more than anyone else made it into the paper; we failed with the results of the ballot. A police sergeant was accused of assaulting a man in his cells at Solihull. The prosecution case on the first day survived, but not the sequel – a legally dangerous omission. Some stories, given up for dead, eventually turned up in alien territory. It was no consolation. A drawing of a Tate Gallery extension I urged the news desk to acquire landed successfully in *The Guardian* two weeks later. Others got through, but badly scarred. One morning in conference, during the protracted civil service pay strike, I suggested we should seek to compare some of their pay rates with outside work. This is what the dispute was supposed to be all about, but nobody was putting out any information on it. I had heard from Denis Hamilton, a trustee of the British Museum, that their civil service rates for shop assistants were much better than outside. The first thing that happened was that I was asked to brief the reporters for fear I had been misunderstood. I did. I mentioned the shop assistants. I underestimated the amount and complexity of the task I had set, but some days later I was told it had been done. The conclusion was that civil servants were not grossly overpaid. When I saw the page with it I was downcast. It was hard to know what we were up to. There were four separate little stories without focus. They were poorly related to each other and to the statistics. In these figures we compared the pay and perks of copy typists, computer programmers, office managers, heads of laboratories, and cashiers – but not shop assistants. Everybody blamed everybody else. The day news people considered the deputy chief sub-editor at night at fault. It was true he had not shown much imagination. But it was too easy to blame a hard-pressed man presented at 6 p.m. with four bits of stories and told by nobody what the exercise was all about, except that the editor wanted it all in. So he put in all in as it was given to him. Murdoch found me slumped over this failure and I told him I probably needed someone like Peter Stothard of *The Sunday Times* to see through a special effort from conception to execution. 'Grab him,' said Murdoch; it was his constant injunction in this period.

This happened to be the issue of the paper in which I looked forward to the results of an effort we were making to disentangle the affair of Sir Peter Hayman, the former British diplomat, who had left some porno-graphic material on a bus and had then been allowed the pseudonym Henderson in some other people's trials. There was an excellent narra-tive which put the whole thing in perspective; but it was in *The Guardian*. We had been badly beaten.

The principal beneficiary of my feelings on these matters was Rodney Cowton, the news editor in charge of the reporters and specialists. What I remarked were his round eyes, which seemed to be in a permanent state of alarm or entreaty. In fifteen years on *The Times* and at the age of forty-seven he had won a reputation as a good administrator. John Grant, the managing editor in charge of administration, thought I should replace him as news editor. I was ready to boil him in oil. I talked to him and looked at the way things happened, and came to the conclusion that it would be unfair to blame him for a complicity of failings. I liked his response to criticism which was, begging your pardon, to defend his reporters when there was a case, but bite his lip and admit they had to do better when there was a clear fault. He was not an imaginative or nimble man, but he was a disciplined, organized person, fair and honest, and these were important qualities in dealing with a daily news room. He suffered from an absence of home news leadership. 'Tell us what you want', he said constantly, 'and we'll do our best.'

Louis Heren, the home editor and disappointed candidate for editor-ship and deputy, was his superior. Heren wanted to rally the reporters, but he lacked the qualities required, and he was anyway bound for a new role. Cowton's chief support was his forty-six-year-old deputy, Clive Borrell, who in a decade of crime reporting had acquired the lugubrious demeanour of a disappointed detective.

They were let down, I also concluded, by the erratic performance of some, but not all, of the dozen or so specialists, most of them hidden behind screens and books along the corridor, and barely in the news desk's control. They had a great deal of freedom. They were not assigned on the general news list for night or Sunday duty. They maintained that any suggestion they should assist the small pool of general reporters would damage their ability to perform their tasks properly and would erode the essential authority of *The Times*. Specialist privileges were justified in the case of someone like Henry Stanhope, the defence correspondent. I thought it was carrying distaste for the new regime a little far when he broke a leg on my arrival; but lying in his hospital bed in traction Stanhope dictated more genuine and original stories in a few weeks than two or three of the others did in months. They had become prisoners of their sources, recyclists of hand-outs. It was a less than jolly lunch when I suggested to them that they would be judged by results.

There was something even more fundamental, which would have defeated wilier people than Cowton and Borrell. It was the nature of the day–night schism at *The Times*. I had come across nothing quite like it before; I had inherited a better system on a provincial morning daily in 1961 in Darlington, when I took over the editorship of *The Northern Echo*.

The hierarchy of *The Times*, working days, was an officer class which drifted home as the non-commissioned sub-editors and warrant-officer night editors settled down for a grubby night's work into the small hours. The latter were crucial to the production of the paper, but they were not part of its inner councils. They bore no resentment. They were happy producing the paper, and the officers were happy to consign these mysteries to the engine-room chaps. The editor, deputy editor, associate editor, managing editor, foreign editor and other senior people had not for years seen a first edition come off the presses. At night the paper was handed over to Michael Hamlyn, the executive editor, and his two night editors. The hand-over was perfunctory. They had grown used to getting on with the job with little guidance from conference and little playback the next day, so long as the stories on *The Times* staff news schedule had a run. There were some capable people at work at night, but imperceptibly the system had been programmed for omission and error.

Hamlyn's two night editors were John Brian and Arthur Gould. They were men in their early fifties steeped in their craft. They had joined *The Times* with solid sub-editing experience when they were in their mid-thirties; Gould and I had unknowingly written banner headlines in rivalry, for he was on the sub-editors' table of the *Manchester Evening Chronicle* at the same time in the 1950s that I was on the *Manchester Evening News*. They were Box and Cox, refusing to accept promotion one over the other and taking it in turns to superintend page one and give each other instructions. The deliberate Brian with oaths like thunder was a conservative force with an iron grip on production. The dapper Gould was more willing to experiment. Gould and Brian (or should it be Brian and Gould?) were highly professional in the business of revising the work of other sub-editors, headline writing, layout and seeing the paper to press. But, like Hamlyn, they were preoccupied with the front page.

They did space deals with the inside pages when stories were moved from the front, but they exerted little influence on the inside pages and none at all on sport and business news. As I sat on the isolated back bench for several nights, I realized what was missing: we were not seeing the reports coming in from the Press Association and all over the world from Reuters and the Associated Press. 'We're flying blind,' I said. No, was the response, the agency news was read at the home and foreign desks, and somebody was sure to call out if there was anything worth bothering about. I watched the home editing desk across the room and saw a man squirreling away teleprinted paper in an open desk drawer. He drew on his pipe as he contemplated the few sheets he had folded and placed on his desk, but for hour after hour he filled the desk drawer. He never bothered anybody. This was where some of the missing stories were going.

What had happened over the years, I concluded, was that *The Times* news schedule had come to be regarded as holy writ. Nobody complained much if anything else was omitted. This had dulled the palate of the men who tasted, which is to say sifted, the news from all sources. Copy-tasting had been downgraded, yet it is a crucial task since the chief sub-editor, who lays out the pages, has not the time to read it all himself. The chief sub-editor who decided what appeared and at what length on the inside home pages was Tim Austin, an earnest craftsman in the Gould-Brian mould, aged thirty-eight, who had come from the *Birmingham Post*; he was intimidated by *The Times*; he was astonished, and responded well, when encouraged to show some initiative. So everyone played it safe, which meant giving space to a story from a *Times* staff man at the expense too frequently of a more important agency story arriving late or unexpectedly. There was little attempt on either the home or foreign desks to make the best out of several reports. With foreign news, in particular, reports arriving late would often be added like bricks under the main structure, so that a story we seemed to have missed could be found tucked away at the end of an earlier and weaker dispatch.

The attitude to late news and especially news in other newspapers or on radio or television had become lackadaisical from a combination of geography and philosophy. A foreign editor had laid it down in the 1930s that nothing was news until it had appeared in *The Times*; a lofty doctrine that had been gratefully embraced until it was declared heresy in the late 1960s in the early days after the Thomson take-over. The ruthless campaign of Michael Cudlipp, then deputy editor, had failed to stamp out this belief. In the late 1970s it had revived. There were open adherents. Just before I arrived, Craig Seton, reporting from Belfast, had telephoned late and urgently with the news that Paisley had assembled a body of armed men displaying guns on a hillside in Ulster. He had been told to save it for the next day; by then it had been overtaken. It has to be said that this question of reports in other newspapers is a tricky business. *News at Ten* on ITV might show a few front pages of the national newspapers, but only in the manner of a Port Said bumboat boy flashing pictures of his sister. Not until well past 11 p.m. are the other national dailies available for close inspection at *The Times*, which is late to be ringing people. *Times* people like to tell the story of how Lord Goodman was rung at midnight in the early Cudlipp days to ask if it were true that the Arts Council had made a grant to Bertram Mills Circus. No, Goodman had replied, but a grant has been made to the zoo to train the chimps to become night reporters on *The Times*. A sense of feeling for other people allies naturally with a sense of feeling for oneself. The story in another newspaper is not a scoop; it is a shallow misinterpretation, a base fabrication, and if it is neither of them, it is something we had months ago but the night staff had failed to realize its importance. There are enough occasions of error and overemphasis and the recycling of old material to make this a fair gambit. It has a natural constituency on *The Times*, which rightly insists that accuracy and authenticity is its stock-in-trade.

For these and other reasons, the system of monitoring the other dailies had become hit-and-miss at *The Times*. The night editors did not see the other dailies as soon as they arrived. They were away in the composing room, a long trek upstairs and across a cold connecting passage to another building. When they got back to their desk, aching for a sandwich and tea, they were a long way from the night news editor, with the sub-editors in between. If the night news editor felt for some reason bullish enough to make the journey and mention a late story to the night editors or chief sub-editor, he had to be able to bear their expressions of pain at breaking into layouts, holding up production or cutting into other material. So it was that, in late March, *The Times* ignored one of the more sensational stories of the year when the *Daily Mail*, relying on a book by Chapman Pincher, reported that Sir Roger Hollis, the director-general of MI5 who retired in 1965, had twice been investigated on suspicion of being a Soviet spy, the last occasion being by the Cabinet Secretary, Sir Burke Trend, in 1974. There was no way *The Times* or any other newspaper could check on all Pincher's work in an hour or two. It would be dishonest to report the story as if it were our own. But there was no reason either why readers of *The Times* should be denied the knowledge that Chapman Pincher had made a startling allegation in the *Daily Mail*. The article was detailed. Pincher had a good reputation. It was bound to produce a major reaction from the government, since it followed only one year after the unmasking as a spy of Anthony

Blunt, Keeper of the Queen's Pictures. I laid down a policy for issues such as this. Attribution was at its heart. If a responsible source made a newsworthy statement it was legally safe to publish, then we could record the fact provided we made its source clear. Other newspapers could be mentioned by title. There was no room in *The Times* for the 'Daily Another Newspaper' syndrome. I saw this as a newspaper-of-record's service to readers, and I carried the policy into effect by reprinting the *Daily Mail* evidence during the rest of the week by arrangement with its editor, David English. Sometimes, I recognized, we would be recording hares that did not run; we had then to make sure we followed up and closed the account. Chapman Pincher's hare did run and had some pace left at the end of the week. It dominated press and Parliament for several days. The Prime Minister confirmed that there had been two investigations. Though it had been impossible to prove a negative, they had concluded that Sir Roger had not been a Russian agent; but the Prime Minister announced that the Security Commission was being asked to review the defences against penetration.

It was easy enough, having found where the bodies were buried, to lay down policies, but carrying them out was another matter. There was lassitude, but there was an area of volatility too. The greengrocery and brewing trades were no doubt enriched by the skills in précis and typography *Times* sub-editors brought to them, but too many experienced men had taken redundancy cheques. They were not really redundant. They had to be replaced by casual sub-editors, who came in for a night or two a week, working on the other dailies on other nights; the paper could not meet its ever earlier deadlines without a certain number of sub-editors to check, edit, revise and headline fifty columns of text in a few hours. It was something Murdoch affected never to understand, giving a sardonic chuckle as he surveyed the troglodytes and asking when I was getting rid of them; and perhaps he did not understand it, since all his experience had been of tabloids with a tenth of the text. What with the loss of permanent men, the casuals and the fact that everybody was on a four-day week, it was a phantom army. A policy explained on Monday had to be re-explained on Tuesday to another keen face which one would not see again for a week. Tim Austin never had four nights in a row as chief home sub-editor. He was transferred to the night editor's table when people there took their days off. It was like producing a play with one half of the cast there one day and the other half the next. No wonder the lines went askew from time to time.

For the news reorganization we embarked on that spring I had three portfolios in my hand: the executive night editorship and the home and foreign departments. Douglas-Home had relinquished foreign on becoming my deputy; Heren had moved from home to associate editorship writing; and Hamlyn had indicated he would like a move from nights. The appointments were crucial, executive enzymes who would change the chemistry of the paper for good or ill. There would be new duties and new hours of work. It was not an experiment in cloning. Day and night had to be linked, energy levels had to be raised. The home side needed a natural competitor with insatiable curiosity, someone who knew the reporters and who would hate *The Times* to miss anything. The foreign department needed someone with a serious interest in foreign affairs, the trends as much as the spot news, but also a cold eye for order and money.

Douglas-Home and I went through the staff. Neither of us had any doubts that Brian MacArthur was the man for the new position of executive editor controlling both day origination and night presentation. I told MacArthur we were offering him the job because of his muscular build, and it was certainly a hard assignment even on four days a week to come in for the noon conference and still think the midnight teleprinter was music. MacArthur, then forty-one, had been education correspondent and later news editor of *The Times* for two years in the mid-1970s; he was one of the signatories of the White Swan protest to Rees-Mogg. In the old days, when we bumped into each other in Gray's Inn Road, he had a habit of rubbing his hands at the idea that *The Times* would have something on Friday that we at *The Sunday Times* had been working on all week. He is a challenger; a slight Manchurian look to his eyes can make him resemble one of those eighteenth-century portraits of a well-fed cardinal, but it disperses with the roar of his laughter. He graduated from Leeds University, and was the founder editor of *The Times Higher Education Supplement*, but he is practical rather than cerebral. Above all, he is a newspaperman roused to Yorkshire ire at the idea that *The Times* can live on its past. Unlike numerous *Times* people, he has seen the inside of other offices. He had been with the *Yorkshire Post* and *The Guardian*, and for a year he was deputy editor of the London *Evening Standard*.

The home editorship was more difficult. Hugh Stephenson, the editor of the business news, wanted it. He was forty-three, judged successful over a decade in restoring the reputation of business news after its wobbly start and had been the driving force behind the JOTT consortium. Rees-Mogg had thought enough of him to veto an appointment at *The Sunday Times*. He was a figure outside the office as an author, *Money Programme* television pundit, and yachtsman with equal coolness charting a course through the City of London money market as a member of the Wilson committee, and across the Atlantic with Peter Jay. His intelligence was high and I knew he would scythe through waffle. He wrote a good analysis of the home department, including the need to 'winkle out' some of the specialists, but I doubted him as home editor and Douglas-Home was strongly opposed. 'He'll not respond to your ideas or mine, you watch.' I had to discount some of this as Eton's estimate of Winchester, but Stephenson is the kind of man who would make Keynes feel he could not count. He had begun in the Foreign Service, as the son of a diplomat, and brought its air of buttoned-up reserve with him to Fleet Street. Business news people swore he was not a cold fish, but he did not communicate easily. I thought he would make an excellent foreign editor, on the other hand, and asked him to do that. He refused and resigned, saying it was nothing to do with me or Murdoch, and later sailed into port at Great Turnstile as editor of the *New Statesman*.

Our choice for home editor came down to one of the longest-serving *Times* men and one of its most celebrated, its political editor, Fred Emery. He was forty-eight, all dash, a fighter pilot on RAF National Service and a presenter on *Panorama* from time to time. He had joined *The Times* in 1958 for a string of foreign beats in Paris, Algeria, Tokyo, Indonesia, Vietnam, Cambodia, Malaysia and Singapore, leading to Nixon's Washington, where he felt his reporting of Watergate had not been appreciated by Rees-Mogg, who objected to what he regarded as the pillorying of Nixon. Emery looks like a Roman emperor whose name has slipped your memory. His head and face in profile cry out for a crown of laurels. Murdoch called him 'Gary Glitter' and more than once suggested it would be a good idea if I could see to it he took redundancy; Long snorted at the mere mention of his name. I thought it was because Emery had been maddeningly insistent in his reporting zeal during Murdoch's take-over. As political editor, I discovered, he had another opponent: he had not endeared himself to Mrs Thatcher in his reporting and occasional television interviews.

This all added up to his being the man for the job, someone not easily deterred from asking questions and who would expect reporters to be no less persistent. His vigour was unselective, perhaps, propelling a body that moved faster than his brain, but he was the man to galvanize the home department and help MacArthur to fuse day and night.

Richard Davy was the leading office figure on the foreign side as chief leader writer. But he was too valuable in that role, a worrier, not an executive. While we were thinking about this position, Long mentioned the name of Brian Horton and I had an immediate series of incongruous images: a large, soft-bodied man and a beautiful ballet dancer, a sauna in Finland with snow around the silver birches and a conversation about espionage. This was where I had last met Horton, then married to a dancer, when we happened to have the same idea about respite from a conference of editors. He was then editor-in-chief of Reuters, having

been a foreign correspondent and chief diplomatic correspondent. I
recalled him as being rather aloof and enigmatic. He had left Reuters in
1974 after a disagreement with Long over the general manager's priority
for the new commercial services, and had set up a small wine business
before going to live in Spain. I asked him to come for a talk. He had
hardly changed: a prominent forehead somewhat more exposed, eyes
screwed up behind heavy-framed glasses on a prominent nose. Yes, he
wanted to come back to journalism and *The Times* was the last great
challenge. He had prodigious experience of organizing foreign reporting
and making every pound count. Douglas-Home had his doubts. Was he
a plant, a Long spy? I pooh-poohed the idea. We fretted about it and
Douglas-Home came round. I agreed with John Grant that the foreign
editor should be paid the same as the other executives in comparable
positions, but Horton told Grant he could not come for that. I returned
to the shortlist. Long, hearing of this, came back and so did Murdoch.
We must give Horton what he wanted. I demurred and was instructed.
'Grab him,' said Murdoch. 'Think of the acquisition of talent for the
company,' he urged. 'Salary structure? Poof!' said Long sadly. 'There's
nothing like it here. It's another job we've got to do.' It was only
later that I learned Horton had known Murdoch as well as Long for
years.

This new troika of MacArthur, Emery and Horton was soon pulling
strongly. MacArthur's good nature and determination impressed itself
on Gould and Brian, now fed with the Press Association copy as a check.
It was comforting to see Emery's beetle brow worrying a morning idea
through into print with the chief sub-editor, and hours later, when most
people had gone home and the news room was dark, to see MacArthur
amid the debris of the back bench eagerly seize the other papers as if he
were just down for breakfast. If we were beaten on first edition, Mac-
Arthur saw that we caught up by final, and we had many more original
reports. Horton had a different style from Emery and MacArthur. He
stayed aloof, looked at the tangles with laser-beam eyes and issued crisp
written instructions. He brought his day and night news editors out of
isolation and into the news room, incidentally saving a post.

All three new men in different ways saw to it that the night staff knew
what the day staff had in mind, but moderated the inflexibility of the
schedule by indicating priorities and options. This meant that stories we
had been missing had more of a chance to be judged on their merits.
Horton carried it furthest with a news schedule that distinguished between stories that must be run at length and those he regarded as having
lesser claims. MacArthur tried to bring stability to the sub-editing staff;
I told him to aim for a smaller permanent body of first-class men and
women. He tried to improve editing standards. He stopped Austin's

musical chairs. Emery put in the eager Huckerby as night news editor and announced he was going on safari down the specialists' corridor. We checked his cleft sticks and snake-bite serum. Word had come back that some of them thought I worried too much about being abreast of the news. 'From the readers' point of view as distinct from specialized people in the field,' one of them commented to Emery, 'it is difficult to see the importance of scoops. The quality of writing is more important.' I hoped it was not megalomania to think we might have both.

The chapel of the National Union of Journalists began complaining formally that people were being worked too hard with too many redundancies and not enough recruitment, and it was true we were stretching people, especially in business news. By the end of May eleven new people had arrived, but thirty-three had left. The chapel officers suspected that there had been a shift in the ratio of chiefs to Indians. There had not been, and nobody could say the new executives were shirking their share of the burden. I had to tell them there was no prize for seeing who could stay in the office longest. I stole the only common day off, Saturday, for a conference at the RAC Club, where new and old *Times* executives thrashed out some of the problems, with squash at lunchtime for those who wanted to take it out on the editor. Fred Emery tried hardest. At the end of the day I asked Douglas-Home to sum up and he struck a pleasant note, saying they were exciting days in which old and new must join together for a better *Times*. 'I pledge myself to be the bridge.'

The story is told and, if it is not true, it ought to be of the butler who met the *Times* crisis of 3 May 1966 by ironing and folding his Lordship's copy of that morning's paper so that the back page was uppermost on the silver salver. The considerate man was attempting to diminish the shock of the decision by Sir William Haley and the Astors to put news on the front page, displacing the personal columns of classified advertising to the back. There is a good deal to be said for conservatism in matters of newspaper typography and layout. When it is not necessary to change, it is necessary not to change. It is no advance for civilization, simply because it is technically possible, to subject the reader to styles and manners of printing type which defy centuries of settled habits of reading. I had become a bore about this with the freer spirits who sometimes turned up at *The Sunday Times* colour magazine and (for instance) set captions impossibly wide or absurdly narrow. The manic experiments on the human eyeball which have been perpretrated in the stretching and squeezing of words in advertisements and in headline displays in photocomposition newspapers are more horrible examples of change for its own sake. It was not a temptation felt by Edwin Taylor, me or any of the others associated in the adventure of seeing how far it was possible to improve the ease and enjoyment of reading *The Times* and enhance its distinction.

We did not feel bound, either, by any unproven convention. Retaining classified advertising on the front page was an example of a bogus historicity. Newspapers began with news and opinion on the front page. It was the advertising which was the intruder, at first a column and then with the expansion of trade so many columns that the printers who made up the paper simply pushed editorial inside. On the other hand, the removal in 1966 of the coat of arms from *The Times* banner was, to me, a destructive radicalism, since it represented the breach of a genuine tradition and the loss of a valuable trade mark which had survived every convulsion since the first issue in 1785. I was as determined to restore this link with the past (though I expected trouble with Murdoch), as I was to bring unimpeded principles of legibility and economy to *The Times* of 1981. I envisaged a redesign effort over two years. I wanted everything from the plan of the paper to its smallest entry to be measured for excellence.

I was fortunate that I had someone who could translate this aspiration with art and practical rigour. Edwin Taylor, the director of design at *The Sunday Times*, had agreed to try to combine the work there with a similar role at *The Times*. I put him in a scruffy old office in a deserted area of the advertising department, where he set up a drawing board and taped pages to the partition walls. I became a little impatient with his approach. I sent him bound copies of *The Times* of the 1930s and 1960s; I marked an immodest page or two in my books on newspaper type and layout. I wanted to sit down and discuss the classic redesign of *The Times* by Stanley Morison in 1932 and its relevance to us. Edwin Taylor always said the same: he was looking at the paper. I discovered he meant it literally. He had schooled himself, even before taking up his appointment, to let his eye wander over the page, testing its legibility and its signposting for the reader, noting its use of space and its dislocations. He was supremely right to do so. By the time the others joined him, he had a series of original observations and he was ready to test them.

It was a characteristic way for Taylor to approach anything; I had forgotten this in the weekly turmoils of *The Sunday Times*. He is a reflective man who had shared the search for effective communication with scientists of the calibre of Julian Huxley, John Boyd Orr and James Fisher, and with J.B. Priestley. He had worked directly with them as a book editor, designer and researcher after graduating from technical college in Johannesburg and the celebrated Central School of Arts and Crafts, in London. He was born in South Africa, where his father was a military engineer and he acquired from him a fascination with making things work. From London he went to be an editor with the *Time-Life*

Science Library in New York and I snatched him from a consultancy with *Readers' Digest* on his return in 1967, and introduced him to the imperfections of newspaper design. He was amazed by its Heath Robinson characteristic of ferrying hundreds of scraps of paper and the lack of a proper visual library for graphic design. It says something about him that, amid the confident dogmatisms of *The Sunday Times*, where he had no direct control of space and no staff at first, he became, without raising his voice, a dominant figure in the paper's presentation and a strong influence on its approach to the more complicated passages of journalism. The experience gave him a glum look. He had dark unruly eyebrows and a big black moustache. Depending on whether or not he wore his glasses, it could have been Zapata or Groucho who came at you down the corridor with a T-square in his hand.

The man who joined Edwin Taylor in his hideaway is the printer's dream of what a newspaper journalist should be. 'Can't you get Oscar to sort this out?' the printers used to hector me at *The Sunday Times*, when a layout became tangled or a big enterprise was entering its agonies. Oscar Turnill did almost every editing task in his many years at *The Sunday Times*. He is a small, polite and pedantic man in his early fifties. Where the run-of-the-mill Fleet Street sub-editor is a butcher with a cleaver in the eyes of the reporters Oscar Turnill is a neuro-surgeon. Writers do not notice his editing: Turnill's stitches disappear. He had been managing editor of *The Times Literary Supplement*, and he was editor-designate of *The Times Health Services Supplement* when I asked him to come to *The Times* as an assistant editor. He sometimes became unduly depressed by the chaos around him, but I knew his standards and dexterity would win the admiration of everyone on *The Times*. He took over the planning of the paper from John Grant and made an immediate improvement in its logic, even while the critical relocation of the leader page away from the true centre of the paper remained undecided. There was a third resource. Taylor and Turnill had call on the services of Walter Tracy. Nobody can contest the details of typography with Tracy, the creator of Times Europa and other typefaces, but for all that a man of insistent modesty.

Surveys of readers of *The Times* and those who had given up showed persistently that they found it hard and uninviting to read. Some of this was due to the reduction in body-type size when Rees-Mogg changed course in 1970 to seek maximum economy of space; some due to the decline in the quality of printing with thinner newsprint. Rees-Mogg had commissioned a new design during his final year, which was to have been launched in the spring of 1981, and Hamlyn had shown us the dummies in the first week. It was certainly a more open and appealing newspaper, but Taylor and Turnill shared my judgement: it betrayed its

American origins, having come from Louis Silverstein of the *New York Times*, where designers graze on vast prairies of newsprint. It was not right for *The Times*, because we could not afford to lavish space on display. The balance in the paper between order and emphasis had gone wrong; we needed less constriction, a little more emphasis. But the central point of newspaper design is that emphasis is a relative matter. If one begins by speaking in a low but discernible voice, extra attention can be aroused by the smallest gradations in volume. Taylor's gazing sessions produced more modest proposals than Silverstein's, but when the subtleties were put together they had a profound effect. I went to his office one afternoon. Turnill and MacArthur had been busy with him, having type set to try out the conclusions and producing it late at night, after the normal paper had gone to press. Their handiwork of page after page of experiment was taped up across the frosted glass panels. The new pages lit up the dreary place. It was an exciting moment.

Taylor's most important single finding concerned the headlines. They were dimly lit, confusing and space-wasting. The technicalities are not difficult to follow. *The Times* style generally had been to lead the inside pages with three lines of headline across three or four columns in a type size known as 30-point. The headline dress was the relatively compact typeface known as Times Roman 334, which is no more than a bold of the body type. It was never designed as the main headline face. In 1932, when Times Roman was introduced, the paper had single-column headlines in titling-capitals only. Stanley Morison had inveighed: 'If ever *The Times* accepts double-column headings, it will not be because they are necessary, but because a generation of readers has been habituated to them by reading journals less scrupulously conducted.' It was right, despite Morison, for *The Times* to use multi-column headlines so as to be able to reflect a richer scale of values, but at these measures the lower-case Times Roman produced a proliferation of characters. The trade journal *UK Press Gazette* once carried a cartoon of a *Times* sub-editor interrupting a reporter: 'Could you possibly let me have a few more facts? I've run out of words for the headline.' The headline in *The Times* of 1981 lost its characteristic as a swift signal, comprehensible at a glance; it was more a letter than a telegram. I knew this was a flaw, but what I did not appreciate before Taylor demonstrated it with trial settings was how, with a wide headline aligned to the left, the residual white space was in the wrong place. It was like having a light in the wrong corner of a room. An astonishing difference was made to all the headlining by two simple measures: choosing two lines at the slightly bigger 36-point, and centring them. The headlines were no longer dim. They were on a placard of white, as if illuminated everywhere by back lighting. What was equally arresting and exciting was that Taylor's proposed new style took up less space: two lines of 36-point (about an inch in depth) saved space on three lines of 30-point. Moreover, having fewer characters forced simplicity on the headline, so that meaning was conveyed at once. Taylor and Turnill had put on their walls the results of other experiments, demonstrating, for instance, how a fractionally stronger column rule stopped the headlines slipping confusingly into each other; and how this failing had been aggravated by the excessively horizontal layouts. There was a further advantage: the proposed new layout styles offered positions for shorter stories which were distinct but did not consume as much space as the old over-headlined style.

They kept to the end Taylor's best surprise for me, which was the parliamentary page. For the first time I could see what it was all about. There was order, instead of chaos. The divisions were logical. Taylor had introduced small photographs of the main speakers, a suggestion that had also been put to me by the Tory minister Kenneth Baker. The faces certainly relieved the page, but, as I was demurring on the grounds that I could not afford to sacrifice a line of parliamentary text, they produced their triumph: even with the photographs they had gained eleven lines of text. Space had been devoured by the old profusion of headlines and a thick black 'tramline' of type rules across the top of the page. We postponed to the autumn dealing with sport and business news, beyond cleansing, because it was enough to see the news page changes through the night staff and the two composing rooms, one hot, one cold, which had been in operation since March. This was only the first stage; on the second I planned moving to six or seven columns on each page instead of eight.

Taylor had photography and illustration also in his brief, and I was called down to look at one final page, which would go through with the others on my approval. It was the page carrying the court circular and obituaries. It was sedate and tidier in those departments, but it was ablaze in the birthdays: there was a caricature of Audrey Hepburn. I was ashamed to feel a little uneasy. I heard Lady Bracknell's voice: 'A cartoon! On the court page!'

'We've saved enough space for light relief,' said Taylor. He was unusually pressing. He was pleased that he had tracked down the artist. It had begun in *Punch*, where he had seen a thumbnail sketch which caught the essence, he thought, of his neighbour and former colleague, the writer Hunter Davies. The artist turned out to be a former Sandhurst cadet by the name of Charles Griffin, and Taylor wanted him to celebrate a birthday every day. I agreed to give it a run. Why not, I told myself. It was a tight page which could do with relief, and caricature had a long lineage in British journalism. I also accepted another Taylor recommendation, which was to engage Ranan Lurie for political cartoons on the news pages five days a week. Lurie is as bold a fellow as his cartoons, a sixth generation Israeli, aged forty-nine, who trained with the French Foreign Legion, parachuted with the Israeli Army, took American citizenship and entered the *Guinness Book of Records* as the most widely syndicated artist, appearing in more than 400 papers in fifty-two countries. He had been drawing for *Time–Life* in New York and *Die Welt* in Germany when he offered Taylor his services for *The Times*. Lurie had intense charm, which he exercised successfully even on those who did not care for his drawings.

In the few weeks following all these decisions, I felt like calling on Lurie and his friends in the Foreign Legion. I was beset again by angry readers. He was one cause, Griffin was another, and, to my surprise, so were the faces on the parliamentary page. 'Why are you keeping your changes a secret?' Gerald Long asked, and I responded by carrying a paragraph on the front page, no more than a polite cough, the day we introduced the new pages. It was provocative. There were five times as many letters as after Reagan, and they kept coming. It was undignified of *The Times* to carry caricatures. A serious newspaper should look serious. The headlines were too big; photographs on the parliamentary page were an insult. *The Times* was read out of a sense of duty, not for entertainment. Griffin was a sadist. Lurie was crude and anti-Semitic. I was an escaped convict from the *Sun*. I felt I could hear Hickey purring in the room next to mine. The staff had been receptive, but Hickey expressed daily disdain for MPs faces and Griffin. A cartoon! On the court page! Taylor defended hotly in conference. Hickey wrote to me: 'The rather coarse cartoon accompanying today's birthdays contradicts the proper formality of that page.' The anti-Griffin forces stopped at nothing. There were sinister late-night telephone calls to Taylor's office. Lord Drogheda, one of the directors of the Holdings board and former chairman of *The Financial Times*, prepared an indictment. He had a new angle. It was cruel to show that people got older. Drogheda's condemnation did not come directly to me. He complained to Murdoch, who passed it on non-committally. This was too dangerous an area, I noted, even for him. I began to regard approving Griffin as important as choosing the front page lead. Was that hair-line right, were we looking at a displaced nostril? This was bigger for *The Times* than the Abdication crisis. But reports came in of schisms in the Establishment. Douglas-Home, hands in pocket, chortled: 'Lord Boyd-Carpenter has rung me up about the drawing of him. He wants the original.' Duke Hussey, whose wife is a lady-in-waiting to the Queen, rode in: 'Funnily enough I saw Queen Elizabeth's [the Queen Mother] private secretary Martin Gilliat at dinner last night and he is a very avid and discerning reader of *The Times* – as is his boss! I asked him what he thought about the Court page and the cartoonist and he was very enthusiastic about it and then commented on how good some of the cartoons had been – Casson for instance. So I don't think you need worry about those letters.' I regarded it as the equivalent of a royal pardon for Griffin, Taylor and me.

I replied none the less to all the letters. I sent the most murderously inclined a complimentary copy of an old *Punch* cartoon which had 1920s clubmen in apoplexy at the hypothetical introduction of a comic strip in *The Times*. I demonstrated that the headlines took less space, but looked bigger because they could be seen in their white space. I sent photostats of the before and after parliamentary page. I began to feel safe when a lady from Dorset, a notoriously sceptical part of the country, said she was persuaded by the examples. Energies were cunningly diverted into the letters page; given the talents of *Times* readers, there was mileage in this. Sir Robert Maclellan posed the issue from Scotland with the right gravity: 'You have taken to slicing the top off so-called head-and-shoulder photographs. Is not the height of a man's forehead of greater significance than how he knots his tie? Please restore to us the politicians we have come to recognise if not to love – scalps and warts and all.' This view was exposed as partial. Sir Robert had no right to complain, said a *Times* loyalist, when his own family inscription bore a head impaled upon a sword. There was a desperate hand-to-hand struggle in the small right-hand corner of the letters page about the whole issue of parliamentary photographs; the good Leon Pilpel referred to it as 'Topless in *The Times*'. The anti-photograph camp was soon dispatched. What was at stake, a leading authority pointed out, was the ability of the scientific community to calculate the depth of the frontal lobes of their leaders, so as to estimate their ability to control their emotions. Opinions were divided about precisely where heads should be sliced. The height of a man's forehead is an accident of birth, a shrewd reader pointed out, but the way he knots his tie is an outcome of calm deliberation and mature reflection: 'Never trust a man whose tie is habitually an inch below his collar.'

While we wrestled with the news organization, features ticked over under Margaret Allen, who had been with *The Times* for eighteen years. Before I arrived, she had decided to leave and build on her success as a writer. My present for her in her final two months was to leave her without her regular outside contributors who had been appointed by Rees-Mogg. It was not that I objected to them all as individuals, though one or two had run their course. I let the retainer payments lapse because I did not like assigning so much of the main feature page to tenant strip farming. It inhibited a flexible and unpredictable response, with opinion and analysis, to the news. And, of course, she still had Bernard Levin.

He, too, had announced that he was no longer prepared to let the blades of the windmill of journalism knock him to the ground every Tuesday, Wednesday and Thursday in *The Times* as well as each Sunday in *The Sunday Times*. But he was in the meantime picking himself up with a song, even though I suspected he stayed on only to get me in difficulties with the law before he scarpered. In his *Times* column he accused Lord Goodman of rambling and M Ps of being drunk in charge of legislation, and the Turkish Ambassador and Gerald Long were at my throat for a piece he wrote on Kemal Ataturk. When these stratagems failed to have me carried off, he produced a noose of a sentence in his final column, so long he failed to get it on a single sheet of foolscap. This was certainly a response to my review in *The Sunday Times* of a book of his collected *Times* pieces on which I had lavished praise, though I compared some of his sentences to the corridors of a Venetian palace: you know there is something good at the end, but occasionally your feet ache getting there. That final Wednesday Levin proposed opening his column in this manner:

There seems to be something about air travel that reduces those responsible for providing any facility required in the course of it to a condition in which they appear to have had the inside of their heads removed and replaced with tinned forcemeat, a view to which I have recently come not because I have undergone any one especially painful traumatic experience but because I have just finished a succession of lesser encounters with its representatives none of which has been irreparably disastrous but which have cumulatively convinced me that there is no point in trying to discover what bizarre form of private logic informs the thinking of airline and airport officials as their behaviour is devoid of any causally connected system whatever, and for that matter of any intuitively based but inexplicably effective method either, the results being a succession of events so entirely random that they demand an explanation that must by definition lie outside the grasp of normal minds.

There was a second mega-sentence in which his nerve or his stamina had not quite carried him through. I was busy, or skulking if you will, and asked Douglas-Home to negotiate. I was prepared, I said, to dig into my personal supplies and give Levin two full stops which he could use in the column. Hours later, when I thought the coast was clear, I found Douglas-Home collapsed in his chair with the diminutive Levin towering over him. I settled for one full stop. He was not content with a draw: that same afternoon I received a memo from him about sentences which trailed into Gray's Inn Road. Rees-Mogg got a knighthood for less.

I announced the appointment of David Watt, the political commentator, and Frank Johnson, on Levin's departure. Readers protested that neither man had a curly, black quiff and an obsession with the North

Thames Gas Board. Johnson was my first recruit for *The Times* and I waited impatiently while he worked out his notice at *Now!* magazine. He graduated in irony under Colin Welch at the *Daily Telegraph*, where I admired his Commons sketches. He is a pale, handsome Cockney who always speaks in a tense whisper. I put this down to his boyhood days in opera at Covent Garden. He joined us just in time to report the reactions of Mrs Thatcher, her husband Denis and William Whitelaw at a charity performance of *Anyone for Denis*. In the Whitehall Theatre, 'which virtually invented the concept of the falling trouser', they were depicted as a henpecker of her husband, a suburban sot, and a generalized buffoon. 'When all three were asked whether they enjoyed the show, there was only one sort of thing they could say under the circumstances: "Yes, certainly, most amusing, excellent, etc."' He might have added that *The Times* had done its best to help in the ordeal: the deputy editor was given the night off to sit with the Prime Minister on condition he noted her reaction every time anyone on stage said something wicked.

I wanted someone young as features editor. Nearly half the readers of *The Times* are under thirty-five. Tony Holden, who was about to sign a new contract as the Washington correspondent of *The Observer*, was thirty-three. He was a former Atticus on *The Sunday Times* and the biographer of Prince Charles. He edited *Isis* at Oxford, published a translation of Agamemnon, slogged his apprenticeship on a Thomson evening at Hemel Hempstead, came top in the Journalists' Training Council proficiency examinations and wrote a book on the St Albans poisoner. Holden had applied for a job at *The Times* while still at Oxford. Rees-Mogg interviewed him between watching the Derby and gave his judgement on Holden's *Isis* notepaper, which John Grant proudly fished out on Holden's arrival fifteen years later: 'Thinks he wants to write. Won't make a writer. Strikes me has much better administrative abilities.' Grant commented to the new features editor: 'There you are, he was right.' Holden brought one American gift with him, a weekly column by the former *Times* man Henry Fairlie, and an American habit of referring to the main feature page opposite the leader page as the 'op ed' page. It caught on.

To support him I brought in as his deputy Peter Stothard, originally with the idea that he would pull together harder political and economic features like the civil service pay analysis. He was another young Oxford man, who had been with the BBC and BP when I spotted him and took him on the *Sunday Times* business news. I promoted Nicholas Wapshott, already five years on *The Times*, to be assistant features editor. He was twenty-nine and a resourceful interviewer who looked like Nicholas Nickleby. This completed what became known as *The Times* kindergarten.

Holden gave me one small tremor before he arrived. With the rest of the press corps he was invited to the White House for the after-dinner entertainment at the banquet the Reagans gave for Mrs Thatcher. He introduced himself to Murdoch and then had breakfast with him the week Reagan was shot. He recounted to me cheerfully how he had discussed his pages with Murdoch, who told him he would like to see strong opinion dominate the page. 'My God', I jumped, 'you must not talk about features policy directly with Murdoch.' Was young Holden naïve or even a little disloyal, I wondered?

It was only prudence on my part. In those first months Murdoch did everything and more to support me editorially. When the Murdoch-watcher, Philip Kleinman, ribbed me in his *Campaign* column in May, he was quoting accurately enough. He said that I rushed back to *The Times* after receiving the 1981 president's award of the Designers and Art Directors' Association, but not before telling several people that Rupert Murdoch was 'marvellous'. Well, Murdoch got things done then that I wanted done at *The Times*. I marvelled at the speed and directness of it.

For all the publicity about the shirt-sleeved newspaperman, Murdoch proved to be much less of a technician than I thought he would be, unsure of typefaces and liable to mix up off-the-stone time (printers finished) and set plate time (foundry finished, and only the machines to roll). Nor does he have the pure editorial flair of Denis Hamilton, who was always dreaming up handsome and ambitious series for *The Sunday Times* review front and colour magazine. He is not an ideas man in that sense: he thinks astutely in marketing terms of publications and news-paper sections that might sell copies rather than, as Hamilton did, of features that might interest and elevate people. His energy is pheno-menal, but peculiar. It does not reveal itself in physical vigour; he slouches, leading with a shoulder, dragging a foot. He doodles and fidgets, seeming to lack concentration, but, as Long said admiringly, his mind is always churning. He tries to hold in his head what other men would commit to paper. Accountants are entranced by one aspect of this. 'If we put up the cover price by x and lose 2% of sale, but cut the trade margin by y, we'll end up net, let's see, with £640,000 in a full year. Work it out, will you?' They do and it is right to within a few thousand. His mind is never in repose, but it also works in displaced time. He picks up something you said two days before without response and challenges it as if the conversation had never been interrupted. The noticeable physical restlessness is deceptive. There is an unbroken, brooding mental process which is secretive and, when revealed, often disconcerting in its violence. It is not temper which produces surprises;

there are no hysterics, shouts and flushed faces. On the contrary, it is the sense of something bottled up. The effect of this was that, when Murdoch was in London, associates were jumpy; you could see the tension relax as he left. I felt it myself. I benefited to the extent that we were moving in the same direction to galvanize *The Times*. I wondered when, in his preoccupation to catch up with events, he would ever catch up with his own reputation.

The dark side of the compulsion to make things happen was manifest in a carelessness about people which Gerald Long aggravated with the intensity of the likes and dislikes of a very clever man. Long ran the office in the absence of Murdoch. Most of the time he was a man on horseback: whip in hand, ramrod back, chin out, aglow in the morning air and ready for anything. Laughter was more frequent than anger, though both alarmingly began in the same way: head back and roaring. One did not know whether to grin or duck. Occasionally the rider vanished, leaving a set of rumpled clothing barely animated by a tired old man. Long's intellect enhanced and diminished him. It gave him supreme confidence and there was bravery in his ambition: remove this debris at once and I will tell you idiots how to build a palace of logic. But the chromosome of tolerance was missing and the intellect was demeaned when it was turned against people.

The most distressing example, one of a number, concerned Denis Hamilton. When Murdoch took his office, Hamilton moved to Ken Thomson's big but remote room on the seventh floor. I called in on him around lunchtime one day and found his secretary near to tears. She had asked the kitchen for a lunch tray for Hamilton, who wanted to work at his desk, and it had been refused on Long's orders: lunch trays were only to be available to the joint general managers on the sixth floor. To do this to the man who invented the company, who only a short time before was its chairman and editor-in-chief, and without whom Murdoch would never have acquired the titles, was malevolence of high order. I told Hamilton I was going to make a fuss about it. He was, typically, mortified. 'Don't do that, dear boy. I'll just never eat another bite in this place.'

Murdoch early on gave the order for an eighty-page *Sunday Times* where we on the old board had hesitated. It deserved to succeed, but union disruption ruined it. The works manager and the overseer were harshly sacked, but, not content with that, the press room overseer of *The Times* was sacked as well, though he had nothing to do with *The Sunday Times* trouble and *The Times* machine room was relatively trouble-free. I protested. He was reinstated an hour before he was due to be given his cards.

I was less successful over Bob Ducas, my energetic associate in the consortium to buy *The Sunday Times* in 1980–81. I wrote a memorandum to Murdoch and Long saying how valuable he was as the New York manager, especially in raising revenue in book deals, syndication and other sales, and I commended him personally. 'Think so?' said Long, looking at me sideways, which was always the crooking of the imperial thumb. Ducas was sacked by open telex from Murdoch and, after nineteen years' service, given an afternoon to clear his office. My petition to Murdoch on his behalf was rejected on the ground that Ducas had tried to define his own duties. His dismissal lost revenue for *The Times*. Months later we were told that North American syndication, which had vanished, could not be discussed by the board 'until the chairman has reached a conclusion'. There was no revenue for *The Times* from our royal wedding efforts; they were given to Murdoch's other papers.

Long was always upbeat during these months about *The Times*. 'Good morning, gentlemen,' he would say at the board meeting. 'We should all congratulate the editor.' Some of this was genuine; he appreciated our new political commentator David Watt and thought his recruitment a triumph. Some of his public praise, though, was calculated as a put-down to Giles, the principal subject of Long's disquisitions when I met him for a weekly lunch. 'Rupert's very worried about *The Sunday Times* and, my God, he's right to be. We'll have to make it a seven-day *Times*. It's the only thing that makes any sense.' If I referred, contrarily, to a mark of *Sunday Times* excellence, Long picked it off as an example of my sentimentality. The war against Giles and *The Sunday Times*, by both Murdoch and Long, was the bleakest counterpoint to the support for *The Times*. Long, an incisive writer, riddled Giles. 'It seems faintly ridiculous to be writing back and forth across Coley Street, the more so since the matter raised in your letter is not an important point of principle, nor a point at all, but an example of what seems to me your abnormal sensitivity about editorial prerogative.' Giles had protested at a Long ukase, saying there was no exception to a ban on increasing pay; he wanted to have the discretion to make merit awards. The ever courteous Giles made the mistake of offering hospitality to Long. For a dinner-party at his St John's Wood home, knowing Long's francophilia, he produced not one, but two, French ambassadors. He might have got away with that, but he also produced an excellent Château Lafite he had bought himself for a derisory few francs in 1964 and laid down. Long regarded it as one-upmanship. He retaliated by ridiculing Giles's wine story and declaring defiantly to the whole table that the French could grow grapes, but they did not know anything about wine. The dinner was not a success.

Soon the whole board was invited to see Giles as an impostor on civilized living. Long prepared a three-page memorandum, circulated to every director: 'Have you a cooking correspondent? What little I have seen on cooking strikes me as amateurish to revolting; I have sent you a note on the subject. Does your wine correspondent write? I remember nothing in the recent past.' There was some pith in the memo, as it happened, comparing food and drink advertising in *The Sunday Times* and *Observer*, and Long mellowed and digressed as a man might do after a banquet:

> I believe it might be possible to attract cognac advertising at this time, since cognac producers face increased difficulties from EC changes in excise duties. If it is of interest a good friend of mine, the German journalist Gert von Paczensky, is a world expert on cognac, which he tastes much as Michael Broadbent does clarets. The country round Cognac is pretty, and not far away is the Marais Poitevin, one of the strangest parts of France, full of canals which the locals use among other things to transport cattle from meadow to meadow, and for a considerable sort of gondola trade in the season. The cooking, especially of the Marais, is very interesting and would look good in colour, including the famous *sauce aux lumas*, a sort of snail soup, which is a dark browny-green ... Such knowledge as I have is, of course, entirely at your disposal.

Murdoch was not often present for meetings of his executive board of Times Newspapers. He was in America or Australia, or in Britain doing deals, though his presence was palpable. It was Long who took the board meetings. We met in his sixth-floor office along the corridor from Murdoch's. He had fumigated it to remove the smell of tobacco and alien thoughts; all the mahogany and leather of Thomson days had gone. It was sprucely, if sparely, furnished in light pine with a small white rug. There was a table for Long's portable typewriter and Vichy water. Seven of us sat in cane chairs in a tight circle above a low pine coffee table, which would have been awkward if there had been papers to manage. Murdoch and Long had both declined to have board meetings in the impressively panelled seventh-floor suite with its long walnut conference tables and oil paintings of the Walters and other *Times* celebrities. I regretted this. In difficult moments in Thomson board meetings I always found solace looking at a painting which showed Geoffrey Dawson upright and in command at his editor's desk with a cowed general manager on the other side and the owner, Col. J.J. Astor, as observer. Murdoch, I deduced eventually, would never have proper board meetings with documents, which was what the seventh floor enjoined. Both men, in any event, wanted the past expunged. Long went to the length of severing the link in the name that Denis Hamilton had preserved with the original site of *The Times* at Printing House Square in Queen Victoria Street, where the paper was produced for 189 years. The new owners there coveted the Printing House Square address, but Hamilton had arranged with the Greater London Council to call his new Gray's

Inn Road building New Printing House Square. 'That is an affectation,' Long pronounced. 'Printing House Square was an address. New Printing House Square is the name of a house like "Dunroamin" and as such irrelevant to its address.' Henceforth we would be known as PO Box 7.

Nomenclature was dangerous ground with Long. He banned the term 'new technology' to describe photocomposition. It was a decade old and our system was obsolete. People gobbled air in mid-speech as they caught Long's eye-flare at 'new tech . . .'. There were many people called director of this or that who did not have a seat on the board. This would cease. Only board members were to be referred to as directors.

I was the only member of the Thomson board to survive to the Murdoch board. The rest came from Murdoch companies. The joint general managers were John Collier and Bill O'Neill. Collier is a former full-time official of the clerical union NATSOPA, who in 1974 turned gamekeeper as a labour manager. O'Neill, the clean-cut apprentice from the composing room in Sydney, personifies Australian directness. He laughed that he was the 'Sydney hatchet man'. I had most to do with him over the agonizing transfer of the paper from hot metal to cold type, which began one week after I took over. The other two department heads were even more contrasting. Ken Beattie, the circulation director, who ran W.H. Smith Wholesale for many years, is a man of two simple moods: up when sales are up, down when sales are down. He carries candour to the point of embarrassment. Michael Ruda, the advertising director, aged fifty, hugs the prevailing contours without marking his elegant suits. The final member was Roy Ekberg, a solicitor from Murdoch's News International where he is company secretary, forever watchful behind his horn-rims.

The notable absentee at every meeting was documentation. In Thomson days the directors for finance, advertising and marketing, circulation, and production all made written reports to the board. The finance reports showed monthly how we compared against all the departmental budgets, highlighted areas of excess cost, and forecast the measure of profit or loss. There was nothing like this in the Murdoch-Long executive boards. Agendas were almost entirely 'any other business', reports brief and conversational. 'I've bagged Selective Marketplace,' was Long's way of announcing the sale of *The Sunday Times* mail order business. The pattern was for the directors to sit in their cane chairs and hear Long proclaim his policies. They were rational and far-sighted. We could save £2 million a year if we could all 'get out of this dump' into the *Sunday Times* building. A new disciplinary procedure was being promulgated. Directors must see to it that written records were kept of misconduct. There would be a house style for all lettering and design from Pentagram.

Nobody else was to place orders. Secretarial resources, 'like everything else in this place', were badly organized. A specialist would visit directors. There would be a review of all management practices. Consultants were being called in.

'Now, let's go round the table. Anything, John?'

The time mostly went on x-rated labour relations stories. Collier and O'Neill seemed to be getting a grip on them.

After a few meetings, I asked for figures. 'I'd like to know how we are getting on.' Beattie and Giles murmured agreement. Long sighed: 'Wouldn't we all. There's no management here. It's hopeless. But give us time.' He cantilevered his chin: 'You know there are only two problems in life. One, knowing what you want to do; two, doing it. Well, gentlemen, we know what we want to do, so we are half-way there.' When I said I would like to know my editorial budget, Long said we would have to begin from scratch. Did I understand the concept of the zero budget? It was built by beginning with nothing and adding only such expenditure as you could not do without. I should begin that exercise. I told John Grant. 'Quite mad,' he said, 'but I'll do as you say.'

I had imagined before I joined *The Times* that I would sit down with Murdoch and Long, if not the whole board, and agree a plan of action. An attack on the ruinous production costs one took for granted, but how could the losses be otherwise contained and gradually turned to profit? An increase in the cover price would help, but would we lose more upper-income readers than advertisers could tolerate, and weaken that source of revenue? Could we charge 25p or 35p, as a premium paper like *The Financial Times*, and keep our essential core of 250,000–275,000 readers? Or how much more would we then have to invest in editorial and promotion? Or should we go all out for circulation, holding the price while improving and promoting the paper? Would that give us sales revenue and an audience for advertisers who could be charged more before we drowned in red ink?

This is the kind of debate there was in the days of Thomson, which had some commercial success before the print unions ruined it. But the discussion I thought might happen any week when Murdoch returned from here or there never took place. When I raised these matters with Long, in our master's absence, he would shrug his shoulders: 'Rupert likes to do these things himself. And he knows a lot more about them than I do.' In view of Long's customary dogmatism this was like the White House spokesman in Joseph Heller's novel who fields a difficult ball for the President by announcing: 'We have no plans and they are all firm.' Long instead focussed on the ignorance of *Times* journalists:

The attached recipe contains a minor illiteracy which is gaining currency.

The Frenglish concoction '*trompe à l'œil*', meaning that which is designed to appear what it is not, is presumably based on two French adjectival phrases '*trompe l'œil*' and '*tape-à-l'œil*'. The active verb '*tromper*' (to deceive) governs the direct object, so that the '*à*' is out of place. The first phrase means 'designed to deceive the eye', the second, vulgarly ostentatious, 'designed to hit you in the eye'. Some Frenglish phrases are merely disturbing and distasteful, such as '*folie de grandeur*' and others which are presumably designed to suggest a knowledge which, ironically, they prove the owner does not possess. This one is also grammatically impossible.

Notes like this from a general manager to an editor must be unique (single, sole, being without a like or equal) in the history of the press. Many were enjoyable. I treated them on merit, discounting Long's contempt for journalists as a breed. *The Times* was not so perfect it could dispense with the services of any etymological vigilante. I had not always noticed the offence. '*Trompe à l'œil*', I confess, had escaped me.

Long's knowledge of the business of newspapers was considerably less. He appreciated serious journalism, he had been a good foreign correspondent, he was a fine writer, and his experience at Reuters had helped him lucidly to frame principles of general management, but his lifetime experience had been in a news agency, which is very different from a newspaper. Its product is information distributed by teleprinter and video to other businesses, notably, but decreasingly to newspapers. At Times Newspapers he was concerned with a more diverse product, made available through a complicated chain of printing and transport, which he was managing for the first time, and which was sustained by sales of newspaper copies and advertising revenue in a subtle relationship wholly new to him. He had the intelligence to master it all fairly quickly, if he had been apprentice to a different master. But Murdoch liked to keep in his direct personal control all central questions of pricing, the multiplicity of advertising rates and promotion.

Murdoch's own board meetings were even more cursory than Long's. 'Yeah, yeah, well let's all get back to work, there's a lot to do.' So I found myself putting to Murdoch directly what had been dealt with before by the board or Hussey and sometimes by Hamilton. He shied away from talking strategy or money, but he was quick and responsive on the other matters. Very early on I told Murdoch that the old company had been thinking of improving the quality of the newsprint, because it was like printing on bread crumbs. Murdoch committed himself to new paper at once and an inquiry into the poor reproduction. I objected to full-page advertisements appearing at the opening of the paper on page 3. Murdoch banned them there. It was his idea – journalism overcoming republicanism – to attempt colour in the paper the day after the Royal Wedding and publish a souvenir magazine, and to have book serials for summer reading. The conversations were sometimes jumpy: 'Johnson's a scream. Know anybody to follow Akass at the *Sun*? Got any ideas who might edit the *News of the World*? Present editor's too nice. Some tough yellow journalist is what it needs.'

Murdoch admittedly did not make my job any easier when he gave an interview to UPI three weeks after I had arrived. 'There are a lot of very ordinary hacks at *The Times*,' he breezed. 'We've just got to sort out the wheat from the chaff.' But he also said: 'We'll get there slowly. The thing about this is that you can't do it overnight. We want more spare forces.' When Murdoch had asked me, during his take-over, for twenty-five redundancies at *The Sunday Times*, he had said it was to appease the other unions and it would be a way of bringing in new blood. He said the same at *The Times*: 'You need more really good people around you. Who is there?' I told him I planned to bring in Bernard Donoughue to help with leaders and Whitehall-Westminster. He wanted to see him, 'if that's all right'. They talked politics. Murdoch pushed his standard line in short restless assertions: the British did not want to work; the Establishment looked down on money-making; Mrs Thatcher was doing the only possible thing, tough but you had to be tough. Donoughue agreed she was right to try to control the public sector unions: 'Her mistake was not to do it right at the beginning.' But he argued the case for more public investment. 'Sure, sure, that's our policy,' said Murdoch. This was a reflection of the drift of low-key discussions we had at Murdoch lunches at *The Times* with the knights of the big state industries: Sir Ian MacGregor, chairman of British Steel, Sir Peter Parker of British Rail and Leyland's Michael Edwardes. 'Get him aboard, can you?' said Murdoch when Donoughue had gone.

He was always probing about key people. Roughly two months after I took over, he beamed: 'Douglas-Home's all right. I met him on the steps and he said you were the best thing that had ever happened to the paper. So you're all right there.' I told Murdoch of all the senior appointments I was making. He had asked for this at the vetting committee, and it had been the rule also with Denis Hamilton. He made only one request, harmless enough at the time I thought. When I listed Michael Hamlyn as the new Washington correspondent to succeed Patrick Brogan, who had resigned predicting Murdoch would 'cut all your balls off', I was asked up to his office next morning.

'This Hamlyn. Can he run things?' Yes, I said, but he also had hidden talent as a writer. How would it be, asked Murdoch, if he stole Hamlyn for News International? 'You're only trying to find him a slot,' he jabbed, 'I can use him.' He had been looking for someone to control the work of News International reporters in New York. His Australian editors were always scrapping about the service. 'Hamlyn can run the bureau, liaise a bit with you. He could do that, couldn't he?' I said he could, but I would still want our own man in New York. 'Yeah, you've got Leapman,' he said knowingly. He and Long kept saying it was time I got rid of Leapman, who was regarded as left and anti-Murdoch. No, said Murdoch, Hamlyn's appointment would not affect *The Times*.

When I communicated this news to Douglas-Home and Horton, they were anxious that *The Times* might none the less lose its own man in New York. Even Long's eyebrow quivered momentarily. I emphasised the point to Murdoch again and, when he promulgated Hamlyn's appointment on 28 May, he met it handsomely: 'News gathering by individual publications within the Group will be undertaken, as always, by the designated correspondents. Their work will continue to be directed by their editors, foreign editors, managing editors or their representatives, through direct contact with correspondents.'

Murdoch made less of an impression on others these days. He had disappointed British Leyland's Michael Edwardes by cancelling Thomson's policy of buying British cars and had a Mercedes himself, but I thought the two men would hit it off as connoisseurs of industrial warfare. Edwardes was a good guest at a *Times* lunch, but Murdoch was off-hand and incurious. He said little, and Long, having surveyed the guest silently for most of the lunch, which was one of his party tricks, laid on a hostile line. Murdoch was uneasy with *Times* executives at lunches. He ate and drank sparingly at any of these affairs, clearly grudging Long's gastronomic flourishes. Sometimes I thought I was missing a joke and Murdoch was imitating a right-winger for their benefit. 'Two kinds of politician in Africa, both chimps, only one has charisma.' When Peter Hennessy talked about rediscovering Delane's passion for truth, Murdoch's face slipped a notch. Leisure, that's where sales were. Of course *The Guardian* had angled it right. He didn't like its politics but they were right in going for the young trendy left aged 20 to 25. We'd go for *Telegraph* readers. We'd get to 400,000, the half million would be a little harder. One day, when I went to Long's office, he had *The Guardian* open and was looking morosely at a feature page of women's knickers. 'Rupert says you've got to give it to *The Guardian*, they know their market.'

Murdoch had British distractions from events at PO Box 7. This was about the time he was relieving Larry Lamb of his long and successful editorship of the *Sun* and gambling brilliantly with its future, cutting its cover price from 12p to 10p and spending millions on bingo to restore it as the best-selling tabloid. I would find him in his office, a vertical furrow in his forehead. 'Sorry, sorry, haven't read your paper much today.' A quick flip would follow. 'Go-od, go-od, fine', and then he would turn to the rack with the tabloids. 'Not a bad *Sun* today. Good spread in the

Star. Wonder who's doing that?' And then: 'Why d'ya keep Grant on?' Gerald Long had told him John Grant was part of the hopeless old guard.

One morning he pulled a face at the 'op ed' page. 'You say Douglas-Home is all right, but he's not much of a journalist.' Douglas-Home had seen Ted Heath during his illness and had come back excitedly to say he thought Heath might join the Social Democrats; he'd told Murdoch this, and then offered me an article canvassing what a catch Heath would be. I thought it was a well-argued, if less than sensational, piece. 'He'll never make an editor,' said Murdoch. 'No idea of news.' Murdoch liked his news bold and simple. Events that qualified were guaranteed to stir him whether in London or New York. He was the first on the phone to me the Saturday a former air cadet brandished a toy pistol at the Queen during Trooping the Colour. He was excited the night there was a clash between the Metropolitan Police and blacks who were marching to protest at the failure to arrest anyone after a house fire killed a party of young blacks at a birthday party. 'Nothing wrong there that a good crack on the head won't cure,' he declared. But political personalities interested him most of all. When he called from New York, it was invariably to ask how the terrible Tory wets were behaving or what that old fool Foot was up to. He loved every minute of the Benn challenge for the deputy leadership, ringing down for the latest when he was in London.

His general demeanour in the office at this period was disarmingly that of visiting fireman. I took him to see Taylor's group of designers at work on our colour magazine for the Royal Wedding. 'Sorry, sorry. Just great. Know you're busy, don't let me stop you. Just great. Sorry.' But he backed the magazine when, for a time, Ruda's advertising people faltered on it, and he was positive in response to new ideas. When I canvassed giving the degree results of every university in the country, and not simply Oxford and Cambridge, he agreed with enthusiasm and sanctioned the additional space at once. He listened to my ideas for the back page which meant displacing classified advertising and told Ruda to co-operate. And on Friday 12 June he emerged from a meeting of the Holdings board for lunch and asked, 'How soon can you start your arts guide?'

These three important developments were like the blades of Levin's windmill. We got up from one to be knocked down by the other; and there was a fourth blade in the effort to reorganize news. Printers and journalists were at full stretch, and I know those with difficulties thought that I had been afflicted by deafness. But newspaper offices are at their best under pressure and good news kept seeping through. The decline in sales had been halted and reversed. It was nothing spectacular, around 284,000 for May against 276,000, but as all newspapermen know, it is stopping a fall which is hardest.

My idea for the new back page began like this: I was apparently the only person in the world who on 2 May 1981 wanted to know the lighting-up time in Bristol, the nature of delays at Heathrow, the latest best-selling novel, and the trend of house prices; and on 3 May was obsessed by the high tide at London Bridge, what was selling at Christie's and the temperature in Venice. Perhaps all these pieces of information could be found by a man in possession of the secret of life. Yet no newspaper dealt consistently or at all with these matters of life and death, assuming our interests to be circumscribed by the fate of the world. I had tried to remedy this deficiency at *The Sunday Times* by starting a service called Noticeboard with the help of Brian MacArthur. But space was against it and I carried the ambition to *The Times*, where it was cordially received. Everywhere there were people nurturing private longings. Mark Boxer, the cartoonist, wanted to know what the other daily papers were saying, without having to go through them all. Peter Watson, the diarist, was downcast daily to find he had missed the last chance to see an exhibition of watercolours. Gerald Long, scenting revolution daily, wanted to be sure the road to Dover was open. And our readers, when there was some disaster, were keen to know where they could send their charity. I had two instruments to hand for this advancement of human knowledge. Cyril Bainbridge, the managing editor of home news, was a cool organizer, and also the author of books on the Brontës and brass bands. Here was a man who understood eclecticism. I asked him to collect the information under about fifty headings and see to it that it was never polluted by error. To execute the scheme I had David Hopkinson, which is like calling on Graham Sutherland for a road map. Hopkinson was the editor of the *Sheffield Telegraph* when he courageously exposed that police were beating people with a rhino whip. He was, from 1964, a distinguished editor of the *Birmingham Post*, then the editor of the *Evening Mail*, and a figure in journalism and the Midlands. He had a disagreement with his company – it happens occasionally – and left, so I snatched him up. He and Turnill come from the same school of master sub-editors. Where Turnill is small and trim, Hopkinson is Mr Pickwick, large, benign, blossoming, the body threatening at all times to burst free of the wide-striped shirt and the straining leather belt. He became a walking symbol of our problem. We could not squeeze all we had into the available space, which was the bottom half of the back page, with the top reserved for news. We could have a weather service improved out of all recognition from the shrivelled paragraphs on page 2; we could list the day's royal engagements, exhibitions, talks, lectures, lunchtime music, auctions, sporting fixtures, tides, lighting-up in the major cities, anniversaries and the state of the pound sterling; we could give space to what the papers say in Britain and overseas; we could predict satellite positions and announce the business of Parliament. But what of Watson's last chance to see, and the times world-wide, today's good cause, and the scores of other items that diligent research had shown were awaited daily?

Eyes lit on space in that bottom half of the back page, but denied to *The Times* information service, as I had decided to call it: the crossword puzzle. The eyes were important ones, since they belonged to Rupert Murdoch. He was visiting me in my office one afternoon when Edwin Taylor brought in a trial setting of the page. 'Ah-ah-em, mmm,' said Murdoch for all of five seconds, and with two quick strokes he had moved the crossword inside the paper. Was the crossword puzzle to be our Rubicon? No. He did not persist when I said I would not move it; but we were not through with the crossword yet. For the sake of an orderly compilation of the information service, Taylor had rearranged the clues to run at the side of the puzzle. John Grant and Philip Howard spoke for England. Grant did more: he demonstrated the posture of a *Times* puzzler on the tube. With crossword and clues in their normal pattern the left hand easily grasped the paper, folded to two-column width, with the right hand ready to enter an answer. The Taylor layout, spreading the puzzle to four columns, doubled the area of grip required from the left hand. It might disqualify from doing the crossword any tube traveller with a fist smaller than that of an orang-utan. Grant's ergonomics showed also that the extra space required by a strap-hanging puzzler would provoke breaches of the peace. I ruled for the *status quo*.

The new page displaced six columns of personal advertisements and up to two columns of births, marriages and deaths; I moved them to the last inside left-hand page with little regret. Sherlock Holmes was a keen reader of the personal column for leads to crime, and in Haley's day one could still pick up in a single day an old coronation robe, a yacht at Monte Carlo, a nanny and a suit of private armour. But the romance fell away in the 1970s and by the end of the decade the personal columns were no more than trade advertising, welcome but not exotic. So on 2 June the new page was launched with *The Times* information service, the crossword exactly as it was, and news at the top. This time I made no announcement of any kind, merely checking that the road to Dover was open. It was a sensible precaution. Once again there was revolt in the shires. There were no fewer than four protesters from Cambridge colleges, led by Philip C. French and Mark Latham of Churchill, obviously a cell. I decided to get to the bottom of this plot on my equilibrium. I telephoned letter-writers. The first I reached reminded me we had met at a legal function. The 'Widgery' was Lady Widgery, the wife of the Lord Chief Justice of England. This was ominous, sentence without trial. Widgery v Evans concerned two lines of scripture which appeared at the top of the births, marriages and deaths column; it was a nuisance to have to turn the page. Did the defendant have anything to say? He did. I ventured that it would be the Lord's work; this was not thought-compelling. I said in cowardly fashion I would consider restoring the two lines to the back page if the Widgerys proved representative in their objections. I was given parole. Four of the other protesters did have the scripture in mind, but two thought it more appropriate above the deaths column. I left it there. I was emboldened to do this by the reception I got on the telephone over several days from a colonel in Winchester, a doctor in Sussex, another in North Wales, a farmer's wife in Kent, about twenty people in all. The strongest line of protest was at the moving of the deaths notices, but letter-writers who had singed their notepaper proved in person to be genial and open to persuasion. I was glad I had phoned, because I learned a lot about the way The Times was read; but what lingered in my mind was their feeling that England had changed for the worst and it was too much for The Times to change as well.

By the end of the second week the correspondence was running favourably and the rise in circulation continued. Couples were spotted reading The Times back to front across the table at breakfast. Bainbridge and Hopkinson were called on to appease insatiable curiosities. So popular did the innovation of the Times Information Service become that, when the grumbles died away during the summer, I began to wonder how the country had staggered on without knowing where to obtain cheap champagne and late petrol. People were not satisfied with being told that at noon in London it was 4 a.m. in San Francisco. What time was it, pray, in the United Arab Emirates? Was Beethoven's violin concerto still outselling Elgar's second symphony; how did one get to Wimbledon, and where could the Queen be seen today? We told them all these things when they needed to know them, solving the problem of space by the way we varied the frequency of entries. The information service became a national bulletin board, an overnight institution. It attracted the scholarly attention of Dr Janet Morgan of Oxford University. She plotted its entries as Sovietologists do those in Pravda and concluded, in a report to Atlantic, that it gave a unique picture of readers of The Times 'ruefully trying to keep up standards, resourceful, self-deprecatory, fond of pottering through almanacs and works of reference, chatty, quietly but proudly aware of taking part in a national rite, an intimate collective experience'.

The new back page was a happy combination of new and old Times men, and so was Preview, the tabloid arts guide launched on 19 June. If the back page was an impressive piece of organization, it was outshone by what was achieved with the launch of Preview. I had introduced a full page of critics' recommendations in the main paper during the *Time Out* strike, but it was no more than limbering up for producing eight pages weekly on films, theatre, music, exhibitions, family outings and a visitor's guide to London. Within days of Murdoch's approval of the expenditure, Edwin Taylor had thought out the structure and detailed design for Tony Holden, Douglas-Home and John Higgins had corralled the critics, and Oscar Turnill, who gave it its name, had seen it through a 2 a.m. difficult cold-type production with Nicholas Wapshott and Richard Williams. The printers said at first that they were too hard pressed to do it, and it was only a direct instruction from Murdoch which persuaded them it might be attempted. I made Williams, formerly of *Time Out*, the editor, impressed by his quiet enthusiasms. Preview was well received. Murdoch grumbled at our choice of the centre spread article, which was John Higgins on Glyndebourne. Long, who was to be Preview's best supporter, rallied in defence of Britten. It was pure chance, though nobody will believe it, that Williams followed up the Glyndebourne centre spread with another on Dracula's rise from the grave.

Then we were into the university results compiled by the imperturbable Bainbridge. We were so short of sub-editors that at 1 a.m., when there were only three or four left, I seized a bundle and discovered it to be my own Durham University, appearing in full in *The Times* for the first time. Altogether we checked and published 16,000 names that summer.

The climax for me and *The Times* was the Royal Wedding on 29 July. We had begun in March, planning a colour magazine. It was no hindrance to have arrive as the magazine's editor the royal biographer Anthony Holden. Douglas-Home wrote on the monarchy's role, Norman St John Stevas of the changes in Britain since the last wedding of an heir to the throne, Antonia Fraser on the idea of a princess, Godfrey Smith on royal Gloucester, and Holden himself on the royal romance. Taylor prepared a spectacular centre fold-out with detailed artwork of St Paul's and Buckingham Palace. The latter would not have been accomplished without the loan of George Darby and Taylor's team of wall-chart artists from *The Sunday Times*. *The Times* just did not have those skills of research and graphic expression. On Tuesday 27 July, the day we made the magazine available with the paper, *The Times* sold 526,000 copies, more than at any time in its history. Not a copy was left even for members of staff who did not place an order.

At about the same time in March we set out to see if we could produce a wedding photograph in colour the next day, something not attempted before. There were no means of printing original colour in Gray's Inn Road. The only possible way it could be done was to print the colour on newsprint reels at a specialist plant and then feed these into the Gray's Inn Road presses carrying the ordinary run of the paper. The technique is familiar in Fleet Street; the timing was against us and it was not the only handicap. We decided to wrap four pages round the ordinary *Times*. The front of the four pages must be a colour photograph of the married royal couple on the day: this would be the problem. The other pages could be prepared in advance. On the back we arranged to reproduce a painting of the marriage of Queen Victoria to Prince Albert in 1840. The inside pages were to be black and white news photographs to add to those in the main paper. At the last moment Brian MacArthur had an inspiration and late at night, with the help of a librarian, I rooted out from a dank basement in another building the bound file of *The Times* of Delane's day. It devoted a full page to the last marriage of a Prince of Wales on 11 March 1863. I had an engraving made of this page: every line of the report by Delane's men could be read as clearly as in 1863.

But how could we manage the front page? East Midland Allied Press at Peterborough said that we could have finished reels in London from around 10.30 p.m. if they received the colour separations of our wedding photograph not later than 3.30 p.m. On the wedding timings this gave us less than two hours to take a satisfactory photograph, develop it, select and scale it for the page, have the transparency broken down into colour separations and get it to Peterborough, and all this in an overcrowded London. Peterborough had space for a helicopter. Rex Features, the processers of the film, and Keene Engraving, who were to produce the colour separations, thought it could just be done, though it left nothing to chance. We made the arrangements in secrecy. Then Keith Smith, the picture editor, reported that we did not have a good position in St Paul's Cathedral for a picture of the ring going on the bride's finger. Picture positions on these occasions are shared on a rota basis between newspapers. Those who had been lucky had an obligation to let us have copy transparencies, but with all the magazines wanting them there was the prospect of a delay of two hours. The ambitious plans were in jeopardy. Edwin Taylor remained sanguine. He argued that there was an even better moment of symbolism, which would occur when the royal couple as man and wife joined their public outside St Paul's, and Smith's foresight had secured us a window on the seventh floor of Juxon House on Ludgate Hill, overlooking the front steps of St Paul's. They tried it out: it was not successful. They tried again with a borrowed 800 mm Nikkor lens and brought me black and white prints of what we might get. It required an effort of imagination to see the photograph of empty steps filled out with pageantry, but it was our only hope.

On the big day, with the streets outside quite deserted, my office filled happily with spectators for the television; the news room television was also playing to a full house with a brisk trade in beer and sandwiches. There were flutters of handclaps and cheers, and I said there was a bottle of champagne for spotting *The Times* literary editor, Philip Howard, who was inside the cathedral in his morning suit. Just checking up. I thought most of the photographer, Peter Trievnor, with his huge lens on the seventh floor of Juxon House. It was all waiting; we had done all the preparation we could twice over. At about 1.15 p.m. there were excited cries of, 'Here he is, here he is.' It was a man in leathers and crash helmet approaching Keith Smith. He was the bearer of the precious transparencies from Trievnor, who had time to take eight frames of Ektachrome 400 before the royal couple moved on from the steps. The first one we looked at had the couple waving but one face obscured, the second had no waves, the third another part of a face obscured, but the fifth and sixth were excellent. They were rushed off to Keenes and by 3 p.m. the motorcyclist was off to Battersea heliport ahead of schedule to hand them to another Evans, the head of editorial services, by the name of Reg. Silence. No sign of the motorcyclist. Evans hopping with consternation. I suddenly realized that for all our planning we had consigned our fate to a solitary motorcyclist finding his way through the dispersing crowds. 'Don't worry, Harry, this is a day when *The Times* luck will count,' said a phlegmatic sub-editor, and so it was. The motorcyclist arrived and we made up the time. Our television crowds had dispersed to their desks just as the wedding crowds were dispersing.

MacArthur had the idea of making a feature of the full formal titles of the royal couple. 'Is this any help?' said a figure in morning dress producing a programme from his pocket. It was the deputy editor, Douglas-Home, who had been in the cathedral as a private guest. I took the formal ceremonial titles from the front of his programme and ran them across the top of *The Times*. At about 10.18 p.m. I went downstairs to shake the grimy hand of a man in blue overalls who had arrived with the first lorry-load of colour reels from Peterborough, fifteen minutes ahead of time. Two hours later, as the other reels arrived, we had enough to stop printing the black-and-white and go to colour. It did not work. There was static in the newsprint and there was difficulty in registration. I stood in the machine room as the quarter hours went by, silently wishing them luck. Finally, at 1.30 a.m., the first colour ran successfully with excitement on every floor of the building. Everyone stopped to admire what had been achieved; happy clusters of people congratulating each other, and a high point for me since it was the culmination of the skills and enthusiasms of old and new members of *The Times*, and there were celebrations as the other dailies arrived without colour. We sold out 400,000 copies. Excluding the Royal Wedding issues there had now been a considerable increase in sales: 291,000 against 269,000 the year before and without any of the conventional expensive television advertising.

There was something else different about *The Times* that day. I restored the Royal arms to the masthead. Originally I had intended to reinstate the arms permanently on the paper's 200th birthday in 1985 – then I thought the Royal Wedding deserved a flourish. I had let these intentions be known well in advance, girded for some last-ditch republicanism from the sixth floor, but there was none. Indeed Long had pre-empted me by having the arms designed into his visiting cards. Murdoch was in Australia. When the staff saw the arms, they clamoured for them to be retained for good. Hickey came to morning conference with a smile. I heard only one note of dissent. In 1966 the Garter King of Arms had congratulated *The Times* on removing the arms 'which for so long and misleadingly suggested that *The Times* had an official character'. Philip Howard said there was displeasure in that quarter and I might be in the Tower by the end of the week. I told him to reply that *The Times* had had the arms longer than the House of Windsor, and fled the country.

I was due on holiday in America. While there, I had the pleasure of reading in *The Times* court page that Tina Brown and I were married on 19 August at Grey Gardens, East Hampton, Long Island, the beautiful summer home of the editor of the *Washington Post*, Ben Bradlee, and his wife, the writer Sally Quinn. With Tina's parents in Spain, the bride was given away by Tony Holden, who had taken a house on Martha's Vineyard with Amanda and his children. The *Sunday Times* foreign correspondent David Blundy, who had just returned from El Salvador, and his daughter. Anna, came in from Manhattan, as did John Heilpern, *The Times* arts correspondent in the United States and his wife, Joan Buck, the writer. The other guests were the novelist Nora Ephron and Mortimer Zuckerman, the publisher of *Atlantic*. The ceremony took place in the Bradlees' Italian garden, on the edge of the Atlantic, with Ben as the best man and young Anna Blundy as the maid of honour.

14
POLITICS
AND MONEY

'I like Reagan,' said Anna Murdoch, looking attractively schoolmarmish in a print dress with a white bow tie. 'At least he knows how to delegate. He decides on the neutron bomb, but leaves times to dance with his wife.'

'Dance with his wife!' Murdoch snorted. 'All PR.' And he gave his sudden, capricious laugh. He almost relaxed when Anna was around and she took the chill out of the air for a few hours that September of 1981, when she came with him for dinner on one of her infrequent visits to London. It was shortly after my marriage to Tina. I had been six months on *The Times*. There were signs that my honeymoon with Murdoch was ending.

The previous day I had arrived at the office feeling pleased with myself about a leader I had written at home on Sunday with the help of Henry Stanhope, the defence correspondent. It argued that the Government should choose the British rather than the American prototype for the new heavy torpedo for Royal Navy submarines; and Mrs Thatcher promptly did that. But when Murdoch sent for me it was not to offer the congratulations of the spring and summer. He was still gouging his ballpoint pen through a report on page 2 by Lucy Hodges: 'Why do you use these Commies?' It was a half-column summarizing evidence to the Scarman riot inquiry from the Brixton Residents' Group. Their lawyer argued that the high crime rate in Brixton before the riots could have been produced by the big increase in the number of policemen on the streets. I replied that it was a good story and Hodges was a good reporter; in any event it was absurd to call her a Communist.

It was in character that Murdoch should dislike carrying an immigrant community's statement critical of the police, but his tenseness and irritability that autumn were not explained by such a small incident. He was tormented by politics and money. It was a bad time for Mrs Thatcher, which we reported, and it was a bad time for Murdoch's finances: how bad nobody knew, because he kept it a secret from his directors at *The Times*.

In tandem with the recession, the Government's electoral slump was breaking all records. At 30% it was eight points behind Labour and lower for a longer period than any government since the war. It was five months since the launch of the Social Democratic Party, and at mid-term in the possible life of the Government the Tories showed no signs of recovery. Murdoch followed all this avidly. In my early months there had been growls about Mrs Thatcher being the only British politician who was any good and 'those pissing liberals' who did not support her. He wanted to know why I thought Holden was any good when he had recruited Henry Fairlie, who was not a fan of Reagan. He lobbed newspaper clippings across the Atlantic, mainly from the American new Right. He asked me to note an article contributed to the *Wall Street Journal* which said there was no plausible alternative to Thatcherism and compared Mrs Thatcher to the wartime Churchill. His head went down and his lips curled in disgust at the first syllables of the names of Sir Ian Gilmour, Jim Prior and Lord Carrington: 'Hypocrites!' But all this was nonchalance by Murdoch's standards.

It was in the autumn that he began to get steamed up. He was on tenterhooks about what *The Times* might say when the Cabinet reshuffle was imminent. He was well informed. He rang through to say that Norman Tebbit was going to be important; Fred Emery was sceptical. Murdoch's hit list was Pym, Gilmour, Prior and Carrington, but he and Long took Prior out to dinner. I was not invited. On the day of the big purge, when I lunched with a Cabinet Minister who was spared, Murdoch was on the phone: 'What do you think?' I could give him only a vague outline of the leader Donoughue was writing which Douglas-Home and I edited. 'Yeah, yeah. Well, I think she's got it right.' Our leader said half right.

There was one ominously enjoyable interlude before the storm, representing the kind of life readers expect editors of *The Times* to lead. I received a gold embossed card inviting me to dinner at 10 Downing Street with the Prime Minister in honour of the French President, M. Mitterrand. I told Murdoch, expecting that he would be there. No, but he seemed to know already about my invitation. 'She likes you,' he said of Mrs Thatcher. It was altogether an agreeable occasion. Mitterrand gave Charles Hargrove in Paris an exclusive interview, which we published on the day of his arrival. In the evening I found the red hand on the placement plan for six tables pointing me to sit with Mrs Thatcher and the President, sharing a small circular table with Gordon Richardson, Governor of the Bank of England, Arnold Weinstock of General Electric, Denis Thatcher, a reticent Ian Trethowan, Director-General of the BBC, and Pierre Dreyfus, the French Minister for Industry, who kept muttering about how wrong it was to have Communists in the French

Government: one of them, the Minister of Transport, M. Fiterman, was blithely drinking the Prime Minister's Krug '64 at another table. I joked with Mitterrand that this man with his ambitions for a Channel tunnel was a subversive red mole. Mitterrand affected to understand what I said. He was warm, witty and fluent; the trouble for most of the table was that it was fluency in French. Two official translators worked in shifts, crouching between the leaders at plate level. In one hand-over there was a gap and an *entente cordiale* on nuclear energy lay in the hands of Arnold Weinstock, manically articulating Mrs Thatcher into fissile French. I congratulated the Foreign Office man who came in for the second half on the quickness and felicity of his translations, which were superior to those of the first-half Frenchman, only to have him say: 'Oh, no, old boy. I'm from the Quai d'Orsay. The other chap was one of yours.'

I asked Mitterrand about Poland. He was firm that the Soviet army would not invade. The difference in Czechoslovakia had been that the official Communist party deviated; so long as the Polish Communist party stayed true to Moscow, the Russians would deal through Poles. He was eloquent about how freedom could only be temporarily put down in eastern Europe: 'The laws of gravity do not apply to rising sap'. There was a good deal of '*mais oui*' and 'of course' between Thatcher and Mitterrand over the imperative of strong defences against the Soviet Union. Mrs Thatcher said to me that she warmed to a socialist who was a patriot prepared to defend his country, 'unlike ours, Harold'. Mitterrand did not spring to the defence of British socialism, but he did express a very Gallic distaste for Reaganomics. His views on the need for currency reform sounded as if he should have been reported to Gerald Long for imbibing Harold Lever. The Governor of the Bank of England would not be drawn; he knew it was dangerous ground. It was the only *frisson* of the evening. We would have had a deal on the Channel tunnel before the *noisettes* of lamb but for the inhospitable activities of Denis Thatcher and Bill Deedes, the editor of the *Daily Telegraph*, who put out propaganda all evening about smelly French lorries driving through Kent hop fields. Sir Peter Parker of British Rail did his best in alliance with the French Transport Minister. The British Cabinet Ministers were a subdued lot; the big reshuffle was imminent. Gilmour was belligerent and asked for space in *The Times*, which I was glad to offer; Christopher Soames sat on the sofa gloomily ruminating on how unjust it would be if he were chopped.

I was not asked to No. 10 again; and when I next saw Mrs Thatcher at a cocktail party at the home of the Attorney-General, Sir Michael Havers, the following February she passed without a word. No doubt it was a multiplication of things. Seven days after the Mitterrand dinner,

Fred Emery came excitedly into my room with a copy of a letter he had acquired on 10 Downing Street notepaper. It was a 'Dear Nick' letter of December 1980 from Denis Thatcher to Nicholas Edwards, the Secretary of State for Wales, asking for a speed-up in the planning appeal on a housing development in Snowdonia. Thatcher declared an interest as the developers' adviser. Edwards scribbled on the corner to his officials: 'The explanation had better be good and quick, i.e. this week.' Murdoch saw the first edition with this story, which was delivered to Woodrow Wyatt's home, where we were having dinner. He looked miserable and said nothing. Every newspaper followed up. Edwards and No. 10 issued robust statements, saying that any citizen was entitled to write to a Minister and use his home notepaper; No. 10 pointed out there was no crest on the paper as there would have been if it were from the Prime Minister. We wrote a mildly admonitory leader, no more than a polite cough. Headed 'Caesar's husband', we said Denis Thatcher had negotiated the pitfalls of being married to the Prime Minister with considerable tact and good humour, but a little more care with notepaper might avoid embarrassing ambiguities. Lord Shawcross wrote to *The Times* to denounce us for a smear, breaching copyright, abetting the receiving of stolen property, and engaging in conduct not previously to be expected from *The Times*, i.e. just a little short of the full Nuremberg charge-sheet. Others said we should be commended for presenting the facts about a matter of controversy in the public domain. I knew publication of a copy of the Thatcher letter would cause offence in No. 10, but I had no hesitation in agreeing with Emery that we had to do it. The ultimate approval of the housing, over the objections of the local authority and the Snowdonia National Park Planning Authority, had caused an outcry in North Wales.

There is no doubt that a great deal of what we published that autumn was discomfiting to Mrs Thatcher and the Government. We gave a full page to a mid-term report on the Government. Ivor Crewe's study of the polls found that Mrs Thatcher was the most unpopular Prime Minister since opinion-poll records began; we reported that Michael Foot was also the most unpopular Opposition leader, but a week before the Tory conference the graph superimposed on a photograph of Mrs Thatcher confronted in the street by an argumentative voter must have looked like a dagger. A series on youth was not good news either. When I arrived at *The Times* I asked Douglas-Home to organize a survey of the attitudes of people between fifteen and twenty-four. I was sceptical of the bromide that unemployment was having no effect. The riots intervened. Dan van der Vat's articles and the accompanying polls provided fascinating, but disturbing, insights. The conclusion was that unemployment was breeding a lumpenproletariat in unique and dangerous isolation. Young people sympathized with the difficulties of the police. Nearly half of them thought they had been too soft with the rioters, only 12% too tough. But no less than 30% thought violence was sometimes justified to bring about political change. They were depressed at not being able to find work and felt a burden on their families. They liked the Queen and were appreciative of their families, but were rebellious about politicians. Tories, Liberals and Social Democrats were all rated lower among these youngsters than in the nation as a whole; only Labour did better. Mrs Thatcher was disliked by 70%.

There was not much balm for the Labour party. Our major political series, published on the eve of the conference, identified the virtually unknown left-wing activists who were winning control of the leadership by changes in the constitution. Bernard Donoughue secured the work of Maurice and David Kogan for *The Times*. Checked and edited in the office, it described in detail how a cool group of lobbyists, using Trotskyist and Militant Tendency muscle, but not part of such groups, had pulled off union and constituency participation of the election of the Labour party leader, and the mandatory reselection of MPs.

However, the Tory news was depressing for No. 10. Edward Heath was on the warpath. Charles Morrison and other leading Tory back-benchers wrote to *The Times* supporting our criticisms of economic policy. Geoffrey Smith even thought it necessary to discuss whether the Tory rebels would run a candidate against Mrs Thatcher (he thought she would win).

Gerald Long exerted himself to get a better press for the Government. He wrote me a 'private and personal' two-page memorandum that I read three times to make sure I had it right. Was he really saying that we should not give prominence to news that was bad for the Government? What produced his outburst was a report by David Blake, the economics editor, based on figures released by the Central Statistical Office. They showed that output had fallen for the sixth successive quarter. It was not much of a fall, about half a percentage point, but it belied the Chancellor's statement in the spring that the recession was over and recovery would begin in the early summer. Blake said the figures were embarrassing for the Government and MacArthur had led the paper with it under the headline 'Recession goes on with sixth drop in output'. Long protested: 'The headline of today's story might be otherwise expressed as "Sir Geoffrey Howe is a liar/idiot." ... This broadside on the unfortunate Chancellor, while not undeserved, seems to me again to be largely irrelevant unless some journalist seeks personal gratification in bringing the Chancellor down.'

What was he on about? The headline was neutral, a straightforward summary of the facts. He was thrusting along a broader front. The key passage in Long's memorandum was this:

> Articles by staff writers in *The Times* and notably by Mr David Blake, who wrote today's lead story, seem to me to have been consistently critical of Government economic policy in recent months. The two articles by Harold Lever on the currency aspects of economic policy and the editorial which followed reinforce the impression that the editorial policy of *The Times* in this matter is to criticise the Government and to consider its economic policies mistaken.

Well, yes. I had no intention of replying. The leaders in *The Times* were consistently critical of economic policy and sceptical of the claims that the recession was over; I had myself written that, if we were turning the corner, it was the longest in the world. But this was nothing to do with the managing director. It was *The Times*'s view. It was temperately and constructively expressed, and we gave space on the 'op ed' page as well for defences of the Government's policy: there was a strikingly bold contribution from Professor C.C. Hague, an adviser to the Prime Minister's policy unit. The articles by Lever, if they were critical of government, were so of all governments, but were really a brilliantly original proposal on how we might end the damage being done to world trade by unstable currencies and interest-rate wars. Long had already harangued me about publishing them, but had no answer to their logic; and later I heard that Murdoch regarded them as one of my crimes.

As for our news reports on the economy and the Government's popularity, I was determined to go on with a proper reporting job, however many memos and threatening scowls there were. It might satisfy Murdoch and Long if *The Times* suggested the recession was over or Mrs Thatcher was doing well in the polls, but that was not what the news happened to be.

Long stood amazed at our effrontery: 'The whole tone of the *Times* story', he wrote, 'is that the figures prove that the recession has not ended.' Guilty again. He wanted an answer from me why our treatment was bolder than other papers. He did not get it. I was not going to let the managing director get me on the run on editorial matters. It was an important story, our report was accurate and fair, and Blake's interpretation was sound. It was certainly vindicated by events. The recession that Long would have liked *The Times* to end went on and on. The Chancellor explained that the end of the recession did not mean the end of the recession; it simply meant that it would continue and with luck would not get worse. But output fell again in the third quarter. By the end of 1981 output was down 6.5% compared with when Sir Geoffrey

Howe took over in mid-1979. And eighteen months after Long's memo it was still down on mid-1979 by 6%.

In October, as the Tory party stirred itself for the big economic debate with Heath, Gilmour, St John Stevas and Rippon on the attack, the Nobel committee announced the winner of the prize in economics. It went to Professor James Tobin of Yale University, and in *The Times* morning conference it was suggested that it would be interesting to see what Tobin had to say about British economic policy. It was an excellent idea and we published Tobin on Britain on the day of the Tory conference debate. I should have checked that Anna Murdoch was around. Murdoch came to dinner at my home in London, and the tirade began in the car as we drew up to the front door.

'Why d'ya run that stuff?'

'Well, it's timely.'

'And it's wrong! Wrong! What does he know anyway?' We spilled out on to the pavement.

'Come on,' I retorted. 'He won the Nobel Prize.'

'Intellectual bullshit!'

'Well, what do *you* know?' I demanded, jabbing the doorbell to my home. 'You said inflation would be down in single figures by now and it isn't. I don't know why you go for this monetarist stuff. All the high interest rates *you're* paying ...'

Tina opened the door. 'Hello!' she said cheerfully, only to discover the proprietor and the editor of *The Times* about to start a street brawl. We abandoned the economic debate there and then, but Milton Friedman and James Tobin hovered over the chicken and soufflé. Tina later remarked that she had never seen anyone so hunched up with resentment as Murdoch. Tobin had trodden on sacred ground. He had declared Britain's economic policy a very interesting but risky experiment: 'The idea that you leave money supply to determine employment and everything we want is burying your head in the sand.... The public never believes that unemployment is a solution to inflation and they are right. It's crazy.'

I had no objections to a political discussion with Murdoch. On the contrary I would have liked to engage him. I was talking policies every day with my colleagues and I was reporting Murdoch's line to Douglas-Home, as I had agreed I would. But Murdoch had no relish for anything more than a couple of colliding assertions. 'What would you do, print, print!' was his contribution on monetarism. He got restless or tetchy with any attempt to engage him further. If he could put the name of a personality to any observation he disliked, he pulverized whoever it was as a wet, an intellectual or a creep, and that was the end of it. He was worse in this way when he came in from America. Of course that was tiring even via Concorde, but Denis Hamilton had an engaging theory that he fell into bad company on the other side. New York dinner-party guests were less likely to look incredulous when Murdoch declared, as he did at one attended by Kathleen Tynan, that Frank Giles was a Communist 'and his wife too'. Gerald Long, of course, was not a restraining influence in such matters. He had the same views or at least those were the ones he wore to the office. They came with a roar, but they did not possess his mind. He could argue abstractly, but he had never bothered to acquire the vocabulary of current economics and I did not blame him, nor did he mingle much with politicians. He left the charnel-house of Gray's Inn Road for evenings with his dictionaries and his music.

The Nobel Prize committee having done its worst, the electors of Croydon North-West fomented more trouble. They voted William Pitt into the Commons, the first candidate to be elected in the name of the Liberal and Social Democratic Alliance approved the previous month. The Tories, who had held the seat, came second, and Labour third. It was a triumph as well for MacArthur and Emery. They organized *The Times* coverage so resourcefully that we were on the presses exceptionally early with the result and a full analysis by the political editor, Julian Haviland. Readers of the *Telegraph* and *Guardian* in comparable circulation areas got either no result in their papers or a skimpy report. It was a pleasure to see four of our presses running with Croydon while the adjacent *Guardian* presses were silent.

I was on my way to Heathrow that happy morning on a weekend visit to see *Atlantic* magazine in Boston – they had the sensational 'confessions' of David Stockman, Reagan's budget director – when the telephone in the car announced that Gerald Long urgently wanted to speak to me. He began by asking when was John Grant going to amalgamate *The Times* and *Sunday Times* libraries and when was I getting rid of him anyway. I was astonished that we were holding a crackling sixty-mile-an-hour conversation on such an issue, and soon found that we were not. Long turned quickly to our report of Croydon North-West. Was he impressed with the speed of reporting? No. He wanted to know why there were ten paragraphs on the front page by Shirley Williams, and Rupert would want to know.

His asking this was part of the autumn's campaign, but this time Long had a point. The Shirley Williams comments were presented under a separate headline down the page with the attribution 'By Shirley Williams'. MacArthur had arranged the contribution in advance in the event of an Alliance victory. Its proper place was inside the paper on a feature page; I voiced my misgivings half-heartedly and too late in the small hours, when the needs of production ruled this out. I should have held the article for a night, but the 'bushy-tailed MacArthur' and 'Gary Glitter' (Emery), as Murdoch called them, were so proud of their whole effort I let it go. Although I regretted the article's position in the paper, I did not say so to Long: I resented the continual pressure. I should have said that in the balance of the news pages a thousand mild paragraphs by Shirley Williams were nothing to the havoc wrought on the Social Democrats week after week by Frank Johnson. His column, which I finally established on the back page, was Murdoch's warm-water port as news depressing for Mrs Thatcher rolled in and seeped through all the defences into the paper. Johnson had unfashionable right-wing beliefs, as he puts it, before they became fashionably fashionable. He carried his column everywhere. I expect to be called to give testimony to a scene at a party at Robin Day's house, when he prodded James Prior with at least a thousand words of solid ridicule as if he were Kerensky. The Social Democrats were meat and drink to Johnson. He followed them everywhere. He travelled on the SDP Moderate Express to Perth: 'The gang of four will be joined by Mr William Rodgers, the former Minister of Transport. That should be enough to end us up in Torquay.' He tracked down Shirley Williams when she fought Crosby: 'Mrs Shirley Williams appeared for her last press conference. She was fresh, bright-eyed, confident, well-briefed, fluent – in a word insufferable ...' When she took her seat as the first elected member of the Social Democratic Party, he was in the gallery: 'Being one of the most senior members of the SDP, she is of course not allowed, under the British Constitution, to make known her political opinions.... She was looking smart. This meant that she had sacked Oxfam as her couturier. The new team had kitted her out in a two-piece which a female colleague in the press gallery informed us was in French blue. That sounded vaguely improper for the representative of so religious a constituency.' Roy Jenkins was 'a Fabergé of an egghead ... shining, exquisitely crafted, full of delights, a much loved gracious figure who is to the liberal classes what the Queen Mother is to the rest of us'. He had a field-day when William Pitt, the Alliance man in Croydon, engaged Lord Goodman to issue a writ for libel:

> It must be emphasised that everyone mentioned from now is a person of unblemished reputation, total integrity and personal freshness, except if Messrs Goodman Derrick and Co, say they are not. Furthermore there is not a jot or tittle of evidence for any suggestion to the contrary or tottle, tittle or bottle. There is not a scintilla, whatever that may mean, or any other evidence. It is all a farrago of untruths and indeed a fandango if required.

It was always a pleasure, whatever the problems, to get back to journalism on *The Times*. I liked the rhythm and the stimulus of news: the daily fix. The team was working well. Douglas-Home edited the paper for two weeks lying on his back on the floor of his office with disc trouble. He greeted me after the summer with a warm letter from his retreat in Berwickshire: 'Mon Général, A word of thanks for the most stimulating five months of my life. It was a ball and I hope we have many more, but in the meatime just a note to say how much I enjoyed working with you and how scrupulously I think you have respected all our private agreements.'

I had kept him abreast of the sagas of the sixth floor. 'Oh, God,' he would laugh lightly, 'rather you than me, old boy.' He was in on all my appointments and staff reshuffles, and all the discussions about the development of the paper. His contribution was steady good judgement. He did not come up with ideas in editorial conception or presentation, but he was positive. He scoffed well. When someone made a silly objection to a change, Douglas-Home's dry snicker, 'Oh, come now, Geoffrey', made the man feel he had dropped soup on the regimental tie. This helped a great deal. He liked 'tasking' people, as he always put it, and he was good at calling meetings to make sure the tasks were done. His style was casual, deprecatory. He was always apologetically laid back about the result when he edited in my absence: 'Not a very good paper, boss, I'm afraid.'

He was concerned in his letter about the pace of work:

> We must, after the holidays, make certain that we are disciplined about time off, otherwise we and the machine will burn itself out. It needed a pause for breath in August, for instance, and I'll bet it will need another by Christmas! But at the everyday level I think we should insulate certain early nights – say three a fortnight each – and see that the other slaves like Brian, Oscar and Edwin learn how to take a break without worrying about it.

He was right. The pace had been intense, not just because I wanted to make changes but because we were short of staff in some areas, and the new production, some hot and some cold, was a nightmare. The worst-hit area was business news. It had been overstaffed, I thought, with fifty-eight people and had too much editorial space. This was a vestigial remnant of the separate newspaper of the early 1970s. It occupied a vast wing of its own with a full panoply of editors and news editors and daily conferences; Murdoch was observed one Sunday afternoon counting the desks. It had a letters column and diary. It was Alexandria to Rome. About a quarter of the staff fled at the sight of the barbarians. It was hard to blame them. They could pick up thousands of pounds in 'redundancy' money and walk into other jobs. Half of them could be spared, the others had to be replaced. Somebody had to write the headlines and compile prices. Recruiting took time. It became a struggle just to produce the section. Insurrection was avoided only because the managing editor,

Denis Topping, played Gandhi. Yet I wanted not merely to produce but to revise Business News.

The new editor who took on the onerous task was Adrian Hamilton, the son of Denis Hamilton. Topping stayed to help him before taking up an appointment with *The Financial Times*. David Blake was disappointed, but stayed. Andrew Goodrick-Clarke, the financial editor, left, so there was another crucial gap. Adrian Hamilton looks just right for a dissident province, much more like a brigadier than his father, who was the youngest in the British army. He is a more solid, squarer Hamilton, the same moustache but less elusive in the eyes. He came to us from *The Observer* business editorship, and before that he made a name for himself as the energy correspondent of *The Financial Times*. Long pulled a face, but Murdoch merely shrugged. It is hard to see how anyone could take exception to Hamilton. He can be determined and occasionally there is a brief flash of temper, but he is transparently honest, open and modest. He is not quicksilver. His father's long, deadpan pauses are celebrated; with his son one can see the wheels working. He is the manifestation of a man in thought. I hoped that some time in the autumn he would have found the right people; he made a good start in the recruitment for Topping's successor with Alan Jenkins, the former editor of the *Glasgow Herald*. Hamilton and I agreed that business news should be more compact, but should be true to its title and not become just a financial section, like the *Daily Telegraph*'s.

My other ambition for the autumn was to improve the arts pages, presided over by John Higgins, a plump, impassively urbane man of forty-seven with a passion for opera and wine. He came to Rees-Mogg's attention in the late 1960s, when he edited the distinctive *Financial Times* arts page, and Lord Drogheda commended him to me – 'though he gives too much, dear boy, to foreign opera'. This was true. When I wanted Higgins, he always seemed to be in the grand circle in Geneva, Paris, Rome or Urbana, Illinois. I thought I would have to get a message slipped on to the end of an aria. I settled for writing him a detailed memorandum commending his principal reviewers, notably Irving Wardle and David Robinson, but asking for more arts news, more relevant features, a sense of enthusiasn and far better presentation. I thought it ridiculous to have John Russell Taylor on George Hoyningen-Huene without showing an example of his photography. I did not like to see the page padded out with inflated interviews with run-of-the-mill actors and actresses – two whole columns on Robert Powell – and I thought that in the 1980s *The Times* should have a daily television commentary. Higgins wrote me an immaculate memorandum in reply. Yes, he sighed, it was 'probably' time to have television reviewed daily. Yes, arts news was weak, it was nothing new, they had been doing it badly for years. There was nobody to do it. I gave him thirty-year-old Brian Appleyard, who wrote financial notes, but pined for the arts. I stole the writer John Heilpern from *The Observer* to cover the American cultural scene for us. I told Higgins that, as he felt hard pressed, I would relieve him of producing the Saturday review. Tony Holden and Oscar Turnill added this to their other duties.

I was able to do something for photography. With Edwin Taylor's help, I restored the tradition of featuring a non-news photograph of quality on Saturdays. Holden suggested birthday portraits. Taylor commissioned a series by Snowdon, Arnold Newman, David Bailey and others; he cross-matched assignments so that Arthur Koestler's was taken, brilliantly, by the glamour photographer Sam Haskins. I took great pleasure in selecting these pictures; with stylish captions by the indefatigable Philip Howard, they were a great success.

Douglas-Home and I agreed that it was now or never for another change, a subject of emotion within and without the office. It concerned the exact position in the paper of the leaders, letters and main features; and I am not sure we got it right. The issue was whether these pages should always appear in the exact centre of the paper. There was great virtue in the fixed centre. It was easy to thumb the paper open for the leaders, and turn it inside out for a settled consideration of the issues of the day. It was a happy coincidence of geographical and mental centre. There was one editorial and one commercial drawback. Editorially, it could be achieved only by abandoning a fixed sequence of departments so that sport, the arts, classified and fashion catapulted about the paper. Commercially, the dispersal of classified was the oldest controversy in *The Times*. Duke Hussey maintained to Rees-Mogg that the fixed centre cost hundreds of thousands of pounds in lost classified revenue, because it led to the dispersal of classified advertisements and the dissipation of the idea of a market-place. The alternative was the floating centre, trying to maintain the regular position but allow the pages to float backwards or forwards to maintain a fixed sequence for editorial and grouped classified advertising.

Douglas-Home was a lifelong floater, Hickey a passionate fixer. In this schism it was too dangerous for anyone else to offer an opinion. Everyone I asked said 'on the one hand' and 'on the other'. Hickey would not refer to a floating centre: it was a *false* centre. 'With a false centre, (a) readers feel something is *wrong* when they open up and meet obits on the left and badminton on the right; and (b) having found the place and folded it back, the damn thing slips and forever become a handling problem.' More importantly, he felt that leaders and letters were central to *The Times* in the sense that they specially characterized it and a fixed position reflected that view. I would have sided with Hickey, but for the commercial case. So I authorized a floating centre and a fixed run of departments, while asking Oscar Turnill to juggle the paper as much as he could to keep the leader page central. He managed it about half the time, Garry Thorne predicted the roof would fall in. It did not, but there were many heartfelt complaints, classified advertising revenues hardly seemed to benefit, and now I doubt the force of that case. Looking back on it, Hickey had the better of the argument.

The complaints about the floating centre, though justified, bothered me less that autumn than the earlier ones. Had I been brutalized? A distinct thickening of the skin certainly developed on receiving letters, which I did every week, protesting about change where none had occurred – on letters, the court page, obituaries, and the law report. I did, it is true, move the science report from the court page to a fixed position on the home page 2 (surely, said a reader, the report on quasars belonged on the overseas page?); but otherwise these departments were unmolested. They ran well. Hickey and Pilpel presided over a splendid correspondence protesting at the Government's abolition of eight of the BBC's thirty-eight foreign-language services. Could Lords Briggs and Harewood, John le Carré, Spike Milligan, Tom Stoppard and the President of the Italian Chamber of Commerce all be wrong? The Governor of Wormwood Scrubs wrote to me to protest that prisons had become 'penal dustbins'. A correspondence began in October and was still rumbling in February about the folly of the Government's decision to withdraw HMS *Endurance* from the south Atlantic. The saving, said Lord Shackleton, Peter Scott, and Vivian Fuchs, 'is likely to be greatly outweighed by the consequences to Britain's future interests in what is expected to become a vital resource area'. Nobody could predict what would catch fire in the letters columns. Every slip in *Brideshead Revisited* was gazetted: sergeant-majors don't wear three stripes, no British soldier would salute a bareheaded Captain Ryder indoors and Oxford undergraduates did not wear mortarboards to lectures. But the chaplain of Sussex University who admitted conducting a marriage service in which the best man was a woman got away with it, and so did Debrett's new rules on etiquette, which declared that it would henceforth be bad form for a person giving country house-parties to offer separate bedrooms to pairs of unmarried young guests who were plainly living together. My interventions in the letters page were almost all to say something should be published which otherwise hovered on oblivion. Hickey and Pilpel were nervous about the risks of contempt of court in allowing Malcolm Muggeridge to propound the New Testament case against legalizing abortion and euthanasia when the Attorney-General was prosecuting the editor of the *Daily Mail* precisely for letting Muggeridge do that during other legal proceedings. I thought time in Pentonville with Muggeridge justified the risk. On another occasion I studied a thick file of exchanges in which a leading physician tried to correct a mis-statement of his position on vaccination. It was months after the original report, but I said the letter should be published. *The Times*, I was sorry to find, was hardly more ready to admit error than lesser newspapers. Graham Greene failed to secure a correction when for one edition we miscaptioned the late Maurice Oldfield as George Oldfield. We said in a leader that all the young black witnesses at the Deptford inquest had been in trouble with the police, which was wrong, and Canon Wilfred Wood had a hard time making us admit it. Nigel Dempster of the *Daily Mail*, with another legitimate correction, was given the run-around for a whole month. It was not Pilpel's fault: he passed complaints to heads of departments. As a dumping ground for apologies and corrections, the letter feature would have constrained interest. I laid down that corrections should appear on the pages of the department which made the original error and that investigations should be immediate. I asked Douglas-Home to monitor all complaints. It took a lot of harrying to improve responses.

The new executives tightened their grip. Emery chivvied the specialists into clusters to support each other and dared to ask a few to change duties. Horton laid an icy hand on the still-palpitating extremities of Greig's special reports department, which had so bothered me on my first day and which Douglas-Home had in the end found too much for him. Horton integrated its staff in foreign and home departments. It saved manpower, but it also gave people more day-to-day involvement in the paper. I put the displaced John Greig to bolster John Grant on controlling spending. Fred Emery's task with the specialists was the most sensitive. Some were models of what a specialist should be, others in Douglas-Home's phrase were 'in a rut – an esoteric rut maybe, but still a rut'. He had longer knowledge of them and supported Emery with memos to me. Donoughue, who was assigned to conduct a weekly policy conference of specialists, was called to Douglas-Home's office and handed a large, brown envelope from a briefcase. 'Don't let anyone at all know about this,' said Douglas-Home. Back in his own office, Donoughue looked inside and was surprised to find himself reading assessments of the private lives of the specialists as well as of their performance: it was the notorious dossier compiled by Douglas-Home that he said he had destroyed. Donoughue handed back the envelope and its contents in the mid-day editorial conference. I never saw it and only learned of this transaction much later.

Some of Emery's and Horton's doings displeased the chapel of the NUJ. They protested, for the second time during my editorship, at disturbance. It was true that the changes were unsettling. MacArthur said he hoped I would stand by Emery, because he had it right. I met the chapel officers in the conference room with John Grant. Paul Routledge, the father of the chapel, who was also the labour editor, led the attack. He had with him Pat Healy, the social services specialist and Michael Prest from Business News. Pat Healy, fifteen years on *The Times*, was said to eat editors for breakfast.

They were belligerent. They resented some of the top jobs going to newcomers. The special reports people objected to a Sunday rota. We should hire more photographers. They were taking legal advice about Emery's moves with specialists; if somebody was appointed to a specialism he had it for life. There was chaos, said Healy. Emery's changes would destroy the authority of the paper, because much of it was vested in the specialists. It would take a specialist six months to get into a new role. The chapel's demand was for stability.

I found myself more angry than I intended to be. I thought Healy was one of the specialists who would benefit from a change, a good news reporter in a rut. I told them I refused to employ more photographers or change Horton's rejig of special reports. I hoped that by the end of the year every department would be properly staffed and there would then be a period of consolidation. It was not yet a question of 'stability', but of arresting the decline of the paper. I saw nothing wrong with inviting people to change their duties. 'Give me one example where someone has been instructed to move from his position,' I said. I should have left it at that, but I added: 'And we changed duties a lot on *The Sunday Times* to great benefit without all this fuss.'

Routledge flared: 'This is not *The Sunday Times*. This is *The Times*. We'll do things our way over here, if you don't mind.'

The pattern of my days was to compare *The Times* with all the daily papers in the morning at home between 7.30 and 8 a.m. We were missing fewer stories (and gaining a few scoops). I went for a run two or three times round St James' Park, while my driver, Syd Markham, took my suit to the RAC club, where I swam. Murdoch said he was going to go too, but I never saw him there. I arrived in the office with notes for news, features and leaders scribbled in the margins of *The Times*. Douglas-Home, who left the office earlier at night, was in before me. There was this odd effect of being approached by an empty suit. He wore loose-fitting hand-ons from large relatives who had died, which was affecting but disconcerting. His wife Jessica, a stage designer, even dressed some of the characters in *Anyone for Denis?* from his extensive wardrobe of cavernous Oxford bags and motorway lapels. Sharp at 11.30 a.m. Horton came in for a quick inquest with MacArthur and Emery bowling in behind, then we joined the fifteen or twenty executives and leader writers gathered down the corridor for a conference. I advanced it to 11.45 to give more time for discussion and leeway for leaders. I wanted everyone there to take part, as they had at *The Sunday Times*. It took a long time to get rid of the idea that it wasn't cricket to make a suggestion for another department. Holden's team bubbled irreverently, but Hickey remained a chilling influence. When I asked if he had any suggestions on a development in Northern Ireland, his constant preoccupation, he uttered the rebuke: 'Just report it.' I choked back saying, 'Report what?' Nobody was going to give us a hand-out. There were five or six aspects we could explore. The reporter had to be briefed properly. During the hunger strike we used our initiative to report in detail on who the men were and what their offences had been; and we gave a page to the victims of violence. I put Hickey's response down to his lack of practical news experience. 'Oh, old Owen, don't bother, that's his way,' Douglas-Home laughed.

The leader conference always ran a close finish with lunch. If I could have a sandwich on the desk, I stayed ahead of the phone calls and the mail. If I had to go out, I might return with a story or leader thought, but I never caught up with Seeber's reproving list of people to call. I often let Douglas-Home take the 4 p.m. news conference. He also had oversight of the planning for politics and features. He did it coolly, delegating well. He did not care to edit and reshape major initiatives like the youth or inner cities series, so often I did this between 4 and 6 p.m., with Turnill, if I was lucky. They were precious hours. I might write or edit a leader or see heads of departments. There was still time in late afternoon to glance at the features layout and headlines, but I would miss what MacArthur called the playpen, the choosing of the main illustrations. Taylor had reorganized the photographic department; there was a marked improvement in quality.

The magic time was 6 p.m. when the home, foreign news and business news barons stood at the back bench to make their offerings for the front page. The system was for the night editors to note and the editor to dispose, with Horton and Emery watching their special interests. These two sometimes clashed. Newspaper pressures on time and space produce a few sparks. Horton, perpendicular man, narrowed his eyes and looked down his nose, de Gaulle style; Emery crouched. It never lasted long.

I enjoyed this period of the day. The pulse of the paper quickened. That single sheet of paper on its way to the back bench might convulse the whole edition. The new arrangement of desks grouped all the executives together in close call with the night news desk and the sub-editors. These anonymous and singularly unappreciated figures hunched over copy paper amidst reference books and plastic coffee cups represented quite a body of learning. Russian, Polish, French, German and

Italian were spoken. There were two barristers, a historian, an expert in watercolours, a qualified psychiatrist who had flown with RAF intelligence on spy missions in the Cold War, and a brilliant impersonator of Charles Dickens. There were three young women sub-editors, very deft at the work, and one woman on the night desk. About half of the sub-editors had been with the paper longer than five years; the widest experience of other newspapers was concentrated on the home desk. The sub-editors earned about the same as general reporters, around £12,000; there was more money in other offices, especially the popular papers. *The Times* was, if anything, a writers' paper, but the better sub-editors made an enormous contribution to the paper in clarity, accuracy and economy. David Hopkinson imposed his bulk benignly on avalanches of copy paper from party conferences and the big trials, and it came out crisp and orderly.

It was companionable working with them. I spent most time on the front and back pages with the breezy MacArthur, and Gould and Brian. We read the more important home and foreign news stories, tried out headlines on each other, and sometimes returned copy to the sub-editor: for instance, I thought the readers ought to know that in the photograph we were publishing the man in white pyjamas next to Mrs Thatcher was the President of Mexico. I let the others draw up the page plans; it was a superhuman effort at restraint on my part which I thought should have had wider recognition.

Murdoch was rarely seen. Long came down frequently. He stood most often talking in Horton's office in a martial stance, back straight, jaw out, surveying the grubby rabble outside. This led to chatter that Horton was Long's spy; there is nothing like a newspaper office for peddling gossip.

Between 8 and 9p.m. I inspected production. It required the gift attributed to the saints of bi-location, since it was necessary to be in two places at once. There was both a hot and a cold composing room. It was always calculated to raise the blood pressure. I might talk with the printer about reducing the number of errors in the paper or with the engraving and foundry departments about the quality of picture reproduction. Around 9.30p.m. I checked the text news service on television and tried the cold supper sent down from the sixth floor. I watched *News at Ten*. By this time Douglas-Home, Taylor, Turnill and Holden might have flopped down on my sofa, coveting the cheese. The first edition arrived at around 10.30p.m. and I went through it, asking for more space for this story and less for that, and changing a few headlines. Sometimes I picked up a copy of the paper on the publishing floor, where the men liked to feel part of the team. I tried to be home by midnight. Occasionally I stayed later than that, so as to see the other nationals;

when I did leave, I could read the paper while being driven home and call in on the radio telephone if there were any howlers. On a newspaper it is easier to get right the big things than the little: the words, for instance.

Every editor tries to keep the language of his paper precise and to maintain a consistent style of spelling and appellation. I regarded *The Times* as having a special position. Literally we might affect the Queen's English. If she said 'honesty pays *off*', it would be the fault of *The Times*. In my first few weeks that appeared, and in a headline we announced that somebody had 'lost out'. I was sure to be blamed. Hickey, to my surprise, took a more relaxed view. 'The days when *The Times* could aspire to be an arbiter in these matters, and consistently apply its own rulings, are past,' he wrote to me. 'All we need are a few dos and don'ts about journalese and headlines.' He was even in favour of doing away with the central section of the *Times* style-book on English usage. Philip Howard, the literary editor renowned for his column on words, had been in this saltmine for years revising the *Times* style-book to relax its old-fashioned rigours. He did not agree with Hickey: 'There is a sentimental case for retaining something that represents the accretion of more than a century of *Times* wisdom on style'.

There were, in fact, three points at issue. The first was a common style of spelling and punctuation for hundreds of choices like NATO/Nato, Cambodia/Kampuchea. *The Sunday Times* proposed, and I agreed, that the *Oxford Dictionary for Writers and Editors* should be adopted.

The second was appellation. This was more tricky. Right at the beginning I had said that if an advertiser wanted to call herself Ms we should accept it. John Grant fought a rearguard action. He told the advertising department that *The Times* would never admit the existence of Ms whoever. I overruled him. Then Long objected: 'Is this nonsense *Times* style?' I overruled him too. This was a sensitive area. Readers complained furiously when we called the Ripper 'Mr' Peter Sutcliffe and referred in a headline to the hunger striker Mr Robert Sands. *Times* style, unlike *The Sunday Times*'s, was titles for everyone in headlines and text, but it was not consistently applied. Much as I used to like 'Mr' Charles Chaplin, it did seem antique and I could understand the crossness about Mr Ripper. I asked Hickey to make recommendations. He was very ingenious about it. In news text *The Times* should call people Mr, Mrs, Lord, Sir, at every mention. But Meryl Streep was all right for the arts and Sebastian Coe for sport. He satisfied liberal decency by stipulating that people on trial should have the benefit of the doubt and be allowed to retain their appellation. But for someone like Sutcliffe, who had pleaded guilty, and for convicted criminals, *Times* style should be Peter Sutcliffe, Myra Hindley at first mention and Sutcliffe, Hindley an option thereafter. We should continue to refuse to anglicize foreigners. They would be Herr, M., Signor, Señor and Senhor. He agreed with my preference to reduce appellations in headlines. We could not abandon them altogether – Princess Anne, the Duke of Devonshire, Lord Glenmara – and he noted there were some difficult problems with women. 'Thatcher is all right and Whitehouse probably all right for Mrs Whitehouse. Some latitude is indicated here.' Many readers disliked seeing Thatcher in a headline; but we stuck with the style.

The third area was the English in the paper. It was easy enough to ban 'gunned down', 'lost out', 'test out', to plead for 'none is' and jump on 'less houses than'. There were times when I thought I was the only man left alive who cared about 'fewer' and 'less'. It was harder, but possible, to rid the paper of 'lone buglers', 'floral tributes' and 'gallant losers'. Miles Kington, the *Punch* refugee I had introduced as Moreover columnist on the court page, helped. He offered a prize for investigative journalism. There were rules:

1   The piece shall be entitled Warehouse Blaze, No Deaths.
2   The subject of the piece must be a warehouse fire on the edge of a large town in which nobody shall die but not less than £50,000-worth of damage be caused.
3   Any firemen mentioned in the piece must toil rather than work, and they should be weary rather than tired. They can, if you like, risk their lives again and again. If an inferno is mentioned, it must be a raging one.
4   The following phrases must appear in the piece: 'Flames shot more than 100ft in the air'; 'Fire brigades from up to 20 miles away were called'; 'Eye witnesses reported a series of explosions'; 'The blaze was eventually brought under control'.
5   Report a comment from either a weary fire officer who had nothing but praise for the magnificent way his men reacted, or a nightwatchman who was lucky to escape with his life, as the building went up like a powder keg.

Here was one of the reasons why readers sometimes had to grapple with mystery:

A witness told the Uganda High Court in Kampala today that Mr Bob Astles, the British-born aide of former President Idi Amin, killed his brother after firing at the canoe in which he and his brother were travelling in May 1977.

Whose brother? The brother of the witness, of Astles or Amin? Who was in the canoe? What does it mean, he killed him 'after' firing at the canoe? Did he miss whoever it was, and come upon him later?
And again:

The battle is on for the alternative bureaucracies which are at the heart of the postwar baby bulge's attempt to run the world in its own image.

When I sat at the back bench I fished diligently for these monsters in the torrents. Other people had their lines out. Philip Howard, the literary editor, and Pat Davis, the foreign manager, looked through the paper. But the biggest catches were landed early on by Long on the sixth floor. He became so engrossed in it, he labelled and shipped them tome:

Times Mindless: 'She had been held at an address in North London.' Detached or semi-detached address?

Times Frankly Muddled: 'The apartments have been made into a single flat on three floors.' The *Oxford Concise* confirms what good sense would suggest and defines a flat as 'rooms on one floor . . .'.

Times Inflated: 'Whatever the case, it avoided what would have been an additionally embarrassing moment in what is already in some ways an embarrassing visit'.

The worst shock was to read Clifford Longley, the religious affairs correspondent, writing about the marriage vows, which came out as follows:

> It retrospectively annuals a vow which the partis may well have kept, for many yers, able; to, for many years, as far as they were able; and it seeks to turn psychological interpretations into hard falts, to give tribunal decisions the apperance of objectivity.

This rendition of a man talking with his teeth out was liable to be imposed on any of the writers. They cried for vengeance; the readers simply wanted their money back. It was an outcome of new methods of producing the paper. Something approaching 150,000 words were in *The Times* each day. The time for setting and correcting them was drastically reduced by a multiplication of things. For a start, old skills were lost in the transfer from setting type in hot metal to producing it by photocomposition machines. This is called cold setting since it produces a bromide for pasting on to a page to be photographed. By the autumn nearly half the paper was cold. These pages required an extra twenty minutes in platemaking, which was one loss of time. More time was lost in the setting. The men who had been fast and accurate with a linotype machine had to learn a new keyboard. They were managing around fifteen words per minute on the visual display units, typewriters with television screens. A typist would easily do three times that speed; one-fingered journalists could have typed in their copy directly much more quickly, but they were barred from doing so by the trade union of the typesetters, the National Graphical Association. To aggravate matters, the proof-reading for cold was done not by the traditional correctors of the press but by men displaced from hot-metal areas. In the meantime, the hot-metal area, still producing half the paper, was robbed of its old skilled operatives and compositors who made up the pages in metal. There was only a thin blue line of make-up wizards.

A third area of delay was pasting up the bromides on the pages. Again, it was a new skill. Some of the men using scalpels on proofs quickly became adept; others in the hot and congested paste-up area were as likely to take out one's jugular as an overset line. On top of all this the phototypesetter was obsolete, distorting Walter Tracy's Europa typeface and producing a heavy black impression.

There were moments in the bedlam when I felt bitter with everyone: with the NGA for demarcation nonsense, with Murdoch for hurriedly acquiescing in 1981 when he held all the cards, with Long who did not understand production, and with Bill O'Neill who did. He made an impact, but he wanted ever faster transfer to cold type and there were limits. 'We'll be old and grey before we hit 100% for *The Times*, never mind *The Sunday Times*,' he complained. I understood his pressure on the printers and on editorial. Cold type cut costs, but the speed of the transfer was a tremendous strain on everyone. George Vowles and Bill Dell, the printers in charge, were grey. It was no help that there was another demarcation dispute in which the messengers would not put the edited copy for the cold area into the vacuum tube. At first, with few pages set cold, sub-editors had to get up from their seats infrequently to do it for them, but, as more and more went cold, the process speeded up so that near edition time they were moving speedily through frame like Keystone Cops. When, after months of this, management finally gave the messengers an ultimatum, the NATSOPA men in the machine room threatened trouble and around 10 p.m. I had a request and advice. 'I'd advise you to cut out other editions, I know it'll please the lads downstairs'. I refused, first because it was a sign of weakness and second because I did not see why the paper should suffer. I like to think I was not over-influenced in this judgement by the source of the request: it was Reg Brady, my old tormentor from the *Sunday Times* machine-room chapel of NATSOPA, now translated by Murdoch into an industrial relations officer.

Editorial did what it could to make up time sacrificed in the transfer to cold type. We advanced deadlines by more than an hour. It always proved a mistake when we tried to save money by not employing casual sub-editors and missed the new deadlines we had set ourselves. Editions then went to press not only without corrections but with 'filler' advertisements in place of unset editorial. I felt a stab of pain for every one of the uncorrected proofs which missed the edition: sometimes there was a pile of 200 or more, each containing at least one error to make the reader choke on his breakfast egg.

The editorial production men were zealots. One of them, Alan Bruce, who had trained in New Zealand, went so far as to come down to the editorial floor to suggest to Paul Feldorf, the revise sub-editor, for thirty years on *The Times*, that it did not matter a damn if 'motor-cycle' took a hyphen so long as the printers got the copy more quickly. The man in charge was Tony Norbury, a Cockney former City office messenger, on *The Times* for fourteen years, whom I promoted from within to take over editorial production from Ernest Russell. He succeeded because he was trusted by the printers not to defend the editorial department when it slipped.

Sadat's assassination put everything to the test. It brought out the best of *The Times*, old and new, though not without a little show of the old dog and it precipitated Louis Heren's resignation. He felt he should have been consulted; but there were a foreign editor, a chief foreign leader writer, and two specialists, and it would have been confusing on a difficult night to add to the chain. I was with an economic group outside the office when it was said that the Egyptian President had been shot and escaped. At the 4 p.m. conference, the flash came that he was dead. The earlier reports had been taken too casually by everybody. Horton commissioned Christopher Walker in Cairo, Robert Fisk in Beirut, Nicholas Ashford in Washington and Michael Binyon in Moscow. The routine I had introduced for editing and laying out these big stories clicked into place, with the hundreds of pieces of paper collated at a special desk, Peter Hopkirk knitting the loose ends and Taylor planning two inside pages. We caught up with ourselves. Holden in features tried to respond in the same way. 'Why have we got to have it for today?' the amiable feature writer Roger Berthoud asked him. 'Why don't we think about this and write for tomorrow's paper?' Holden was stung: 'I thought this was supposed to be a daily paper.' He was swiftly put down: 'No, it's *The Times*.'

It was unthinkable to Holden that he should go to press with features that had been planned without knowledge of the news, and by 6 p.m. he had negotiated a memoir from James Callaghan, and the rights to extracts from both Sadat's autobiography and Henry Kissinger's forthcoming memoirs. In London we drew on the special knowledge of Richard Owen and Edward Mortimer for the leader and analysis of Mubarak and the implications for Middle East peace. All the material in the paper was of high quality. The antithesis suggested by Berthoud between the rushed imperfect and the delayed perfect is plausible but delusive for newspapers. Readers look for guidance, and publishing at once does not necessarily mean publishing something inferior. It might – that is where the challenge lies. At its best, as Phil Graham of the *Washington Post* once said, it is a first rough draft of history.

Murdoch was in London. Everything worked so well that I kept my dinner appointment with him on the sixth floor. Despite our money problems, which I will describe, he urged me to 'grab' a sports columnist and a financial commentator I had been eyeing. He came down and looked moodily at the page proofs, saying nothing. But in the composing room, when Holden approached me with an op-ed proof and a query about Lurie's cartoon on Sadat, Murdoch interrupted him.

'Is it a question of fact or of taste?'

'Well, taste.'

'Bugger taste,' said Murdoch irritably without looking at the cartoon. 'We want to sell newspapers. Print it!'

Holden looked loyally at me. I nodded him away. It was an instruction to a journalist, but I chose to regard it as a hot flush, like the time Murdoch marked *The Sunday Times* leader proof. There were graver issues. Murdoch was tightening a noose.

After politics, finance was the crucial difference between us. It was the way he sought control of areas that were my responsibility. When he came to seek my dismissal, as I will relate in due course, one of his principal lines of attack was to say that I had overspent. Long issued the first decree in the summer. 'All executives of the company', said his pink circular, 'are reminded that written authorisation is required for any proposed action of whatever nature. There is no exception to this rule. Verbal authorisation can never be accepted. All executives must make themselves familiar with the channels for seeking authorisation for any proposal and must follow them invariably.'

When first distributed, the circular was unsigned and thought to be a hoax. A signed repeat followed. I ignored it anyway. The paper would have seized up at once if we had taken it seriously. News does not wait upon written authorisation, and the ruling would also have meant that the Murdoch management was effectively editing *The Times*. As the pressure on the paper's political opinion and reporting mounted in the autumn, so too did this additional challenge over finance and the editorial independence of *The Times*. I had then edited the paper for seven months without being given the budget that I was promised and to which I was entitled. As a director of Times Newspapers I had not been informed of the financial state of the company. To understand the thrust and nature of Murdoch's method, it is necessary to describe what happened in Thomson days.

For fourteen years as a director of Times Newspapers and editor of *The Sunday Times* under Roy and Ken Thomson, Denis Hamilton and Duke Hussey, I knew month by month where we were on our road map of the year. This was our budget or financial plan. We drew it up in the autumn, trying to calculate our revenues from sales and advertising, and what our costs would be for editorial, production, distribution and newsprint bought with uncertain sterling. Directors for production, advertising and circulation, and the two editors as well had to have their spending budgets agreed by their colleagues. The collective process was beneficial. The budget process was not one of saintly harmony; editors and advertising directors, for instance, both had claims on limited space, and quotas for editorial and advertising space had to be fixed. But the plan that emerged was the better for the arguments, and we had a common will to stick to what was hammered out. Every month we had operating statements which showed how we were doing. Directors and editors had to account to their colleagues if they went off plan.

The business sense of this is obvious. It was one of the reasons why Times Newspapers was a successful company until it was wrecked in the battle with the print unions. When the oil price explosion transformed everyone's economic prospects overnight, we carried out a very successful collective retrenchment, not excluding editorial. This was not just our way of doing business; it is a commonplace in most of the larger companies. The aspect of it crucial to me, Rees-Mogg and the editors of the Literary and Education Supplements was that within our agreed budgets we had editorial freedom.

Management had the central say in general wage settlements, as distinct from individual merit awards; but never once in fourteen years did management otherwise attempt to intervene in the allocation of editorial resources. Creative editing would have been impossible if they had. How we spent the editorial budget determined the kind of newspaper we produced. It was up to us to reconcile our priorities between home and foreign, business news, sports and the arts. If we sent a correspondent on an unexpectedly expensive trip through Africa or spent more than we intended on acquiring memoirs for serialization, we knew something else would have to be sacrificed. Within the newspapers the system worked as it did for the financial plan. Every section editor was responsible for controlling the budget he had helped to formulate. Rees-Mogg and I knew each month how our department heads were performing against their budgets, just as the chief executive and the board knew how the editors were managing.

One of Murdoch's guarantees was that this sytem of editorial budgets would continue. Two pictures of the autumn of 1981 come to mind:

SCENE ONE: St John's Wood, dinner at Woodrow Wyatt's house. Murdoch, Frank Chapple of the electricians' union and Arnold Weinstock, head of General Electric. Weinstock explains his system of running General Electric in which everyone down the line knows his costs and revenues, cf. Times Newspapers in Thomson days. Murdoch nods approvingly. Atmosphere is one of mutual congratulation.

SCENE TWO: Same week, Gerald Long's office. He has a sheet detailing the finances of *The Times* which I have never seen. 'May I look?' He hesitates. 'Rupert is very funny about figures. You must not say you have seen this.' He lifts the corner for a quick peep.

What he meant by 'funny' was 'secretive'. Murdoch on his take-over sent for the chief accountant David Lawson. 'You are working for *me*. You must show figures to nobody.' This for a time included Long. He was running a company without a map or speedometer. An accountant from News International Peter Stehrenberger, was brought over, and Roy Ekberg from News International instituted new systems. Accounts were told each month what payments to make to News International but not for what services.

I did not know all of this at the time. At the board meetings I asked a second and third time for financial figures. Long raised his palms to the ceiling in a Gallic gesture and the bristles on his walrus moustache wilted. 'Wouldn't we all? It's such a mess.' Nobody else joined me. The Murdoch people probably knew the score; Giles was too unfamiliar with what had gone before. I noted that nothing appeared in the minutes. The excuse was partially true. Murdoch and Long had sacked experienced people in accounts as they had in advertising, and the clerical union was obstructive. Two men had been hiding invoices so that they could accumulate overtime in dealing with outraged creditors. It still did not explain the incident of Long's statistical peep-show. The occasion for this was a long-awaited meeting in which the editorial budget would be agreed. Two hours were set aside in Long's office. Grant had done some work on the concept of the zero budget. He complained he could not get the figures he wanted, but I was ready for a discussion. I told Long I could not understand Murdoch's secrecy. 'He just says tell everyone to spend less,' said Long mournfully. Vague exhortation went against all Long's rational principles of good management, but he was clearly not going to fight about it. 'Rupert works by weekly figures. He takes them on the plane with him. I've told him it's deceptive. But who are we to argue with him? He's very successful. He has a brilliant financial brain.'

David Lawson arrived with various folders. Long glanced at them contemptuously. He was abrupt with Lawson. What assistance did he think he was giving? These figures were no use. He should go away and prepare proper figures on which we could work out the editorial budget. Lawson, a conscientious man with great experience as a newspaper accountant at *The Times* and in the provinces, looked bewildered. Shortly afterwards he was sacked. I never saw his figures, nor received a copy of the ones Long had. The budget exercise went into limbo.

What we had instead was a series of fiats from Murdoch. The origin of the first followed a lunch on the sixth floor which Horton also attended. Murdoch asked us to drop into his office on the way back. He did not seem to have anything to say and Horton volunteered the observation that we could probably save money by cutting down on the use of the telephone. Murdoch got very excited about this. I was asked to tell everyone that we were going to have a drive on excessive telephoning, especially for personal use. I agreed with that. But the next day, 16 September, at a board meeting in Murdoch's office, with Long on holiday, Murdoch ordered that except for directors all private lines should be removed forthwith. He was surly. Giles risked decapitation by piping up in his proper manner to Mr Chairman that foreign correspondents might not be able to get through with messages when the switchboard was jammed. I supported him. I was glad he had taken the heat; I was tired of being singed. Murdoch scowled. It was left unresolved. I tended to think it might be the kind of order Nixon gave Haldeman: a safety valve for pent-up feelings rather than something to be acted on literally. The next day, however, O'Neill gave orders to remove direct lines, and The Sunday Times was stricken in a military-style operation. The news desk and Insight were cut off in mid story. I told O'Neill I refused to take out any line until I had examined what ours were doing. I knew the order was impetuous. Immediately I checked, I knew it was impractical as well. There were sixteen direct lines, used 90% for receiving incoming calls without delay. The Times switchboard was obsolete. At peak times of day it could not cope and at others it was undermanned. Callers gave up. The direct line to the prices clerks in business news was essential for about a hundred calls between 3.30 p.m. and 6 p.m.; so was the sports-desk line for late results. Horton said the foreign desk saved money with its direct line by an immediate sanction or refusal on reverse-charge calls from overseas. I approved the removal of one line only, and waited for Murdoch to explode.

It did not happen. Long came back from holiday and saw the futility of the exercise. He called in IBM to study our telephone system. The truth was that our system gave us no way of stopping abuse; removing direct lines lost more than it gained. The sensible course was to have an electronic switchboard to enable proper control and swift answering. This was Long at his best, though The Sunday Times did not get back its lines. Tony Dawe, the news editor, protested in writing to Murdoch and Long at what had been done. He was sent for by Long and given a dressing-down for being nasty and rude.

Simultaneously with the absurd telephone edict, the editors and managing editors received another directive from Murdoch, which had not been discussed at the board or mentioned at all.

Editorial spending is reaching intolerable levels and it is now necessary to exercise extreme restraint in all areas. . . .

1 Authorisation of any fee in excess of £100 must be obtained from the editor or managing editor before the commitment is undertaken. Anything in excess of £1,000 is to be submitted to the managing director.

Schedules of *all* items of expenditure must be prepared weekly for review by both myself and the managing director.

2 *All* expenses for staff and contributors must be countersigned by the relevant managing editor after first being approved by the head of department. This will also be reviewed on a weekly basis by myself or the managing director.

Instead of having freedom within a budget, we were being ordered to submit, on the basis of assertion, to *ad hoc* personal control by the managing director answerable to Murdoch. It was not in line with Murdoch's guarantees and it was not efficient either. If editorial spending on both papers had reached 'intolerable levels', one wanted to know where and how, to see how it could be contained and with what damage to quality. He was, no doubt, genuinely concerned about levels of expenditure throughout the company, but there was more to it than that. An editorial budget against which my performance could be measured would have given him financial control; but it would not have permitted the personal interventions on any item of editorial expenditure.

This was a point at which I might have gone to the national directors. The case was sound, the tactic questionable. One appeal to the national directors, I argued to myself, and it is goodbye to any remaining hope of a practical working relationship with Murdoch. Hamilton advised me the difficulties would probably blow over when Murdoch had dealt with his New York *Post* battles in America. Murdoch had not discussed his new edict with his editors and had left at once for New York. I decided I would tackle him head on. I placed a transatlantic call for when he arrived.

'I cannot edit the paper in this way. You must give me a budget.'

'Sure we'll get your budget in place. This is temporary until we do.'

'I do not want to go to Gerry with editorial requests.'

'Sure. Talk it over with Gerry. What's Benn up to?'

I was caught on Murdoch's fork. If I went to Long, I would sacrifice the principle of freedom within a budget. If I did not, I could be accused of disobedience and 'overspending', even though there was no level by which to judge 'over'. I decided that editorial freedom was more important than any flak that might come my way. If I asked Long's financial approval for an investigation we were contemplating into the connection between the Pope's assailant and Bulgarian intelligence, or into allegations that the Soviet Union had used yellow rain chemicals in Laos, Cambodia and Afghanistan, he would have to form an editorial judgement on their importance. He could not do this without considering other editorial claimants. He would be editing the paper.

So I did not prepare Murdoch's weekly schedule of all items of expenditure, which I regarded as unrealistic in a newspaper. It was unusual for *The Times* to wish to spend more than £1,000 at a time, but when I had to go over this sum to tell the story of the Labour party's unknown activists who had captured the constitution I did so without reference to Long or Murdoch; nor did I ask permission later when Oriana Fallaci offered me her sensational interview with the Polish Deputy Prime Minister. Nothing was said. I supposed the authorizations I had signed were all being knitted into hemp on the sixth floor. I started two drives. The first was to wring a budget out of Murdoch and Long sooner than later. In a note to Murdoch I wrote on 22 September I said: 'I do find it difficult to accept the principle of day-to-day approval for detailed items. I can't, honestly, edit the paper properly without having discretion *within an agreed budget*. We have a very urgent task in getting budgets agreed and monthly operating statements so that we can know how we are performing and we, for our part, can know if anything is going wrong. Hit me as hard as you like on budgets and their control, but do leave me responsibility for controlling the people who report to me and controlling their departmental budgets. Believe me, everybody here is desperately anxious to make a go of things.'

I said much the same thing to Long – that a budget system was more effective than random checks and general squeezes. 'It is not really practicable or even desirable to be referring individual items of expenditure – while it is essential that the editor and the editor alone be held accountable to the chairman and the managing director and board for the efficient control of the budget.'

My second drive was to cut costs where we could without damaging editorial quality. The instrument for the attack on costs resembled an irascible country doctor, a red Turkey-cock face with owlish bifocals half-way down his nose. He was a man of settled routine who wore tweeds and left the office at 6p.m. without fail. His passion in life was the crossword puzzle. This was John Grant, the managing editor. He had been Rees-Mogg's right-hand man in the battle with the left-wing leader of the journalists' chapel, Jake Ecclestone, who took them on strike. To the strikers, Grant was the Svengali of *The Times*; others thought he created Ecclestone. It was extraordinary for me to find him in this Gradgrind role. He was a reporter with the *Guardian* when I was with the *Manchester Evening News* and we sometimes lunched together with others from the *Guardian*. He was then an incisive writer, as the

Bedside Guardian testifies. He went on to be defence correspondent of *The Times* and at the time of the Thomson take-over his name was mentioned as a possible editor of the paper. Perhaps it was one disappointment after another which had soured him. 'Never write a line now,' he said. He was my Cassandra. When I told him in the summer of the plan to run feature serials for two months, he rolled his eyes: 'Where's the money coming from?' I told him: 'Murdoch has asked me to do it and he's finding the money. Cheer up.' He looked down his glasses and gazed at me for a long time before pronouncing: 'It'll all end in tears. Mark my words.'

I had made it clear to Grant right at the beginning that I regarded him as a keeper of the purse, and I expected him to run a tight ship. He brought his proposals on salaries to me, always asking would I 'do the necessary'. I asked him on arrival for the budget and he said there was no budget. I found this odd, since I had left Giles at *The Sunday Times* a budget and I expected Rees-Mogg to have left me with one. 'It's all chaos upstairs,' Grant explained. He reported that there was not much fat on editorial. I urged him to control the costly appointment of casual labour, secretarial overtime, contributors (where there was overpayment) and the bill for newspapers and magazines, and I called a conference of senior executives. Afterwards Donoughue and Horton, who got on well together, came to see me. They were not impressed by Grant. They volunteered to take over the cost-cutting drive. It was very generous of them. Long was always telling me Grant was a washout, but I wanted to keep some of the old guard in place and I defended him. I asked Douglas-Home what he thought of the Horton-Donoughue offer and he brushed it off. 'They'd only get in John's hair. You can leave it to Grant. He's jolly good is old John when he gets going.'

I asked Horton and others to consider reporting the European Parliament without the expense of staff flying from London, doing without a second man in Washington, pulling out of Spain and Tokyo. I told Holden his freelance feature payments were too high. I told Horton to take a grip on foreign travel, essentially to make sure there was no duplication. He took it further, ticking off anyone, leader writers and home staff, who caught a plane without a Horton pass. Emery leapt like a tiger. Hickey wrote a stylish rebuke to the effect that it was not done at *The Times* for colleagues to behave to each other in such a peremptory fashion. Douglas-Home sent me a worried note: 'There are echoes of GL in all this by the look of things.' It was also a demonstration of the difficulties that arise when department heads have no agreed budgets.

At the beginning of October I asked Long to assign editorial a management accountant so that we could work out proper budgets. I asked again at the end of October. A new chief accountant arrived, confusingly called Godfrey Smith and very different from the *Sunday Times* Falstaff. When I met him in Long's office to see how we might proceed, he announced that *The Times* did not need so much business news. Could he tell me how much it cost? No.

The budget was my main target, but I had not given up trying to find out how the company was performing. I did not know then how determined Murdoch was to keep the board a eunuch. For months the 'board' meetings has been termed by Long 'executive committees'. An executive committee, unlike a board, had no legal status.

When both papers were closed by the NGA in September, the *Times* staff asked me how much the paper was losing. I had to say I had no idea. Figures of £10 and £20 million were bandied about, but the executive directors were presented with nothing to sustain such figures or explain them. Nobody knew whether Murdoch was charging Times Newspapers a rent for the building and putting the proceeds to News International or what was the distribution of overheads. Having failed with repeated verbal requests at the board meetings, I sent Long a note on 2 November outlining the crucial variables we should have before us every month: profit and loss, revenue from advertising both display and classified, by volume and by column yield, our market share of advertising revenue and sales, and our costs split between editorial, newsprint, ink, production, overtime, administration, and compared with the previous year. 'This may be old hat to you, but I find it exceedingly difficult to make a constructive contribution on our commercial problems without figures like these.'

Long would not challenge Murdoch's secrecy and methods. 'We've just got to give him good figures, that's all,' he would say when he came down to my room. How can we, I demanded of him time and again, when we are not allowed to have a say on revenues and management? He came down frequently that autumn, mostly depressed, sometimes on a high with Murdoch's latest telephoned order. 'Rupert says he wants 30% off staff all round immediately. 30%! He's in great form by the way, says *The Times* is doing well.'

John Grant said it would mean closing sport and parliament, and half of business news. I recognized careful staff cuts would have to be considered, but '30%' was another rush of blood to the head, not a strategy. Long was being ridden hard by Murdoch. His great head bore itself with dignity for the most part. Late one afternoon he relapsed a little. He came into my office saying, 'Nothing, nothing, just got to get away from that madhouse', meaning the sixth floor. Politics apart, I appreciated his desire for *The Times* to succeed. He supported me with the new preview section. Beattie said it should be ended, because it had not led to increased sales on Fridays. He had already said this to Murdoch, who was grumpy about preview having too much theatre and music, and not enough about films: 'Give all the cast names, lots of them, that's what people want.' I bit Beattie's head off and regretted it. I told him he overlooked the possibility that preview had attracted some of the thousands of new readers of *The Times* and they would show up in the weekly, not the Friday, figures. Long pressed Ruda to sell more advertising for it, and told an incredulous Beattie that he would sell more if he put out posters in French and Japanese. 'Preview is just right,' he explained, 'for thousands of tourists.' Long conducted the executive meetings well, but we were all dummies. Every single commercial decision of any importance was taken along the corridor in Murdoch's office, while we went through our charades.

I wrote Murdoch two memos on the conduct of the company. In the first I gave him some figures on costs from recent research which showed that the British press spent 30% of its revenues on production and the American metropolitan daily 20%. This was the source of our unknown losses, and I urged him to have a showdown with the unions to achieve the manning levels in production and clerical departments which he should have achieved the first time round. In the second, in December, I canvassed policies on advertising rates and cover prices as I would have done at a Thomson board meeting, offering to go along with an increase in the price of *The Times* to preserve its quality. I suggested he should re-examine the merging of the advertising departments of *The Times* and *Sunday Times*, which had demonstrably not worked.

I received no replies from Murdoch to my analysis and suggestions.

During the spring and summer he had never stopped praising the paper; not infrequently I could see little to praise. Then he suddenly stopped. One evening there was a dinner at the White Tower with Nigel Grandfield, his plump and urbane new advertising agent, glowing in the success of the launch of the *News of the World* magazine *SunDay*. (His predecessor Garry Thorne had been abruptly sacked without a word from Murdoch.) The purpose of the dinner, said Murdoch, was how to get *The Times* sale to 400,000. I found it uncomfortable sitting there with Ken Beattie, Michael Ruda, Long and Grandfield, while Murdoch rattled off one-liners about the paper. Tombola for *The Times*, that would do it, he said. Up-market Bingo! And more sport! Forget women's features. Kill the diary. Sport sells papers! Gransfield had his turn. It was Omo time: we should add brightness to lightness. Grandfield, the advertising man, became expansive over brandy. The real trouble with *The Times* was the leaders: too long, not hard enough, who read them anyway? It was an offensive little scene.

The next afternoon Murdoch asked me up to his office. Ruda was there. 'Sport, I told you! Where's the sport?' Murdoch's biro was going through a copy of *The Times*, clearing space for sport and matching it against the *Guardian*. Unhappily he had hit on a day when sport had been deprived of four or five columns of space it should have had for the sake of business news. In my absence, Douglas-Home had dismissed the sports editor's claims which I had twice defined in a memo, so as to preserve the right balance between sport and its neighbour business news. But Murdoch was not satisfied with the Rhineland. He annexed more pages of business news for sport. 'Four pages for sport, every day,' he demanded. Ruda was having the time of his life watching the editor get his orders. I said that was going too far. I wanted more sport as he did and we were getting it in within the relatively small papers. I had already cut back business news a lot. There was a minimum service we had to give: he had just crossed out the unit trust prices, which we ran only twice a week anyway. He became annoyed. 'I'm telling you four pages minimum for sport. What do you want this crap for anyway? Two pages is plenty for business news.'

This assault on business news had been brewing for weeks. I had a tank trap ready. 'Look at the advertising revenue business news is bringing. That's the best paying display in the paper. It won't be there unless there's business editorial.' He rounded on me: 'You let *me* worry about the revenue! You get the sport in!'

I looked expectantly at Ruda. He knew that business advertisers wanted business pages. Murdoch turned on him. 'Anything wrong with that?' Ruda bobbed and smiled that it was all right. I protested: 'But you're always asking for these ads to go in business news. Are you saying they can go anywhere?' Ruda licked his lips and smiled, yes, yes, it would be all right. The first thing I did when I got back to my office was to write a note in longhand to Murdoch saying that I strenuously objected to the editor of *The Times* being placed in the position he had been last night with Grandfield and this afternoon with Ruda.

There were moments of exhilaration working with Murdoch; the debilitation, I reflected, was in seeing how his pressures made people behave. There was, however, some light relief: I even had the nerve to accept an invitation to Buckingham Palace.

Twenty-one editors of national newspapers, the BBC and ITN were asked in by Michael Shea, the press secretary to the Queen, a writer in his spare time of engrossing thrillers. It was the first meeting of its kind in twenty-five years. We walked from the snow-covered forecourt along the red carpets, past the marble busts of monarchs and into the white and gold of the 1844 Room, named because of its occupation that year by the Emperor Nicholas of Russia. In this setting, suitably reminiscent of incipient tragedy, Michael Shea revealed that one body was missing, that of Kelvin MacKenzie, who was last seen alive in an office in Bouverie

Street. Everyone protested their innocence, but Shea had it all worked out. MacKenzie, the editor of the *Sun*, was being held in his office by his employer. He had sent word, obviously under duress, to say that he put a meeting with this unnamed employer ahead of a meeting at the Palace! We all cheered up when Shea said that his (Shea's) employer – again unnamed, but we were beginning to cotton on to the code – would be joining us for a drink after our meeting.

Shea's message was that the Queen and other members of the Royal Family were worried about invasions of privacy; the Princess of Wales in particular felt beleaguered. I thought he was putting the finger on me. *The Times* that day, said Shea, had no fewer than ten separate Royal stories. But this was no more than his way of illustrating the interest in the Royal Family among all classes of the press. This was legitimate and understandable. He acknowledged the argument, which was more than some others I knew did, that these were times of economic depression and the stories provided happy, pleasant relief. But if anything about the Princess of Wales was 'good news', the strain on her was beginning to tell. She had come through the public engagements with flying colours, but she was a young woman of twenty, expecting her first child, who was entitled to a private life. She was more than usually affected by morning sickness 'because of her age and build', yet she was under siege at her home in Highgrove in Gloucestershire. Camouflaged photographers were bivouacked in the bushes; they were in ambush in Tetbury High Street, if she went out to buy a paper or some wine gums. She welcomed the public photographs, but she was increasingly despondent at the idea she could not go outside her own front door without being photographed. She had not asked for this meeting herself, but the people who loved and cared for her were growing anxious for her immediate happiness and for her longer-term attitude; Prince Charles was becoming angry. She would be part of the history of the country, said Shea, 'longer than any of us' and it would be a tragedy if her worries about the media were to continue into mature life, when she and her husband would play an even more important role than today. What could be done to allow the Princess of Wales a peaceful and unharassed pregnancy, and also respect the privacy of the Queen and her family at Sandringham?

There is no more fissile substance than a conglomerate of editors. The daily competition to be different is pursued after office hours with a perverse dedication, and with the ostentation when any other editor is in the vicinity. I knew that we would be hard put to agree that we were all sitting round a table in Buckingham Palace on a snowy day. Michael Shea was attuned to this fear of being compromised. He put it all with brilliant diffidence: on the one hand the attitude of the photographers, on the other the views of an anxious mother-in-law, a human dilemma rather than an issue of state. 'I cannot say you must do this or that; I hope you'll think about it.' Bellisario, he said enigmatically, had been a helpful precedent. Bellisario? It was the name of a freelance photographer, I recalled, who surreptitiously stalked the Queen and Princess Margaret at picnics and water ski-ing in the grounds of Sunninghill Park in the dark days of 1964. Two of the editors present, John Junor of the *Sunday Express* and Bob Edwards of the *Sunday Mirror* but then of the *Daily Express*, published the Bellisario pictures; a staff photographer of Edwards's was discovered by a forester hidden in the undergrowth with his camera trained on a hut where Princess Margaret was changing her clothes. The Press Council, invited to pronounce by the Queen's Press Secretary, accepted that the two editors were deceived into believing Bellisario's pictures were taken from a public place. They apologized and had their knuckles rapped for not taking enough care with intrusive photographs. Fleet Street followed up by shunning Bellisario. I regarded the two editors surreptitiously. Was there the smallest of winces, the tiniest of blushes? Both had gone straight for seventeen years. Shea would have no trouble there. But he took no chances; he did not name them or their papers. The Rehabilitation of Offenders Act may have been in his mind, but I regarded it as part of his skill. He was clever enough to endorse the aesthetic judgment of Mike Molloy, the editor of the *Daily Mirror*. His picture of the Princess coming out a sweet-shop in her parka was lovely; it was just the feeling of media claustrophia which was distressing the Princess. And clearly some of the intruders were foreigners.

Despite Shea's therapy, it was none the less edgy for a little while. The first to speak murmured that it would solve only part of the problem if his people agreed 'a self-imposed embargo', with the implication that they may as well solve none of it at such a price. The fear of being scooped showed. I chipped in that we all knew what was public and what was private, and if we individually exercised our ideas of restraint it would make a big difference. Barry Askew of the *News of the World*, speaking perhaps for the whole of Bouverie Street, clearly thought the 'next Queen of England' got what she deserved if she went out to buy wine gums. Didn't it mean, he hazarded, she was having a miscarriage? John Junor jumped all over him. They had been told it was just a little morning sickness, no one had the right to make more of it. The mood of the meeting developed co-operatively thereafter. The only flutter was when someone asked how it was to be reported. The editor of *The Times*, it was protested, had been taking advantage of his ability to write shorthand. I volunteered to forgo my notes for an on-the-record summary by David Chipp of the Press Association. Passions were cooled.

We moved into the Carnarvon Room, hung with paintings of the

Spanish guerrilla war against the armies of Napoleon, and we were joined by the Queen and Prince Andrew. I found myself conversing with the Queen about Leonid Brezhnev and Henry Kissinger's account of what he said about world peace when he was stuck with him up a tree on a bear shoot. I was struck, as everyone is, by her superior knowledge of affairs. Nobody in our rather stiff semi-circle raised the questions of the morning's conference. It seemed not on. But Barry Askew of the *News of the World* had not given up his campaign that this Royal Princess must learn to accept personal restrictions as the others had done. He came over and with characteristic boldness challenged the Queen point-blank: 'If Lady Di wants to buy some wine gums without being photographed, why doesn't she send a servant?' The semicircle of editors froze, and then collapsed in laughter as the Queen with a smile replied: 'What an extremely pompous man you are!'

When I came to write a leader that night I sympathized with the captive Princess, snapped and pinned like an errant butterfly to the front pages of public prints. Whether or not there was illegal trespass, the surveillance at Highgrove was immoral intrusion. Tetbury High Street was more difficult. No ordinary citizen could expect to be protected from photography in a public place, but a different view should surely be taken in the light of the knowledge that it caused distress. I wrote in a sentence for private amusement: 'The idea that the Princess might send a servant for the wine gums is pompous if not preposterous.'

Murdoch was not in a mood that night for jokes. When he received the first edition of *The Times*, he came on the telephone. 'Why are you picking on the *Sun*?' Pages in the *Sun*, the *Daily Mirror* and the *Daily Star* were cited as helping to precipitate the request from the Palace; we reported that MacKenzie 'who did not attend the meeting was not available for comment'. I told Murdoch that I could not see what he was getting at. That was the news. 'You're always picking on the *Sun*,' said Murdoch.

He was sufficiently relaxed the next day to make a sally. I had asked if he had any objection to my going off to receive an honorary doctorate from the University of Stirling. 'I suppose', he replied, 'I will have to live with the unquenchable thirst of editors for notoriety and titles. After this morning's editorial, I feared that we might be heading for a more serious breach, and I hope that I will not have these misgivings confirmed on January 1!'

There were far more serious matters. On the day of our conference at the Palace, 8 December, it was unexpectedly announced that Denis Hamilton was resigning as chairman of Times Newspapers Holdings board and as a national director. His successor as chairman was Rupert Murdoch.

Denis Hamilton represented the highest aspirations of journalism. His abrupt departure severed the last link with the values and achievements of the Thomson era. He had been the editor of *The Sunday Times* for six years, the editor-in-chief of Times Newspapers for fourteen and associated with *The Sunday Times* for thirty-five years. It was on the understanding between him and Roy Thomson that the political independence of *The Sunday Times* had been founded in the 1960s and 1970s, and its cultural horizons extended. It was his intergrity which had induced the Astor family, in 1966, to merge *The Times* with Roy Thomson's *Sunday Times*; and over fifteen years he had been as true to the inherited ideas of *The Times* as he was to those he himself established for *The Sunday Times*. He had brought me to *The Sunday Times* and made me its editor. He had resisted pressures himself as the editor, and he had sustained me in difficult passages with government and the law. He was the man I expected to turn to first for counsel in the current difficulties over politics and budgets which threatened the editorial independence of *The Times*.

He had endorsed Murdoch's acquisition of Times Newspapers, seeing it as the way of preserving the company he had created. He was a constitutionalist and, with the editorial guarantees in place, he had trusted Murdoch. His reward that December had been a visit from Gerald Long, deputed by Murdoch to tell him it was time to go after barely nine months in the chair. Hamilton had said on his appointment in February 1981 that he saw himself as a bridge to the news, but it was my understanding that he intended to serve at least two or three years, certainly not less than the full year. He was just sixty-three. His chairmanship of Times Newspapers Holdings board was more symbolic than operational, but as his appointment had symbolised continuity and trust so his removal was dismaying.

Denis Hamilton was too proud and too hurt to do other than bow out with customary dignity. When I went to see him that bleak December day, he was quietly assembling his papers. He gave me a farewell present. It was his handsomely bound set of volumes of the official *History of The Times*.

Shortly afterwards I went on holiday for Christmas. There was deep snow and silence around our home in Kent; we were cut off for several days. Only the track of a fox marked the whiteness stretching to the larch at the end of the garden and into the woods. I sawed silver birch logs and in front of the fire read the volumes Hamilton had given me, as beautiful in their craftsmanship as their language. I felt safe with the Walters and Barnes and Delane, wrapped in a tranquil time-warp.

15
PLOTS

A man in English cricket flannels was an incongruous figure in the sub-zero temperatures in Warsaw over Christmas and New Year. Roger Boyes, the man from *The Times*, had travelled lightly for a few days' reconnaissance when the military cracked down on Solidarity in December. Freezing but unmolested, he saw the riots and sifted the rumours of bloodshed, and day by day he wrote it all down in his diary in the hope that somehow he could get something back to London.

Sending a staffman to Warsaw had been my first foreign priority when I arrived at *The Times*. Richard Davy and Dessa Trevisan did good work as visiting firemen, but leaving that political and social drama to random trips was like dipping into *War and Peace*: the struggle of ten million people involved in Solidarity to create a plural society was so extraordinary it demanded a sustained effort to report and understand it. It took longer than I hoped to find the right man. Boyes was twenty-eight and had been educated at military school in Dover. He had experience for Reuters in Moscow and three years on *The Financial Times* in eastern and western Europe. He impressed me as an unflashy man of resource and good judgement. I appointed him in November and Horton gained accreditation for him just in time.

The censorship was draconian. A sentence such as 'The situation is calm apart from persistent reports of localized violence and widespread labour unrest' would be cut after four words. Boyes tried to send a truer picture in 'Dear Harry' letters addressed to me which he gave to 'pigeons', friendly travellers on their way back to the West. He typed up three or four copies of every letter; there was no carbon paper, still less photocopying. We exercised discretion extracting news from the pigeon mail. We were anxious not to compromise him. For this reason I vetoed a proposal by Fred Emery to send a reporter without a visa with one of the food lorries from the West. The loneliness and frustration, not surprisingly, told on Boyes; in the communications black-out he had no idea whether we had received his clandestine messages. Should he come out and tell the story? Brian Horton thought it a feasible risk; he had a visa and might get back in again. I decided against it and we were all rewarded in the middle of January when the cruder censorship was lifted. We asked Boyes to empty his diary and from these jottings, his notes and smuggled letters we set about trying to compile an authoritative narrative of the events since the midnight coup.

It made two pages and it was ready for 13 January, one day after the easing of censorship. It was the first perspective in the press on the climactic month of martial law which had been so confused by rumour and speculation. Its conclusions have proved sound. I was proud of it. I sent a note to Murdoch and Long suggesting it should be advertised, and I mentioned it to Murdoch when I passed him in the foyer of the *Times* building the night we did it. There was no publicity. A day or two later, when I was in Murdoch's room, he went over to his reading rack and flicked open a copy of the *Sun*. 'There,' he said, '*that*'s all you need on Poland', and he put his hand on a few paragraphs of his *Sun*.

I was not provoked to respond. This was all part of the warfare that Murdoch had started after Christmas. It had a variety of expressions, some personally offensive, some hostile to *The Times*; I was convinced its roots lay in his sense of obligation to Mrs Thatcher. In the autumn his campaign had been to provide comfort for a government at the nadir of its fortunes and a cold climate for the buoyant Alliance. In the New Year it was to get rid of me. There was something approaching panic in right-wing circles. A general election could not be more than two years away and she was still massively unpopular. Only a quarter of the population expressed satisfaction; the Falklands war was no more than a fever in the mind of an obscure general in Buenos Aires. The recession, which was supposed to have ended in midsummer, was deepening. Unemployment and interest rates were rising, industrial production was still falling and Tory backbenchers were restive. *The Times* did not go out of its way to give undue prominence to any of these trends, its editorial attitude to the Government was critical but not hostile, and it faithfully tracked the squabbles between the Social Democrats and the Liberals over the allocation of seats. But Murdoch had made up his mind over Christmas. The first sign was the curious affair of the dinner engagement at my home. Murdoch accepted but, as soon as he heard that Roy Jenkins was to be one of the guests, he cancelled at once without explanation. He had a small circle of friends in London, including Woodrow Wyatt, Paul Hamlyn and Paul Johnson. He went into a huddle for a long afternoon with Johnson in the study of Johnson's home in Iver, Bucks. Johnson, one of Mrs Thatcher's most fervent acolytes in the press, used his *Spectator* column to expose my sinister influence on *The Times*. He detected a revolutionary drift in headlines

before I had been at *The Times* a week. Murdoch's meeting with Johnson, which was followed up by Gerald Long with lunch at the Savoy,
was the first of a series of Murdoch conversations with maverick right-
wing figures of journalism which gradually filtered back to me and were
not good news. The usual shorthand was applied, conviction and conscience being a monopoly of the Right. I ran into the opening barrage on
Thursday 7 January.

On New Year's Eve I travelled to North Wales to see my mother and
father, and on 2 January flew to the United States to fulfil a longstanding
commitment. MacArthur, Emery and Hickey were in charge at the
office; Douglas-Home went on a month's sabbatical at the end of December. I planned to return after five days. 'Gerald Long', my secretary, Liz
Seeber, reported to me by transatlantic phone, 'is rampaging round the
office asking for you. He says, "Who's editing this paper, a computer?"'
I scoured the paper to see what had given offence in the time between my
departure and Long's return from holiday. Could it be the article by me
discussing readers' views on the Scorpian short ski which was provocatively headlined 'Equal rights for short skiers'? No, a more inflammatory
entry in *The Times* was that by Robin Young, the consumer affairs
writer. He had form: he had been denounced by Long previously for
conducting a blind tasting of British and French shop food. Only a
charlatan, Long had declared, would conduct a blind tasting. This time
the recidivist Young had given a list of caterers who would cook for
private dinner parties, and he had commended bourgeois cooked meats
and unhealthy fruit tarts that Long was sure to have found distressing.
I returned at once to England.

Murdoch was back as well, a day earlier than expected. I learned that
he had telephoned the office on 30 December and had been told by the
duty secretary that I was at home in London. He had telephoned again
on 4 and 5 January, both times to complain to MacArthur about 'leftist'
headlines which were 'EEC snubs Reagan over Poland' and 'Peace breaks
out in the Labour party'. MacArthur defended the first one and changed
the second to say 'Peace breaks out, claims Labour party'. Were these
'instructions to a journalist' about which I should protest, I wondered,
as I went up to see Murdoch on the afternoon of 7 January? Neither
MacArthur nor Emery, who heard MacArthur deal with Murdoch,
thought so.

'Where the hell have you been?' said Murdoch as I entered.

'In America. I told you I would be away.'

'Nobody could find you. And where's Douglas-Home? And whad d'ya
stand for? Nothing! *The Times* has no convictions.'

I accepted the provocation. I was glad to have it out in the open. I
outlined five policy lines on defence, trade union reform, public invest-

ment, individual liberty, the Western alliance. 'They're strong and clear,' I declared. 'And I'm never going to accept monetarist dogma.'

He let them all go by, except for the Western alliance. 'I don't see *that*,' he stabbed; and then he added acidly: 'Of course, I'm not supposed to speak to you like this. . . . I'm supposed to ask the national directors.'

That concluded the worst formal encounter with Murdoch in ten months. The political challenge was not upsetting in itself. The bitter sterility of it was. Against his accusing one-liners, a reasoned exposition sounded long-winded and weak. It was only the beginning. He followed up with a note reiterating that I had not told him or Long I would be away. I was reduced to sending him a photocopy of the memo addressed to both him and Long advising him of my absence. Then he complained about the reception he had received when he telephoned my office on 30 December. 'I was treated like an outsider. If I am treated like an outsider, I may start behaving like one.'

That afternoon I had an agitated Richard Davy in my office. 'We don't have to change our line, do we?' the chief foreign leader writer asked. I had no idea what he was talking about. 'Our line on Poland and the Russians as Mr Murdoch says,' he explained, and he rattled off a Murdoch diatribe about conscience requiring an economic war on the Soviet Union. It transpired that Murdoch had sent for Hickey and accused *The Times* of being soft. We should end détente and co-existence which amounted to appeasement. The Soviet Union was a rotten apple and if we cut off all trade and diplomatic relations it would fall. 'I don't accept that, I can't agree, I detest their system, but that's too simple,' Davy expostulated. I was boiling with impatience to speak to Hickey, but I heard Davy out, reassured him that I was not about to take orders and, when Davy had gone, sent for Hickey. He came in blinking shyly, but volunteering nothing. We sat on the sofa and I said I understood he had been sent for and would he mind telling me what happened. 'Certainly, certainly.' It was perfectly in order, wasn't it, for the chairman to ask him up for a chat? 'It's his point of view,' he said of Murdoch's Cold War rhetoric. But there was more. Murdoch had objected to our giving space on the op ed page to Ray Buckton of the ASLEF rail union to write an open letter to the commuters he was inconveniencing. We had done that the day previously and followed it up that very morning, 12 January, with a reply headed 'Where Ray Buckton got it wrong' by British Rail's negotiator. 'I told Mr Murdoch that this was good journalism,' said Hickey. 'I said *The Times* had a duty to provide a platform for varying views, while maintaining its own editorial position.'

He seemed to doubt whether he had carried his point. I liked the image of Hickey's polite tutorial for Murdoch in elementary principles of ethical journalism, but he should have told me about the audience. 'Oh,

I was careful to watch', he said demurely, 'that it didn't amount to instructions to a journalist.'

Douglas-Home was in Gloucestershire, writing a book on the British monarchy. I interrupted his historical reveries. We canvassed whether, in his phrase, I should put down a marker, and concluded uneasily that there was little to be gained by making a noise at this stage. It so happened a leader had been commissioned that morning on the Polish crisis. It was written by Richard Owen under the supervision of Richard Davy and it developed *The Times* policy which, after a hesitant response on the first Sunday of the crisis, was critical of dithering in the West. It renewed a call we made on 5 January for selective sanctions until General Jaruzelski freed those interned in Poland and resumed a dialogue with Solidarity and the Church. I took the opportunity to reject Murdoch's line and wrote:

> It is sometimes suggested that cutting off all trade and diplomatic relations with the Soviet Union would precipitate the collapse from the edges inwards of an imperial system already over-stretched by nationalist unrest, economic difficulties and a guerilla war in Afghanistan. This is a romantic notion. It almost certainly underestimates the flexibility of the Soviet system and the capacity of the Russians, if not the East Europeans, to endure it, even in extremis. More importantly, it would introduce a dangerous unpredictability in to East–West relations which would return to the Cold War with thermonuclear knobs on. There may come a time when high risks have to be run – the resolve must always be maintained – but it is premature to take the gamble with the stability of the entire continent, east and west, which is implicit in such apocalyptic strategy.

I expected some come-back from Murdoch, but he was off on a bombing run. The target was *The Sunday Times*. When he asked me to see him on the morning we published the leader it was to say that he had done 'something terrible' to me: 'I'm taking Brian MacArthur to be deputy editor and editor-designate at *The Sunday Times*. He's bushy-tailed. He'll put energy in over there.' I knew I would miss MacArthur; his exuberance had dispelled a lot of stale air. It was a promotion for him and I could not stand in his way. But the next piece of information was genuinely stunning. He had sacked Ron Hall, said Murdoch, both as joint deputy editor and editor of the magazine; he was demoting Hugo Young; and to replace Hall he was bringing in Peter Jackson, the editor of the *News of the World* colour magazine *SunDay*. He added with a grin: 'I'll tell the national directors at lunch Frank Giles has asked for it all.' Was the remark a bravura display or a frightener to indicate his contempt for the whole paraphernalia of national directors, editors and guarantees? When the Secretary of State, John Biffen, agreed to Murdoch's acquisition a year before, condition 4 (b) (iv) of his consent said:

'The editor of each newspaper shall retain control over the appointment, disposition and dismissal of journalists.' Well, here in Hall, Young, Jackson and MacArthur were rude gestures for every sub-clause of 4 (b) (iv).

I knew some of the background and I pieced the rest together later. Murdoch sent for Giles on Tuesday 12 January, on the eve of a lunch with the national directors, and told him what was to happen. Giles was troubled by it. Overnight he accepted Hall's sacking and steeled himself to do it; there had never been much love between the two men. But he felt that Jackson, whom he had never met, was being foisted on him and he remained upset at the idea of demoting Young, the man he favoured as his own successor. He arrived early at Murdoch's office, but found him engaged. Instead of waiting in the ante-room, he went down the sixth floor passage and ran into Long, who ushered him into his office. There Giles confided his misgivings to his old adversary – a measure of his unhappiness – and then – a measure of his faith in mankind – allowed Long to get ahead of him into Murdoch's office on the understanding that he would be a mediator. As an ambassador, Long was an excellent executioner. Giles did not see Murdoch. Long's shuttle diplomacy merely produced ultimatums. If he did not accept the *News of the World*'s Jackson as editor of the magazine, Murdoch would go to the national directors and say he, Giles, should be dismissed because he was impeding a vital commercial decision. Yes, he really would. Ditto for his request that MacArthur should be No. 3 to Young's No. 2. Giles asked him if he could have lunch with Jackson before announcing his appointment, which was graciously granted, as was his appeal to be able to tell Young he was still in the running for the editorship. It was, as Giles said later, the worst day of his life. He believed it was 'his head or mine', and he went back to summon the wholly unsuspecting Young and Hall to tell them that he had just made certain decisions concerning them which he plainly had not. It could not be anything but a miserable farce. 'I want your job,' Giles said with wounding ambiguity to Hall, and by this time had half-convinced himself he did. Young was told he was too much like Giles and the No. 2 slot had to go to a news and production man. At a meeting of the colour magazine staff, Giles denied that Jackson had been imposed on him; he had had a long talk with him at lunch. He tried again to put a brave face on it all when he met heads of departments. No one really believed him. Some wanted to, others were openly, if politely, incredulous. Giles later told Young he had 'a very nice call' from Murdoch to thank him for being so helpful in a difficult period.

Young's consolation was a visit from Long to dilate on Murdoch's qualities: 'I admire Rupert tremendously. We should all admire him. His only interest is in excellence, excellence in all things. He does not like it when people are unable to see excellence in the *Sun*, and he equally wants *The Times* and *Sunday Times* to be excellent. *The Sunday Times* is flabby, unexciting, lacks an element of surprise. Rupert says so and I agree.' Young was told he should not feel down. No slight had been intended, none at all. It was just that Rupert felt a new mix was necessary. 'The real trouble is Giles. He's terrified of Rupert. It's quite pathetic. He has no idea how to deal with Rupert, which is openly and directly, and ready for an argument on equal terms.'

Long was still talking about Giles when I entered his office a few days later to press, yet again, for my budget. He motioned me to stay as an eavesdropper to his telephonic instruction of Bruce Page at the *Statesman* in the matter of correct form. Mr Page should please understand that the changes were not only announced by Giles but decided, yes *decided*, by him. Only the editor could decide such matters, that was clear. A decision had been taken. Therefore only Giles could have taken it.

'What can one do about Giles?' Long moaned, when he had finished unconvincing Page. 'Just look at this.' It was a piece of rococo embodied in a letter from Giles to *Sunday Times* journalists. It should have appealed to Long's concern for accuracy, if not to his taste in prose, for it was one of the more accurate statements of the period: 'I, as editor,' wrote Giles, 'was involved in the discussion with higher management that led to these decisions.'

Long's irritation was as much with *The Sunday Times* as with Giles. This was partly a loyal reflection of Murdoch's views. Neither man understood the paper. Murdoch's attitude was exactly as H.G. Wells described Northcliffe's to *The Times*. He was a big bumblebee puzzled by a pane of glass. All these individuals with their different views, and the editor listening to them. Anarchy! Long's passionate endorsement was not the sycophancy the *Sunday Times* staff thought it was. No syncophant would have behaved as Long did after a private preview of the film *Gallipoli*, which Murdoch backed and which had such associations with his father. Long dismissed it as cheap sentiment.

Long's attitude was a complex of intellectual views about authority and an emotional yearning to be seen and admired as something quite special, an intellectual who had also seen the world. This was in conflict with his doctrine on authority, which was that it had to be demonstrated all the time, in size of office and style of address. His normal manner was so aggressive it provoked reaction. It was derived from reading books rather than observing men. It was self-conscious. He tested himself against the wisdom of Norman Vincent Peale, Dale Carnegie and the Power of Positive Thinking. Long's appreciation of Murdoch as someone with more natural authority was, therefore, sincere and he really did think Murdoch had a magic touch with newspapers and numbers. So why did the *Sunday Times* staff go on about their wretched independence and not jump to Murdoch's orders about Hall and Young? They were stuck-up layabouts. 'They all hate me over the bridge,' he sighed. He had a soft spot for Hall, a fellow Yorkshireman, similarly strong-minded, clever and musical, and he was baffled why he had not seized his chance to dominate Giles and oust Young.

'Use your elbows, Ron,' Murdoch had said to Hall. The idea was that Hall kept an eye on the colour magazine in the week, but came in on Saturday, as joint deputy editor, and elbowed aside the editor and other deputy editor who had spent the week on the paper. 'How are those elbows going?' was Murdoch's constant greeting, tightening into a complaint. Hall is a forceful person, but the idea that he could impose himself on the newspaper in this way over Giles, Young and the other senior executives, even if he had wanted to, which he did not, was a delusion that could only be held by someone who had an imperfect understanding of how *The Sunday Times* worked and what it was all about. It was not a paper created in an authoritarian manner, still less in a one-day rush of superficial judgements. Hall was more vulnerable to the second complaint, which was the quality of a dummy prepared for a women's magazine within the main magazine, to be called *Look*. Murdoch flung it down in front of me: 'Just look at the garbage your friend Hall has produced. It's disgusting.'

Peter Jackson of the *News of the World* was a rum choice to succeed Hall. Murdoch had been impressed by the way he introduced cleavage in colour into his *News of the World* magazine. He made him edit both magazines at the same time, which no doubt explains why Jackson, examining transparencies at *The Sunday Times*, thought Laurence Olivier was Spike Milligan. Jackson introduced commercial supplements common to both papers and directed the minds of the staff to test beds, reader traffic and target audiences. It was a far cry from Hamilton's founding aspirations to engage the readers in cultural adventure with the finest writers and photographers. Jackson guilelessly made it clear that he took his instructions and his inspiration from 'the chairman', not the editor, of *The Sunday Times*. Women's editor Suzanne Lowry told him that a feature would shortly be ready on the women in the SDP with specially commissioned photographs. No, said Jackson, that will have to be killed. 'The chairman does not like the SDP.'

The blunt Hall and the cerebral Young have different talents and different styles, but they have one thing in common: they are not yes-men. The sacking of Hall deprived *The Sunday Times* not just of an outstanding technician but also of a tough original intellect. Young's demotion was a blow to the idea of a paper of principled, unpartisan vigilance. The message of the Murdoch *putsch* was clear: use your elbows and bend with the wind. And there are ways round guarantees. Roy Hattersley's hope, expressed in his *Punch* column, that the affair would lead to the appearance of Murdoch, Long and Giles in the Pentonville exercise yard was frustrated by Giles's unsuspected ability to swallow hard. The Secretary of State was relieved of having to deliver.

I thought Murdoch was most fair, however, in the 1981 annual report of his News Corporation. He referred to the 'exciting results' on *The Times*, where everyone recognized that a return to profitability required a long-term effort. 'Mr Evans has begun, in a number of ways, to improve *The Times*, while increasing its authority,' said the News Corporation document, and it listed on two pages what it saw as the achievements: the emphasis on the primacy of first-hand reporting; the expansion of *The Times* position as a paper of record, notably by featuring the results from all the universities, and the innovation of the Times Information Service; the new senior editorial team and columnists; the redesign of the paper.

> The results of this energetic editorial programme have been extremely gratifying. With no promotion, circulation has begun to move upward from 276,000 at the time of the take-over to more than 300,000 today.... *The Times* will continue to incur losses for some time to come but the improvement in its editorial product and its circulation growth provide the basis for optimism.

In the early months of 1982 I spent considerable time kneeling on the carpet in my office, which might in the circumstances have been taken for a posture of prayer. The devotion, however, was to Mammon. I was trying to make a further improvement in the 'editorial product', not a term to set the blood racing, by revising the business section. Spreading trial pages on the carpet proved the most convenient way to try permutations of content and design. I was joined in these exercises by Adrian Hamilton, the editor of business news, and David Driver, recently appointed as Edwin Taylor's deputy and working under his guidance. He was a good choice. He was a precise designer-editor from the *Radio Times*, his pink bow-tie precisely tuned to pick up 1215Hz/247m. He perfectly understood the havoc that could be created across the country by a careless attitude to digits. None of us was interested in what is called in the trade a 'tarting up' exercise, making pages look prettier. That could have been done overnight. The difficulty was to make sure we were providing the right services in the right way for the *Times* reader. How many of their lives turned on soyabean meal? Who cared about rubber physicals? One day we lost, by accident, a line devoted to

meat commissions and apparently threw numerous traders into angry
indolence. There was a plethora of material. We could not compete with
the comprehensive *Financial Times*, but were we making good use of
forty-five daily columns? This was around twenty columns more than
the *Telegraph* or *Guardian*. It was a lot of newsprint spiked with all
manner of statistics. Hamilton flung himself on the barbed-wire thickets
with great gallantry. He explored miles of muddy print. He went on
patrol through hundreds of unit trust and commodity prices. He sub-
orned the best young talent on the specialist journals. He found some
surprising gaps in the paper of record, and waste as well. *The Times* did
not record the number of daily bargains on the Stock Exchange (20,000
plus), though to do so took only one line. It published rather more than
a thousand unit trust prices every day, 150 more than the *Telegraph*. But
it was not a full list compared with *The Financial Times*'s 1,842 prices.
This was because a small fee was charged for entry, and not all the trusts
were willing to pay. Hamilton recommended that we include all the
prices on editorial grounds, which would make *The Times* the only
paper, other than *The Financial Times*, to give a complete service. I
accepted this. But we could save a great deal of space as well, for there
was no need to give four or more columns daily to the prices. They did
not change as frequently as equities. Twice weekly publication of the
full list was adequate. This was a saving of sixteen columns of space
weekly, which could be used by other departments. In the smaller papers
of the recession it did not make sense to maintain forty columns or more
for business, while restricting home news and the law report to twenty-
five, and overseas and sport to under twenty, especially when some of
this space was squandered on a duplication of main paper features such
as letters, the diary, and a big title piece. Hamilton thought he could
produce a section more closely integrated with the paper in 30–34
columns, which still made it the largest in the dailies other than *The
Financial Times*. We were both sure it would be wrong to emasculate it
into a *Telegraph* specialist City review. Murdoch did not quite say he
wanted that, but it was the drift of his wrangle with me in the autumn,
when for the sake of sport he wanted to squeeze business news further
than I was prepared to go. I laid it down that business news must have
a minimum of thirty columns daily. For a highly successful businessman,
Murdoch had a surprising antipathy to news about business. His interest
stopped at his rivals' take-over battles. When we recruited Anthony
Hilton from New York as Hamilton's deputy, he asked Maxwell Newton, the financial editor of Murdoch's *Post*, for his views on *The Times*.
Newton sent Murdoch a copy of them and Murdoch sent them on to me
with a scribbled note: 'This is worth reading *carefully*!' Newton's notes
were long on Murdochspeak, calling for the pages to be exciting, con-

tentious, provocative, fiery, but there was some sound observation and the coverage suggested was broad, not narrow.

I expected a new argument about space with Murdoch every day when we relaunched the business section, but it never came. It was satisfying working with Hamilton and his business news staff. They took their opportunities without a backward glance. I turned to sport, which had been as starved of space and staff as business news had been surfeited. To say they were cowed would not be quite right, but under Nicholas Keith they carried into newspaper work the fortitude of gallant losers on the field. There was never a full team on the night desk. They had to call in casuals, the work was unduly rushed and inevitably there were mistakes; there was no one to revise and copy-taste. The writers were of high quality, but there were only eight staff men including two racing correspondents. There was still no one to do a form guide, an omission presumably due to the theory that *Times* readers were always lunching with the owners. When Geoffrey Boycott abandoned the MCC tour in India, there was no one to follow up the story in his home county. There was no general columnist like Frank Keating of *The Guardian*. He agreed to join us, then succumbed to the entreaties of his editor Peter Preston. Hunter Davies, the biographer of the Beatles and Tottenham Hotspur FC, filled the gap but blanched at the way his masterpieces were hammered into small holes.

My ambitions for the arts pages were unfulfilled. They remained dull and respectable. I wished to make them more enjoyably responsive. In John Higgins, the arts editor, I was up against a man who raised procrastination to an art form. I came to think of him as journalism's *Yes, Minister*. I had raised with him very early on the question of whether it was prudent to devote his own time and four columns of the paper to an opera in Geneva when it led to the neglect of other happenings. I fretted about a succession of serious omissions. Higgins was not readily on hand to put these matters into consoling perspective. He was still devotedly in a grand circle somewhere between Basel and Valparaiso.

Editorially it was a rewarding period. The seductive challenge of newspaper editing is that you can never get it all right, but you keep thinking you can. I had distractions. There was John Grant's thumb for a start. I was always interposing my body between Long and Grant. One of the Uriah Heeps who flourished in the atmosphere of suspicion whispered to Long that Grant approved expenses by stamping them with an engraving of his signature. Long pounced: this practice must cease immediately. He might have had a point, but he had not bothered to inquire the reason for the curiosity and the mischief-makers had not told him its history. It was that Grant was disabled in the thumb. Both his joints had degenerated with gout. He had lost the bone of one thumb and was threatened with the loss of the bone in the other, which would mean he would not be able to write at all for six months. To have to countersign up to 300 expense claims weekly was impossible for him, yet it was his duty as managing editor, so the stamp was devised. It was kept under lock and key. All this was well known to the accounts people. I told Long so in a suitably composed memorandum and commended Grant's thumb to his mercy. He relented at the cost of a formal undertaking, readily given, that no one would ever apply the stamp except the said Grant.

The matter of New York was graver. It was the first of a series of new issues touching the independence and quality of *The Times*; and there was a combined assault by Murdoch and Long. *The Times* staff reporter in New York, Michael Leapman, left towards the end of 1981 to join the *Daily Express*, and I considered who should succeed him from the staff. It was an important and well-established position. Murdoch sent me a note on 16 December saying it should not be filled. I was 'very wrong' to replace Leapman: 'We are already over-staffed there. The expense of this is enormous and I must protest.' But there was no *Times* man in New York, and filling the vacancy did not represent an increase in staff; indeed, in a reshuffle of posts we were saving two. That was not the point: Murdoch was trying to insist on *The Times* being serviced by the reporters he employed indiscriminately for his British, Australian and American newspapers and magazines, the vast bulk of them trivial publications. It was this bureau, not *The Times* at all, he was referring to when he said we were already over-staffed. There were three issues here, each of them reinforcing me in my determination to keep a *Times* staff man in New York. The first was the quality of the service, the second its control, and the third, almost incidental, was that Murdoch was breaking two promises: one he made to the Secretary of State to secure the titles and one he had made to *The Times* only eight months before.

I went ahead and announced the appointment in January, moving Peter Watson from the diary. (It so happened that he had an apartment in New York and the costs were less than for Leapman.)

Long sent me a bristling memorandum, copy to Murdoch. New foreign postings were banned on grounds of cost. But it was not a new posting and cost was a red herring. The cost of what they were trying to enforce was to excellence, and to the excellence Murdoch had pledged himself to maintain. If I knuckled under to the Murdoch-Long ruling, I would be accepting that *The Times* was no different from the Sydney *Daily Mirror*. An individual reporter in the agency might perform well one day, but the distinction and discrimination which were supposed to be the hallmarks of *The Times* would be gambled. Second, the bureau was Murdoch's, answerable directly to him. Once *The Times* was serviced by a Murdoch bureau in New York, why not Washington and elsewhere? A distinction would have been blurred, one deep in the history of *The Times* and central to its independence. There were two symbols of the struggle for me. The first was the sight of a Murdoch man in New York tearing a news agency message from the teleprinter, changing a few words and sending it off to Australia in his own name. The second was Murdoch on the telephone in his office at the New York *Post* 'reworking' a leader for the *Sun* in London, then telling the waiting Robert Ducas of Times Newspapers: 'I'm not having two or three journos go to something like the space landing. One journo can write for all my papers.'

The attempt to veto my appointment was, finally, a breach of a pledge Murdoch made the previous April that his incidental appointment of a *Times* man, Michael Hamlyn, to run the Murdoch bureau would not carry the implication that *The Times* could dispense with its own man answerable to London. Hamlyn knew *The Times*, but he had his hands full, not least with the Australians with different deadlines, styles and interests. Whatever Hamlyn might have been able to do, the principle was crucial, as Murdoch acknowledged himself in his note of 28 May: 'News gathering by individual publications ... will be undertaken, as always, by designated correspondents ... directed by their editors, managing editors, or their representatives through direct contract with correspondents.'

So I rejected Long's attempt to veto my New York appointment.

Murdoch came back himself. He switched the attack: 'Hamlyn, whom you recommended, is far too weak for the job, and we will have to move him *unless he stands up for his rights and makes all editors and foreign editors work through him.*'*

This was harsh on Hamlyn, but revealing, for this is what the argument was all about – Murdoch's determination to funnel *The Times* service through his News bureau, again contrary to his pledge. It would have meant that the editor of *The Times* and his foreign editor could commission articles from New York only with the approval of Murdoch's man. 'I wonder sometimes', his letter said, 'what we would lose in all our papers if we simply shut the New York office down. There would be moments of loss, but they would not be fatal. At the moment we have the biggest staff there and quite the worst coverage of any Fleet Street newspaper.' But it was not *The Times* which had the biggest staff. When he wrote his letter we had nobody there.

---

* My italics.

I confirmed the appointment. Brian Horton made life more difficult. He had been the first person the previous May to raise the alarm, but for some reason he changed his mind: 'Let's give the bureau a chance.' It all became heated when Tony Holden, himself a former Washington correspondent of *The Observer*, returned from a visit to New York and Horton accused him of a 'whispering campaign'. Holden's offence was to make it clear he believed *The Times* must maintain its own New York man and that, in any event, the News bureau was not able to provide all *The Times* needed: 'Maybe once in a hundred years, they'll by accident write a report of a White House press conference which would pass the NCTJ* proficiency certificate, but I rather doubt it.' But he was an assistant editor and it was his duty to say what he thought.

Horton drew himself up to his considerable full height and said to me: 'If you want to persist with this New York appointment, you'll have to overrule me.'

'Consider yourself overruled,' I said.

When Long challenged over New York, he also questioned whether *The Times* should spend money on a diary. There was not an item in the paper, not a writer or area of interest, he could not question in this way. Ostensibly it was a management cost query; in practice it was an expression of a quasi-editorial judgement which was becoming oppressive. As Bagehot said of the supply power of the House of Commons: 'It could absolutely control the money, and thereby the policy, of the State.' The editor shapes his paper by the way he allocates resources within a budget. Without an agreed total I was exposed on every item if expenditure, subject to Murdoch's impulsive personal control, which was precisely why we had insisted on a budget as a crucial element in his guarantees of non-interference. I emphasized this yet again in my reply to Long: 'An editorial budget with regular operating statements, which I have been seeking for eleven months, is the realistic way to control costs, providing both of us with the financial monitoring we require and the editor with the freedom essential to editorial creativity.' He gave the standard excuse: 'You know that we have been hampered in our efforts to produce editorial budgets by the lack of an efficient system for recording costs.'

It was on 20 January, eleven months after my appointment, that I finally got some figures from the chief accountant, Godfrey Smith, via Long. It was very curious. Smith's note to Long said the current total of spending on *The Times* was £9,710,600 'compared to Mr Murdoch's budget of £7,723,000'. What was this? It was the first I had heard of 'Mr Murdoch's budget' or the sums of £9 million and £7 million. How could budgets have been set without consultation with the editor? The

* National Council for the Training of Journalists.

guarantees said the budget would be agreed, and this one had merely been proclaimed and sprung on me. Not only that, it had been a secret figure. I was going to be told I had exceeded a total nobody had admitted existed and which I had no part in forming. Long followed up by asking me to meet with Smith, as a matter of urgency, 'to reduce editorial spending at The Times by £2 million p.a.' Why stop at £2 million? Why not £10 million? How were these sums worked out? It was a far cry from Long's ultra-rational approach of the zero budget. But I was more than willing to save money. I did not regard editorial spending as sacrosanct. I was eager to wrestle with some figures at last, infinitely preferring a smaller budget I created and controlled to secrecy accompanied by commando raids. Also The Times was in trouble. The principal causes were Murdoch's eagerness in the take-over of 1981, which tempted him to a soft compromise with the print unions, and lack of advertising revenue. Only in Long's note, however, was I at last informed of the scale of the Times Newspapers losses, running between £12 and £15 million. The board meetings had still had no figures, still less any discussion of them. To cut £2 million was a tall order but, if it could be done, we would do it. This was what I told Long.

Grant rolled his eyes when I told him. 'They're quite mad. Can't be done, just can't be done.' I discovered the figures were deceptive. In 1980 Rees-Mogg's editorial budget was £7,364,000. In December 1981 money that was £8,615,880. So Murdoch's secret editorial budget of £7.7 million represented a cut of nearly £1 million in real terms on Rees-Mogg's Times. No wonder it had been kept under wraps. How could it have ever been built into anyone's plans when, on Murdoch's own authorization, we had spent on columnists, serials, university results, and Preview? Nor was the overshoot of the secret budget quite what it seemed. For the first time the editorial department had been allocated the costs for non-journalist labour in messengers, the wire room, dark room and other service areas. This came to £600,000. So the strictly editorial spending for 1981 was, in real terms, an additional £400,000, rather less alarming than £2 million. I asked Smith and Long on 26 January if they accepted these calculations, and the exclusion of non-editorial items from the editorial budget, so that we could proceed. I also asked John Grant to see if he could work out what had happened to expenditure, in real terms, in the different departments since 1978. He was not expeditious. He had carried out the routine tasks, but now, at the first big test, he did not seem to have a grip of things.

I did not have a reply to my budget questions from Smith or Long. At Long's request we had begun to examine where it was possible to reduce staff numbers. This led to a scene with Murdoch. He asked the editors for 'a total freeze' on recruitment while negotiations were proceeding with NATSOPA to reduce the number of clerks. In theory this was easy; in practice judgement was necessary, because an editorial staff is constantly in flux. Certain critical vacancies must be filled if the paper is to maintain its service and meet its deadlines: failure to meet deadlines can cost thousands of pounds on a single night. Murdoch reluctantly acknowledged this at a board meeting on 12 January. Essential appointments could be made, but only with Long's approval. It was another limitation on the editors, but we went along. It was one of the frustrations of a crisis period and I expected I would soon be operating with normal hire-and-fire powers. Long approved the hiring of two sports sub-editors, and a replacement for Stanley Muir, a skilled home news sub-editor who sadly had died. On 19 January I had a furious note from Murdoch. It was a disgrace that we were advertising for a reporter for the parliamentary gallery. I did not know we were. It turned out to be something John Grant had prepared in December for *UK Press Gazette*. Grant, in one of the quirks of *Times* administration, had reponsibility, which he jealously guarded, for seeing that the parliamentary staff of thirteen was up to strength to produce its eight columns daily and have a man in the House at all hours of day or night when it sits. I stopped the outside recruitment. It was essential to maintain the quality of the report, but the gallery would have to manage for a few weeks with a man down. I went to see Murdoch. I wanted to satisfy myself he would not take my action as acquiescence in the permanent enfeeblement of the gallery, and I was angered by the erosion of my editorial authority. He got up from his desk as I walked in. He would not keep still, ducking and weaving as I circled for an opening.

'I want you to understand, Rupert, that running the gallery a man short is a temporary measure. The quality of that report is crucial to *The Times*.'

'The freeze is a freeze. No, it's not just for the NATSOPA talks. It's a *freeze*. Period.'

'This is a very grave situation, chairman,' I replied. 'I am entitled to a budget and the freedom to make decisions within it. When will I have that budget?'

He flushed. 'You'll get a budget,' he said irritably. 'Soon. Then you can hire and fire as you like.'

I told Long at once: 'Great, I've just been promised my budget at last.' I expected merely a nod, but Long looked down his nose at his moustache and he grimaced: 'You'll be lucky!'

This sudden spark of pity for the idea that I was to have the freedom of a budget was the nearest Long got to an indiscretion. It was extraordinary, because it was an admission that we were locked in a charade.

Long was unpredictable. In the office I had my head down on a legally complex story and looked up to see him lugubriously settling himself opposite me at the desk. He paused.

'We're very different. I've wondered if we can be friends . . .' He did not wait for a response. 'But we're *too* different. We can never be friends. We have to be enemies.'

I sought the sanity of the news room. He came with me. I paused, inviting him to admire the industry, and said by way of a gesture to ease the awkwardness: 'I trust you to look after us, Gerry.'

'I wouldn't do that if I were you. Don't trust me. I can be very mean,' he said, and walked off into the night.

He was clearly under pressure himself from Murdoch. I no longer knew when he came to my office which role he was playing. There was the ramrod autocrat who in the New Year reissued his decree that nothing at all of any description could be done unless it was first approved in writing. There was a stream of memos announcing that this or that new system or study would begin immediately. Everything was announced with immediate effect. And there was Thurber's sad walrus. 'My God, it's tough,' he said with a short bitter laugh, pacing the room with shoulders sagging. When, to draw him out, I murmured that Murdoch seemed depressed of late, he replied: 'Rupert does not change. It is something in us that is different.' Like a private seeing the CO approach, he straightened his back. He was a trapped man. He had not the slightest influence on revenue, and the area of significant cost-cutting involved a confrontation with the unions which only Murdoch could orchestrate. Murdoch had brought in as deputy to Long a hardened newspaper manager, Bill Gillespie, with experience in Thomson and News International. Long's own authority was in question. By chance it was I who handed him an instrument for self-inflicted wounds, to wit, a cheese knife. It happened like this.

Long was in the habit of sending me copies of his literary efforts in speeches and radio talks. They were always vivid. In November I received a bundle of correspondence between Long and Albert Roux, the proprietor of the London restaurant Le Gavroche. Long had dined there and did not like it. It was at about the time inspectors from the *Guide Michelin* were dining there. They did like it: in January they awarded it three stars, the first restaurant in Britain to receive this accolade, indicating it worth a special journey. Who was right, Long or Michelin? The people had a right to know. I took out the letters again.

He had begun with the turbot. The sauce was heavy, according to Long, completely masking the taste of the fish and, being opaque in a dim light, also masked the fish itself. 'In my view fish served in a heavy sauce, usually an error, should not contain bones; my turbot did. It was present in very small quantity and appeared to be over-cooked. I drew that conclusion from its rather hard consistency; it had no taste.'

However, it was the more enduring issue of fraudulent cheese varieties which moved Long most. He was offered a large selection of 'French farmhouse cheeses'. He smelt an imposter. Was that not a St Paulin, which was produced industrially? 'If Monsieur knows cheese better than I do, then of course Monsieur is right,' said the waiter. It was, Long told Roux, 'a quiet arrogance typical of most of the service'. He went home and checked his Androuet *Guide de Fromage*. He was right. What was Roux going to do about it?

Roux pleaded that the waiter, Jean-Claude, had one hobby in life, wine and cheese, and got very emotional about it. Then he brought on the hard man, Maître Philippe Olivier. The St Paulin was an unpasteurised cheese lovingly moulded by hand or with a ladle by monks at Belleval de St Paul; it was a cheese entirely made by craftsmen on the scale of a cottage industry. Long riposted that he was being asked to accept that a cottage industry was not an industry. As for Maître Olivier he knew him of old. He had a shop in Boulogne, yet the disputed cheese was a Picard cheese, it was spelled Belval, not Belleval. 'If it is indeed the cheese I saw it belies its artisanal origin through an appearance very close to that type of French nursery cheese known disparagingly as "Bonbel" or "Vache qui rit".' Roux gave up with a French gesture. Would Mr and Mrs Long care to be his guests for lunch or dinner and have endless pleasure talking about food? Long would not: 'I eat very rarely in restaurants in this country, even less than in France.'

I offered to publish Long–Roux as a prelude to a series on eating out in Britain by Robert Courtine of *Le Monde* and Gert von Paczensky, one of the leading German gastronomic journalists. This had been Long's idea, and despite his friendship with Paczensky it was a sparkling one. Paczensky sounded a good man to have around. He once successfully sued for assault a restaurant owner who shook him by the lapels. Long and Roux both agreed to their letters being published. Holden had his doubts. On the eve of publication Long, as author, checked the proofs and asked Holden what he thought. He hummed and hawed a bit.

'Ah well, Gerry, the grand tradition of British eccentricity.'

'Eccentric?' bridled Long, 'What's eccentric about it?'

I knew the letters would arouse interest in Long as much as in farmhouse cheese. Some might take him as arrogant, others as a worthy champion of the British against French snootiness in culinary matters. Murdoch did not regard the letters as entertaining when he read them in the paper. He regarded them as incendiary. They were published on 6 February, two days before his ultimatum to the unions that 600 jobs must go because Times Newspapers was bleeding to death. He was sure they would be used against him as evidence of the good life led by the managing director, the faces of the poor ground down in St Paulin. This was surely a misreading of cheese for cake. In any event he bawled out Long, he ordered him not to introduce Paczensky and Courtine in *The Times*, and then he struck at his very vitals: he closed the kitchens and dining-rooms on the sixth floor. That Saturday, when Murdoch and Long did their tour of *The Sunday Times*, Long dragged his heels two paces behind. 'I seem to be out of favour with the proprietor today,' he lamented.

The sight of Long in disgrace lightened the days of some people. There was not much else. At *The Times* the night staff was depressed and exhausted by the frustrations of production. Most of the paper was now set cold, but the system could not cope. The pleasure of creating the new business news was eroded by the way it was flung together. Night after night it went to press without full pages of editorial; anything was put in to get to press, old advertisements, hastily written promotions. The quality of the output from the obsolete phototypesetters gave all the paper the appearance of being printed in cold treacle. I felt let down by management. O'Neill was back in Australia, Long had no knowledge, and Murdoch was on the move. Yet his returns to London gave me none of the uplift they used to do. I was reading Evelyn Waugh's letters for weekend relaxation and felt now about Murdoch as Waugh did writing to his wife about Randolph Churchill: 'I have got to the stage of disliking Randolph, which is really more convenient than thinking I liked him and constantly trying to reconcile myself to his enormities.' There was a board meeting around this time which was symptomatic for me. All the directors were kept hanging about in Murdoch's outer office. When the door opened, it was to let out Brian MacArthur, who was flushed with pride. He had been stroked while his editor Frank Giles was kept waiting for a meeting that was sure to be less relevant to his paper than what had transpired in the previous ten minutes. And so it was. There were no papers; discussion of any of the serious issues facing the company was unthinkable. Murdoch was drained by all his jet travel. His face had an embalmed quality. He chewed the end of his glasses, conveying mounting impatience to anyone who spoke more than a sentence. It was two weeks after his promise of a budget. There was still no sign of it. Smith and Long had still not replied to my questions.

I envied Douglas-Home his country idyll. He had only the Plantagenets to deal with. I told him by telephone of all these encounters. 'The blighter has no regard for his promises,' he observed. The blighter hadn't. Douglas-Home was due back on Wednesday 3 February, but he turned up early on the Tuesday and I greeted him warmly. 'I've got a mistress,' he said. 'My book. I did 40,000 words. Jolly good papers you put out.

You see *The Times* differently in the country. We get too close to it in the office.' He went on to talk about warriors, but it was not the Wars of the Roses. 'I've been up to see *him*. Thought I better had, things seemed bad between you both and that isn't good for the paper. I told him frankly he's an absentee landlord, problems of credibility and all that. "Rupert," I said, "you're a warrior king who should lead from the front, join us more on the paper" ... My God, how do you cope, Harry? He bounces you in and out.'

Douglas-Home was so laconic I felt I was falling in slow motion. I was shattered at how ingenuous he seemed.

'But, Charlie, you might have told me you were going to see him. And the warrior king is the last thing we want. We'll have him all over the editorial floor. For Pete's sake don't do it or say it again.'

'Oh, by the way,' he added brightly, 'he says you can always tell the paper when Harry's here. So much better. I nearly said to him you're always here.'

I asked Douglas-Home to organize a weekly arts conference in the hope that we might net the exotic Higgins and also to look ahead to our spring promotions. These were happy pursuits, but I had also to tell him I had misgivings about John Grant's performance. We were under pressure to cut staff and he was dilatory. 'Oh, John will sort it all out,' Douglas-Home replied. 'He's a good egg.'

Murdoch's original theme had been that we should give *The Times* a blood transfusion. That policy was abruptly reversed without discussion. When Long asked me how many staff we could lose if pressed, I said twenty-five, but they had to be the right twenty-five. The trouble with voluntary redundancy was that some volunteers had to be replaced, in parliament and sub-editing for instance, and some writers were irreplaceable. Long authorized a general offer of terms and eight swiftly took the opportunity. Four days later Murdoch said we had to withdraw it, and Long raised talk of a cut of thirty-five jobs with the journalists' chapel, without first mentioning it to me. The escalation and confusion were not good for morale.

The strain of all this and the long days without a deputy took their toll. On the second afternoon after Douglas-Home's return I ran a temperature and told him to take over. I sent Murdoch a note saying I was going home. They were a fateful few days of sickness. Within minutes of my departure, checking that I had gone, Murdoch was prowling the editorial floor saying to various people that morale was bad, wasn't it? The senior staff were unhappy, weren't they, and Harry did not know how to lead, did he? He tried this line on Adrian Hamilton in business news, adding that the paper had no conscience. Hamilton knocked him for six in his dogged manner and was henceforth a marked man. 'Harry's fine, the paper's fine. It's the management that's the trouble. It doesn't know what it's doing.'

Murdoch took his subversive thoughts to the back bench. Douglas-Home was in my chair talking with Fred Emery and Alan Jenkins opposite. Murdoch sat on the desk top, picking up bits of copy and grimacing at a Lurie cartoon. Douglas-Home told me later he had to 'kick Emery under the table' to stop him involving Murdoch in editorial issues. I was glad that he appreciated the limits of the warrior king thesis. The next day Murdoch had Frank Johnson in his room. He had rung him at the *Times* room at the House of Commons and a message had been stuck in Johnson's typewriter. He thought it was a hoax. Murdoch asked him what he thought about the paper. 'I don't like discussing such things when the editor is not here,' said Johnson. 'That's just why we are discussing them,' replied Murdoch. He played his record about the Cold War, and how wrong it was to let E.P. Thompson write on disarmament. It was more appealing to Johnson than Hickey. Roll back Communism; it could be accomplished in a few paragraphs of irony. Johnson essayed that the paper had done a lot on Poland. 'All over the place,' snapped Murdoch.

I heard nothing from him until the Sunday. Then there was a sudden solicitude for my well-being. Long rang me up in the country and so did Murdoch. I must take a proper rest, not come back in a hurry. He was going to give an ultimatum to the unions on Monday 8 February that he would close Times Newspapers unless he got immediate job cuts. He rang again on the Monday to read me his letter to staff and unions. 'Now', he said, 'I'm pissing off to New York.' But he was not. He arranged to meet the *Times* senior staff, under Douglas-Home, in the editorial conference room.

Over sandwiches and coffee he read them the ultimatum and told them that Times Newspapers was losing £15 million a year and would close for good in ten days unless he got 600 redundancies. He added that thirty-five journalists would have to go. The news was a bombshell to everyone, the questioning shellshocked and inadequate. When he had gone, with everyone deep in gloom about the possible closure and the certain loss of journalists, there was a discussion about whether the thirty-five included the eight who had just recently opted to take redundancy. At *The Sunday Times* early redundancies were being allowed against the total of cuts; the word from Long was that this did not apply at *The Times*, which would mean we were being asked to lose forty-three altogether. Fred Emery piped up. Douglas-Home, he said, had better take it up with Murdoch: 'You're the editor.'

The remark disturbed some people, others wrote it off as a product of Emery's excitable nature. The threat to the paper and to jobs was a strain on everyone. The tension and despair were always present in the following two weeks, and I regarded stress as the explanation for the way Douglas-Home began to behave. Our first difference was over a story that was brought to my office on the day I fell ill by Des Wilson, the chairman of CLEAR, the Campaign for Lead-Free Air. He had told Tony Holden he had something important but would reveal it only to the editor. Wilson produced a confidential letter written by Sir Henry Yellowlees, the Government's chief medical officer of health, a year before but never made known. It made me jump. Hundreds of thousands of children were at risk from brain damage, said Sir Henry, because of lead in petrol getting into the air and into food. Lead is a known neurotoxin affecting the brain and central nervous system. What was new about the Yellowlees letter was the seriousness of his expert assessment and his belief that it was an issue of such importance that he had to write to the permanent secretaries of all the relevant government departments. His letter was written on 6 March 1981, at the height of a battle in Whitehall over what should be done about lead poisoning. Wilson argued that if Sir Henry's views had been made known at the time there would have been a public outcry and the Government would have been forced to order the phasing out of lead in petrol as the United States, Japan and Australia were doing. Instead, Ministers effected a weak compromise between competing Whitehall departments to reduce, but not abolish, lead in petrol; and in doing this they relied on data Yellowlees demonstrated had been overtaken by later research.

I told Wilson at once I regarded the Yellowlees letter as important enough for the front page of *The Times*, possibly its main report, and for a leading article. It was disturbing in itself and it was another example of the disastrous furtiveness of government in Britain. I asked Holden to have the letter verified and a report prepared for Monday which we would have to ourselves.

When Murdoch rang me at home on the Sunday, I said we had one important report for the next day's paper. This was a mistake. He asked what it was and his lack of interest put a frost on the lines to London. Later I rang Douglas-Home and asked how the paper was shaping.

'Nothing much doing,' he replied. 'It's going to be rather a dull paper, I'm afraid.'

'Well,' I said, 'you have the report about children at risk and that will give you a front page lead on a slack night.'

'I hardly think so,' was his response.

'What else do you have, then?'

'Nothing at the moment, but we'll find something.'

I was angry. I told him he was wrong, quite wrong, to be so condescending about the Yellowlees letter. The poisoning of children was not a matter for nonchalance. If we showed we took it seriously by the fullness and prominence of our report and with a leader, the Government would have to take it seriously and something might be achieved. I instructed him to use the full text of Yellowlees and front-page prominence for the story. I was reluctant to go further and say he should lead the paper with it: anything might happen in the night. I had, in any event, always made it a practice to give freedom to the judgement of the acting editor on the spot. 'Well, you're in charge tonight, Charlie, but I'll have a beady eye on the lead in the morning.' He led the paper that Monday with a report from Washington on President Reagan's budget proposals of the previous Friday. It was a good background message rather than news. But the Yellowlees letter was the second lead and the text was given on page two, with a feature article by Des Wilson. I would have reversed those front-page priorities, but it was not a major issue. I would have thought no more of it but for the exchanges at the conferences on Monday morning.

'Is this a campaign?' asked Rodney Cowton, the news editor.

'What do you mean, a campaign?' said Douglas-Home in the chair, very much in the manner of a judge affecting puzzlement at a manifestation of pop culture.

'I mean,' replied Cowton, 'do we go beyond normal news values?'

'No, we don't,' said Douglas-Home.

The same indifference prevailed in the leader conference. Only Donoughue's persistence, unbidden by me, secured a top leader which he wrote. The conference exchange was revealing. What are these normal news values? Is it abnormal to regard the poisoning of children as a subject for persistent inquiry and for vigorous comment? This was the implication and it perfectly reflected the moral torpor of the Douglas-Home horizontal school of journalism: it waits on events. Speeches, reports and ceremonials occur and they are rendered into words in print along a straight assembly-line. Scandal and injustice go unremarked unless someone else discovers them. I saw reporting Yellowlees as only the beginning. What was the research between 1980 and 1981 which influenced Yellowlees? What evidence had accumulated in the twelve months since he wrote his letter? What had been happening in America, Australia and Japan? What would Ministers say now?* The effort to get to the bottom of things, which is the aspiration of the vertical school of journalism, cannot be indiscriminate. Judgements have to be made about what is important; they are moral judgements. The vertical school is active. It sets its own agenda; it is not afraid of the word 'campaign', which can mean anything. As I brooded on these matters at home, I

---

* The Government committed itself a year later to phasing out lead in petrol.

imagined a man writing in a small room in the rabbit-warren of old Printing House Square: 'What is the use of a commission to enquire whether a child ought to work more than ten hours? They might as well institute an enquiry into whether the health of children would be injured by cutting off their legs or putting out their eyes.' Thomas Barnes, daily exposing the abuses of child labour, would not have understood the suggestion that his news values were 'abnormal'. The fastidiousness of the conference exchange was contrary to the oldest traditions of *The Times*.

Douglas-Home's behaviour was disturbing because it was in such contrast to the first nine months. It was as if in amateur dramatics he had grown tired of playing the loyal adjutant and was now backstage trying on the insurrectionary's wardrobe. 'I have countermanded your instruction,' he announced on the telephone one evening, when all he meant was that he had changed a photograph I had chosen. He baffled subordinates with remarks meant to be vaguely critical, such as that the editor was too receptive to ideas. It was all done with such lethargic charm that I did not take it seriously. Still, I invited him home to see if there was any misunderstanding between us. He was as affable as ever. He had no grievances or comments on the paper; I would have been surprised if he had, since he had been back in the office only a few days after his sabbatical. We chatted for a while and, lying on the sofa, he suddenly volunteered: 'I don't want your job, you know, Harry. I couldn't do it.'

It had never occurred to me that he could; not had I envisaged any vacancy in the editorship. 'I would never work for that monster Murdoch,' he added.

I had not mentioned Murdoch or asked Douglas-Home for any such assurances. I knew that my resistances to Murdoch were hazardous as well as disagreeable, but I told myself I was protected by my record at *The Times* as well as by the national directors. When I returned the following day to an office gripped by fear as the days of the closure ultimatum ticked away, Adrian Hamilton told me of Murdoch's newsroom backbiting. 'Well, at least,' he said, 'you're safe from being sacked. He can't do that because he has no grounds.'

Douglas-Home, who was always curious about Murdoch, was meanwhile volunteering the unsolicited advice that I should forget about him. Then four days after my return he told the economics editor, David Blake, who had an editorial suggestion for me: 'Don't bother with him. He's finished.'

I heard of this at home, so I telephoned Douglas-Home and invited him to elaborate. 'Yes, let's face it, you *are* finished,' he said equably. 'You are not getting on with the proprietor.'

When I put it to him face to face that the proprietor was the man we had both agreed to hold to his guarantees, he repeated that he did not wish to be editor: 'Murdoch is a monster.' I told him, furthermore, that I had myself protected him from Murdoch's criticism of his skill as a journalist. Donoughue, one of the wariest of men, came to see me later: 'Charlie's all right. I've just been talking to him. He says that Murdoch is a monster.'

Over a depressed evening meal with Tina, I explained grandly to her that it was a very stressful time for us all and Murdoch made people jumpy. I called on Rees-Mogg at his home in Smith Square: 'Can I trust Charlie?' I asked him. 'Of course,' he replied. 'Charlie won't let you down.'

It was, of course, true that I was not getting on with the proprietor. I was not a petty barrack-room lawyer looking up every sub-clause of the guarantees. There had to be a rough flexibility. However, the freedom of the staff from direct political pressure, the independence of the foreign service, the freedom within a budget and the allocation of space were all vital rights. Douglas-Home took a more relaxed view. 'It doesn't amount to a *casus belli*,' he said, shrugging his shoulders. I could not then understand how on the one hand he seemed genuinely to regard Murdoch as a wrecker of institutions and yet on the other could not grasp the nature of the threat. I could not 'rub along', as he suggested, on essential freedoms. I did not enjoy offending Murdoch. It was a personal strain and it also carried the risk of alienating him altogether from *The Times*. It was unrealistic to think I could cut him out of the paper altogether. 'If I am to be treated like an outsider, I'll start behaving like one,' he had said over that holiday fracas. I felt that the only sensible course was to make him feel part of the paper, while politely and firmly fending him off from editorial decisions. Surely, when the union confrontation was over, we would begin a new chapter. But one had already opened that second week of February. It was a campaign and it was against me.

The first intimation I had had of it was a telephone call from William Hickey, the *Daily Express* diarist, while I was ill. Was I leaving *The Times*? I said, 'No'. I presumed they had heard something of an offer I had received to go into television; such was my naïvety, it did not occur to me they were exploring the possibility of my ejection from *The Times*. That happy complacency was broken on Wednesday 10 February when *The Guardian* carried a report that the Holdings board had inconclusively discussed my dismissal, and there was something similar in *Private Eye*. I called Eric Roll at once. He was about to leave on a European trip. The *Guardian* report, he said, was not correct, but he needed more time than he had to explain the background. Could we talk, he asked, when he was back at the end of the following week? I called Peter

Roberts of *The Sunday Times*, the only staff man on the Holdings board, since Murdoch had not filled the vacancy created by Heren's departure. Roberts was as surprised by the *Guardian* story as I was. There had been no board discussion at all. I called Murdoch at the New York *Post*. I was told, after some delay, that he was not around, but, when I went upstairs to have it out with Long, his secretary delayed me at his door: 'Mr Long is engaged; he's speaking to the chairman.' I waited. Long seemed to be purring with pleasure in the fifteen minutes of our interview which followed.

'I must have an explanation of this *Guardian* story,' I said. 'Were you present at that meeting?'

'It's not correct. It was just a lunch. You know how Rupert is, always probing. He only raised the question whether he had the right editor for *The Times*.'

'But what's the criticism?'

'Oh, Rupert wants you to put your thumbprint on the paper.' He stroked his moustache. 'Hasn't he told you that, Harry? He's always saying he wants to see an editor's thumbprint on a newspaper.'

'And the others?'

'Well, Pickering wondered if there was a featureish element in the news columns, that's all. Rupert's a remarkable man, you know. Not many people can stand up to the force of his personality.'

I insisted on a statement that day. I said I was prepared to fly to New York to get it. Twenty minutes later Long called me back to his office and asked if I would be happy with the following statement he and Murdoch had drafted which would be issued immediately: 'Reports in competitive newspapers that Harold Evans is about to be replaced as editor of *The Times* are malicious, self-serving and wrong. Mr Evans's outstanding qualities and journalistic skills are recognized throughout the world, as are his improvements to *The Times* over the past twelve months.'

The statement went out, but the rumours were another turn of the screw in the tensions of the office. Two days later they exploded when it was discovered that Murdoch, who was threatening to put the company in the hands of the official receiver, had removed the titles from Times Newspapers and into his News International company. It plunged me into a new distracting confrontation with Murdoch and Long, and it completed the process of demoralization of the staff. More than forty of them were threatened with redundancy, all of them were working under the threat that in seven days there might be a closure, and now there was the prospect that, if this happened, the titles would not be available for a new ownership. *The Times* would go into a commercial coma. There would be no compensation for anyone. We had been so recently back at work after the year's suspension it was all too much. This was the background against which I continued to fight my private battle; and also to explore new ownership for *The Times* should Murdoch shut down.

There was, despite the statement, no relief from harassment. Reports came back to me of Murdoch unflinchingly exposing his right-wing views of the paper to journalists like Colin Welch (a writer I admire) and Andrew Alexander, the entertaining Poujadist of the *Daily Mail*, who was invited to see Murdoch after an interview for an article whose suffocating sycophancy finally broke surface in a New York magazine. Murdoch was pointedly not talking to me in mid-February. Then, in the third week, on his return to London for the final show-down with the unions, he became, for him, a prolific writer of memos. I received a 'Dear Harry – Yours sincerely, Rupert' letter pressing me again on political policy. He wrapped it up, but Brian Horton made it clear it was the message of the autumn and New Year about party politics. He had been in New York with my agreement, seeing what he could do for Murdoch's News bureau, and, when he came back, he was pleased to reveal his closeness to Murdoch.

'I had some chats with Rupert. He's getting in a mess fighting on all fronts at once. I said, "Look, Rupert, one battle at a time. Don't go banging on about Harry and the SDP. Leave that until you've beaten the print unions."'

I asked Horton later to expound a bit on Rupert and the SDP. He thought better of it. He could not remember talking about the SDP.

Murdoch's way of putting it was in a memo: 'My chief area of concern about the paper is one I have raised with you several times: the paper's stand on major issues. Of course it takes attitudes, but I fail to find any consistency in them, anything that indicates the clear position of conscience that a great newspaper must be seen to hold. Just what that position is, it is your duty to define, and it cannot be defined. But it must be defined with clarity and authority and even repetition.'

I replied formally:

Dear Chairman,
    I note what you say about clear policies for *The Times*. I am not accustomed to being accused of lacking a conscience, rather the contrary. You have not, as it happens, made this criticism on several occasions to me but only once (7 January 1982), though I have been made aware of what you have said to other members of the staff when I have not been present.
    I would contend that *The Times* has given consistently clear leadership on a number of central if contentious issues.
    Allied unity in the *defence* area (Trident being a particular); Western co-operation in the economic area, especially to stabilise *currencies* and prepare

the way for new economic growth, an original view on which we have led opinion internationally.

Consistent support for the Government's approach to *pay*, especially in the public sector, which the Chancellor has acknowledged was crucial in winning the civil service pay battle.

Campaigning to improve the *banking* and financial support for industry and for competition in banking as in industry. (We gave the clearest lead of all the British press over the Royal Bank of Scotland and we did get the legislation against foreign banking stopped.)

Specific reform on the *trade unions*.

Campaigning for *free trade* against protection.

Consistent opposition to *Marxist infiltration* of British politics and industry.

Support for President Reagan in his ultimately strong response to *the Polish crisis*, and a concerted effort to revitalise Allied unity.

Running through these and other editorials is a continuous concern for the individual and for the values of free societies, independent of party and vested interest. Interestingly, you will recall that the *New York Times* feature on the new *Times* particularly picked out the improved strength and clarity of the editorials. Would it not be better to discuss such matters?

But of course, while being consistent in our editorial position, we have deliberately opened the paper to a diversity of views in the belief that truth will triumph and that our readers, especially, want a fully informed debate rather than a monolithic line of propaganda.

He was not looking for debate. He was looking for weapons. His next complaint was that the 22 February report by the *Times* labour reporter, David Felton, on the Times Newspapers crisis 'contained at least eleven errors of fact'. I asked Arthur Brittenden, the publicity officer luxuriating under the title director of corporate relations, to identify the eleven errors. He could not. It came down to one denial of a statement by a trade union leader that Murdoch had told them his companies would be in trouble with the banks if he did not get the 600 job cuts he wanted in the five days left of his ultimatum. Even this was repeated by Owen O'Brien, the NATSOPA leader, on 2 March, when he said on *Panorama*: 'He told us that he was bleeding to death; that he was under pressure from his bankers to put matters right.'

Murdoch had better luck with another line. The fact that *The Times* was on the brink of closing again meant it was a subject for journalism of sorts. Louis Heren, asked to comment on BBC's *Newsnight*, chose not to discuss the crisis but to suggest he had been elbowed out of *The Times* and the paper was going downhill. I allowed myself to be irritated by Heren and an article in the *Spectator* by an old *Private Eye* adversary, Patrick Marnham, which lamented the departure of three journalists, Roger Berthoud, Marcel Berlins and Peter Hennessy. (The first two of them were among the eight who had taken the opportunity for redundancy money.) I should have kept on ignoring the harassment. I did publicly, but in my second six-monthly private report to Murdoch I let off steam, describing it all as a manifestation of old-guard reaction, and he saw the chink of vulnerability for which he is always alert. His note of 22 February said: 'You know that I have been concerned about the fluctuations in the *Times* staff of journalists that had so much attention recently. I am frankly disturbed by the decision of Messrs Hennessy, Berthoud and Berlins to leave you.'

This came at the time Murdoch and Long were harrying me for a cut of no fewer than forty-three in the number of journalists. It was a close question whether it could be done without grave damage to the paper. (Douglas-Home, finally agreeing with me that Grant was not up to the task, was reviewing staff in every department for me.) I had only just shot down Long for raising with the journalists' chapel the question of *The Times* maintaining its own staff to report parliament, instead of using the Press Association, which did not maintain full cover. I replied to Murdoch: 'Your main message to me on staff was originally to hire talent to renew the paper. Lately it has been to get staff numbers down urgently. All the new recruits have settled down well. I cannot understand, therefore, why you should say you are concerned about the fluctuations in the staff. They are an inevitable consequence of what you encouraged and what indeed was required.'

Murdoch had no personal knowledge of the three men or their work, any more than he would have of the forty other *Times* journalists he wanted me to lose, though he successfully pumped the sale-room correspondent, Geraldine Norman, when she went to see him as chairman of JOTT. I wondered where the next attack was coming from. There was a whispering campaign about Evans profligately exceeding his budget, taking on too many journalists, losing too much advertising revenue, having no policies, and morale being bad at *The Times*, etc. A man with the art of second sight, as Swift wrote, might have admirably entertained himself round town by observing the different shapes, sizes and colours of the swarm of lies which buzzed about the heads of some people like flies about a horse's ears in summer. I ignored them and immersed myself in the paper: a meeting I had with Oriana Fallaci on the night Reagan was shot bore fruit in two interviews with Poland's Deputy Premier, Mieczyslaw Rakowski, which Douglas-Home declared the best thing the paper had ever published. I sorted out the legal and editorial problems of a multimillion banking fraud which I had first heard about when prone on a physiotherapist's couch and had asked Stewart Tendler to investigate. I superintended the new sports pages. But I was not to be left alone. One of the larger lies of the period came at me from BBC Television.

It was incubated in an otherwise excellent *Panorama* report on Times Newspapers. The programme was triggered by Murdoch's ultimatum to the print unions, but extended to editorial matters. Elwyn Parry-Jones said that in more than ten years' reporting the affairs of Fleet Street for the BBC he had never before come across such an atmosphere of suspicion and fear. 'Among those who work here are some of Britain's most eminent journalists, dedicated seekers after truth, protagonists of the public's right to know, yet none will reveal in public the accusations they make to me in private. Off the record they talk about editorial interference by Rupert Murdoch, of managerial incompetence and rockbottom morale among the journalists.' *Panorama* did have critical interviews with three *Sunday Times* journalists – Phil Jacobson, Peter Lennon and Tony Dawe – all of them at or past the point of departure from the paper. Then he went on to *The Times*. 'Harold Evans has been Rupert Murdoch's first editor of *The Times* and clearly he has his fans . . . but he has been in conflict with his management and there's evidence of direct interference by Rupert Murdoch in his editorial control of *The Times*.'

Pictures of two pages of an earlier *Times* were shown. They featured artist's sketches of the faces of Libyan terrorists supposedly sent to shoot President Reagan. I remembered the pages well. Jones commented: 'On 11 December *The Times* carried this story about a Libyan hit squad on an inside page. But after a phone call from Rupert Murdoch in America the story was promoted to the front page. It's this sort of interference that people feared.'

The lying insect itself was trivial and contemptible, but the sting was poisonous. It damaged my credibility and my authority, and it was bound further to depress the staff. Somebody else was watching the programme and had the same reaction as I did. It was Brian MacArthur, the new deputy editor of *The Sunday Times*, who sent me a copy of a letter he wrote the next day to Elwyn Parry-Jones to say they had it wrong:

> At that time I was executive editor of *The Times* and on that night I was running the back bench. Earlier that evening I had chosen the identikit pictures of the suspected Libyan hit squad for a foreign page. When Harold Evans saw the page at about 9.15 p.m., he immediately suggested, in his usual style, that this was (a) a marvellous story and (b) a marvellous picture, and that it should go on the front page. This was done for our second edition, which has to be ready and off the stone at 10.45 p.m. There was a call to the office from Rupert Murdoch that night. It came to me first and was then put through to Harold Evans. It should be noted, however, that that call came

about two hours after the decision to change the position of the story had been made.

This was entirely correct, if unavoidably incomplete. Murdoch was not in America as *Panorama* said. At the time he was, according to *Panorama*, telling me what to do, he was in Concorde on his way to London. He flew in to join a group of *Times* staff on the morning on 11 December for a visit and private talk I had arranged with the US Defence Secretary, Caspar Weinberger. The first and only time he came on the phone that evening was after he had received the first edition of the paper at his home at Eaton Place and it would not have got there earlier than 10.45 p.m.

The *Panorama* lie, which went uncorrected, came from within the editorial department of *The Times*, but it was endemic in Murdoch's way of working. It thrived on the suspicion and fear to which Parry-Jones rightly referred. It accused me of acquiescing in the very thing I was resisting.

At this critical point Douglas-Home handed me a letter:

Dear Harry,

In the separate notes I am sending you on the exercise in reduced manpower you will see that I have recommended merging the home and foreign departments and putting them under the deputy editor, saving two assistant editors. I have not done this with myself in mind since I want to apply for redundancy.

I won't go into the many reasons which have brought me to this decision and would not dream of walking out on you at this critical time. The accountant says it would be better for me to stay until the start of the new financial year in April and that would also enable you to have a holiday after this crisis is over in March.

So I would like to work about six weeks of my eighteen months' notice period and then take cash in lieu of the remaining notice along with my redundancy for seventeen years' service.

A sad but necessary decision. We had some good times together, for which thanks.

Yours sincerely,
Charlie

My eyes lingered on the final sentence: 'We had some good times together, for which thanks.' I had not imagined that our recent difficulties merited this. I asked him to withdraw his application and resignation with it. *The Times* was in turmoil with its threatened closure. We were fighting for survival. I understood how attractive a new life might be compared to the stresses of Gray's Inn Road, but this was not the time, I thought, to be rocking the boat still more. I asked him to hold his letter; Murdoch seemed close to winning his fight with the clerical union – he did – and everything might look different quite soon. If not, I would see to it that he could still take redundancy. He agreed to put his resignation on ice and not say anything to anyone. I got on with editing the newspaper.

Two days later, on the morning of a memorial service for Lady Pamela Hartwell, I was asked by Long to stay behind in his office after the executive committee meeting.

'Aren't you unhappy?' he asked, pursing his lips. 'We have been together for a year. Rupert is thinking of changes, fresh beginnings. I'll be having a change myself.'

It was my cue, I suppose, to say that I was so miserable I would like a change too. I felt not the slightest inclination to put my foot on this escalator to a vacant lot. I told him, over his raised eyebrows, that I relished editing The Times, but that I did not like the way I was being 'frozen out'. I knew Thatcherite politics were involved and I was not shy about arguing politics robustly. In some things, I said, to demonstrate the infinite possibility of debate, I might be to the right of Rupert Murdoch. Long looked incredulous, as well he might. Half an hour later I saw a gaunt Murdoch across the aisle in St Margaret's, Westminster. In the afternoon there was a note from him. He wrote: 'I don't see why we should be writing notes to each other when my door is always open to you. Gerry Long has told me of his talk with you this morning and we must have a serious talk as soon as we get through the present troubles.' There was a PS: 'The sports pages look terrific.'

I had decided I must consult the national directors. Two weeks previously I had written memoranda for them on the threats to The Times, instancing Murdoch's harassments and my lack of a budget. I held back sending them to Robens, Roll, Greene and Dacre, because I was due to see Robens at a long-arranged lunch and I thought it better to take his counsel first. With the threat now to my own position as well as to the guarantees, I invited Robens, as the leader of the original four, to come to my office. I took pleasure in showing him how we had displayed in the editorial offices the paintings of Times men which Long had banished from the sixth floor. I would have been glad to have Douglas-Home in on the conversation because of the challenges to The Times, but Robens gently took my arm in a dissuasive gesture and we went into my room. Under the benevolent gaze of Henri de Blowitz, who always had a way of eavesdropping on news, I told Robens what had been happening. 'Oh, that's his game, is it?' he said. The political pressure was news to him and we talked for a little while about politics: there was very little difference between us, not least on monetarism, as I knew from previous talks, and he had anyway an appreciation of the issue of independence. He was enormously sympathetic. He had no time for Murdoch's methods, 'the way they carry on here'. This was all uplifting, marred

only for a few moments by an imperfect understanding of our constitution. Robens had not appreciated that the national directors could refuse
to approve the dismissal of an editor. He was under the impression that
their power was restricted to the right of approving a newly-nominated
editor and hence only in a filibuster. I showed him the Articles of
Association. He said that I must not let Murdoch and his men get me
down. The first thing was for me to meet for dinner with all four of the
original directors – 'not Pickering, mark you'.

I decided I should put the fifth national director on his mettle; a sixth
had not then been appointed to take Denis Hamilton's place. Edward
Pickering represented Murdoch on the board of the publishing house of
Collins, which was owned 42% by Murdoch. Hamilton had said at the
time that the other national directors at *The Times* raised an eyebrow,
but Murdoch had defended it as a journalistic charity: Pick needed the
money. Pickering is not a man of vivid affections and is slow and heavy
in speech, but we had always had friendly relations. He was a Middlesbrough boy who had been a sub-editor on my beloved *Northern Echo*
under Reg Gray. When I came to London, we had lunch at the Garrick
and he happily reminisced about those days and his less happy editorship
of the *Daily Express* under Lord Beaverbrook. I met him later, after he
had retired from IPC, when we were all trying to rouse the Government
to resist the moves in UNESCO that would inhibit the development of a
free press in the Third World.

I was surprised to find him in *The Times* a great deal after his
appointment. He always seemed to be wandering around. I did not ask
him what he was up to. I feared he might buttonhole me about UNESCO.
He saw the dummy pages in Edwin Taylor's office during the redesign
exercises the previous spring and suggested that, instead of photographs
of MPs on the parliamentary page, we should have caricatures, a bright
idea but also a stratagem to ruin me for ever in Hickey's eyes. Then I
learned that Murdoch had given him an office. Except on one occasion,
when he wondered if there were any books I could put Collins's way, he
never asked to see me. But recently he had taken Douglas-Home to
dinner at the Garrick and there he endorsed a definition of Murdoch's
ideal editor. Douglas-Home had reported it to me with stunning casual-
ness. 'What you are saying,' Douglas-Home said to Pickering, 'is that
Murdoch wants as editor of *The Times* someone who is technically
competent but politically compliant.' Pickering replied: 'That sums it
up.'

When Pick came into my office, a stooping, unwrinkled man in his
seventieth year with a hippodrome of a bald head, I said I'd heard he
thought the news pages were too featureish. Had he anything in mind?
He washed his hands loosely. 'The paper is fine, fine,' he said in his

heavy voice. I hoped he would tell me directly if he had any criticisms. 'Of course, Harry.' He was uncomfortable. I put it to him straight: 'What protection can I expect from you as a national director against improper pressures?'

His big, round eyes looked at me through his big, round spectacles. He smiled faintly.

'You have to remember,' said the fifth independent national director, 'that I worked for Beaverbrook ... that's the way things are.'

16

THE VANISHING TITLES

Richard Henry Searby QC is thought in Melbourne to be rather grand and slightly mysterious. His practice in commercial and company law is conventional enough, but he also moves with skill and stealth in the grey area where politics can enrich business. He has directorships of three corporations and is said to have turned down an opportunity in 1981 to become Chief Justice of Australia. He gave advice to the Liberal Prime Minister, Malcolm Fraser, who was at Oxford at the same time in the 1950s; his wife, Caroline, is a personal friend of Tammie Fraser and stayed with her at the official residence, The Lodge, in Canberra. He is a member of the Melbourne Club and he is renowned for his prowess at real tennis, in which you smash a ball of tightly wound cloth about the floor, walls and ceiling of a concrete indoor court, 32 ft longer than a tennis court, and into holes in the wall. He is also Rupert Murdoch's 'problem solver'. In the week of 14 February he was called to London to deal with a loose ball of Murdoch's, something that Gerald Long told me with a touch of hyperbole, before Searby arrived, 'could put us all in the clink'.

Searby travelled as the chairman of News Corporation, Murdoch's Australian holding company, and as a director of Times Newspapers Holding Company, on which the national directors have their seats. At fifty-one he is tall and polished with alligator eyes and sharply defined, sensuous lips. His Australian accent is sharper than Murdoch's, but his voice is softer, thickly textured. He met Murdoch when the two of them shared a study at Geelong Grammar School, a misleading name for a private school favoured by the establishment rich; the Prince of Wales went there too. Murdoch and Searby became close friends at Oxford where Searby studied classics at Corpus Christi and became an enthusiast and a scholar of the history of the crusades, Jane Austen and Latin, in that order. He was fancied to get a First and managed only a Second, but it was one better than Murdoch at Worcester. When Murdoch went back to his father's newspapers, Richard Searby went to the Inner Temple. He fitted in well there, but decided the opportunities were better back in Melbourne, where he had a chance to become judge's associate to Australia's great jurist and influential high court judge, Sir Owen Dixon. Searby's father was a doctor in a fashionable Melbourne district. His own career was remote from Murdoch's in these years. Murdoch was raising heat in tabloids, Searby refrigerating hot commercial doings on behalf of corporations brought before the Trade Practices Tribunal. Convergence occurred after Fraser became Prime Minister in 1975. Searby introduced him to real tennis and began advising him on legislative ricochet as well, a connection with government which was not unnoticed. Murdoch asked Searby to join the board of News Ltd in December 1977; he was already on the boards of Shell Australia and Cozinc Rio Tinto. When Murdoch's purchase of Melbourne's Channel 10 television station was declared not to be in the public interest by the Australian Broadcasting Tribunal in September 1980 on grounds of his excessive power in the media, it was Searby who solved the problem, though not without embarrassment all round.

Fraser's then Minister for Communications, Ian McCahon Sinclair, proposed revisions of Australia's Broadcasting and Television Act which had the effect of helping Murdoch. Murdoch, now chairman of Times Newspapers, flew to Australia to give evidence to the Administrative Appeals Tribunal and on 13 May was asked if he had had 'discussions, direct or indirect' with the Government on matters affecting his interests in Australia.

'Not regarding television,' said Murdoch.

'Never?'

'Never.'

'Have you had any discussions, direct or indirect, through the medium of any of your associates or employees with Cabinet Ministers in Australia?'

'No,' Murdoch replied.

The next day he denied that Searby, chairman of News Ltd, the Australian operational company and a subsidiary of Murdoch's holding company, News Corporation, had ever been a vehicle, to his knowledge, for communication between News Corporation and Government. Later *The Financial Review* revealed that drafts of the proposed amendments had been supplied to the News group, and Sinclair agreed in Parliament there had been extensive discussions 'with lawyers'. Murdoch had to go back to the tribunal and on 16 July 1981 said that after his earlier evidence Searby had told him 'that I ought to know that over the years he has been consulted from time to time by the Government in a private capacity on many issues and that he was indeed asked on one or two occasions about this Act in the first two or three months of this year, and he was doing it in a private capacity'. Searby, said Murdoch, had told him nothing about this. Fraser put out a statement saying he had sought Searby's advice in Searby's private capacity and Searby put out another saying he had not understood himself to be consulted in the role of chairman of News Ltd. All of which was rather spoiled by a third statement from the Minister, Sinclair. Searby had been to see him about the Murdoch amendments, said Sinclair, and he had seen him as being an official of the News Ltd group 'and found it hard to see that he could be there in any other capacity'. Furthermore, said the dogged Sinclair, he believed that when Fraser had talks with Searby it was with Searby in his role as a News Ltd director.

By this time Searby's remarkable gift for dissociation was academic. The legislation got through the Australian Senate on 10 June, removing concentration of media interests as a criterion of public interest, and three months before his rescue mission to London, Searby became chairman of Murdoch's holding company. His relationship with Murdoch is such that when he has business in Sydney he occupies Murdoch's private office with its reproduction antiques, and in London in Murdoch's absence he moves into Murdoch's suite on the sixth floor in Gray's Inn Road. He does not have a natural affinity for newspapers or notions of editorial independence. His political views are unsurprisingly right-wing and he has several times written directly to editors of The Australian suggesting 'a chat' on their political line. Searby's general attitude to newspapers including The Times was perfectly caught one night at dinner in London. I went outside the restaurant to collect a first edition of The Times brought round by my driver. Apropos of me and Murdoch, Searby said to Tina: 'Of course they actually believe the be all and end all of life is bringing out their smelly rag. In fact, of course, if it disappeared no one would miss it.' I was intrigued later in the year to read in the Sydney Morning Herald of Searby's sensitivity about his views on newspapers. Someone referred to as 'one of Searby's most up-market friends' was reported as saying: 'Every time I see him he tells me how he hates newspapers and how grubby he finds the whole thing. I always look at him and think: "You're having the time of your life." ' Searby went to the trouble of issuing a lawyer's comprehensive denial. The report, he said, was wholly incorrect both in words and in substance or content: 'It does not represent my views and any person who believes he (or she) heard me say them or anything like them must have either misapprehended a remark of mine or taken something I said out of context.' But Searby certainly believes Murdoch would do better to put his energies and money into something else, and has demonstrated how. In 1980–81 he helped to put together a consortium which involved News Ltd in making a bid in tenders invited by the Government for oil and gas exploration in the Bass Strait. They won the most favoured site.

I had met Searby on several occasions with Murdoch since that bitter and hectic night in January when the price was fixed for Thomson's sale. Searby was brought into that, in the words of a Thomson negotiator, to 'nickel and dime' the deal, and did a good job for Murdoch. He had an effortless contempt for the other side. Searby is a man who finds it difficult to express esteem.

The matter which brought this cool operator urgently to London in the third week of February and which so troubled Long was the owner-ship of the titles of *The Times* and *Sunday Times*. Murdoch had moved them out of Times Newspapers and into News International, the com-pany which controlled the *Sun* and the *News of the World*. This raised issues of morality and of law. It was something he had promised from the very beginning he would not do, and it was something he did not have the legal right to do. It was all arranged, and it was all discovered, in a manner that was symptomatic of the way Murdoch's Times News-papers was run.

The origins of the crisis went back to autumn 1981 when *The Times* was stopped by a dispute at *The Sunday Times* involving 101 members of the NGA machine managers' chapel. Murdoch responded by suspend-ing the entire staff of *The Sunday Times*. The NGA retaliated, in turn, by calling out all its members at *The Times*. None of this had anything to do with *The Times* and the NGA men in all departments wanted to work normally, but they obeyed their union and we were unable to produce the newspaper. The penalty for being in the same company was still further dramatized when Murdoch announced that he would put Times Newspapers into liquidation, closing *The Times* as well as *The Sunday Times*.

At this point Gerald Long raised the question of whether it was possible to confine the closure to *The Sunday Times*, the source of the trouble, and attempt to continue *The Times*, where it was thought the NGA men would rebel against their union. The economics of this were upside-down, since *The Times* lost money and *The Sunday Times* made it, but the idea was attractive to *The Times*, so frequently plagued by *Sunday Times* trouble. Those of us who had heard the suggestion, including Douglas-Home, were disappointed when Long reported that it was stymied by 'technical problems in company law'. Murdoch quickly won the NGA dispute and both papers resumed publication.

Three months later, in Long's office, we had one of our desultory weekly meetings of executive directors. There were seven of us, including Roy Ekberg, who was doubling as company secretary at Times News-papers and Murdoch's News International, publishers of the *Sun* and the *News of the World*. Long, mentioning the control of journalists' expen-ses, gave throttle again to the always idling engine of his animosity for

John Grant, the managing editor of *The Times*. Long and I had one of our routine altercations about Grant, and moved on to matters we could agree, such as 25 December being Christmas Day. Holiday publication arrangements were agreed. Giles asked for promotion for *The Sunday Times* serialization of Patty Hearst's book, Beattie submitted a job specification for a publicity manager. Michael Ruda said he would try to find another sponsoring partner for *The Times* crossword competition. We were shuffling our bits of paper to leave when Long said: 'Do you mind staying for a moment or two? Roy wants formal approval for something.' We sat down again. Long murmured that we might recall how, during the NGA dispute, we had found we could not carry out the threat to shut *The Sunday Times* while continuing to publish *The Times*. Well, we had now got over the problem. We had taken full legal advice and assigning the titles to News International gave us freedom to produce one paper if the unions took action against the other. 'Of course, it's a technicality,' said Long with a shrug. News International were paying our debts and we would have to shut down if we got a 'one-line letter from Roy' saying they were not lending us any more money. Ekberg gave one of his thin smiles and said yes, all the proper steps had been taken. Nobody asked any questions. We were on our way again within a couple of minutes.

There was no announcement of the transfer of the titles. At the time I regarded the transfer simply as a tactic for any repetition of the previous September, when both papers were closed because of trouble at one. The implications of the move were, in fact, far more profound. The perfunctory nature of our transaction had made us careless. I was wrong not to ask questions, and wrong to take anything on trust at Times Newspapers, but we had been misled. Long, the managing director, and Ekberg, the company secretary, had assured us that the move had full legal approval. A legal transfer of the titles could come only from the six national directors sitting on the Times Newspapers Holdings board. They had never been asked for that approval and they had never given it. This was a breach of the conditions laid down by the Secretary of State when he accepted Murdoch's acquisition of Times Newspapers without a reference to the Monopolies Commission. Murdoch had promised to honour those conditions. Apart from the conditions laid down by Parliament, our own company Articles of Association made it quite clear that the executive directors had no powers to do what we had been asked to do except on terms approved by and with the prior consent of the Times Holdings board. The national directors were the custodians of the editorial guarantees, along with the titles. Nobody had satisfied themselves that these guarantees were unaffected by the move.

The awakening occurred two months later, in February 1982. Mur-

doch had again threatened to liquidate Times Newspapers in his ultimatum to the unions demanding a cut of 600 jobs. When on Monday 8
February, he briefed *The Times* editorial conference on his ultimatum
– the one I missed through illness – he was asked by Douglas-Home if
the titles would be available to a liquidator. He had replied vaguely that
they 'might not be'. The next day, when Long attended a meeting of *The
Sunday Times* editorial conference to brief them on the threatened
shut-down, he attempted to brush aside questions about the titles. 'He
treated us like pygmies,' said one of those present. 'He said he didn't
know the status of the titles. We were bothering our heads with a matter
of no consequence.' The *Sunday Times* men persisted and Long finally
said that he would, if they liked, have a word with the lawyers. *Sunday
Times* staff checked the records at Companies House and noticed that,
in contrast to previous records, there was no mention of 'titles and
copyrights' among the assets of Times Newspapers.

During my absence from the office recovering from influenza, Donald
Macintyre of *The Times* labour staff began piecing together a story for
the paper about the titles. He asked for information from Arthur Brittenden, the corporate relations director of News International, a diffident and shy man who was once editor of the *Daily Mail* and had
recently been brought into Gray's Inn Road from Bouverie Street. Brittenden had nothing to say to Macintyre nor to *The Times* chapel of the
NUJ. Long was not available. Macintyre tried Brittenden every day and,
after four days, he got an answer. Was it true, Macintyre asked again,
that the titles had been transferred to News International. Yes, it was,
said Brittenden. Now back at the office, I had four sheets of copy paper
from Macintyre put into my hand by Cowton, the news editor, and I
learned for the first time that the national directors had been by-passed.
'We were not consulted,' said Lord Dacre in Macintyre's story. '*Prima
facie* this seems to me a violation of the terms on which the papers were
secured to News International and in any sense I regard it as a gross
breach of civility. The proprietor met the national directors on 12
January and he said nothing about it. The national directors will take
note of this.'

The failure to consult the national directors was not an oversight of
manners: it was an act of defiance. Murdoch was in New York, but,
speaking for him, Brittenden said that the titles were 'not within the
authority or discretion of the independent national directors'. This was
plainly wrong. I had been one of the vetting committee with the national
directors exactly a year earlier when Murdoch had assured us that he
accepted the superior power of the national directors over the ownership
of the titles. I had seen Hamilton insist on the importance of separating
Times Newspapers as a company from News International. However,

inside knowledge was not required. When the Secretary of State, John Biffen, gave his consent to the sale, one of his conditions stated: 'News International shall not without the consent of a majority of the independent national directors procure or permit anything to be done which shall result in Times Newspapers selling or otherwise disposing of any interest in *The Times* or *Sunday Times*.'

Roy Ekberg, Murdoch's company secretary at both newspaper groups, fastened on the word 'interest' in Biffen's conditions. He said legal advice had been given to the board that the national directors had a veto on the disposal of an 'interest' in *The Times* and *Sunday Times* – but titles and assets did not amount to 'an interest'. But no such legal advice had been given to the executive board. None could have been given to the Holdings board because there had been no such meeting. Not only was Ekberg's statement false about what the board had been told the previous December, it was demonstrably wrong about the powers of the national directors. There was no escape in the word 'interest'. The title of a newspaper inescapably represents an interest in the business of publishing it. Murdoch had broken Biffen's condition and he had also violated the constitution of the company. Paragraph 89 of the Articles of Association of the Times Holding board specified that the consent of a majority of the national directors was required for the disposal of 'either *The Times* newspaper or *The Sunday Times* newspaper or the business of publishing either newspaper.' There was no scope for casuistry. All the silks of the Inner Temple could not devise a way of publishing *The Times* and *Sunday Times* without their titles. Yet this was what we were being asked to accept.

The day that *The Times* published the news story about the transfer of the titles and the failure to consult the national directors, I had a call at my home from Long. How could I have passed our report for publication? Macintyre had written that the news of the transfer of the titles had been 'announced' by Times Newspapers. It was not announced, said Long. Did I not read the story before it went in? Did I not understand there was a difference between something being announced and something being made known in response to questions? It was a subtle difference, but an important one in the circumstances and I ought to know it.

'The important thing', I rejoined, 'is that the national directors should have been consulted.'

'No reason why they should have been,' he said.

I thought we were in for one of our unpleasant wrangles, but suddenly the steam ran out of him. It was the melancholy Long who continued: 'I don't know ... the lawyers now say they may have got it wrong, so we'll all be in the clink.' This was a reference, I took it, to the penalty for a breach of the Fair Trading Act. Biffen had said that criminal sanctions would apply if Murdoch broke any of the conditions of the sale or changed the Articles of Association without the consent of the Secretary of State. The law specified a fine or up to two years' imprisonment, or both.

Grave issues were now laid bare. There was the repudiation of the authority of the national directors on whose powers depended the ultimate integrity and character of the papers. There was the furtive way the transfer had been conducted. There was the unabashed attempt to find loopholes in the small print. This was all conduct which betrayed Murdoch's hostility to the constitution. But the crisis was deeper even than that. It lay fundamentally in the power Murdoch had given himself over the destiny of *The Times* and *Sunday Times*. This went beyond respect or contempt for the editorial guarantees. He was, in fact, saying to the press, for what it was worth, that the editorial guarantees would continue in the same way, because it was News International which had made the promises in the first place. But that was no longer the main issue. If the titles stayed with News International, and Murdoch liquidated Times Newspapers, then he was free to follow a number of strategies. He could close and re-open on his own terms. He could re-open only *The Sunday Times* and keep *The Times* closed for a longer period on grounds of cost. He could say that economics dictated a seven-day newspaper. He could move the titles to his Australian or American companies with unforseeable complications for parliamentary supervision in Britain. On the other hand, if the titles remained in Times Newspapers, they would, on liquidation, be available to the official receiver. He would be legally obliged to dispose of them to bidders. There was no question that there would be bidders for both papers who would maintain them in excellence and independence, and who might in those circumstances also strike better deals with the unions. As a protection for the future of *The Times* I had, in February, been to Jim Sherwood, the chairman of Sea Containers, who bid £4 million for *The Times* title in 1981. He had confirmed to me that he was still a buyer, and on 9 February he wrote to Murdoch to say so. He was turned away. Neither he nor anyone else would be able to keep *The Times* going if its title were in a safe in the *News of the World* offices with only Murdoch holding the key.

This was an intolerable prospect. A year ago such fears would have seemed unrealistic, such distrust ungenerous, but fear and distrust were precisely what Murdoch's conduct over the titles generated. If he got away with this, he could get away with anything. The mood of the company was to bluff it out. The protection of the papers called for a public row.

I called Denis Hamilton who had been chairman of Times Holdings board until a few days before that cursory December meeting in Long's office. He confirmed that the question had never been referred in any way to the Holdings board or the national directors or to him as an individual. He was shocked, but he concluded that he should not make a public statement, because he thought he might be called in as an envoy between the national directors and Murdoch. The newly knighted Rees-Mogg made a strong critical statement. He asked me for help in documenting the breaches of the law and of trust, so that he could be more effective, and I had no hesitation in giving him the material. He wrote to Biffen to say the transfer was illegal. I called Lord Robens and told him how we had been misled, and I read him the relevant paragraphs from the Articles of Association. He commented on the 'shambolic' way Murdoch had behaved. He promised that the national directors would have a meeting, excluding Edward Pickering, whom they regarded as a Trojan knight. I did not ask if this would be an appropriate meeting for them to consider my own position, as we had previously arranged. The titles were a more immediate and more important battle.

I also tried to enlist the help of Charles Douglas-Home. I wanted him to tell Dacre about the titles and the general harassment of *The Times*. Douglas-Home was barely interested. He said it was not a major issue. Rees-Mogg had gone too far in his criticisms, and I was wrong to pick a fight with the proprietor on such an issue. He exhaled his favourite phrase: 'It's not a *casus belli*.'

I went into the office, though it was my night off, to superintend our news report. I wanted to be sure we gave the fullest background possible. I was glad I did go in. Nobody could find a copy of the Articles of Association. I was able to provide one and to remedy the omission of a list of national directors. I was engaged in this when my private line rang.

'How's your father, Harry?'

It was Murdoch – the first contact for weeks. He had not asked about my father since I had told him eleven months earlier of a heart attack he had suffered one weekend in London, while staying with me; he had recovered, but seven days previously he had had a stroke and was in coma in a hospital in North Wales. I had not seen him and I was not about to share my anxieties with Murdoch. The real point of his call followed immediately: 'You're not running much on this titles business – *are you*? I'd play it down.'

I told him *The Times* was to carry a very detailed story.

'What do you want to do that for?'

'Well,' I said, 'for one thing, how is it going to look if *The Times* of all papers does not do proper justice to a story concerning itself? It would look bad and it would be bad.' He grunted, made the usual lunge or two about party politics and rang off.

I made the report on the titles the second lead on the front page, which was justified on the night's news. The Opposition was seeking a Government inquiry into what John Smith, the shadow Trade Minister, called a 'breathtaking subterfuge'. A spokesman at the Department of Trade talked about a possible reference to the Monopolies Commission. Murdoch himself was unyielding. He was reported as saying that the transfer had been made on legal advice to 'protect' the titles.

The attempt to bluff it out continued: when I told a staff meeting that the national directors should have been consulted and that I had assumed they had been, I was visited by Long.

'You will not say that again,' he ordered.

I refused. Two hours after his visit, on Tuesday 16 February, I came upon evidence of such deceit in the company that I closed my editorial door and called in legal advice.

The previous Friday, as soon as I first discovered that the national directors had been ignored, I had called Frank Giles at *The Sunday Times*. His memory of the meeting had been exactly the same as mine. 'Let's check the minutes,' he suggested. He called back: he could find no record of the title transaction and neither could I. All we had received were the minutes of the discussions we had had as executive directors before we moved briefly into a session of the board. The executive meeting had no legal status; our discussions on Christmas holiday publication and the like were faithfully recorded. The board had legal status; there were no minutes for it. Giles said he would pursue them. He rang Long and Ekberg. Three days after his calls there were still no minutes. I made my own requests to Long and Ekberg. It was not until the evening of Tuesday 15 February that Giles and I received the minutes of the meeting of 16 December.

They revealed that the minutes, which had not been presented for approval or signed, had been falsified. They recorded transactions that had not taken place, resolutions that had not been passed.

There were two other sets of minutes with those for 16 December. They were for two subsequent meetings of the board of Times Newspapers of which Giles and I had no knowledge. They had been held, not at Times Newspapers, but at the offices of News International in Bouverie Street. As directors we were entitled to notification of these meetings and had been available to attend. We had received none.

These two clandestine meetings had been attended by only two of the nine directors. They were John Collier (in the chair) and Roy Ekberg, acting as secretary; G. W. Richards of the solicitors Farrer & Company was 'in attendance'. This was a further breach of the Articles of Association of Times Newspapers. Two directors did not form a quorum. Additionally, Ekberg was also a director of both Times Newspapers and News International, and the business they decided concerned matters where his duties as a director could be held to be in conflict.

The business of the meetings was to complete financial transactions falsely recorded as having been set in train at the board meeting of 16 December. At that meeting there had been no mention of putting a price on the titles, whereas the resolution we were wrongly recorded as having passed said the titles would be assigned 'if a reasonable price for the same could be agreed'. Ekberg and Collier on 23 December at 10.30 a.m. had considered a letter of that day from News International saying no more money would be advanced unless News International immediately had security for its money in ownership of the titles of *The Times* and *Sunday Times*. It offered £1 million for *The Times* and £2 million for *The Sunday Times*, and offered to lease them back for £50,000 and £100,000 a year respectively. The minutes said: 'The Directors considered the offer (in total) of £3 million for the trade marks and associated goodwill was or was likely to be considerably in excess of their open market value'. When Murdoch acquired the papers from Thomson the value of the titles was set at £4 million in a £12 million transaction.

Ekberg and Collier had also agreed that 'certain freehold and leasehold properties', plant and machinery should be the subject of a mortgage debenture, giving News International a first claim on their value in the event of liquidation. At 11.15 a.m. the same morning, at a second improper meeting of Times Newspapers Ltd, Collier reported that News International had agreed to the proposals from the first meeting. The documents were duly executed.

All this was not simply a breach of the constitution of Times Newspapers; it was open to challenge by a liquidator as 'fraudulent conveyance'. The Companies Act of 1948 enables creditors to challenge the sale of assets within six months preceding the liquidation. The Times Newspapers transactions were made in December with the threat to put the company into liquidation two months later. News International, of course, was the major creditor. The sale could have been defended on the grounds that without this credit Times Newspapers was threatened with closure, but how much money News International was lending we, as directors of Times Newspapers, did not know. Accounts were never presented to us.

Taking legal advice, I wrote a formal letter of protest that same evening to Long as chairman of the board meeting on 16 December with copies for the other directors, Giles, Ekberg, Collier, Beattie, Ruda and Peter Stehrenberger, the new finance director, and Bill Gillespie, recently transferred from News International as an assistant managing director.

I arranged for the letters to be delivered by hand before the board meeting scheduled for the morning of 17 February. Giles wrote his own letter of objection from *The Sunday Times*.

I took my letter to Long to his office shortly before the meeting was due to start at 10.30 a.m. He was melancholy. Despite my outrage at what had happened, I suddenly felt sorry for him wasting his brilliance in the sterile air of Gray's Inn Road. It had been a long time since the building had reverberated to one of his volcanic laughs. 'I'd like you to read this before the board meeting, Gerry,' I said. 'I've sent copies out.' He stood by the window, thumbed the letter open and froze.

'I'm not reading any more of this. Take it back.' His melancholy had vanished. He was engorged.

'No, I can't take it back, I won't.'

'Withdraw it. You can't do this. Rupert's not going to like this. I'm not reading it.' He put it back in the envelope, paced the room and suddenly was gone through his side door. He had gone along the corridor to Murdoch's room.

The other directors drifted in, all having received my letter. 'Quite right, quite right,' said Ken Beattie, as uncalculating and candid as ever. Ekberg and Collier said nothing, but took their seats at the hexagonal pine coffee-table. O'Neill was relaxed, talking about production. Gillespie, the new man, looked bewildered. Giles came in last. Fifteen minutes passed with messages that Mr Long would be in shortly.

When he arrived, he made a short announcement. Richard Searby, chairman of Murdoch's News Corporation, would be attending our meeting as an observer, if that was agreeable. Searby came in a few minutes later. The contrast between the two men was remarkable. It was Long who looked as if he had flown in from Australia, liable to disintegrate or ignite. He poised himself on the edge of his cane chair, and kept the fingers of both hands stretched out on the papers in front of him like a concert pianist waiting for a cue. Searby settled himself back at one side, elegant and composed. Long, staring straight down at his fingers, asked me to withdraw my letter. He made no reference to a letter from the editor of *The Sunday Times*. I refused, but suggested we discuss it. All the people who had been at the original meeting were present.

'Will you withdraw?'

I said the letter must stand. But could we not discuss what had happened? What did the other directors have to say? There was a long silence. Then Giles murmured that he had sent a letter . . . the minutes of the December meeting had just arrived. 'Mine arrived all right,' interjected Long. Ekberg made a fluttering gesture with his hands by way of apology for any lateness there may have been. Long bore down yet again on me for a withdrawal. This time Giles began to reply, 'Well, no,

chairman. . . .' Long cut him off: 'Very well, this matter is adjourned to
a further meeting which the chairman [Murdoch] will take on his return
from New York this week.' I persisted: we ought to have a discussion at
this board meeting. Still none of the others said anything. Long moved
on tensely to other items.

Searby now took over. He sat at Murdoch's desk. He summoned Long
and Ekberg, and he spoke with officials at the Department of Trade. He
went through the minutes and the Articles of Association. And without
grinding a gear, he slipped the company from forward into reverse.

I saw Searby in his office on the afternoon of the board meeting. He
relaxed in an easy chair. I should understand that he had to protect
Rupert. Somebody might go to 'some judge', some hillbilly he implied,
who, without knowing the first thing about it, would grant an injunction
and then where would we be? He spoke not as a man with a vision of his
employer and friend sharing a cell in Wormwood Scrubs but as a lawyer
saving the time of important people set upon by cranks. The way to do
it was to rescind the transfer of the titles and then begin again with the
'oi-en-dees', the acronym his Australian accent had coined for INDs, the
independent national directors. He would clear up other matters. He
presumed I was happy with this.

Searby tried to give the impression that it was all a bore, that the oi-
en-dees would approve on the nod, but his languid manner could not
conceal that an important battle over the rights of the national directors
had been won. It was up to them how they consolidated the position.
Retreating and regrouping may have been Searby's view of the prudent
course from the beginning; if not, the stand Giles and I had made that
morning would have tipped the balance. I could imagine the reaction of
a hillbilly judge on being told that the relevant minutes of Times Newspapers Ltd had not been signed because in one case the two editor-
directors did not agree with them as a true record and in the other case
there was no quorum.

The next day Searby came down to my office with everything all but
tied in red ribbon. He had worked out resolutions for the boards of
News International and Times Newspapers. G. Long in the chair at *The
Times* was to say that 'certain doubts' had been expressed about the
legality and effectiveness of what had been done. He had been informed
subsequently that the board of News International had therefore resolved to rescind the assignment, the agreement and the mortgage debenture so that the independent national directors of Times Newspapers
Holdings and their board could be given 'the opportunity to consider
these matters afresh'. We, on the Times Newspapers board, were to ask
the Holdings board to consent to the title transfer in view of our need
for further funding from News International. It was proposed that News

International would pay £3 million for the assignment of the titles and lease them back. Searby covered the non-meeting of 23 December with another resolution asking the board of Times Newspapers to adopt the minutes 'notwithstanding the fact that at that meeting two directors only had been present'.

The Searby scenario was enacted at a board meeting on Thursday 18 February, neatly in time for it to be announced in the Commons by John Biffen, the Secretary of State for Trade, who was due to face a demand for action. He said he had satisfied himself that the purpose of the transfer was not to avoid the editorial safeguards and that it had all been done with the legal advice that it did not breach the conditions he had laid down. 'Nevertheless it is now accepted that the validity of a transfer, albeit within the same group, without the consent of the independent directors, may well be open to doubt.' A meeting had been arranged at which the consent of the national directors would be sought, subject to suitable safeguards. John Smith, for the Opposition, thought Biffen had been extremely indulgent in letting Murdoch off the hook: the episode smacked of 'sharp practice' and showed how lightly Murdoch regarded any inconvenient obligations. Biffen's response was that it was all up to the national directors.

They were supposed to meet Murdoch, Searby and the rest of the Holdings board the following Monday, 21 February, the day Murdoch had said he would close the paper unless he got a cut of 600 jobs. That weekend senior *Sunday Times* men set out to lobby the national directors, backed by a unanimous vote of the chapel asking for the transfer to be rejected. They had developed their argument in a letter to Giles, and it was rather more principled than the inability of Times Newspapers, stripped of its assets, to pay them their redundancy in a liquidation. They were concerned about the survival not only of something called *The Sunday Times* but also of a newspaper staffed by a body of journalists dedicated to certain standards. It was quite unrealistic for Murdoch to think that title transfer and liquidation would enable him to close and re-open on his own terms: 'News International with its past record and with the hostages the unions hold at the *Sun* and the *News of the World* may be the least well placed of any owner to carry out this strategy ... All other strategies involved the closure of *The Sunday Times* and the sacking of its staff. If that situation obtained for more than a week or two, it would become impossible to assemble the core of the journalistic body which now produces the paper ... It will not be remotely like the 1978 shut-down. Very quickly the collective entity will be dead.'

On the other hand, said the *Sunday Times* men, if the company were liquidated still in possession of its titles, they knew there would be bidders who would retain the journalists and uphold the paper's standards. It was a point which attracted Lord Dacre, when they met him at the Savoy: 'Murdoch is saying an awful cad might buy them on liquidation, but an awful cad has already bought them.' Lord Roll, who had been in Europe, exercised his prudence on *The Sunday Times* arguments. Why did they think the titles were more likely to survive outside News International than inside? Would another buyer accept the same editorial guarantees Murdoch had given? He conceded he did not know whether Murdoch, by shifting the titles, could slip out of the guarantees. It was one of the things he was going to look into, but he felt Murdoch was treating the national directors badly and his general attitude towards them was worrying.

All four of the original national directors were angry by this time at the way Murdoch railroaded them into meetings without proper notice or papers, taking them by surprise for quick approvals. Pickering was the agent of these impromptu summonses. They had begun to take care not to be present at a meeting with Pickering as the only other national director. 'About three weeks ago there was a nasty smell in the air,' Dacre told *The Sunday Times* delegation. 'I wrote to Roll and urged him to have a meeting of the national directors, excluding Pickering, to clarify in our own minds our understanding and responsibilities. We kept being summoned without an agenda and faced with a *fait accompli*. It is time for us to define our own power.' This was about the time I had invited Robens to my office to tell him of my own disquiet and he had suggested I might go along and talk with them at some stage.

The upshot of the weekend of telephone calls was that the original four agreed to have their long-planned private meeting on Monday morning, 20 February. They had taken legal advice. It would be a breach of company law, they were told, for them to approve anything that looked like preferential dealings in advance of a bankruptcy. Dacre argued strongly that Murdoch's duplicity was such that they should not accept the Murdoch–Searby assurances that the position of the national directors would be unchanged by a title transfer: 'The wolf has started sucking lozenges to sweeten its breath.' With a bold line from Robens the four decided on rebellion, a gesture first followed by substance. When the Holdings board met in the seventh-floor suite later that same Monday, Murdoch found he had only one national director present, Edward Pickering. The original four had 'prior commitments'. The Holdings board was, therefore, unable to proceed on the Searby plan. Having made their point, the four agreed to go to Murdoch's second Holdings board meeting that week. It went on for more than two hours. I had time to write a leading article before I was called to adjudicate on how we played the company statement. I placed it as the main story on the back page and wrote two headlines of fair summary: 'Times titles stay where they are'. And an overline: 'Directors support Murdoch job cuts'. The statement was brief. The question of transferring the titles had been deferred until the crisis on job cuts had passed.

The oi-en-dees were not behaving as Searby thought they ought to behave; but Murdoch had other work for the man about Melbourne.

March was the cruellest month. On the first day of it my father died in North Wales. He had been in a coma for nearly a month and he was in his eighty-second year, but he was the hero of my life and I was deeply affected. He was proud of his craft as a steam-engine driver on the old LMS and his fifty years on the railway, and so was I. When the Queen visited Manchester in the 1950s, he had driven the royal train; I had my head down on the *Manchester Evening News* sub-editor's table, and Jimmy Entwisle, handling the royal story that day, convulsed the room at my expense by declaring in the manner of a station announcer what was happening at every stop to the precious Evans train. I often thought, though, of what my father might have done if his family had not been so poor. His own father, a railway platelayer, could write only his own name; shortly before his stroke, Dad stood in the sunshine in Kent saying what a rum thing it was that the grandfather of the editor of *The Times* was illiterate.

He himself had been picked for grammar school when he was a boy in Coppenhall, Cheshire, near Crewe. He had a remarkable head for figures; even at eighty-one he liked to do mental arithmetic for fun, such as calculating what day 28 June would be in 1992. But his family was too poor to do without his wages while he went to high school, and so, at thirteen, he left the countryside at 6 a.m. each day for the foundry at Crewe works. My mother left school even earlier for a cotton mill, but when I was 10 she started a grocery shop which thrived. Both my parents were determined that the four sons, of whom I was the eldest, would stay at school. They enabled me to start in newspapers by saving to buy me a shorthand and typing course after I matriculated, and then seeing me through university. My father's mind had been stimulated by politics and geography lessons run by the Labour party. He regarded knowledge as some kind of secret you had to wrest from the ruling classes. Yet he had not the slightest bitterness or envy in him. He was an idealistic socialist of the Jimmy Maxton school; his only fantasy – and he nourished it all his life – was to be a cowboy on the western plains. He had us all on pins with his liking for a friendly argument. When everyone else in our street in Manchester was saying that the German tanks were made of cardboard and we would be hanging out our washing on the Siegfried Line, he cornered my mother's grocery customers with figures on Germany's steel production culled from his battered encyclopaedia *Everything Within*. All this makes my home sound like a political schoolroom, but it was not. My father's main grievance was football players who could not kick the ball with both left and right feet. We always drifted back to these iniquities when we failed, as we often did later, to agree on politics.

I conducted the conferences at *The Times* that Monday, and on the Friday we buried my father on the hill of Bluebell Wood cemetery overlooking the sea at Prestatyn. My mother was too ill to be there, but all four sons were, from publishing in the west country, insurance in Canada and government service in Hong Kong. It had been a poignant moment, forty-eight hours before he died, for the four of us to visit him in hospital and see the flutter of an eyelid acknowledge our presence together for the first time in many years. His friends had said, 'He's waiting for all four sons', and I think he was.

Murdoch had written me a note of condolence, saying it was thirty years since his own father died and he remembered it as yesterday. 'A good father and son relationship is one of the best experiences in life. You must take any time you need to attend to the necessary family arrangements.' Twenty-four hours after my return from the funeral he summoned me to his office. 'I want your resignation today,' he said. I replied: 'You cannot have it. I refuse.'

It was Tuesday 9 March, about thirty minutes before the Chancellor was due to rise in the Commons and announce the 1982–83 Budget. I had planned to publish the most ambitious coverage in the history of *The Times*.

I was astonished, and still am, at how calmly I took Murdoch's demand for my resignation. I am not phlegmatic by temperament, and I had given everything I had to *The Times*. I suppose it was like a deep cut, seeing the blood flow freely but feeling no pain until much later. What case could he possibly produce for a resignation? He leaned back behind his desk, tilting his chair. Then he leaned forward, took off his glasses and stared at me. I noticed how red the rim of his left eye was.

'The place is in chaos,' he said. 'You can't see the wood for the trees. Yeah, sure, Donoughue and Holden will stand by you, but your senior staff is up in arms.'

'What senior staff? Who?' I grabbed at air. 'The only thing approaching chaos is in *your* production and we've done wonders there advancing deadlines....'

He waved his hand: 'We're getting that right. Bill O'Neill is going to stay till it's sorted out.'

'You talk about people up in arms,' I said. 'People are miserable because of management. What do you expect with so many redundancies and the threat of closing?'

He was sitting back in his chair again. 'Yeah, I know Gerry has been roughing people up a bit, but I've told him to ease off.'

'I'm proud of what we've achieved,' I said now. 'If senior staff is an issue, they're with me,' and I began ticking off the names of executives – Hamilton, editor of business news; Emery, home editor; Horton, foreign editor; Donoughue, assistant editor; Hopkinson, chief night editor; Holden, features editor; Gould, night editor; Turnill, assistant editor; Brian, night editor; Taylor, head of design.... And then I added: 'Of course, there's Douglas-Home.'

He lunged forward: 'He *resigned.*'

'What criticisms do *you* have of the paper?' I asked.

'Oh, you've done a good job with the paper, sure ... We haven't signed your contract, you know, but we'll honour it. Of course.'

And then he veered: 'You've said I put pressure on you. I haven't put any pressure on you. I've always made it clear political policy is yours to decide.'

'Come on! You attacked the policy of the paper. You've tried to put pressure on me through Hickey and others. You've done it through them.'

'Hickey! I can't understand a word the old fool says. And his long boring leaders!'

It was Murdoch's way to evade an issue by assaulting a personality. In the midst of the bitter exchanges a remarkable thing happened: he began to say how much harder it was for him than for me. No need for me to worry, I'd get lots of offers. He had wondered if I would take another job in News International, but guessed I would refuse. It was tough to have to do things like this, really tough. I should understand. Then his voice suddenly wavered. For a few incredible seconds I was convinced he wanted me to break down and sob with him. The moment passed, but it had been real enough. I saw it as standard manipulation, but even if there had been something genuine in his emotion I was incapable of responding. The long glacial period between us, the smears and the manœuvring had left me feeling hardened and I had experienced too much real grief to join in a few cheap tears.

Murdoch stayed put for twenty minutes. He was prepared to prolong the meeting for the time necessary to secure my resignation. It was me who broke it off by saying, a trifle absurdly, that I had to get back to see to the Budget. He did not have my resignation. I would think about my position. He murmured about calling a meeting of the independent national directors. He had picked up Searby's oi-en-dees *patois*. As I left, I asked who had been in his mind as my successor. 'Douglas-Home,' he replied.

In the light of the low opinion he had expressed of Douglas-Home, he was defensive: 'Can't bring in an outsider at this stage. He'll be all right for the time being.'

So I returned to edit *The Times*.

When I entered my outer office, I could hear someone talking about resisting pressures. It was Geoffrey Howe on the position of the pound sterling. His voice was coming from the radio in the deputy editor's office, where Douglas-Home was presumably following the Budget speech. Before I could enter my own office, he emerged from his, rocking forward slowly in his stiff-legged walk. It looked particularly odd because he had his thumb held upwards in the air like someone transfixed in the act of pressing a doorbell.

'Been upstairs, have you?' One ceilingward jab of doorbell thumb.

'Seen him?' Another thumb jab. 'Too bad.'

He followed me into my office and sat at one end of a sofa. I had nothing to say.

'He had me up before you,' he began. 'He offered me the editorship of *The Times* and I have accepted.'

'But I have not resigned the editorship,' I replied.

The features of his face tightened.

'And tell me, how could you accept the editorship when the editor has not resigned?'

Now he replied in a clipped voice: 'He asked me if it would make any difference your resigning on Budget Day. I said, "No, Rupert, the paper is bigger than any individual. We've got out a Budget paper before without Harry and we can do it again".'

Was I now supposed to say, 'Well done, Charlie, and let's drink to that'? I reminded him forcefully that I was still the editor of the paper and that we had a Budget to report. He was less cheerful when he left than when he came in.

As soon as he had returned to his office, I called Lord Robens, Lord Roll, and Denis Hamilton. I told Robens what had happened and of my need to consult the independent national directors: the meeting he had promised with them had never materialized because the titles row had intervened. Neither of us, I imagined, had expected events to move so quickly. Robens counselled that I do nothing further without talking to him. He would meet me the following morning at the Reform Club.

Hamilton was startled by the news. At Christmas, when he had left the company as chairman, he had said I should not worry about the pressures, because I was in too strong a position for Murdoch to attempt anything against me. Over the phone, he said he was taking the chair the following day at a Reuters board meeting which Murdoch would attend. He volunteered to try to find out what was in his mind. He could not understand what Murdoch might have against me. 'It's best to take a lead from Alf,' he advised. 'He will carry the original four directors with him.'

Before speaking to Roll, I checked on business news and the Budget operation. Not only were we reporting more of the Budget than ever before but we had to cope as well with earlier deadlines imposed by new methods of production. It buoyed me to see Adrian Hamilton at the radio surrounded by his team of financial specialists listening to the Chancellor. He was coolly detaching them one by one to revise the articles they had written and already set in type in anticipation of what the Chancellor would do. The sight of the operation with Murdoch's bogus charges still ringing in my head made me speak with some bitterness to Roll. I had called him early in February, when Murdoch had started his campaign against me, and it was agreed that we would have a discussion when he returned from his extended business travels for S. G. Warburg. He had told me then that press leaks about the national directors favouring my dismissal were untrue. Now he was anxious that I should not make an immediate public statement. He, too, said that Robens was the person best placed to decide what to do next.

I wondered if I should phone the other two national directors of the original four, Lords Greene and Dacre. It was borne in on me once again what an amateurish system we had created: no chairman for the national directors, no secretary, imperfect communication between them and each other, and between them and the editor, and no procedure to summon them except as members of Times Newspaper Holdings board. Greene would follow Robens's lead, I knew, and though Dacre had just written to congratulate me on becoming Editor of the Year, I regarded him as an unlikely campaigner on my behalf. It was out of the question to make representations to Murdoch's man, Pickering. John Gross, the former editor of the *Times Literary Supplement*, had only just been appointed as the sixth national director by Murdoch and would know little or nothing.

For the next six hours I edited the special Budget edition. It was one year to the day since I had begun my editorship. It marked also the fulfilment of the prophecy of the seer of Auchtermuchty, John Junor, editor of the *Sunday Express*, that Murdoch would fire me after twelve months: 'One year. You'll see. One year. . . .'

Everyone had a gruelling night producing the Budget special and I shared it with them; none could share my inner torment. Nobody knew that Murdoch had that afternoon asked for my resignation, except Douglas-Home, who sat at the back bench leafing through proofs as the deputy editor. Our new early deadlines required copy and page plans to start arriving in the composing room almost as soon as the Chancellor sat down. In previous years the Chancellor's speech had been given in full over some two pages, but there had been short shrift for the accompanying financial statement and report – the so-called Red Book – and it had all been dispersed with typography that mumbled. The detailed income tax tables, showing the effect on families with different incomes, had also been skimped. All this and more was edited into our special eight-page report. The ambition was to justify the reputation of *The Times* as the paper of record.

By the end of the night we had achieved that and I felt proud. I was congratulating Adrian Hamilton, when I became aware of an incandescent glow at the back bench. It emanated from Rodney Cowton, the news editor, holding a sheaf of stories and protesting furiously that not enough space had been given to his reporters' follow-up stories. They had wasted their time. The whole point of the operation had been to document the Budget properly and follow up the next day. I looked to Douglas-Home to respond since I had asked him to supervise this arrangement. He said nothing. I asked him to deal with Cowton's complaint. He moved his hands without a word. Hamilton came over and got a singeing from Cowton. I understood Cowton's frustration; he was an honest man. It had been an unnecessary blow-up.

By this time one was clearly necessary with Douglas-Home. I went to him in his room and told him he had behaved despicably in colluding with Murdoch. I was no longer cool. He had no integrity, no honour. 'I thought you'd take that view,' he said, affecting to be languid, stretched out in a chair. It was a day when physical characteristics kept impinging on my consciousness. I noticed the scimitar line of his mouth.

'How could you betray your editor? How could you do it when you think what you do about Murdoch?'

His reply had the merit of candour. 'I would do anything to edit *The Times*,' he said. 'Wouldn't you?'

Saying 'No, I wouldn't do anything to edit *The Times*' seemed wan in the glare of his ambition, but he had no intention of boring me. He made a counter-attack so manifestly ludicrous I wondered how he could keep a straight face. The trouble was, he said, that I was too close to Murdoch, too desirous of his approval, too ready to do his bidding. 'Look at your budget memo to him.' Douglas-Home had seen that memo, of course, as part of my agreement that he would have daily access to my file of copies of letters and memos. It had lain innocuously on a file open to him for weeks; he had said never a word about it before and I would have been amazed if he had. The memo he referred to was one I had sent to Murdoch asking if he agreed with my idea for producing our budget special as a separate section. This was not something I could decide as editor. It was a costly operation and was the responsibility of management. The responsibility for its content was mine. Was Douglas-Home expecting me to ignore the issue of production costs? He had no answer. I thought his aimless shaft had fallen to the ground; I underestimated the universal appeal of rationalization for men of troubled conscience.

He tried another defence, working himself into indignation: 'I've worked fourteen years for this company. It's about time I was rewarded.'

'But you have been. You are deputy editor of *The Times*.'

'And *you* offered *my* job to Hugo Young of *The Sunday Times*.'

This was more absurd every demeaning second. When he gave me his resignation letter he knew, of course, that I had asked him to stay and he knew and had approved of an invitation to Young as an insurance policy against his departure. He rattled on: 'That was your big mistake that Sunday telling me Murdoch had been critical of me. That's when I decided to resign. What was the point of staying on if I was not to be editor? That's what has led to this. Once Murdoch knew I was leaving. . . .'

It was par for the course and long past time for me to go home after fourteen hours in the office.

It was approaching midnight. My wife was waiting for me at home with her father, George Brown, the film producer, who was staying with us. It was felicitous to have someone around who had spent all his life supervising the manufacture of melodrama, intrigue and farce. It all sounded to him just like Hollywood in the days when they rotated studio heads on a spit; he had no doubt that editing in defiance of an owner like Murdoch was an experience I should forgo. It had scarcely been the happiest of times for Tina. The long hours, the disruptions and the vapours of Gray's Inn Road spilled over into our home, but she was so incensed by the cynicism and injustice that she was ready to support me in the challenge to continue in the editorship. She had little confidence in the national directors against the wiles and pressures of Murdoch but, like Hamilton, had no doubt that the record would speak for itself if I really wanted to go on. Murdoch pushed and pushed wherever he found a weakness; against a determined editor he might retreat.

We debated it into the small hours until exhaustion overcame us. My resolve of the afternoon had weakened. I had maintained a physical resilience all year, but I was undoubtedly at an emotionally low ebb. I brooded on the corruptions of personality I had seen in the Murdoch year. I had invitations to take up appointments in the United States and in television in Britain. Yet was it not my duty, as the first Murdoch editor of *The Times*, to make a stand of some sort? I went to bed and heard the thud of the papers arriving at 5 a.m.

It is strange: in that morning's edition of *The Times* was a distinguished obituary of Lord Butler. On his birthday, 13 December, Rab Butler had written me a letter in his own hand from Trinity College, Cambridge: 'I have for some time been meaning to tell you how well I think *The Times* is going under your leadership. I shall be going away for a month or two after Christmas and on my return look forward to getting in touch.'

I went for the appointment with Robens, which he had made for 11 a.m., a discreet time at the Reform Club in Pall Mall.

'My goodness,' a voice boomed as I entered, 'your Budget coverage today is fantastic.' It was, but Murphy's law of the clandestine had placed on sentry-go in the deserted foyer of the Reform one of the most acute men in London, Nicholas Faith, a former *Sunday Times* business news specialist and now a broadcaster and writer. If anybody could make something of the editor of *The Times* meeting the most celebrated national director, it was Faith. Happily he moved away from the strategic point before the unmistakable burly form of Alf Robens appeared, and we sought out an upstairs corner we judged to be at the furthest remove from the ears of Faith. But we were not yet through with slapstick. We were pursued up the stairs and into our alcove by a woman with a vacuum cleaner, who hoovered up every remark before it reached Robens's less than perfect hearing. Only when we transferred to the library did we have a chance to begin our crucial talk, and even then we were taking a risk that the elderly clubman with a dictionary at the far end was only feigning death.

I have a regard for Robens as a bold man of some vision. He comes from humble beginnings in Manchester, which naturally gives him a head start, and sat in the Commons for Blyth, in Northumberland, as a centre-right Labour man and Minister of Labour. He might easily have been Prime Minister instead of Harold Wilson. In the 1960s when I was editor of *The Northern Echo*, the miners' daily in Durham, he was chairman of the National Coal Board, and I knew from solid Sam Watson, the Durham miners' leader, how forthright he had been in guiding the industry. Robens, never one to beat about the bush, told me what had been happening. At a meeting of the national directors in the first week of March, Murdoch, after some earlier complaining, had asked them to dismiss me and put in a new editor. He had told them the reason was 'staff *malaise*'. The senior staff was disaffected, morale was low, Douglas-Home was resigning and 'some fellow called Grant' had said he could not work with me. Dacre, I learned later, had caught sight of a document in Searby's possession with the name of Douglas-Home on it as the nominated successor. Robens said the national directors had refused to approve the sacking. If Murdoch dismissed me, however, then I had a right of appeal to them. Murdoch had then said that I was unhappy and I might well wish to resign. The national directors had to say that they had no standing on the question of a voluntary resignation; they did not object, but they did not advocate it either. It was a matter between Murdoch and me. I learned later that at this point Roll put in the caveat that any forced resignation would be a different story altogether; no pressure must be brought on the editor to resign. Murdoch concluded by saying to the directors he would approach me for an agreed settlement on the basis of my contract. All very gentlemanly.

A week later, on Budget Day, Murdoch had called them in again after a meeting of the Holdings board. He said he had not asked me to resign in the intervening week but had talked to me about the paper. He was going to ask me to go and if I resigned he would put up Douglas-Home to them. Again the national directors told him they could not approve a sacking except on appeal and could not be asked to approve a resignation.

It was both an encouraging and a disturbing story. It was good as far as it went that the national directors, if with varying degrees of resolve and excluding Pickering, had foiled the Murdoch coup. But it was a glimpse of how easy it was for Murdoch, meeting them alone, to tell them anything he liked. It was untrue that Murdoch had talked to me about the paper, whatever that meant, in the preceding week. There had been no contact whatsoever. But more insidious than falsehood was the way Murdoch had obviously exploited the procedure in the name of selective truths. How were the national directors, remote from the paper, to know whose testimony was fair or relevant or representative of more than self-interest?

I told Robens that I would certainly have critics on the paper, some of them because I had changed it, but so would the head of any organization of 270 people. Robens expressed a vivid contempt for Murdoch and his methods. All the original four directors were of the same mind: 'We've had enough of this way of carrying on.' They had a duty imposed on them by Parliament – 'Parliament, my lad' – to preserve the editorial independence. When he asked me what I proposed to do I rehearsed, not altogether coherently, the considerations I had debated the previous night. 'You're in a strong position because us four, with Dacre maybe a little' – he wobbled his hand – 'will support you. But is it worth it? You'll be in a lunatic asylum at the end of six months the way they go on in that place.' It was not a prediction I could contest with much conviction.

The harassment of the last few months had been nerve-racking. 'It's your choice, but I know what I'd do in your place, lad.'

Perhaps if I had not been stricken by my father's death I would have been in more robust spirits, but that sad Wednesday morning I told Robens I had asked his advice and I would take it. 'Very wise, Harold. You can have a new career away from that madhouse. Nobody will ever forget what you did for those children.' Robens, in his fatherly manner, made the whole thing seem simple, dignified and right. I told him I had been planning a holiday the following week, returning in April. 'That's right. Go on holiday, don't talk to Murdoch. Leave everything to your lawyer. Relax. We'll stand by you.' The national directors were so fed up with Murdoch, he said, that they'd be resigning next. At the conclusion of our talk I gave him a memorandum of about a thousand words I had written on 26 February for the national directors but not delivered, in anticipation of the Robens dinner meeting. It outlined Murdoch's breaches of his guarantees: the persistent refusal to give *The Times* an editorial budget, his attacks on the political policies of the paper, and his personal harassment.

I went into Pall Mall with Robens. When he left me I had nearly two hours before lunch in Whitehall. I did not go back to *The Times*. I walked around St James's Square, past the handsome headquarters of my old adversary Distillers and the gloomy Department of Employment, where I had once been to protest to Michael Foot about the closed shop in journalism, and I walked around again and into the Park. I had told Robens I would go, but it had been too swift and simple. I had leaned too easily on Robens's friendly shoulder, allowing a bluff old politician to lift a decision from me that only I could take. And I had, I knew, not yet taken it with head and heart. It had been surreal. I had stood aside from myself and watched the editor of *The Times* casually say he was going to resign, as if only the shock of seeing him do this would force me back into myself to resolve the inner torment. All I had observed in myself in the Reform Club had been a reflex action to remove anxiety, an evasion of the considered assessment of duties and risks of the kind I had tried to take all my professional life. Was it wrong to go? Why should I yield to Murdoch when I had resisted years of intimidation and more than once seen off a better class of bully boy? Why should I be so downcast when I had relished the manœuvres in the confrontation with the Government over publication of the Crossman Diaries? What did I have to fear when I had risked prison and disgrace in the exposure of Philby and the Thalidomide campaign? I had seen those conflicts and so many others, rightly or wrongly, as an editor's inescapable duty, with the possibility of benefit to society. So why did I hesitate? A fight now to protect *The Times* was surely the last campaign I should undertake.

I knew how I would go about it. I would bring everything out into the open, beginning with a full briefing of the staff on the facts and the issues, then MPs and the press. I would make a formal presentation to the national directors of Murdoch's breaches of his undertakings, with a copy to the Secretary of State. I would call on them to enforce the Articles of Association and the pledges to Parliament. They had the power to instruct Murdoch to respect the editor's authority. They would have to insist on the right of the editor, as embodying the independence of *The Times*, to be free of political harassment, direct and indirect. There was no doubt I would be within my legal rights in making these demands. I could go to law to have them enforced. Murdoch might fight dirty, but I had nothing to hide, and I could prove his bad faith. I could win.

There was a glimmer of sun through the clouds in St James's Park, but it was as evanescent as the exultation I felt for a moment at the prospect of such a battle over the body of *The Times*. There were crucial differences between this crisis and those others, and they had to be weighed. I might be thought of as mercurial and impetuous, but in reality I had never entered a campaign without calculation and preparation. Not one of those at *The Northern Echo* and *The Sunday Times* had been mere gestures of defiance. They had not been quixotic acts of individualism, petitions for martyrdom. They had all been the product of deliberation based often on research by brilliant and skilled journalists, and advice by seasoned lawyers. At *The Sunday Times* in particular there had been that remarkable unity of purpose, varying in its expression but unshakable in its conviction. There had been Denis Hamilton's honour and prudence, and the fierce integrity of Bruce Page and the moral rigour of Hugo Young and the loyalty of Frank Giles and all the benevolences that flow from a community where individuals, in all the fractious moments and rivalries, hold each other accountable to certain ideals. It was with pride, bitterness and sadness that I brooded during my walk on how different my calculations would have been if Douglas-Home had been true to our pact, and to his family motto 'True to the End'. I had to reckon instead on my deputy being Murdoch's weapon and possibly an agent for disaffection. How cleverly Murdoch had played things. I had made a crucial mistake: I had put the paper first and not protected my back.

And this was surely the turning-point. Nothing in my experience remotely compared to the atmosphere of intrigue, fear and spite at Murdoch's *Times*. Life at the *Manchester Evening News*, and *The Northern Echo*, and the years at *The Sunday Times*, had not been all sweetness and brotherly love but it had a rough decency to it. If I fought and beat Murdoch this time, despite the odds, I would have to endure an endless assault. His record betrayed no taste for repentance; Graham

Perkin's inner idealist had died for lack of nourishment. I would be subjected to a thousand humiliations, challenged on every paperclip. My energies would be absorbed not in journalism but internal politics, seeking alliances, suspecting every man's hand. I would have to keep in constant touch with the national directors and their successors, ready to justify and vindicate every editorial decision Murdoch chose to challenge or misrepresent. It would be Russian roulette. I would become frightened to pull the trigger on an empty chamber. I feared for my own character and self-respect. I had seen what had happened to others, the courtiers apprehensive on his arrival, hoping for the boyish grin, fearing the scowl, demeaning and coarsening themselves. Perhaps I would make one accommodation with Murdoch to win favour and then another, or subconsciously begin to guess what he wanted and give it to him. It was a challenge to myself I thought I could endure; but there was the contrary danger implicit in that flash of vanity. There was the certainty, it seemed, that I would become obsessed with either Murdoch or my own introspections. Neither was an attractive prospect.

I tried these thoughts in different combinations, running through my mind on tracks swift and slow, upbeat and downbeat, but unable to avoid the melancholy collision with the worldliness of Lord Robens. I was miserable that my dreams for *The Times* were ending in this way in St James's Park on the edge of Parliament Square and Downing Street, and perhaps my career in journalism, too, but it seemed better that morning than a morally debilitating war of attrition. Had Robens or Hamilton encouraged me otherwise I dare say the conclusion might have been different. But as I emerged into Pall Mall, after heavens knows how many circuits of the park, I was clear. I thought yes, I could countenance resignation after all; but what I would not be able to bear was complicity in the pretence that it was amicable. I determined that when I went I would put it on record that it was because of policy differences between me and Murdoch. I would go, but I would not go quietly.

And with that I reassumed my duties as editor of *The Times*, which meant going to lunch at the Institute of Directors in Pall Mall with the American Ambassador John Louis, Cardinal Hume, the chairmen of BP and Rothmans and Sir Donald Maitland, the Permanent Secretary to the Department of Energy. Unaccustomed to my impending role as an ex-editor, I pumped Maitland on the state of Cabinet play on the proposals for a major coalfield at Belvoir and discussed a *Times* leader on the Papacy with Cardinal Hume. It was a trying lunch, group conversation treading down the sods again on the State of Britain, but better than being the menu for Murdoch and Searby.

That afternoon I had a message from the Chancellor via the economics editor, David Blake. 'He was full of praise for the Budget coverage which

lived up to the standards of *The Times* as a newspaper of record for the
first time for many years. Our coverage was competitive with *The
Financial Times* in a way it had never been and he was particularly
complimentary about the clarity of it.' Those follow-up contributions
by specialists which had preoccupied the news editor were scheduled for
a second-day page of reaction and analysis. There was no question it
had been the right order of priorities for *The Times* to report first in
detail. But any notion I might have had that morning that I could get on
quietly editing the paper in a valedictory month was soon dispelled. My
secretary marched in with an envelope from 'the chairman'. It arrived
when I was consulting my solicitor, Peter Mimpriss, and there was
enough astonishment for two. The letter, in Murdoch's hand, read:

> Dear Harry,
>   We all want to be understanding of your position and, more important,
> *generous*.
>   However, it is of paramount importance that this change be made at once.
> There is no way to prevent the news leaking and *both* of us being wrong-
> footed. In your interests as well as ours an announcement *has* to be made
> tonight. You should know this before you see your solicitor in a few minutes.
> It may even be necessary tonight to agree a statement in advance of and
> without prejudice to the financial settlement.
>   Richard and I will hold ourselves free until we hear from you.
>
> Sincerely,
Rupert

I wrote a note of refusal. It was just twenty-four hours since he had
demanded my resignation. Now he was trying to hustle me into agreeing
that afternoon. There were two principles at stake: my right to decide in
my own time or go to the national directors; and my right to fair
compensation. I had been with the company for sixteen years and I was
in no mood to trust Murdoch. I was damned if I was going to be rushed
out of the building and at his mercy on terms. 'Leave everything to your
lawyer,' Robens had told me. 'Relax. We'll stand by you.' Murdoch's
answer was Richard Searby.

I had already called in Peter Mimpriss from the solicitors Allen and
Overy. Murdoch objected to them: of all things, they turned out to be
his lawyers as well. So they concluded that they would act for neither of
us. Mimpriss, who was making other legal arrangements for me, stayed
in my office as an observer when Richard Searby entered: 'Rupert wants
your resignation at once,' he demanded. 'He's had my answer,' I replied.
He persisted. It was the old-established firm of coax, wheedle and bully.
I insisted that if I were to resign it would not be until the following
month, subject to agreement on terms and on the statement. 'That won't
do', he said. I told Searby I had several reasons for refusing to be

railroaded and, if they carried on in this intolerable manner, I would stay, a massive illogicality which failed to register. The arguments went on. He kept returning to the theme that unless I resigned immediately 'it' would leak. To which I replied: 'How can there be anything to leak when I haven't resigned?' The confrontation lasted for almost an hour. I told Robens about it. 'Typical', he said. 'Take no notice.'

The next morning, Thursday 11 March, I went to see the solicitor who had agreed to stand in for Peter Mimpriss and who would have to endure my agonizing as well as Richard Searby. Richard Eddis, with his tufted silver hair, his stiff white collar and his manner of punctilious courtesy, was a senior partner of Stephenson Harwood, a most distinguished firm that had warmed up for these talks by negotiating for the release of the American hostages with the Ayatollah Khomeini. Peter Mimpriss acquainted Eddis with the terms of my seven-year contract which Murdoch had postponed signing since it was ready the previous summer. It reiterated the guarantees of editorial freedom. 'He's taken it with him on Concorde to study', was the message Murdoch's solicitors, Farrers, kept giving Allen and Overy. I told Eddis that I was not committed to resigning. The terms were separate. Once he thought they were fair, I would accept them as the basis for a possible resignation. If I did decide to go, I would insist on making an honest statement of my differences with Murdoch. With that we moved to his office in Saddlers' Hall and with a colleague he went in to meet Searby.

An hour later Eddis came in to say they had got nowhere on terms or the statement. Searby wanted me to restrict myself to a statement they had drafted, and he had offered terms Eddis regarded as insulting. Fundamentally, the Searby–Murdoch offer was without any provision for the pension rights I had accumulated over sixteen years with Times Newspapers. Eddis advised me he could not possibly agree to such terms. He went back in again.

It was a miserable time sitting alone in a featureless side room, churning over and over again the events of the last two days. Now that the legal talks had begun I wanted to get them over as quickly as possible. Eddis came back around noon, shaking his head as much at Searby's arrogant manner as what he had to say. They were nowhere. Searby had not moved at all and was saying he would call a meeting of the national directors for that afternoon to ask for my dismissal. Our side welcomed a meeting and made it clear we would insist on being present to contest the Murdoch–Searby case. If we were going before the national directors, I would fight to keep the editorship. Murdoch had in the meantime opened his own salient. When I returned to the office to see what was moving on the news wires, I discovered that I was.

My secretary announced that she had a list of reporters in press and broadcasting who wanted to talk to me. 'It' had leaked. I was about to have a lesson on what it is like to be the subject of press interest. The origin of this was Murdoch taking the morning Concorde to New York for a party to celebrate his fifty-first birthday.

'Asked about rumours that Mr Evans was to leave the editorship of *The Times*, Mr Murdoch said, "I cannot make any comment at all. You must ask Harold Evans. It is not for me to say anything." Mr Murdoch said the future of Times Newspapers is now secure after the manning cuts agreed with the unions.'

It was a set up. The 'rumours', originated by Murdoch, had died down with his denial of them on 10 February and my award as Editor of the Year. The leak, having failed against me as a theoretical weapon the night before, had been turned into a reality with a planted question and a carefully devised answer. The Press Association had not dreamed of asking a reporter to question Murdoch about me that morning. What happened was that there was a telephone call to the picture desk of the *Standard* with a tip-off 'from the inside'. It was to the effect that there had been a stormy meeting at *The Times* in which I had been sacked and that Murdoch was catching Concorde. The *Standard* picture desk got in touch with Brenards, the news agency at Heathrow, and Alan Walker, in all innocence, did his stuff and then filed the Murdoch quote to the Press Association.

I reflected, as my office reported more and more calls, that it served me right in a way: when a year earlier Murdoch wanted to bring pressure on Denis Hamilton to stop arguing over the release of Gerald Long from Reuters he had said to me with a big grin: 'Leak it for me, will you, that Long is coming. That'll do the trick.' And I had.

No sooner had I read the Press Association message than three of the best reporters on *The Times* came into the outer office and seeing me at the door pressed forward. 'What's happening? You mustn't resign! You mustn't!' The three were the doughty education correspondent Diana Geddes, whom I was considering for Paris correspondent, having nearly sent her to Washington; Lucy Hodges, an apparently frail girl in round silver spectacles, who had kept close to the grassroots in the tough business of reporting race; and Frances Gibb, shy unraveller of many a tangled legal story and a possible successor to Marcel Berlins as legal correspondent. I was touched by their spontaneous reaction. They had all been on *The Times* when I arrived, and were something of a cross-section, I guessed, in terms of office politics. I had not been easy on them. Diana Geddes had been the most worried at first that change might mean lower quality for the paper she loved: she talked of *The Times* as their birthright. But she had thrived on the challenge for authority and detail; they all had.

I was not able to say much. I could not deny I was under pressure to resign. I told them I was considering my position, and I was not unmoved in this by their appeal. That was true; I had not expected the issue to be made public, of course, but if I had I would not have counted on any uprising of support in the light of the low morale over redundancies and the enemies within. Now that the news was out it was unthinkable that I should canvass support; it would be demeaning to turn the editorship of *The Times* into some kind of popularity poll. When the three asked what they could do, I said it had to be up to them to decide whether to do anything at all. 'But why should you resign', they said impatiently, 'when there are no grounds?' I could only shrug, though I was beginning to feel like shouting. They said the NUJ chapel was not the right forum for a protest. They were going to collect signatures for a staff petition to the national directors and I was to hold fast.

In the middle of the afternoon I learned that Searby had got a raspberry from the original four national directors. Pickering had been joined only by John Gross. 'We're not responding to their beck and call,' Robens told me. 'You sit tight.' I was finding it hard to do that. The cancellation of the meeting, though a snub to Murdoch, was anti-climax. We were back to negotiation, and I disliked it. Eddis had come over to *The Times* for the national directors' meeting and stayed to respond to Searby's wish for more meetings. He was a bit more co-operative, but not much. Eddis was in and out of my room; so were members of staff, mixing outrage and encouragement with queries about the following week's paper. The place was buzzing with gossip. My mood was unstable. Perhaps I could talk to Murdoch as a reasonable man? He could end Searby's stonewalling and I could be free. The call to New York, which I made with Eddis present, was the dash of cold water I needed to get a grip of myself. As soon as I heard his belligerent rasp of a response I felt better.

'What are you doing in the office? You should be at home, not editing the paper.'

'I am the editor and editing is what I'm doing.'

'You're damaging the paper being there.'

'You're damaging it by leaking that story.'

I turned to the early page proofs of Friday's paper for relief; the experience was at once gratifying and tormenting. There on the second feature page was a reminder of why I was in journalism and why I was finding it hard to leave. It was a report by George Hill and Lucy Hodges, which I had commissioned weeks earlier, on what progress had been made in the four years since Lord Pearson's royal commission called for reform of our system of damages for victims of accidents. *The Sunday Times* had prompted Ted Heath to set up the Pearson inquiry in the early 1970s when we had demonstrated that the Thalidomide children symbolized a grievous double fault in our way of dealing with all kinds of accident. The victim on the road, in the operating theatre or at work needs help quickly; the public needs as quickly to establish what went wrong so as to prevent it happening again. Both needs are frustrated by a system which offers compensation for injury only by the lottery of a long process of litigation to determine fault, if any. In 1978 Pearson proposed that we adopt the principle of no-fault compensation, beginning with road injuries, funded by a levy of 1p a gallon on petrol. In March 1982 the Government was bringing in a Pearson Bill, but the Hill–Hodges report, harrowingly documented with personal case histories, demonstrated how feeble it was. Pearson's radical and significant proposals had been ignored.

I decided that, if this was to be my last issue of *The Times*, it ought to have a leader by me on some of the values an independent paper might espouse. Donoughue had put the idea into my head and, stimulated by the feature pages, I began to make a few notes. Then my office private line rang and I discovered that I was myself a candidate for grievous bodily harm.

'You little fucker, I'll come in there and wring your neck,' said the voice. It was Douglas-Home, rather excited. 'You've told people Larry Lamb will be the next editor if you go, you bastard, you.'

I told him to seek first aid. I had said nothing of the kind. It was unthinkable that I should say anything about a possible successor. He should go home if he could not control himself. He could not. He was up and down the stairs to the sixth floor to see Murdoch's 'independent' national director Edward Pickering, his first employer. The atmosphere belied the institution. That afternoon, within minutes of the trio of *Times* reporters leaving my room, Diana Geddes was sought out by Douglas-Home. He wanted everyone to know he would be the next editor. He followed it by saying that I was their enemy. I had criticized them to management; to get up a petition would be divisive. He had been hotfoot in the news room, and was to be remarkably well informed about any of my callers. He had recruited his own Mata Hari with the promise of a new life when the old tyranny had been swept away. My private secretary, Liz Seeber, was in the starring role. Whenever someone entered my office, Seeber in these critical days called Douglas-Home: 'He's got Hopkinson in there now . . . he's on the phone to Lord Robens . . . Donoughue has been to see him.' Douglas-Home recognized that Seeber was an ambitious woman: she was certainly able and thought secretarial work was below her. He had told her that if he became editor she would be promoted to an executive assistant (and so she was).

I was happily in ignorance of these farcical games. I read and approved

March 1982: the editorship of *The Times* was front-page news for a week in the rest of the press.

'Rupert who?' Jak's view of the March 1982 crisis.

'Just for fun, Harry – we've buried your golden handshake somewhere in Britain and the clues are all in today's paper' – Mac in the *Daily Mail*.

Harold Evans and his wife, Tina Brown, face press and television each morning on leaving home.

Charles Douglas-Home, deputy editor of *The Times*, at his London home on 13 March 1982.

GOLD MEDALLIST   (O.K. for Front Harry.?) Garry

Scarfe's caricature for a *Sunday Times* staff celebration of Harold Evans's award of the gold medal.

the extract we were carrying from Henry Kissinger's memoirs. My leader was headlined 'The Deeper Issues':

Sir Geoffrey Howe has rightly had a good press for his budget, including from *The Times*. In terms of the fruit machines, whose taxes he varied, he might be said to have scored three pears for its politics, and two oranges for its economics, which may represent a lot of votes in Hillhead. Sir Geoffrey has also done a power of good for Tory morale. It would be a pity, however, in the general approval of the Budget, if sight was lost of issues of concern in Britain today of much greater significance than a scatter of items of tax reform and the insulation of lofts. The condition of the country is only partly amenable to Government action – there are some deep-rooted sicknesses in society in attitudes to merit, class and family – but there are areas where so far Government has done nothing to ameliorate life and in some cases has damaged its tone and quality.

Unemployment is a social scandal. The prospects remain about as dismal after the Budget as before, not least for the young but especially for the chronic long-term unemployed – skilled and unskilled men and women whose dignity is reduced on the dole. For the young there is some hope, perhaps the certainty, that thousands will be marked in their character by the debilitation of a life of subsidized idleness, one of the reasons, but not the only one, why *The Times* recently reopened a debate about National Service. It is in this context that the cuts in training and in higher education remain a matter for regret and puzzlement.

Life in the inner cities, despite the brilliant flourish provided by a Barbican arts centre or two, has diminished in its civilization. Crime and racial tension are part of this but so is the destruction of the old community life in which businessmen and teachers and bankers shared the community's hopes and privations. Only Mr Michael Heseltine, of the leading ministers, seems fully to have appreciated the disaster that has occurred over several administrations.

There is no quick solution here, as high-rise blocks of the post-war years are demolished, but there is an overwhelming need for investment in the social infrastructure and so far little has been committed relative to the scale of the problem. The predicament of the Health Service is worse with polarisation between an adequate private sector – which must be preserved – and the increasing squalor of the public sector. And when something goes wrong in our hospitals wracked by idiot union abuse and starved of funds, as has happened in some dramatic recent cases, we are back to the evils exposed by the Thalidomide scandal – the afflicted are left to try their luck by sueing for negligence in the courts. They face delay, secrecy, cost and anxiety when least able to endure it. The report by Lord Justice Pearson, provoked by Thalidomide, would have ended this particular injustice but it remains unenacted.

Where there has most been an erosion of hope and a collapse of vision is in the role of Britain as a leading member of the international community. None of the economic problems of this country, or of others, can be solved in isolation. It is international cooperation in currency reform, free trade, and

North–South issues, which is required here. The political damage in the division of the West is palpable in its uncertain response to Soviet aggression, but the damage is as real in every area of economic activity. Here we give the impression of a bored insularity.

Underlying the view of *The Times* on these matters is a conviction of the value of the individual free spirit and of free debate. We favour a more competitive society as against one which is subject to the monopoly powers of capital or the trade unions, or too great a concentration of power in any one institution: the national press itself, to be fair, is worryingly over-concentrated. Yet we also want to see a more considerate society with greater social harmony.

No single British party has a programme which matches the needs of this great but troubled nation. It is because of this that *The Times* in its long history has resisted attachment to any particular party. We can believe, as we do, that it would be a great loss if Mr Roy Jenkins, a man of some stature, were not elected at Hillhead, without now or in the future committing ourselves to the SDP Alliance. Every case must be judged on its merits, robustly but without malice, and with respect for dissent. But what is necessary at this time is leadership and vision that will lift the British people beyond the current dogmas and disputes. A society is judged not only by what it achieves but by what it aspires to achieve.

The rhetoric was all very well. The reality was a hectoring Searby in Murdoch's office, an immaculately patient Eddis, and Douglas-Home establishing squatters' rights in my chair on the back bench where the paper is put together. Eddis proposed to catch the train to Sevenoaks. It was an attractive idea. He could see no purpose in further meetings with Searby. Then there arrived a letter to me signed by Gerald Long:

> Richard Searby has discussed with your Mr Eddis the terms which News International Limited is prepared to offer in consideration of your resigning.
> I now ask you formally on instructions from Mr Murdoch whether you are prepared to resign on those terms.
> Would you please inform me or Mr Searby by 8 p.m. in writing whether you are now prepared to resign forthwith?

There was about an hour before 8 p.m. I had had enough of deadlines for one day. I reminded Eddis of the train to Elysium. I told him I intended to ignore this latest ultimatum and I did. I involved myself in the production of the paper. The night staff rallied round; it was very heartening. Tony Hilton, the deputy editor of Business News, urged me to go out on the floor and rouse people from their depression: everybody would acknowledge that the paper had been transformed in my year. I told all the well-wishers that I had decided against addressing the staff because I thought it would look like playing to the gallery. Perhaps, in the light of later disinformation, I was wrong in that.

At about 10.30 p.m. a peaked cap showed around my door. It was a demand for money but only for fish and chips. My driver, Syd Markham, had become obsessed with the damage being done to my health by the nightly tray of wilted salad left for me and had campaigned for the nourishment to be offered by an establishment in Theobalds Road. I gave in. Then without announcement, while I was going through the first edition, Searby appeared. He asked for the return of the Long ultimatum letter; they were still dealing. All he wanted was an agreement in principle that evening and he settled down on the sofa to get it. I should have asked him to leave, but I had no intention of yielding. He produced press statements already prepared for both sides.

It was just as I feared. On my resigning that evening, the company's hollow-laugh department had produced:

> In the past year since he took over the editorship Mr Evans has made a significant personal contribution to the re-shaping of the paper and setting it on course for future development and expansion.
>
> Mr Murdoch said from New York tonight: 'I wish to pay tribute to Harold Evans for all that he has done professionally and personally in his fifteen years of devoted service to *The Times* and *The Sunday Times*. As I have written to Harold Evans today, his successes in investigative and campaigning journalism have won him the admiration of his colleagues in Britain and beyond.
>
> 'His contribution to all aspects of his craft has been immense and he has put a distinctive stamp on each of the newspapers he has edited.'

The lines written for me to say were:

> The past year has been one of tremendous effort and achievement. Without doubt *The Times* is now in a position to build on the strong foundations that have been laid. This has only been achieved by tremendous efforts by everyone concerned in the enterprise – by Rupert Murdoch, by management and by the loyal staff in every department of *The Times*.

I demurred. Everyone was entitled to know that, if I was resigning, it was because of differences; but Searby was now the soft policeman. We put his statements aside and he started jotting down figures, first on one sheet, then another. I did not want to talk about money. It made no difference. Here was another formula, and another, and another. Here was a way with tax paid. Here was a way with a pension fund. It was like watching someone play Find the Lady. Markham came back in the middle of it with fish and chips wrapped in paper – inelegant, but appropriate. Searby, sitting on my sofa, helped himself. Unfortunately it gave him new zest for arithmetic and advocacy. He was the honest broker, he was acting without authority, he was the detached adviser, he was my best friend, he was everybody except Richard Searby who had come all the way from Melbourne to sort things out. I was exhausted. It was past midnight. When the second edition of my 'smelly rag' arrived I ushered him out.

The Times was scooped that Friday morning. The *Standard* had carried only a few lines after Murdoch's airport interview but all the morning papers had worked hard and their front pages reported, as we did not, the news that Murdoch had asked me to resign and I was still editing the paper. *The Times* said cryptically that its editor had no comment to make on reports circulating about his future. The *Express* front page had it as '*Times* editor in job riddle' which they all found it to be. The confusion, which I well understood, was exemplified by a report in *The Financial Times*: 'According to some reports the then five independent directors unanimously agreed at a meeting on 25 February to accept the resignation of Mr Evans and the appointment of Mr Douglas-Home to the post. However, they did not agree to Mr Evans resigning against his wishes.' Murdoch's PR machine had been busy with suggestions from unnamed sources in Gray's Inn Road that the dispute was really over my exceeding my editorial budget and hiring too many highly paid journalists. I had not spoken to anybody in the press, so I could not complain. Stephen Cook in *The Guardian* got it right about Murdoch's desire for a more right-wing political direction. *The Guardian* also said Douglas-Home was telling staff he had been appointed the new editor.

There were television crews and photographers outside my home and office that morning. I told them that reports of my death were greatly exaggerated and I was going in to edit *The Times*, which is what I proceeded to do. I was about to dictate memos before the conference when Long came magisterially into my room, erect, bristling, and red in cheek. What did I have to say, he demanded, about the fact that one of my secretaries had answered a press inquiry with the comment that he, Long, might be the one who was leaving his job? I do not think I had ever lost my temper with Long; I did then. Whatever anyone might have said, I told him, it was nothing to the pressure I was under. I objected strongly to it. 'You know it and you know it's wrong.' He turned on his heel. He did know the pressure, he did know it was wrong and I think he was privately ashamed of it. He is a hard man, but with scruples; he was himself travelling only in a better class of tumbril.

John Grant turned up in the observers' seats at the news conference like one of Madame Defarge's knitting companions. 'I am breaking the habit of a lifetime,' he giggled. 'Wouldn't miss this for the world.' I did not feel uncomfortable; Douglas-Home was slumped at my side but there were a lot of friendly faces and Grant was doomed to disappointment in expecting my resignation. I made a brief statement to the effect that this was going to be a difficult time for them. We would all wish to congratulate two *Times* staff that day named in the British press awards, one a newcomer, Frank Johnson the columnist, and the other, Diana Geddes, eight years on *The Times*, and note that they represented a happy marriage of the new and the old *Times*. When we got to our own story on the news list, I told Cowton that *The Times* should try to treat it as news like any other story and he assigned two good straight reporters from the labour staff, Donald Macintyre and Dave Felton. By this time it seemed to me as if the story was being pursued by every reporter from Fleet Street to Melbourne. I was saying nothing and I was not asking anyone to say anything for me, but they were doing so – and how. Petty crises, as much as great events, illuminate character in surprising ways. I expected that Donoughue or Hamilton would speak out if there was occasion; I was mildly surprised when I heard that the quietly reflective Edwin Taylor had collected a petition for the national directors of most of the senior staff, but nothing surprised me as much as the emergence of Tony Holden as my champion. I would never have thought that the companionable Holden, an excellent but apolitical features editor, would throw himself into a fight of this sort. But when the press and radio sought someone to go on the record and say something, Holden did it boldly. In view of later events it has to be said that his exercise of the right of free speech consisted of taking pride in what had been achieved in the year, rejecting the story that the senior staff were up in arms, and critically reciting the Murdoch complaints against giving a place for dissent on the features pages. Holden spoke for himself. It was none the less rapidly put about by Murdoch's men that Holden was only my mouthpiece, an understandable error since the only principles they were acquainted with were those of ventriloquism.

Around lunchtime that Friday the clamour suddenly seemed remote. Eddis had been called back in by Searby and he came to my room to say that there had been a change of position. Searby was still insisting on statements being mutually agreed: 'We'll have trouble with that.' But the compensation for loss of office would now include my pension rights if I agreed to resign that afternoon. Eddis advised that a court would award higher compensation, but it was, as he put it, 'acceptable at this stage in view of the strain you are under'. I hesitated. He pressed the case. He was right about the strain. I hated as well what the intrigue was doing in the office. It was hateful for the staff. I would resign. That was the mood in which I took Eddis to lunch at the Garrick Club, to which Tina came later. She was worried at my volatility; after Searby's midnight visit I had been talking of forcing a showdown with the national directors and staying on. When I went back into the office in the afternoon I accepted non-press calls and was plunged into a confusion of guilt and uncertainty at the warmth of the goodwill and the urgings to stay on and make even more of an issue of it. I was told of a petition which the *Sunday Times* staff was also sending to the national directors; other *Times* staff in different departments had sent letters.

Eddis had gone to see Searby at 3 p.m. I rang him while he was there and asked him to convey the message that I would not resign that afternoon. I wanted the weekend to think about it. I told him, for his own peace of mind, that I would not prolong things beyond Monday one way or the other, the choice being resignation or rejection of the terms and a formal hearing with the national directors. I sent him a note upstairs to the same effect. Eddis came downstairs to say that Searby would not agree. The terms were for my resignation today. He had called executive board meetings for 5 p.m. I asked Lord Roll by telephone to tell Searby this was not acceptable and he called him, but it made no difference. I went upstairs to see Searby myself. He was sitting in his braces at Murdoch's desk, half-moon glasses down his nose, a pencil at his lips. He looked washed out, the debonair riverboat gambler smudged and haggard after all-night poker. Mark Twain had upset him.

'What's this,' he said hoarsely. 'Rumours of your death are greatly exaggerated?'

'I am not going to resign this afternoon,' I told him.

He brought his fist down on Murdoch's desk.

'You talk about your mother. I left my family in Australia for a week in February. I'm still here!'

The man from Melbourne, beleaguered in London, stared down at the *Standard*. It was open at the page with an overline '*Times* battle over editor's independent stand' and Holden's quotes about Murdoch's political pressures.

'And where's all this coming from?' he choked. 'We can't have a weekend of more of this stuff.'

We wrangled for half an hour. In retrospect it seems absurd: it was nothing to a confrontation with Murdoch, and Searby was as jittery as I was, but I found I could hardly speak. I was dry with nervous tension and had to go outside for a glass of water. I heard a small voice giving in, agreeing to resign on Friday with an announcement on Saturday. I stood up to go with that and was overwhelmed by revulsion for the whole proceedings, by shame and by anger. I shouted at Searby: 'No! No! And you can stuff your pound notes.'

Still shaking, I left to tell Eddis how I had put his handiwork at hazard. As I went down, Beattie and Ekberg went up to the board meeting suitably composed for my funeral. Eddis took my news as he would an announcement that the train for Sevenoaks was running three minutes late; but he was anxious at the risk I was taking. He had the papers for me to sign. I suggested that he call Lord Robens there and then. Robens was a rock. Four national directors at least, he told Eddis, would not agree to my dismissal. I was to do what I thought fit but take my lawyer's advice before I signed anything. That helped to restore perspective. So did the arrival in the office of Tina and cool counsel from Donoughue. I left Eddis to deal with Searby, who was soon on the phone; Eddis was heard rebuking him for shouting and ranting.

I went to the back bench to check on the progress of the night's paper. I told David Hopkinson, the unflappable new chief night editor, that I was going for supper but would call in to check our story on events at *The Times*. At 8.30 p.m. it had not arrived at the back bench so I went to our cottage in Kent and thought I would watch *News at Ten* before calling in: Macintyre and Felton could be trusted to handle the story fairly anyway. I had reckoned without Murdoch, Searby and Douglas-Home. Alistair Burnett read a statement from Murdoch in New York issued by Searby in London which was so distant from the truth that I put in calls at once to David Nicholas, the editor of ITN, and *The Times*. What Murdoch said is worth quoting as an example of the art form:

> It is true that I asked Mr Harold Evans for his resignation. This was done on Tuesday 9th March [accurate so far] with the unanimous approval of the independent national directors. [With their knowledge, yes. With their approval, no. 'Unanimous' and 'approval' carefully chosen to suggest a board resolution which he did not have. Robens called it 'sloppy'; there are other terms.]
>
> Mr Evans agreed to give his resignation [untrue] but has been negotiating terms for his departure. These have now been agreed [the terms, yes, but not the departure].
>
> At no point has there been any difference, stated or otherwise, between Mr Evans and myself about the policy of the paper [lie: 'Stated or otherwise' attempts to give it an air of precision and honesty].

As a statement it was revealing of Murdoch's contempt for truth and the public record as was his statement of 10 February denying that there were any plans to replace Harold Evans whose outstanding qualities, etc. But Friday night's was sinuous in its deception and dealing with it quickly was hard. I concentrated on denying that I had agreed to give my resignation and denying that it was an argument about money. I spoke to David Nicholas in the commercial break and the extraordinary skill and speed of ITN gave me at least the satisfaction of hearing my rejection of Murdoch's statement in the second half of the programme. I said I had no argument about money but I had about the principles of conducting *The Times*. I did not know at the time that Robens was making a statement: 'I don't understand why Mr Murdoch says that the unanimous approval of the independent directors has been given to Mr

Evans' resignation when our approval is not even required. And I do not recollect sitting down and having the resolution that he should be replaced as editor put to us.'

When I called *The Times*, the reaction was very different from that of ITN. David Hopkinson had gone home. I found myself speaking with Charles Douglas-Home, who would normally have gone home too. They were carrying Murdoch's statement and one by Douglas-Home saying there had never been any political pressure from Murdoch. But Douglas-Home refused to carry my denial in *The Times*. I told him it was an instruction from his editor, and if he was going as far as to defy that he might consider fairness. He was dismissive and I was melting the telephone line. I told him to put me on to the night editor, John Brian. He was in the composing room. Finally, he handed me to Denis Archdeacon, saying to him for my benefit that I was emotional. Archdeacon, a relatively new and capable sub-editor, took down my denial and, in the absence of Brian, I spoke with the night editor's assistant, Christine Long. Poor girl, she did not know what to do. Here was the editor saying publish, and here was the deputy saying hold out. Fortunately the soldierly John Brian returned to take command and sent my paragraph to the printer.

Douglas-Home was desperate. He saw the prize slipping away. Like Searby he was worried at the impression Holden was making. He was complaining to people all day that he was being handed 'a poisoned chalice'. He had his Macbeth confused; I think I was Duncan. When Holden approached him shortly after his telephone conflict with me he was eager to talk. They withdrew to the darkened diary area adjacent to the main news room and in this cramped and gloomy setting had exchanges which haunted Holden for the collision of sentiment and cynicism. 'Half of me loves Harry,' said Douglas-Home, his face intense in the shadows. But how could Douglas-Home do what he had done when only the previous month he had said he would never edit a paper owned by 'this destructive monster Murdoch'?

'But you would have done what I have, wouldn't you?'

'No.'

'Oh yes you would if you had worked for this paper as long as I have and if all your life the only thing you wanted was to be the editor of *The Times*. You would have done anything to get it.'

It was a familiar refrain, but there was a mysterious twist. Douglas-Home asked Holden if he played bridge. Holden, a poker player, had to acknowledge that he did not. 'Ah, if you played bridge', said Douglas-Home, 'you would understand.'

Douglas-Home was indeed doing anything he could. In a statement to the *Daily Telegraph* he made later he said: 'I know of nobody acting on my behalf. I would discourage divisive operations in the office.' But later that Friday night in great secrecy Douglas-Home urgently telephoned Geraldine Norman at her flat in Great Portland Street to do something on his behalf which was furiously divisive in the office. Norman was the sale-room correspondent. She had limited newspaper experience, but she had built up a strong position with items from Christies and Sothebys, and exposed Tom Keating's art forgeries. A widow in her forties, she could be taken for a grammar school headmistress fretting over going comprehensive. The permanent anxiety in her case is change in *The Times*. She holds it in awe as an institution rather than a newspaper. She fears that anything new must be a threat to the tradition and gentility she regards as the heart of *The Times*; to her news on the front page had been the slippery slope to the ultimate horror of 'quali-pop'.

Norman's usefulness to Murdoch was that, when she conveyed some of the old guard's unease, she gave him an idea of a constituency that might be mobilized against me. Norman's usefulness to Douglas-Home was that she was the chairman of Journalists of *The Times*. JOTT had naturally ceased to be very active when Murdoch bought *The Times*, though it still had rather more than 200 *Times* staff as shareholders at £4 a head. Douglas-Home made the right appeal to Norman. The good name of *The Times* was at stake because Harold Evans was at the Garrick Club spilling the beans to Donald Trelford, the editor of *The Observer*. The origins of this assertion probably lay in my receiving a friendly letter from Trelford that Friday commending The Deeper Issues editorial I had written and saying, like everyone else, that they would like to know what was going on: another candidate for Seeber's dead-letter drop. Norman's imagination was inflamed by this menace to public decency. It was, as they say, a farrago of nonsense with not a jot or tittle of truth in it, but Norman took Douglas-Home at his word. She saw him as an old *Times* man who would preserve the inner citadel of sameness, and she resented the attention being paid to new-comers like Holden who could not begin to understand the paper's traditions.

She drafted a statement for JOTT as a refutation of 'misleading comments by journalists who had recently joined *The Times*'. It welcomed Douglas-Home as a new editor on the grounds that Murdoch and I had threatened the paper's editorial integrity and its traditional character. I had made some genuine improvements, but the paper's stability had been destroyed. On Saturday morning Norman had her statement approved by six *Times* people on the eleven-member JOTT board. In fact, the six did not consult their 200 members.

The six were the two leader writers Geoffrey Smith and Edward Mortimer, David Blake, Gabriel Ronay (a foreign sub-editor) and Tim

Austin. Austin was the only name that surprised me: as chief sub-editor on the home side he had welcomed the changes Geraldine Norman distrusted and I had promoted him to be an assistant foreign editor. (He later wrote me a letter of regret.) There were furious protests by many JOTT members at the statement that was released as representing their views. A counter statement was drafted. Geraldine Norman apologized – too late – with another statement saying, 'I am sorry there was no opportunity for consultation'.

Geoffrey Smith followed up the first statement by asking to go on BBC Radio Four's *The World This Weekend*, on which he accused me of compromising my editorial independence. It was rich. He read out the memo I had sent to Murdoch about the production cost of the Budget separate section and represented it – as Douglas-Home had done to me – as evidence that I was in the habit of asking Murdoch to approve editorial content. His action set everyone guessing where he had got it from, which was certainly more interesting than the memo. Roy Hattersley in his *Punch* column painted a picture of Smith breaking into the building late at night wearing a Dick Turpin mask, a black and white hooped jersey, armed with a jemmy and a bag marked 'swag'.

Fortunately for my composure I had resolved to cut myself off from print that tense weekend. It took something of a campaign to do so because of press efforts to get me to talk. The story was now splashed as soap opera. 'Power Struggle!' proclaimed the *Daily Mail*. 'Dirty Tricks at *The Times*.' The *Daily Express* spoke of 'Two men of power in a clash of wills' and *The Guardian* of 'Warfare as Evans hangs on'. I was ambushed on a foray to the village grocer's by a *Sunday Express* man secreted inside a van though I had gone to the trouble of disguising myself with a country walking-stick. Of course Murdoch's men were busy. The owner of *The Sunday Times* and *News of the World* got in touch with the former owner of *The Observer*, Robert Anderson, to see what could be done to angle that paper's report; Kenneth Harris relayed the message to the editor, Donald Trelford, who put it on the spike. Eddis was so enraged by the distortions he threatened to seek an injunction to restrain the other side, which I would not have liked. Through Long, Robens sent a protest to Murdoch at the caricature of the attitude of the national directors. 'Murdoch's not right, not right,' Greene said to me. I spoke with all four original directors, dragging Robens from his orchids, and with John Gross, who told me he wanted to associate himself with Robens. I gave them accounts of the way I had been pressured. Dacre and Roll thought they should put out a statement to clarify their role and correct Murdoch, but Robens disagreed. He was as reassuring as ever. He went a bit far, I thought, in saying on the radio on Sunday that the editor had not appealed to the national directors in any shape or form, but I supposed this was a better posture in the event of their becoming some sort of appeal court.

It was this final step I was now deliberating. It had taken every resource from me to refuse to resign on Friday. From Friday lunchtime there were terms on the table that I was advised I could accept. They would be the ones on which I would resign if I so chose. The press was still being briefed that I was holding on for better terms, which was another invention. I stuck it out through the weekend and into Monday for two reasons: to clear my own mind about going or staying, and to write it in every day's banner headlines that editors of *The Times* were not to be as casually discarded as had the thirteen editors in fifteen years on *The Australian*. I had succeeded in that. Murdoch had helped. I had been shocked by his leak on Wednesday and felt beleaguered. He had certainly calculated that I would resign promptly under pressure; there was plenty of precedent for that belief and he knew I was low. But the weapon he had sought to use against me had turned in his hand. I was never going to go quietly, but any statement by me that it was due to differences would have made little impact by comparison with the spectacle of a daily public fight. Donoughue had predicted that, much as I hated it at the time, I would be glad I had held out and he was right. On Sunday evening I conceived the idea of giving in my resignation not to the management but to the national directors, still further to emphasize their role. Having been on the phone incessantly to them, and knowing how conflicting their own schedules were, I asked Donoughue if he could test the practicability of this with his old friend John Gross.

I felt composed on Monday when I went in to resume editing the paper. I was borne up by scores of messages to my London home. Henry Kissinger and Harold Lever telephoned to express bewilderment. Kissinger had to acknowledge that his common testimony that the foreign news and opinion in *The Times* had been improved was not worth much since international right-wing figures had put it to Murdoch that I was a closet Communist just like him. Jack Ashley, the Labour MP for Stoke and my old Thalidomide ally, rang to say he was putting a question down in the Commons. In the office Long suggested a meeting, which I refused; Searby had gone to see Murdoch in New York.

Geoffrey Smith did not attend the leader conference. There was feeling among all sections of the staff, I learned later, that Smith had let the side down by indulging in what the *Mail* splashed as 'Dirty Tricks at *The Times*', and members of JOTT were angry at what had been done in their name. Edward Mortimer, one of my JOTT critics, was heard saying on the telephone: 'We've blown it'. Brian Horton, who had stayed detached, was ventilating displeasure in his icy manner, though he was widely regarded as Murdoch's man on the editorial floor. Douglas-Home even thought it necessary to say he deprecated what Smith had done.

The production of the paper was not at all disrupted, as I had feared it might. John Greig scuttled past me in the corridor head down, as if eye contact would turn him to stone, but everyone outside the inner JOTT group was friendly, if bemused. I agreed with the news editor Cowton when he remarked that he hoped our own story could be wrapped up fairly soon. I knew I would either resign during the day on Monday or insist on a showdown; in any event I was determined to edit the paper. I was reinforced in this when Horton told me, which I did regard as being a frightener from Murdoch, that in the deadlock he could threaten to pull out financial support for *The Times*.

I was a few minutes late for the leader conference. Douglas-Home, sitting palely in my position at the top of the table, looked as if he realized it was Sweeney Todd's chair. 'You're editing,' he said. He dropped out of a discussion on a Labour document on prices and wages which David Blake was outlining. Donoughue was in good form here, delineating its main weaknesses, and so was Richard Davy, who was ready to write on a French call for closer European co-operation on defence. I deputed Blake to write the economic leader and went to lunch; on the way the Attorney-General, Sir Michael Havers, laid his hand on my shoulder. It was the first time in my career as an editor that it was well meant.

It seemed like a normal day. In the afternoon, while I was reading feature proofs, Donoughue suggested it would be interesting to see if there had been any letters on the affair. I called in Leon Pilpel, the letters editor. He is a man in his mid-fifties, a former chief sub editor who has been with *The Times* for thirty years. He is a stickler for accuracy, form and the genuine traditions of *The Times*. Some people in the office thought he was an infuriating pedant; I had respect for his skill and his standards.

I asked him if he had any letters on the *Times* affair. He put in front of me a proof of a letter already in type from Lord Shawcross. It read as a defence of a proprietor's right to dismiss an editor. He who paid the piper called the tune. That was fair enough. 'Is this all?' I asked Pilpel. He looked embarrassed and left the room. He returned with a sheaf of about forty letters and telegrams. I skimmed through them. They were a mixture of reasoned argument and anger, a few from well-known people. They had one thing in common: they were all favourable to me and hostile to interference by Murdoch. I asked him what was the principle by which the one letter unhelpful to me had been selected for publication and all the favourable ones rejected. He looked even more embarrassed. Mr Hickey had made the selection; Hickey normally did make the final choice and had beseeched me to let him retain this responsibility when I took over.

I sent for Hickey. He sat facing my desk. I asked him the same question. Had he considered the Shawcross letter so eloquent and conclusive that it silenced everything else? He wriggled in the chair, avoiding my eye. 'You didn't think that we would ...' his voice trailed off. 'You will understand', he said, 'that we are all at present in a difficult position.'

'Of course. I hope it is not prolonged. But I am responsible for editing the paper. Can you tell me the principles on which the choice of letters has been made?'

He could not. Did he think the other messages were so inadequate? He did not. How could we reconcile his selection with the tradition of *The Times* for fair debate? He had nothing to say. It was not enough to leave it at that. I had an editor's interest in fairness and would have been appalled at such a singular choice on any subject at any time. But I was also Harold Evans, the subject of the debate. It seemed best to give Hickey a second chance to be the conscience of *The Times*.

'We can do one of two things,' I said. 'You and I can make a fair selection from all the letters, Shawcross plus perhaps two from the others. And daily we can reflect the changing balance in this way. Or we can wait and publish letters when the dust has settled a bit. You decide.'

Hickey said on reflection he thought it wiser to publish nothing for now, and that is how it was left.

I was now leading a double life, editing the paper as if I was there for life and preparing myself to resign that day. I gave Eddis a text of what I proposed to say if I did resign. I knew that psychologically I would go right up to deadline before deciding whether to do it or not. I would have to wait until Wednesday for a formal meeting with the national directors: Donoughue told me in mid-afternoon that with the best will in the world the national directors could not be got together before then. Tina had arranged for friends to come for supper, not knowing herself whether it would be a resignation party or a battle party.

Sometime in the late afternoon I heard that my text was not agreed by Murdoch. Long in London was keeping in touch with him and Searby in New York with Farrers in attendance. I told Eddis I was unshakable on my statement and got on with the next duty in editing the paper, which was seeing to the leaders. Blake's needed revision. It was loosely written and he had omitted some of the central points Donoughue had made. Davy suggested the European leader should be the top and I needed no persuading. I went to Adrian Hamilton's business news night conference. After the 6 p.m. back-bench conference on the main news I stayed with the night editors. They were examining a photograph of an exhausted foam-covered London fireman, wondering if it was strong enough for the front page. In one of those happy inspirations which make newspaper work so stimulating the assistant picture editor, Tom Galvin, defended it by saying firemen had been conspicuously active recently, and I asked the news desk to write 300 words of caption telling us that story. Emery, back from holiday, insisted on turning my attention to rape and obscenity. Only the editor, he declared, could decide how much of the descriptive detail of stage buggery we should run in a report by David Nicholson-Lord on the Mary Whitehouse prosecution of the National Theatre's *The Romans in Britain*. It took my mind off the attempted censorship of my statement. Then the news desk delivered a poor caption on Galvin's fireman, missing the point completely. I asked for it to be redone: in the previous ten days London's firemen had tackled 2,929 fires and they merited a better effort.

Around 8 p.m. Eddis arrived at my office. I read the documents. Murdoch had stopped trying to put words in my mouth. If I would confine myself to my paragraph, they would confine themselves to theirs. Long had the directors upstairs ready to receive my resignation. I was not ready to give it.

I went out to the news department. I read Donald Macintyre's report on the editorship and suggested he call the national directors for some quotations. It said I was still firmly in charge of the paper, but quoted Donoughue as saying he doubted whether I would wish to stay once I had established the principle that the editor of *The Times* could not be railroaded out of his editorial chair by the proprietor.

It was a poignant tour. In the nearly deserted hot-metal area where I checked on production with a long-serving *Times* overseer, Phil Barton, the lines of Linotypes were shrouded in dust-sheets, their productive lives at *The Times* at an end. I did not like the idea that mine was. This was where we had seen some of our big efforts, Reagan, Brixton, Poland, come jaggedly to triumph, where I had fretted over the tricky launch of the new back page, and followed Haley in the tradition of seeing my own leaders to press. I thought then I would go on editing *The Times*, and that was my mood when I joined the night staff in the photo-composition area. The new sports and business pages were over their teething troubles and everyone cheerfully engaged. Douglas-Home was there, off by himself leaning bleakly against a cabinet. He had been limping all day. 'I think I'll go to the national directors on Wednesday,' I said, to cheer him up. And then I went back to my office, through the back bench area where the pace had slackened with the first edition finished and people were drifting out to supper, and I was overwhelmed by the outrage I had bottled up for the week. All the thoughts of St James's Park gathered. Why should I give my energy, my ability and my experience and one more minute of my time to this man Murdoch? I had done what I could to establish the principle that an editor of *The Times* was not to be shoved around. Why should I expose myself and my family and friends to the sure recurrence of similar ordeals in an atmosphere which engendered betrayal?

I signed. Not trusting the management with my own press release – and in the event they did not keep the understanding to restrict themselves to their own announcement – I called *News at Ten*. I said I would make an unspecified statement to camera. While I waited there was a call which I took in the outer office. 'Hello, Charlie, it's Pick here . . .' I put the phone down on the independent director. The door opened and Long, lugubriously muffled for the night, looked in: 'Well done, Harry,' he sighed. I asked him to leave me alone. Meanwhile, at home, Tina's forty-five guests were circulating uneasily round the sitting-room not knowing what they were celebrating.

Around 9.30 p.m., just after our scheduled first edition, the ITN crew came up the stairs at the double. The interviewer coaxed me into position. 'Please stand over here, Mr Murdoch . . .'

This may have partly accounted for the pained expression when, with my back to a souvenir of our colour front page of the Royal Wedding, at 9.40 p.m. on Monday 15 March I read:

> Mr Rupert Murdoch on Budget Day asked me to resign as editor of *The Times*. I refused. At no time have the Independent National Directors sought my resignation but, in the circumstances, the differences between me and Mr Murdoch should not be prolonged. I am, therefore, resigning tonight as the editor of *The Times*. I have enormously enjoyed my fifteen years as editor of *The Sunday Times* and *The Times*, and I look forward to a future as exciting and interesting.

Only later did I recognize the significance of the date. It was 15 March. It was chilling to remember that 'Beware the Ides of March' was one of the passages from Shakespeare that my father knew well and liked to declaim.

# AFTERWORD

The difference between the Thomson era and my experience of the Murdoch era is that in *The Sunday Times* years all our energies were directed outwards, and at *The Times* they were turned fatally inwards. It was the external restraints of the law and executive secrecy that tried to constrain the editorial freedom and excellence of *The Sunday Times*. But at *The Times* the pressures came from within: from a proprietor in breach of his guarantees to Parliament and from a debilitating intro-spection about the role and identity of the paper.

The press is a frail vessel for the hopes it is meant to bear. The best that it can do can never be quite good enough to illuminate what Walter Lippmann called the 'invisible environment', the complexity of forces and agencies we cannot monitor for ourselves, but which affect all our lives. A free, cultivated, diverse, resourceful and honest press can only try, and if we ever get one it will be interesting to see what it achieves. In the meantime, the nature of the two distinct areas of restraint is central to our understanding. The first is external: the accumulation of laws and conventions which limit and punish free inquiry – the chapters on *The Sunday Times* in this book offer example. The second is internal: the vulnerability of an editor to a proprietor, the resources available for serious journalism and the unity and purpose of the staff, including the print unions. It was only on the basis of internal freedom with a skilled and united staff, and a proprietor willing to support editorial judgement, enterprise and risk-taking that *The Sunday Times* was able to be effective in areas of public policy. Without internal freedom there is little hope of producing a newspaper of quality and none at all of challenging the external restraints.

Ultimately, all stands or falls on the values and judgement of the proprietor. A newspaper of entertainment and propaganda may be commercially successful where editorial authority is diluted and there is capricious intervention by the proprietor – the *Daily Express* of Beaver-brook is the classic example. But no newspaper dedicated to public affairs has ever succeeded in this way. There has to be constancy of purpose, and a commitment has to be shared by a proprietor, editor and staff. One thinks first of the Walters and their editors of *The Times*, but also of the Ochs-Sulzberger families and their editors at the *New York Times*; of *The Guardian*'s editors' responsibility to the Scott Trust; of the Grahams and their editors at the *Washington Post*; of Pearson Longman and Sir Gordon Newton and Geoffrey Owen at *The Financial Times*; and, of course, of the Astors and the Thomsons, all providing an environment for the pursuit of excellence. Every great partnership has recognized the importance of viability and profit, but also the primacy of the editorial objective: there need be no conflict, as the profitable *Sunday Times* demonstrated for very many years until it was stricken by industrial unrest. At its highest levels, a great newspaper is not simply a personal possession but a public trust. That was the tradition of *The Times* for a century and *The Sunday Times* for a generation, and that was why Parliament and the Thomson ownership asked Rupert Murdoch for guarantees that editorial independence would continue to be honoured under his proprietorship.

He guaranteed that the editors would have control of the political policy of their newspapers; that they would have freedom within fixed annual budgets; that the editors would not be subject to instruction from either the proprietor or management on the selection and balance of news and opinion; that instructions to journalists would be given only by their editor; and that any future sale of the titles would require the agreement of a majority of the independent national directors. In my year as editor of *The Times*, Murdoch broke all these guarantees. He put his point of view very simply to the home editor of *The Times*, Fred Emery, when he summoned him from holiday on 4 March to his office shortly before asking for my resignation: 'I give instructions to my editors all round the world, why shouldn't I in London?' He was reminded of the undertakings to the Secretary of State. 'They're not worth the paper they're written on,' Murdoch replied.

Murdoch is right. The guarantees are not worth the paper they are written on – unless the proprietor shares the spirit of them. If he does, they are merely ornamental; if he does not, they are unworkable. There is no point in trying to make them stronger. Internal freedom cannot be acquired by external rules, and at Times Newspapers and *The Observer* the State has gone as far as it ought in attempting to lay down rules for the conduct of a private enterprise. The true role for the State must be to administer the anti-trust laws honestly and effectively. Once an acquisition has been agreed, it is too late for petty bureaucracy. There is justification for firmness here, since there is a universal recognition that monopoly power represents a danger, in the words of the Fair Trading

Act, to 'the accurate reporting of news and the free expression of opinion'. The Act should be used, by amendment if necessary, to impose a clear obligation to procure diversity of ownership of existing titles, consistent with viability, at least until the day when it is easier to start new national titles. Here the major restraint remains another monopoly power, that of the print trade unions. They have made the launching of new enterprises prohibitively expensive, frustrating the opportunities created by the revolution in printing technology.

Editorial guarantees are a paltry defence and they may be delusive as well. At Times Newspapers their invention enabled an air of respectability to be given to an unnecessary and hazardous extension of monopoly power, and they suggest that *The Times*'s tradition has been maintained when behind the fake ivy it can so easily be plundered. The theory of the constitution is that the independent national directors would not permit this to happen. As one of the architects of the constitution, I believed this too. I found in reality that the national directors are incapable of monitoring the daily turmoil of a newspaper. This has nothing to do with their theoretical powers, and increasing or entrenching them would make no difference. In a crisis, such as in the titles row I have described, they can be effective. At the same time any intervention on editorial matters inevitably hazards the future relationship between the complaining editor and the aggrieved proprietor. It is like telling tales. On the other hand, arbitration is impossible on the innumerable issues which may arise in many different ways every day between editor and proprietor. What it amounted to with Murdoch was for me symbolized on the day he placed his hand on a few paragraphs of the *Sun* and, comparing it to *The Times* coverage, exclaimed 'There! That's all you need on Poland.' Does one complain to the independent directors? Or accede to the proprietor's 'advice'? Or do battle? There is no system of external supervision which can protect an editor from proprietorship of this kind.

In contrast, I remember now Roy Thomson's 'creed', which he produced from his pocket whenever he was challenged on editorial independence, and I think it bears repeating:

> I can state with the utmost emphasis that no person or group can buy or influence editorial support from any newspaper in the Thomson group. Each paper may perceive this interest in its own way, and will do this without advice, counsel or guidance from the central office of the Thomson Organisation.
>
> I do not believe that a newspaper can be run properly unless its editorial columns are run freely and independently by a highly skilled and dedicated professional journalist.
>
> This is and will continue to be my policy.

A proprietor of commercial and political instinct who interferes in the running of a quality newspaper will inevitably erode its standards. This need not be obviously dramatic. It can happen in ways as apparently innocuous as insisting that sport has extra columns at the expense of news, or closing a foreign bureau on grounds of cost, or offering guidance on the state of economy. It is like a drip effect, however: in time the authority and quality of the paper will be undermined and sometimes dramatically so. The Hitler diaries story was a demonstration of a deeper erosion at *The Times* and *The Sunday Times*. The credibility of both quality papers was seriously damaged. Their separate identities were confused. It happened because the proprietorial energy was engaged at the cost of editorial judgement and editorial experience. There were individuals on *The Sunday Times* who warned that the diaries were deeply suspect and required more tests and investigation. The editor of *The Sunday Times* himself was initially highly dubious about their authenticity. Blame attaches, of course, to Dacre for his hasty confirmation that the diaries were 'the real McCoy'. (He was also a director of Times Newspapers.) My former colleague Charles Douglas-Home, editor of *The Times*, was a trifle gullible too. 'I have smelt them,' he announced in affirming the authenticity of the diaries on BBC Television. 'I am a minor historian and we know about the smell of old documents. They certainly smelt.' But, once Murdoch himself became involved in the excitement of negotiation and of sensational scoops, all serious journalistic standards were swept aside.

Enormous energy was expended by Murdoch and his executives flying from New York to London to New York to Hamburg and back to New York; incessant ingenuity was exhibited over wheeling and dealing on matters of price, release dates, and the need for secrecy; Gerald Long from News International in London was sent into the vault in Zurich; Murdoch men unconnected with Times Newspapers jetted in and out, conferring on how Murdoch's other outlets in his press and television empire could syndicate the material; the editor of *The Times* went into the vault; the scoop of the century was switched from *The Sunday Times* to *The Times* and back again to *The Sunday Times* just two days before its launch; the headlines were written: 'Hitler's Secret Diaries to be Published', 'Documents of Momentous Historic Significance', 'Sensational Disclosures', 'The Tenderness of His Love for Eva Braun', 'New Light Shed on Hitler's Character'.... But in the compulsive process an elementary tenet of journalism was sacrificed by two great newspapers: the facts were not confirmed.

Murdoch's apologists have suggested that the Hitler affair was no different from 1968 when, it is said, *The Sunday Times* published Mussolini's fake diaries. This is not so. Mussolini's diaries were bought by a Thomson subsidiary. The diaries were never announced as being genuine by *The Sunday Times*. On the contrary, it was *The Sunday Times* which first broke the news in Britain that the diaries were fake. The affair of the Hitler diaries will no doubt become an amusing curiosity piece, along with the other great hoaxes in history – but an important principle was at stake. There are those who believe it was an affront to history. It was certainly within serious newspapers the unacceptable face of commercialism. My point is that in no sense does Rupert Murdoch appreciate this. When he was told that the diaries were fake, he reassured the worried editorial men at Times Newspapers who feared for their credibility: 'After all,' Murdoch said, 'we are in the entertainment business.'

Are we?

When I left *The Times*, there were friends and colleagues of mine who were fired or who resigned, and I should like to name them: Bernard Donoughue, assistant editor; Fred Emery, home editor; Henry Fairlie, us columnist; Adrian Hamilton, editor of business news; John Heilpern, us arts editor; Anthony Holden, features editor; Edwin Taylor, head of design; Oscar Turnill, assistant editor; Richard Vines, home sub-editor; Peter Watson, New York correspondent; and Dr Jonathan Wills, Scottish correspondent.

Good times, bad times.

 # SEQUELS

David Blake, economics editor, succeeded Rodney Cowton as home news editor, Cowton becoming defence correspondent

Dr Bernard Donoughue, assistant editor, became partner in stockbrokers Grieveson Grant

Charles Douglas-Home, appointed 13th Editor of *The Times*, 18 March 1982

Fred Emery, became a presenter of BBC Television's *Panorama* on resigning as home editor

Frank Giles, retirement as editor of *The Sunday Times*, due July 1984, took place September 1983. Appointed 'editor emeritus'

John Grant, appointed as deputy editor by Douglas-Home in March 1982, later succeeded by Colin Webb

Michael Hamlyn, succeeded Peter Watson as New York correspondent, later India correspondent

John Heilpern, writing plays

John Higgins, promoted to executive editor (arts and features) assisted by Peter Stothard as features editor

Anthony Holden, freelance journalist and author

Brian Horton, succeeded John Grant as managing editor *The Times*, later made Director of Development, News International

Frank Johnson, resigned to join *The Observer*

Gerald Long, replaced as managing director March 1982 by Bill Gillespie; made deputy chairman, News International

Andrew Neil, editor of UK section of the *Economist*, appointed Editor of *The Sunday Times*, overtaking 'editor designate' Brian MacArthur and deputy editor Hugo Young

Sir Edward Pickering, appointed by Rupert Murdoch in March 1982 as his executive vice chairman of Times Newspapers. Resigned as independent national director

Lord Robens and Lord Roll, both resigned as independent national directors June 1983

Peter Strafford, moved from leader-writing to obituaries

Edwin Taylor, freelance designer

Oscar Turnill, freelance editor

Richard Vines, assisting *China Daily*, Peking

Peter Watson, freelance journalist and author filming his book on art smuggling, *Double Dealer*

Dr Jonathan Wills, producer BBC Radio Scotland

BIBLIOGRAPHY

Historical sources include:

History of The Times, vols I–IV (Times Publishing Co., from 1935)
The Story of The Times, William Dodgson Bowman (Routledge, 1931)
Thomas Barnes, Derek Hudson (C.U.P., 1943)
Delane of The Times, Sir Edward Cook (Constable, 1915)
British Newspapers and Their Controllers, Camrose (Cassell, 1947)
The March of Journalism, Harold Herd (Allen & Unwin, 1962)
Lord Northcliffe, R. Macnair Wilson (Benn, 1927)
Northcliffe, Hamilton Fyfe (W. H. Allen, 1930)
Northcliffe, Reginald Pound and Geoffrey Harmsworth (Cassell, 1959)
Northcliffe, H. J. Greenwall (Wingate, 1957)
Geoffrey Dawson and Our Times, John Evelyn Wrench (Hutchinson, 1965)
In The Chair: Barrington-Ward 1927–48, Donald McLachlan (Weidenfeld, 1971)
A Man of The Times, Iverach MacDonald (Hamish Hamilton, 1976)
Growing up on The Times, Louis Heren (Hamish Hamilton, 1978)
The Times Newspaper and The Sunday Times Newspaper, report by the Monopolies Commission (HMSO, 1966)
Thomson of Fleet, Russell Braddon (Collins, 1965)
After I Was Sixty, Lord Thomson (Hamish Hamilton, 1975)
The Pearl of Days, Harold Hobson, Phillip Knightley and Leonard Russell (Hamish Hamilton, 1972)
The Press Inside Out, Bill Grundy (W. H. Allen, 1976)
Newspapers, Simon Jenkins (Faber, 1979)
The Prerogative of the Harlot, Hugh Cudlipp (Bodley Head, 1980)
The Rise and Fall of the Political Press in Britain, Stephen Koss (Hamish Hamilton, 1981)
Powers of the Press, Martin Walker (Quartet, 1982)
The Life and Death of the Press Barons, Piers Brandon (Secker, 1982)
Barefaced Cheek, Michael Leapman (Hodder, 1983)
The Stuart Case, K. S. Inglis (Melbourne University Press, 1961)

PRINCIPAL SUNDAY TIMES BOOKS

The Zinoviev Letter by Lewis Chester, Stephen Fay and Hugo Young (Heinemann, 1967). How the famous 'Red letter', which helped to defeat Ramsay Macdonald's Labour Government, was forged by White Russians and circulated by Conservative Central Office with Secret Service help.

Philby, The Spy who Betrayed a Generation by Bruce Page, David Leitch, Phillip Knightley, with an introduction by John le Carré (Deutsch, 1968).

An American Melodrama by Lewis Chester, Godfrey Hodgson and Bruce Page (Deutsch, 1969). History of the US Presidential election of 1968, during which Richard Nixon elected and Robert Kennedy murdered.

The Secret Lives of Lawrence of Arabia by Colin Simpson and Phillip Knightley (Nelson, 1969). Documentation of Lawrence's sado-masochism and unsuspected role in Middle East politics.

Journey to Tranquillity by Hugo Young, Bryan Silcock and Peter Dunn (Cape, 1969). History of man's assault on the Moon.

The Strange Voyage of Donald Crowhurst by Nicholas Tomalin and Ron Hall (Hodder, 1970; Penguin, 1973). The mystery of lone sailor Crowhurst, who vanished from his trimaran during the *Sunday Times* single-handed non-stop race round the world.

The Pound in Your Pocket by Peter Wilsher (Cassell, 1970). Century of Sterling 1870–1970.

Do You Sincerely Want To Be Rich? by Charles Raw, Bruce Page and Godfrey Hodgson (Deutsch, 1971). Subtitled 'Bernard Cornfeld and IOS, An International Swindle'. Investigation of the rise of Investors Overseas Services (IOS) and its creator, Bernie Cornfeld, how it operated as an 'offshore' company responsible to the law of no single nation and what it did with the £1,000 million entrusted to it by a million savers.

Ulster by the *Sunday Times* Insight Team (Deutsch and Penguin, 1972). Results of four months of inquiry into the origins of the troubles.

Hoax by Lewis Chester, Stephen Fay and Magnus Linklater (Deutsch, 1972). The forgery and retailing of Howard Hughes's autobiography by Irving.

On Giant's Shoulders by Marjorie Wallace and Michael Robson (Times Books, 1976). The story of Thalidomide victim Terry Wiles.

The Thalidomide Children and the Law, The Sunday Times (Deutsch, 1973). Documents and texts.

Watergate by Lewis Chester, Stephen Aris, Cal McCrystal and William Shawcross (Deutsch, 1973).

Nicholas Tomalin Reporting (Deutsch, 1975). Ron Hall introduces reporting by his colleague and friend, killed on duty for *The Sunday Times* on the Golan front October 1973.

The Yom Kippur War by the Insight Team (Deutsch, 1975). Sequel to *Sunday Times* 1974 book *Insight on the Middle East War*, published in 1974.

The Exploding Cities by Peter Wilsher and Rosemary Righter (Deutsch, 1975). Foreword by Barbara Ward. Stimulated by *Sunday Times* conference with United Nations Fund for Population Activities at Oxford University.

Insight on Portugal (Deutsch, 1975). Portugal's return to democracy.

The Crossman Affair by Hugo Young (Cape, 1976).

Death of Venice by Stephen Fay and Phillip Knightley (Deutsch, 1975). Investigation of threat to survival of Venice.

Destination Disaster by Paul Eddy, Elaine Potter and Bruce Page (Hart-Davis, MacGibbon, 1976). Investigation of Paris DC-10 crash.

Slater Walker by Charles Raw (Deutsch, 1977). Jim Slater tried to prevent publication of Charles Raw's four-year investigation, which concluded that in all its various forms Slater Walker was really about one thing, the manipulation of share prices.

The Abuse of Power by James Margach (W. H. Allen, 1978). The war between Downing Street and the media from Lloyd George to Callaghan by veteran *Sunday Times* political correspondent.

The Fall of the House of Beaverbrook by Lewis Chester and Jonathan Fenby (Deutsch, 1979). How Trafalgar House acquired the *Daily Express*, *Evening Standard* and *Sunday Express*.

Jeremy Thorpe: A Secret Life by Lewis Chester, Magnus Linklater and David May (Deutsch and Fontana, 1979).

Suffer The Children by the Insight Team (Deutsch, 1979). Thalidomide story.

Stop Press by Eric Jacobs (Deutsch, 1980). The inside story of the year of the suspension of Times Newspapers 1978-9.

Siege! by the Insight Team (Hamlyn, 1980). How the SAS rescued hostages at the Iranian Embassy, London, 1980.

The Vestey Affair by Phillip Knightley (Macdonald, 1981).

OF SPECIAL INTEREST:

First Casualty, Phillip Knightley (Deutsch, 1975). *Sunday Times* writer on war correspondent as hero, propagandist and myth-maker from Crimea to Vietnam.

Lawsuit, Stuart M. Speiser (Horizon Press, New York, 1980). Lawyer in the DC-10 case opens his files on celebrated cases including Nader, Onassis, Entebbe, Tenerife.

APPENDIX

MORGAN GRENFELL & CO. LIMITED

23 Great Winchester Street
London EC2P 2AX

S.G. Warburg & Co. Ltd.,
30 Gresham Street,
London EC2P 2EB.

31st December 1980

Dear Sirs,

We are writing to you on behalf of Mr Harold Evans, Editor of *The Sunday Times* and Chairman of *The Sunday Times* Executive Committee, and his close associates on the Staff of *The Sunday Times* ('his Associates') in response to your letter to Mr Evans of 4th December 1980. They intend to put forward a firm proposal as soon as practicable for the purchase of *The Sunday Times* from Times Newspapers Holdings Limited ('TNHL'). This letter is to inform you of the intentions and aims of Mr Evans and his Associates regarding the matters raised in your letter.

Mr Evans and his Associates are aware that it is Thomson British Holdings Limited's ('TBH') preference to dispose of TNHL as a single unit. It is their view however that *The Sunday Times* is capable of being separated and operated independently of the other publications of TNHL. They consider that, in many ways, it would then be a more manageable operation.

This letter is written on the assumption that TBH and TNHL will be making alternative arrangements for *The Times* and The Supplements and that they will not continue to be published in the New Printing House Square, 200 Gray's Inn Road complex.

The proposal set out in this letter is based on the information contained in the Information Memorandum and the Appendix and Addendum thereto sent to us on 16th December 1980.

The basis of the proposal will be that a newly formed company ('the Company'), which has not previously traded, will offer to acquire the title, assets, business and undertaking of *The Sunday Times*. Subsequently, the Company will change its name to The Sunday Times Limited. At the time of purchase the shareholders of the Company will consist principally of substantial and reputable investment institutions. Shares will be made available to the employees of the Company generally as well as to Mr Evans and his Associates. It is possible that there will be at least one significant trade investment in the shares of the Company but such holdings are not expected to represent a majority of the share capital.

The assets to be acquired will be the title, assets, business and undertaking of *The Sunday Times*, including:

(a) the title and trade marks of *The Sunday Times* and *The Sunday Times Magazine*;

(b) the issued share capital of The Sunday Times Limited and Selective Marketplace Limited;

(c) the whole of the production plant and equipment located in 200 Gray's Inn Road, excluding only the equipment required exclusively for the production of *The Times* and The Supplements, and including the proportion of the Text II photo-composition system necessary to produce *The Sunday Times*;

(d) fixtures and office equipment in 200 Gray's Inn Road together with certain of the office equipment located in New Printing House Square being used by *The Sunday Times*;

(e) such motor cars as are required by the employees of the Company; and

(f) the freehold of 200 Gray's Inn Road and the lease of the industrial basement in New Printing House Square.

It is intended that the Company should not own 200 Gray's Inn Road but that it be the subject of a sale and leaseback. The industrial basement in New Printing House Square will, if possible, be dealt with in similar fashion. Alternatively, the Company would be in a position to lease both under new leases from TBH or its subsidiaries.

We envisage that the price to be offered will be realistic as between a willing buyer and a willing seller for the business being acquired after taking account of such liabilities as are assumed by the Company. TNHL will be responsible for all redundancy payments in respect of employees not being offered employment with the Company. The Company will assume responsibility for payments arising from redundancies that will arise subsequent to the purpose as a result of the agreed introduction of photo-composition. We are, of course, not aware of TBH's requirements as to the treatment of redundancy payments.

It is intended that the Company should introduce a pension scheme for its employees similar to that presently available to the employees of *The Sunday Times* through The Thomson Organisation (1968) Pension Fund. Arrangements will be made for the pension scheme to assume that part of the assets and liabilities of The Thomson Organisation (1968) Pension Fund applicable to the employees of the Company.

The offer will be subject to normal terms and conditions. It will be conditional inter alia upon:

(a) there being no reference to the Monopolies and Mergers Commission;
(b) the assignment to the Company of material contracts relating to the business of *The Sunday Times*, including the printing contract with Sun Printers (Watford) Limited and the agreement with *The Guardian* and Manchester Evening News Limited;
(c) agreement with the Unions to new manning levels, comparable to those set out in the Information Memorandum, and working practices and to the introduction of photocomposition;
(d) there being no discontinuance of production of *The Sunday Times* or *The Sunday Times* Magazine prior to completion; and
(e) satisfactory arrangements with TNHL for an orderly transfer of the business of *The Sunday Times* to 200 Gray's Inn Road.

The consideration will be paid in cash on completion of the purchase or at a later date as agreed with TBH. The consideration will be financed by the Company from the subscription of shares in the Company principally by institutional investors and from term debt or its equivalent. Full details of the sources of finance to the Company will be provided at the time of making a firm offer.

Mr Evans and his Associates expect the Company to be managed in its day to day affairs by an executive management committee closely resembling the present Executive Committee of *The Sunday Times*. This has been found, during its short life, to provide successfully the close communications necessary to manage this publication.

It is presently intended that the Board of the Company should include the Editor and the Chief Executive. Other directors would include representatives of shareholders and of employees; and independent persons familiar with the newspaper industry.

A trust will be formed to protect editorial independence and integrity. It alone will have powers to appoint and remove the Editor after due consultation with the Board of the Company. It will also be required to approve any disposal of the title or right to publish the title. The trustees will not be employees or directors of the Company. They will comprise persons embracing certain specified interests, including the former editor of *The Sunday Times*; a journalist of *The Sunday Times*; a distinguished journalist not connected with *The Sunday Times*; representatives of public life; a representative of the printing unions; and a representative of the shareholders.

Details of the composition of the management committee, the Board and the Trust will be given when appropriate.

We consider that, for this proposal, the single most important factor in the future operation of *The Sunday Times* will be the relationship between the Company and its employees. Mr Evans is well known and respected by the workforce and we believe will provide an environment of personal trust in which satisfactory negotiations can proceed. The single title, smaller unit size, shorter lines of communication and direct responsibility and a new ownership should all contribute towards an improvement in the general level of labour relations within *The Sunday Times*. It is intended that employees be given incentives, including an Inland Revenue approved profit-sharing scheme, to reach realistic performance standards that will be set for uninterrupted production. This should ensure the backing of employees.

Mr Evans and his Associates consider that the extra commitment from staff, together with financial incentives and more harmonious labour relations promise to provide the Company with the benefits of continuous production. This would give *The Sunday Times* the scope in both financial and managerial terms to increase pagination beyond the present 72 pages to which it has been limited for so long despite the ability to attract advertising in excess of 80 pages, and to utilise fully the opportunity to develop the Magazine offered by the new contract with Sun Printers (Watford) Limited. In the longer term, the available resources of a powerful editorial team and the surplus plant capacity would be used to develop other publishing activities.

Mr Evans and his Associates consider that these proposals when translated into a firm offer would provide the best prospect for a smooth transition of ownership of *The Sunday Times* and justify their conviction that *The Sunday Times*, as an independent newspaper again, will be entirely viable and will continue to make a contribution to British life.

Our clients' proposal may be briefly restated as being the offer of a fair price, the ownership by a new and independent company, and the safeguarding of editorial independence and quality which is central to the criteria laid down by TBH. There will be the support of a proven creative team in editorial and revenue raising and the prospect of improved labour relations.

We look forward to meeting you at your earliest convenience.

Yours faithfully,
For MORGAN GRENFELL & CO. LIMITED

INDEX